The Myth of the Machine:

THE PENTAGON OF POWER

Books by Lewis Mumford

THE STORY OF UTOPIAS 1922

STICKS AND STONES 1924

THE GOLDEN DAY 1926

HERMAN MELVILLE 1929

THE BROWN DECADES 1931

TECHNICS AND CIVILIZATION 1934

THE CULTURE OF CITIES 1938

MEN MUST ACT 1939

FAITH FOR LIVING 1940

THE SOUTH IN ARCHITECTURE 1941

THE CONDITION OF MAN 1944

CITY DEVELOPMENT 1945

VALUES FOR SURVIVAL 1946

GREEN MEMORIES 1947

THE CONDUCT OF LIFE 1951

ART AND TECHNICS 1952

IN THE NAME OF SANITY 1954

FROM THE GROUND UP 1956

THE TRANSFORMATIONS OF MAN 1956

THE CITY IN HISTORY 1961

THE HIGHWAY AND THE CITY 1963

THE URBAN PROSPECT 1968

THE MYTH OF THE MACHINE:
  I. TECHNICS AND HUMAN DEVELOPMENT 1967
  II. THE PENTAGON OF POWER 1970

INTERPRETATIONS AND FORECASTS:
  1922-1972 1972

FINDINGS AND KEEPINGS 1975

MY WORKS AND DAYS 1979

The Myth of the Machine

THE PENTAGON
OF POWER

by LEWIS MUMFORD

A Harvest/HBJ Book
HARCOURT BRACE JOVANOVICH
New York and London

Chapter 14 appeared in *Challenge for Survival* by Pierre Dansereau, copyright
© 1970 by Columbia University Press.

A substantial portion of this book appeared originally in *The New Yorker,* in
somewhat different form. Parts of some of these chapters originally appeared in
AV Communication Review, Garden Journal, Horizon, Proceedings of the American Philosophical Society, and *The Virginia Quarterly Review.*

The lines by Robert Frost are from "A Considerable Speck," from *The Poetry
of Robert Frost,* edited by Edward Connery Lathem, copyright 1942 by Robert
Frost, copyright © 1969 by Holt, Rinehart and Winston, Inc., copyright ©
1970 by Lesley Frost Ballantine; reprinted by permission of Holt, Rinehart and
Winston, Inc.

Library of Congress Cataloging in Publication Data

Mumford, Lewis, 1895-
The pentagon of power.

(His The myth of the machine, v. 2)
(A Harvest/HBJ book)
Bibliography: p. 439
1. Technology and civilization. I. Title.
[CB478.M783]   901.9   73-13626
ISBN 0-15-671610-0

CONTENTS

1: NEW EXPLORATIONS, NEW WORLDS *3*

2: RETURN OF THE SUN GOD *28*

3: THE MECHANIZED WORLD PICTURE *51*

4: POLITICAL ABSOLUTISM AND REGIMENTATION *77*

5: SCIENCE AS TECHNOLOGY *105*

6: THE POLYTECHNIC TRADITION *130*

7: MASS PRODUCTION AND HUMAN AUTOMATION *164*

8: PROGRESS AS 'SCIENCE FICTION' *197*

9: THE NUCLEATION OF POWER *230*

10: THE NEW MEGAMACHINE *263*

11: THE MEGATECHNIC WASTELAND *300*

12: PROMISES, BRIBES, THREATS *321*

13: DEMORALIZATION AND INSURGENCE *346*

14: THE NEW ORGANUM *378*

EPILOGUE: THE ADVANCEMENT OF LIFE *414*

BIBLIOGRAPHY *439*

ACKNOWLEDGEMENTS *471*

INDEX *473*

ILLUSTRATIONS

GRAPHIC SECTION I

Between pages 148 and 149

1: MECHANIZATION OF THE WORLD PICTURE
2: ABSOLUTISM, MILITARISM, AND MECHANIZATION
3: POWER
4: SPEED
5: REMOTE CONTROL
6: COMPUTERDOM
7: PENTAGONS OF POWER
8: DIVINE KINGSHIP: NEW STYLE
9: MAGNIFICATION AND MUMMIFICATION
10: AUTOCRATIC TECHNOCRACY
11: SPACE ROCKETS AS POWER SYMBOLS
12: HOMICIDE, GENOCIDE, AND BIOCIDE
13: BARBARISM
14–15: ENCAPSULATED MAN
16: MECHANIZATION TAKES COMMAND

GRAPHIC SECTION II

Between pages 340 and 341

17: TECHNOLOGICAL INTUITIONS
18–19: TECHNOLOGICAL EXHIBITIONISM
20: HOMAGE TO GIANTISM
21: ENVIRONMENTAL DESICCATION

22: ORGANIZED DESTRUCTION

23: INDUSTRIAL POLLUTION, COMMERCIAL FALLOUT

24: MEGALOPOLIS INTO NECROPOLIS

25: THE ACADEMIC ESTABLISHMENT

26: MASS MOBILIZATION OF YOUTH

27: RITUALS OF 'COUNTER-CULTURE'

28: THE AGE OF MONSTERS

29: PASSAGE TO BIOTECHNICS

30: ETHERIALIZATION OF THE WORLD PICTURE (GABO)

31: THE RENEWAL OF LIFE (MOORE)

32: NAUM GABO AND HENRY MOORE

'The Myth of the Machine' was planned originally as a single volume; and this book, Volume Two, is the fourth of a series that opened in 1934 with 'Technics and Civilization.' Though perhaps the most original contribution of these books was their treatment of technics as an integral part of man's higher culture, they were equally audacious in denying that man's departure from animalhood and his continued development rested solely on his propensity for tool-using and tool-making. Furthermore, in defiance of contemporary dogma, they did not regard scientific discovery and technological invention as the sole object of human existence; for I have taken life itself to be the primary phenomenon, and creativity, rather than the 'conquest of nature,' as the ultimate criterion of man's biological and cultural success.

Though the basic ideas of 'The Myth of the Machine' were present, at least in outline, in 'Technics and Civilization,' I have been driven, by the wholesale miscarriages of megatechnics, to deal with the collective obsessions and compulsions that have misdirected our energies, and undermined our capacity to live full and spiritually satisfying lives. If the key to the past few centuries has been 'Mechanization Takes Command,' the theme of the present book may be summed up in Colonel John Glenn's words on returning from orbit to earth: "Let Man Take Over."

Amenia, New York   —L. M.

The Myth of the Machine:

THE PENTAGON OF POWER

CHAPTER ONE

New Explorations, New Worlds

1: THE NEW VISION

The period that opened at the end of the fifteenth century has been called The Age of Exploration; and that characterization covers many of the events that followed. But the most significant part of this new exploration took place in the mind; and what is more the cultural New World that was opened up still was attached in fact, even in the Western hemisphere, to many obscure ramifying roots in the Old World, roots that pushed through heavy layers of soil into the debris of ancient cities and empires.

What was truly new for Western man was the exhilarating sense that, for the first time, every part of the planet was accessible, and offered opportunities for daring adventure, for active economic intercourse, and even, at least for more reflective minds, for self-enlightenment. Both the earth and the skies lay open to systematic investigation, as never before. If the bright starry heavens invited exploration, so did the dark continents across the seas; and so, eventually, did the still darker continent of man's cultural and biological past.

Broadly speaking, then, two complementary kinds of exploration beckoned Western man. While they were closely related to their point of origin, they moved in different directions, pursued different goals—though often crossing—and at last merged into a single movement, which increasingly sought to replace the gifts of nature with those more limited fabrications of man which were drawn from a single aspect of nature: that which could be brought under human domination. One exploration focussed mainly on the sky and on the orderly motions of planets and falling bodies, on space-measuring and time-keeping, on repetitive events and determinable laws. The other boldly traversed the seas and even burrowed below the surface of the earth, seeking the Promised Land, lured partly by curiosity and cupidity, partly by the desire to break loose from ancient ties and limits.

Between the fifteenth and the nineteenth centuries, the New World opened by terrestrial explorers, adventurers, soldiers, and administrators joined forces with the scientific and technical new world that the scientists, the inventors, and the engineers explored and cultivated: they were part and parcel of the same movement. One mode of exploration was concerned with abstract symbols, rational systems, universal laws, repeatable and predictable events, objective mathematical measurements: it sought to understand, utilize, and control the forces that derive ultimately from the cosmos and the solar system. The other mode dwelt on the concrete and the organic, the adventurous, the tangible: to sail uncharted oceans, to conquer new lands, to subdue and overawe strange peoples, to discover new foods and medicines, perhaps to find the fountain of youth, or if not, to seize by shameless force of arms the wealth of the Indies. In both modes of exploration, there was from the beginning a touch of defiant pride and demonic frenzy.

Moved by this New World vision, audacious sailing ships breached the geographic barriers that had too long kept the peoples of the earth apart: through these openings during the next few centuries the first trickle of explorers turned into a torrent of emigrants who poured into the Americas, into Australia and New Zealand, into Africa, to seize and settle in their own style great areas of the earth, whose indigenous inhabitants had hitherto led a relatively self-centered life.

From the outset in the sixteenth century the leaders of European society fervently believed that a great cyclical change in the life of man was about to take place. Poliziano, the imaginative Florentine humanist, promptly declared that the discovery of the New World by Columbus would bring about a beneficent change in human existence: while only a century later the Calabrian monk Campanella, excited by Bacon and Galileo, hopefully hailed with equal fervor the new world of astronomy, physics and technology, embracing in fantasy the still nameless mechanical and electronic inventions that were bound, he felt sure, to transform human society. After outlining the main features of his ideal commonwealth, 'The City of the Sun,' Campanella observed that according to contemporary astrologers the coming age would have more history within a hundred years "than all the world had had in the four thousand years before."

Granted a little charitable latitude, that prophecy proved remarkably correct: the wildest imaginary inventions fell far short of the actual achievements that in a few centuries came to pass. From the beginning this subjective faith in a New World that would transcend all past human achievements took hold of the most sober minds: it had the same effect upon Western man as the flinging back of the shutters and the opening of windows in an ancient house that had been sealed up for many winters and had fallen into disrepair. Those who breathed the fresh air of spring were not content to live longer amid the moldy rafters and the cobwebs, even when the heirlooms in their ancient quarters were still serviceable and beautiful. Though they might hesitate at first to demolish the entire dwelling, they began to throw out old furniture, renovate unoccupied rooms, install new conveniences. And the more daring were ready to abandon the old mansion altogether in order to start life afresh—at least spiritually—in the wilderness or even on the moon.

Writing to his friend Michel de Montaigne, Etienne de la Boétie said: "When at the threshold of our century a new world rose out of the ocean, it happened because the gods wished to create a refuge where men under a better sky can cultivate their fields, while the cruel sword and ignominious plague condemn Europe to perish." A similar mood, a similar desire to make a fresh start united the scientists with the inventors, starry-eyed writers of utopias with swaggering pioneer backwoodsmen. The New World vision seemed to enlarge and exalt every human possibility, even though the explorers and pioneers, in turning their backs on the Old World, did not in fact leave the 'cruel sword' or the 'ignominious plague' behind them, for their smallpox, measles, and tuberculosis decimated those natives whom their guns did not exterminate.

When the active period of discovery and colonization was over and the promised land still lay below the horizon, much of the original faith and fervor was transferred from the exploitation of the indigenous 'New World' to that of the machine. But in fact these two different approaches to the New World—one aimed at natural resources to be discovered and appropriated, the other at mechanical power and artificial wealth, to be fabricated and profitably sold—had never from the beginning been far apart. Both impulses had sprung out of a militant medieval background, just as the ascetic, life-renouncing, orderly habits of early capitalism had sprung out of the medieval monastery.

2: THE MEDIEVAL PRELUDE

The official date for the opening of the New World has long been fixed as that of Columbus' first voyage; though by now one has reason to suppose that sundry other blinder, more tentative thrusts were made in the same general direction—possibly by Irish monks, Norse rovers, and Breton fishermen, and finally by sailors from Bristol between 1480 and 1490, as

Carl Sauer has recently pointed out. Certainly the Greek cosmographers' picture of the earth as a globe had become known, if not generally accepted, even before the fifteenth century; and significantly, the abstract model of the mechanical New World was framed in lines of latitude and longitude on fifteenth-century maps well before 1492. It was through a similar set of pre-cartesian coordinates that the Renascence painters, a whole century before Descartes, began to look at the world and plot with accuracy on their canvasses the relation between near and distant objects, defined by receding planes in space.

In turn Columbus, though in no wise an intellectual leader, commanded the scientific means to plot his voyage and ensure his return through the astrolabe, the magnetic compass, and the existing sailing charts: means that gave him the self-confidence to set forth on his tricky voyage and hold to his course in the face of his doubting crew. Thus long before the industrial changes brought about by coal and iron, by the steam engine and the automatic loom, these earlier technical advances—which, like the extensive use of windpower and water in mills, originated in the Middle Ages—had wrought a far more significant change in the human mind. The latter-day practice of dating this cultural change from the seventeenth century is a parochialism due originally to lack of historic information among technicians and lack of technical information and insight among historians. From the thirteenth century onward there was persistent, fruitful intercourse between these two areas.

Our current views of both the terrestrial and the mechanical New Worlds have been falsely colored by the opaque religious prejudices of the leaders of the eighteenth-century Enlightenment. Thinkers like Voltaire and Diderot, judging medieval institutions by the decayed survivals of their own day, took for granted that the Middle Ages were a period of besotted ignorance and superstition; and in their desire to throw off the influence of the Established Church, they converted the High Middle Ages, one of the great moments in European culture, into a neo-Gothic horror story, assuming that no serious progress had been made in any department until their own period. This anti-Gothic obsession resulted not only in the devaluation of medieval achievement but also in the wholesale destruction of buildings and institutions that, if preserved and renewed, might have helped to humanize the rising power system.

Now that competent medieval scholarship has removed these blinders, we can appreciate that the groundwork for the Age of Exploration was laid by a series of technical advances that began in the thirteenth century, with the introduction of the magnetic compass and gunpowder from China: indeed, from the tenth century onward European society staged a kind of dress rehearsal for the period that followed. This had started with the clearing of the forests by the monastic orders and the founding of feudal

pioneer settlements and new cities on the eastern and southern border-
lands; and the first settlers in the New World, so far from starting life
anew, carried with them their typical medieval institutions and continued
the same processes: even the 'American' log cabin came from Sweden.
(See the chapter The Medieval Tradition in 'Sticks and Stones,' 1924.)

On this view, the bold sorties and bloody conquests of the Norsemen,
raiding Ireland and England, seizing the Orkneys, settling in Iceland, invading Sicily, conquering Normandy, finally reaching Persia, were the first
wave of later conquests and colonizations; and set the same pattern of
ruthless intimidation and berserk destruction. So, too, the series of Cru-
sades in the Near East must be regarded as the earliest manifestations of
Western imperialism, culminating in the Fourth Crusade, which, without
the faintest pretext of pious purpose or self-defense, went out of its way to
sack and devastate the Christian realm of Byzantium. Again, the exploration of the perimeter of Africa by the Portuguese, beginning with Prince
Henry the Navigator (1444) set another ugly precedent, for it brought
back Negro slaves. This resuscitated slavery, an institution that had been
dying out along with serfdom in feudal and urban Europe; and thence this
inhuman practice was spread by the Portuguese, the Spaniards, and the
English to the New World.

As for the equipment that made these conquests and exploitations and
enslavements possible—the armor, the crossbows, muskets and cannon—
these new technical facilities gave the Europeans who commanded them,
though vastly outnumbered, the power to overcome the aborigines: their
grim audacity and their utter ruthlessness were not only supported but
magnified by their superior weapons. What is more, the easy successes this
achieved re-enforced the new power complex that was coming into existence.

If the New World exploration did not come to anything like its happy
expected fulfillment even in North America, where the odds were more
favorable, it was because the new colonizers and settlers brought so much
of the Old World in their refined equipment and their brutal customs with
them. The wonder is rather that the hopeful dream has remained alive for
so long, for some of its original luminosity still dazzles and blinds the eyes
of many of our contemporaries who continue to pursue the same archaic
fantasies, planning further voyages through outer space. Contemporary
'space age' prophets, who proclaim space exploration as the endless
frontier and astronauts as the coming pioneers, throw an unrealistic
glamour over both the past, and even more, the future of such efforts.

To cap this whole process, the increasing sale of indulgences within the
Roman Catholic Church, farming out the concession to dispense these to
international financiers on the best capitalist principles, enlarged a practice
that was already a scandal in the time of Boccaccio. This system announced more brazenly than by words that henceforth there was nothing

on earth or in Heaven that could not be bought for money. That very belief, in words that tied together financial and spiritual profit, issued forth in so many words from the mouth of Columbus: "Gold is excellent, gold is treasure, and he who possesses it does whatever he wishes in this life and succeeds in helping souls into paradise." This utterance needs no italics.

From the beginning there was an inner contradiction in Western man's attitude toward the New World: not merely between the dream and the muddy reality, but between the desire to extend the influence of Christianity—under royal power and command—to distant parts of the world, and a seething dissatisfaction with these same institutions at home, which nourished the hope that at least on the other side of the planet a fresh start might be made.

On one hand the Christian missionaries sought to convert the heathen, by fire and sword if need be, to the gospel of peace, brotherhood, and heavenly beatitude; on the other, the more venturesome spirits wished to throw off the constraining traditions and customs, and begin life afresh, levelling distinctions of class, eliminating superfluities and luxuries, privileges and distinctions, and hierarchical rank. In short, to go back to the Stone Ages, before the institutions of Bronze Age civilization had crystallized. Though the Western hemisphere was indeed inhabited, and many parts of it were artfully cultivated, so much of it was so sparsely occupied that the European thought of it as a virgin continent against whose wildness he pitted his manly strength. In one mood the European invaders preached the Christian gospel to the native idolators, subverted them with strong liquors, forced them to cover their nakedness with clothes, and worked them to an early death in mines; in another, the pioneer himself took on the ways of the North American Indian, adopted his leather costume, and reverted to the ancient paleolithic economy: hunting, fishing, gathering shellfish and berries, revelling in the wilderness and its solitude, defying orthodox law and order, and yet, under pressure, improvising brutal substitutes. The beauty of that free life still haunted Audubon in his old age.

Nowhere were these contradictions more flagrant than in North America. The very colonists who threw off their allegiance to England and justified their act in the name of freedom, equality, and the right to happiness retained the institution of slavery and exerted constant military pressure upon the Indians, whose lands they systematically seized by fraud and force, shamelessly described as 'purchase,' sanctified by treaties the United States government has repeatedly broken—and still keeps breaking—at its own convenience.

But an even more tragic paradox sullied the New World dream and made it impossible to begin life afresh under a new sky. For the high cultures that were already established in Mexico, Central America, and the

Andes were not in any sense primitive or new, still less did they represent more acceptable human ideals than those the Old World cultures had put forward. The conquistadors of Mexico and Peru found a native population so rigidly regimented, so completely deprived of initiative, that in Mexico, as soon as their king, Montezuma, was captured and unable to give orders they offered little or no overt resistance to the invaders. Here, in short, in the 'New' world was the same institutional complex that had shackled civilization since its beginnings in Mesopotamia and Egypt: slavery, caste, war, divine kingship, and even the religious sacrifice of human victims on altars—sometimes as with the Aztecs on an appalling scale. Politically speaking, Western imperialism was carrying coals to Newcastle.

As it turned out, the wilderness that Western man had failed to explore was the dark continent of his own soul, that very 'Heart of Darkness' which Joseph Conrad depicted, released by its distance from Old World sanctions, throwing off archaic taboos, conventional wisdom, and religious inhibitions, and obliterating every trace of neighborly love and humility. Wherever Western man went, slavery, land robbery, lawlessness, culture-wrecking, and the outright extermination of both wild beasts and tame men went with him: for the only force that he now respected—an enemy with equal power to inflict damage on him—was lacking, once his feet were firmly established on the new soil. Within half a dozen years after Columbus' landing the Spaniards, a contemporary observer estimated, had killed off one and a half million natives.

Emerson noted, significantly, in his 'Essay on War,' that the celebrated Cavendish, who was thought in his times a good Christian man, wrote thus to Lord Hunsdon, on his return from a voyage round the world: "Sept. 1588. It hath pleased Almighty God to suffer me to circumpass the whole globe of the world, entering in at the Strait of Magellan, and returning by the Cape of Buena Esperanza; in which voyage I have either discovered or brought certain intelligence of all the rich places of the world, which were ever discovered by any Christian. I navigated along the coast of Chile, Peru, and New Spain, *where I made great spoils*. I burned and sunk nineteen sail of ships, small & great. All the villages and towns that I ever landed at, I burned and spoiled. And had I not been discovered on the coast, I had taken great quantity of treasure."

For one humane Captain Cook, who saw no point in imposing Britain's savage penal laws upon Polynesian natives—"that thieves are hanged in England I saw no reason why they should be shot in Otaheite"—there were uncounted Vasco da Gamas, who cold-bloodedly hanged from his masthead the fishermen of an East Indian port he visited—innocent people he had hospitably invited aboard his vessel—in order to terrorize the population on shore. These ferocities remained a stigma on New World methods, and they continued through the centuries along with forced labor and outright enslavement. The treatment of the natives of the Congo under King Leopold or those of South Africa under Verwoerd and his successors, are fossilized mementoes of this original terror and brutality.

Not merely slavery but genocide gained ground with the New World exploration. Again, this practice was not unknown in Europe, for it had been employed with the sanction of the Church against the Albigensian heretics of Provence in the thirteenth century and has continued to recur, without producing any sufficient moral reaction, into our own time: witness the Turkish massacre of the Armenians in 1923, Stalin's deliberate starvation of millions of Russian peasants in 1931–32, the German massacres of the Jews and other vilified nationalities in the nineteen-forties, to say nothing of the indiscriminate attacks on urban populations in the Second World War, initiated by the Germans in Warsaw in 1939 and Rotterdam in 1940, but also sedulously imitated, in contravention of the once-accepted rules of war, by the de-moralized leaders of Britain and the United States.

These New World practices (enslavement and genocide) formed another secret link with the anti-human animus of mechanical industry after the sixteenth century, when the workers were no longer protected either by feudal custom or by the self-governing guild. The degradations undergone by child laborers or women during the early nineteenth century in England's 'satanic mills' and mines only reflected those that took place during the territorial expansion of Western man. In Tasmania, for example, British colonists organized 'hunting parties' for pleasure, to slaughter the surviving natives: a people more primitive, scholars believe, than the Australian natives, who should have been preserved, so to say, under glass, for the benefit of later anthropologists. So commonplace were these practices, so plainly were the aborigines regarded as predestined victims, that even the benign and morally sensitive Emerson could say resignedly in an early poem, 1827:

> "Alas red men are few, red men are feeble,
> They are few and feeble and must pass away."

As a result Western man not merely blighted in some degree every culture that he touched, whether 'primitive' or advanced, but he also robbed his own descendants of countless gifts of art and craftsmanship, as well as precious knowledge passed on only by word of mouth that disappeared with the dying languages of dying peoples. With this extirpation of earlier cultures went a vast loss of botanical and medical lore, representing many thousands of years of watchful observation and empirical experiment whose extraordinary discoveries—such as the ancient Indian use of Rauwolfia serpentina as a tranquillizer in mental illness—modern medicine has now, all too belatedly, begun to appreciate. For the better part of four centuries the cultural riches of the entire world lay at the feet of

Western man; and to his shame, and likewise to his gross self-deprivation and impoverishment, his main concern was to appropriate only the gold and silver and diamonds, the lumber and pelts, and such new foods (maize and potatoes) as would enable him to feed larger populations.

Years passed before objects of art like those presented by Montezuma to Charles II would be exhibited in Europe for their value as works of art—or even shown in an American museum of art. Yet Albrecht Dürer, who examined this Spanish collection, had no doubt about their esthetic value. "Never," said Dürer, ". . . have I seen anything that warms my heart so much as these things." Those who turned these works of art into ingots of gold did not share his insight or enthusiasm.

Unfortunately the hostility that the European displayed toward the native cultures he encountered he carried even further into his relations with the land. The immense open spaces of the American continents, with all their unexploited or thinly utilized resources, were treated as a challenge to unrelenting war, destruction, and conquest. The forests were there to be cut down, the prairie to be plowed up, the marshes to be filled, the wildlife to be killed for empty sport, even if not utilized for food or clothing.

In the act of 'conquering nature' our ancestors too often treated the earth as contemptuously and as brutally as they treated its original inhabitants, wiping out great animal species like the bison and the passenger pigeon, mining the soils instead of annually replenishing them, and even, in the present day, invading the last wilderness areas, precious just because they are still wildernesses, homes for wildlife and solitary human souls. Instead we are surrendering them to six-lane highways, gas stations, amusement parks, and the lumber interests, as in the redwood groves, or Yosemite, and Lake Tahoe—though these primeval areas, once desecrated, can never be fully restored or replaced.

I have no wish to overstress the negative side of this great exploration. If I seem to do so here it is because both the older romantic exponents of a new life lived in accordance with Nature, or the later exponents of a new life framed in conformity to the Machine, overlooked the appalling losses and wastages, under the delusion either that the primeval abundance was inexhaustible or else that the losses did not matter, since modern man through science and invention would soon fabricate an artificial world infinitely more wonderful than that nature had provided—an even grosser delusion. Both views have long been rife in the United States where the two phases of the New World dream came together; and they are still prevalent.

Yet the hopes so often expressed in the sixteenth century, later idealized by the Romantic movement in the eighteenth century, were not without a foundation: indeed there was a moment in the nineteenth century when they seemed, in the North Atlantic states, to be almost on the point of realization in a new type of personality and in a type of community that offered its gifts to all its members: "to each according to his need, from each according to his ability."

The New World, once its incoming inhabitants had found their roots, captured their imaginations. In its vastness, in its ecological variety, in its range of climates and physiographic profiles, in both its teeming wildlife and in the hoarded treasure of food plants and trees, the New World was a land of promise, indeed a land of many promises for both body and mind. Here was a natural abundance which promised to lift the ancient curse of slavery and poverty, even before the machine lightened the burden of purely physical toil. The coastal waters teemed with fish, clams, oysters; and game was so plentiful that in the frontier settlements domestic beef and pork sold at a premium. Those who were at home in the wilderness, like Audubon, never lacked food, despite mortgages and debts. The belief that a better society would be possible in the New World stirred many a company of immigrants, from the Jesuits of Paraguay to the Pilgrims of Massachusetts and the later Hutterites in Iowa. Thus almost until the end of the nineteenth century the secret name of the New World was Utopia.

For four centuries the intellectual leaders of the New Exploration prospected and ransacked every part of the planet. Through Captain Cook or Darwin they went on long, difficult voyages, making oceanic and meteorological observations and bringing to light the countless marvels of marine zoology; through Schoolcraft and Catlin and Lewis Morgan, as with Spencer and Gillen in Australia, they surveyed and made graphic records of the indigenous cultures, already gravely disturbed by the intrusion of Western man; through Layard they uncovered 'Nineveh,' or with Stephens made known through description and drawing the first great Mayan ruins; while through Aurel Stein and Raphael Pumpelly remote Turkestan and Inner Mongolia, once the seat of thriving cultures, became known again.

Though this first exploration was swift and necessarily superficial, it uncovered ways of life that reached back into a distant past, bringing to light forgotten cities and neglected monuments, revealing the vast variety of languages and dialects, to be numbered by the hundreds even in small tracts like New Guinea, along with the myths, the legends, the forms of plastic and graphic art, the systems of notation, the rituals and laws, the cosmic interpretations and religious beliefs of mankind. Thus, during the centuries when the agents of mechanical uniformity were steadily gaining the upper hand, reducing or defacing natural variety in the interest of speed, power, and financial gain, these other explorers moved toward the opposite pole, and early and late revealed for the first time the immense cultural variety of mankind: the rich compost of human history, which almost matches the original abundance and variety of nature.

As a by-product, almost by accident, this worldwide exploration in space was complemented by an equally decisive historic exploration in time: that which was mischaracterized by Jacob Burckhardt, an historian of genius, as the 'Renascence.' The unearthing of both Greek and Roman antiquity from its surviving documents and monuments was only a single incident in a much wider survey of the human past. As geographic exploration loosed the spatial bonds to a particular soil and culture, so these new temporal explorations loosed the bonds to the immediate present: for the first time the human mind began to move about freely in both past and future, picking and choosing, anticipating and projecting, released from the provincial presence of an over-insistent here and now. Through both natural history and cultural history Western man discovered many significant aspects of his nature that have been left out of the purview of quantitative scientific investigation. If the present generation has now lost the sense of this liberation, it is because all too soon seventeenth-century science imprisoned the mind in an ideology that denied the realities of biological self-transformation and historic creativity.

Though other cultures—like the Sumerian, the Mayan, and the Indic—coupled human destiny with long vistas of abstract calendar time, the essential contribution of the Renascence was to relate the cumulative results of history to the variety of cultural achievements that marked the successive generations. By unburying statues, monuments, buildings, cities, by reading old books and inscriptions, by re-entering a long-abandoned world of ideas, these new explorers in time became aware of fresh potentialities in their own existence. These pioneers of the mind invented a time-machine more wonderful than H. G. Wells' technological contraption.

At a moment when the new mechanical world-picture had no place for 'time' except as a function of movement in space, historic time—duration, in Henri Bergson's sense, which includes persistence through replication, imitation, and memory—began to play a conscious part in day-to-day choices. If the living present could be visibly transformed, or at least deliberately modified from a Gothic to a formalized Classic structure, so could the future be remolded, too. Historic time could be colonized and cultivated, and human culture itself became a collective artifact. The sciences actually profited by this historic restoration, getting a fresh impetus from Thales, Democritus, Archimedes, Hero of Alexandria.

For the first time, it would seem, the future, however untried, was more attractive than the past, as the experimental and the novel took precedence over the well-tested and the traditional. Even a monk like Campanella, in the heart of the Church, would express this new sense to perfection in a letter to Galileo: "The novelties of ancient truths, of new worlds, new systems, new nations are the beginnings of a new era."

The fantasy of a 'New World,' which seized Western man in so many forms after the fifteenth century, was, then, an attempt to escape time and the cumulative effects of time (tradition and history) by changing it for un-occupied space. This took many forms: a religious form by breaking away from the established church and its orthodoxies, a utopian form by found-ing new communities, an adventurous form by conquering new lands, a mechanical form by substituting machines for organisms, and trading physical changes, in which time exists only as wear and tear, for organic changes, in which time leaves a permanent record: finally, the 'New World' took a revolutionary form: an attempt to make over the ways and habits and goals of a large population, in which all these modes of escape were more or less combined in a single complex—the new heaven and earth that would come into existence once royalism, feudalism, ecclesiasticism, and capitalism should pass away.

This attempt to make a new beginning rested on the valid perception that at various points something had profoundly gone wrong in man's development. Instead of accepting this as ineradicable, as an integral defect for which the theological name had been original sin, and instead of sub-mitting to it as fatally ordained by the gods, Western man, in his growing self-confidence, wanted to wipe the slate clean and begin all over. And therein lay a trap; for in order to overcome time, in order to begin anew, it was imperative for him not to run away from his past, but to confront it, and literally to live down its traumatic events within himself. Until every generation did this consciously, examining its hoary tradition in the light of new experience, evaluating and selecting every part of its heritage, man could make no fresh start. In one mind after another that effort was begun: but at too early a point it was abandoned. So it remains an urgent task for our own day.

3: OUTER CONFLICTS AND INNER CONTRADICTIONS

There is always a disparity between ideal professions and actual achieve-ments, at very least, a gap in time. This is part of the natural history of human institutions and should not give rise to callow cynicism. But in the case of the gap between the vivid New World dream and its actual transla-tion, the contradictions are so numerous and the achievements so spotty and smirched that they almost defy any systematic treatment. Part of the difficulty springs from the fact that the explorers and adventurers carried with them a heavy admixture of Old World traits, many of which in the course of thousands of years had proved lethal, without inciting any serious attempt to weed them out. Neither cutting loose from the Old World in space, nor making a breach with its past, proved easy.

Looking back we can now see that the proposal to wipe the slate clean and begin afresh in the New World was based on an illusion, or rather a series of illusions. As in the typical myth of Robinson Crusoe, the treasured Bible of both land pioneer and industrial enterpriser, survival in the New World was possible only if valuable lumber and tools could be salvaged from the Old World wreckage. In the act of conquering the Americas and establishing trading posts and colonies elsewhere, from the Cape of Good Hope to Java, the invaders could maintain themselves only by drawing heavily upon the new technology, with its guns, steel knives, machetes, and hardware of all kinds. From the beginning the mechanical New World sustained them; and with every fresh invention their debt to the machine became heavier, as the canal, the steamship, the railroad, the telegraph brought the two New Worlds ever closer together. The more prosperous the New World settlement, the less use it had for its own primitive foundations, once dearly prized, later sentimentally over-celebrated.

In the United States this contradiction between ideal aim and act characterized the westward march of the pioneer: one sees it even in the career of Audubon, a spirit deeply enamored of the wilderness, devoting his whole life to observing and depicting the birds and mammals of North America—but almost wrecking these intentions by sinking all his working capital into a steam sawmill, a premature mechanical enterprise that landed him in bankruptcy. The very immigrants who turned their backs to the seaboard settlements in search of independence and freedom, not merely demanded the active aid of the central government in establishing canals, highroads, and railroads; but called upon national troops to protect their settlements and to extrude, expropriate, and, when resisted, exterminate the aborigines who stood in their path. What were the Indian 'reservations' but early concentration camps?

Though the philosophers of the eighteenth-century Enlightenment, Diderot no less than Rousseau, believed in the natural goodness of man, the actual conduct of the New Exploration had demonstrated too often the Biblical truth that "the imagination of man's heart is evil from his youth." What Jehovah told Noah and his sons was equally true of New World man: "the fear of you and the dread of you shall be upon every beast of the earth, and upon every fowl of the air . . . and upon all the fishes of the sea; into your hands are they delivered."

These ancient words, as applied to the Americas, strike an ominous note whose significance was brought home by one of the greatest of exploratory scientists, Alexander von Humboldt. "In this paradise of the

American forests," he wrote, "as well as elsewhere, experience has taught all beings that benignity is seldom found together with power." That statement has universal application. Yet in the present century it was possible for the American historian Walter Webb to write a history of the American frontier, regarded by some eminent scholars as a classic work, emphasizing the frontier's contributions of wealth, freedom, power, with only two sentences on slavery, as a 'Secondary Windfall' in the whole work.

Nevertheless both the economic and the cultural gains from the new exploration were genuine, and one would do ill to belittle them, any more than to make light of the accompanying gains of technology. For the first time, in spite of all the ensuing errors and mischiefs, modern man became conscious of the planet that he occupied as a whole, in all its richness and diversity of habitats, ways of life, cultural achievements, ecological partnerships. Even the most brutal whaling voyage brought back, not merely oil and whalebone, but some knowledge of climates and ocean currents, of tropical fruits and vegetables, of Indians and Polynesians and Micronesians, who lived a different life, at a different tempo, and for a different purpose than the heirs of 'snivelization,' as one of Melville's characters in 'Redburn' called it.

Through this exploration the abstract cosmos of space and time and gravitation, established independently by scientific observations, with scientific instruments, was brought down to earth, an earth teeming with life. As the range of settlement widened, the astonishment and delight over nature's gifts grew: once the planet was opened up mankind proved far richer than the stay-at-homes had ever supposed. Von Humboldt, exploring the Orinocan forest, cannot conceal his excitement: within three months he had collected 1,600 plants and found 600 new species!

As never before, it would seem, a new curiosity, a new passion for discovery, a new delight in unearthing rare minerals, identifying strange plants, sampling exotic fruits and vegetables and collecting their seeds, seized Western man. The old paleolithic quest, with its finding and picking, its searching and collecting, its tasting and sampling, began anew on a grand scale. In North America passenger pigeons by tens of thousands blackened the sky; and in the prairies the strawberries grew so thick that the horses' fetlocks, one traveller reported, seemed covered with blood. For the New World man was first of all a prospector; and as a food gatherer he had an appetite for wild and gamy things. Even before A. R. Wallace, Audubon had tasted and sampled all the birds he killed: and reported that he found flickers disagreeable because they fed on ants, herring gulls too salty, but starlings delicate.

Once more Western man peered more intently and searchingly into what lay under his feet: not only seeking veins of marble or pockets of gold and silver, but likewise seams of coal, pools of mineral oil, mines of metalliferous ore; and in the course of these probings he uncovered and pondered over bones he had not had the wits or the scientific background to notice before, such as the bones of elephants in Siberia, where no wild ones were known. Looking farther afield, he found the huge remains of reptiles that, he later realized, had roamed the earth eons before the mammals appeared.

Though it was long before these scattered findings could be brought together and intelligently digested by the empirical and historical sciences, the story of the technical and scientific advances that were made after the sixteenth century cannot be properly told, still less evaluated, without reference to this exhaustive exhibition of the contents of the earth—an exploration that is still far from ended, since we have only begun to tap the depths of the earth and the sea, or to reckon with the vast but long-invisible world of microorganisms. To equate all our many-sided technical advances with the invention of the power loom, the steam engine, and similar mechanical agents, is to cover up a large part even of utilitarian progress.

From the sixteenth century on, the capital accumulation of first-hand knowledge of nature easily matched the increasing capital investments in ships and mines and mills and factories: and who shall say which brought higher returns? Many of the best minds in the arts joined in this search. Leonardo da Vinci, finding fossils in the Tuscan hills, laid the foundations for both geology and evolution, for he surmised that where the shells were found, the ocean in which they flourished must once have covered the land; while Dürer, according to Panofsky, collected bones, shells, quaintly shaped nuts, rare plants, and stones; and many other contemporaries established similar collections. Here, too, a start had been made in the Middle Ages, in terms of course of its own supernatural ideology: for what were the relics of saints, bits of hair and bone, patches of garments, vials of blood, wood from the true Cross, but examples of the same indiscriminately acquisitive spirit—and even the same appreciation of the magic and wonder of life through its most concrete if superstitious manifestations.

In the fifteenth century such collections became secular, and their patrons exhibited their 'cabinets of curiosities,' which kept on increasing and expanding until they became the public institutions we now call museums. The early Tradescant collection became famous, as did that of Sir John Soane, the London architect, in the eighteenth century, with its great variety of architectural objects. Living collections, in zoological gardens and botanic gardens, vied at the same time with those of inanimate objects. The voyages of Captain Cook to the Pacific Ocean—significantly, first planned for astronomical observation of the transit of Venus—brought back a rich store of botanical and anthropological information, as did Darwin's famous voyage in the 'Beagle.' Captain Cook would record that, even in the bleak Tierra del Fuego, his scientists, Mr. Banks and Dr.

Solander, returned from shore "with above an hundred different plants and flowers, all of them wholly unknown to the botanists of Europe."

In their fixation on the feats of the physical sciences and their related technologies, Victorian interpreters and many of their latter-day successors overlooked the immense importance for the later processes of industrialization performed by the new exploration. The organic sciences, zoology, botany, paleontology, with their exhaustive inventories of forms and species have been given a lower status than those that fall within the abstract framework of mathematics, mechanics, and physics. But it is time to redress this one-sided view: at every point in development the two modes of science, the concrete, the empirical, and the historical on one hand, and the abstract and mathematical and analytical on the other, have both been necessary for forming an adequate picture of reality. If anything, the finders and collectors have served the needs of life more fruitfully than the fabricators and the manipulators.

In short, long before the age of terrestrial discovery had reached a barren climax in a few daring acts like the ascent of Mount Everest or the on-the-spot identification ('discovery') of the North and South Poles, the adventurers and prospectors, the miners and hunters and collectors, the geologists and botanists and zoologists, had begun to put together, for the first time, a picture of the earth as not merely the dwelling place of man, but as the seat of organic evolution and the home, a rare and wonderful home, of life itself in all its concrete immensity and diversity. They brought forth long-buried achievements, to which the archaeologists and the paleo-anthropologists have been adding, during the last century, a crowning touch. Without this exploration, which brought together man's hitherto unplumbed past existence, and thereby opened up even greater future potentialities, man's sense of his own dignity and destiny would have been permanently overshadowed by the astronomical discoveries of the sixteenth century.

In the perspective of history, the cultural gains from the new exploration should count more heavily than the immediate material gains that came through trading beads and trinkets for furs, hides, and ivories, or through controlling the markets of decadent kingdoms and empires. The eventual economic wealth, through the opening up of immense areas of unexhausted land for cultivation, the cutting down of vast quantities of timber, and the exploiting of mineral resources of every kind was, of course, indisputable: but all these advances were only continuing—if at a faster pace—a movement already begun in the Middle Ages, and up to the nineteenth century had been little affected by New World wheat, maize, or cotton, or Australian wool. In the long run, it was the cultural interchanges that would prove important, and it was Western man's unreadiness for cooperative two-way intercourse—his egoism, his vanity, his reluctance to learn from those he conquered, and not least his calculated ferocity—that actually wiped out many of the potential advantages of the New Exploration.

Even from the standpoint of industry, Western man needed to explore the whole planet to make the fullest use of its technological potential. Turgot in the eighteenth century believed that Europe's 'mission' to colonize and civilize the world was a necessary requirement for its own development; and that belief, Frank Manuel points out, was shared even by such later reformers as Condorcet and Saint-Simon. And though in time Western man accomplished this, he would probably have been far more successful had he paid closer attention to the cultures he disrupted and destroyed; for in wrecking them he was reducing his own intellectual working capital. Though eighteenth-century industrialism did not need New World products to fabricate its new machines or utilize coal as a source of power—just the reverse, at first—by the nineteenth century the New World's contributions of maize and the potato and the yam made it possible to shift an increasing number of workers from farming to manufacture. In turn it was the New World market for textiles, brummagem jewelry, glass beads, and hardware that offered the most profitable outlets for mass production.

As for the debt of our present technology to primitive societies, it would remain huge if only a single contribution were taken into account: that made by the obscure tribe of Amazon Indians who had learned the uses of their native rubber plant and had produced, before the White Man encountered them, not merely rubber balls, but syringes and raincoats. No twentieth-century invention is more remarkable than this imaginative utilization of the rubber tree's sap: a feat even more spectacular than the first extraction of metals or the melting of glass. Without this primitive exploitation of the wild rubber plant, originally limited in its botanical distribution, the modern world would possess neither natural nor artificial rubber, for which the natural gum served as a model. And without rubber, obviously, all motor transport would screech to a halt. Still another contribution of 'primitive' cultures—Peruvian bark, the source of quinine—made it possible for Western man to gain a hold in the malaria-ridden areas of America, Africa, and Asia.

In sum, the last four centuries of prospecting and exploring have been fully as important to our major technological development as the fabrication of power machines or the development of electric communication. With the standard picture of 'the' Industrial Revolution as an affair primarily of coal, iron, and steam, the significance of this search has been belittled or completely overlooked. But only a small portion of the metals and rare earths necessary for an advanced technics exists on any one continent: manganese, magnesium, chromium, thorium, tungsten, platinum, iridium, aluminum, helium, uranium, to say nothing of petroleum and coal, have only a spotty planetary distribution. The discovery of these elements by chemists, and the opening up of these resources, was the necessary preliminary to any wider system of invention and fabrication. Even today, despite the near miracles performed by synthetic chemistry, manufacturing molecules to order, chemists and biologists are renewing the practice of systematically prospecting the seas, suspecting with good reason that the denizens of the ocean, some of whom learned to produce high-tension electricity long before man, have kept many other valuable secrets to themselves.

A few of these discoveries, be it noted, had a regressive side. Two of the oldest plants, the opium poppy and hemp—not discovered but spread further—had long been a bane to man. And though the new stimulants, tea, coffee, yerba maté, must be largely counted as benefits, perhaps even as active contributors to the intellectual vivacity of Europe from the seventeenth century onward, the worldwide adaptation of tobacco, not as a ceremonial incense as with simpler peoples, but as a chronic addiction, if not a neurotic compulsion, deliberately inculcated for commercial profit, must be put on the debit side. So, too, the abundance of grain and potatoes, which lowered the cost of making gin, whiskey, and vodka, encouraged periodic bouts of drunkenness, among the poor and exploited, as a means of offsetting the brutal industrial regimen.

But even with such qualifications and deductions, the advantages that accrued from this far-reaching territorial exploration and interchange were immense. And many of these redoubtable advantages owed little at first to mechanical industry: rather, the other way round. Without this vast increase in mineral resources, raw materials, and food plants, the changes usually attributed solely to the physical sciences and invention would have been retarded, or in some cases have proved impossible.

While all too little noted, the transoceanic explorations of Western man had still another effect: namely on the development of the exact sciences themselves. Long-distance sea voyages, out of sight of land for weeks at a time, demanded for their success more than a courage close to foolhardiness, though even the latter, as in the case of both the Norsemen and their Hawaiian contemporaries, seems to have been possible mainly through a close observation of the flight of land-based birds.

Navigational skill required exact science; it was on the sea that the main procedures of the scientific method itself were first worked out. It was the mariner's need for astronomical information, quite as much as the demands of astrological prediction, that turned the European mind to exact solar and stellar sightings. And it was the need for safety in approaching land, to take soundings and accurately record their measurements, that made quantitative observation a habit among seagoing peoples; while the need to respond to, and if possible forecast, the changes of weather led to constant observation of the clouds, the winds, the color and motion of the water. The plotting of the ship's course and the transcription of topographic data to maps instituted the higher bookkeeping of science. And finally, the keeping of the ship's log, the prompt record of observed events, set the meticulous pattern of the laboratory notebook, while the constant cartographic correction of hypothetical or sketchy information by closer firsthand observation again predated the methodology of the experimental sciences. All these practices were registered and re-enforced in the scientific mind. Modern science's original debt to navigation is no less than its debt to capitalist accountancy; and it was on that double foundation that the abstract structure which the seventeenth century identified with cosmic reality came into existence.

4: NEW WORLD UTOPIA

At the beginning, I suggested, the two forms of exploration, terrestrial and technological, had a common source, and for long remained in constant interplay. For a few centuries, Western man, or at least a wakeful minority, believed it would be possible to make the best of both worlds. We are now sufficiently far away from the original New World pictures, which linger only as after-images, to see that they did in fact have much in common.

Both movements, to begin with, were characterized by an unconcealed hostility to the past—though to different parts of the past: they openly gloried in discontinuity, if not in outright destruction. In the eighteenth century these contrasting attitudes were summed up in the personalities of Jean-Jacques Rousseau and Denis Diderot, the first exalting the primitive, the unsophisticated, the older peasant folkways, despising formalized order and favoring spontaneity and simplicity: the second, though personally hankering after the open sexual freedom of the Polynesians, trusting rather to the intelligence than to instincts and natural feelings, and eagerly investigating the processes of mechanical invention and production. The fact that these two men began as friends only underlines their symbolic roles.

Beneath both attitudes toward the past was the sense, which had appeared at earlier points in history, notably in the sixth century B.C., that formal civilization had somehow gone wrong; and that its most successful institutions had retarded and restricted, rather than furthered, the full development of man, though it had made possible great collective assemblages of manpower that transformed the environment and energized the mind—enterprises that no earlier tribal community or village had even dared to conceive.

The state, the official religion, the bureaucracy, the army, these resurgent institutions of civilization were capable indeed of effecting great constructive transformations of the environment, but the human price of their success was heavy: the class structure, the lifetime fixation of function, the monopoly of land and economic and educational opportunity, the inequalities of property and privilege, the chronic savagery of slavery and war, the fears and obsessions and paranoid ambitions of the ruling classes, culminating in mass destructions and exterminations. In short, a nightmare. Such constant miscarriages of power and organization offset the genuine claims that could be made for this system, and raised serious questions, at least in the minds of the oppressed and the enslaved, about the value of civilization itself. These doubts encouraged the notion that if only the past institutions and structures of civilization were destroyed, men would be happy, virtuous, and free. Rousseau expressed this idea in its most extreme form in his prize essay for the Academy at Dijon, in which he castigated the demoralizing effects of the arts and sciences, those features of civilization about which people had the fewest doubts.

The notion that many of the ways of civilization are in fact not beneficent but injurious had been expressed in one way or another in many of the Axial religions and philosophies, and had taken the form of a yearning for a more elemental mode of life—a return to the village, the bamboo grove, the desert, seeking detachment from the compulsions and harsh regimentations demanded by the megamachine as the price of wealth, 'peace,' and victory in war.

Once the traumatic effects of civilization were acknowledged, the elder prophets taught, one might be born again, and begin life over on a sound basis, defying sterile tradition, framing new laws, exploring strange environments, throwing off old restraints. These impulses were reaffirmed in that great migration to the wilderness areas that marked the colonization of the New World: for the pioneers perforce left civilization behind them and acted, as Longfellow put it, so that "each tomorrow finds us farther than today." That retreat, unfortunately, was open only to a venturesome minority.

The underlying notion of 'improvement by movement' curiously bound together both the roving frontiersmen of the New World and the mechanical pioneers, who have for the last three hundred years devoted no small part of their energies to speeding every form of mechanical transportation. 'The more rapid the movement the greater the improvement' was accepted as axiomatic. Behind both efforts was the belief that 'farther' meant not only farther away in space but farther away from the past. That part of the environment which came under the influence of Rousseau and his followers was, in so far as it sought primitive environments and simpler modes of getting a living, a return to a deliberately archaic existence: it was in effect an attempt to begin all over again at that point in paleo- and neolithic cultures before the new institutions of civilization had conquered and overwhelmed the small scattered farming communities.

For a brief period, almost a century, it looked as if this latter effort might partly succeed; and even when it succumbed to the new forces of industrialism, it left traces on American life that have not yet entirely disappeared—though they are now happily sublimated in the conservation movement, and in efforts to preserve residually some portion of the near-primeval wilderness.

The evidence for this brief success is known to all students of pioneer settlements. There, the class distinctions, the regimentation, the legalized inequalities of Old World institutions were, if not absent, at least only faintly and intermittently present. Not merely was arbitrary political power, as exercised under kingship and feudal authority, curbed by representative government, but in New England at least there was a healthy development of communal autonomy, alike in the congregation-governed churches, the free schools and libraries, and the Town Meeting that handled local public affairs. Living in small, partly self-contained communities, where each member was forced to count on his neighbors for help, whether to raise a roof or to shuck corn, or to band together, as in a mining camp, against desperadoes, they seemed for a while to have found a way to overcome the basically one-sided modes of class exploitation introduced by civilization. Even the economic division of labor tended under these conditions to disappear.

George Perkins Marsh, the linguist and geographer, one of the extraordinary minds that emerged from this background, observed in a lecture on the English language: "Except in mere mechanical matters, and even there far more imperfectly, we have adopted the principle of the division of labor to a more limited extent than any modern civilized nation. Every man is a dabbler, if not a master, in every knowledge. Every man is a divine, a physician, and a lawyer to himself, as well as a counsellor to his neighbors, in all the interests involved in the sciences appropriately belonging to these professions." Emerson's 'Essay on Self-Reliance' confirmed this attitude.

Marsh did not exaggerate, nor did he over-idealize, this condition. For a brief period, roughly between 1800 and 1860, or at latest 1880, it seemed that the principles of Rousseau and Diderot might, at least in a few favored areas, be effectively reconciled: the romantic and the utilitarian personality were learning to live side by side, not merely co-existing but prospering together. The typical figures of this period did not recoil from science, mechanical invention, or industrial organization: on the contrary, they embraced all these new potentialities within the framework of a larger life that included man's natural and his humanistic inheritance. While Thoreau, for example, responded to the natural environment, exploring every wood, field, and riverbank around Concord, he furthered his family business, pencil-making, by utilizing a new process for purifying graphite which he found in a scientific review. This same ready wholeness of response characterizes and unites the other leading minds of this New World galaxy: Audubon, Olmsted, Emerson, Marsh, Melville, Whitman. They were neither hermits nor primitives; but in their minds at least they had thrown off the frayed and soiled clothes of all previous civilizations.

This New World utopia, this promised land, was soon buried under the ashes and cinders that erupted over the Western World in the nineteenth century, thanks to the resurrection and intensification of all the forces that had originally brought 'civilization' itself into existence. The rise of the centralized state, the expansion of the bureaucracy and the conscript army, the regimentation of the factory system, the depredations of speculative finance, the spread of imperialism, as in the Mexican War, and the continued encroachment of slavery—all these negative movements not only sullied the New World dream but brought back on a larger scale than ever the Old World nightmares that the immigrants to America had risked their lives and forfeited their cultural treasures to escape.

As a result of this setback, the mechanical New World displaced the 'romantic' New World in men's minds: the latter became a mere escapist dream, not a serious alternative to the existing order. For in the meanwhile a new God had appeared and a new religion had taken possession of the mind: and out of this conjunction arose the new mechanical world picture which, with every fresh scientific discovery, every successful new invention, displaced both the natural world and the diverse symbols of human culture with an environment cut solely to the measure of the machine. This ideology gave primacy to the denatured and dehumanized environment in which the new technological complex could flourish without being limited by any human interests and values other than those of technology itself. All too soon a large portion of the human race would virtually forget that there had ever existed any other kind of environment, or any alternative mode of life.

5: THE CONTRAST WITH MEDIEVAL NATURALISM

To grasp the nature of this approaching ideological transformation one must contrast it with that which prevailed in Europe toward the end of the Middle Ages. Such rudimentary scientific knowledge as the Middle Ages possessed, beyond the elements of geometry and astronomy, was largely passed on through the medical schools, beginning with the most influential, that of Salerno. Apart from the direct experience of the organism that physicians necessarily have, the desire for knowledge of nature largely took the form of a series of questions, put almost at random, about the natural world.

Brian Lawn, in his treatise on the Salernitan Questions, referring to a late manuscript that seems to date from around 1300, observes that though these questions derive from many ancient sources, "not more than ten deal with abstract, Aristotelian physics and metaphysics, and only two deal with the soul or intellect." The questions as a whole, he points out, "are almost entirely confined to mundane subjects, such as anthropology, and medicine, zoology, botany, mineralogy, and alchemy experiments, meteorology, and geography. . . . Emphasis is laid on experiment and alchemy."

Only scholarly courtesy led Lawn to group these questions under what would now be the appropriate scientific disciplines, for positive science was still centuries away. The questions range from "Why does the resounding echo repeat words" and "Why is dry old age still prone to sleep?" to "How is it that milk or fish is changed into nourishment?" "Why does the savage unicorn curb his fierce wrath with the virgin's embrace?" or "What causes rain, winds, and lofty clouds?" These questions characterize minds that were only beginning to awaken to the natural world: still confused, still unable to take their bearings, still largely dependent upon Greek and Roman tradition, even for the questions themselves. Compare these questions with the medieval artist's accurate answers: This is ivy, this is a hunting dog, this is a peasant mowing, this is a sly old priest. Though in both cases the mind was handicapped for lack of an abstract framework and method, the craftsman was nearer to nature and a science based on nature than the learned scholar, putting these random questions in Latin verse.

Not that the medieval mind lacked facility for dealing with abstractions: quite the contrary. In 'Science and the Modern World,' A. N. Whitehead, himself a distinguished mathematician and philosopher, pointed out that the extraordinary refinement of abstract thought among Christian theologians, with their deep faith in an orderly, coherent, and intelligible world, provided the strongest possible underpinning for rational science: since scholastic theology not only presumed a corresponding rationality in the universe, but assured the investigator who took it for granted of his ultimate success. What distinguishes the system of the logical abstractions developed by the scholastics from those that scientists later developed was that the real world, for the medieval mind, was the invisible one: that toward which all earthly life was only a preparation.

The ultimate concern of the Axial religions with death, with non-being, with an 'after-life,' deprived these religious abstractions of any immediate application to technology—though no small part of the mental energy of the great minds of this period was spent in forging ingenious links, or rather weaving gossamer threads of connection, between these ultimate abstractions—God, the Holy Ghost, angels, immortality, Heaven, Hell— and the concrete civic and domestic practice of the community.

Science itself, and with it, later, a science-oriented technology, did not begin to flourish until the medieval ability to deal logically with imaginary entities and hypothetical relationships came back through fresh developments in mathematics. The question of how many angels could dance on the point of a pin no longer is absurd in molecular physics, with its discovery of how broad that point actually is, and what a part invisible electronic 'messengers' play in the dance of life. What medieval theology lacked was not rigorous abstractions but a coeval ability to enter into and understand concretions, in all the richness and density and integrity that organized life presents.

Here esthetic naturalism had a contribution to make. The most limited handicraft worker, if he wished to qualify for his guild, still had to report to his masters on coming back from his travels what he had seen with his own eyes and copied with his own hands. Artist-craftsmen transferred this new knowledge to images in stone, wood, and painted parchment: on church porches and pews, in calendars and Books of Hours, one finds scene after scene from daily life, not treated as an evidence of some more ultimate spiritual revelation, but enjoyed immediately as direct bearers of both esthetic form and spiritual meaning.

"The sculptors of gargoyles and chimeras," as Lynn Thorndike observed, "were not content to reproduce existing animals but showed their command of animal anatomy by creating strange compound and hybrid monsters—one might almost say, evolving new species—which nevertheless have all the verisimilitude of copies from living forms. It was these breeders in stone, these Burbanks of the pencil, these Darwins with the chisel, who knew nature and had studied botany and zoology in a way superior to the scholar who simply pored over the works of Aristotle and Pliny."

This recovery of nature through observation and exact representation preceded the 'revival of learning' and was far closer to the original Greek tradition of science than the sedulous imitations of dead classic forms or the pious reading of time-worn and mangled Greek texts. Arising out of daily work in the free cities, under the guidance of autonomous guilds which had evolved high standards of workmanship and competence, this process of naturalization continued to grow; and it is not surprising that by the sixteenth century it had developed further in the transformation of the craftsman into the full-fledged artist, alike a worker, a thinker, an organizer, and a creator, exploring every aspect of experience in or outside his trade by the same method.

The artists of the Renascence opened a direct passage from 'naturalization' to 'humanization': first the Holy Trinity takes on purely human form, then the saints and the pagan gods begin to disappear, too, leaving the natural landscape of Ruysdael and Constable, the natural man of Rembrandt or Hogarth, or even the lowly peasants of the brothers Le Nain, as a sign that every part of the natural world open to human culture had been entered. In this process the craftsman and the artist had preceded by whole centuries the natural philosophers or scientists. What is more, the new mechanical inventions of the clock and the printing press exercised a profound influence upon the scientific mind.

Not surprisingly, in the final articulation of the New World picture, it was an earlier advance in medieval technics—the development of glass lenses—that brought about the decisive change; for the astronomical observations that were first made with such difficulty by Copernicus and Tycho Brahe, using the naked eye, were vastly widened and the process itself was lightened, through the invention of the telescope. Heliocentrism was accepted slowly: indeed it had little effect upon the learned world for a century after Copernicus: even today the common-sense view, that the sun moves around the earth, suffices for most men. But the telescope and the microscope made a profound difference; for the infinite and the infinitesimal, the macrocosm and the microcosm, ceased to be merely speculative concepts: they revealed, at least potentially, the ideal limits of significant visual experience.

These two artifacts of glass technics wrought a far more radical transformation of human life than did the steam engine. What had once been purely religious concepts attached to an after-life—infinity, eternity, immortality—were now related to actual time and space. With that, the once enclosed, self-contained and self-centered world of Christian theology was no longer credible. But religion itself was not excluded: for a new religion had in fact secretly come into existence: so secretly that its most devout worshippers still do not recognize that it is in fact a religion.

CHAPTER TWO

Return of the Sun God

1: SOLAR THEOLOGY AND SCIENCE

So much for the long series of technological changes that, beginning perhaps as early as the eleventh century, came to a climax in the 'Age of Exploration.' But as it happened, the most decisive technical improvements that took place in the sixteenth and seventeenth centuries lay outside the immediate province of technology: for the great event that presided over all other activities and transformed the Western outlook upon life was a religious phenomenon: the return of the Sky Gods, and especially the Sun God.

Not that the religion of the Sun God had ever entirely disappeared: in the new institutional practices derived from solar theology, which took shape in the Pyramid Age, the major outlines of the great civilizations had been traced, and the practice of this religion of the Sky Gods, centered in the person and authority of the Divine King, had spread, whether by spontaneous re-invention or by actual human contact through persons or ideas, over the entire earth: exercising political and military control, and performing by means of great collective machines astounding feats of geotechnics: building canals, irrigation systems, massive walls, temples, and cities.

The deity that presided over the new religion and the new mechanical world picture was no less than Atum-Re, the self-created Sun, who out of his own semen had conceived the universe and all its subordinate deities—except more ancient Nun or Ptah—without the aid of the female principle. To establish the directness of this succession one need only remember that it was in the course of correcting the astronomical calculations of the Greco-Egyptian astronomer Ptolemy (second century A.D.) that Copernicus arrived at the notion that the earth, instead of being the center of the universe, actually swept in a predictable orbit around the sun. By giving the sun a central position, Copernicus was in effect a better Egyptian than Ptolemy.

If there is any one point at which one may say the modern world picture was first conceived as the expression of a new religion and the basis of a new power system, it was in the fifth decade of the sixteenth century. For not merely was Nicolaus Copernicus' 'De Revolutionibus Orbium Coelestium' published, but likewise Vesalius' treatise on anatomy, 'De Humani Corporis Fabrica' (also 1543), Jerome Cardan's algebra, 'The Great Art' (1545), and Fracastoro's enunciation of the germ theory of disease, 'De Contagione et Contagiosis Morbis' (1546). Scientifically speaking, that was the decade of decades: unrivalled until our own century. If the reader doubts that this was a religious as well as a scientific and ultimately a technological revolution, let him withhold his dissent till I have assembled the proofs.

The usual way of interpreting the Copernican revolution is to assume that its most shattering effect was to break down the theological assumption that God had made the earth the center of the universe and that man was the ultimate object of his attention. If the sun was actually the center, then the whole structure of dogmatic Christian theology—with its unique act of creation, with the human soul as the central interest of God, and man's moral probation on earth in preparation for eternity as the divine consummation of God's will—threatened to collapse.

Viewed through the new glasses of science, man shrank in size: in terms of astronomical quantities the human race counted for little more than an ephemeral swarm of midges on the planet itself. By contrast, science, which had made this shattering discovery by the mere exercise of common human faculties, not divine revelation, became the only trustworthy source of authentic and reputable knowledge. But such conclusions, however obvious they may seem now, were not immediately made by those who were most deeply captivated by the new religion. For three centuries Western man tried to make the best of both worlds without transcending in thought their self-imposed limitations.

The immediate effect of the new theology was quite different: it helped to bring back to life, or to rejuvenate, the old components of the power system deriving ultimately from the Pyramid Age in both Egypt and Mesopotamia. As in the first volume of 'The Myth of the Machine,' I do not confine the term Pyramid Age strictly to Egyptian culture, or to the four centuries (2700–2300 B.C.) when pyramids of increasing size were actually built. I use it rather as a brief way of referring to the changes that took place during the Fourth Millennium B.C., both in Egypt and Mesopotamia, marked by a typical constellation of institutions and cultural inventions: the cult of Divine Kingship, astronomical time measurement, the written record, the division and specialization of labor, organized conquest by war, and the building of imposing monumental structures, temples, palaces, walled cities, canal and irrigation systems: not least the assemblage of the once-invisible Megamachine.

While Egypt is the classic locus of the Pyramid Age, this usage does not imply either unique Egyptian leadership or the direct influence of Egypt on any other culture. Yet the fact that this complex of institutions, if not always the Pyramid form itself, is found later in widely separated cultures, not only in China, Turkestan, and Iran, but in Cambodia, Thailand, Peru, and Mexico, would seem to justify this special designation.*

By resuming its ancient central position in the minds of the ruling classes, the sun actually became God once more. This took place not merely because the sun was the chief source of power on earth, as it actually is, but because the sun was the central point of reference in the motions of the planets, including the earth; the mechanical regularity already achieved in machines, above all, in clockwork, provided the miniature replicas of absolute cosmic order. In the course of less than a century the sun changed its position in the minds of learned observers: it was no longer a satellite or servant, but the master of human existence.

In terms of the new deity all complex phenomena must be reduced to the measurable, the repetitive, the predictable, the ultimately controllable; first in the mind but eventually in the organization of daily life. The Sun God, the symbol of centralized power, became the model of perfection for all human institutions; and the priesthood of science, whose mathematical measurements had first disclosed and utilized this source of cosmic order lacked the faintest premonitions of the possible consequences. In all innocence, astronomy and celestial mechanics laid the foundation for a more absolute order, political and industrial, similar point for point to that which underlay the Pyramid Age. But four centuries were needed before the great pharaonic invention of the Pyramid Age, the megamachine, could be assembled again.

The association of the new astronomy with the revival of divine kingship and centralized political power was no mere accident, still less is it a meretricious conceit. The greatest Western monarch of the seventeenth century, Louis XIV, despite his piety as a Catholic prince, dramatized his absolute authority by calling himself Le Roi Soleil, the Sun King. And even before Louis XIV, Norden, in 'A Christian Familiar Comfort' compared the State to Heaven and Queen Elizabeth and the Council to the Primum Mobile or controlling sphere. "The roi soleil is indeed," adds Tillyard, "one of the most persistent of all Elizabethan commonplaces." Once this central authority was established, the other functionaries of the ancient

* For a fuller discussion, see the section Archetypes or Genes? in 'The City in History,' page 90, and Chapters Eight, Nine, and Ten in 'The Myth of the Machine,' Volume One.

system all reappeared, dressed in only slightly different costume: the priest-hood, the army, the bureaucracy. With their assistance, the whole cult became operative again, working toward a system of absolute power capable of conquering and controlling great masses of men, widening the bounds of "humane empire," as Francis Bacon said, to the "effecting of all things possible."

The first mark of the Sun God's ascendancy, then, came not in tech-nics, but in government: the new religion re-enforced both ideologically and practically the belief in power, inordinate and unqualified power. "Scientific thought," Bertrand Russell once observed, correctly interpreting 'The Scientific Outlook,' "is essentially power thought—the sort of thought that is to say whose purpose, conscious or unconscious, is to give power to its possessor." The worship of the Sun God was the outcome of the same constellation of interests that had prompted and revived observation of the planets in astrology.

Now astrology had long before been condemned by Saint Augustine and other Christian theologians as a pagan superstition, incompatible with belief in God's exclusive providence and man's free will. With the later corrosion of Christian faith, astrology assumed a special role as a supple-mentary religion; and the pursuit of occult information, based on the correlation of the exact hour of a person's birth with the conjunction of the planets, demanded not merely exact time measurements but close observa-tions of the heavens. Thus astrology fostered astronomy, as alchemy fostered chemistry. These pursuits were more important by reason of the method than for their reputed results. Copernicus and Kepler both cast horoscopes; and it was by such close observation of planetary movements, as well as by tedious mathematical calculation, that Tycho Brahe con-firmed Copernicus' conclusions and made possible Kepler's final correction.

From the beginning astronomy had flourished under court patronage. The establishment of the solar calendar was from the outset one of the substantial attributes of royal authority wherever kingship spread; and it was a generation after Copernicus' treatise that in 1582 the spiritual monarch of Christendom, the Pope of Rome, ordered the latest revision of the calendar. It is not for nothing that the Vatican still maintains its own astronomer, if only to regulate its movable feasts. Every European court had its 'astrologer in residence,' just as their predecessors had done in Egypt and Babylonia thousands of years before. Without this intense inter-est in astrology, science would not have received the support that it enjoyed from kings and men of affairs: a support that belies the popular notion that modern science originally had a difficult uphill fight.

But astrology made still another contribution to exact science: it established as a canon of faith a belief in the strictest sort of determinism; for it interpreted singular life events in terms of collective statistical probabilities, based on data originally gathered from a mass of individual biographies, collected and collated, it is reported, by royal mandate. Thus royal patronage had not merely promoted star-gazing but laid the groundwork for the more austere and pragmatically useful determinism of the physical sciences. Once firmly embedded in the mind, this unprovable assumption would even lead a proud mathematician to boast that from a sufficient knowledge of a single event the position and state of every other particle in the universe could be predicted. That unfortunate exhibition of intellectual *hubris* laid the foundation at an early date for the dubious alliance between scientific determinism and authoritarian control that now menaces human existence.

What astronomy did under the original influence of astrology was to transform a purely religious concept of Heaven, attached to an after-life—infinity, eternity, immortality—to the observable movements of physical bodies travelling through boundless space whose distance increased with each further improvement of the telescope. The enclosed, self-contained, man-centered world of Christian revelation was in this new perspective no longer credible. That this new world, which gave primacy to light and energy and motion, was quite as subjective and anthropomorphic as the older view remained to be discovered. But there is no doubt about the immediate effect upon the astronomers themselves. As Butterfield observes: "Copernicus rises to lyricism and almost to worship when he writes about the regal nature and central position of the sun." It was in this state of emotional exaltation that the Sun God was reborn and the ancient megamachine reassembled and eventually rebuilt.

Though Galileo was no mystic like Johannes Kepler, and though he was reluctant to disturb the prevailing Ptolemaic description of the planetary movements, he shared the same emotions as Copernicus, all the more because the newly invented telescope brought him much closer to the fixed and moving objects in the sky. "He who gazes highest is of the highest quality," said Galileo; and in the dedication of his 'Dialogue on the World Systems' he proudly added: "The turning to the great book of nature, which is the proper object of philosophy, is the way to make one look high. . . . Hence if ever any persons might claim to be signally distinguished for their intellect from other men, Ptolemy and Copernicus were they that had the honor to see farthest and discourse most profoundly of the world systems."

Unfortunately, in seeking to read the book of nature more faithfully, the new thinkers repeated the error made by Thales and Aristarchus: unthinkingly, they banished the thinker himself from the picture as peremptorily and arbitrarily as Socrates, and after him the Christian theologians, had turned their backs on nature. Not until astronomers discovered that a source of error in their observations was the length of time it took the nervous system to transmit a message from the eye to the brain did they realize that no part of the external world was wholly extraneous to man, or could be investigated except by utilizing man's physiological aptitudes and cumulative cultural inventions—that the very notion of a universe independent of man was itself a peculiarly human achievement, dependent upon human history and human consciousness.

Plainly, it was not the new truths that astronomy disclosed about the vastness of physical nature, but old truths man neglected about himself that diminished his stature and importance. Those who looked upward and outward and forward, and were prepared to traverse astronomical distances, forgot to look downward and inward and backward: the Sun God had dazzled and blinded them into conceiving scientific reality as a landscape without figures—forgetting the artists who had spent countless generations painting it, and without whom the universe in its vastness was literally unthinkable.

The new world that astronomy and mechanics opened up was in fact based upon a dogmatic premise that excluded from the outset not only the presence of man but the phenomena of life. On this new assumption the cosmos itself was primarily a mechanical system capable of being fully understood by reference solely to a mechanical model. Not man but the machine became the central feature in this new world picture: hence the chief end of human existence was to confirm this system by utilizing and controlling the energies derived from the sun, reshaping every part of the environment in conformity to the Sun God's strict commands. In the acceptance of this mechanical orthodoxy man was to find his salvation.

Though the religion of the Sun God, which shaped the new power complex, was to have immense practical consequences—political, military, economic—it would be an error to believe that these were the motives originally in view: it was the numinous and luminous aspects of astronomy, achieved by its very detachment from pressing human concerns, that seemed to offer a new promise of salvation, not tainted by corrupt human motives. In a world still embattled in relentless theological controversy and enmeshed in ideological confusions, the new astronomy brought a clarifying order that in itself evoked—to use a then-current phrase—the "music of the spheres."

This new world of light and space, disinfected of the human presence, was until our own time a refuge from the dogmatic brawls and savage religious persecutions that characterized the sixteenth and seventeenth centuries. As late as the eighteenth century, indeed, the words most often on the lips of scientists, when they contemplated the new system of nature so majestically revealed by Newton, were "order" and "beauty." Though the silence of infinite space frightened Pascal, it was this very silence and distance that gave comfort to many harassed spirits.

If one ignores the religious aura that hung over the great scientific discoveries in the period between Copernicus and Newton and never entirely faded away, one misses the hidden subjective contribution of the new outlook and its great source of sacred power. While the Christian Heaven shrank, the astronomical heaven expanded. Such mighty changes as have taken place during the last three centuries could proceed only from a profound religious re-orientation, one that permeated every aspect of existence. Only on such assumptions can one account for the immense authority that the astronomical and mechanical world picture exerted—and still exerts—over many of the most able minds.

Unfortunately, just as behind the terrestrial exploration stalked demonic and criminal impulses that crippled its utopian hopes, so behind the benign order and geometric beauty of the new science an ancient power system had begun to re-establish itself, on a scale never before conceivable. So far from reducing human affairs to insignificance and discouraging all worldly ambitions, the new cult paradoxically promoted an immense concentration on the mastery of earthly life: exploration, invention, conquest, colonization, all centered on immediate fulfillment. Now, not the hereafter, was what counted.

In fixing their gaze on the sky and on the movements of physical bodies, the scientific revolutionists were only continuing an austere religious tradition that goes back to the beginnings of civilization, if not before: and more immediately, they were resuming a practice that looks back to the Greeks. When Pythagoras was asked why he lived, he answered: "To look at heaven and nature." That struck the new scientific note. Similarly, Anaxagoras, de Santillana points out, when accused of caring naught for his kind and his own city, replied by pointing at the heavens and saying: "There is my country." The exchange of the Christian's universe, focussed on man's existence and his ultimate salvation, for a purely impersonal universe without a God except the blazing sun itself, without a visible purpose or desirable human destination, might seem a bad bargain: indeed, a pitiable loss. But it had the compensatory effect of making science the only source of meaning, and the achievement of scientific truth the only ultimate purpose.

Dr. Henry A. Murray has given this skyward orientation a name, Ascensionism: he associates it not only with the practices of astronomy, but with a general psychal orientation toward brightness, levitation, flying, climbing, upward pointing and moving, perhaps even with hierarchic order in which the highest unit or the highest person represents the utmost in power, intelligence, or numinous authority. But Murray has also pointed

out that the actual environment becomes more empty of living organisms
as one ascends toward the symbolic mountaintop, and the air likewise
becomes rarer and harder to breathe: less capable both physically and
figuratively of supporting human life. It is not by accident but by inner
necessity that, in order to do justice to the forces of life, in the Egyptian
pantheon the Sun God, Atum-Re, was counterbalanced by Osiris the
friend of man, the teacher of agriculture and handicrafts, the god of life
and death, of burial, resurrection, and renewal: that god who in another
form became the center of the Christian universe.

For those who may still feel that I am exaggerating the subjective,
emotional, religious attractions of the new cosmic order that centered in
the sun, let me cite the words of Kepler. They are all the more persuasive
since, in his scientific capacity, Kepler was able to overcome an old ideological bias in favor of a perfect figure like the circle sufficiently to discover, after many efforts to evade this conclusion, that the actual orbit of
the earth about the sun was an elliptic one. Listen, then, to his description
of the sun, in which the two heavens, the ancient one of Christian theology
and the new one of astronomy and exact science, merge and become one.

"In the first place," he says, "lest perchance a blind man deny it to you,
of all bodies in the universe the most excellent is the sun, whose essence is
nothing less than the purest light, than which there is no greater star: which
single and alone is the producer, conserver, and warmer of all things: it is a
fountain of light, rich in fruitful heat and most fair, limpid, and pure to the
sight, the source of vision, portrayer of all colours, though himself empty
of colour, called king of the planets for his motion, heart of the world for
his power, its eye for his beauty, and which alone we should judge worthy
of the Most High God, should he be pleased with a material domicile and
choose a place in which to dwell with the blessed angels."

Much of this description is of course factual; but Kepler's rhetoric is
the language of religious adoration, perfervid, exalted. And it does not
weaken the case for regarding sun-worship as the renascent religion to
discover that Copernicus and Kepler were not alone. Tillyard, again, points
out that the sun in Elizabethan times was widely considered the material
counterpart of God. The contemporary author of the 'Cursor Mundi,'
indeed, came close to downright heresy from any Christian view, for he
described the sun as God the Father, the sphere of the fixed stars as the
Son, and the intervening 'etherial medium' as the Holy Ghost.

By a queer accident, the time-span between Copernicus' treatise on the
revolution of the planets and Newton's law of gravitation was roughly the
same as that between the building of the first Step Pyramid in Egypt
and the construction of the Great Pyramid at Giza. "Where history is on the
march, thanks to kings, heroes, or empires," Mircea Eliade observes, "the
sun is supreme."

No one can doubt that history was on the march in the Western world from the sixteenth century on, or that it was the kings of Portugal, Spain, England, and France, monarchs by 'divine right,' who seized the initiative in conquering and colonizing with their own peoples large portions of the planet. Meanwhile the more circumscribed ventures of the Venetians, the Genoese, the Florentines, or the Hansa cities, the leaders in the first wave of migrations and conquests, faded away, for they were unfavored by the magic of divine kingship, and therefore unattached to the new cosmic seat of power and the myth that supported it. In establishing the sun as the center of the planetary system, Copernicus unwittingly had likewise made Europe the center of the twin New Worlds that had come into existence at the same time: the New World of geographic exploration and the New World of the machine. The latter proved to be an even greater and richer empire, open to colonization by the mind, than that claimed by military conquest and settlement.

Eventually one particular place in Europe, the astronomical observatory at Greenwich, became the recognized fixed point for time reckoning in both new worlds; and by the opening of the twentieth century Britain was the center of the only global empire in history, since, unlike Genghis Khan's domain, it was the only one that could honestly boast that the sun never set on its territory. But the claim was presumptuous and, as with all the other contemporary colonial dominions, the new establishment proved ephemeral: as it turned out, the recent removal of this observatory from its original site has coincided, with poignant if unintended symbolism, with the decline of the British Empire. This historic parallelism is almost too exact.

Three centuries passed before the full consequences of this transformation were worked out, or could be taken in as an interrelated whole: that is, before the regularities observed in the heavens, even in such an event as the predicted trajectory of Halley's comet, which duly returned on schedule, could be transmitted to every mode of organization, mechanical or human. In order to understand the immense consequences of the changes that confront us today, some of which threaten to arrest or even totally destroy the possibilities of further human development, we must trace in detail the subjective and ideological foundations of these twin New World explorations. In the chapters that follow I purpose to center attention almost exclusively on the New World of the machine, and on the human consequences of this technology to the "life, prosperity, and health" of modern man.

Now, the seeds that suddenly flowered in the sixteenth century had long been buried in the soil, ready to sprout at the right moment. There was not a single idea in the new scientific and mechanical system that had not existed in some form before. Celestial mechanics, astronomical measurement, heliocentrism, empirical observation and experiment, the discovery that the earth itself was a spheroid, the belief that change alone is real and stability an illusion (Heraclitus), that matter, however massive, is composed of minute particles like motes dancing in the sun, the atomism of Leucippus and Democritus, of Epicurus and Lucretius—in short the main assumptions of post-sixteenth-century science—had all been formulated, if only crudely, by the Egyptians, Babylonians, Chinese, Greeks, Romans, Arabs, before the separate shards were dug up again and pieced together. What is more, the two key sciences, astronomy and geometry, were an integral part of medieval higher learning with its special gift for handling metaphysical abstractions.

But a moment came—a 'moment' prolonged for perhaps two centuries —when these valuable insights interacted and coalesced under direct influence of the Sun God into a single system of power and organization: represented in diagrammatic form by the depersonalized mechanical world picture. That diagram, so widely applied in technics—and so usefully applicable—was then mistaken for reality itself. In turn, purely mechanical forms were superimposed upon every manifestation of life, thereby suppressing many of the most essential characteristics of organisms, personalities, and human communities. This mechanistic conversion proved all the easier because the older myths and confused collective dreams were themselves fading away before the rising sun itself. All this had far-reaching consequences.

Whereas many of the older ideologies had mistakenly accepted a static, earth-centered world, with only the most limited possibilities of change, mostly of a cyclical or apocalyptic order, the new ideology fostered an intense interest in space, time, motion, in their widest cosmic setting, not the setting in which organisms actually function in their earthly habitat, intermingled with other organisms, and pursuing their own further life-potentialities. Abstract motion took possession of the Western mind. The rotation of the earth, the majestic geometric path of the planets, the swing of the pendulum, the arc described by hurtling projectiles, the exact motions of clockwork, the rotations of water wheels, the accelerated motion of sailing ships or land vehicles—all these now commanded interest in their own right. Speed shortened time: time was money: money was power. Farther and farther, faster and faster, became identified with human progress.

The language of daily speech no longer sufficed to describe this insistently dynamic world or served to direct it. For this purpose new symbols and logical operations were needed, those of algebra, trigonometry, the differential calculus, vector analysis. While there is no real analogy between a planetary system and a machine, they share the properties of motion and measurability; and so the abstract advances first made in astronomy and mechanics proved serviceable, both in direct and roundabout ways, to mechanical invention in every department; for in both it was necessary to exclude qualitative organic factors and concentrate upon quantities. This relation was reciprocal: the increasing use of artillery in warfare called for better scientific data to make sighting more accurate, and this in turn called for the spyglass to supplement the naked human eye. Precisely the same kind of military demand led to the development of the computer today.

So it is hardly strange that the arsenal at Venice served as one of Galileo's best laboratories and that his observation of the swaying lamp in the cathedral at Pisa brought about the application of the pendulum to the improvement of time-keeping in clocks. In turn, metaphors and analogies derived from the machine were applied shrewdly, if coarsely, to organisms: to reduce life to its quantitative mechanical and chemical components seemed an infallible method of eliminating the ultimate mystery of life itself. Among the most original and fruitful contributions to the study of living organisms in the seventeenth century were Harvey's observations on the circulation of the blood, whereby he described the heart as a pump with pipes called veins and arteries, whose blood flow was regulated by valves; while Borelli made similar efforts to interpret the locomotion of animals in equally mechanical terms. Both were admirable contributions, as long as their descriptive limitations were not taken as those of the living organism itself; for life was the 'filterable virus' that teasingly escaped through the pores of this new mechanical container.

This new outlook did not take possession of society by any sudden break-through: it is only in retrospect that events of the sixteenth century assemble themselves in a recognizable 'mechanical' pattern. Rather, the new ideology seeped into the common mind through a thousand cracks and fissures, against which no peremptory prohibitions of ecclesiastical edicts, aimed at a single book or a special doctrine, could in the long run have any effect.

Actually, despite conflicts and skirmishes with the Church, science produced no martyrs—though there were in fact religious martyrs, like Michael Servetus, and humanist martyrs, like Giordano Bruno. The fate of the latter, who defiantly challenged the Church's doctrines, contrasts with that of Copernicus, Galileo, Kepler, and Descartes, who discreetly side-stepped martyrdom, and who therefore could not be effectively silenced. Fear of the implacable Inquisition, it is true, often delayed publication and retarded the circulation of fresh knowledge; but pride and vanity on the part of individual scientists, seeking to establish priority and concealing fresh discoveries in anagrams and similar disguises, played a similar part in the retardation of new ideas. Whatever the Church might say or do, the fact is that kings and emperors, from Frederick II of Sicily onward, repeatedly accorded scientists their favor.

Once, indeed, scientists decided to exclude theology, politics, ethics, and current events from the sphere of their discussions, they were welcomed by the heads of state. In return—and this remains one of the black marks against strict scientific orthodoxy with its deliberate indifference to moral and political concerns—scientists habitually remained silent about public affairs and were outwardly if not ostentatiously 'loyal.' Thus their mental isolation made them predestined cogs in the new megamachine. Aware of this political neutrality, Napoleon I, while he favored mathematicians and physical scientists, distrusted humanists and excluded them from his circle as troublemakers.

Even under the provocation of the military misuses of nuclear power as an instrument of genocide by the United States government in 1945, the nuclear physicists, however humanly apprehensive and morally concerned not a few of them were, never went so far as to propose a general strike of scientists and technicians. Only a brave minority disdained the patronage and the rewards that the government offered for their acquiescence, if not their active cooperation. Science, I repeat, produced many 'saints,' dedicating their lives with monastic devotion to their discipline—but no notable rebellious martyrs against the political establishment. Yet, as we shall note later, that alienation and renunciation are at last perhaps under way.

2 : NEW WORLD DREAMS VERSUS OLD WORLD REALITIES

These, then, in barest outlines, were the two New Worlds that took possession of Western man in the sixteenth century, the geographic New World and the mechanical New World. And to these I have ventured to add a third New World, the New World of historic time, which has during the last few centuries widened the entire human horizon. This conquest of time has in subtle ways changed modern man's perspective and opened new possibilities of releasing him from the grip of his unconscious past, with its buried traumas and its futile repetition of attested errors. But that consummation still lies ahead.

What I purpose to account for now is the way in which the first two initiatives went wrong, in their translation from imagined possibilities and projects to their actual expression. How is it that the period of terrestrial exploration and settlement was conducted with such flagrant brutality, with such disregard for traditional human values, with so little regard for the future, though it was usually in the name of a better future that so much of this effort was made? And how is it that the development of science and invention, with its intent to liberate man from the burdens of heavy toil on a meager subsistence level, imposed new burdens, new diseases, new deprivations, in a routine that lacked all direct contact with the sun and the sky and other living creatures, including his own kind?

In short, how did the brave new world of Shakespeare's 'The Tempest' become the derisive 'Brave New World' of Aldous Huxley—now vulgarly pictured as the inexorable destiny of modern man? To these questions no one can yet give more than a tentative and imperfect answer. Yet certain clues to this gross miscarriage are not lacking. Both movements came during a period when in Europe the great fabric of Christian belief, embodied in the ceremonies, rituals, dogmas, and daily practices of the Church, had begun to disintegrate. By the seventeenth century conditions in Western Europe had so far improved that the morbid fear and anxiety, the despair and disillusion, that had prompted the spread of Christianity throughout the Roman Empire no longer tallied with reality. For the moment, the Dance of Death seemed over: so it was no longer in Heaven, but on earth, that men began again to look for salvation; and it was not by prayer and good works and divine grace, but by their own strenuous and systematic efforts that they sought to improve their condition.

Gradually Heaven, that shining place in the mind, faded from the sky: it was to the stars and planets that kings, councillors, and learned men turned to foretell their fate and map their courses accordingly. Even earlier, when Louis XI asked his trusted courtier, de Joinville, whether he would rather be healthy in this life and be damned for eternity, or be a leper and be saved, Joinville unhesitatingly rejected salvation at the price of leprosy. That was a secret turning point.

Whatever their adhesion to the outward ceremonies of the Church or their belated profession in the panic of their deathbeds, more and more people began to act as if their happiness, their prosperity, their salvation were to be achieved on the earth alone, by means they themselves would if possible command. If God was not dead, man at least had become alive with new bodily vigor, confident, audacious, sexually exuberant, climbing mountains he had once feared, traversing seas that had never before beckoned him, and in general, as I have observed before, translating five of the seven deadly Christian sins into positive virtues, topped by pride, the special sin that caused Lucifer's fall from Heaven.

Centuries passed before the New World ideology displaced verbal professions of Christian faith; and to make the passage to the New World of the machine slower, a counter movement to recover the inner life took place, beginning with the Franciscans and the Waldensians, then with later protestant sects, while saintly rebels within the Church managed, at the height of New World aggression, in Peru, in Yucatán, in Paraguay, to recapture, in their care for the pagan natives themselves, some modicum of Christian grace and even began there to preserve some written memorial of the life they had once lived.

But in the end the new forces triumphed: power in all its forms went to men's heads like the strong drinks, brandy and whiskey, they had recently learned to distill.

Freed from the Christian superego—or too often perversely incited by this superego—murder and lust became rampant under the guise of missionary zeal. Exploration was merely the first stage of exploitation; and with it came back war, slavery, economic pillage and piracy, and environmental destruction: the ancient trauma of 'civilization,' which has been imprinted upon every 'advanced' culture ever since. The discovery that the world is always at the mercy of merciless men had been made by those Fifth Millennium hunting chiefs and proto-monarchs whose bloody maces had subdued the unarmed gardeners and farmers of Egypt and Sumer; and in the very act of inventing, organizing, and diffusing the genuine goods of civilization, some of which, like iron tools, eventually benefited the conquered groups, the new power complex only repeated and magnified the errors of the old.

Yet with every step forward that Western man made into the New World, with its promise of natural abundance, social equality, personal autonomy, mutual aid—and all these brave, vivid promises, newly made, seemed within the pioneer's grasp—he took two steps backward into his 'civilized' but savagely brutalized past, and repeated methodically all the sins that had accompanied the otherwise valuable achievements of the Pyramid Age. The promise of a great forward movement was authentic: but the regression into the past, the sinking back into the original perversions of power, was no less real. Against such forces, the salutary romantic reaction that began in the eighteenth century proved hopelessly naïve—and eventually impotent.

By the middle of the nineteenth century a considerable part of this new culture nevertheless had escaped many of the disabilities encrusted in all previous civilizations, without forfeiting the residual advantages of the Old World traditions. In the free states and territories of North America slavery was banished. Gone, too, were lifetime labor at a single occupation, watertight divisions of labor, excessive caste divisions between occupations and professions, between mental and manual labors; gone was the secret knowledge confined to a restricted, self-favoring group; gone the authority of an inviolate priesthood and an all-powerful monarch; gone remote control through a bureaucracy whose own prosperity depended upon the life, health, and prosperity of the divinely appointed king; gone—at least after the American revolution—were the compulsions of an alien army cold-bloodedly executing the will of the sovereign.

All these burdens had been removed or greatly lightened, if not everywhere, still in large patches; while thanks to the printed book and improved direct communication by telegraph, the forerunner of other forms of instantaneous communication, the tribes and nations began to sense—and, to a degree, experience—their interdependence. Not least, with the eager use of many labor-saving and energy-multiplying devices, and with the spread of automatic machines, the burden of life-cramping overwork, was lightened. Early in the nineteenth century an English observer had calculated that a stevedore, unloading bags at a Liverpool dock, staggering under a heavy load, might trot some forty-eight miles in the course of a day. But in every industry, that inhuman load was slowly being lifted: machine power was replacing muscle power.

In short, there were large areas in which the mechanical New World had joined with the terrestrial New World to modify, if not completely undermine, the practices of all ancient power systems. If the latter gain brought a loss of specialized efficiency in certain areas, it promised, in return, an increase in human dignity and self-respect.

These were not little benefits and ameliorations; and they largely explain the confident exultant note that one finds at the climax of this movement in the mid-nineteenth century, in the writings of Emerson, Whitman, and Melville; for the latter, even in the darkest pages of 'Moby Dick,' still felt that "the Declaration of Independence"—independence from the past and its constraints, not just from the British rule—had made a vital difference. But one might easily spoil one's case by making the New World achievement seem more complete and more permanent than it actually was: so various qualifying admissions remain to be made. Let me then give full weight once more to the ways in which the Romantic dream had fallen short or betrayed its own promises.

By formal declaration the Northern American states had abolished slavery; but the shovel gangs of the Irish and Chinese immigrants who built the railroads were, during their working span, hardly to be distinguished from slaves, if only temporary slaves. Republican government had promoted civil justice, along with law and order, to such an extent that the Commonwealth of Massachusetts showed such a low rate of violence or crime that Daniel Webster could boast without exaggeration that no one had to lock the door of his house at night. But these democratic communities were nevertheless part of a National State that waged merciless war all through the nineteenth century upon the rightful original occupants of the soil, the American Indians; that still shamelessly robs and mistreats their descendants; and that had despoiled Mexico of millions of acres of land in an infamous war.

Theoretically, the New World polity favored equality and actually distributed freely vast tracts of land to those who would work them: but it surrendered public lands for the benefits of private lumber, railroad, mining, and oil magnates, thus increasing economic inequality and promoting the rich and unscrupulous at the expense of all other citizens. In short, war, oppression, human alienation, and economic exploitation all remained.

One need not pile up these negative examples. Enough to say that there was hardly an ideal possibility or achieved benefit that was not endangered, even in such a self-governing country as the United States, from 1830 on, or that was not effectively subverted by 1890. New World man, if one may put the case paradoxically, dug his own grave before he was out of the cradle. So when one considers the three components of the New World dream, the utopian, the romantic and naturalistic, and the mechanical, one must realize that the first two had vanished as tangible possibilities well before the last frontier had been conquered. This left the mechanical power impulse dominant. Even in the New World itself it was the other part of the New World vision, the possibility of enlarging human powers through systematic scientific investigation and mechanical invention, that actually conquered: not merely conquered, but sought to gather to itself the prerogatives of nature and the promises of utopia.

Until the nineteenth century, the geographic New World and the mechanical New World had seemed to offer equal benefits. To many, indeed, the territorial New World seemed a more attractive alternative: an escape route into a realm of effortless abundance and wealth, or a return to primeval simplicity and good-natured felicity; while if the mechanical New World seemed to lead to the same destination, it was by an altogether different, somewhat duller route. As long as the territorial refuge was open, at least as a possibility, the growing regimentation of life could be accepted as a temporary inconvenience, not necessarily a permanent oppression: the frontiers beckoned to those who preferred to get their living from the land. For long the territorial New World thus served as a safety valve at least in the mind; and when it was most open, between 1814 and 1914, even the poor, the exploited, the desperate were not without hope: they could not only dream of a promised land across the ocean, but could even freely migrate thither.

In the nature of things, it was impossible to maintain this balance between the two New Worlds, for as the population of the planet increased and as all the good land in the sparsely occupied continents was taken up by farmers and herders, the province of the machine widened, and it dominated increasingly not merely the process of manufacture but every other aspect of life. The original New World dream thus faded away: or rather it retained a hold on the mind only by conforming to the demands of the machine. Among North American scholars it has become customary to smile patronizingly at the Romantic idea of believing that both wild nature and the cultivated countryside are essential foundations for a full human development. This 'bucolic' or 'pastoral' ideal, as the apologists for Megalopolis like to call it, is supposed to contrast unfavorably with their own inverted romanticism of living not according to nature, but according to the machine.

Yet even these missionaries of mechanical progress cannot entirely ignore the older passion for nature that still survives as an essential part of our New World heritage; for they have invented a prefabricated substitute for the wilderness, or at least an ingenious equivalent for the hunter's campfire. That ancient paleolithic hearth has become a backyard picnic grill, where, surrounded by plastic vegetation, factory-processed frankfurters are broiled on an open fire made with pressed charcoal eggs, brought to a combustion point by an electric torch connected by wire to a distant socket, while the assembled company views, either on television or on a domestic motion-picture screen, a travelogue through an African game preserve, or scenes with the grizzly bears in Yellowstone. Ah! Wilderness. For many of my own countrymen this is, I fear, the terminus of the pioneers' New World dream.

The alternative was more sophisticated, more capable of being rationalized in terms of scientific exploit; but ultimately just as barren: the reinstauration of the old cycle of exploration and discovery and colonization with the solar system, or more distant planetary objects—a sterile moon, a coy Venus, a lethal Mars—as the terminal point. That this dream should now be revived, just at the point where many minds have discovered for themselves the essential limitations—indeed, terrifying consequences—of this whole one-sided process, is a sign that a large portion of our leaders have lost contact with living realities and have ceased to be concerned with the human consequences of their cherished ideas and exploits.

Nevertheless the animus behind both New World explorations deserves respect. The original visions of the New World and the institutions and activities that have made these visions come to pass have opened new and important realms of human experience; and no project that attempts, as this one does, to trace the continued interactions of technics with human development can fail to take account of them. Though some of the hopes awakened have come to grief, many of the most extravagant expectations—instantaneous communication, flight, transmutation of the elements, nuclear power—have been fulfilled, with a swiftness and fullness that has often surprised and even shocked those responsible for their success.

3: KEPLER'S DREAM

One of the reasons for the general failure to understand the radical weaknesses of both aspects of the New Exploration is that their subjective side has been neglected, indeed not even recognized as existing: chiefly because scientists, in overcoming the subjectivism of earlier systems, resolutely denied the many evidences of science's own subjectivity. Yet at the very outset, this subjectivism was expressed with classic clarity in Kepler's 'Dream,' which anticipated by more than three centuries the world in which we are now actually living: its empirical knowledge, its practical devices, its compulsive drives, its mystic aspirations—and finally, most remarkably now, its rising disillusion.

Kepler, born a century after Copernicus, but only a few years after Galileo, embodied in his own person the three great aspects of the New World transformation: the scientific side, in his classic discovery of the unexpectedly ellipsoid course taken by the planets around the sun: the religious side, in his open adoration of the sun itself and the starry sky as a substantial visible equivalent of the fading Christian Heaven: and finally, his untrammeled technical imagination; since in a day of sailing ships and short-range, inaccurate cannon he dared to depict in vividly realistic terms the first power-driven journey to the moon.

If Kepler was a sun-worshipper, he was also as moon-mad as any of the contemporary technicians in the National Aeronautics and Space Administration (NASA). As a student he devoted one of his required dissertations at Tübingen University to the question: "How would the phenomena occurring in the heavens appear to an observer stationed on the moon?" He already saw in his mind what the first astronauts beheld with hardly greater vividness from their space capsule; and Plutarch's work, 'The Face of the Moon,' so fascinated him that in 1604, in his 'Optics,' he drew from it fourteen quotations.

For three centuries Kepler's 'Somnium' (Dream), published only after his death, remained a literary curiosity, largely unread; partly because it existed only in its original Latin, supplemented in 1898 by an equally obscure German translation, but even more because it seemed too fanciful to be taken seriously. Kepler himself, however, had no hesitation in putting his projected moon flight before Galileo, for he wrote out his plan for a moon landing as early as the summer of 1609, and justified his interest in exploring that satellite on the same grounds that justified similar explorations by sea. "Who could have believed [before Columbus]" he wrote, "that a huge ocean could be crossed more peacefully and safely than the narrow expanse of the Adriatic or the Baltic Sea, or the English Channel? . . . Provide ships or sails adapted to the heavenly breezes, and there will be some who will not fear even that void [of interplanetary space]. So for those who will come shortly to attempt this journey, let us establish the astronomy."

Note the word "shortly." In 'Typee," Herman Melville predicted, in 1846, that by the end of the nineteenth century people on the West Coast would, thanks to air travel, be spending their weekends in Honolulu. But Kepler's impatient prediction was even more audacious. Those who have seen in scientific and technical advance only a cautious hardheaded series of steps from one solid tuft of observed facts to another, have not reckoned with these hot subjective pressures. The quick leap in Kepler's mind from purely scientific astronomical exploration to this staggering practical exploit surely helps explain the vulgar engulfment in space fantasies today, now that their realization has proved feasible.

The fact that these fantasies should have appeared, fully fleshed, in Kepler's mind at the very moment when the first halting theoretic advances were being made, would seem to indicate that they issued from deep common sources in the collective psyche. The same self-confidence, the same ambitious or aggressive impulse that sustained a Cortes in the subjugation of Mexico, was also working in the leading minds in astronomy and mechanics, though in a more subtle and sublimated form.

Kepler was far from being alone. These space-centered adventurers felt the future in their bones, as people used to say—that is, in their unconscious; and to the extent that their own work helped to bring that future nearer, their predictions became self-fulfilling. This animus was far more widespread than most scholars have until recently recognized, awakened largely by Marjorie Nicolson. A century and a half before Edgar Allan Poe's description of Hans Pfaall's trip to the moon in a balloon, a report of an airship's journey from Vienna to Lisbon appeared in a current newspaper without greatly outraging popular credulity. And in the eighteenth century Dr. Samuel Johnson, in 'Rasselas,' giving a reasonable account of the possibility of aerial navigation, even coupled it with the possibility of space flight, once the aeronaut reached a point beyond the earth's gravitational field, so that he might behold the rolling earth passing beneath him.

Now the remarkable fact about Kepler's moon exploration, apart from the audacity of the conception itself, was his keen grasp of the embarrassing details. He had already canvassed in his mind some of the most serious obstacles to its accomplishment, though he knew quite well that the solution of these problems was beyond the technical equipment of his age. "On such a headlong dash," he pointed out, "we can take few human companions. . . . The first getting into motion is very hard on him, for he is twisted and turned just as if, shot from a cannon, he were sailing across mountains and seas. Therefore he must be put to sleep beforehand with narcotics and opiates, and he must be arranged, limb by limb, so that the shock will be distributed over the individual members, lest the upper part of his body be carried away from the fundament, or his head be torn from his shoulder. Then comes a new difficulty: terrific cold and difficulty in breathing. . . . Many further difficulties arise, which would be too numerous to recount. Absolutely no harm befalls us."

This last bit of reassurance was again premature; but Kepler was obviously moved by interior compulsions that would not be daunted by seemingly insuperable difficulties, still less, possible failures. Like the artist in 'Rasselas,' he might have said: "Nothing will ever be attempted, if all possible objections must be first overcome."

That this extravagant dream was not so easily translated into the practical world as Kepler impatiently anticipated, is far less surprising than the fact that it took possession of Kepler's mind at such an early date. Kepler, steeped in sun worship, seems to have realized that powers derived from the Sun God would open new possibilities and would have no difficulty in imposing the huge sacrifices necessary to make a lunar journey possible. All the forces that had been set in motion by the exploration of our own planet were eventually transferred, with no loss of momentum and no great change of method or goal, to interplanetary exploration—but accompanied likewise by the same defects: the same exorbitant pride, the same aggressiveness, the same disregard for more significant human concerns, and the same insistence upon scientific discovery, technical ingenuity, and rapid locomotion as the chief end of man. What we also know now, as Kepler could not know, is that space exploration would require a megamachine of far larger dimensions than any previous one to ensure its success; and this megamachine would take centuries to assemble.

Kepler's 'Dream' passed beyond the borderline of prudent speculation; yet by that very fact it draws attention to another characteristic of his age: the science-stimulated fantasies of the seventeenth century have often proved closer to our own twentieth-century realities than the more humanly fruitful but relatively pedestrian enterprises of eighteenth- and nineteenth-century industry; for their boasted mechanical improvements in general only applied new sources of energy and a more militarized type of organization to the most ancient neolithic industries: spinning, weaving, pot-making, or to the later Bronze and Iron Age industries of mining and smelting.

In the seventeenth century Joseph Glanvill, who still believed enough in witchcraft to write a book denouncing it, also looked forward to such other practical consequences of science as the phonograph, and instantaneous communication at a distance. Even more remarkable, an English bishop, Dr. John Wilkins, sometime Master of Trinity College, Cambridge, wrote a book in 1638 proposing travel to the moon; while in a work entitled 'Mercury or the Swift Messenger' (1641) he predicted a series of new inventions, such as the phonograph and the flying chariot. A year later, in 'A Discourse Concerning a New World,' he suggested that "as soon as the art of flying is found out some of [our] nation will make one of the first colonies that shall transplant into that other world."

What is perhaps just as important as Kepler's realistically fanciful description of a moon flight, which he hopefully thought would be a mere matter of hours, is his description of the kind of organisms that might, under the permanent conditions of extreme cold and extreme heat on the opposite sides of our satellite, have developed on the moon. For he rounds out that journey with a nightmare of no little psychological significance. With marvellous ecological insight Kepler translated the physical conditions of life on the moon into appropriate biological adaptations. He imagined that 'Prevolvan' creatures would inhabit the cold side of the moon, and 'Subvolvans' the hot side, where plants would grow visibly before one's eyes, and likewise decay in a single day; where the infra-human inhabitants would have no fixed and safe habitation, where they would traverse, in a single day, the whole of their world, following the receding waters on legs that are longer than those of our camels, or on wings, or in ships; where those that remain on the surface would be boiled by the midday sun and serve as nourishment for the approaching nomadic hordes of Prevolvans rising up from cavernous interiors.

Kepler, be it noted, had no romantic illusions such as legend attributes to Ponce de León, exploring America to find the Fountain of Youth: Kepler presents nothing less than a painful phantasmagoria of organic deformation and degradation, of grotesque creatures in a fever of insensate activity and purposeless travel: the ultimate lunar 'Jet Set.' In contradiction to his hypothetical one-day limit of maturation and death, Kepler allows the Subvolvans to build cities—but mainly, be it noted, for a characteristically technocratic reason: *to solve the problem of how they could construct them!*

One must grant Kepler not merely truly remarkable powers of scientific deduction, but an equally realistic imagination in dealing with biological conditions: for he did not for a moment suppose that any organic forms comparable to those that exist on earth could flourish in such a hostile environment. Unfortunately, this fact opens up a serious question that it is impossible to answer and fruitless to speculate upon: *Why did Kepler suppose that a journey to such a planet was worth the effort?* Why did the utmost achievements of technology, which are symbolized even today by a journey to distant planets, terminate in fantasies of shapeless monsters and cruel deaths, such as often haunt the cribs of little children? If we had an answer to this question, many other manifestations of the life-negating irrationalities that now threaten man's very survival would perhaps be sufficiently intelligible to be overcome.

Kepler's 'Somnium' has only to be translated into rational contemporary terms to serve as an urgent warning signal. What did Kepler's sky-searching mind foresee in the new world created by science and technics? It saw a world that had escaped organic limits, a world in which the processes of growth and decay had been reduced to a single day, and in which its emphemeral creatures existed only to be promptly devoured. In this world the only protection against a savage environment would be retreat into deep underground shelters; and the chief occupation of its unfortunate inhabitants would be continuous motion. A monstrous habitat, in short, in which only monsters could be at home. In cutting loose from the earth, Kepler had left behind two billion years of organic existence, with all the immensely creative activities and partnerships of living species, culminating in the mindfulness of man. As far as life values are concerned, one might trade all the planets of the solar system for a square mile of inhabited earth.

If this nightmarish conclusion were peculiar to Kepler, it might be treated as a personal aberration; but as it happens, it has been a recurrent theme of later technological kakotopias. In H. G. Wells' 'The Time Machine' the narrator realizes that the technological progress toward leisure and luxury had proved self-destructive: and he travels farther into time only to find all life gradually waning on the planet. He sees in the growing pile of civilization only a "foolish heaping that must inevitably fall back upon and destroy its makers in the end." This premonition was so deeply at odds with Wells' conscious commitment to scientific progress that he came to a startling conclusion: *"If that is so, it remains for us to live as though it were not so."* In other words, we had better close our eyes and shut our minds. A fine terminus for the scientific pursuit of celestial truth that Copernicus and Kepler had instituted!

So far what I have sought to explain is how it came about that the territorial New World, with its seemingly boundless opportunities, suffered from the beginning from the moribund institutions and obsolescent aims that, in principle, the New Exploration attempted to escape.

Now I have to examine, in far greater detail, the nature of the 'mechanical' New World that still increasingly dominates the consciousness and the daily activities of modern man. I shall show how the very assumptions about man and nature that once proved so helpful in enlarging the scope of technology were also responsible for misinterpreting, and therewith suppressing, essential organic and human functions, and, what is worse, distorted human purposes by subordinating all other activities to the expansion of power. These assumptions betrayed the ideal promise once held forth by both New World explorations—that of enlarging the boundaries and deepening the foundations of human existence.

CHAPTER THREE

The Mechanized World Picture

1: THE DE-NATURED ENVIRONMENT

The cult of the Sun God gave the ultimate authority of cosmic fitness and rightness to every earthly manifestation of order, regularity, predictability, and—because of the sun's own position and influence—of centralized power.

Behind this cult lay an ancient perception whose truth further scientific inquiry has demonstrated: that the phenomena of life are actually influenced by remote forces, many, like cosmic rays, long unperceived, some doubtless still to be identified, over which man himself can have little, if any, control. What was lacking in this original picture was the realization that man himself was also a cosmic event, indeed a culminating one, and possessed powers of mind derived not alone from the sun but from his own highly evolved nature.

Astronomy prepared the ground for the great technical transformation that took place after the sixteenth century: for it provided the frame for a depersonalized world picture within which mechanical activities and interests took precedence over more human concerns. The organization of this world picture was largely the work of a series of mathematicians and physicists who count among the great luminaries of all times. Beginning with Copernicus, Kepler, Galileo, and Descartes and culminating in Leibnitz and Newton, their systematic descriptions of space, time, motion, mass, gravitation eventually brought about a major shift in technology: from the workshop to the laboratory, from the tool-using craftsman and artist, himself a prime mover as well as a designer, to the complex power-driven automatic machine under centralized direction and remote control. And it was this world picture, not individual mechanical inventions alone, that contributed to the final apotheosis of the contemporary megamachine.

51

The central figure in this galaxy was Galileo Galilei; for he embodied in his own person the two great attributes of the new science: empirical knowledge, based on close observation, and theoretical knowledge, based on an ability to formulate and manipulate symbolic abstractions of quantity, number, relationship, structure—an ability that disentangled the mind from the often impenetrable and indescribable confusions of concrete existence. In effect, Galileo brought Copernicus down to earth; yet in doing so, he exiled man himself from this new realm of clarified knowledge as completely as the new astronomy had exiled the pious Christian from his hoped-for Heaven.

Given the fossilization of official Church doctrine, based on Aristotle via Saint Thomas Aquinas, Galileo's reaction was inevitable and indeed salutary. Yet the form it took was not merely a justifiable attack on the authority of Aristotle in areas where more satisfactory interpretation was possible: it also exhibited an indifference to areas of biological behavior and human experience where Aristotle, as a first-hand observer, was still superior in insight to those who equated science with mechanics, and organisms with machines.

Aristotle was no mathematical physicist; and he published untenable reports about the behavior of physical bodies which he had never taken the trouble to check by experiment. Moreover to regard him as an infallible authority on all matters of science was a lazy vice of official theological thought. Reprehensibly, in the formulation of medieval science, the printed text, though perhaps originally based on experience, had taken the place of that experience, and prevented any further inquiry. This is well illustrated by Galileo's story in his 'Dialogues' (Second Day) wherein he tells about a physician who dissected a corpse to demonstrate that the nervous system had its origin in the brain and not the heart—exposing the mass of nerves that proceeded from the brain and the single nerve coming from the heart. But the Aristotelian observer present, confronted with this proof, said: "You have made me see this business so plainly and sensibly that, did not the text of Aristotle assert the contrary . . . I should be constrained to confess your opinion to be true."

Thus, too, had spoken the obstinate doctors Galileo had encountered at Padua. When rational thought had stiffened into this corpselike state, embalmed in obsolete texts, it was plainly time to bury such authorities and begin all over again, going over the same ground as earlier observers, but with fresh, self-confident eyes and minds eager for new discoveries.

This was what in fact took place with the new instauration of science; but unfortunately, instead of covering as wide a territory as Aristotle had done, the inquiry into the immediate nature of the 'physical world' took precedence over that into the nature of life and the environment of life. Aristotle had been the philosopher of living organisms endowed with autonomy and purpose, capable of self-organization and self-replication. Galileo and his later disciples were the philosophers of the non-living processes then being incorporated in the new machines.

I purpose to deal with only that part of Galileo's work which radically modified man's sense of his own unique place in the cosmos and contributed to the exploitation of every manner of technical facility.

Galileo took up and developed an observation that his younger colleague Kepler had made in the first volume of his 'Opera.' "As the ear is made to perceive sound," Kepler observed, "and the eye to perceive color, so the mind has been formed to understand not all sorts of things but quantities. It perceives any given thing more clearly in proportion as that thing is close to bare quantities as to its origin, but the further a thing recedes from quantities the more darkness and error inheres in it." Roger Bacon in his 'Opus Majus,' Part IV, had long before taken the same position: "All that is necessary for physics can be proved by mathematics, and without them it is impossible to have an exact knowledge of things." But in both cases, exact knowledge was identified with sufficient knowledge, and the truth that applied to things was applied without amplification to organisms—though it did not suffice there until *they* were reduced to things.

In 'The Assayer' Galileo repeated Kepler's idea in his own words. "Philosophy," says Galileo, "is written in this great book, the Universe, which stands continually open to our gaze. But the book cannot be understood unless one first learns to comprehend the language and to read the letters of which it is composed. It is written in the language of mathematics, and its characters are triangles, circles, and other geometric figures, without which it is humanly impossible to understand a single word of it; without these one wanders around in a dark labyrinth." Following Kepler's clue, Galileo constructed a world in which matter alone mattered, in which qualities became 'immaterial' and were turned by inference into superfluous exudations of the mind.

Galileo's spirit was so close to that of Kepler, with whom he was in active, friendly correspondence, that he did not suspect how many fallacies lay embedded in what seemed to both thinkers a quite obvious statement. And even now, so firmly have their views become entrenched, indeed popularly accepted as unchallengeable axioms, that I shall find it necessary to expose these fallacies before tracing their consequences. Fortunately, this effort has been lightened by the criticisms of a growing group of mathematicians, physicists, and biologists, from Stallo and Lloyd Morgan and Whitehead to Planck, Schrödinger, Bohr, and Polanyi: they have not merely anticipated this analysis, but carried it further, each in his own department.

First one must note that the 'universe' both men were talking about was composed only of isolated physical bodies, destitute of life: 'dead' matter. But we know now that this utter absence of life—or at least of life potentiality—is an illusion. 'Matter' has in the constitution and most intimate structure of certain elements that which is capable, at some far point in its own evolution, of fulfilling its potentiality for becoming 'alive'; and it is with the emergence of living organisms that the qualities that Galileo rejected as subjective and unreal, because indescribable in mathematical terms alone, came into existence. There is indeed an underlying unity between the astronomical cosmos and man's nature: organic life conforms to cosmic periodicities, such as night and day, the phases of the moon, the change of seasons, and doubtless responds to many other more obscure physical changes, for man himself in his own right is a representative sample of the cosmos. So Galileo was correct in surmising that the language of geometry would help in understanding even the behavior of organisms—as the concept of the double helix in DNA has notably done in our own generation.

But no organism could survive in the rarefied world that the physicist, up to the present generation, regarded as the real one, the abstract area of mass and motion—any more than man could survive without massive equipment on the life-forsaken moon. The actual world occupied by organisms is one of literally indescribable richness and complexity: a life-furthering accumulation of molecules, organisms, species, each bearing the impress of countless functional adaptations and selective transformations, the residue of billions of years of evolution.

Of these vast transformations only an infinitesimal part is visible or can be reduced to any mathematical order. Form, color, odor, tactile sensations, emotions, appetites, feelings, images, dreams, words, symbolic abstractions—that plenitude of life which even the humblest being in some degree exhibits—cannot be resolved in any mathematical equation or converted into a geometric metaphor without eliminating a large part of the relevant experience.

The second fallacy in the new mechanical world picture issued from the first, Galileo's dismemberment of the human organism; for he treated the mind as if it could function without all the other members of the body, as if the eye saw by itself and the ear heard by itself, and as if the brain, equally isolated, was dedicated in its most perfect state to the specialized function of mathematical thinking.

Recent experiment shows that on the contrary, the human brain, so far from having the limitations of a computer, which can work only with definite symbols and exact images, has a marvellous capacity for coping with vague, indistinct, and confused data, making sense out of information so incomplete that it would paralyze a computer—as in translating a wide range of sounds, tones, different pronunciations into the same intelligible words. It is these unifying properties of the human mind, with its ability constantly to bring together symbolically relevant portions of the past, the present, and the future, that has made it possible for man to react with some measure of success to a diversified environment and an open world, instead of retreating into a safe niche, with a limited range of opportunities and responses, like all other species.

Against Kepler, then, one may justly say that the further the scientific world picture recedes from sound and color and odor and the animal functions they derive from, the more darkness inheres in its treatment of the unique properties of organisms and living human beings; though many properties that the organism actually shares with other physical bodies can be handled with equal effectiveness on Kepler's principles.

Both Kepler and Galileo held that organisms cannot, so to say, become respectable citizens in the commonwealth of scientific knowledge until they are dead. This curiously dogmatic discrimination against living phenomena had no ill results at first upon the pursuit of experimental physics and mechanics; but for long it retarded biological investigations and diverted them into blind alleys. It has taken the scientists the better part of three centuries to see through this faulty analysis. Recent experiments fortunately have demonstrated, according to Dr. Lawrence Hinkle, that to cut the mind off completely from qualitative stimuli of light, color, sound, muscular tension, even under laboratory conditions, is to bring about psychological disintegration; for it is only through maintaining constant intercourse with his complex surroundings, including his own organs, that man's delicate mind can be kept in balance. To reduce events solely to their quantitative elements is to make the practitioner of this method unfit for dealing with any kind of organic behavior.

What was implicit in this whole formulation was something that Galileo would hardly have dared to put into words, even if he had been aware of it. To understand the physical world, and ultimately man himself, who exists in this world as merely a product of mass and motion, one must eliminate the living soul. At the center of the new world picture man himself did not exist, indeed he had no reason for existence: instead of man, a creature with a long history on a planet whose inhabitants and habitats have had an immeasurably longer history, only a fragment of man remained—the detached intelligence, and only certain special products of that sterilized intelligence, scientific theorems and machines, can claim any permanent place or any high degree of reality. In the interests of 'objectivity,' the new scientist eliminated historic man and all his subjective activities. Since Galileo's time, this practice has been known as 'objective science.'

By his exclusive preoccupation with quantity, Galileo had in effect *disqualified* the real world of experience; and he had thus driven man out of living nature into a cosmic desert, even more peremptorily than Jehovah had driven Adam and Eve out of the Garden of Eden. But in Galileo's case the punishment for eating the apple of the tree of knowledge lay in the nature of knowledge itself: for that tasteless, desiccated fruit was incapable of sustaining or reproducing life. One vast tract of the real world, the world of living organisms, was excluded from the province of the exact sciences: those transactions and configurations that belonged most clearly to that world, along with human history and human culture, were dismissed as 'subjective,' since only a minute part could be reduced to abstract 'sense data' or described in mathematical terms. Only cadavers and skeletons were suitable candidates for scientific treatment. At the same time, the 'material' world, that is, the abstract world of 'physical objects,' operating in an equally abstract space and time, was treated as if it alone had reality.

What this conception has come to mean in its final twentieth-century vulgarization can perhaps best be demonstrated by citing Buckminster Fuller's sublime description of the nature of man: a description which, if not authentic, I might be accused of having wantonly invented for the purpose of exposing the crudity and absurdity of the original doctrine:

Man, observes Fuller, is "a self-balancing, 28-jointed adapter-base biped, an electro-chemical reduction plant, integral with the segregated stowages of special energy extracts in storage batteries, for subsequent actuation of thousands of hydraulic and pneumatic pumps, with motors attached; 62,000 miles of capillaries, millions of warning-signal, railroad, and conveyor systems; crushers and cranes . . . and a universally distributed telephone system needing no service for 70 years if well managed; the whole, extraordinarily complex mechanism guided with exquisite precision from a turret in which are located telescopic and microscopic self-registering and recording range finders, a spectroscope, *et cetera.*"

Fuller's parallels are neat; the metaphor is superficially precise, if one discounts the airy, pseudo-exact statistical guesses. Only one thing is lacking in this detailed list of mechanical abstractions—the slightest hint, apart from his measurable physical components, of the nature of man.

One can guess what Galileo would have said to this callow description. In his personal behavior, Galileo, a true exemplar of baroque culture, with its dazzling mixture of the mechanical and the sensual, delighted in the multi-dimensional world that his own intellectual analysis denigrated and rejected. He himself was an ardent lover and a prolific sire; and he allowed erotic passion, esthetic delight, poetic feeling to be exiled from his world only as long as his technical and scientific interests were uppermost. As de Santillana has emphasized, he was as proud of his literary skill as a humanist as he was of his scientific discoveries. Though Galileo's own limited concepts helped to establish the machine as the ultimate model for scientific thought, his actual environment was still richly furnished with traditional esthetic forms, religious rituals, and emotionally charged symbols: so he could have no anticipation of what the world would be like if his standards were universally accepted and if the machine and machine-made men succeeded in de-naturing or banishing every organic attribute. He never suspected that the ultimate consequence of the mechanical world picture would be an environment like our present one: fit only for machines to live in.

2 : THE CRIME OF GALILEO

Though Galileo's interpretation of planetary movements led to a charge of heresy by the Roman Catholic Church, the heresy that he was accused of was one he did not utter. As he plaintively put it at the end of the 'Dialogues on Two Worlds,' he could not be justly convicted of a crime he had never committed. Like so many eminent later colleagues in science, such as Pascal, Newton, and Faraday, he was a theological conservative; and even in science he had no notion of bringing about any revolutionary overthrow of previously established truths: his error there, if anything, was to attempt clumsily to shore up and repair Ptolemy's traditional structure.

But actually, Galileo committed a crime far graver than any the dignitaries of the Church accused him of; for his real crime was that of trading the totality of human experience, not merely the accumulated dogmas and doctrines of the Church, for that minute portion which can be observed within a limited time-span and interpreted in terms of mass and motion, while denying importance to the unmediated realities of human experience, from which science itself is only a refined ideological derivative. When Galileo divided experienced reality into two spheres, a subjective sphere, which he chose to exclude from science, and an objective sphere, freed theoretically from man's visible presence, but known through rigorous mathematical analysis, he was dismissing as unsubstantial and unreal the cultural accretions of meaning that had made mathematics—itself a purely subjective distillation—possible.

For the better part of three centuries scientists followed Galileo's lead. Under the naïve belief—exposed by Stallo a century ago—that they were free from metaphysical preconceptions, the orthodox exponents of science suppressed every evidence of human and organic behavior that could not be neatly fitted into their mechanical world picture. They thus committed, in reverse, the error of the early Christian Fathers who had suppressed any interest in the natural world in order to concentrate upon the fate of the human soul in eternity. That 'mass' and 'motion' had no more objective existence than 'soul' and 'immortality' apart from their derived relation to other human experiences, was not even suspected by those who strained at the theological gnat and swallowed the scientific bat. Galileo, in all innocence, had surrendered man's historic birthright: man's memorable and remembered experience, in short, his accumulated culture. In dismissing subjectivity he had excommunicated history's central subject, multidimensional man.

Galileo committed this crime with a cheerful heart and open eyes. He had no notion that his radical distinction between the external world and the internal world, between the objective and the subjective, between the quantitative and the qualitative, between the mathematically describable, and thus knowable, and the irreducible, inaccessible, unanalyzable, and unmeasurable, was a false distinction, once human experience in its symbolized fullness—itself a deposit of countless ages of organic life—is left out of account.

What was worse, Galileo introduced a dualism between the objective and subjective worlds that was even grosser than Christian doctrine had imposed by separating the heavenly, perfect, and eternal from the earthly, the imperfect, and the sinful; for at least the Christian's subjective Heaven became an operative part of his daily life, made visible in splendid churches and cathedrals, charitable acts and communal celebrations. In the anti-historic utilitarian order through which the mechanical world picture became validated, what was left of subjective experience was either impoverished or deformed by loss of contact with man's past, and by lack of prudent forethought for his future.

Under the new scientific dispensation it was the organic world, not least man himself, that demanded redemption. All living forms must be brought into harmony with the mechanical world picture by being melted down, so to say, and molded anew to conform to a more perfect mechanical model. For the machine alone was the true incarnation of this new ideology: however complicated any particular mechanism might in fact become, it was still a simple artifact disparagingly compared to that which Buckminster Fuller's description of the human body caricatures. Only by throwing off organic complexity, purifying it by abstraction and intellectual sterilization, eviscerating man's inner organs, and wrapping the remains in ideological mummy cloth, could man become as flawless and as finished— finished in every sense!—as his new mechanical artifacts. To be redeemed from the organic, the autonomous, and the subjective, man must be turned into a machine, or, better still, become an integral part of a larger machine that the new method would help to create.

This view, curiously, did not even do justice to the 'physical' properties of natural phenomena, as Kepler himself was quick to perceive when he meditated on the complex geometry of a snowflake and observed that a similar order, *as if mind were at work,* pervaded other parts of nature, as in the structure of a flower. Atoms, too, physicists now hold, have their own innerness, impenetrable to the eye, puzzling to the mind; and each atomic element has its own definite character, dependent upon the composition and arrangement of its various hypothetic particles or charges. Some aboriginal tendency to organization and association seems, accordingly, to have been engrained at the lowest level of existence, billions of years before living organisms appeared: a profound intuition expressed by both Leibnitz and Stallo that was too long ignored.

What is more, these 'ultimate' particles elude direct observation: so what is innermost and inaccessible, even in physics, cannot be said to be unreal, much less may it be called wholly subjective, however well preserved its secret. In short, innerness is as objective as outerness. One does not have to perform surgery to be objectively certain that all the essential inner organs exist in a living creature—if one allows for possible extirpation or artificial replacement. As for what we call the external world, it is a necessary part of each organism's internal world, and only by internalizing it in some degree can the organism remain in existence.

All this critical analysis would be a flogging of a dead horse, but for the fact that these original misconceptions and misinterpretations have left a heavy deposit of bias and error in scientific, and even more in popular, thought and technological practice. True, the mechanical world picture, as first put together by Kepler, Galileo, Descartes, Newton, and Boyle, has long ceased to be acceptable in advanced science: through the reasoning and the experiments of Faraday, Clerk Maxwell, Planck, and their successors, every part of the classic 'physical world' has become de-materialized: more insubstantial, more subtle, more complex, and therefore ultimately more elusive than ever—but also more ready to come to terms with the complexities and mysteries of life. The seventeenth-century world of spinning planets, swinging pendulums, hurtling cannonballs, falling stones, hard atomic pellets no longer embraces all observable or conceivable existence; for electro-magnetic radiation, spreading in every direction, cannot be plotted on a two-dimensional surface, and many ultimate 'physical' phenomena, physicists tell us, cannot be visualized at all.

Despite this, the world picture of the scientist, even today, still bears the faded impress of Galileo and Kepler; for, as Schrödinger observed, it still remains without "blue, yellow, bitter, sweet, beauty, delight, sorrow" —in short, without the most vivid reports of human experience. Existentially, the scientific world picture is still under-dimensioned; because at the outset it eliminated the living observer and the long history recorded in his genes and his culture.

Unfortunately, the ultimate effect of the methodical seventeenth-century advance in clarity of description and fidelity to observed fact was to devaluate every aspect of human experience that could not be so treated; and its final result was to eliminate all other products and by-products of the human personality: so that the technological world, which prided itself on reducing or extruding the human personality, progressively displaced both nature and human culture and claimed indeed a higher status for itself, as the concrete working model of scientific truth. "In 1893," Loren Eiseley reminds us, "Robert Monro in an opening address before the British Association for the Advancement of Science, remarked sententiously . . . 'imagination, conceptions, idealizations, the moral faculties . . . may be compared to parasites that live at the expense of their neighbors.' " To have pointed the way to this devaluation of the human personality and its eventual exile was the real crime of Galileo.

3: DETAILS OF THE CRIME

The great merit of Galileo's method, once it was widely applied, was that it opened an important part of the visible world to systematic public observation, while the method itself, accessible to all who were competent to master it, lifted the results above private dispute. Positive science, in the sense that Galileo exemplified it, was a reaction against the medieval notion that such truths as had not been established by Divine revelation were to be arrived at by purely verbal reasoning between opposed sides, in open debate. This is the dialectic method, still largely used in courts of law; it puts a premium upon personal force and forensic skill, but easily descends in the course of argument to empty verbal pyrotechnics and ill-natured wrangling. As Renaudot, a French popularizer of science in the seventeenth century put it, such discussions "not only obscured all eloquence and pleasure of the discourse, but usually ended in riots and pedantic insults."

Galileo accordingly deserves the approbation he has won by helping to establish a method that would induce open minds to correct their personal bias and faulty reasoning, and, through careful observation and well-planned experiments, skillfully interpreted, to arrive at common conclusions equally open to all who would repeat the same operations. Not merely strict reasoning but reasonableness, not merely brilliant intuitions but humility in accepting the cooperation or the contrary findings of other minds, working under the same orderly discipline, were the great moral fruits of the new scientific method; and in time these mollifying intellectual courtesies spread from the sciences to other departments. The high reputation that the scientific vocation once rightfully enjoyed was largely due to this selfless detachment, this open-mindedness, this willingness to discard untenable hypotheses, to correct errors—even to revise basic postulates: in short, to the absence of ulterior motives and willful passions.

That new discipline was not easily imposed. From the kind of opposition Galileo awakened, we can infer how necessary his innovations were. "Oh, my dear Kepler," Galileo wrote to his colleague, "how I wish that we could have one hearty laugh together! Here at Padua is a principal professor of philosophy, whom I have repeatedly and urgently requested to look at the moon and planets through my glass, which he pertinaciously refuses to do."

This eye-opening had begun, we have seen, at least three centuries before; notably in the Franciscan friar Roger Bacon, who observed: "He who wishes to rejoice without doubt in regard to the truths underlying phenomena must know how to devote himself to experiment. For authors write many statements and people believe them through reasoning which they formulate without experience. Their meaning is wholly false. For it is generally believed that the diamond cannot be broken except by goat's blood, and philosophers and theologians misuse this idea. But fracture by means of blood has never been verified, although the effort has been made; and without that blood it can be fractured easily; for I have seen this with my own eyes."

"I have seen this with my own eyes." This was the new note, now struck more emphatically and decisively by Galileo and his successors. Once the method was firmly established, angels, devils, ghosts, not visible to an unbelieving observer, became suspect, unless indeed these entities had been smuggled, in scientific costume, as 'phlogiston' or 'the ether,' into the mechanical world picture. Every true scientist became professionally a Doubting Thomas, like the disciple who demanded to see for himself Jesus' wounds before he would credit his resurrection.

The satisfaction of this demand for authentic information was made possible by the systematic opening up of the two 'new worlds' we have already explored, the terrestrial and the mechanical. And for that change of temper which Galileo had helped to bring about his contributions deserve our qualified respect. Unfortunately, in achieving these results, and attempting to make them more austerely objective, Galileo accepted Kepler's baseless notion that the brain was a specialized organ peculiarly adapted to handling mathematical information; and that to achieve such intelligible order, all other avenues of information must be sealed off.

"As soon," Galileo wrote, "as I form a conception of a material or corporeal substance, I simultaneously feel the necessity of conceiving that it has boundaries of some shape or other; that relatively to others it is great or small; that it is in this or that place, in this or that time; that it is in motion or at rest; that it touches or does not touch another body; that it is unique, rare, or common; nor can I by any act of imagination disjoin it from these qualities. But I do not find myself absolutely compelled to apprehend it as necessarily accompanied by such conditions as that it must be white or red, bitter or sweet, sonorous or silent, smelling sweetly or disagreeably; and if the senses had not pointed out these qualities, language and imagination alone could never have arrived at them. Therefore I think that these senses, smells, colors, etc. with regard to the object in which they appear to reside are nothing more than mere names. These exist only in the sensitive body, for when the living creature is removed, all these qualities are carried off and annihilated. . . . I do not believe that there exists anything in external bodies for exciting tastes, smells, and sounds, etc. except size, shape, quantity, and motion."

This judgement was not, be it noted, the result of any experimental demonstration: it rested solely on the postulates of astronomy and mechanics, backed by a hypothetical operation performed by the observer, which removed all physiological data except those necessary for describing size, weight, 'force,' or, even more abstractly, 'mass' and 'motion.' Not merely human personalities and organisms, but likewise the chemical elements—themselves as yet unidentified and undescribed—were absent from Galileo's universe. "I think," said Galileo, going back to this thought in another place, "that if ears, tongues, and noses were removed shapes and numbers would remain, but not odors, nor tastes, nor sounds." But why did he halt his hypothetical surgery with ear, tongue, and nose? What would become of shape and numbers and motion if the eyes and hands and brains were removed, too? Absolute entities that exist by themselves are only plausible figments of the human mind: all that can be called 'real' is the outcome of a multitude of sustained transactions and interrelations between the human organism and the environment.

Galileo never explained how his so-called primary qualities, size and shape, would have any more tangible existence or meaning than color and odor if the human brain that reacted to them, and translated the phenomena into symbols, should vanish. Nor did Galileo face the equally baffling problem of how mass and motion could produce even the illusion of qualities. All the supposedly objective components of the physical world are inferences, by now highly probable inferences, at least for man, from a multitude of historic and biographic experiences.

Galileo's mechanical world was only a partial representation of a finite number of probable worlds, each peculiar to a particular living species; and all these worlds are but a portion of the infinite number of possible worlds that may have once existed or may yet exist. But anything like a single world, common to all species, at all times, under all circumstances, is a purely hypothetical construction, drawn by inference from pathetically insufficient data, prized for the assurance of stability and intelligibility it gives, even though that assurance turns out, under severe examination, to be just another illusion. A butterfly or a beetle, a fish or a fowl, a dog or a dolphin, would have a different report to give even about primary qualities, for each lives in a world conditioned by the needs and environmental opportunities open to his species. In the gray visual world of the dog, smells, near and distant, subtle or violently exciting, probably play the part that colors do in man's world—though in the primal occupation of eating, the dog's world and man's world would approach each other more closely.

What applies to the biological background applies likewise, and perhaps even more, to human cultures, as a whole series of observers, from Immanuel Kant to Benjamin Whorf, have in one way or another sought to show. The only world that human beings move about in with some confidence is not Galileo's 'objective' world of primary qualities but the organic world as modified by human culture, that is, by the symbols of ritual and language, by the diverse arts, by tools and utensils and practical activities, by geotechnic transformation of landscapes and cities, by laws and institutions and ideologies. As soon as one moves in time to another epoch, or steps into another culture, this subjective familiarity and seeming objectivity disappear: disparities, anomalies, differences, contradictions disclose themselves, and along with these the irreducible richness of human experience, and the inexhaustible promise of human potentialities: not to be contained within any single system.

When Galileo's successors pulverized this immense cultural heritage into that which was measurable, public, 'objective,' repeatable, they not merely falsified or obliterated the basic facts of human existence, but curtailed the possibilities for human growth. Even worse, they created split personalities, whose private and subjective life never could, on the accepted postulates, modify or be modified by their public, objective life. By the nineteenth century, that split opened an unbridgeable gap between the artist and the scientist: a gap not to be closed, on Lord Snow's prescription, simply by making the artist more receptive to science.

Galileo's distinction between primary and secondary qualities was, he believed, a distinction between verifiable reality and mere sensory illusion. The first was an aspect accredited by the heavenly bodies and independent of man, while the latter was a subordinate kind of experience, since it rested upon the private reports of an ephemeral human personality. This was a faulty distinction: object and subject are inseparable.

Anger, for example, is a private subjective state, in so far as it directly affects consciousness: it becomes more public, but not more real, when it is open to external observation, in the tone of voice, the color of the skin, the contraction of the muscles; and this could, if necessary, be further objectified instrumentally by taking the blood pressure, the heartbeat, and analyzing the contents of adrenin and sugar in the blood. Both aspects of anger are real: but the public report would be unidentifiable without reference to the private emotional state that accompanied these events, since similar bodily changes are also produced by fear. On pseudo-objective terms, anger and fear would be virtually identical, except that in some instances—but not always or inevitably—the first may lead to attack and the second to flight.

As for Galileo's belief in the objective reality of shapes, without reference to the contribution of the observer, this, too, has no foundation. The boundaries that Galileo so clearly envisaged as a proof of independent objectivity disappear when the electromagnetic field is taken into account, just as the smooth edges of a sharp knife become jagged under a high-power microscope. The experience of reality in the higher organisms, particularly man, involves a continued oscillation between the inner and the outer, the subjective and the objective fields, and this reality is not only limited but falsified by a one-sided account. "Nature," as Adolf Portmann wisely observes, "comprises every aspect of life—subjective experience no less than structure."

Needless to say, it was not Galileo's commitment to primary qualities and mathematical analysis that alone brought the mechanical world picture into existence: he was abetted by both the theoretic pronouncements and the actual experiments of a succession of fellow scientists, who, so far from correcting his bias, deliberately exiled a large part of human experience from the realm of science.

The documents that establish this general acceptance of the mechanical world picture are so numerous that I will take a single example from the eighteenth century to stand for the rest.

The classic summation of Galileo's conception was made by David Hume, a brilliant mind that, under the cover of complete skepticism, established the new outlook as a dogma. "When we run over libraries," Hume noted, "persuaded by these principles, what havoc must we make? If we take in our hand any volume, of divinity or school metaphysics, for instance, let us ask, Does it contain any abstract reasoning concerning quantity or number? No. Does it contain any experimental reasoning concerning matter of fact and existence? No. Commit it then to the flames; for it can contain nothing but sophistry and illusion."

Those who took these injunctions seriously found it easy to wipe out every mode of theology and metaphysics other than their own, which they mistook for common sense and reality. Lived and recorded history suffered the same fate. On his own terms, Hume's 'History of England' would have been among the first works to be destroyed. Science in fact so completely lost any respect for the immediately non-observable or non-repeatable, that it is only recently that scientists and technologists have begun to be interested in their own history. More than one scientist has lately said that any work of science more than ten years old is not worth considering. This indicates more than the inordinate inflation of the scientific ego that the great theoretic and experimental advances of the last generation have produced: it indicates an effort to discredit an essential part of organic experience, memory, which establishes continuity with a longer past and a wider environment than a ten-year mind can encompass.

That attitude was responsible for the tardy following through of Faraday's penetrating insight into the electronic aspects of 'matter,' and it explains how the computer was so belatedly developed by scientists and engineers who might have proceeded with this invention at least a generation earlier, if they had ever heard of Babbage's calculating engine. At a lower level, the same attitude accounts for the anti-subjective views of the behaviorist 'psychologist' B. F. Skinner, who observed in 'Walden Two' that "we do not take history seriously." And no wonder: if man knew no history, the Skinners would govern the world, as Skinner himself has modestly proposed in his behaviorist utopia.

4: VALIDATION BY THE MACHINE

The new scientific philosophy took over and carried further two processes that were already at work in society, and were partly responsible, indeed, for the renewed interest in science itself. One was the invention and multiplication of machines, composed of closely articulated, finely measured, standardized, and replaceable parts, as in the mechanical clock and the printing press. The other was the wider use of coined money, stamped uniformly by machines, which in itself was partly due to the increasing practice of attaching a price—an abstract numerical notation referring to weight or number—to goods offered for sale. The maxim of Franklin's Poor Richard, "Time is money," symbolized this change; and the transactions of science resembled those of the marketplace in that they both required a neutral medium of exchange.

As mechanical power increased and as scientific theory itself, through further experimental verification, became more adequate, the new method enlarged its domain; and with every fresh demonstration of its efficiency it shored up the shaky theoretic scheme upon which it was based. What began in the astronomical observatory finally ended in our day in the computer-controlled and automatically operated factory. First the scientist excluded himself, and with himself a good part of his organic potentialities and his historic affiliations, from the world picture he constructed. As this system of thought spread into every department, the autonomous worker, even in his most reduced mechanical aspect, would be progressively excluded from the mechanism of production. Finally, should these postulates remain unchallenged and the institutional procedures remain unchanged, man himself will be cut off from any meaningful relationship with any part of the natural environment or his own historical milieu.

Those who created the mechanical world picture foresaw many actual inventions and discoveries, and were passionately eager to bring them about: but they could not, even speculatively, anticipate the dismaying social outcome of their efforts.

The immediate outcome, indeed, of the new system of thought and de-emotionalized statements, was temporarily a happy one, for it cooled off the overheated atmosphere of theological controversy left over from the Reformation and the Counter Reformation. Interest of the poets in science, from Milton and Johnson to Shelley and Wordsworth, and beyond, to Whitman and Tennyson, testifies to the liberating effects of the new world picture, for poets, Homer reminds us, tell us of things as they really are. Minds that were divided about the nature of the cosmos and man's ultimate concerns, were drawn together by their appreciation of the new world picture and the new machines that translated this picture into operative realities, useful products, social improvements. This of course was a gain.

What was generally helpful about this attitude toward the 'external world' was that it made constant reference to common experiences in which everyone could in some degree participate; and it gave confidence in man's ability to understand nature's operations. No longer could the mind be content with imaginary maps, fanciful histories, tenth-hand explanations, cherished hallucinations, in the fashion still prevalent in the Middle Ages, and then acceptable to all but the keenest minds. Accurate knowledge, even if unduly isolated and restricted, was better than muddled and inaccurate general knowledge that pretentiously professed to embrace everything. The provision of such useful knowledge temporarily offset, if it did not cancel out, the underlying errors. Thus, in the seventeenth century, the application of the thermometer to register the body's heat, Galileo's suggestion to Sanctorius, furnished a diagnostic aid to medicine, as the use of both the thermometer and the barometer offered the first quantitative clues to describing and predicting the weather.

All these achievements made the mechanical world picture highly acceptable: and many parts of that picture happily remain so. Hereafter, in every department, the sign of quantity or magnitude would, ideally, become a necessary part of every qualitative judgement. Up to a point, then, the new method was self-validating. It was only when it concentrated on quantity to the exclusion of quality, and upon piecemeal knowledge to the exclusion of form, pattern, functional organization, design, that the weakness of the original emphasis on so-called primary qualities would become a handicap. Those who developed the mechanical world picture further ignored Leibnitz's salient distinction between accurate knowledge and adequate knowledge, and were too easily content with accuracy, even if at the cost of leaving out or even denying the existence of relevant data. This practice was made all the easier because function and purpose, both essential in describing organic processes and human behavior, were transferred to the machine.

E. A. Burtt, commenting on the consequences of giving special status to the so-called primary qualities, observed correctly that this was "the first stage in the reading of man out of the real and primary realm. . . . Man begins to appear for the first time in thought as an irrelevant spectator and insignificant effect of the great mathematical system which is the substance of reality."

In effect, when the new scientist eliminated man from the picture he presented, he was seeking to let nature itself make the direct impression, much as the photographer allows light and chemicals to leave a 'neutral' record on a film. But those who use such a metaphor for a process seemingly independent of human bias disclose the speciousness of this conception: for before such a neutral procedure can be set in motion, the photographer must load his film, choose his subject, focus his camera; and of course before the camera could come into existence, a long process of human discovery was necessary, in optics, chemistry, glassmaking, plastics. In short, a multitude of human needs, interests, and choices must be reckoned with before the impression of light on a sensitized surface can be recorded and preserved. So with exact science. If man could have actually pushed himself and his culture completely out of the picture, there would have been no picture and no reason for taking it—certainly no mechanical world picture and no fresh generation of machines!

Yet for all its ideological weakness, the mathematical-mechanical method resulted in a clarification of 'physical events' which gave the inventor and the engineer confidence in their ability to arrive at predictable results. As for the 'physical world' that was described in these simple terms, what was this in itself but a plausible abstraction; for, as A. N. Whitehead pointed out, "the concrete enduring entities are organisms, so that the plan of the whole influences the very characters of the various subordinate organisms which enter into it. . . . Thus an electron within a living body is different from an electron outside it, by reason of the plan of the body." And, one may now add, an electron within an oxygen atom is different from one in a carbon atom, again by reason of its plan. Thus the scientific method, when it ceases to deal with statistical probabilities must pass from positivism to platonism.

What made the new world picture so potent was that its method of deliberately ignoring the complex reality of organisms was an immense labor-saving device: its pragmatic efficiency counterbalanced its conceptual superficiality. The universe as a whole, the whole that contains all other wholes, is immeasurable and unthinkable in its infinite variety and multifold concreteness. Only by samples and abstractions can one put together in the mind a playtoy model.

The ecological complexities of existence overwhelm the human mind, even though some of that richness is an integral part of man's own nature. It is only by isolating some little part of that existence for a short time that it can be momentarily grasped: we learn only from samples. By separating primary from secondary qualities, by making mathematical description the test of truth, by utilizing only a part of the human self to explore only a part of its environment, the new science successfully turned the most significant attributes of life into purely secondary phenomena, ticketed for replacement by the machine. Thus living organisms, in their most typical functions and purposes, became superfluous.

5 MACHINES AS DEFECTIVE ORGANISMS

Again, it was the philosopher E. A. Burtt who, a generation before Erwin Schrödinger, put his finger most decisively upon the consequences of the new system of analysis.

"Man's performance could not be treated by the quantitative method except in the most meagre fashion. His life was a life of color and sounds, of pleasures, of griefs, of passionate loves, of ambitious strivings. Hence the real world must be outside the world of man: the world of astronomy, the world of resting and moving terrestrial objects. The only thing in common between man and this world was his ability to discover it, a fact which, being necessarily presupposed, was easily neglected, and did not in any case suffice to exalt him to a parity of reality and causal efficiency with that which he is able to know. . . . Along with this exaltation of the external world as more primary and more real, went an attribution of greater dignity and value. Galileo himself proceeds to this addition. 'Sight is the most excellent of the senses, because of its relation to light, the most excellent object; but as compared with the latter, it is as inferior as the finite in comparison with the infinite.' "

To treat as ultimate and supreme the physical phenomenon of light, and to forget the light of consciousness, itself the highest manifestation of life, shows if anything how effectively the Sun God had stricken his worshippers with blindness. How much was lost by this exaltation of the mechanical world picture one may gather from an account of a recent invention, by the biologist Pumphrey.

The Bell Telephone engineers, Pumphrey tells us, "found that all intelligence could get through a system called a Vocorder, which instead of transmitting a continuous but limited spectrum, squeezed as it were all the sound energy of speech through ten narrow gates, thirty-two cycles wide . . . with the economic consequence that, with sufficient paraphernalia at the sending and receiving ends, ten intelligible messages can now be simultaneously transmitted over a channel where one would go before.

"The interesting feature for us," continues Pumphrey, "is the effect of this process on the character of speech, for in discarding or blurring the detailed structure, it has effected a completely mechanical separation of the emotive and informative functions of speech. The output of this infernal machine is perfectly intelligible and perfectly impersonal. No trace of anger or love, pity or terror, irony or sincerity, can get through it. The age or sex of the speaker cannot be guessed. No dog would recognize his master's voice. In fact, it does not sound as if a human agent was responsible for the message. But the intelligence is unimpaired."

"The intelligence is unimpaired." That is only another way of saying, in fact, that this sort of intelligence is, in terms of life, innately defective, since it can never receive or respond to a sufficiently full and comprehensive report of the actual world as experienced by fully activated organisms and mindful human personalities. Ironically, it was originally pride in man's new mechanical inventions, a very human pride exalted with justification by the telescope, that led the great thinkers of the seventeenth century not only to exile man from his own many-dimensioned world, but to reduce his scientific voice, so to speak, to the equivalent of a Vocorder.

The same reduction and isolation took place indeed with all his other organs: today even the erotic life, at the hands of all-too-eager geneticists and physiologists, has not proved immune from such violation. Witness the speciously objective reports of Johnson and Masters on human sexual acts. This progressive reduction of the dimensions of life involved far more serious humiliations than the discovery that the earth was not the center of the universe. Christian humility supposedly brought the soul nearer to God: but scientific humility brought it closer to self-annihilation.

Now compare this mechanical world view, with its exclusive emphasis on the quantitative, the measurable, the external, with that of one of the most primitive of known races and cultures, the Australian aborigines. According to a recent interpreter, Kaj Birket-Smith, "The fundamental idea in the Australian's concept of life is that there is no sharp division between man and nature, between the quick and the dead, nor even a gap between past, present, and future. Nature can as little exist without man as man without nature, and yesterday and tomorrow, in a manner inexplicable to us, merge into today."

Whatever the deficiencies in the Australian aborigine's habits of observation or in his symbolic formulation of his experience, it will become plain, as the theme of this book develops, that the Australian's 'primitive' view is in fact far less primitive, biologically and culturally speaking, than that of the mechanical world picture, for it includes those many dimensions of life that Kepler, Galileo, and their successors intentionally excluded, as spoiling the accuracy of their observations and the elegance of their descriptions.

All through the nineteenth century, the major voices in science proclaimed, as confidently as Huygens and Newton had done, not simply that the laws of mechanics are among the laws that govern all phenomena, but that these laws are the only laws needed for an adequate explanation even of life and mind, and that no other non-mechanical behavior need be looked for. Even such an emancipated physicist as Clerk Maxwell would say in 1875 that "when a physical phenomenon can be completely described as a change in the configuration and motion of a material system, the dynamical explanation of that phenomenon is said to be complete"; while Helmholtz, a little earlier (1869), said confidently: "the object of the natural sciences is to find the motions upon which all other changes are based, and their corresponding motive forces—to resolve themselves, therefore, into mechanics." The notion of Boscovich and Faraday that non-mechanical behavior might exist, even at the level of the atom, then lay far outside the pale.

This explains the contempt, indeed the shudder of theological horror, as over a damnable heresy, that is still expressed by many biologists when asked to give rational consideration to 'vital,' 'organismic,' 'teleological,' or 'parapsychological' phenomena. The ultimate result of this mechanistic doctrine was to raise the machine to a higher status than any organism, or at best to admit grudgingly that higher organisms were supermachines. Thus a set of metaphysical abstractions laid the groundwork for a technological civilization, in which the machine in the latest of its many incarnations would in time become the 'Supreme Power,' an object of religious adoration and worship.

During the last century, in particular during the last generation, the weaknesses in this original formulation have been exposed, and in many places corrected: most decisively, not without irony, by the direct heirs of Galileo, the nuclear physicists, for their world of minute particles or charges cannot be described or handled on purely mechanical or geometrical terms, or made coherent and visible by being re-assembled in some work-performing machine.

For all this, the mechanical image, by reason of its very concreteness, has remained dominant—even though the actual experience of our contemporaries includes X-rays and the electronic transmission systems of images and sounds. To illustrate the hold that the mechanical world picture still keeps, I shall confine myself to two examples, both fortunately a little comic.

In a recent book a biologist of note has dismissed the real existence of pain on the ground that it is an inner experience, privately reported and therefore, scientifically speaking, inaccessible and indescribable. In order to eliminate this factor which, by its very existence, defies the method he reveres, he goes so far as to say: "We have been talking about pain as if it was some horrid little demon sitting inside you. Let us now talk about it by comparison with machines and other objects, in terms of nerves and their impulses, and above all in terms of brains and the way they react to it. Then at least we *may* be able to teach ourselves not to feel pain."

If effective, this would of course be a desirable kind of instruction for, let us say, a cancer patient: though it might be quite imprudent on many other occasions, when a sharp pain, as when a child's hand touches flame, teaches him to avoid more serious bodily damage. There is no doubt that hypnotism, which is a valid form of such teaching, under certain circumstances serves as an admirable anesthetic, as was long ago demonstrated; and even stoic self-discipline or auto-suggestion may be an excellent anesthetic for many pains. But what shall one say of the theoretic limitations of a scientist who goes on to say "that it is absurd to try to express the existence of something that cannot possibly be described"? Is it not far more absurd to deny that existence?

To dismiss as non-existent what happens to be indescribable is to equate existence with information. Can a color be described solely in terms of its mathematically determinable wave length? No matter how accurate this abstract description may be, it gives no indication of color as a subjective experience. So with pain. To deny the existence or importance of pain because it is too private to be described—is that an example of scientific objectivity?

This attempt to make pain scientifically disreputable is in reality an attempt to keep organic reactions coupled to machinelike behavior; and since machines do not have any means of registering pain, an organism that does so becomes an anomaly, or, worse than that, a technological anachronism. What is perhaps even more exasperating to those who cling to this obsolete mechanical model is that pain itself points to something for which no biological answer is as yet available—although the fact itself has long been staring our evolutionary doctrines in the face. How is it that such a gross maladaptation as intense pain, which serves no purpose that lesser degrees of pain might not equally serve—indeed, often gets worse when the condition it calls attention to is entirely beyond remedy—has become an *inherited* trait? This would seem a heavy price to pay for the exquisite sensitivity and over-responsiveness of the nervous systems in higher organisms. What 'selective pressure' produced and transmitted such a disserviceable reaction?

Today this almost pathological fear of what cannot be directly examined and brought under control—external, preferably mechanical, electronic, or chemical control—survives as a scientific equivalent of a much older atavism, fear of the dark. And if, on the contrary, at the end of four centuries devoted to filling in the outmoded mechanical world picture, we now overvalue the machine, is it not because the mechanistic doctrine which has made us competent to design machines and control them also promises to give the scientist an equal hold over the living organisms he unfeelingly identifies with machines? In a world of machines, or of creatures that can be reduced to machines, technocrats would indeed be gods.

True: those who have seen most deeply into the problem have found reason to suppose that if man actually succeeded in fabricating such machines he would not be able to control them, since if they were truly alive they would not only be autonomous but subject to other influences, including their own caprices, besides those of man. Norbert Wiener even feared this might happen in a not-too-distant future with computers: a point the scenario of the film '2001' followed up when its infallible spaceship computer, on being crossed, became hostile to its astronauts. Would not electronic omniscience, if indeed it possessed like man an equivalent of subjective life, prove as crazy, cruel, and murderous as the powerful deities of the Bronze Age in fact were?—all the more hostile because totally lacking in the cultural safeguards that even then man had built up for his own self-protection against his unconscious.

That an up-to-date scientist should still be committed to the archaic mechanical world picture to the point of resenting organic events that take place outside this limited frame shows how attractive and how potent that over-simplified model was—and unfortunately remains even now. But the absurdity of using the machine to explain the autonomous processes of organization and growth and reproduction comes out best, perhaps, in the story Frank O'Connor tells of his mother's effort to explain to him as a boy how babies are conceived, without going into embarrassing physiological and emotional intimacies. Concerned, she explained that "mummies had an engine in their tummies and daddies had a starting handle that made it work, and once it started it went on until it made a baby." But of course! What could be more '*natural*,' that is, more mechanical, more 'objective'?

Thus by the end of the nineteenth century a simple woman, confronted with the facts of life, was driven by sexual embarrassment to adopt the same kind of explanation, cruder but substantially similar, that scientists had been making, to reduce organic behavior to a 'mechanical' process—as if machines were more primordial than the 'innate' tendency toward organization that must be posited at the very beginnings of pre-organic existence to account for even the evolution of the atomic elements.

6: ABSOLUTION FOR GALILEO

One task of this book will be to trace out the unfortunate consequences of Galileo's 'crime.' Yet that crime proved so successful, and the intellectual booty it brought in was so huge, that those who have followed in Galileo's footsteps, so far from having to bow to the Inquisition in order to avoid torture, have by now extended Galileo's methodology and metaphysics to every phase of human activity. As a result, the masters of the scientific guild, with their many imitators, and disciples, now wield more influence and power than any older priesthood. What is more, the religion of this new priesthood, propagated by a succession of attested miracles, has a firm foothold in every mind, and even those areas of scientific knowledge and technical facility that owe no direct debt to the Sun God nevertheless bow to his authority.

In pointing out these insufficiencies in the mechanical world picture, I have no wish to disparage the many beneficent results, particularly in the realm where they could be applied most directly and vigorously—that is, in technics itself. Every fresh quantum of scientific truth, however dismembered or minute, was precious. In a period of bitter political and theological conflicts, when in defense of dogmatic positions intense feelings were aroused, when conversation had become impossible between a Catholic and a Protestant, or for that matter, between the adherents of two different Protestant sects, the new mechanical ideology performed a unique service: it provided a common language, and it opened up a field of practical endeavor in which people with widely different inner worlds could nevertheless collaborate. This common world of intelligent intercourse and cooperation has, in the face of national egoisms and jealousies and self-isolating totalitarian ideologies, continued to widen. Scientists are more at home among their colleagues in every part of the world than any other vocational group, for they speak a common language and pursue a common aim. That unity, though it has been frequently interrupted, is too precious to be lost.

Admittedly the sciences so created were masterly symbolic fabrications: unfortunately those who utilized these symbols implicitly believed that they represented a higher order of reality, when in fact they expressed only a higher order of abstraction. Human experience itself remained, necessarily, multi-dimensional: one axis extends horizontally through the world open to external observation, the so-called objective world, and the other axis, at right angles, passes vertically through the depths and heights of the subjective world; while reality itself can only be represented by a figure composed of an indefinite number of lines drawn through both planes and intersecting at the center, in the mind of a living person.

But let us, at the end, give the Sun God his due: the order that he established is indeed fundamental to all other manifestations of life; and in a culture open to disorganization and disintegration, then as now, his worshippers introduced a necessary respect for order itself. Let us then in addition give Galileo a graceful post-mortem absolution: he knew not what he did, and he could not possibly guess what would follow from the splitting apart of objective and subjective experience. He himself was not a concealed heretic but an open-minded naturalistic humanist, or humanistic naturalist, and he could not guess that the abstract conceptual world he had helped to create would eventually displace all traditional values and reject all experience and knowledge that did not conform to the dominant mechanical pattern. Galileo must have taken for granted that the culture which had formed his own life and mind would continue in existence more beautifully ordered, enriched—not devitalized, impoverished, and reduced —by his new way of looking at the world.

In denying the importance of subjective factors, that is, human propulsions, projections, and autonomous responses, the followers of Galileo unfortunately fended off any inquiry into their own subjectivity; and in rejecting values, purposes, and non-scientific meanings, fantasies, dreams, as irrelevant to their positivist methodology, they failed to recognize the part such subjectivity had played in creating their own system. What they had actually done was to eliminate every value and every purpose but one, the one they regarded as supreme: the pursuit of scientific truth. In this pursuit of truth, the scientist sanctified his own discipline and what was more dangerous placed it above any other obligations of morality. The consequences of this dedication have only begun to appear in our own age. Scientific truth achieved the status of an absolute, and the incessant pursuit and expansion of knowledge became the only recognized categorical imperative.

Now, if the history of the human race teaches any plain lessons, this is one of them: *Man cannot be trusted with absolutes.* When the Romans said "Let justice be done though the ceiling fall," they did not for a moment suspect that the ceiling might fall; but the physicists who so steadfastly pursued the splitting of the atom were, in fact, endangering the human race. With the invention of nuclear bombs, they placed all life on earth in danger, for not just the ceiling but the heavens might now fall. In the old game of truth or consequences, the consequences turn out to be as important as the truth, and must be warily examined and re-examined with every extension of truth into new areas. For lack of this wariness today not only do millions of human beings live in the shadow of a total catastrophe, but the air they breathe, the water they drink, and the food they eat are being poisoned by other misapplications of scientific knowledge.

If the new science had begun with the observer himself, as an essential component in its own scheme, the insufficiency of his mechanical model and his de-natured and de-humanized universe would have been apparent—indeed, inescapable. Without intuitions and memories, without ancient cultural landmarks, the intelligence is enfeebled, and the report it gives on its own say-so is so incomplete, so qualitatively inadequate, so structurally distorted that it becomes downright false. Percy Bridgman, in his 'Introduction to Stallo,' did well to point out that it was the scientist's active experimentation and selection that enabled him to overcome the basic theoretic weaknesses of his mechanistic formulations.

No one who is familiar with scientists, or who has read biographies of creative scientists, will imagine that the prevailing canons of objectivity, complete impersonality, mechanical precision, austere repression of feeling apply to anything but the handling of apparatus or the final presentation of the results in the form of careful, systematic descriptions. In playing the scientific game, the scientist must follow its strict rules, or he will be penalized—and, if necessary, disqualified. But the game itself is played by human beings open to subjective promptings of every sort, from pride and vanity to intellectual playfulness and intense esthetic delight. Without these subjective underpinnings in one combination or another, it is doubtful if some of the best work in science would have been done.

Though the full personality is a necessary basis for creative activity in science as elsewhere, nothing except a radical transformation in the method and purpose of the scientist can overcome the persistent limitations that spring from its absence from the original mechanical world picture itself. Man cannot, even in theory, eviscerate his necessary organs and reduce the whole field of his activities to that which is observable and controllable without presenting a defective picture of both his own nature and the world he lives in.

To dismiss the most central fact of man's being because it is inner and subjective is to make the hugest subjective falsification possible—one that leaves out the most critical half of man's nature. For without that underlying subjective flux, as experienced in floating imagery, dreams, bodily impulses, formative ideas, projections, and inventions—and above all with increasing lucidity in language—the world that is open to human experience can neither be described nor rationally understood. When our age learns that lesson, it will have made the first move toward redeeming for human use the mechanized and electrified wasteland that is now being constructed, at man's expense and to his permanent loss, for the benefit of the megamachine.

CHAPTER FOUR

Political Absolutism and Regimentation

1: LORDS OF NATURE

The transformation begun in theory by Copernicus, Kepler, and Galileo was carried further by René Descartes, for he coupled the new world picture to the two new phenomena that gave it immense authority: the behavior of clockwork automatons and the claims of monarchical absolutism. He proved to his own satisfaction that all the manifestations of life could be explained on a purely mechanical basis, and that except in the case of man organism and mechanism were interchangeable terms.

Descartes' 'Discourse on Method' stands as a landmark in the history of Western thought: through its elegant style and its fusion of mathematical and mechanical modes of reasoning, it left a permanent imprint on later scientific formulations. This work, as short and readable as Rousseau's later 'Social Contract,' was Descartes' substitute for a more comprehensive book that he suppressed when he saw what trouble his contemporary, Galileo, had gotten into with the Holy Inquisition. As such, it serves almost as a prefatory 'Summa' to modern thought: a neatly articulated skeleton that contrasts with the corpulent, over-detailed synthesis of Thomas Aquinas.

At the time Descartes wrote there was still no part of the world that did not seem open to adequate scientific investigation by a single mind. Alone, like a royal despot, he ventured to lay the ideological foundations for a new age. In that sense, Descartes was still in the older Aristotelian tradition, and had not yet made the great submission his older contemporary, Francis Bacon, prophesied; for the latter realized that science, to become more productive and immediately serviceable, must accept the specialized division of labor and a standardized piecemeal mode of investigation.

From Descartes, nevertheless, one gets a clear account of the underlying motives for scientific investigation, apart from its oldest and noblest impulse, the sheer delight of using the mind to discover ordered relationships and to create intelligible symbolic structures that reveal the underlying causal sequences or the emergent patterns of seemingly haphazard events. Without that bottomless curiosity and wonder, man could hardly have advanced beyond the animal state of muscular exercise and mindless enjoyment. What Thorstein Veblen used ironically to call 'idle curiosity' once served to attach the best minds to the passionate pursuit of science, often to the exclusion of other more tangible rewards. That disinterested commitment to universally sharable truth was perhaps science's most enduring bequest.

But in addition more egoistic ambitions and utilitarian lures played a part from the beginning in the development of science, as earlier with magic; and these concerns come out even in the austere statements of Descartes. "I perceived it to be possible," he observed, "to arrive at knowledge highly useful in life; and instead of the speculative philosophy usually taught in the schools, to discover a practical [method] by means of which, knowing the force and action of fire, water, air, the stars, the heavens, and all the other bodies that surround us, as distinctly as we know the various crafts of our artisans, we might also apply them in the same way to all the uses to which they are adapted, and thus render ourselves the *lords and possessors of nature*." (Italics mine.)

The language of this last sentence is obviously not the language of the disinterested speculative scientist: it was attached rather to the social motives that from the sixteenth century on had begun to play an ever more active part in the whole development of Western civilization: in exploration and colonization, in military conquest and mechanical industry. To become the "lords and possessors of nature" was the ambition that secretly united the conquistador, the merchant adventurer and banker, the industrialist, and the scientist, radically different though their vocations and their purposes might seem.

Even at the beginning, science and technics played a part in furthering these extravagant ambitions and arrogant claims. Without the magnetic compass, astronomical observations, and cartography, the circumnavigation of the globe would have been long delayed, if not impossible. But from the nineteenth century on, science's preoccupation with man's one-sided mastery over nature took another turn: that of seeking artificial substitutes for every natural process, replacing organic products with manufactured ones, and eventually turning man himself into an obedient creature of the forces he had discovered or created. Ironically, the duplication of urea, an animal waste product, was the first great triumph of such research! But many other substitutes—fibers, plastics, pharmaceuticals—followed; some excellent in their own right, some merely producing larger profits for bigger organizations.

Descartes could not of course foresee that this one-sided effort to 'conquer nature' would bring a special danger, the closer it approached realization: that of dispossessing and displacing man himself. But though we must now confront this ultimate threat, I mention it here only to exonerate Descartes and proclaim his relative innocence. Like Galileo he could have had no notion of what would happen when the control of external phenomena and the increase of physical energies available for altering the environment and commanding time and space should take precedence over the effort to humanize man himself, to discipline and direct his own development, and to explore the abounding potentialities of his culture and personality.

In Descartes' time, the physical and mathematical sciences had not yet achieved anything like their present position of superiority. Descartes himself, though a gifted mathematician, was not exclusively immersed in mathematical problems or physical phenomena; for he made a close physiological study of the motion of the blood in the heart and arteries, along the lines that Harvey was to carry to a more successful conclusion. Though Descartes conceived of man's becoming a lord of nature, that overlordship remained for him, despite his experience as a soldier, chiefly in the mind. His best hopes lay, not in increased physical power or productivity, but in achieving knowledge of the human organism, which he hoped would provide a rational foundation for a more healthy regimen.

Thus, while Descartes, like Bacon, saw that science was practically desirable, as leading to the "invention of an infinity of arts, by which we might be enabled to enjoy without any trouble the fruits of the earth and all its comforts," he felt that "if any means can ever be found to render men wise and more ingenious than hitherto . . . it is in medicine that they must be sought for." He was confident that "we could free ourselves from an infinity of maladies of the body, as well as the mind, and perhaps also of the debility of old age, if we had sufficiently ample knowledge of their causes, and of all the remedies provided for us by nature." For him the direct human benefits still counted for more than the gross increase of material goods or power.

As modern man has reason gratefully to acknowledge, that confidence was not altogether misplaced. The increased number of people in the Western World who live out their normal life span today, as a result of hygienic care, preventive medicine, skillful surgery, and antibiotics—to say nothing of the universal use of soap and water—shows that Descartes' sanguine hopes were justified. But as with all those minds, scientific or utopian, that were elated by expectations of endless improvements, Descartes overlooked the negative results that would accompany and insidiously undermine these achievements, often in proportion to their success. Among them we now begin to recognize biological errors of great magnitude. These unforeseen consequences have partly nullified the genuine advances and left the ultimate balance in science's favor increasingly doubtful, unless massive measures are now taken to halt the scientifically and financially expedited forces of destruction and extermination.

2 : THE PASSAGE TO ABSOLUTISM

Though Descartes was an assiduous scientific experimenter in more than one area, the cartesian method itself was most immediately applicable to 'physical,' that is to pre-organic, nature. Descartes deliberately concentrated on this aspect because it seemed to him "the most common and simple, hence the easiest to know"; while the mathematical advances that delighted him seemed at first serviceable only because they "contributed to the advancement of the mechanical arts."

Despite the wide range of Descartes' investigations, the baroque culture of his time stamped his thought with two identifying marks that were to have a serious effect upon later technics through re-enforcing practices that were already in operation. The first was Descartes' belief in political absolutism, as a means of achieving and maintaining order. As opposed to all those processes that involve tradition, historic continuity, cumulative experience, democratic cooperation and reciprocal intercourse with others, Descartes favored the kind of external order that could be achieved by a single mind, like that of a baroque prince, detached from precedent, breaking with popular customs, all-powerful, acting alone, commanding unqualified obedience: in short, laying down the law.

This destruction of organic complexity was the prime condition for effecting mechanization and total control in every department. The workings of such minds were already visible in the buildings and cities of the period: structures designed by engineer-architects, working in the service of an autocratic authority, according to a predetermined plan, ready for instant execution.

In Part Two, Descartes singled out this order of planning for praise, and in contrast disparaged those buildings and towns that had gone through a longer period of growth and exhibited, along with their imperfections, the revisions, the adaptations, the happy second thoughts and the fresh innovations of later generations. He even praised Sparta, not because he thought its particular laws and customs were necessarily good, but because they had been "originated by a single individual" and "tended to a single end." No wonder he used the plan of the baroque city as the model for his philosophical system: mechanical order and inflexible control is written all over it, as I have shown at length in 'The City in History.' If one removes the trimmings from the Palace of Versailles, one has, in effect, the shell of a modern extended factory unit.

Descartes' soloism was a natural expression of baroque absolutism in other areas than government: to act alone, to occupy the center of the stage, to displace all rival personalities or groups—this was the underlying tie between the princely despot, the musical prima donna, the monopolistic financier, and the reflective philosopher. The final effect of this movement was to reduce to a whirl of decomposed atomic particles all the constituent elements of society, and to leave to a single polarizing element, the king or the 'state,' the function of giving some sort of order and direction to the alienated and fragmented individuals that were left. This stripping away of the constituent groups that compose any real community—the family, the village, the farm, the workshop, the guild, the church—cleared the way for the uniformities and standardizations imposed by the machine. We can witness this process most clearly in the analysis of reality for which Descartes long was famous.

Seeking to clear out of his mind all knowledge, true or false, that it contained, in order to build again from rock bottom, Descartes was left with what seemed to him an indisputable proposition: the famous, "I think, therefore I am." This equation of thought with being removed it from all qualifying limitations: thinking itself tended to become unconditional and absolute: in fact, the sole imperative demand of existence. In order to reach this point Descartes forgot that before he uttered these words, "I think . . . ," he needed the cooperation of countless fellow-beings, extending back to his own knowledge as far as the thousands of years that Biblical history recorded. Beyond that, we know now, he needed the aid of an even remoter past that mankind too long remained ignorant of: the millions of years required to transform his dumb animal ancestors into conscious human beings.

"I think, therefore I am" had meaning only because of this immense mass of buried history. Without that past, his momentary experience of thought would have been undescribable; indeed, inexpressible. Perhaps the greatest defect of all world pictures up to now is that the transformation of history, except in the cloudy form of myth, has played so little part in their conception of reality. In Jewish tradition almost alone is history regarded as a necessary and meaningful revelation of universal forces, or as theology would put it, God's will.

In trying to make a fresh start, Descartes had in fact swept away nothing. For without his collectively stored and individually remembered experience, Descartes' lips and tongue and vocal cords could not have framed his triumphant sentence. "Man is only a reed, but a thinking reed," said his contemporary Pascal. Descartes had merely restated this conviction, which most seventeenth-century intelligences shared and regarded as axiomatic: namely, that thinking is man's most important activity. But this itself is open to question, since sexual reproduction is more essential to thought, biologically speaking, than thought is to reproduction; for life not merely encompasses but transcends thought.

Descartes' contemporary Gassendi saw the weakness of his position. "You will say," he wrote Descartes, "I am mind alone. . . . But let us talk in earnest, and tell me frankly, do you not derive from the very sound you utter in so saying from the society in which you have lived? And, since the sounds you utter are derived from intercourse with other men, are not the meanings of sounds derived from the same source?"

Beneath Descartes' equation of thought with existence another idea was implicit which derived from the social style of the baroque period. Under a rational system of ideas, all minds would be forced to submit to scientific 'laws' as the subject of an absolute ruler to his edicts. Law in both instances, as Wilhelm Ostwald was later to point out, established the realm of predictable behavior: this simplified choices and economized effort. Thus the ultimate aim of science, the proof of both its truth and its efficacy, would be to make all behavior as predictable as the movements of the heavenly bodies.

To many scientists, even today, this is not only an unchallengeable axiom but a moral imperative. If scientific determinism operated everywhere, then human lives, too, might ultimately be brought under perfect control. This of course assumed, as in any absolute system of government, that there were no unruly elements that were not known to the police, or could not be rounded up and imprisoned indefinitely without further investigation.

In rejecting the cumulative contributions of history, Descartes lost sight, then, of both the significance of nature and the nature of significance, and failed to understand their interdependence, since the mind that explores nature is itself a part of nature and exhibits otherwise hidden or inaccessible characteristics. Without this larger time-span to sustain it, life would shrink and shrivel into nothingness; and the ego would lack the very words needed to deny the mind's existence or to curse its own impotence. It is in such a state, incidentally, that many of our contemporaries actually find themselves today, since they accept the momentary reports of their senses as final revelations—however hideous—of truth.

What was implied by way of renunciation in Descartes' rational scheme comes out in the following brief passage. "Because our reasonings are never so clear or complete during sleep as when we are awake, though sometimes the acts of the imagination are lively and distinct, if not more so, than in our waking moments, reason further dictates that, since all our thoughts cannot be true because of our partial imperfection, those possessing truth must infallibly be founded in the experience of our waking moments rather than in that of our dreams."

This again was a valuable counsel for checking perverse fantasies: yet it did not do justice to the arcane forces that were themselves helping to produce a technical and social order that corresponded closely to Descartes' own subjective assumptions. Here the reason carefully protected and hid its own tendency to unreason, when divorced from the whole tissue of organic experience. Three centuries later Dr. Sigmund Freud, by intention a rigorous 'materialist,' strictly committed by his medical training to an austere mode of investigation that had no need for Descartes' God even as a hypothesis, returned to the world of dreams to discover how much of the human reality Descartes had rejected in adhering strictly to those waking moments favorable to rational investigation.

What Descartes necessarily lacked the perspective to see was that his own interpretation of life as a purely mechanical phenomenon, comparable to the strictly regulated motions of an automaton, was not as transparently rational as it seemed to him and to many of his successors.

Note, finally, the implications of Descartes' mechanistic absolutism. For the sake of clarity and predictable order, Descartes was ready to set aside the most characteristic function of all organisms: the capacity to enregister and hoard experience and continuously to reinterpret present activities in relation to both remembered and prospective or imagined events: above all to act for themselves without outside instruction or control in pursuance of their individual purposes or those of their species or group. For the same reason Descartes was oblivious to all those complex symbiotic interactions that demand empathy, mutual aid, and sensitive accommodations, for which Aristotle at least could have given him homely illustrations.

True to the principles of absolutism, Descartes preferred a predeterminded design, laid down by a single mind, to fulfill a single end at a single point in time; and he thought that in matters of mind, as well as in government, the best communities "followed the appointments of some wise legislator." He characterized as "restless and busy meddlers" reformers who sought to alter these appointments. No active organism, no historic group, no living community could without protest be successfully imprisoned in that cartesian framework: Descartes was in fact writing out the specifications for a successful machine.

In his conception of science's method and role, then, Descartes openly followed the style of the Renascence despot; he preferred absolute government, with its Procrustean simplifications, to democratic government, with its divided powers, its tenacious traditions, its embarrassing historic contradictions, its confusions and compromises and obscurities. But the acceptance of the latter is in fact the necessary price for a method capable of embracing the complexities of life without leaving any function or purpose unrecognized, uncounted, or uncared for. By his penchant for political absolutism Descartes paved the way for the eventual militarization of both science and technics.

Descartes did not perceive that the complex processes and singular events of history and biography, most of which remain unobservable and are by definition unrepeatable, are no less important manifestations of nature than mass phenomena that are open to observation, experiment, and statistical description. As a result, mechanical order, with its clarity and predictability, became in the minds of Descartes' followers, the main criterion of reality and the source of all values, except those that Descartes preferred to leave entirely in the care of the Church.

3: THE SCIENTIST AS LAWGIVER

In effect, Descartes elevated the scientist into an absolute lawgiver, not of course in his individual capacity, but in his collective role. By turning man into a "machine made by the hands of God," he tacitly turned into gods those who were capable of designing and making machines. As long as those powers were extremely limited, as they indeed remained until the present century, this yearning for godlike powers did little harm: if anything, it buttressed confidence in the face of difficulties with its assurance that, 'with the help of God' (Science) any project, however audacious, might finally be accomplished.

As a healthy reaction against superstition and pseudo-knowledge, this cartesian clarification was at first beneficial: it had the effect of a flowing river of fresh water, loosening the barnacles of encrusted superstition and subjective error that had impeded the movement of the ancient vessels of thought. But as a permanent contribution to thought and life, the mechanical mode has turned out to be an auxiliary at this juncture to political absolutism, for the two were in perfect harmony.

"The body of man," observed Descartes flatly, "is nothing but a statue or a machine made of earth." The long quarrel between organicism and mechanism centers on this dogmatic "nothing but." In order to prove that the nature and behavior of living creatures, with the exception of man, could be fully accounted for on purely mechanical principles, Descartes turned naturally to the special model that had always exercised a fascination over kings: the automaton. This fascination was by no means capricious or accidental; for automatic figures, in animal or human shape, 'animated' as we say by clockwork, were the perfect embodiment of the royal demand for unconditional obedience, absolute order, push-button control—qualities that such rulers, from the Pyramid Age onward, sought to implant in their subjects. The success of even the simplest automatons gave point to Descartes' question: May not living organisms be satisfactorily explained, and so governed, as if they were machines?

The specific attributes of life seemed to Descartes "not at all strange to those who are acquainted with the variety of movements performed by different automata or moving machines fabricated by human industry." This superficial resemblance closed his eyes to the immense gulf between man-made machines, composed of separate mechanical parts, and organisms, in which no cell, tissue, or organ has any existence or continuity except as a dynamic member of a unified self-renewing whole, most of whose essential characteristics vanish as soon as life ceases.

Though Descartes took care to exempt man from his mechanical explanation, he made the specious error declaring that if machines were manufactured exactly resembling in organs and outward form an ape or any other 'irrational' animal, we would have no means of knowing that they were in any respect of a different nature from these animals. Logically, this error would seem too flagrant to demand refutation: for Descartes was taking as a hypothetical basis the very possibility he was trying to prove. If any machine *exactly* resembled an organism, it would be an organism, not a machine: which means, among many other things, that it would be capable of designing and manufacturing itself without human help.

What is generally regarded as a timid hedging on Descartes' part when he came to man was, in fact, a recognition of the claims of the subjective life, the superiority of human reason, and the creativity of man's unique achievement: language. Nevertheless he had little use for any other principle of explanation than that which the machine supplied; and it was this emphasis, not his discreet qualifications, that carried over into the methodology of science. "I want you to regard these functions," he wrote, "as taking place naturally in this machine because of the very arrangement of its parts, neither more nor less than do the movements of a clock or other automaton from the weights and wheels, so that there is no need on their account to suppose in it any soul vegetative or sensitive or any principle of life other than its blood."

This passage reveals the deep impression that lifelike clockwork mechanisms made on Descartes' contemporaries, and not least on Descartes himself. Kepler shared that reaction. In a letter written in 1605 he said: "I am much occupied with the investigation of physical causes. My aim is to show that the celestial machine is to be likened not to a divine organism but rather to a clockwork." But it was easier to reduce the organism to such a machine than to reverse this process and turn 'machines' into organisms. That alternate ambition was left for our own age to express.

To Descartes' credit as a thinker, he realized better than many of his followers that his over-simplified mechanical model broke down in the case of man because of "two most certain tests." Men had the ability to use words and signs "in order to declare their thoughts to others." And men had freedom of will in a sense that is absent, or at least not fully developed, in other animals. Though a creature built on mechanical principles alone might, Descartes said, perform various individual acts even more perfectly than man—as many machines now do—the limits of its behavior are set by its organs, and those organs are not sufficiently diversified to meet, by their set response, all the occurrences of life "in the way in which our reason enables us to act."

This was a generous admission and a significant partial correction; but it still does not do justice to capacities that even many lower organisms possess. Animal instincts and reflexes, physiologists and ethologists now tell us, are not so strictly programmed genetically and so inadaptable in their behavior as post-cartesian theory for long held. Descartes' early overcommitment to the machine was his theoretic undoing; though in his unwillingness to treat man as a behaviorist automaton he escaped the chronic errors of later generations of behaviorists. Descartes' failure to apply to man the same reasoning he applied to other organisms has often been dismissed as a cowardly precaution against persecution by the Church. But was it not rather the example of truly scientific circumspection?

4 : THE MACHINE MODEL RE-EXAMINED

What Descartes did by equating organisms with machines was to make it possible to apply to organic behavior the quantitative method that was to serve so efficiently in describing 'physical' events. To know more about the behavior of a physical system one must isolate it, disorganize it, and separate out its measurable elements, down to the minutest particle—a necessary feat for understanding its operation. But to pass beyond the limits of a physical system into the realm of life, one must do just the opposite: assemble more and more parts into a pattern of organization that, as it approaches more closely to living phenomena reacting within a living environment, becomes so complex that it can only be reproduced and apprehended intuitively in the act of living, since, at least in man, it includes mind and the infra- and ultra-corporeal aspects of mind.

Reductionism reverses this process: for it dares not even hint at such a primal thrust in the direction of organization as would account for the specific nature of atoms or the self-replication of crystals: aspects of matter that contradict the old views of a mindless universe of 'dead' atoms colliding at random. On any pure theory of causality or statistical probability, organization would be completely improbable without the external aid of a divine organizer.

Newton in his 'Optics' did not hesitate to reach that conclusion, even with reference to the physical universe alone. But this inescapable condition can be stated, as Szent-Györgyi suggested, without resorting to any theological subterfuge: namely by locating the 'organizer' within the cosmic system from the 'beginning' and attributing design, not to any *original* plan but to the increasing tendency of organized processes and structures to combine with the selective aid of organisms into more purposeful emergent wholes.

Here Descartes' original recognition of the lifelike qualities of clockwork, which exhibit a highly advanced form of mechanical organization, tempted him to introduce the extraneous notion of mechanism into his analysis of organic behavior. This was a pseudo-explanation for it undermines the very point he was trying to make. Organic design (finalism) and causal determinism are antithetic concepts, which actually stand at opposite poles. As Hans Driesch long ago pointed out, no one ever succeeded in building a house by throwing stones at random on the site: at the end of a century one would still have only a pile of stones. To account for the orderly behavior of living beings Descartes introduced the concept of the machine which, more than any conceivable organism, is the product of design from start to finish. Even more than Newton's divine organizer, the machine model introduced teleology or finalism in its classic form: a purposeful organization for a strictly predetermined end. This corresponds to nothing whatever in organic evolution.

Actually, the gap between pure causality, or its statistical team-mate, pure chance, and any form of working mechanism is unbridgeable. Machines, however crude, are embodiments of a clearly articulated purpose, so firmly fixed in advance, both with respect to the past and the future, that even the lowest organism, if similarly organized, would be unable to utilize fresh genetic mutations or meet novel situations.

Organisms, on the other hand, unlike stones, cannonballs, and planets, have a future that is partly pre-determined by all that has happened to the species and to organic life in general, back to their very beginnings, and even before that in the constitution and 'speciation' of the elements themselves. Past events a billion years gone are still present in living cells and organs, like the salt in the blood that records the origin of primordial life in the seas; while future potentialities, equally remote, may likewise be present, in unrecognizable subjective form, in a given organic constellation. The purely causal analysis of what is immediately visible in a fertilized ovum would give no clue to its later development unless the observer already knew the natural history of the species: not only embryogeny and ontogeny, but even phylogeny.

History unfortunately played no part in the Galilean-Newtonian world picture, though by now physicists tell us that even in the physical universe a theoretic historic sequence, beginning with the hydrogen atom, must be posited. By introducing the concept of a man-made mechanism in describing organic behavior, Descartes was in fact secretly restoring those very subjective attributes: design, purpose, *telos*. Ironically, Galileo and Descartes himself had supposedly eliminated these concepts as outside the realm of positive science.

The interpretation I am making openly reverses the conventional reading of causality, chance, statistical order, and purposeful design, and gives to the organism as a working whole in all its indescribable capabilities the role that Descartes gave to the machine. To clarify this position, I propose to examine the actual nature of the machine—any machine—to see if it can be adequately described and understood by the purely analytical method in the restricted terms that have been applied to animate organisms. If it cannot be so described, then the reference to this model in interpreting organic behavior conspicuously misses the one significant trait that actually binds mechanisms and organisms together—purposeful organization and subjective intention.

For convenience let us follow Galileo's own frequent practice, that of making a hypothetical experiment. Take a clock that has 'fallen from the sky,' and let us suppose that the history of time-keeping and the function of a clock are as completely unknown as the origins and functions of living organisms were four centuries ago. Let this strange instrument be passed around a group of diverse specialists, with each one extracting a single part: the glass, the face, the hands, the springs, the wheels and ratchets, and so forth, until the clock is completely dismantled. Then let each part be accurately measured, photographed, and analyzed by qualified physicists, chemists, metallurgists, mechanics, each working in his private laboratory. When their reports are assembled, every part currently open to scientific investigation will be accurately known in 'objective' reductionist terms. In making such an analysis, the principle of causality will suffice unless the investigators penetrate to the core of the various individual atoms.

But meanwhile, the clock itself has disappeared. With this disappearance, the design that held the parts together has vanished, along with any visible clue to the function each part performs, how the assembled mechanism interlocks, and for what purpose the clock once existed. Under these circumstances, who would dare to suggest that anyone who knew only the separate parts would be able to put the parts together again, or understand how they worked, and above all what purpose they served? Only history could provide an answer sufficient to enable a competent mind to assemble the works and tell time.

Now, the design of the clock, and the functions performed by the parts can be taken in only when the clock is considered as a dynamic working whole. A purely causal analysis of the individual components would throw no light on the purposeful nature of the going mechanism. Though conceivably a re-assemblage of the parts might be achieved by a series of miraculous strokes without a subjective knowledge of its ultimate purpose—time telling—the dead mechanism would remain mysterious, and its purpose baffling. Even the twelve numbers on the dial would mean nothing in a culture that had never divided the day into twice twelve hours. So if by lucky accident and shrewd experiment the parts of the clock could be put together, the movement of the hands would still be unintelligible and the need for regulating the speed of the movement in conformity to a planetary time-keeper would never occur. Causal analysis, by definition, has no concern with final ends or human purposes.

What, then, becomes of the attempt at causal (non-teleological) explanation of living organisms through 'mechanism'? Plainly the working of the clock cannot be accounted for without re-introducing those human factors the scientific method has resolutely eliminated: astronomers and time measurement and time-oriented activities, as well as mechanics and clockmakers. In other words, the mechanical metaphor is not in itself a satisfactory device for eliminating purely human concerns, for mechanisms are themselves subjectively conditioned fabrications and their own peculiarities, which counterfeit certain aspects of organisms, are precisely what must be explained. Taken by themselves, machines present a puzzle, not an explanation. The answer to that puzzle lies in the nature of man.

Now, no one who knows the history of time-keeping should be tempted to invoke a superhuman clockmaker, comparable to Archdeacon Paley's God, and suppose that the idea of a clock was present in His mind from the beginning. The cold facts of history do not support this view. The earliest time-measuring devices—sundials, candles, clepsydras, hourglasses—give hardly a hint in their physical structure or mode of operation of the eventual mechanical clock.

To end up with such a time-keeper, the clockmaker would have to be concealed in each successive invention and improvement; and in fact this invisible and unidentifiable clockmaker was present in precisely the subjective form that guaranteed his concealment: as an idea in the human mind. The key to all these devices, including the final mechanical clock, is the conception of time and time-keeping: a subjective phenomenon antedating any time-keeping contrivance. That idea of time cannot be located in space, though it has endless spatial manifestations, both physical and symbolic.

In short, the purpose of telling time is what alone accounts for this lengthy sequence of inventions and improvements; and likewise for the specific characteristics of each part of the time-keeping mechanism. Though at no point does this purpose promote anything but the next appropriate step, without this persistent underlying aim there would be no next step, other than the dissipation of energy and the eventual disorganization of the parts that had once been assembled.

To say this is to say something deeply shocking, I fear, to those who cling to cartesian doctrine, whether in dealing with the physical elements, with machines, or with organisms: namely, that 'identification,' 'speciation,' association, organization, purpose, and transcendence are not accidental by-products of mass, energy, and motion, but are aboriginal components of the same system. True, these organic properties emerge only at later stages of cosmic development, and become visible only through the human mind at its highest point of evolution. Though undetectable and unrecognizable in the earliest state, the properties of life must, as Leibnitz held, be present as potentiality from the beginning. The fact that each element in the periodic table has definite characteristics that establish its identity and define its range of associations and organizations indicates that 'speciation' exists even in pre-organic forms, with similar restrictions as to the combinations that make organic forms possible.

As with the sequence of time-keeping inventions, neither an external creator nor a predetermined plan is needed in order to account for the increase of organized creativity and self-actualizing design. The total result of this process is a beautiful and unimaginable surprise: "If God knew the answer he would not bother to work it out." Yet at the very heart of the hydrogen atom the physicist confronts the fact that its behavior pattern cannot be accounted for except by invoking an invisible agent that we recognize only in its human form: namely, mind. The specific nature of the elements, themselves seemingly evolving out of the primordial charges dynamically held together in the hydrogen atom, defy any mode of explanation except in the equally inexplicable terms of mind itself. Between that Alpha and Omega, the beginning and the end, lies the mystery of life. Destroy the undefinable subjective component, and the whole cosmic process, like the process of time-keeping, becomes meaningless—indeed unimaginable.

I have gone into this matter in detail, though it seemingly lies outside the scope of technology, because Descartes' analysis of the machine, and his admiration for its automatism had, and still has, a potent effect in causing Western man to misinterpret and underestimate the unique subjective quality of organisms, and above all of man's own symbolic performances in crowning mere existence with meaning and purpose. No machine, however complex its nature or however ingenious its human inventor, can even theoretically be made to replicate a man, for in order to do so it would have to draw upon two or three billion years of diversified experience. This failure to recognize the importance of cosmic and organic history largely accounts for the imperious demands of our age, with its promise of instant solutions and instant transformations—which turn out too often to be instant destructions and exterminations.

The missing elements in Descartes' grossly over-simplified mechanical model, and in the scientific outlook that, consciously or unconsciously, has taken that model over, are history, symbolic culture, mind—in other words, the totality of human experience *not simply as known but as lived;* for every living creature knows something about life that even the most brilliant biologist cannot discover except by living. To heed only the abstractions of the intelligence or the operations of machines, and to ignore feelings, emotions, intuitions, fantasies, ideas, is to substitute bleached skeletons, manipulated by wires, for the living organism. The cult of anti-life secretly begins at this point, with its readiness to extirpate organisms and contract human wants and desires in order to conform to the machine.

Now it is against the evolutionary background of organic complexity, complemented by the totality of human experience as lived and recorded that the artful simplicity and clarity of the mechanical world picture and its derivative institutions must be critically appraised. The notion that if objective investigation becomes sufficiently refined and is carried far enough it will reveal all that we now have only fitful subjective access to is sheer illusion. The "machine in mummy's tummy" and "the handle that starts it" are only a forgivably comic caricature of the mode of explanation that Galileo and Descartes made plausible when they excluded subjective, remembered, or unrepeatable phenomena from the world they were attempting to describe. In doing so they rejected what could only be experienced, but never accurately observed, since the observation itself deforms—as biologists and physicists have now discovered—the nature of what is observed.

The remedy for this embarrassment is a human one, and it was left to a poet to express it. In 'A Considerable Speck' Robert Frost tells about his encounter with a paper mite, crawling over the page on which he was writing, who observed Frost's lifted pen and visibly panicked. This behavior awakened sufficient fellow feeling in Frost to spare the speck's life.

"I have a mind myself and recognize
Mind when I meet with it in any guise."

What the poet is in fact saying is that neither power nor knowledge should undermine one's own humanity nor obliterate one's sense of active fellowship with all other forms of life.

Let me submit a final example that will perhaps reveal how far the 'objective' methods of science still are from presenting a comprehensive and unified description of the phenomena of life. Until half a century ago dreams were regarded as scientifically disreputable, despite the fact that every culture before our own day was concerned with dreams, and sought, however ineffectually, to interpret them. The first systematic scientific attempt to penetrate this world of subjective fantasy was made by Sigmund Freud, examining his own dreams, listening to those recited by his patients, and attempting to correlate dream images with known impulses and pathological reactions.

Though the kind of knowledge so gained often proved illuminating, it was uncertain, and difficult to validate, for different dream interpreters would often attach different values to the same images and plots. In reaction against this method, a group of contemporary scientists, using a method of recording electric brain waves that has proved useful in the diagnosis of brain disorders, has sought to correlate subjective occurrences in sleep with eye movements and with the waves registered on an electroencephalograph.

These findings constitute objective public knowledge, and for this reason the investigators regard their results as more authentic than the verbal report of a dream. But the hope of directly eliciting information about the contents of dreams from data so gathered is baseless: as impossible as deducing the sensation of color by counting its vibrations. Only someone who can subjectively identify individual colors can correlate experienced color with its name and wave length. So with dreams: even if their contents should be accurately read from a graph, the investigator would still have to rely upon the confirmatory testimony of the dreamer as to whether his 'objective' reading was true—and without that elusive subjective verification—itself unverifiable!—his own claims would remain dubious, if not worthless.

This is a test case; and I present it at this early point in tracing the technological consequences of the new world picture because it shows how self-defeating the bias against subjectivity in the under-dimensioned mechanical model actually was. Should we wonder, then, that a world that has been constructed deliberately to accommodate machines and mechanized men has proved increasingly hostile to organic realities and human needs? Without a more organic ideological framework it is hardly remarkable that our one-sided technology has cut man off from his biological potentialities and alienated him from his historic selves, both past and future.

Nevertheless, a generous qualifying admission must be made. Once established, the habit of analytical thinking, with its dissociation from organic complexities, was immensely beneficial not only to science but to technics; for this liberation from the organic was a first step in creating efficient machines. To reduce a complex object to its elements made it possible to recombine those elements in a relatively simple machine; and the habit of dissociating physical components from their usual concrete manifestations greatly facilitated invention.

The first crude efforts to create an airplane were unsuccessful because the physical conditions for flight were too closely associated with the flapping of wings. Ader's large-scale model for a plane, which still hangs in the Conservatoire des Arts et Métiers in Paris, not merely has movable wings, but its wings and propellers have a featherlike form. No wonder it never flew. Similarly, no efficient automaton could be modelled after a human being with arms and legs, though in fact the first robots were given this quasi-human form.

Analysis, dissociation, and reduction were the first steps toward creating complex technical structures. Without the mechanical world picture to keep together the various aspects of the physical world that were thus described, without machines themselves to translate the parts into purposeful pseudo-organisms, the wholesale effort at mechanized control which has characterized the last three centuries might have foundered.

Perhaps the most radical fault in Descartes' philosophy was that he accepted the division of the "two cultures." Although he was prepared to examine all the phenomena of external nature, he did not apply the same method to man's subjective life, where its crudity would have become obvious, but took the Christian Church's monopoly of that sphere as unchallengeable and final. In abandoning the human soul entirely to the 'theological arm,' Descartes turned his back upon the possibility of creating a unified approach to every part of nature, including those events that were private, singular, non-repeatable, personal: the world of memory and futurity, of history and biography, of the entire evolution of species.

This was a fatal handicap to an integrated and universally applicable system of thought: for it still causes the orthodox scientist automatically to seal his mind against any shadowy phenomena—such as those of parapsychology—that cannot yet be accounted for within science's present framework. The scientific method left every tentative truth open for further examination and correction: provided that one accepted without question the assumptions of the system itself. Since science opened no path into private and subjective experience, it was forced to deny either its importance or its existence.

Knowing the culture of the seventeenth century, one need not be surprised that its representative thinkers, from Galileo to Newton, were unwilling to abandon altogether the domain of religion and dismiss the traditional interests and experiences it embodied. But even centuries later, when the Church had lost its old dogmatic hold, when people like Freud were beginning a methodical inquiry into the manifestations of subjectivity in dreams, fantasies, and unconscious projections, those who were trained in science took pride in excluding feelings, emotions, and evaluations from their routines. 'Cold' and 'dispassionate' still remain words of praise for the scientific personality.

Even Freud felt forced to emphasize his strict scientific 'materialism,' in order to give a cloak of respectability to the demons and monsters of the unconscious whom he was bringing up to the surface. In contrast, Lord Russell, after depicting the austere renunciations demanded by scientific procedure, felt it necessary to introduce, as a corrective, the mystic, the lover, the poet, with "their heritage of culture and beauty." If science as conceived in the seventeenth century had embraced all the phenomena of nature, including man himself, neither the theologian, the mystic, the lover, nor the poet would have been so peremptorily exiled at the beginning; nor would it have seemed possible to suggest, as many besides Herbert Spencer have since done, that science, if pursued more universally and rigorously, would finally eliminate them.

In a real sense, then, Descartes' claims for the scientific method were too modest; for if this method provided a key to understanding every aspect of the universe, it should be capable of embracing in its own special way the whole territory of moral values and religious ends, and be able to formulate and utilize whatever truths they had in fact recognized and partly embodied, while liberating the mind from undisciplined and disordered subjectivity, with its misplaced animism, and its unsorted set of moribund errors, too carefully embalmed and coffined over the ages.

To accept the Church's monopoly of the subjective life, or to surrender it to muddled magic and vulgar superstition, was to set limits to the examination of human experience and the pursuit of truth. The inner life could not remain forever a no-man's land, where saints, gypsies, lords, beggars, artists, and lunatics had established squatters' rights and wasted precious human energy erecting an endless series of crazy, flimsy structures. In turning his back on the realities of subjective life, Descartes rejected the possibility of creating a unified world picture that would do justice to every aspect of human experience—that indispensable pre-condition for the 'next development of man.'

5: THE FAILURE OF MECHANOMORPHISM

From Descartes' time on until the present century, to all but the most penetrating minds in science, a 'mechanistic' explanation of organic behavior was accepted as a sufficient one. And as machines became more lifelike, Western man taught himself to become in his daily behavior more machine-like. This shift was recorded in the changing meaning of the word 'automaton,' which was used in English as early as 1611. At first this term was employed to describe autonomous beings with the power to move alone; but it soon came to mean just the opposite: a contrivance that had exchanged autonomy for the powers of motion "under conditions fixed *for* it, not *by* it" (New Oxford Dictionary).

Now, though all the components of machines are found in nature— mass, energy, motion, the chemical elements and their processes of combination and organization—no machines or purposeful mechanical structures of any kind exist in pre-animate nature: even the simplest mechanisms are solely the products, internal or external, of organisms. If individual processes within the organism can be described, conveniently and accurately, as 'mechanisms,' *it is precisely because the fabrication and elaboration of mechanisms as functional working units is a specific organic trait:* one that no pre-organic combination of elements can by random collisions, accretions, or explosions, however often repeated or prolonged, bring about. If machines are sufficiently simplified to help us understand better how organisms behave, it is because the mechanisms involved in organic behavior are too dynamic, too complex, too qualitatively rich, too multifold to be grasped except by some such simplification. But it is not the machine that explains purposeful organization: it is organic functions that explain machines.

The distinguishing mark of actual machines, even the most lifelike of computers, is that its powers and functions are derivative: their increasingly lifelike qualities are all secondhand. No machine can invent another machine, nor yet, though it may undergo a 'humiliating' breakdown, can it express humiliation willfully by committing suicide. Neither hope nor despair are a part of its equipment. Still less can a machine persist indefinitely in its activities, once it ceases to elicit human interest and human cooperation. True, inventors of computers have introduced random elements to simulate creativity, or at least the pseudo-creativity associated with electronically created 'poems' or 'music,' but the instrument itself does not possess this capability until the human mind introduces it.

Such a limitation holds equally for the attempt to give the machine one of the main traits of living organisms, the ability to reproduce itself. Though, given a sufficient number of parts and a sufficiently detailed program, self-replication by a machine is theoretically possible, this supposed feat rests on an innocent self-deception. Who gives those directions for self-replication to a machine? Certainly not the machine itself, or an ancestral model. No machine finds the necessary impulse to reproduction in its own original design, or appropriates the necessary materials and shapes them. Nothing like reproduction can happen in a machine except through the providence of the human mind. In this critical matter of reproduction, essential to any simulacrum of life, Samuel Butler's inverted definition of man remains central: on the lowest terms, he is "a machine's way of making another machine."

Thus, though 'mechanical' processes (tropisms, reflexes, hormones) are among the essential properties of much organic activity, the opposite notion, that the organism can be reduced 'simply' to a bundle of mechanisms, can hardly be applied even to a bacterium, much less to any higher organism. Organisms most closely resemble machines in those lower functions that have passed out of consciousness, while machines resemble organisms in those higher functions associated with purposive designs. For millions of years organisms existed without benefit of any mechanisms except those which the creature itself could fabricate: man himself survived without complex machines until some five or six thousand years ago, and even then his first elaborate machines, as I demonstrated in Volume One of 'The Myth of the Machine,' were composed mainly of human parts, mechnized and organized by the mind. The conscious development of mechanism is a specifically human trait, as visible in the organization of language and ritual as in machines of wooden and metal parts. Mind itself might almost be defined as the organism's mode of creating, utilizing, and transcending its own mechanisms.

If Descartes had only looked closer at the actual nature of automatons, instead of being hypnotized by their superficially lifelike movements, he would have discovered why they bore so little resemblance to higher organisms: for the most generous description of the most highly evolved type of mechanical-electronic apparatus is that it is a defective or under-dimensioned organism. Yet the underlying desire to reduce man to a machine, for the purpose of establishing uniform behavior in the army and the factory, or any other potentially disorderly collection of men, was so strong by the seventeenth century that Descartes' description, while odious to Christian dogma, was taken for granted by progressive scientific minds.

By 1686 Robert Boyle, the 'Sceptical Chymist'—though he remained a pious Churchman—could refer to "these living automata, Human Bodies." And two whole centuries later, Thomas Henry Huxley could still say, in his paper on 'Animal Automatism,' that "In men, as in brutes, there is no proof that any change of consciousness is the cause of change in the motion of the matter of the organism." Huxley was still so deeply committed to Descartes' theoretic mechanical model that he completely overlooked abundant contrary data available to anyone—such as the fact that a few words in a telegram may contract the muscles of the cheek into a smile, or cause the reader to drop dead of a shock.

This transposition of the specific characters of organisms and machines actually elevated the mechanical creature above his creator. That error has brought catastrophic potentialities in our day, in the willingness, on the part of military and political strategists, to give to agents of extermination they have created—nuclear weapons, rockets, lethal poisons and bacteria—the authority to exterminate the human race.

But this radical misinterpretation has also had a more amusing consequence in biology itself: for instead of doing away with teleological or purposeful explanations of organic behavior, it brazenly smuggled in, under the disguise of 'mechanism,' the very trait it professed to exclude; embracing in fact the most disreputable and indefensible form which the Christian theologians had taken over from Aristotle.

Unlike an organism, which is an open system, subject to chance mutations and to many external forces and circumstances over which it has no control, mechanisms are closed systems, strictly contrived by the inventor to achieve clearly foreseen and limited ends. Thus a full-fledged automatic machine is a perfect example of pure teleology, and every part of it bears the same imprint: no machine, however rudimentary, was ever put together by chance or random accretions or natural selection. By contrast, even the lowest species of organism, according to the doctrine of evolution, has remarkable potentialities that no machine can boast: it can alter its species' character and re-program itself, so to say, in order to seize new opportunities or resist unwanted external pressures. That margin of freedom no machine possesses in its own right.

Unfortunately, the favored machines of Descartes' period, the clock and the printing press, left such a deep imprint on the scientific mind, and Descartes' deceptive metaphor made it so easy to accept as rational a 'mechanical' (supposedly non-teleological) explanation of far more complex, subjectively conditioned, organic behavior, that this decrepit and obsolete model is still trotted out, sometimes by distinguished scientists, as if it were unchallengeable, even when the data themselves contradict the description. Such an austere and careful investigator as Sherrington has demonstrated that a unifying pattern constantly presides over each separate physiological activity and keeps it in harmonious relations with the rest of the organism: but that platonic pattern—invisible except in operation— gains not a scintilla of meaning by being attached to the concept of mechanism. By now all this should be plain. Yet only recently a well-accredited scientist stated in so many words that "man is born a machine and becomes a person."

On what planet does this take place? Certainly not on earth, where machines are never born but fabricated: what is more, a baby, from the moment of its conception, exhibits many traits not found in any observed or conceivable machine. If a machine should become a person that would be an infinitely greater miracle than any recorded in the Bible or the Koran.

Now the underlying implications of Descartes' baroque absolutism must not be forgotten. By accepting the machine as his model, and a single unifying mind as the source of absolute order, Descartes in effect brought every manifestation of life, ultimately, under rational, centrally directed control—rational, that is, provided one did not look too closely at the nature and intentions of the controller. In doing so, he set a fashion in thought that was to prevail with increasing success for the next three centuries.

On Descartes' assumptions, the work of science, if not the destiny of life, was to widen the empire of the machine. Lesser minds seized on this error, enlarged it, and made it fashionable. And as often happened before in the history of slavery, the obedient slave first made himself indispensable to his master, then defied him and dominated him, and finally supplanted him. But now it is the master, not the slave, who must, if he is to survive, devise a scheme to recover his freedom.

6: ENTER LEVIATHAN ON WHEELS

From Descartes' platform it was easy to take the next step; and that was to outline a set of principles favorable to a political order that would deliberately turn men into machines, whose spontaneous acts could be regulated and brought under control, and whose natural functions and moral choices would all be channeled through a single responsible center—the sovereign ruler or, in the bureaucratic jargon of our own day, the Decision Maker.

Descartes had taken this step in reverse, by drawing his theoretic picture from the example of absolute rulers. But the thinker who saw the full political implications of the new mechanical world picture was Thomas Hobbes. Though Hobbes did not become acquainted with geometry till he was over forty, he was a cartesian at heart even before he met Descartes personally. Both men shared an interest that also, we have seen, delighted princes: they were equally impressed by automatons.

Hobbes expressed his political position in two books, 'De Cive' and 'Leviathan.' Though the basic doctrine is the same in both books, the one that made him famous, 'Leviathan,' is the more dramatic in style, and, not accidentally, the one that is dominated by the mechanical world picture. Its basic errors were repeated and refined by Rousseau, who made each individual both a potential despot and a victim of a collective totalitarian despotism which he confounded with democracy.

Hobbes started from two contradictory but related assumptions. One was that men were virtual machines; the other that they were just the opposite, incurably wild and disorderly, in constant strife and conflict, perpetually troubled by fear, and incapable of even the rudiments of orderly social behavior until they surrendered to a single external source of power, the sovereign, accepted his commands, and under threat of punishment learned the arts of social intercourse and cooperation sufficiently to make life and property safe.

Primitive man's life in Hobbes' famous words, was short, brutish, and nasty; and this very savagery and anxiety became the justification for an absolute order established, like Descartes' ideal world, by a single providential mind and will: that of the absolute ruler or monarch. Until men were incorporated into Leviathan, that is, the all-powerful state through which the king's will was carried out, they were dangerous to their fellows and a burden to themselves.

Complete and utter submission to the sovereign was accordingly for Hobbes, as it was for the Egyptians of the Pyramid Age who had originally deified the office of Kingship, the sole key to earthly salvation. The fact that we have encountered this doctrine before, as the ideological foundation and pre-condition of the megamachine, only makes its resurrection in the seventeenth century more significant. This submission to absolute authority was for Hobbes the condition for enjoying as isolated individuals the benefits of civilization, including the dubious benefit of collective warfare, which Hobbes shrewdly held to be the inevitable price for protection against civil violence at home.

Hobbes' dissertation on the Sovereign State springs from the same common source as Descartes', and rounds out the latter's analysis of the nature of animals by cheerfully passing on the same attributes, without any further additions, to men. This scientific zoömorphism has led to even greater distortions and suppressions than the anthropomorphism it has reacted against. In his introduction to the Leviathan—itself a sort of political 'Moby Dick'—Hobbes observed: "Nature is by the art of man, as in many other things, so in this also imitated, that it can make an artificial animal. For seeing life is nothing but a motion of the limbs . . . why may we not say that all Automata (Engines that move themselves by springs and wheels as doth a watch) have an artificial life? For what is the heart but a spring; and nerves but so many strings; and the joints but so many wheels, giving motion to the whole body." This is already the authentic claptrap of technocracy.

Note the cool manner in which Hobbes puts forward his most vulnerable statement, as if it were an unchallengeable axiom: "Life is but a motion of the Limbs." That is not even a minimal definition of life, for, if accepted, it would bestow the attributes of life on the limbs of a dead tree moving in the wind. But this is obviously a suitable doctrine for those who would condition men to absolute obedience: another man-trainer and conditioner, a behaviorist psychologist in the employ of an advertising agency, three centuries or so later, would identify not only speech but thought itself with the muscular movements made in the larynx.

That wild leap of Hobbes' from automata to organisata brought the desired conclusion—automatically. If indeed automata are artificial organisms, why cannot man, whose life is "but a motion of the Limbs" be brought equally under the control of external forces initiated and operated by the sovereign? Predictable behavior and remote control from the center—this is the ultimate goal of megatechnics, whether mechanical or electronic, though it has taken a long time to perfect the inventions and assemble the organization that would make this final outcome possible.

Hobbes' distinction was to join together the new science and the old politics of the seventeenth century and to address them to the fabrication of human beings that could be used to enhance the power and glory of Leviathan—above all to transfer autonomy from each individual member and group in the community to the organized whole in which they would function only as obedient, machinelike parts. From this effort many institutions directly followed: to begin with, the regimented mass army, in which every part was regulated and standardized, starting with the newly standardized uniform itself; likewise, the new bureaucracy, that efficient product of Italian despotism; in the eighteenth century, the factory; and in our own time, the new educational and communications systems. These were the new components. Thus the ultimate product of Leviathan was the megamachine, on a new enlarged and improved model, one that would either completely neutralize or eliminate its once-human parts.

Hobbes' Leviathan was a fabulous monster, conceived for the purpose of magnifying fear and inspiring collective awe: deliberately concocted, indeed, to justify and confirm the powers that were being gathered together once more in the unified territorial state and in the new empires that were spreading Western law and order, in all its forms, legal and mechanical, over every part of the planet. This system, we know now, was founded on a purely fictional account of the evolution of human society: one that bears little resemblance at all to any observed condition among surviving 'primitive' peoples, though it has enough likeness to the events and institutions of civilization, at sundry points, from the Fifth Millennium B.C. on, to have a certain air of plausibility. Hobbes' mythic picture cast aside every positive evidence of spontaneous order, morality, mutual aid, and autonomy: at the same time it magnified, by treating it as an original necessity, the absolute authority that the state was newly seeking to re-establish, against the resistance of many other more functional forms of corporate unity and voluntary, cooperative association.

In the light of present anthropological knowledge, Hobbes' fanciful picture of primitive man was even further from historical reality than Rousseau's subsequent description of man in an innocent state of nature. Early observers of simpler societies—such seasoned minds as James Cook and Alfred Russel Wallace—had actually found many admirable customs and practices in Indonesia and the South Seas that corresponded closely to Rousseau's more idyllic picture, and much that flatly contradicted Hobbes, for the latter treated the latent fears and calculated aggressions of the upstart oligarchs and the commercial magnates of his day as if they had pervaded all previous human societies.

Hobbes' account was nevertheless mixed with shrewd observations on human motives and desires in the strife-torn political establishments of his own day; and his doctrine had the singular virtue of justifying absolute sovereign power, no matter whether it was held by a king or a Roundhead parliament, a popularly elected president or a self-elected dictator: it could even, by extension, justify any arbitrary exercise of power when derived from 'sovereign authority,' if exercised by a government administrator, a factory owner, a business executive, or a computer.

Hobbes had done nothing less in fact than re-instate the ideological premises upon which Divine Kingship had originally been based, for that charismatic idea had never been completely obliterated, though it had long become but a shadow of its ancient self, enfeebled by failure of faith and cut down to human size by practical experience. Even Jean-Jacques Rousseau, Hobbes' chief rival as a political thinker, did nothing to exorcise Hobbes' absolutism: on the contrary, his doctrine of the Social Contract showed how, indeed, the sovereign might be legally replaced—but only by another sovereign power, one that rested on the 'general will.' The actual passage from kingship to representative government and collective authority—seemingly a liberation—proved only how little had been changed. For in the meanwhile the original concept of kingship, always too dependent upon identifiable and vulnerable human agents, was now being reinforced by a multitude of mechanical aids.

Hobbes' justification of power as the source of all other goods helped to magnify both the state and the machine, in their dual efforts to establish law, order, and control, and to widen the whole system by further conquests of nature and other human groups. And the aftermath of Hobbes' thought became even more brutal than its original expression. Passing through the minds of other men, joined to their experiences in war, territorial conquests, and colonization, Hobbes' one-sided picture of life as a constant struggle for power motivated by fear, became the foundation of both the practical doctrines of imperialism and the ideal doctrine of machine-conditioned progress, as both were carried into the nineteenth century as the Malthus-Darwin 'struggle for existence.' The latter was liberally interpreted by Darwin's contemporaries as the license to exterminate all rival groups or species.

7: THE MACHINE AS PEDAGOGUE

Almost every classic philosophy terminates in a system of education; and this holds for the mechanical world picture: indeed, its first and perhaps its clearest expression accompanied the treatises of Descartes and Hobbes. I refer to 'The Great Didactic' of John Amos Comenius, the Moravian teacher and theologian. As a philosopher Comenius established his general theory of teaching on the necessity of order, in its most generalized aspects, but he was completely under the spell of the new mechanical models. Note his description of the clockwork "movements of the soul." "The most important wheel is the will; while the weights are the desires and affections which incline the will this way or that. The escapement is the reason, which measures and determines what, where, and how far anything should be sought after or avoided."

With that ideological basis, it is not surprising that Comenius' whole conception of education is based on the requirements for mass production. In his endeavor to make education cheap enough to include the poor, he sought to effect economies by the skillful arrangement of time. Long before Lancaster and Bell in England, Comenius invented the monitorial system of teaching, as a means of reducing costs. "I maintain," he said, "that it is not only possible for one teacher to teach several hundred scholars at once, but that it is also essential." On no account, Comenius warns, was the teacher to give individual instruction. In the light of contemporary educational theory, we must now recognize Comenius, in fact, as the precursor if not the inventor of mechanically programmed education: nothing separates him from those who now have at command the necessary electronic and mechanical apparatus for carrying his method out. Is it surprising that he also provided for the eight-hour working day and the forty-eight-hour week?

"As soon as we have succeeded in finding the proper method," Comenius elsewhere explains, "it will be no harder to teach schoolboys in any number desired, than with the help of the printing press to cover a thousand sheets daily with the neatest writing." Close upon this follows another revealing sentence: *"It will be as pleasant to see education carried out on my plan as to look at an automatic machine, and the process will be as free from failure as these mechanical contrivances when skillfully made."* Precisely: and what Comenius formulated in the seventeenth century, Gradgrind and M'Choakumchild would carry out clumsily and brutally in the nineteenth century, to be followed by the more facile pigeon-conditioners and programmers of the present age, equally captivated by their own automatisms.

For Comenius, as for his fellow-encyclopedist J. H. Alsted, and later for John Locke, the mind of man was a blank sheet of paper. The task of education was to leave on this sheet the desired uniform imprint: again the image of the printing press. Like the inventor and the physical scientist, the new educator sought to achieve perfect mechanical order—but eliminated the spontaneities of life and all the intangible and unprogrammable functions that go with life.

In 1633, when Comenius published a treatise on physics divided into twelve chapters, he began with the sketch of creation and followed an ascending hierarchy, from the physical order to that of plants and animals and man, till he finally, as theologian, reached his ultimate category, angels. But in 'The Great Didactic' he reversed this; for though he began with (1) time, his illustrations were (2) of the human body, (3) of mind ruling body, (4) king or emperor; and then—(5) Heron of Alexandria moving weights by means of cleverly devised machines, (6) the terrible operations of artillery, (7) the process of printing, (8) another example of mechanism, a wheeled carriage, (9) a boat, with keel, mast, rudder, and compass, and (10) the clock. The clock was both basic and climactic.

Comenius' work makes plain the interweaving of inventions, mechanical experiences, regimented institutions, and, underlying them all, exorbitant magical expectations, which produced the new industrial and political fabric. The combination of astronomical regularity, absolute political authority, and lifelike automatism proved increasingly irresistible. We need hardly be surprised, then, that when Comenius finally reaches the clock in his enumerations his words become nothing less than ecstatic: "Is it not a truly marvellous thing that a machine, a soulless thing, can move in such a life-like, continuous, and regular manner? Before clocks were invented would not the existence of such things have seemed as impossible as that trees could walk or stones speak?"

Comenius' emotional involvement was typical, and it did not subside with the later invention of a vast variety of machines, many of them with fabulous capabilities beyond that of any clock: the same sentiments may now be encountered, in even louder and more ecstatic tones, among cybernetic theorists, perhaps because what is left of their emotional life is now being channeled into the Big Brain with which they have identified their residual selves.

If punctuality, that is, clockwork regularity, was once deemed the courtesy of kings, all the prerogatives of the Royal Establishment—above all, that of commanding strict obedience from its subjects—have now become increasingly the property of automatons. To meet their set requirements soon became the whole duty of modern man, while to keep on expanding these requirements has become the privilege of the ruling groups. By the end of the seventeenth century, then, the stage of Western civilization, emptied of its historic properties and scenery and its traditional cast of characters, was set for a new technodrama, the restoration and triumph of the megamachine.

CHAPTER FIVE

Science as Technology

1: THE 'NEW INSTAURATION'

Between the sixteenth and the twentieth centuries the new scientific world picture became increasingly unified, though the various sciences that took part in this change had different points of origin, developed different methods of investigation, and were governed by different, sometimes contradictory, aims. Random exploration, severe mathematical analysis, piecemeal discoveries, organized experiment and invention, even historical exploration in geology, paleontology and phylogeny—all these eventually took the name of science and contributed to its growing authority. By now the original ideological foundations have given way, yet the deceptively simplified superstructure remains intact, seeming to float in air.

If the world picture that emerges from these disparate efforts presented any coherent image, it was that which could be traced back ultimately to the Ionian philosophers, and more immediately to the ascendancy of the automaton. As the fields of investigation were parcelled out very much in the way that the territories of the planet were parcelled for exploitation among the great powers, the pattern of knowledge reflected this division; and soon it became considered impermissible for anyone, even the professed philosopher, to deal with human experience as a whole.

The last grand effort to achieve this feat in accord with the canons of positive science was that of Herbert Spencer's voluminous 'Synthetic Philosophy.' His explication of evolution as the passage from indefinite, unorganized homogeneity to definite organized heterogeneity was too thin to be very useful, and yet too provincial in its evaluations to be applicable to any culture but that of Western European origin. But Spencer's failure only proves how useful cartesian mechanism had once been, in its innocence and simplicity, in holding the fragmented world of thought temporarily together. If Spencer gave undue authority to a kind of automatic finalism, he helped to establish, even before Darwin, a central idea that had been lacking: historic evolution itself.

In retrospect, Spencer's failure brings out by contrast the practical triumph of Francis Bacon in his attempt earlier, and with much poorer equipment, to "take all knowledge for his province." This is all the more striking because they shared the same utilitarian principles and were buoyed up by the same hopes. Though Bacon flourished before Descartes, he made the working partnership between science and technics an even more binding one, by linking it to the immediate human desires for health, wealth, and power.

In a real sense, the success of the mechanical world picture was ensured in advance by Francis Bacon, whose very lack of any qualification as either a mathematician or an experimental physicist perhaps made him readier to extend the scientific method to every department of life. Bacon deserves a special place, not for any fresh scientific discoveries he made or even contributed to, but for outlining an ideal institutional foundation for the systematic achievement and application of ordered knowledge. In addition, Bacon declared in no uncertain terms that the final goal of science was "the relief of man's estate" and the "effecting of all things possible." Thus, in the characteristic vein of British empiricism, he outlined the pragmatic justification for society's commitment to modern science as technology. No sky-gazer like Galileo, no sun-worshipper like Kepler, Bacon brought science down to earth.

Now, however high-flown modern scientific theory may be, and however much subjective delight it may give to its adepts, the scientific establishment from the beginning has been encouraged and promoted chiefly because of its hoped-for or promised applications to practical affairs: warfare, manufactures, transportation, communication. The belief that science developed solely out of a pursuit of knowledge for its own sake is at best only a half-truth, and at worst, mere self-flattery or self-deception on the part of scientists. As with the holiness of saints, which has bestowed unwarranted authority on the grosser worldly claims of the Christian Church, the total effect of scientific ideology has been to provide both the means and the justification for achieving external control over all manifestations of natural existence, including man's own life. If science and technics have not been officially married, they have long lived together in a loose common-law relationship that it is easier to ignore than to dissolve.

In reviewing Bacon's work and influence, it is natural perhaps that one should over-emphasize those aspects of modern civilization that have confirmed his predictions and surpassed his none-too-cautious expectations. This is particularly true when we consider 'science as technology,' for it is in this department that his most startling intuitions have been realized.

Three centuries before Jules Verne and H. G. Wells, to say nothing of later writers of science fiction, Bacon had anticipated the multifold uses that technology would make of science, though his imagination failed him, as it did not fail later utopian and kakotopian writers, when he tried to describe the kind of world we would actually live in; for quaintly enough his future world in 'The New Atlantis' was still, in costume, manners, and religious belief, the familiar world of Elizabethan legal and court circles. I shall use kakotopian [kakos = bad] as the opposite of utopian for an under-dimensioned, over-controlled 'ideal' community.

The title of the present chapter would not have surprised or shocked Francis Bacon, for perhaps his most original contribution to the enlargement of the province of science was his understanding of its great future role in transforming the material conditions of life. But I am sure that some of the results I shall point to would have profoundly disturbed him; for his faith in science as a source of invention, and in technology itself as the final justification of science, foresaw only the goods that would come from this pursuit, and did not anticipate the negative end-products of which the modern world is now becoming acutely conscious. Yet Bacon had a singularly capacious mind, open to self-examination and correction; and as his life had been shattered by his acknowledged malfeasance in public office, he might have been among the first to revaluate the results, and to introduce intellectual safeguards whose need he did not originally anticipate. In a real sense, the present chapter might be characterized as a Baconian feedback.

Though Bacon was undoubtedly expressing, in fantasy, as sensitive artists often do, the changing temper of his age long before it was visible in the streets, his dynamic predictions proved self-fulfilling, for they turned men's minds in the direction of the machine and gave confidence in the new scientific orientation toward the physical world. This became the common meeting ground for minds otherwise ideologically separated. Men who could no longer agree upon the nature of God or the conditions for human immortality could come to terms by making a god out of Nature, and by worshipping the machine as man's highest product. By following through the practical consequences of science, Bacon sought to show that even those who were engaged in abstract observations or experiments might ultimately confer great benefits upon the human race—greater than those who sought to improve it by morals or government, or who were content to change the environment solely by manual labor and art.

Now the notion that the scientific investigation of 'air, earth, water, and fire' might have fruitful practical applications occurred to many minds before Bacon. All the advances in past technology, such as the discovery of glazes, glass, and metals, had been due to just this kind of observation, still scattered and empirical, but nevertheless a step to more adequate knowledge and more effective practical applications. Some scientists today have expressed pride in the fact that there are more scientists alive today than existed in the whole course of human history before. But this is an empty boast: there are also now more priests in the Christian Church than ever before. It may be doubted if scientific knowledge, despite popular education, is even now as widely diffused in any effective form as was the rich empiric knowledge utilized in a pre-scientific era in metallurgy, pottery, brewing, dyeing, plant selection, animal breeding, agriculture, and medicine.

To assume that accurate, positive knowledge did not exist until the scientific method was invented is to overpraise contemporary achievements by belittling those of a different order that laid the solid foundations for them. As I have pointed out elsewhere, the watchmaker's or even optician's standard of accuracy imposed in cutting the stones of the great Egyptian pyramids was, considering the few crude tools at the disposal of the workers, quite as remarkable an achievement as anything in rocket-design today—all the more because rockets too often misfire.

But Bacon deserves our respect for helping to close the gap between the separate spheres of science and technics, one long considered 'liberal' but practically useless, the mental play of a sophisticated minority, the other, however useful, cursed by its servile and debasing nature, except perhaps in medicine and architecture. Bacon held that science in future would rest increasingly on a collective organization, not just on the work of individuals of ability, operating under their own power; and he held further that instruments and apparatus were as necessary in the technology of systematic thought as they were in mining or bridge building. He foresaw, as the baroque soloists and prima donnas of science did not, the coming impact of science as a corporate activity.

"The unassisted hand," observed Bacon, "and the understanding left to itself possess little power." This was an even more revolutionary conception than Leonardo da Vinci's aphorism: "Science is the captain, practice the soldiers," for it implied that the captain himself had something to learn from the men in the ranks. And it was no less revolutionary, no less effective, because from the standpoint of the scientific method it was, by overcompensation, too one-sided. Bacon's very over-emphasis on the collective apparatus of science, his close concern for the operational and instrumental aspects of scientific thought, were probably needed temporarily to overcome the traditional bias of an isolated leisure-class culture, theological and humanistic, operating by choice in a self-sealed social vacuum.

In this respect, Bacon's teaching was exemplary, and helped break down prejudices that go back at least to the Greeks. Science, Bacon pointed out in his 'Preface to The Great Instauration,' must deal not only with lofty matters, but with things "mean or even filthy . . . such things, no less than the most splendid and costly, must be admitted into natural history. . . . For whatever deserves to exist deserves also to be known." Bravo! That declaration freshened the air.

Bacon's place as a philosopher of science has been disparaged during the last half century on the ground that he had little grasp of the methods by which science was beginning to make orderly advances in his own generation. In so far as Bacon had no practice as an experimental scientist, unlike Galileo or Gilbert, this criticism is well founded: but to deny him credit because he did not give sufficient weight to the mathematical innovations is less than fair; for Bacon specifically said that "many parts of nature can neither be invented—that is observed—with sufficient subtlety, nor demonstrated with sufficient perspicuity . . . without the aid and intervening of the mathematics."

In compensation Bacon had, at all events, an almost clairvoyant intuition as to the ultimate destination of science: he saw its social implications and applications in detail more clearly than any of his contemporaries. Bacon was undoubtedly expressing certain fundamental though still hidden tendencies in the temper of his age, much as Shakespeare was expressing, in the figure of Caliban, the growing awareness of man's animal origins and of the underlying primitive creature lurking within. Coming at the turn of the tide in Western civilization, Bacon's predictions helped his followers ride on to fortune.

The timeliness of Bacon's contribution should have saved him from a little of the patronizing deflation that he has been subject to in recent years. Without doubt he was blandly indifferent to the actual procedures followed by the successful scientists in his own time; and further, it is no doubt true that he grossly overestimated the fruitfulness of mere fact-collecting and fumbling empirical observation, though there are still areas, like taxonomy in biology, where this kind of systematic preparatory effort has yielded certain theoretic rewards. By the same token Bacon seriously underestimated, one might almost say entirely ignored—with the exception just noted—the immense liberation that would be effected in both science and technics through the audacities of pure mathematics, emancipated from empiric details, dealing with probabilities and abstract possibilities that remain, until experimentally verified, entirely outside the realm of sensory experience and direct observation.

On his own terms, Bacon would not and did not anticipate the sweeping transformations of the entire framework of thought effected by single minds, using little corporate aid, like Newton, Mendelejev, or Einstein. Even Galileo's quantified world, a world conceived solely in terms of primary qualities and measurable quantities, was an almost unthinkable abstraction to Bacon. But to offset these disabilities which, in contrast to William Gilbert's, plainly reduce Bacon's importance as a representative of the new outlook, he had a strong sense of the social context of science, and of the appeal that its practical achievements would make, not only to scientists, to inventors, to engineers, but to the countless human beneficiaries of their work. He foresaw finally—far in advance of his age—that science would materially prosper by becoming a collective enterprise, subject to systematic organization on a worldwide basis; and that the social goal of science, as he phrased it in 'The New Atlantis,' would be "the enlargement of the bounds of humane empire."

What Bacon did was to close the gap, at least in the mind, between science and technics. He realized that the direct application of systematic thought to practical problems would open up many new possibilities, while in turn new instruments of research, arising from the magical experiments of alchemy, like the glass alembic, the retort, and the high-temperature furnace, would make it possible for trained minds, utilizing small samples, to draw large conclusions about the gross behavior of materials and forces.

Bacon was, all too obviously, still vague as to how to go about this research. At times, doubtless, he not merely fumbles in his thinking but seems to advocate fumbling as a method: thus raising into a principle the empiric British method of 'muddling through.' Yet even blind sailing may open up territory more effectively than reliance on a well-drawn chart that reveals only the mapmaker's own preconceptions. It was not by systematic effort but by happy accident that Fleming discovered the possibilities of penicillin as an antibiotic, and it was in a dream that the Benzol ring first appeared to its formulator. At the very least, Bacon broke down the mental barrier between theory and practice: he put them on speaking terms, and opened up a new continent for their joint exploitation.

2: BACON'S TECHNICAL INSIGHT

Curiously, what is most fresh and original in Bacon, his conception of the role of science as the spiritual arm, so to speak, of technology, is the hardest part for our contemporaries to appreciate today. Partly, they are put off by the fact that he arrayed these new conceptions in an elaborate metaphorical court dress; but even more they are alienated, or to speak more frankly, bored, because the ideas themselves have become so engrained in our life that most of us can hardly realize that they had a specific point of origin and were not always 'there.' But if Bacon failed in describing the methodology of science as it was taking shape in his own time, he leaped ahead four centuries to the mode and milieu in which science and technics both flourish, in their peculiar fashion, today.

When Benjamin Franklin founded the American Philosophical Society, he felt it necessary, in the sober utilitarian spirit of his age, to stress its aim of promoting "useful knowledge": but if he had been even closer to Bacon's spirit he would have realized that usefulness is implicit in every kind of scientific knowledge, almost, it would seem, in proportion to its degree of abstraction and its isolation from immediate practical concerns. The most dynamic gift of science to technics is what A. N. Whitehead termed the greatest invention of the nineteenth century: "the invention of invention." Purely theoretic and experimental discoveries repeatedly suggest outlets and applications that could not even have been conceived until the scientific work itself was done.

In the past, certain branches of science, like geometry, had developed out of practical needs, as in the Egyptian need for surveying the boundaries that had been effaced in flooded fields; and some of that interplay between practical needs and scientific investigation of course still goes on, as in the classic instance of Pasteur's researches on ferments in response to the pleas of French wine growers. But the enormous advances of science in every field have not waited for such direct stimuli, though it may very well be that they are indirect responses organically connected with the needs and purposes of our society at a hundred different points. Quite possibly it was not by accident that the electronics of radar location coincided with coordinate advances in high-speed flight. Increasingly, however, it is the advances of science that suggest a new technological application: witness laser beams. Indeed the by-products seem to multiply in direct relation to the scope and freedom of scientific research. So ready are we now to accept the inventive consequences of science that we have almost lost the safeguard of common sense or the braking device of mocking laughter against freaks and follies unrelated to human need, but technologically attractive because of their very difficulty.

Bacon's interest in the practical applications of science naturally endeared him to Macaulay and the other smug utilitarians of the nineteenth century, for in his 'Novum Organum' Bacon boldly asserted that "the legitimate goal of science is the endowment of human life with new inventions and riches": indeed the idea of riches and material abundance pervaded his thinking about science. Taken as the main object of science, this is, of course, a more questionable goal than Bacon thought; but it is because of the accelerated fulfillment of these promises by the sciences, especially during the last half century, that national governments and great industrial corporations have vastly augmented their financial contributions to scientific research. Bacon's merit was to make plain that there was no aspect of nature that would not lend itself to transformation and possibly improvement through the confident application of the scientific method.

Necessity had always been a most reluctant mother of invention: Bacon understood that ambition and curiosity were far more fertile parents, and that the inventions so promoted would become the mother of new necessities. True, a large part of Bacon's prophesied inventions and discoveries, it now turns out, would not so much alleviate poverty or satisfy basic needs as open up a vast realm of superfluities and luxuries. But this makes them all the more a reflection of his own inordinate taste for display: a taste that, when he put on a masque for Gray's Inn, in 1594, almost bankrupted him, even as the array of extravagant, gold-brocaded clothes he ordered for his future wife for their wedding heavily depleted her dowry. In this regard, Bacon's personal tastes again singularly anticipated the meretricious affluence of our own day.

Now, Bacon did not rely upon the individual's passion for scientific inquiry alone. He saw that curiosity, to be effective, must enlist not just solitary and occasional minds, but a corps of well-organized workers, each exercising a specialized function and operating in a restricted area. By a technological organization of science, as he portrayed it in 'The New Atlantis,' he proposed to fabricate an engine capable of turning out useful knowledge in the same fashion that a well-organized factory would, a few centuries after Bacon's prediction, turn out textiles, refrigerators, or motor cars.

Bacon's description of this division of labor strikes us as quaint and finicking because of its static, ritualistic assignment of tasks; but those who would dismiss it altogether are wider of the mark than was Bacon; for part of the immense quantitative output of contemporary science is surely due to its ability to make use, not only of a few great directive minds, but of a multitude of specialized piece workers, narrowly trained for their tasks, deliberately discouraged from exploring a wider field, indeed often denied any opportunity to do so: workers whose part in the whole process increasingly resembles that of a factory worker on an assembly line. As in a factory, many of their tasks are now being assigned to cybernetic substitutes. Quite naturally, Charles Babbage, the designer of the earliest computer, in his 'Philosophy of Manufactures' (1848) backed up Bacon's proposals.

The broad division of labor in science, with its logical separation into the main categories of mathematicians, physicists, chemists, biologists, and sociologists, did not become firmly established until the nineteenth century. But once it was started, it led progressively to minuter subdivisions within each category. As such it proved an effective formula for accuracy, speed, and productivity; likewise, it had the further advantage, from the standpoint of mass production, that it provided for the employment of a whole army of workers incapable of personal initiative or original thought. The smallest discovery, the least significant experiment, may nevertheless fill up gaps in knowledge and lead others to some larger results. In itself the method of analytic dismemberment favored such piecework: but by the same token, it resulted in the dissociation, segmentation, and insulation of knowledge: failure to realize the importance of the over-all pattern: the organic correlation of functions and purposes.

Unfortunately, if "meaning means association," as Gray Walters observes, then dissociation and non-intercourse must result in a decrease of shared meanings. Thus in time, specialized knowledge, "knowing more and more about less and less," finally turns into secret knowledge—accessible only to an inner priesthood, whose sense of power is in turn inflated by their privileged command of 'trade' or official secrets. Without faintly suspecting it, Bacon had rediscovered the basic power formula of the megamachine and laid the foundation for a new structure that all too closely parallels the ancient one.

The corporate scientific personality has thus taken over the attributes of the individual thinker; and as science comes more and more to rely for its results upon complicated and extremely expensive apparatus, like computers, cyclotrons, electronic microscopes, and nuclear piles, no work along present lines can be done without close attachment to a well-endowed corporate organization. The dangers that this technological advance offer to science have not yet been sufficiently canvassed; but in the end they will perhaps nullify no small part of its benefits and rewards.

This conception of institutionalized science appeared three centuries before its practical realization. For Bacon's scientific contemporaries, science was still one large field: except in a vague way, there were no boundaries between the sciences, or if there were, the scientist could step over them without even apologizing for trespass. A physician like Dr. William Gilbert devoted himself to the study of magnetism, while Paracelsus, for all his mining background and his alchemical experiments with mercury, prided himself mainly on being a physician, devoted to curing the body. It was Bacon's peculiar genius to think of a hierarchic organization for scientific research, comparable to the standard organization of an army.

To Bacon's credit, his conception of the hierarchic organization of science did not altogether overlook the part played by individual creative minds: he even had a name for such luminous investigators, for he called them 'Lamps,' and indicated that their function was to "direct new experiments of a Higher Light, more penetrating into nature." But his peculiar contribution was to sense that, if the insights of creative minds were to have the widest kind of application, they would need abundant collective support: government aid, corporate organization, systematic conferences and publications, and, finally, public exhibition and celebration in museums of science and industry. It was these features of collective organization and governmental regimentation, not perhaps entirely unknown in pre-Christian Alexandria, that Bacon so presciently recognized, advocated, and exalted.

So it was not only the Royal Society or the American Philosophical Society that Bacon actively influenced by his anticipations. His quaint account of the future in 'The New Atlantis' provided in imagination for our present-day foundations for scientific research and our specialized institutes and laboratories, which utilize hundreds and even tens of thousands of workers in what has increasingly become a factory system for the mass production of knowledge—technologically exploitable, financially profitable, bellicosely employable. What Bacon did not foresee is that science itself might in time become demoralized by its very success as an agent of technology, and that a large part of its constructive activities might be diverted, by heavy government subvention, to destructive anti-human ends on a scale that mere empirical day-to-day technics could never achieve.

3: THE NEW ATLANTEAN WORLD

In the few years immediately before his death in 1626 Bacon assembled his leading ideas in his unfinished utopia, 'The New Atlantis.' There he more than rectified his failure to interpret the scientific method practiced by his contemporaries by showing in detail its possible collective organization and its tangible goals. Within a generation—a short time in the history of ideas—his dreams began to materialize, partly no doubt because they were already shared by many other men. Though the French scholar, Théophraste Renaudot, for example, could hardly have been familiar with Bacon, in 1633 or thereabouts he set up his 'Bureau d'Addresse.' Here he held weekly conferences to discuss questions of the most encyclopedic nature: from which "all discourses of Divinity, of State-Affaires, and of News were banned."

In 1646 a similar group began to meet regularly at the Bullhead Tavern in Cheapside, London. Their object, like Renaudot's, was at first "no more than only the satisfaction of breathing a freer air, and of conversing in quiet tones with one another, without being engaged in the passions and madness of that dismal age." Science, particularly mechanics, with its deliberate divorce from human reactions, provided a welcome sanctuary for politically harassed and troubled minds. Originally, they called themselves the Invisible College, a name that later became inappropriate for a publicly sanctioned society. Two years later they received a royal charter from Charles II. The earlier Accademia dei Lynxei, founded in Florence in 1603, may have given Bacon his germinal idea, since he was invited to become a member. But in 1630 that academy was shut down; so the members of the original group made a fresh start in 1660, with the aim "to improve the knowledge of natural things, and all Useful Arts, Manufactures, and Mechanick practices, Engynes, and Inventions by experiments."

In the light of science's later development, it is pertinent to note that the original Baconian bias was visible from the beginning. In 1664 the Royal Society had constituted itself in eight permanent committees; and first of all, be it noted, a mechanical section, to consider and approve all mechanical invention. The other committees were: Astronomical and Optical, Anatomical, Chemical, Surgical, History of Trades, a committee for collecting all phenomena of nature hitherto observed; and, finally, a committee for correspondence. The last two committees lingered on sufficiently into the nineteenth century to suggest to Dickens the constitution of the immortal Pickwick Society, and produced Mr. Pickwick's own noteworthy contribution to science: "An Inquiry into the Source of the Hampstead Ponds, with some Observations on the Theory of Tittlebats." But what is most remarkable, in view of the later developments of science, is that three of the committees, on Invention, on Technical History, and on 'Georgics' (Agriculture) were directly concerned with "the relief of man's estate."

Even more to the point, since it had a profound influence on the entire development of the scientific method, was a condition laid down in Robert Hooke's original memorandum on "the business and design of the Royal Society," namely, its engagement not to meddle with "Divinity, Metaphysics, Morals, Politicks, Grammar, Rhetoric, or Logick." This reservation not merely discouraged the scientist from critically examining his own metaphysical assumptions: it even fomented the delusion that he had none, and kept him from recognizing his own subjectivity—a theme only recently, and reluctantly, opened up. But in turn it protected the scientists from being exposed to attacks by the Church and the State, so long as they kept close to their own rabbity thought-warren.

The scientists' aloofness from the social scene, though an excellent temporary protective device, also prevented the body of scientists from concerning themselves about the political or economic uses to which their seemingly disinterested pursuit of knowledge might be put. Under the new ethic that developed, science's only form of social responsibility was to science itself: to observe its canons of proof, to preserve its integrity and autonomy, and to constantly expand its domain. Three centuries would pass before a society to "promote social responsibility in science" was even conceived; and though growing numbers of scientists today have become aware of their moral obligations, awakened from their somnolence or self-absorption by the first nuclear blast, it is doubtful if a majority as yet subscribes to this conception. As for the possibility that science, by excluding politics and religion, was excluding from consideration a vast field of human experience significant for interpreting events that cannot be reduced to mass and motion, it is only today that even a minority of scientists is willing to consider this as a defect. So a large residue was left unaccounted for by orthodox scientific theory—indeed, most of the phenomena of life, human consciousness, social activity.

Thus the Baconian emphasis on the utilitarian applications of science was present from the beginning, despite all professions of detachment, neutrality, studious isolation, theoretic 'otherworldliness.' This is not a reproach: many of the great improvements in the human condition, from the domestication of plants to the massive engineering works of early civilizations, had been due to an increase in ordered knowledge; and such advances as had long been made in medicine and surgery demonstrated this fruitful interplay of theory, close observation, and practice. Three centuries before Francis Bacon, his namesake Roger, a Franciscan monk, had been stirred by the same prospects; and his chief scientific treatise, appropriately, was one on optics. There is no proof that Francis Bacon had read the works of his predecessor: but their intellectual brotherhood comes out in Friar Bacon's account of future inventions; as witness:

"Machines for navigation can be made without rowers so that the largest ships on rivers or seas will be moved by a single man in charge with greater velocity than if they were full of men. Also carts can be made so that without animals they will move with unbelievable rapidity; such, we opine, were the scythe-bearing chariatons with which men of old fought. Also flying machines can be constructed so that a man sits in the midst of the machine revolving some engine by which artificial wings are made to beat the air like a flying bird. Also a machine small in size for raising or lowering enormous weights, than which nothing could be more useful in emergencies. . . . Also a machine can be easily made by which one man can draw a thousand to himself by violence against their wills, and attract other things in like manner. Also machines can be made for walking in the sea and rivers, even to the bottom without danger. For Alexander the Great employed such, that he might see the secrets of the deep, as Ethicus the astronomer tells. These machines were made in our times, except possibly a flying machine which I have not seen nor do I know anyone who has, but I know an expert who has thought out the way to make one. And such things can be made almost without limit, for instance, bridges across rivers without piers or other supports, and mechanisms, and unheard of engines."

This sounds, of course, like a clairvoyant revelation in a trance: the sources are as confused, the means as indescribable, the objects themselves as vivid. Certainly the coming mechanical apparatus and the concrete results had already been assembled in dream. What Francis Bacon did in 'The New Atlantis' was to suggest for the first time the kind of organization that would make it possible for these dreams to come true; not merely to fulfill them, but to enlarge their whole province.

In Alfred Gough's edition of 'The New Atlantis,' the utopia itself occupies less than forty-seven pages; but of this his list of new discoveries and inventions, and the resulting achievements, takes up a full nine pages. As Gough remarks, though the theoretic end of Solomon's House, 'the knowledge of causes,' stands first, almost every experiment performed there has an obvious relation to the needs or pleasures of man. Some of these experiments are of uncertain value; some are still in process of technical elaboration and will soon doubtless come forth; but merely to list those that have already been achieved gives one a new respect for Bacon, though none of his best dreams began to be realized till the nineteenth century. Let me cite only the well-tested fulfillments, chiefly in Bacon's own words:

"The prolongation of life: the restitution of youth in some degree: the retardation of age: the curing of diseases counted incurable: the mitigation of pain: more easy and less loathsome purgings: transformation of bodies into other bodies: making of new species: instruments of destruction as of war and poison: force of the imagination either upon another body or upon the body itself [auto-suggestion and hypnotism, if not telekinesis]: acceleration of time in maturations: acceleration of germination: making rich composts for the earth: drawing new food out of subjects not in use: making new threads for apparel, and new stuffs such as paper, glass, etc: artificial minerals and cements: "Chambers of Health where we qualifie the Aire" [air conditioning]: use of Beasts and birds for dissections, and the sting of poisons and other medicines: means to convey sounds in trunks and pipes in strange Lines and distances: engines of war, stronger and more violent, exceeding our greatest cannons; 'degrees' of flying in the air: ships and boats for going under water."

With a little further exegesis, this list might easily be lengthened. And not the least of his anticipations, already doubled in height in the plans left behind by Frank Lloyd Wright, was that of a skyscraper half a mile high. In addition, as part of the apparatus of science, as early as 1594, in a preface to a masque at Gray's Inn, he had already provided for a botanic garden, a zoo, a natural history museum, a technological museum, and a technical laboratory.

Perhaps the most remarkable fact about Bacon's canvass of scientific and technological possibilities is that he alone among the seventeenth-century philosophers of science escaped the cartesian limitations of the mechanical world picture; or, to speak more accurately, he never accepted it as the exclusive key to truth. Even when he was thinking about the future, Bacon's world was not merely that of the mechanical arts, but one embracing a larger technology, a true polytechnics, that of agriculture, medicine, cookery, brewing, chemistry. His very incapacity for abstract mathematical exercises only made him more receptive to that large province of human activities that could not be handled in this manner. Thus even subjective phenomena, like auto-suggestion, which the 'objective' scientists excluded, had a part in his coming sphere of organized investigation.

In this sense, Bacon cannot be reproached for scientific backwardness and inadequacy: he was, rather, in advance of the more specialized scientific minds that accepted the current interpretation of mass and motion as giving a complete—or at least sufficient—picture of the real world. By heeding Bacon the humanist, Bacon the extoller of science and technics pointed the way, indeed, to a post-Baconian world: the world that the present essay seeks further to open up: one in which the arbitrary restrictions and limitations of the religious, the humanistic, and the scientific outlooks will be transcended.

Behind all Bacon's expectations, however, there was a little-noted factor that was to mark the inauguration of an age committed increasingly to the pursuit of science and the perfection of machines: an ambition for conquest that coincided with a growing sense of power which the machines already in existence, particularly cannon and firearms, had greatly stimulated. According to Bacon, there are three kinds of human ambition. The first is that of extending one's personal power in one's own country—the ambition of princes, lords, soldiers, merchants. The second is the increase of the power of one's country over other countries—more dignified than the first, according to Bacon, but not less covetous and selfish. Finally, there is the ambition to enlarge the power and the dominion of the human race "over the universe of things." This last seemed to Bacon a more disinterested and noble ambition than the other two, for "the empire of man over things depends wholly on the arts and sciences."

Bacon's aphorism, "Knowledge is Power," must not be taken as a mere descriptive figure: it was a declaration of intention, and it meant emphatically that power was important. Though Bacon was, apart from his personal lapses, a studious moralist, he did not have sufficient insight to realize that the attempt to extend "the empire of man over things" might have even more terrible consequences for the human race than a too compliant adaptation to nature's conditions. If the conquest of nature on the purely physical level was a less bloody achievement than any form of military conquest—at least until this conquest began, in the nineteenth century, to have a disruptive effect upon the ecological balance of all organisms, including man—the same ambitions, the same drives, indeed the same neurotic compulsions to sacrifice all the other occasions of life to the displays and demonstrations of power, gradually took possession of its exponents. This created special ties with more vulgar forms of conquest, those of the trader, the inventor, the ruthless conquistador, and the driving industrialist seeking to displace natural abundance and natural satisfactions with those he could profitably sell.

Since the conversion and utilization of energy is an essential characteristic in the growing and working of all organisms, this drive has a biological basis: to increase power is one of the prime ways of increasing life. What was embarrassing in the social application of power was that once energy is released from its organic setting, escaping the limits imposed by the habitat, by other parts of man's own nature, and by other organisms, it knows no limits: it expands for expansion's sake. Thus the vulgar form of imperialism, which resulted in the temporary subjugation of the major territories of the planet by Western industrial and political enterprise, had its ideal counterpart in both science and technics. The nobler ambition that Bacon approved has in fact never been free from the baser egoisms of the individual and the tribe.

This utilitarian preoccupation was the side of Bacon's thought that was to exert the greatest influence. Yet there was another side of him that kept its tie to traditional knowledge, and retained an appreciation of those modes of life that were, from the beginning, deliberately excluded from the mechanical world picture. Much though Bacon valued invention and practical achievement, he still left a place for history, psychology, and religion. Was not his ideal Bensalem a Christian state converted to the 'true faith' by a wholly supernatural visitation? In the sense that Bacon's philosophy still had a place for the incommensurables, the elusive indefinables, and the irrationals, his subjectivity was more robustly objective than the kind of one-sided scientific 'objectivity' which chose flatly to ignore phenomena that could not be described or accounted for by its own system of explanation. Thus Bacon, after giving a major place to science and invention, could still say: "The contemplation of things, as they are, without superstition or imposture, error or confusion, is in itself more worthy than all the fruit of inventions."

To that view most scientists would have subscribed, without reserve, right through the nineteenth century; and it still remains the underlying motive and the highest reward of science, even today. But before long, it was Bacon's pragmatism and his intellectual imperialism that gained the upper hand, spreading the desire for physical conquest and human control, and raising to the nth power the pursuit of power itself.

4: THE BACONIAN FULFILLMENT

In looking back over the outcome of Bacon's expectations, it is plain that there were three critical points. The first occurred at the very beginning, when the activities of scientific investigation were transferred from the University, seemingly their natural home, to the workshop, the dissecting room, the laboratory, and the astronomical observatory, and thence to whole societies for the promotion of scientific research. It was first at the meetings of these bodies that new reports, expositions, and demonstrations were reviewed by their members.

The sciences that remained in the University were those that had been part of the curriculum in the Middle Ages: arithmetic, geometry, and astronomy, while the descriptive sciences of botany and anatomy continued to hold their own mainly in the medical schools. The medieval universities, with their orientation toward theology, jurisprudence, and the abstract humanities—areas with which science professed to have no concern—were uncongenial environments for science: right into our own time chemistry was popularly known, in one of the most venerable universities, as "stinks."

In establishing headquarters outside the University, the exponents of science not merely asserted their independence from traditional knowledge, but turned their backs upon any effort to present a unified and inclusive view of the world. Hence the mechanical world picture, as finally perfected by Newton, existed as an independent entity, unmodified by other modes of human experience, however much a Pascal or a Newton might personally be concerned with more ultimate questions of cosmic destiny or of religious experience, and personal salvation. This resulted in a loss on both sides. The Church and the University took their stand on arrested, if not utterly obsolete and false, conceptions of nature.

Though at every point in its development science has disclosed wonders and miracles far more astounding than any religious vision, except perhaps that of the Hindus, had dared to conjure up, science, in the name of objectivity and certainty, clung to the explainable, the communicable, and ultimately the useful—not realizing that the finer the analysis and the better the explanation of the parts, the more mysterious and wonderful the whole universe actually became. DNA may account for the organizing process in organisms: but it leaves the mystery of DNA itself totally unaccounted for.

Walt Whitman's proclamation that a leaf of grass was a miracle to confound all atheists did more justice to the findings of science than a positivism that stopped with the breaking down of the chemical reactions between sunlight and chlorophyll. This isolation of science from feeling, emotion, purpose, singular events, historic identity, endeared it to more limited minds. But it is not, perhaps, an accident that most of the great spirits in science, from Kepler and Newton to Faraday and Einstein, kept alive in their thought the presence of God—not as a mode of explaining events, but as a reminder of why they are ultimately as unexplainable today to an honest enquirer as they were to Job. (That thought has been admirably translated in Conrad Aiken's poetic dialogue with 'Thee.')

One of the consequences of organizing science was that, with the aid of the printing press, a new means was available for the systematic circulation of knowledge, through the periodical publication of scientific papers. Analytical knowledge grew by an accumulation of details: yet curiously, this rapid circulation of ideas was impeded by a counter-movement in culture, derived from the Renascence academicism against which Leonardo railed. For the new humanists scrapped the universal language of the learned world in Europe, Scholastic Latin, to return to a more cumbrous Ciceronian vocabulary and grammar.

Had Scholastic Latin remained acceptable and been further simplified—as Professor Peano the mathematician was later to attempt—it might have served as the second language of learned discourse throughout the world. The failure by the moderns to realize in time what was lost through abandoning a common language for national tongues is difficult to explain since it limited the range of communication. Today desperate efforts have been made to program computers to translate scientific reports into other native languages: but the crude, inaccurate translations so produced have already demonstrated that, whenever qualitative judgements are involved, an electronic brain is no substitute for the human mind.

The second critical point in Bacon's program came in the nineteenth century. At this juncture, for the first time, scientific experiments in physics by Volta, Galvani, Ohm, Oersted, Henry, and Faraday resulted almost within a single generation in inventions that derived almost nothing from an earlier technology: the electric telegraph, the dynamo, the electric motor; and within two generations came the electric lamp, the telephone, the wireless telegraph, and the X-ray. All of these inventions were not merely impracticable, but technically inconceivable, until pure scientific research had made them live possibilties. The methods that had proved so fruitful in mechanics and electronics were then applied, with growing success, in organic chemistry and biology; though, significantly, those parts of technology with the oldest accumulations of empiric knowledge, like metallurgy, for long remained almost impervious to the advances of science.

While in England fresh technical inventions were protected, from the seventeenth century on, by royal patents, so that the inventor, or those who took advantage of the inventor, would have a monopoly in exploiting the idea economically for a limited period, it was originally an honorable point of pride among scientists to claim no personal advantage from their discoveries. Though there might be occasional sordid squabbles over priority, aggravated sometimes by national antagonisms, like the deplorable quarrels between Newton and Leibnitz or later between Pasteur and Koch, science was by definition public knowledge, and its publication and circulation without restriction was essential to its critical evaluation and validation.

Pascal pointed out that people often spoke of 'my ideas' as complacently as middle-class people talked of 'my house' or 'my paintings,' but that it would be more honest to speak of 'our ideas.' This trait became so deeply a mark of the finer scientific mind that my own master, Patrick Geddes, was pleased rather than offended when others put forth his most original ideas as their own. He gleefully described his habitual practice as that of the cuckoo bird who lays her eggs in other birds' nests, and gives them the trouble of hatching and caring for the offspring.

The third radical change came in the twentieth century, through a change in scale, magnitude, and eventually of purpose: this was brought about, almost automatically, by the expansion of new facilities for communication, and the exploitation of new modes of reproduction in printing, photography, and motion pictures. This series of transformations lifted once inviolable limits on human activities. A shot could be heard around the world by means of radio more than eleven times faster than it could be heard by the unaided ear only a mile away.

Scientific discoveries in new fields no longer remained aloof and inert: they lent themselves to immediately profitable exploitation for industry or war. At this point, science itself became the master model, the technology of technologies. In this new milieu the mass production of scientific knowledge went hand in hand with the mass production of inventions and products derived from science. Thus the scientist came to have a new status in society, equivalent to that occupied earlier by the captain of industry. He, too, was engaged in mass production; he, too, dealt in standard units; and his product increasingly could be evaluated in terms of money. Even his separate scientific papers, his prizes and awards, had 'exchange value' in pecuniary terms: they determined university promotions, and raised the market price of lectureships and consultantships.

The old image of the self-directed scientist, abstemious, even ascetic—in the laboratory, if not at the dinner table—still remains popular, surviving particularly among 'old-fashioned' scientists. But with the expansion of science as mass technology, the scientist himself no longer need practice self-denial in any form: his scientific status rises in proportion to his contributions to the affluent society; and his success may even be measured quantitatively by the number of assistants in his laboratory, the total annual budget for apparatus, mechanical aids, computers; and finally in the mass output of scientific papers to which his name may be unblushingly signed.

As an operator in this power-oriented technics, the scientist himself becomes a servant of corporate organizations intent on enlarging the bounds of empire—by no means always Bacon's "humane empire"! Increasingly the 'gross national product' of industry reflects the gross national product of science. Every theoretic innovation, however innocent in intention, automatically multiplies the number of practical products—and, more significantly, profit-making wants. By participating in this transformation, the scientist has forfeited the qualities that were exalted in the past as his special hallmark: his detachment from worldly gains and his disinterested pursuit of truth.

To the extent that the scientist's capacity for pursuing truth depends upon costly apparatus, institutional collaboration, and heavy capital investment by government or industry, he is no longer his own master. Even the mathematician no more remains as disencumbered as was an experimenter like Faraday who, with a few bits of glass, iron, and wire, had the makings of all the apparatus needed for his basic discoveries in electro-magnetism. This physical simplicity perhaps helps explain the fructifying originality and daring of contemporary mathematical thought. But a growing corpus of scientists has lost the capacity to stand alone or to say no, even on grave matters that threaten the existence of the human race, like the exploitation of nuclear or bacterial knowledge for mass genocide.

Graphically though Bacon was able to anticipate the immense potentialities of a corporate organization of science, he was still too remote from their actual development to be able to foresee any but favorable consequences. It would be foolish to blame him for his lack of either historic perspective or foresight: most of our contemporaries are still destitute of both. Bacon could not guess that the Fellows of Solomon's House would, through their knowledge of the secret causes of things, disclose forces of nature that had never been suspected, and perfect apparatus of fantastic complexity and refinement capable of utilizing them. Nor could he anticipate that this very ability to augment human power mechanically and electronically would result in resurrecting the ancient myth of the machine: or finally, that it would create a perfected twentieth-century megamachine, far surpassing in all its evil potentialities the archaic model.

This is only another way of saying that the best minds of the seventeenth century could not imagine what life would be like once their 'objective' mechanical world picture had helped to bring into existence a society that conformed strictly to its limited premises and lived in accordance with its prescribed terms. In conceiving a social organization that could make a fuller use of machines, they failed to foresee that society itself might take

on the characteristics of an increasingly automatic machine, run by machine-conditioned personalities, in a machine-fabricated habitat, for purely
abstract mechanical-electronic ends. These leaders could not, in short,
picture the dismaying nightmare of twentieth-century existence, in which
almost no malign hallucination or psychotic impulse would be technically
impossible to carry out, and in which no product of technics would, if it
filled its own specific requirements, be regarded as humanly undesirable,
if only it promised increasing money or power or prestige to investors,
fabricators, or financial and political exploiters.

Bacon, even more than Galileo or Descartes, was still living bodily and
mentally in an earlier world, not yet stripped of its historic achievements or
its human traits. Bacon's references to theology, philosophy, and humanistic learning continued to balance off his preoccupations with material
advances and scientific audacities. Unlike some of his more rigorous
successors, Bacon was even ready to admit some cogency in dreams, or
some reality in the hypnotic powers of the imagination—elusive and
dangerous though he might feel all these phenomena to be. This was the
saving grace of Bacon's radical empiricism. His philosophic system, more
than Galileo's, was still an open one: despite his strong emphasis on
science and technics, he did not restrict his own conception of reality to
this realm alone. In the twentieth century, science itself, led by Sigmund
Freud and his disciples, would have to reclaim some of the territory that
Bacon, in his own person, had never entirely abandoned. Curiously, Freud
believed that his daring interpretations of dreams and other forms of
psychal symbolism were still strictly in the spirit of 'objective' scientific
materialism.

But if anything proves how deeply the myth of the machine was stirring
again in the Western mind, Bacon's own personality and his work would
testify to it, for his concern to explore the new world of the machine was
not the result of his mature reflection, but was the earliest intuition of his
youth. Admittedly, he was no mechanical genius, like Leonardo, no keen
mathematical mind, like Kepler, no skillful anatomist and dissectionist,
like Vesalius. Far from it: no one better appreciated the gallantries and
intrigues of courtly life; no one could have been farther from the classic
scientist's renunciation of the pomps and vanities of the visible world than
this worldly courtier. Yet no other contemporary was more vividly conscious of the prospective triumphs of a science in its now dominant mid-
twentieth-century form, pursued relentlessly for practical ends: material
wealth, political control, and military power, all ostentatiously dressed up
and prettified as "the relief of man's estate." Did Bacon not die as a result
of pneumonia brought on by an experiment in preserving a chicken by
packing it with snow? A first effort at swift refrigeration for preserving
food. Bacon had lived in the style of the past: he had pursued his ideas in

the new style of his own day: but he died in the style of the future: a style he himself had helped to create.

Within this generous Baconian synthesis, unfortunately, the serious metaphysical errors later made by Galileo, Descartes, and their fellow-travelers in scientific exploration were already deeply embedded. Hidden within this whole movement of thought, we can now see—but for long disguised by the variety of immediately fascinating discoveries and serviceable practices that it furthered—were two guiding aims whose magical nature has only now become apparent, and whose undeclared ultimate goals are now at last visible.

First: he who creates a perfect automaton is in fact creating life, since, according to mechanistic doctrine, there is no essential difference between living organisms and machines, provided that they work. Even such a percipient and sensitive mind as that of Norbert Wiener came increasingly to endow his Golem with the ultimate properties of life. But, second, beneath this magic wish was a more insidiously flattering idea: *he who creates life is a God*. Hence the very idea of a creative deity, which science from the sixteenth century on had regarded as a superfluous hypothesis in analyzing matter and motion, came back with redoubled force in the collective persona of organized science: all those who served this God participated in his power and glory, and for them was the ultimate kingdom, too.

Even a few years ago this interpretation might have seemed unacceptable except in an avowed science-fiction tract. But in 1965 the president of the American Chemical Society, a Nobel Prize laureate, in a parting address put this ambition into so many words. "Let us marshal all our scientific forces together," he urged his colleagues, "in order to create life!" Thus the alchemist's rejected dream of creating a homunculus in a test tube has now been translated into the sober chemist's dream of creating, not a little man, but at least a virus . . . perhaps eventually a bacterium. . . .

On the surface this seemingly audacious proposal suggests a deadly bit of Swiftian irony, coming from the sciences which have put all modes of life in jeopardy by their misapplications in the production of herbicides, pesticides, and homicides. The leading minds of science, it seems, would cover this devastating threat by beginning all over again in the hope of turning a large complex molecule into an organism. What an audaciously stultifying proposal! One would hardly guess from this project that life already exists and has penetrated every nook and corner of this planet.

Observe: billions of dollars, thousands of hours of valuable time, the best brains in science, would be marshalled together to bring into existence by artificial means something that already exists in abundance in billions of different forms, in the air one breathes, the soil one walks on, in the ocean

and the seashore and the forest. To begin organic evolution all over again
in the laboratory would be, to say the least, a redundancy—though the virus
so produced might prove in addition to be as lethal as the 'Andromeda
Strain'!

These fantasies of creating life have taken hold, not only of many
members of the scientific elite, but even more of younger minds who have
been sedulously conditioned to regard the expansion of science and megatechnics as the ultimate reason for human existence. When the distinguished biochemist George Wald addressed a university audience recently,
some of the students demanded eagerly that he comment on the prospect of
creating an artificial human being within the next ten years; and when he
dismissed this callow fantasy, even allowing for a far longer period, as
laughably improbable, they were openly disappointed and would not accept
his verdict. But neither they nor their science-fiction mentors had asked
themselves why they regarded such a feat as desirable on any conceivable
rational grounds. Nor, granting for a moment the impossible prospect that
such an artificial organism could be created, did they ask themselves what
kind of behavior could be expected of an organism without a history—
though if they had read Mary Shelley's description of Frankenstein's
monster, they might have found out.

But if the creation of life in the sense proposed by our distinguished
chemist would be a backward step—more than three billion years backward—the creation of life by increasing the number of automatons and
fabricating whole societies of automatons that would take over, one by
one, the functions now exercised by man is actually in operation. Most of
the technical difficulties in the way of such creation have been overcome;
but the psychological and cultural results have still to be reckoned with.
Complete success here, I propose to demonstrate, has already drastically
lessened man's own sense of his worth and his significance, and deprived
him of the resources, external and internal, needed for his further development. That outcome, already visible, would wipe out all the putative
immediate benefits.

5: ANTICIPATIONS VERSUS
REALIZATIONS

Now if the fulfillment of Bacon's dream deserves our respectful recognition
of his prophetic insights, it also imposes upon us a special duty—that of

dissociating ourselves from the mythology he so largely helped to promote. Only thus shall we be able to appraise, in the light of historic experience, his unexamined premises. These premises are now so thoroughly institutionalized that most of our contemporaries continue to act upon them without even a quiver of doubt. But we proceed further at our own risk, for science as technology now presents a series of problems that science as the disinterested examination of nature in search of rational understanding never confronted. Already the scientific establishment shows the same irrationalities and absurdities that mass production in other fields has brought about.

The chief premise common to both technology and science is the notion that there are no desirable limits to the increase of knowledge, of material goods, of environmental control; that quantitative productivity is an end in itself, and that every means should be used to further expansion.

This was a defensible position in the seventeenth century, when an economy of scarcity still prevailed everywhere. Then, each new facility for production, each fresh increment of energy and goods, each new scientific observation or experiment, was needed to make up the terrible existing deficiencies in consumable goods and verifiable knowledge. But today our situation is precisely the opposite of this. Because of the success of the sciences in widening the domain of prediction and control, in penetrating the hitherto inviolable mysteries of nature, in augmenting human power on every plane, we face a new predicament derived from this very economy of abundance: that of deprivation by surfeit. The quantitative overproduction of both material and intellectual goods poses—immediately for the Western World, ultimately for all mankind—a new problem: the problem of regulation, distribution, assimilation, integration, purposeful anticipation and direction.

As science approximates more closely the condition of technology, it must concern itself with contemporary technics' great weakness: the defects of a system that, unlike organic systems, has no built-in method of controlling its growth or modulating the enormous energy it commands in order to maintain, as every living organism must, a dynamic equilibrium favorable to life and growth.

No one questions the immense benefits already conferred in many departments by science's efficient methodology: but what one must challenge is the value of a system so detached from other human needs and human purposes that the process itself goes on automatically without any visible goal except that of keeping the corporate apparatus itself in a state of power-making, profit-yielding productivity. What is now called 'Research and Development' is a circular process.

In the exploding universe of science, the scattered parts are travelling at an accelerated rate ever farther from the human center. Because of our concentration on speed and productivity, we have ignored the need for evaluation, correction, integration, and social assimilation. In practice this results in an inability to use more than a small fragment of the existing corpus of knowledge—namely that which is fashionable or immediately available, because it can be commercially or militarily exploited. This has already worked havoc in medicine, as any competent and morally trust-worthy physician will testify, and the results are increasingly visible in every other professional activity.

Is it not time, then, that we began to ask ourselves certain questions about science as technology that Bacon, by reason of his historic position, was too uninformed to put to himself? Are we sure that the control of all natural processes by science and technics is by itself an effective way of relieving and improving man's estate? Is it not possible to have a surfeit of inventions, like a surfeit of food—with similar distress to and derangement of the organism? Have we not already evidence to show that science as technology may, through its inordinate growth, become increasingly irrele-vant to any human intent whatever, except that of the technologist or the corporate enterprise: that, indeed, as in the form of nuclear or bacterial weapons, or space exploration, it may be not merely coldly indifferent but actively hostile to human welfare?

But I would go further. By what rational canon do we seek, on purely Baconian premises, to save time, shrink space, augment power, multiply goods, overthrow organic norms, and displace real organisms wth mecha-nisms that simulate them or vastly magnify some single function they perform? All these imperatives, which have become the very groundwork of 'science as technology' in our present society, seem axiomatic and absolute only because they remain unexamined. In terms of the nascent organic world picture, these seemingly 'advanced' ideas are obsolete.

Just because science as technology has begun to dominate every other aspect of science, we are bound, if only in self-preservation, to correct the mistakes Bacon sanctioned and unwittingly fostered. Science now makes all things possible, as Bacon believed: but it does not thereby make all possible things desirable. A sound and viable technology, firmly related to human needs, cannot be one that has a maximum productivity as its supreme goal: it must, rather, seek as in an organic system, to provide the right quantity of the right quality at the right time and the right place in the right order for the right purpose. To this end, deliberate regulation and direction, in order to ensure continued growth and creativity of the human personalities and groups concerned, must govern our plans in the future, as indefinite expansion and multiplication have done during the last few centuries.

Has the time not come, then—in technology as in every other aspect of the common life—to re-examine our accepted axioms and practical imperatives and to release science itself from the under-dimensioned mythology of power that Galileo, Francis Bacon, and Descartes unguardedly subscribed to and helped to promote? With this aim in view I shall now turn to the development of technics itself.

CHAPTER SIX

The Polytechnic Tradition

1: THE MEDIEVAL CONTINUUM

For the last century, even before Arnold Toynbee coined the term "the Industrial Revolution," the whole history of modern technology was misinterpreted by the Victorian over-valuation of the mechanical inventions of the eighteenth century and after. Those who believed that a radical departure had taken place at this point not only overlooked the long series of preparatory efforts, dating from the twelfth century, but they attributed an immediate result to changes that were not fully established till the second half of the nineteenth century, when they wrote.

Curiously enough, the scholars who first popularized the notion of medieval backwardness read their documents with spectacles first invented in the thirteenth century, published their ideas in books produced on the printing press of the fifteenth century, ate bread made of grain ground in windmills introduced in the twelfth century, sailed by sea in three-masted ships first designed in the sixteenth century, reached their destination with the aid of the mechanical clock, the astrolabe, and the magnetic compass, and defended their ships against pirates with the aid of gunpowder and cannon, all dating before the fifteenth century, while they wrote on paper and wore woolen and cotton clothes fabricated in watermills that date back at least to the third century B.C. in Greece.

Since many scholars still persist in treating the eighteenth century as an unmistakable watershed, it will be useful to give a more accurate characterization of the technological complex that existed before "mechanization took command." As it happens, the current attempt to amend the first budget of errors by dividing a single industrial revolution into two periods —one of mechanical invention, preceded, and now finally completed, by a scientific revolution—is equally misleading in that it ignores the impression that the earlier technical changes had themselves made on the scientific thought of the sixteenth and seventeenth centuries.

A more careful reading of the evidence shows that the most radical technical mutations that came into existence, before those introduced by scientific discoveries in electricity, came about early in the Middle Ages; and if one is to understand under what conditions they flourished one must follow them back to their source. What we have to do is to trace the stages by which the rich and varied polytechnics that was available in the late Middle Ages—thirteenth to fifteenth centuries—with its masterpieces of art and engineering and its first essays in mass production through printing, was transformed under the influence of political absolutism and capitalist enterprise into the present system of high-speed megatechnics, out of which a new type of megamachine, more powerful than that of the Pyramid Age, is coming into existence.

Now one of the most significant facts about the great transformation of mechanical industry which took place in the eighteenth and early nineteenth centuries was that its effective inventions apart from the steam engine—notably the spinning jenny, the flying shuttle, the power loom—occurred in the ancient neolithic industries: spinning, weaving, and pottery. In these areas the large-scale application of power to mass production in huge factories came mainly, not from the steam engine, but through the increased use of watermills. The early term for a factory, 'mill,' testifies to its source of power.

This utilization of waterpower was what confined the textile industries so long to the fast-flowing streams of England and New England: indeed, hydraulic energy was used in many mills to the end of the nineteenth century and even later: it thus paved the way for hydro-electric installations. So slow was the introduction of the steam engine as a prime mover that even in Britain, the home of James Watt, where coal and iron were available in quantity, in Thomas Martin's 'Cyclopedia of the Mechanical Arts' published in London in 1818, there is not even a mention of the steam engine; while in the United States the first use of steam power in cotton mills was in the Naumkoag Steam Cotton Mill at Salem, Massachusetts, in 1847.

The other great inventions of the nineteenth century, the Bessemer furnace and the open-hearth furnace, were likewise end-products of the Iron Age, whose vastly improved techniques in mining had been introduced, not in the eighteenth century, but in the fourteenth and the fifteenth centuries, in response to the military demand for iron for armor and cannon. The great and rapid changes that did in fact take place in the eighteenth century were due, not alone to its absorption in mechanical improvements but to a loss of concern with many other aspects of life that had kept technology in balance with other institutions. The mere fact that medieval technology cherished other interests and pursued other aims than those focussed on mechanical expansion has long been treated, without rational justification, as an evidence of technical ineptitude.

From the eleventh century on, all over Europe, beginning in Italy, there was a resurgence of technical activity, stimulated by contact, direct and indirect, by trade and war, with the more advanced technological cultures of the East: Byzantine (mosaics, textiles), Arabic (irrigation, chemicals, horse-breeding), Persian (tiles, rugs, and possibly, if Arthur Upham Pope is right, the Gothic arch and vault), Korean (wood-block printing), finally, Chinese (porcelain, silks, paper—paper money, wallpaper, toilet paper).

After the fifteenth century, the opening up of the New World, along with the Near and Far East, immensely increased the supply of raw materials and technological resources: not merely large quantities of gold, silver, lead, silk, cotton, along with a wide variety of woods such as teak and ebony, but also the food plants, florals, and medicinals, from Persian lilacs and tulips to the South American potato, maize and cocoa, cinchona bark (quinine), and tobacco. *Long before rapid transportation and communication became mechanically possible, this polytechnics had broken through national barriers and drawn upon a planet-wide culture.* Since this vital agricultural revolution owed nothing to later mechanization till the middle of the nineteenth century, its significance has been played down, or completely overlooked.

The basic source of energy and the chief mode of production, right down to the middle of the nineteenth century, even in 'progressive' machine-committed countries like Britain, was agriculture, and the crafts and prime-movers directly associated with agriculture. In Britain in the fifteenth century more than ninety per cent of the population lived in the countryside; and though the proportion varied from region to region, as late as 1940 four-fifths of the population of the planet, according to the French geographer Max Sorre, lived in agricultural villages. As late as 1688, when fairly reliable estimates became available, some seventy-six per cent of the entire population of England was engaged in agriculture and related rural activities.

Until the nineteenth century, in fact, when one speaks of crafts, trades, and technologies one must give first place to agriculture; and it was the many botanical advances made here that laid the basis for the later machine economy, long before machines became available for plowing or reaping. To equate technical improvement with the machine alone is literally to place the cart before the horse. The very term we still use for units of work, horsepower, betrays this original debt to medieval technics, with its improved shoeing and harnessing of horses. Where water and wind-power could not be developed, horsemills were common.

The careful breeding of horses—doubtless stimulated by early contact

with the Arabs, and later by the introduction of a Persian fodder, alfalfa—
went on during this whole period, as a series of specialized breeds, from
Percherons for military uses and heavy dray-wagons to high-tempered fast
horses for hunts and races, bears witness. Inventions for transport and
weight-lifting freed manpower for other tasks, as did the series of improvements brought about in pulley hoists and derricks, which finally resulted in
the maneuverable and seaworthy three-masted sailing vessels. More significantly this increase of horsepower, waterpower, and windpower created for
the first time in history an advanced economy based entirely on 'free' (non-
slave) labor. By the seventeenth century that economy prevailed over the
better part of Europe, except for backward pockets where serfdom lingered
into the nineteenth century.

The prime agents of this industrial freedom were the craft guilds:
independent self-governing bodies, established typically in equally self-
governing cities, which provided for the education, the discipline, and the
sustenance of their members, from youth to old age, in sickness and in
health, and cared for the widows and orphans of their brothers when in
need. Not least, the guilds set for themselves standards of qualitative performance: quantity production, as such, did not play a part except where
the guild system itself had broken down. As late as the eighteenth century,
it is interesting to note, the builders of the Carpenters Company of Philadelphia were paid for their work *after* the building was constructed, on the
basis of an evaluation made by an independent assessor of both the labor
consumed *and* the quality of the workmanship. Quality deliberately held
quantity in check.

Even before the mechanization of production, some of this freedom
had been whittled away by mercantile practices that favored the bigger
masters in the wholesale trades, who formed a ruling oligarchy and who,
after the sixteenth century, farmed out work to unprotected handicraft
workers in the rural or even suburban areas outside the jurisdiction of the
guild. The legal abolition of the guilds, which followed, opened the way for
the dehumanized practices of early machine industry. Thus the new freedom proclaimed by the advocates of 'laissez-faire,' like Adam Smith, was
freedom to abandon the medieval system of guild protection and social
security and to be exploited by those who owned the costly new machinery
of production.

By a mental sleight of hand, this accompaniment of mechanical progress was minimized by those committed to the system: in proclaiming the
immense economies of mass production, they ignored the fact that the
landless and the homeless proletarians, forced into the new factories by the
price-undercutting of handicraft labor were worse off, in food, sanitary
facilities, water supply, and environmental amenities than the agricultural
workers of their own time: a fact established by the English life-insurance

tables, which show that farm laborers still have a notably higher expectation of life. The factory system degraded the worker into a wage slave instead of using its power machines to abolish slavery.

As it happens, these depressing social consequences were most visible in the very departments where great technical improvements were being made. The undoubted gains, through organization and mechanization, visible from the very beginning, were offset by the merciless regimentation and exploitation of the workers, particularly the child laborers and women. These facts are still glossed over by those who believe that technological progress automatically brings social improvements, without bothering to appraise the actual results. In this they only imitate the Victorian apostles of industrialism, like Andrew Ure, who dismissed the now scientifically established fact that the prevalence of rickets in factory children working fourteen hours a day was due to lack of sunlight: gaslight, he ignorantly proclaimed, was quite as good—and more progressive!

2: THE POLYTECHNIC HERITAGE

Because the era before the eighteenth century is mistakenly supposed to have been technically backward, one of its best characteristics has been overlooked: namely, that it was still a mixed technology, a veritable polytechnics, for the characteristic tools, machine-tools, machines, utensils, and utilities it used did not derive solely from its own period and culture, but had been accumulating in great variety for tens of thousands of years.

Consider this immense heritage. If the watermill went back to pre-Christian Greece and the windmill to eighth-century Persia, the plow, the loom, and the potter's wheel went back two or three thousand years further; while its grains, fruits, and vegetables derived from a much earlier period of paleolithic food-gathering and neolithic domestication. The bow that won the battle of Crécy for the English was a paleolithic invention, once used in hunting Magdalenian bison. As for the paintings and sculptures in public buildings, these issued from an even more ancient paleolithic past: the Aurignacian caves. The introduction of new inventions like the clock did not necessitate on principle the discarding of any of these older achievements.

Not the least significant fact about this 'backward' technology is that the areas in which technical skill and engineering audacity were highest, namely, in the massive Romanesque and the towering Gothic cathedrals, drew on the oldest parts of our technical heritage, and were associated directly, not with any utilitarian purpose, but solely with attempts to add significance and beauty to the necessitous round of daily life. It was not the need for food or shelter, or the desire to exploit natural forces, or the effort to overcome physical obstacles that raised this constructive technics to the highest pitch of effort. To express their deepest subjective feelings, the builders of these monuments posed for themselves the most difficult technical problems, often beyond their mathematical insight or craft experience, but calling forth a daring experimental imagination, so daring that it sometimes fatally outran their capacities—as more than one toppled tower revealed.

To build these monumental structures, groups of workers of diverse capabilities and talents were assembled, to perform a wide variety of tasks, from the monotonous shaping of stones into square blocks, small enough for a single man to handle, to the acrobatic feats needed to place the carved stones on the topmost pinnacle. Not merely muscular strength, mechanical skill, and physical courage went into the fabrication of these buildings: emotions, feelings, fantasies, remembered legends—in fact, the community's total response to life—took form in these supreme technological achievements. Technology itself was a means to a greater goal: for the cathedral was as near to Heaven as any earthbound structure could get.

Such mastery of the complex processes of architectural creation was not for the purpose of either "making work," as in ancient times, or of doing away with work, as under today's automation: neither was it just to increase the personal prestige of the Master Mason or the incomes of the workers, still less to 'expand the economy.' The ultimate end of such a magnificent technical effort was not the building alone but the vision it promoted: a sense of the meanings and values of life. This achievement has proved so valuable that successive generations of men, with far different religious beliefs and aspirations, have nevertheless felt a fresh infusion of spiritual vitality on beholding these buildings, even as William Morris did, as an eight-year-old boy, when he first confronted, breathlessly, the marvel of Canterbury Cathedral.

Not every aspect of handicraft, it goes without saying, offered such happy working conditions or such ultimate rewards. There was backbreaking drudgery, hardship, crippling organic maladaptation, and chronic disease in occupations such as mining, smelting, dyeing, and glass-blowing: yet today, despite our superior medical diagnosis and treatment, many of these disabilities still exist, and have even been magnified in technically 'advanced' industries where the workers are exposed to radioactivity, to lead poisoning, to silicate and asbestos dust, or to malign pesticides like malathion and dieldrin.

The other human weakness of some handicraft industries, like weaving, their fixation in routine motions and unrelieved monotony, paved the way for mechanization: but the effect of the latter, until automation took over, was to intensify the boredom, while the speeding up of the processes took away the soothing effect of repetition that makes such crafts so useful to the psychiatrist in the concluding phases of psychotherapy, as William Morris discovered by personal experience during a troubled period in his own marital life.

In certain departments of handicraft, the rewards and the penalties were, admittedly, almost inextricable. In some of its highest reaches, as in the Persian rug-making of the sixteenth century, the perfection of both the design and the process of work, demanding as many as four hundred knots to the square inch, might call for a lifetime enslavement of the worker, to reach such a pitch of artifice. There is no need to conceal these ugly blemishes: but also no excuse for hiding one of the great compensations—the work itself was prized and preserved. One of the beautiful rugs that now covers a wall in the Victoria and Albert Museum in London demanded the whole lifetime of the temple slave who made it. But this slave was an artist, and in his art enjoyed the freedom to create. At the end of his task, he proudly signed his name to the masterpiece. He had not lost his identity or his self-respect: he had something to show for his working life. Compare the death of this slave with Arthur Miller's 'Death of a Salesman.'

To understand the older polytechnics, partly mechanized by the sixteenth century, but not wholly committed to mechanization, one must remember that its dominant arts were solidly based on ancient neolithic foundations: mixed farming—grains, vegetables, orchard crops, domestic animals—and buildings of every sort, from houses and barns to canals and cathedrals. All these occupations required an assemblage of craft knowledge and skills; and the work, in the very process of growth and construction, changed from hour to hour and from day to day. The process itself did not demand staying in the same position, performing a single uniform task, accepting monotony and uniformity, without at least the relief of a change of weather or seasons, or a change of pace.

Consider the performance of the old-fashioned Japanese craftsman cited by Raphael Pumpelly in his 'Reminiscences.' Pumpelly wanted a door that could be locked, so he called in a metal-worker to make screwed-in hinges; but unfortunately this craftsman had never seen a screw. When Pumpelly presented him with an iron screw, the worker went away and next day brought a dozen brass screws, beautifully made and polished, after being ingeniously molded. "He also asked permission to copy my Colt's revolver. Before long he brought an exact duplicate working well in all its parts, and it was more highly finished." One would look far to find such confidence and resourcefulness in a modern machine shop: it was long ago exiled from the assembly line.

In the workshop and the household there were plenty of tedious tasks, no doubt: but they were done in the company of one's fellows, at a pace that allowed for chatting and singing: there was none of the loneliness of the modern housewife presiding over a gang of machines, accompanied only by the insistent rumble and clatter and hum of her assistants. Except in servile industries like mining, playful relaxation, sexual delight, domestic tenderness, esthetic stimulation were not spatially or mentally separated completely from the work in hand.

Though hand labor brought many skills to the highest point of perfection—no machine can weave a cotton as fine as Dacca muslin with number 400 thread—an even more important characteristic was its wide diffusion, which is another way of referring to the tool-user's essential autonomy and self-reliance. Nothing proves this better than the annals of overseas exploration, with their repeated record of building seaworthy ships to take the place of a wrecked vessel. "The ship's carpenter who marched in Cortes' army, directed the building and launching on Lake Texcoco of a whole fleet of brigantines big enough to carry cannon." Such a mode of work was equal to any emergency: neither the skill nor the overall knowledge of design was restricted to a few specialists. That our present gains in horsepower have been diminished by a loss of effective manpower, and above all *cooperating* mindpower, widely distributed, has still to be sufficiently appreciated.

Karl Buecher gave an account of this inter-relation between handicraft work and esthetic expression in his classic study, 'Arbeit und Rhythmus,' unfortunately never translated into English; and I have emphasized, in 'Art and Technics' and elsewhere, the fact that mechanical invention and esthetic expression were inseparable aspects of the older polytechnics, and that, down to the Renascence, art itself remained the principal field of invention. The purpose of art has never been labor-saving but labor-loving, a deliberate elaboration of function, form, and symbolic ornament to enhance the interest of life itself.

This ancient reciprocity between folk work and folk art reached its apogee in music between the seventeenth and the nineteenth centuries: witness Samuel Pepys choosing a serving-maid partly for her qualifications in holding her part in song around the family dinner table—or Franz Schubert, who, according to legend, translated the work song of the pile drivers on the river into the melody and rhythm of his Nocturne in E-flat Major. If orchestral music reached its climax in the symphonic works of Haydn, Mozart, Beethoven, and Schubert, it was perhaps because it still obviously drew upon the wealth of folk songs and dances that were tied to the rural crafts: a heritage that Verdi, in an industrially 'backward' country like Italy, could still draw on.

Had this craft economy, prior to mechanization, actually been ground down by poverty, its workers might have spent the time given over to communal celebrations and church-building on multiplying the yards of textiles woven or the pairs of shoes cobbled. Certainly an economy that enjoyed a long series of holidays, free from work, only fifty-two of which were Sundays, cannot be called impoverished. The worst one can say about it is that in its concentration on its spiritual interests and social satisfactions, it might fail to guard its members sufficiently against a poor winter diet and occasional bouts of starvation. But such an economy had something that we now have almost forgotten the meaning of, leisure: not freedom from work, which is how our present culture interprets leisure, but freedom *within* work; and along with that, time to converse, to ruminate, to contemplate the meaning of life.

Aside from agriculture and building, the most radical weakness of the older handicrafts was their excessive craft-specialization, which prevented the free circulation of knowledge and skill, and deprived the individual crafts outside the building trades of the great corporate assemblage of knowledge that had made the engineering feats of the cathedral builders such marvellous vehicles of cultural expression. At the end of the Middle Ages, this excessive specialization began to break down through an invasion from above. Note that Rabelais made the study of arts and crafts part of Gargantua's education: on cold and rainy days he devoted himself to carving and painting and went with his tutor to observe "the drawing of metals or the casting of cannon, or paid visits to jewellers, goldsmiths, and cutters of precious stones; or to alchemists and coiners, or to tapestry makers, printers, musical instrument makers, dyers, and other craftsmen of that sort; and everywhere . . . they learned and considered the processes and inventions of each trade."

In this description, Rabelais was recording, in effect, the great innovation effected in person by the Renascence artist: the audacious all-round amateur who, though he might still have to attach himself to the Goldsmith's Guild, was actually breaking through a cramping and obsolescent craft isolationism; for this new figure was equally ready to paint a picture, cast a bronze, plan a fortification, design a pageant, or construct a building. Whatever he could think he could draw: whatever he could draw he could do. Through defying the constrictions of craft specialization, the artist restored the full exercise of mind.

This facility was not the product of a special genius: was Vasari a genius? It was due, rather, to a disruption of older municipal, guild, and ecclesiastic institutions by princely despots and patrons. This gave an opportunity for detached, non-specialized minds to move freely from one craft to another, utilizing their hoarded skills, but not having to invent them alone, *de novo,* as the machine designers after James Watt were largely forced to do. But note: the most successful of these artists, Brunelleschi, Michelangelo, and Christopher Wren, derived their strength mainly from the ancient, if highly organized, building crafts—as a later industrial giant, Joseph Paxton, did from horticulture.

3 : TECHNICAL LIBERATION

However slow in pace, pre-mechanized industry and agriculture relied so largely on manual labor that this gave it a freedom and flexibility that a system more dependent upon a permanent assemblage of specialized machines demanding a heavy capital investment ceased to enjoy. Tools have always been personal property, selected and often re-shaped, if not directly made, to fit the needs of the individual worker. Compared with complex machines they are cheap, replaceable, easily transported: but worthless without manpower. With his kit of tools, the urban journeyman, once his apprenticeship was over, could and did travel abroad, surveying new scenes, learning new technical tricks, overcoming in some degree the traditional craft stratifications.

So far from being stagnant, medieval technics not merely introduced new inventions like the silk-reeling machine (1272), block printing (1289), the spinning wheel (1298), and the wire pulling machine (1350), but it expanded and perfected older industries, like glass-making and glass-blowing—as before noted, skills that provided the indispensable flasks and alembics for later chemical experiments. But here again, be it noted, the first large-scale use of glass was not for utilitarian but for esthetic purposes: the great windows of the Lady Churches of the thirteenth century.

Thus, until the seventeenth century, this polytechnic tradition performed the feat of transmitting the major technical heritage derived from the past, while introducing many fresh mechanical or chemical improvements: sometimes inventions as radical in technical conception and as profound in social effects as the printing press.

The rapid success of the printing press, which made the transition from manuscript writing to printing from types in less than a century, was in itself a proof of how effectively handicraft had prepared the way for this further step, and showed no inherent hostility to such improvements. Apart from the passing resistance of the old manuscript copyists, the new invention could spread swiftly because the initial step in mechanization, the creation of perfectly standardized hand-lettering, had long been achieved in the monastery, where a deliberately mechanized habit of life laid the groundwork for wider mechanizations.

As a contribution to the growing sense of liberation and autonomy that accompanied the first mechanical innovations, the hand-operated printing press had a central place. No one worthy of respect seriously doubts the social advantages of multifolding the printed word, for this invention broke down the class monopoly of written knowledge and opened the world in time as decisively as the new explorations that were contemporary with it opened the world of space. Until the sixteenth century the enormous amount of empirical knowledge that had been preserved within each craft had lain under this limitation: it never was transferred to the permanent record; and when, unfortunately, the human links were broken by plague or war, essential elements in the tradition might disappear.

With the invention of printing, it was possible to collect and diffuse technological knowledge on a great scale; and it is not without significance that one of the greatest of technical compendiums, Agricola's treatise on mining and the metallurgical arts, appeared within a century of Gutenberg's innovation, conveying not merely accurate scientific information, abundantly illustrated, but displaying an extraordinary grasp of many other crafts. In time 'De Re Metallica' was followed by other useful handbooks and recipe books, as well as by series of wood engravings, such as those of Jost Ammann, illustrating the progress of the arts.

With the technological portions of the great French 'Encyclopédie,' done under the personal supervision of Denis Diderot, this movement came to a temporary climax. This increased consciousness of technology seems to have been part of a synchronous worldwide movement, hardly to be accounted for by direct contact; for Chinese and Japanese prints, from the sixteenth century on, strangely show a similar interest in craft skills, in technical processes, and even, in many cases, in the characteristic environment of the worker.

The great feat of medieval technics, then, was that it was able to promote and absorb many important changes without losing the immense carryover of inventions and skills derived from earlier cultures. In this lies one of its vital points of superiority over the modern mode of monotechnics, which boasts of effacing, as fast and as far as possible, the technical achievements of earlier periods, even though the result, as in the case of monotransport by motor car or jet plane alone, may be far less flexible and less efficient than the more diverse and many-paced system which preceded it. Some of this polytechnic advantage was due to the fact that the skills, the esthetic judgement and appreciation, and the symbolic understanding were diffused throughout the whole community, not restricted to any one caste or occupation. By their very nature, polytechnics could not be reduced to a single, standardized, uniform system, under centralized control.

Not the least part of polytechnic tradition lay in the arts derived from neolithic culture, where woman's interests and woman's modes of work continued to play a part: not only in pot-making, basketwork, and spinning and weaving, but in the specifically domestic arts which account for such a large part of human work: cooking, preserving, brewing, dyeing, washing, even soap-making. Many of the prime inventions in this area remained unaltered for thousands of years, like the shapes of pitchers and vases, and four-legged furniture, because they had achieved a satisfactory form at an early date. When one is counting up the accumulated richness of this tradition, one must remember, too, the wealth of recipes for cooking and baking that each separate regional culture produced: the endless combination of nutrients and tempting flavors that helped turn the animal process of private maceration into the social art of enjoyable eating. This, too, is part of our technical tradition, as much as the medical pharmacopoeia.

In a period such as the present, which takes pride in its ability to produce ever larger quantities of food—pasteurized, homogenized, sterilized, frozen, or otherwise reduced to an infant's standard of tastelessness—the disappearance of this heritage has become a necessary condition for meekly accepting the space capsule's requirements for nutrition as the standard human diet. Here again, the polytechnic tradition stands for variety and esthetic discrimination as essential conditions for heightening organic activity. In cooking, clothing, bodily ornament, and gardening, as in painting and sculpture, no culture had to wait for the "industrial revolution" for endless modifications and qualitative improvements.

The medieval social order could not be completely mechanized or depersonalized because it was based, fundamentally, upon a recognition of the ultimate value and reality of the individual soul, a value and a reality that related it to equally identifiable groups and corporate associations. The relation between the soul and its God, between the serf, the armed retainer, and the lord, between the apprentice and his master, between the guildsman and his city, even between the king and his people, was a personal relation, too complex and too subtle to be confined to a specific function or limited to a specific contractual agreement, since it involved the entire life. One of the favorite themes of medieval folk tales is that of the brave peasant or miller who talked back to the king and told him off: such a tale as I once heard the Lord Mayor of The Hague repeat, with a twinkle in his eye, on a great civic occasion when the Queen of the Netherlands was present. But who has ever told off a computer?

In countries like England and Holland, moreover, written constitutions and parliamentary rules of order were established in many informal local units before they were passed on to bigger organizations. At the very moment that the great crafts and merchant guilds, already corrupted by wealth, or made subservient to the State, ceased to exercise their old functions, the English working classes, in desperation, revived the Friendly Societies and the Burial Societies for the support of the sick, the widows, and the orphans—associations that had long before originated in the Roman Empire and had never been entirely obliterated, it would seem, in the mind, even when they disappeared from the historic scene.

This social background of medieval polytechnics is too often overlooked by the specialized technical historian, who treats technology without reference to either the political or the personal forms that it helps to bring into existence.

As late as the sixteenth century, this dynamic and enterprising polytechnics was not only intact, but was still developing, as the wider exploration of the planet brought into Europe both natural resources and technical processes it could use to advantage. For the first time in history, the arts and technics of the world as a whole were ready to intermingle, to learn from each other, to increase the range of both their practical effectiveness and their symbolic expression. Unfortunately at that point, a change came about that fatally arrested this growth: a system of one-sided political and military domination produced its counterpart in a system of mechanization and automation that ignored the human premises upon which the older agricultural and handicraft technologies had been founded.

Not that the handicrafts died out quickly. The great improvements in fabricating automatic spinning and weaving machinery, in clocks and watches, could not indeed have taken place except with the aid of handicraft workers, who shifted from wood-turning to metal-turning and pattern-making, and who used their craft experience to interpret the instructions of engineers or scientists. For the new complex machines could not be designed in detail on the drafting board, even in outline. Before this could happen, the working parts themselves had to be re-worked and shaped by hand.

England's leadership in the production of automatic machines from the beginning of the nineteenth century onward derives from a succession of such master craftsmen, beginning with Joseph Bramah and Henry Maudslay, and continuing through Nasmyth, Whitworth, Muir, Lewis, and Clement, men who made inventions like the screw-cutting lathe (Maudslay), which in turn made more complex machines possible. One of Maudslay's fellow-workmen bore testimony to the qualities of his art: "It was a pleasure to see him handle a tool of any kind, but he was *quite splendid* with an eighteen-inch file." As with the meticulous craftsmanship that went into the building of the Egyptian pyramids, the last refinement of accuracy was that achieved by the human hand.

By the middle of the nineteenth century, this form of craftwork had in some departments reached a higher pitch of technical perfection in the metallurgical arts than ever before. With the aid of power machinery, harder steel, a wider range of metals and alloys, accurate lathes and dies, increased control over temperature and speed, there was no mechanical problem that the craftsman could not master. Until all this was achieved, machines could not produce machines. The great proof of that skill and resourcefulness was the construction of the Crystal Palace in London in 1851: a building pre-fabricated and put together with a speed that could hardly be equalled, if starting from scratch today. The point I am making is that if craftsmanship had not been condemned to death by starvation wages and meager profits, if it had, in fact, been protected and subsidized as so many of the new mechanical industries were in fact extravagantly subsidized, right down to jet planes and rockets today, our technology as a whole, even that of 'fine technics' would have been immensely richer—and more efficient.

What is not generally recognized is that, during the long transitional period from handicraft to complete mechanization, the crafts themselves had been multiplying and becoming more differentiated, and had taken advantage of small-scale mechanization in power-driven fulling mills or in precision machines like lathes. In 1568, Jost Ammann enumerated ninety different crafts: but two centuries later Diderot's encyclopedia counted as many as two hundred and fifty. As late as 1858, in England, in the little town of Lincoln alone, at a time when machine-goods were beginning to invade every market, Norman Wymer reports that there were still over fifty crafts and trades being actively practiced; though by the end of the century all had dwindled and many of them had disappeared.

In another half century, the physical lot of the surviving workers had notably improved, with unemployment insurance, social security and the new health services, while their children's school education was assured by government-operated schools: in addition, they had, for intellectual or emotional stimulus and diversion, the radio and television. But the work itself was no longer as various, as interesting, or as sustaining to the personality: and in the case of any large breakdown in the mechanical system, there would not be enough craft-skill left, or the necessary tools and self-confidence to improvise even a temporary substitute. Seebohm Rowntree's successive surveys of York in 1901, then in 1941, amply document this change.

Whatever the advantages of a highly organized system of mechanical production, based on non-human sources of power—and as everyone recognizes there are many advantages—the system itself tends to grow more rigid, more inadaptable, more dehumanized in proportion to the completeness of its automation and its extrusion of the worker from the process of production. On this matter, I shall have more to say at a later point. Here I would only emphasize that the deliberate maintenance of a widely diffused and varied group of handicraft occupations would have been a guarantee of human autonomy and an essential factor of economic safety; and that the recovery of many of these all-but-lost arts, which William Morris began in the middle of the nineteenth century, was—and still remains—an indispensable counterbalance to over-mechanization. Where surplus manpower is available—in a world indeed threatened by an overproduction of manpower with millions misemployed or out of work, in either case, demoralized—manual labor should still perform important productive tasks and human services that the machine must either leave undone or accomplish only at an excessive cost.

Felix Greene's film on Vietnam made this point with startling impact. In North Vietnam, between 1965 and 1968, the United States air forces destroyed villages and attacked industrial installations, along with railroads and highroads—not once, but again and again—with the object of making it impossible to manufacture weapons, build up supplies, or transport troops and munitions to the south. In the course of three years this effort proved utterly unsuccessful in achieving its objective. The North Vietnamese government, by calling on the diffused manual labor and craft ingenuity of its people, by enlisting human muscles rather than machines, by using simple weight-lifting and water-transporting devices, worked by hand, were able rapidly to repair the damage and not merely have refused to accept defeat, but continued to carry the war itself into the south.

Thus this residual craft culture and almost neolithic economy, utilizing home-grown materials and home-taught skills, all still available in a farming community, were able to counteract the powerful mechanized instruments of the invader, and to make fools out of the Pentagon strategists who were sure they could terrorize the Vietnamese into surrender, or paralyze their military effectiveness by destroying their means of production.

If, as many anthropologists still hold, the making and using of tools was one of the chief sources of primitive man's intellectual development, is it not time that we asked ourselves what will happen to man if he departs as completely as he now threatens to do from his primal polytechnic occupations? Since they can no longer be pursued at a profit, perhaps they will have to be restored as modes of sport and recreation, even more as helpful—increasingly essential—forms of personal service and mutual aid.

4: SUBVERSION OF POLYTECHNICS

The common habit in the nineteenth century of equating technical improvement exclusively with power-driven machines, increasingly automatic, led to an under-estimation of the amount of improvement that actually had been made between the twelfth and the eighteenth centuries through the fabrication of more adequate containers: both individual containers, like pots, pans, sacks, bins, and collective containers, like canals and ships. That containers may transmit power, like a millrace, or utilize power, like a sailboat, is one of those obvious facts that concentration on a purely mechanical world picture has led historians to overlook—partly because containers themselves, being static and passive, do not noisily call attention to themselves.

Not the least contribution of medieval polytechnics, however, was that it demonstrated how to maintain a balance between the static and the dynamic components of technics, between utilities and machines; and, as it happens, the first notable improvement that made worldwide transportation possible was the design of the three-masted sailing ship, in which windpower was more effectively applied than ever before to move a large container laden with goods from port to port. Similarly, the first step in speedy transport, with regular deliveries, came through the building of canals in Europe, from the sixteenth century on; and the network of canals that spread up the rivers from the Low Countries, finally covering great distances, like the Rhone Canal, brought steady improvements in both shipping and agriculture. Because the Netherlands took the lead in this development it became, according to Adam Smith's calculations, by far the richest country in Europe, in proportion to the extent of the land and the number of inhabitants—the richest and the best fed.

One might indeed compile a long list of the non-mechanical improvements that antedate by two or three hundred years the so-called Industrial Revolution. This list would include the introduction of domestic glass windows on a large scale after the sixteenth century, typified by the three-windowed Dutch urban dwelling; the introduction of wallpaper and toilet paper; and the functional organization of the dwelling house into specialized rooms for dining, cooking, sociability, and sleeping. Add to this the multiplication of pots and pans, of iron stoves and ovens, of earthen and glass ware: the metal piping of water for domestic use, and finally the use of water pipes and waste drains in that most decisive of domestic improvements, the water closet, invented by Sir John Harrington, in 1596.

All this was accompanied by a vastly increased application of non-human energy to industries like brewing, dyeing, pottery-making, brickmaking, salt manufacture, and transportation. John Nef points out, for instance, that from 1564 to 1634 the recorded shipments of coal from the Tyne increased nearly fourteen times over, from 32,952 tons to 452,625 tons. Similarly Braudel estimates a comparable increase in shipping: the volume of shipping between 1600 and 1786–87, when reliable statistics were available in France, increased five times: so that it would be more correct to say, he notes, that the steam engine was launched by the Industrial Revolution rather than that it was the cause of it.

The change of mind that underlay this earlier technical transformation was that which likewise underlay the coalescence of the mechanical world picture: a transfer from ritual regularity to mechanical regularity, with an emphasis upon orderly time-keeping, space-measuring, account-keeping, thus translating concrete objects and complex events into abstract quantities; and it was this capitalistic devotion to repetitive order and mechanical discipline and financial rewards that helped to undermine the lively, diversified, but finely balanced polytechnics that came to such full fruition in seventeenth-century Holland.

Meanwhile, mechanization itself had assumed formidable proportions before the seventeenth century, hastened no doubt by the processes that were bringing about absolutism in government, and capitalistic organization into all the industries where heavy capital investments, for ships or machinery, were essential. Long-distance control through numerous agents favored the enterprises of those who commanded money and were capable of exercising a ruthless, semi-military control over men: the *condottiere*, the piratical sea captain, like Sir Francis Drake, or the slave snatcher, like Sir John Hawkins, the efficient organizer and money-maker, like Jacob Fugger the elder, or his rivals, like the Welsers, who already had investments in Venezuela. The mechanization of money-making, and the making of money by mechanization were complementary processes. Impersonal authority and submissive obedience, mechanical regimentation and human control, went hand in hand. The miner, the soldier, the sailor, eventually the factory laborer performed their tasks on the most harsh and inhuman terms, forced by starvation to accept conditions that provided a minimum amount of social security, human fellowship, or physical health.

And first, the increased use of armor in warfare, with the later invention of cannon and muskets, made fresh demands on the metallurgical industries: mine, furnace, foundry, and forge. By the sixteenth century, as Agricola vividly demonstrates, mining and smelting had become advanced industries, in the sense that many operations were now highly mechanized, and some of them, like machinery for mine drainage, became, where waterpower was available, completely automatic. In the mines of Saxony, in Agricola's day, it was possible to sink deep mines and use water pumps for removing underground water; while tracks shod with metal (railroads) were laid for hauling ores over the otherwise rough surface of the tunnels. Forced ventilation, fans operated by waterpower, was used to clear away noxious gases, and waterpower was used, too, for crushing ores. Again in the mine, possibly for the first time in history, wage laborers were used, instead of criminals or slaves.

Thus many of the principal mechanical inventions were derived from the mine, including the railroad, the mechanical lift, the underground tunnel, along with artificial lighting and ventilation, and were all in existence centuries before the "first" industrial revolution; and the steam engine, which was perfected by Watt in 1760, had first been used in Newcomen's cruder form to pump water out of mines. The eight-hour day and the twenty-four-hour triple shift had their beginning in Saxony.

Actually mining operations in early nineteenth-century England had not yet reached the point, either mechanically or socially, that had been attained in late medieval Germany. If this fact had been generally known, the pious Victorian belief in automatic mechanical progress century by century might have been slightly shaken.

Mining originally set the pattern for later modes of mechanization by its callous disregard for human factors, by its indifference to the pollution and destruction of the neighboring environment, by its concentration upon the physico-chemical processes for obtaining the desired metal or fuel, and above all by its topographic and mental isolation from the organic world of the farmer and the craftsman, and the spiritual world of the Church, the University, and the City.

In its destruction of the environment and its indifference to the risks to human life, mining closely resembles warfare—though likewise it often, through its confrontation of danger and death, brings into existence a tough, self-respecting personality, with capacities for heroism and self-sacrifice, not unlike that of the soldier at his best. But the destructive animus of mining and its punishing routine of work, along with its environmental poverty and disorder, were passed on to the new industries that used its products. These negative social results offset the mechanical gains.

If mining involved speculative economic risks, it also brought huge returns; and this, too, served as a pattern for both capitalist enterprise itself and later mechanization. The readiness to make heavy investments in mining was stimulated by this possibility of making extraordinary profits. Agricola took pains to point out the chances for easy gains in mining, as compared with normal commerce; and Werner Sombart in 'Der Moderne Kapitalismus' calculated that in the fifteenth and sixteenth centuries German mining earned as much in ten years as trade in the old style was able to in a hundred. In the capitalist attack upon polytechnics, war was the spearhead and mining the shaft: both were inured to methodical destruction, both sought to 'get something for nothing,' both placed physical power above any other human need. In the traditional industries, the older concepts of the just price, based on time and skill, normalized by use and wont, still held: but in mining, as in the wholesale trades and long-distance commercial adventures, the highest price possible, regardless of justice or equity—"what the traffic will bear"—was the object. Let the worker cringe, let the buyer beware!

As capital gains increased, more capital was available for investment in mines, ships, and factories, as well as in the costly machinery that, from the eighteenth century on, competed with hand labor and drove it out of the market. This general movement was in turn abetted by two other inventions, both social, which gave the advantage to machine operations over the small surviving workshops. that utilized local materials and local hand labor. I refer to the patent system, first established in England, which bestowed on the inventor, or, rather, the exploiter, of a new invention, an effective temporary monopoly; and the other was the joint stock company, with limited liability, which widened the number of possible investors and relieved them of the burden of individual responsibility for bankruptcy that single ownership or partnership entailed. These changes completed the depersonalization of the whole industrial process. After the seventeenth century an increasing number of anonymous workers were exploited for the benefit of equally anonymous and invisible and morally indifferent absentee owners.

Thus the various components of mechanized industry conspired to remove the traditional valuations and the human aims that had kept the economy under control and caused it to pursue other goals than power. Absentee ownership, the cash nexus, managerial organization, military discipline, were from the beginning the social accompaniments of large-scale mechanization. This removal of limits had the effect of undermining—by now almost totally destroying—the earlier forms of polytechnics, and of replacing it with a monotechnics based on maximizing physical power, contracting or expanding or diverting human needs to those that are required to keep such an economy in operation. Warfare, the activity that had first made such heavy demands on the mine, in turn contributed further to mechanization by reverting in industry to a military discipline and daily drill, in order to ensure uniform operations and uniform results. This reciprocal interplay between warfare, mining, and mechanization was ultimately responsible for some of the most vexatious problems that must now be faced.

From the beginning, I must emphasize, if we are to understand technology's increasing threats to mankind, the murky air of the battlefield and the arsenal blew over the entire field of industrial invention and affected civilian life. The war machine hastened the pace of standardization

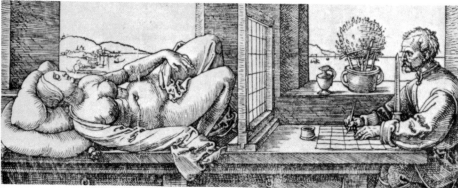

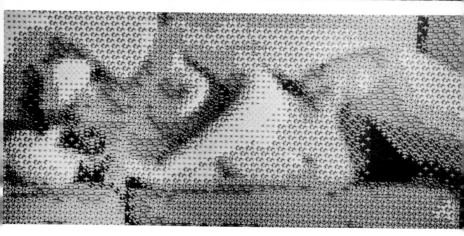

1: Mechanization of the World Picture

(Top) Woman as seen and felt by a twelfth-century craftsman (Saint-Lazare d'Autun, France). (Center) Woman as mapped by a Renascence painter, using cartesian coordinates before Descartes. (Bottom) Woman as translated into fashionable computer language as a pseudo-photograph. (See also Plate 29.)

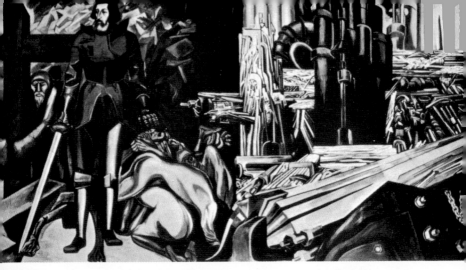

2: Absolutism, Militarism, and Mechanization

The increasing centralization of political and military power in Europe, beginning in the fourteenth century, made heavy demands upon the metallurgical industries. Thus the industrial foundations of the modern power regime were laid, not in the eighteenth-century cotton mills, but in the sixteenth-century mines, foundries, and arms works. Technical improvements attributed to the later factory system were introduced in the Arsenal and shipyards of Venice centuries earlier, including the prefabrication of standardized parts of ships and mass production. The economic policy misnamed mercantilism was a premature mockup for the present centralized, State-dominated complex. Orozco's painting (top) epitomizes all these forces of dehumanization: the 'religious' drive, the mechanical processes, the military assault—and the human outcome.

3: Power

The increase of energy available for both constructive and destructive social uses has been one of the main marks of technological progress, not only from the thirteenth century onward, as Henry Adams pointed out, but from the earliest beginnings of 'civilization' in the Fourth Millennium B.C. The first great advance came through the use of fire to obtain heat and light from organic materials: this goes back some five or six hundred thousand years. But the most massive increase resulted from cultivation of plants which captured energy directly from the sun, and with the cultivation of the hard grains—wheat, barley, millet, rice—made storage and more equable distribution throughout the year possible, with a great increment of manpower no longer wholly absorbed by agriculture. On this advance all other forms of human power still depend.

The major constructive transformations of early civilizations, almost up to the Christian era, rested on the harnessing of animalpower and manpower. Except for foodpower, windpower, and waterpower, all later sources of energy, dependent upon chemical transformations (coal, petroleum, uranium), have increased productivity at the price of degrading the environment, more or less in direct proportion to the quantity used. The hydroelectric plant shown here (left) comes closest to the ideal requirements for a clean, efficient, non-toxic form of energy. The jet plane, on the other hand, as befits a machine originally designed for strictly military purposes, produces the maximum amount of environmental injury and social disruption. The notion that there are no limits to the expansion of extra-organic energies, since granite rocks, if broken down, hold enough uranium to meet human needs indefinitely, takes no account of the ecological and human effects of such over-exploitation. Even carelessly planned hydroelectric installations can despoil precious recreational areas and disrupt wildlife. A bio-technic economy would foster modes of production, transportation, and human settlement that would deliberately reduce the amount of non-organic energy required to the lowest possible level. An economy of plenitude would prudently seek only the optimum amount for daily use, and store surplus power for special uses or emergencies.

4: Speed

Increase of speed in construction, production, transportation, and communication has from the outset been one of the definite marks of the power system. Speed in locomotion was first accelerated by the domestication of the horse, an animal in royal military use from the Second Millennium on. But apart from horse racing, popular interest in speed as a mode of recreation is a modern development, manifested in the seventeenth century in the sail wagon, shown here (left), and in the early nineteenth-century chute-the-chute. With the motor car, speed—here shown (right) in the early form of the steam omnibus—was, like so many royal prerogatives, 'democratized.'

Though the speed achieved in tobogganing or skiing or motoring brings a certain playful exhilaration, partly derived from tension and danger, partly from a sense of bodily release, speed more widely serves as an ostentatious symbol of power and prestige: part of a more general effort to escape organic limits. Whatever its contribution to social status or recreation, speed in transport and communication has practical political and economic uses: it not merely confirms the authority of the ruling elite but makes it possible for them to exert more effective control over distant territories, tributaries, and markets. From the eighteenth century on, power and speed became the chief criteria of technological progress, along with quantitative productivity. This raising of the tempo of change, allowing less time for the assimilation of new experience, for feedback and rectification, accounts for many of the worst misdemeanors of industrialization in its destroying valuable parts of the historic heritage and doing permanent damage to the environment. The salutary truth of the old proverb 'Haste Makes Waste' was over-ridden by the new principle: 'Haste and Waste Make Money.'

While motor cars are still built with brakes, reverse gears, and steering wheels, as well as accelerators, the power complex today is preoccupied only with acceleration; and cannot concede that it may be necessary, for the preservation of life, to reduce the tempo, to alter the direction, or to bring a profit-making but dangerous process to a halt. In a biotechnic economy, in contrast, speed would be a function, not of power or pecuniary advantage, but of social purpose; and in the interest of health, welfare, or creativity this would, on many occasions, call for deceleration, or even complete stoppage, to ensure the enhancement of more important human values.

5: Remote Control

Central to the power complex from the beginning was remote control. As long as the main components of the megamachine were human beings, this required doglike obedience from every human unit in the chain of command. Such one-way hierarchic order was secured by severe punishment for the slightest disobedience. The transition from this cumbrous and laborious method was facilitated by the introduction of a national educational system, first in autocratic Prussia in the eighteenth century: afterward in France under Napoleon. National military conscription, imposed first by the 'democratic' French Revolution, completed this process.

The translation of these sometimes inefficient and recalcitrant human automatons into purely mechanical and electronic units made instantaneous remote control practicable: this was the largest possible gift to centralized authority, not only in government and military affairs, but in the widened operations of the great industrial corporations and financial conglomerations that now increasingly operate on a continental or global basis. The control room of the Houston Space Center, here shown, demonstrates this system at its superhuman best—though without the active cooperation of still semi-autonomous astronauts its space missions would have been repeatedly bungled or aborted.

Even before the computer and television were in operation, Hitler's direct interference in military battles on the Russian front, by direct contact with even lower field officers, demonstrated one of the inherent disadvantages of remote control: misguided interference. But the basic weakness of remote control is that it is not, and cannot possibly become, a two-way system open to feedback and revision, without the aid of intermediary units. While electronic processing of information makes instant decision possible at headquarters, the absence of responsible local units with sufficient authority to form independent judgements, to correct misinformation, and to add unprogrammable data, enlarges the probability of human error. This calls for the rebuilding of decentralized, semi-autonomous if not independent, groups and agencies as an imperative safety device, as well as an essential condition for responsible human participation.

6: Computerdom

As an instrument for organizing large quantities of information, or performing extremely complex symbolic operations beyond human capabilities within a normal lifespan, the computer is an invaluable adjunct to the brain, though not a substitute for it. Since the computer is limited to handling only so much experience as can be abstracted in symbolic or numerical form, it is incapable of dealing directly, as organisms must, with the steady influx of concrete, unprogrammable experience. With respect to such experience, the computer is necessarily always out of date. The computer's lack of other human dimensions is of course no handicap to it as a labor-saving device, whether in astronomy or bookkeeping: but such creativity as the computer may simulate is always in the first place a contribution of the minds that formulate the program.

The utter absence of innate subjective potentialities in the computer makes the contemporary art exhibition shown here (top), in all its pervasive blankness and artful nullity, an ideal representation of its missing dimensions. Those who are so fascinated by the computer's lifelike feats—it plays chess! it writes 'poetry'!—that they would turn it into the voice of omniscience, betray how little understanding they have of either themselves, their mechanical-electronic agents, or the potentialities of life. A city of even three hundred thousand people, ten per cent of whom have access to regional or national libraries with as few as a million volumes, would actually have a total capacity for storing, transforming, integrating, and not least applying both symbolic information and concrete experience that no computer will ever rival.

7: Pentagons of Power

Power, like a desolating pestilence,
Pollutes whate'er it touches; and obedience,
Bane of all genius, virtue, freedom, truth,
Makes slaves of men, and, of the human frame,
A mechanized automaton.

Percy Bysshe Shelley

Though the power system can be adequately represented by abstractions, the concrete form of the Pentagon in Washington serves even better than its Soviet counterpart, the Kremlin, as a symbol of the absurdity of totalitarian absolutism: all the more because this particular megastructure combines a pathetically outmoded Renascence plan with the current wasteful and inefficient facilities for monotransportation by private car.

Not the least mark of Pentagonal authority is its imperviousness to information coming from outside sources and expressing human desires and purposes that have no status in the power complex. This in itself helps explain, perhaps, the increasingly desperate human reactions that the system is now provoking throughout the world. Never before has such a vast number of human beings, virtually the entire population of the planet, lived at the mercy of such a minuscule minority, whose specialized knowledge seems only to increase the magnitude of their incompetence in the very areas of their professional specialization.

8: Divine Kingship: New Style

During the last three centuries, absolute power was brought under partial control by the restoration of the old Greek device of voting by secret ballot, and by the gradual extension of this franchise to the whole adult population. Even single-party totalitarian governments find it necessary to go through the mummery of fake democratic elections. With the new dictatorships in Russia, Turkey, Italy, Germany, and China since 1918, the once-banished cult of divine kingship was resurrected and made more effective by the new technologies for mass control. By terror and electronic magic, the Leader is inflated into the semblance of a God: the Führerprinzip or Personality Cult.

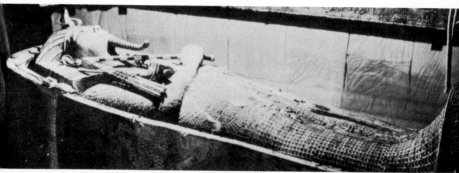

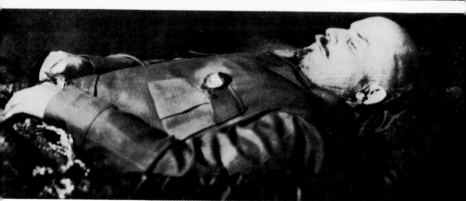

9: Magnification and Mummification

The pathology of the Power Complex expresses itself publicly in two forms: magnification and mummification. As with the colossal statues that dominated the palaces of ancient Egypt and Babylonia, the same effect is produced for the more ephemeral absolute rulers of our own time in blown-up photographs, while by radio, television, and telephoto the image of Big Brother, by sheer repetition and multiplication, becomes inescapable. But the end product of this fraudulent inflation is a mummy: a corpse preserved in the Egyptian fashion, placed in a tomb for public worship. Even Lenin, who according to his widow "wanted no memorials to him," could not escape this ignoble deification.

10: Autocratic Technocracy

As was demonstrated in Volume One of 'The Myth of the Machine,' part of the immense productivity of the Pyramid Age was devoted to pyramid building itself, including the extensive mortuary cities that were necessary to ensure the performance of the required rituals. But this ancient power complex likewise produced masterpieces of architecture and engineering: dams, irrigations works, canals, reservoirs, temples, palaces, and cities, the latter often built in Mesopotamia on man-made mounds, high above flood level. As in our own age, these genuine benefits must be balanced off against the use of the same engineering skill in destroying cities, ruining soils, exterminating innocent civilian 'enemies,' and mercilessly exploiting the mass of workers whose forced labor, disciplined to machinelike precision, made these feats possible.

Historically, autocracy and technocracy are Siamese twins; and there are many present indications that their nature has not changed. But what archetypal fantasy erupting from the unconscious caused a contemporary technocrat to conceive his ideal collective habitation in the imitative form of a pyramid, big enough to entomb the population of a whole town? There are many contemporary variants of such dehumanized megastructures, apart from Buckminster Fuller's other project of a city under a geodesic dome: plans for underwater cities, underground cities, elevated linear cities, cities a mile high, all compete for attention as the City (read Anti-City) of the Future. Whatever their superficial difference, all these projects are essentially tombs: they reflect the same impulse to suppress human variety and autonomy, and to make every need and impulse conform to the system of collective control imposed by the autocratic designer. Small wonder that signs of revolt against the megamachine have broken out, ominously like those which ended the Pyramid Age in Egypt.

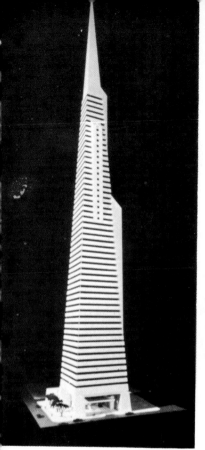

11: Space Rockets as Power Symbols

The moon rocket is the climactic expression of the power system: the maximum utilization of the resources of science and technics for the achievement of a relatively minuscule result: the hasty exploration of a barren satellite. Space exploration by manned rockets enlarges and intensifies all the main components of the power system: increased energy, accelerated motion, automation, cybernation, instant communication, remote control. Though it has been promoted mainly under military pressure, the most vital result of moon visitation so far turns out to be an unsought and unplanned one—a full view of the beautiful planet we live on, an inviting home for man and for all forms of life. This distant view on television evoked for the first time an active, loving response from many people who had hitherto supposed that modern technics would soon replace Mother Earth with a more perfect, scientifically organized, electronically controlled habitat, and who took for granted that this would be an improvement. Note that the moon rocket is itself necessarily a megastructure: so it naturally calls forth such vulgar imitations as the accompanying bureaucratic obelisk (office building) of similar dimensions, shown here (left). Both forms exhibit the essentially archaic and regressive nature of the science-fiction mind.

12: Homicide, Genocide, and Biocide

The ancient practice of exterminating the population of a conquered city was restricted by the amount of hand labor required. Modern technics has removed such limits: nuclear blasts and chemical poisons have been treated by professedly humane governments as a justification for returning to indiscriminate attacks, not on armies but on whole populations, as practiced by Ashurbanipal and Genghis Khan. Such atrocities are all the easier to achieve because they can be conducted from rocket centers or from planes by obedient Eichmanns who do not hear or see their tortured victims. This spread of homicide, genocide, and biocide mocks all our boasted life-saving advances in hygiene, diet, medicine, and surgery.

From the total destruction of the buildings, as of Coventry in the 1939 war, it is only a step to the defoliation and destruction of a whole countryside by the American army in Vietnam. The latter practice, too, has an ancient precedent: the salting of the enemy's fields by the Assyrians to ensure starvation. But the same indiscriminate attack upon life, through defoliants, pesticides, and herbicides, has been accepted and even boastfully acclaimed as a progressive contribution to highway upkeep and large-scale corporate farming—despite the immediate danger to human life through eating food, drinking water, or breathing air contaminated by these poisons. Thus the military atrocities committed in Vietnam are sanctified by the commercial atrocities committed daily upon our own native population. Witness the near-deaths of a number of children in Fresno, California, from phosdrin, a deadly pesticide accidently impregnated in the new blue jeans they wore.

13: Barbarism

14–15: Encapsulated Man

Behold the astronaut, fully equipped for duty: a scaly creature, more like an oversized ant than a primate—certainly not a naked god. To survive on the moon he must be encased in an even more heavily insulated garment, and become a kind of faceless ambulatory mummy. While he is hurtling through space the astronaut's physical existence is purely a function of mass and motion, narrowed down to the pinpoint of acute sentient intelligence demanded by the necessity for coordinating his reactions with the mechanical and electronic apparatus upon which his survival depends. Here is the archetypal proto-model of Post-Historic Man, whose existence from birth to death would be conditioned by the megamachine, and made to conform, as in a space capsule, to the minimal functional requirements by an equally minimal environment—all under remote control.

Dr. Bruno Bettelheim reports the behavior of a nine-year-old autistic patient, a boy called Joey, who conceived that he was run by machines. "So controlling was this belief that Joey carried with him an elaborate life-support system made up of radio tubes, light bulbs, and a 'breathing machine.' At meals he ran imaginary wires from a wall socket to himself, so his food could be digested. His bed was rigged up with batteries, a loud-speaker, and other improvised equipment to keep him alive while he slept."

But is this just the autistic fantasy of a pathetic little boy? Is it not rather the state that the mass of mankind is fast approaching in actual life, without realizing how pathological it is to be cut off from their own resources for living, and to feel no tie to the outer world unless they are connected with the Power Complex and constantly receive information, direction, stimulation, and sedation from a central external source, via radio, discs, and television, with the minimal opportunity for reciprocal face-to-face contact? The stringent limitations of the space capsule have already been extended to other areas. Technocratic designers proudly exhibit furniture planned solely to fit rooms as painfully constricted as a rocket chamber. Even more ingenious minds, equally subservient to the Power Complex, have already conceived a hospital bed in which every function from the taking of temperature to intravenous feeding will be automatically performed within the limits of the bed. Solitary confinement thus becomes the last word in 'tender and loving care.'

Except for meeting emergencies, as with an iron lung or a space rocket, such mechanical attachment and encapsulation presents a definitely pathological syndrome. Increasingly, the astronaut's space suit will be, figuratively speaking, the only garment that machine-processed and machine-conditioned man will wear in comfort; for only in that suit will he, like little Joey, feel alive. This is a return to the womb, without the embryo's prospect of a natal delivery. As if to emphasize this point, *the actual position of the astronaut here shown, under working conditions, is on his back,* the normal position of the foetus.

16: Mechanization Takes Command

Not merely machines but mechanical order and regimentation spread through the entire environment. Even the drafting room of a large architectural office, despite individual draftsmen not yet computerized, resembles an assembly line. With the mechanization and prospective automation of farming, the aim is not to improve the life of the farmer but to augment the profits of the megatechnic corporations that supply the machinery and the power needed for large-scale monoculture, with the smallest possible use of human labor. Though this monoculture, through excessive use of chemical fertilizers and pesticides, deteriorates the environment and creates health hazards, it produces crop surpluses that then draw forth from a compassionate government extravagant subsidies for *non*-production. A biotechnic economy would reverse these irrational methods by restoring *manpower* for mixed farming, horticulture, and rural industries, reclaiming the countryside for human occupation and continuous cultivation.

and mass production. As the centralized territorial state increased in size, efficiency, and command of taxable wealth, larger armies were needed to reenforce its authority. By the seventeenth century, before iron had begun to be used in large quantities in the other industrial arts, Colbert had created arms factories in France, Gustavus Adolphus had done likewise in Sweden, and in Russia, as early as Peter the Great, there were 683 workers in a single factory: a heretofore unheard-of number.

Within these factories, the division of process in serial production had already begun, each worker performing only part of an operation; and the grinding and polishing machinery was worked by waterpower. Sombart observed that Adam Smith would have done better to take arms manufacture, rather than pin-making, as an example of the mechanization of the process of production, with its specialization and fixation of human effort before the machine itself was sufficiently organized to take over the whole job.

Standardization, prefabrication, and mass production were all first established in state-organized arsenals, most notably in Venice, centuries before the "industrial revolution." It was not Arkwright, but Venetian urban officials in command of the arsenal, who first established the factory system; and it was not Sir Samuel Bentham and the elder Brunel who first standardized ship production, with various tackle blocks and planks cut to uniform measure; for centuries before, the arsenal at Venice had so well mastered the process of pre-fabrication that it could put together a whole vessel within a month. And though the priority for fabricating machines with standardized and therefore replaceable parts belongs to the inventors of printing with movable type, it was in the production of muskets that this method first became widely adopted: first in LeBlanc's innovation in France in 1785, and then, in 1800, in Eli Whitney's factory at Whitneyville, under contract with the United States government. "The technique of interchangeable part manufacture," as Usher observes, "was thus established in general outline before the invention of the sewing machine or harvesting machinery. The new technique was a fundamental condition of the great achievements realized by inventors and manufacturers in those fields."

But there was still another place where war forced the pace of invention and mechanization, not for the first nor yet the last time. Not merely was gun-casting "the greatest mutant of improved technique in the foundry," and not merely was the "claim of Henry Cort to the gratitude of his countrymen . . . based primarily on the contribution he had made to military security," as Ashton says, but the demand for high-grade iron in large quantities went hand in hand with the increase of artillery bombardment as a preparation for assault even on the open field. The effectiveness of this concentration of firepower was demonstrated by the brilliant young artilleryman Napoleon Bonaparte, who was to scourge Europe with his technological genius while he liquidated the French Revolution.

The mathematical calculations and physical experiments that increased the precision of artillery fire reflected the military preoccupations rather than those of the current industrial arts, with their cut-and-try methods; and this influence was so universal that the roles of the military, the civil, and the mechanical engineer were at first almost interchangeable. Let us not forget that the same demands for accurate artillery fire resulted in the invention of the modern computer.

It was in the army, finally, that the process of mechanization was first effectively applied on a mass scale to human beings, through the replacement of irregular feudal or citizen armies, intermittently assembled, by a standard army of hired or conscripted soldiers, under the severe discipline of daily drill, contrived to produce human beings whose spontaneous or instinctive reactions would be displaced by automatic responses to orders. "His not to reason why," was the motto for the whole system: the doing and the dying followed.

Military regimentation proved the archetype for collective mechanization, for the megamachine it created was the earliest complex machine of specialized, interdependent parts, human and mechanical. Though perfected for military purposes in Macedonia and the Roman Empire, that power unit had partly lapsed in the West until it was re-introduced in the sixteenth century and perfected by Prince Maurice of Orange and Nassau. Thus the pattern of the new industrial order first appeared upon the parade ground and the battlefield before it entered, full-fledged, into the factory. The regimentation and mass production of soldiers, to the end of turning out a cheap, standardized, and replaceable product, was the great contribution of the military mind to the machine process. And not strangely, the first important by-product of this transformation was the military uniform itself.

Though special liveries had been used to designate the servants and guards of great princes and municipalities—Michelangelo's design for the uniform of the Papal Guards is still worn—armies hitherto had not boasted identifiable uniforms. But with the increase in the size of the army, it was necessary to create an outward sign of their inner unison, to correspond to the uniformities of the daily drill. The military uniform was an early example of a general tendency to uniformity, which characterized the barracks architecture and street façades of the seventeenth century, with their uniform rooflines and repetitive windows. Each soldier must have the same clothes and the same equipment as every other member of his company. Drill made them act as one, discipline made them respond as one, the uniform made them look as one.

With an army of 100,000 soldiers, such as Louis XIV had brought together, the need for uniforms made no small demand upon industry. This was in fact the first large-scale demand for standardized "ready-made" consumer goods. Individual taste, individual judgement, individual needs other than the dimensions of the body, played no part in this new mode of production: the conditions for complete mechanization were present. The textile industries felt this solid demand, anticipating in the end product the sewing machine that was tardily invented by Thimonnet of Lyons in 1829—though one is not surprised to find that it was the French War Department that sought first to use it.

From the sixteenth century on, then, the army furnished the pattern not only of quantity production but of ideal consumption under the machine system: rapid standardized production for equally rapid standardized consumption—with built-in waste and destruction as a means of averting financial bankruptcy through overproduction—the latter a recurrent threat to the capitalist system during the transitional era of competition in the free market.

The great change produced by this whole process of mechanization was to shift the balance of economic power from agriculture, with its accompanying industries—textiles and pottery and building, all neolithic in origin—to mining and warfare and machine production. The application of mechanical inventions to textiles, which went on so rapidly after the seventeenth century, only increased this imbalance by undermining the old hand-workers and drawing a largely unskilled labor force into the new factories, organized on the same principles that governed mines and arsenals. The new industries, glass-making, iron mining and smelting, weapons manufacture, as well as the new water-driven textile mills, lay usually outside the old towns where the arts and crafts had flourished under guild and municipal protection. Printing, too, had grown up without being subject to guild regulations.

Late medieval national legislation in England, following the example of the town guilds, sought to limit quantitative growth and give social protection to the established workers. The Statute of Edward VI prohibited gig mills, and the English Statute of Apprentices of 1563 likewise sought to limit the opportunities for human exploitation: even the Statute of William and Mary limited the number of looms that might be employed by one master. But in the name of 'economic freedom' all these regulations were repealed in England in 1809. Symbolically, this marked the end of domestic production by independent artisans, free to come and go as they pleased. From this time on, freedom for the manufacturer meant freedom to exploit labor: freedom likewise to ignore qualitative standards, personal obligations, human needs.

Thus facility in making automatic, power-driven machines, which

resulted in enormous gains in productivity in essential industries like textiles, was accompanied, as it had been in the Pyramid Age, by the practice
of debasing the worker to the level of the machine: depleting health,
deforming the body, shortening the life of the worker, and driving the
unemployed into pauperdom and beggary, starvation and death. This
dehumanization of the living worker was complemented, paradoxically, by
the progressive hominization of the machine—hominization in the sense of
giving the automaton some of the mechanical equivalents of lifelike motion
and purpose, a process that has come to a striking consummation in our
own day.

This is not the place to reckon up the net gains and absolute losses that
came about through the unrestricted process of mechanization. There are,
indeed, not enough data to support even gross guesses until, in a few
countries after the eighteenth century, the statistics of births and deaths
and diseases, of industrial output and consumption, become available. How
indeed can one compare a mainly handicraft polytechnics, whose slow rate
of production is matched by an equally slow rate of consumption, with a
system that matches its extraordinary output of energy and goods with
equally rapid consumption and destruction: that indeed deliberately forces
consumption or waste, through incessant, superficial changes of fashion,
of otherwise durable goods? If the first was in fact inherently a scarcity
economy, how was it that it could afford to put so much energy into works
of art and religion, that it could waste so much manpower in war, that the
wealthy could retain such large armies of retainers and menials?

All this would indicate, not technical insufficiency, but rather the fatal
absence of a just system of distribution: a conclusion that is re-enforced by
Benjamin Franklin's estimate, well before megatechnics had taken hold,
that if work and reward and consumption standards were more evenly
distributed, a five hour day would suffice to supply all human needs. If, on
the other hand, the machine economy has now transcended these limitations, how is it that in the United States more than a quarter of the
population lacks an income sufficient to provide a minimum standard of
living?

Of only one fact we may be sure; and this is that although the material
resources of the world have been immensely increased by our high-energy
technology, the net gain has not been nearly as great as is usually reckoned,
when the constant factor of wanton waste, premature obsolescence, organic
deterioration through environmental pollution and depletion, and premature death by war and genocide are taken into account.

That there have been considerable gains in many old areas is beyond
doubt; and that there has been a creative enrichment through many new
technological processes and products is equally evident. But the nineteenth-
century exponents of 'progress,' and their old-fashioned disciples today,

falsified the picture by failing to take account of the accompanying losses—above all, losses brought about through the deliberate extirpation of the handicraft tradition itself, with its immense storage of human experience and skill, only a small part of which has been passed on in the design and fabrication of machines. On this score, Leibnitz's observation still holds: "Concerning unwritten knowledge scattered among men of different callings, I am convinced that it surpasses in quantity and in importance anything we find in books, and that the greater part of our wealth is not yet recorded." Most of that unrecorded wealth, deplorably, is now lost forever.

Those who are committed to megatechnics regard as reprehensible the repeated attempts made, at various times and places, to retard or halt the process of invention. There was, indeed, a long tradition of such resistance: Friedmann instances the story of the Emperor Vespasian refusing to accept a labor-saving device for lifting building stones up the Capitoline Hill, because it would deprive the "little people" of their work and wages; and a more selfish kind of resistance to invasion of vested interests was offered to other inventors: such as the reputed inventor of a mechanical ribbon loom at Danzig, who was condemned to death as a public menace for his invention. The machine-wrecking of the Luddite rioters in England has become proverbial as an example of futile opposition—though what they sought by their rioting was only to maintain their living standard.

But what shall we say of the counter-Luddites, the systematic craft-wreckers, of the machine: the ruthless enterprisers who, during the last two centuries, have in effect confiscated the tools, destroyed the independent workshops, and wiped out the living traditions of handicraft culture? What they have done is to debase a versatile and still viable polytechnics to a monotechnics, and at the same time they have sacrificed human autonomy and variety to a system of centralized control that becomes increasingly more automatic and compulsive. If, two centuries earlier, they had fully succeeded in extirpating the handicraft traditions of the primitive peoples, rubber would not play the part it now does in our advanced technology. Were these craft-wreckers afraid to let handiwork survive lest it join forces, against their financial interests, with the human heart?

5: THE TECHNOLOGICAL POOL

As late as the middle of the nineteenth century an immense technological heritage was still in existence, widely scattered among the peoples of the earth, every part of it colored by human needs, environmental resources, inter-cultural exchanges, and ecological and historic associations. This heritage already contained not merely a greater accumulation of past inventions and technical skills than had ever achieved a worldwide provenance before, but as a result of fundamental discoveries about nature, physical and biological, it had disclosed fresh potentialities for a marvellous future—a future already initiated by the invention of the electric telegraph, the dynamo, and the electric motor. In terms of this variegated, infinitely rich planetary heritage, the prospects offered by the bare mechanical world picture were already outmoded.

The major part of this technical equipment had been passed along for thousands of years, and had consciously drawn into a common pool, more or less accessible through books and printed publications, many precious components that had hitherto been confined to the widely scattered communities where they originated, passed on intermittently only by imitation and word of mouth. The diffusion of this store of knowledge in Western Europe, after the twelfth century, provided in itself the equivalent of many new inventions and was in no small part accountable for the technical dynamism that made still more sweeping technical changes—later misidentified as "the" Industrial Revolution—possible. During these fateful centuries (A.D. 1200–1800) mankind learned more about the earth itself as a habitable globe, about the organisms that inhabit it, and about human cultures than had ever been known before.

Biologists have coined the term "gene pool" to describe the immense amount of genetic material available, in ever fresh combinations, in a large population. Though over a long period certain genes will tend to disappear because they are lethal, and others will undergo modification and selective development through continued transactions with their environment and with each other, there are many genetic traits and organic properties that go back far into our mammalian past, whose absence or deficiency would undermine man's higher development.

Similarly, one may talk of a technological pool: an accumulation of tools, machines, materials, processes, interacting with soils, climates, plants, animals, human populations, institutions, cultures. The capacity of this technological reservoir, until the third quarter of the nineteenth century, was immensely greater than ever before: what is more, it was more diversified—and possibly quantitatively larger, as well as qualitatively richer—than that which exists today. Not the least important part of this technological pool were the skilled craftsmen and work teams that transmitted the colossal accumulation of knowledge and skill. When they were eliminated from the system of production, that vast cultural resource was wiped out.

This diversified technological assemblage not merely contributed to economic security: it permitted a continuous interplay between different phases of technology; and for a time this actually happened. Though the water-turbine was a late eotechnic invention (1825), coming at a time when water was being widely replaced by coal as a steady source of energy, it came back at a higher level in the turbines of hydro-electric power stations; and the turbine principle was still later applied to the airplane motor in an advanced type of jet propulsion. A reverse reaction, in which an older technology benefited from new scientific advances, is exemplified in the altered cut of mainsail and jibs in modern sailing vessels: a change resulting from the closer analysis of air flow for the purpose of improving airplanes.

Western man's pride over his many real achievements in mechanization made him too easily overlook all that he owed to earlier or more primitive cultures. So no one has yet attempted to make an inventory of the massive losses resulting from both the neglect and the deliberate destruction of this craft heritage, in favor of machine-made products. While the population of complex and technically superior machines has enormously increased during the last century, the technological pool has actually been lowered as one handicraft after another has disappeared.

The result is that a monotechnics, based upon scientific intelligence and quantitative production, directed mainly toward economic expansion, material repletion, and military superiority, has taken the place of a polytechnics, based primarily, as in agriculture, on the needs, aptitudes, interests of living organisms: above all on man himself.

Both the tool and the tool user, with their wide range of aptitudes, have almost disappeared in many areas. To get a simple job of repair done on a rake, William Morris once presciently predicted, with only a pardonable exaggeration, one would eventually need to transport a whole crew with their mechanical equipment. That day is already here. What cannot be done by a power machine or replaced by the factory must be scrapped, for nothing can be repaired by hand. The very ability to use simple tools with patience and skill is fast disappearing.

It was not technological insight and adroitness but cupidity, power-hunger, overweening pride, and indifference to the future that kept Western peoples from maintaining their own craft traditions and their tool-using habits. If there had been any appreciation of the immense technological treasure that was being wrecked, or of the powers of the human personality that were thus being sapped, the growing commitment to a monotechnics, based on the displacement of man, might have been publicly challenged and slowed down, or, when necessary, arrested.

There was no reason whatever to make a wholesale choice between handicraft and machine production: between a single contemporary part of the technological pool and all the other past accumulations. But there was a genuine reason to maintain as many diverse units in this pool as possible, in order to increase the range of both human choices and technological inventiveness. Many of the machines of the nineteenth century, as Kropotkin pointed out, were admirable auxiliaries to handicraft processes, once they could be scaled, like the efficient small electric motor, to the small workshop and the personally controlled operation. William Morris and his colleagues, who almost single-handed salvaged and restored one ancient craft after another, by personally mastering the arts of dyeing, weaving, embroidering, printing, glass-painting, paper-making, book-binding, showed superior technological insight to those who scoffed at their 'romanticism.'

The nearest our machine-oriented culture came to preserving some of its immense wealth of technical traditions was to install a limited number of sample specimens in museums of art and natural history, and to collect a trickle of information—rarely adequate—about processes and methods from travellers, and later, from trained archaeologists and anthropologists. So one-sided has this effort been, however, that the article on crafts in the current International Encyclopedia of Social Sciences (1968) treats the subject as if it could be confined to the working traditions of primitive peoples! One could hardly guess from that article that the crafts are a basic heritage of the entire human race, not least in the higher cultures, and that many unexplored potentialities will be destroyed if they are allowed to lapse. There is no new contribution of mechanics or electronics that cannot be readily absorbed in this great technological pool. The only thing that cannot be absorbed is a system that would destroy the pool, in all its immense historic variety, in favor of a humanly underdimensioned monotechnics.

6: THE SUBJECTIVE TRANSITION

If I have dealt at length with the late-medieval background of modern technology, it is in order to bring out two points that have usually been overlooked. And first, the period between the twelfth century and the eighteenth was not one of technological stagnation: far from it. Nor was it a period when only hand labor was available and the function of machines was despised or minimized. On the contrary, this was increasingly a power economy, and machines themselves, beginning with the watermill, the windmill, the mechanical clock and the lathe, were an integral part of it. This combination of extra-human energy with polytechnics enlarged the area of human freedom; yet the pace of production, the constant involvement in works of art, and the conservative traditions of the old handicrafts, kept any one part of this economy from becoming heedlessly dynamic, or lopsidedly dominant.

By the sixteenth century in the more advanced Western countries the outlines of a balanced economy, based on a resourceful technology, had come into existence; and if all the parts had been kept in being then, its further mechanization might have taken place with great human profit at many points, without upsetting this balance.

The other point is that the power elements in this technology began, from the fourteenth century, to get out of hand, as feudal stability, based on use and wont, custom and ritual, was undermined. This was mainly the result of the new principles and incentives of capitalist finance, with its acquisitive appetites, its love of numbers and quantitative increase, themselves symbols of a new kind of status, with its new seizures of power. All these motivations were in turn augmented through the imperious demands of militarism for weapons and armaments, in a period of national unification and colonial expansion.

The assemblage of the mechanical world picture, from the sixteenth century on, gave all these disparate efforts the subjective unity needed to ensure their eventual dominance; and meanwhile technics itself, so long rooted in agriculture, in every sense the basic industry, and in the regional environment, cut loose from these old ties and turned progressively into a monotechnics, concentrating on speed, quantity, control. One by one the factors that tended to limit the overgrowth of technics itself disappeared; and a machine-centered economy flourished as the Canada thistle once flourished on the Argentine pampas, when its invasion destroyed the ecological complex that had kept the environment in balance. In this changeover, the mechanical world picture, in all its many subjective manifestations, played a part perhaps as significant as the whole assemblage of new inventions.

For those who responded to the mechanical world picture, the extension of the machine to every possible human activity was far more than a practical device to lift the burden of labor or increase wealth. As the otherworldly concerns of religion faded, these new activities were what gave fresh meaning to life, no matter how unfortunate the actual results on any cold rational appraisal might seem to be. Here again one sees, as long before in the Pyramid Age, how the process of mechanization was furthered by an ideology that gave absolute precedence and cosmic authority to the machine itself.

When an ideology conveys such universal meanings and commands such obedience, it has become, in fact, a religion, and its imperatives have the dynamic force of a myth. Those who would question its principles or defy its orders do so at their peril, as groups of rebellious workers continued to discover for the next three or four centuries. From the nineteenth century on, this refurbished religion united thinkers of the most diverse temperaments, backgrounds, and superficial beliefs: minds as different as Marx and Ricardo, Carlyle and Mill, Comte and Spencer, subscribed to its doctrines; and from the beginning of the nineteenth century on, the working classes, finding themselves helpless to resist these new forces, countered the capitalist and militarist expressions of this myth with myths of their own—those of socialism, anarchism, or communism—under which the machine would be exploited, not for a ruling elite, but for the benefit of the proletarian masses. Against this machine-conditioned utopia only a handful of heretics, mostly poets and artists, dared to hold out.

What hastened the pace of mechanization was the fact that it not only represented but actualized the new world picture: engaged on a conscious mission—that of spreading the empire of the machine—the demands of mechanical progress had the effect of a divine ordinance, sacrilegious to challenge, impossible to disobey. Confronting such an ideology, poly-technics was helpless: it had no corresponding ideology to draw on: when forced to face this fact, William Morris, the archetypal craftsman, turned to Marxist communism.

Since all the scattered trades and crafts and vocations had grown up over the ages, their underlying inner unity was largely an unconscious traditional heritage, and their values had not yet been translated into a philosophy—much less a common systematic method. The contrast Des-cartes had made, already cited, between a town that has grown up gradually, house by house, street by street, and the city that has been projected as a unified structure by a single mind, would stand for the similar contrast between the diffused polytechnic tradition and that of monotechnics. The power system admits only one kind of complexity, that which conforms to its own method and belongs to the current period: a system so uniform that its components are in effect interchangeable parts, conceived as if by a single collective mind.

This quasi-religious cult of mechanization was furthered, from the seventeenth century on, by some of the best talents available in England, France, and America: its leaders were at work everywhere, not merely expounding its merits, but demonstrating them in practice in the counting-house, the factory, the army, and the school; and as they increased in number, they solidified their ranks and brought theory and practice closer together. Against this united ideological front the exponents of the older arts and crafts and humanities were helpless: poor in resources, scattered, fighting a rear-guard action, often clinging out of their weakness to obsolete practices and ideas. What was gravely lacking in both camps was historical perspective—and it still is lacking. The choice open was never that between a moribund and irretrievable past and a dynamic, irresistible future. In putting the case in those terms, both parties were at fault.

There were in fact many profitable and feasible alternatives to the course actually followed in the leading countries of Western civilization, and now rapidly enveloping the entire world. One of the great benefits of individualized national and regional cultures is that, if the opportunities are consciously seized, these potential alternatives can be experimented with under varied conditions and their advantages compared. Any philosophy of history that takes account of natural and human diversity must recognize that selective processes in nature have reached a higher stage in man, and that any mode of organizing human activities, mechanically or institutionally, which limits the possibilities of continued trial, selection, emergence, and transcendence, in favor of a closed and completely unified system, is nothing less than an effort to arrest human cultural evolution.

Unfortunately, history could teach no lessons in a culture that had eliminated history from its basic premises. Hence the benefits of mechanization, so far from being absorbed into the existing polytechnics, were partly forfeited in order to make its own system more watertight.

The results of this concentration are now painfully visible: every error, every defect, is now repeated—often instantaneously—on a worldwide scale. The more universal this technology becomes, the fewer the alternatives that will be available, and the less possibility to restore autonomy to any of the components of the system. But this is to anticipate: the substantiating details will come out in the next chapter. Enough to point out here that though much of the polytechnic heritage has been lost forever, the concept of a diversified polytechnics will remain a necessary one in any humanly oriented system. In such a system the organism and the human personality, not the machine, will provide the master-model.

7: THE BURIED RENASCENCE

There was a moment at the beginning of the sixteenth century, before the new power system, exemplified in capitalism and in colonialism, had taken form, when it might have seemed that a new order was taking form, in which the older modes of polytechnics would be reconstituted and re-enforced by the contributions of a science-oriented technology.

This possibility was expressed in the personality and the achievement of more than one great artist of the period: indeed, it was visible in the working life of many lesser artists like Vasari and Cellini. But above all, it was present in Leonardo da Vinci, in whose mind this new order struggled to come into existence—only to be frustrated by other forces that were moving in the opposite direction. Those forces were in fact to dominate the next four centuries. In a sense, as I shall explain in the final chapters of this book, Leonardo's vision and work foretold a later mode of integration that has still to be achieved.

There are many ways of looking upon the life of Leonardo da Vinci. One may see him as the meticulous painter whose passion for perfection lowered his output of art, as the extraordinary engineer whose inventions and improvements upon existing inventions (including the flying shuttle) rank him as one of the greatest technicians of all time, as the frustrated genius whose capacities were never sufficiently called forth by contemporary patrons—or, finally, as the wide-ranging mind that took all existence, if not all knowledge, as his province.

On the whole, present-day interest in Leonardo centers increasingly upon his vast range of mechanical proposals and exploits. I accept all these characterizations for what they are worth. But there is still another way of looking at Leonardo; and this is as the forerunner of an age that has still to dawn: an age different from his own period, and in sharp contrast to that we live in today. The very traits that seem to mark him as a failure, and are taken as a reproach, give Leonardo, from the point of view developed here, a special distinction.

If Leonardo's example of diversification had been more widely followed, the whole tempo of mechanical and scientific development would have been slowed down. This means that the pace of change might have been established in relation to human need, and that valuable parts of man's cultural heritage might have been kept alive, instead of being ruthlessly extirpated in order to widen the empire of the machine. Instead of rapid advances, on the basis of uncoordinated knowledge, in specialized departments, mainly those concerned with war and economic exploitation, there would have been the possibility of a slower but better-coordinated advance that did justice to the processes, functions, and purposes of life.

Had Leonardo's example in fact been followed, naturalization, mechanization, organization, and humanization might have proceeded together. Thus one method could have influenced and sustained the other, maintaining continuity with the past, yet alertly absorbing useful or significant novelty, constantly reviewing and correcting past errors, and seeking a wider selection of possibilities; introducing new values, not to destroy but to enrich and fortify those already achieved by other ages and other cultures. Such a practical syncretism of technologies and ideologies would have been an open one, open indeed at both ends, to past and future—constantly absorbing and refining more of the past while projecting and remodelling in a richer design ever larger tracts of the future. Unlike the technocrats of a later day, Leonardo was full of admiration for his predecessors. (See Volume One.)

The facile way of disposing of Leonardo's genius is to ally it with a supposedly vanished characteristic of the Renascence mind: to treat it as the product of a culture so intellectually undeveloped, so lacking in scientific specialization, that a single mind could master every part of it. This is both a false compliment to Leonardo and a gratuitous disparagement of the cultural resources available. For the fact is that no culture, at least since the invention of writing, has ever been at the disposal of a single mind: even an Aristotle, an Ibn Khaldun, or a Thomas Aquinas must necessarily have left out large tracts of human experience.

Despite his wide range of interests, Leonardo was extremely sensitive, indeed highly susceptible, to new technical possibilities and new motives, and more than once they threatened to throw him off balance as badly as they did later enterprisers. Like any Victorian inventor, he too sometimes had dreams of quick financial success. "Early tomorrow, Jan. 2, 1496," he records in one of his notes, "I shall make the leather belt and proceed to a trial. . . . One hundred times in each hour 400 needles will be finished, making 40,000 in an hour and 480,000 in 12 hours. Suppose we say 4000s which at 5 soldi per thousand gives 20,000 soldi: 1000 lira per working day, and if one works 20 days in the month, 60,000 decuates the year." Even the shorter work week lay embedded in this wild dream of freedom and power through a successful invention; but happily this too-easy type of success evaded him.

Except for these temporary aberrations, Leonardo never succumbed completely to such utilitarian projects; and despite the intensity of his studies in painting, sculpture, engineering (military and civil), geology, and anatomy, he never allowed any single interest to dominate him: in fact he sacrificed practical success, because of his slowness in delivering the final product, possibly because the process itself engaged him more fully than did the ultimate result. At all events, he maintained his many-sidedness and his balance. Had his moral sense not been awake, he would not have suppressed his invention of the submarine, because he felt that the soul of man was too devilish to be trusted with it. Just as, in the world of organisms, ecological complexity and variety prevents any single species from achieving complete dominance, so in human society, Leonardo's mode of thinking—had it prevailed and governed our system of education—would have prevented megatechnics from taking command.

Leonardo's practical failures, so far from being a fault, were rather the price of his achievement as a feeling, thinking, value-weighing, acting human being. In an age when the printing press was open to him, this indefatigable recorder and writer published nothing. He was assembling first in his own mind, with a fullness that no one since Imhotep, that master pyramid-builder, had perhaps ever achieved, the necessary ingredients for a culture that would do justice to every aspect of organic life. Again, this synthesis was nowhere consciously adumbrated, it found expression only in Leonardo's works and days: but that expression—though imperfect—pervaded his whole life.

Significantly, he was not alone: minds of the same caliber, like Dürer's and Michelangelo's, surrounded him, and similar minds came into existence in later generations, from Christopher Wren to Goethe and George Perkins Marsh. But success and honor came most readily to those who concentrated on the service of the power system and obeyed its instructions.

Yes: it is futile to dwell on ifs and might-have-beens. But if the spirit of Leonardo had influenced the modern age, the whole process of invention, exploration, colonization, and mechanization would have gone on more slowly, with a less ruthless suppression of many rival human propensities, with a less savage dismissal of rival interests and cultural forms. On the positive side, this would have ensured a more effective assimilation and coordination of the new knowledge. In so far as these missed potentialities are still available in man's redoubtable brain, and still stored—if widely scattered—in all man's organs of mind, in language, tradition, history, architecture, books, records, the synthesis outlined in Leonardo's life still beckons us, all the more since the Sun God's reign threatens to be terminated, not only by human failures, but by its own colossal but self-negating success.

One has only to look through Leonardo's Notebooks to realize that he had assembled in his own mind the main components of the modern world picture. He was already aware, through his willingness to inspect his own dreams, of the terrible potentialities for destruction and dehumanization that might lie in store for modern man unless his self-knowledge and his historic insight matched his accurate observations of external nature, and unless his ethical principles held in check the insolent egoes that had already shown how little fit they were to be in control of the new forces now at modern man's disposal. Even gunpowder, steel armor, and advanced mining technology had opened up powers of destruction and conquest that enabled small gangs of resolute men to perform acts of both construction and destruction that had hitherto called for tens of thousands of brawny bodies.

Not the least notable thing about Leonardo's mind was the lurking doubts beneath his ardent experiments and imaginative trials. While making meticulous anatomical dissections, which preceded Vesalius' studies by almost half a century, he recorded his wish for power to know the mind and social institutions of man as well as his body. There were countercurrents running in Leonardo's anxieties and inhibitions that may account for the fact that despite his immense creative energies he did not turn to early publication: perhaps these reluctances made him the more willing to leave his work tentative and incomplete. Success might have come easily through specialization and publication, but at the price of forgetting wholeness, of becoming crippled and unbalanced, perhaps irrational and destructive.

What I am saying here in praise of Leonardo must seem a mere mockery to the busy specialists of today, addressed from the beginning of their careers to some early application of newly achieved knowledge or technical expertise: each eager to jump with all possible speed to a post of authority, to the direct application of his knowledge to some overt form of control over the physical environment or over organic reproduction, and finally over other human brains—*as soon as possible!* For such minds to follow Leonardo's example, to spend a whole lifetime in their work with only a handful of small projects or publications to show for it would be an act of vocational suicide. Such diversification of interests as Leonardo practiced, such continence and self-control, such voluntary censorship, lie beyond the Power Complex's intellectual horizon. To hold Leonardo as a model before the success-prone scientists and technicians of today would be to invite scorn. In no sense was Leonardo their model or their forerunner.

It is an error, nevertheless, to hold that Leonardo's example is an impossible one for our age. The example is impossible only because those who seek power are unwilling to pay the price of achieving balance and are unattracted by the human reward. What one must give up, in any effort to achieve a many-dimensioned and coherent world picture, is the idea of early achievement and instant exploitation. Whatever the field of invention, or organization, one must be ready to go forward at a slower pace, looking before and after; to make fewer discoveries, to spend as much time assimilating knowledge as in acquiring it; to do less, perhaps, in a whole lifetime in any one department than the concentrated specialist is able to do in a decade. From the standpoint of the power system this demands an impossible sacrifice: the sacrifice of power to life.

CHAPTER SEVEN

Mass Production and Human Automation

1: THE PENTAGON OF POWER

So far I have attempted to expose the interplay of human interests and technological pressures that conspired after the sixteenth century to dominate Western civilization. In time these forces coalesced in the unconscious as a replenished Myth of the Machine. As with the earlier myth, this social and technological transformation might be duly rationalized as a massive practical effort to fulfill human needs and increase material wealth: but beneath it was a deeply subjective and more obsessive drive toward the 'conquest' of nature and the control of life, to the "effecting of all things possible."

I have now to show how the new ideas of order and power and predictability that dominated the new mechanical world picture made their way into every human activity. Within the last four centuries the older tradition of polytechnics was replaced by a system that gave primacy to the machine, with its repetitive motions, its depersonalized processes, its abstract quantitative goals. The later enlargement of these technical possibilities through electronics has only increased the scope and coercive absolutism of the system.

Part of this story is now so familiar that one hesitates even briefly to recapitulate its main features. After the sixth century A.D. in Western Europe some of the harsher features of the older megamachine were eliminated largely by 'etherializing' the power motive in the Roman Catholic Church, and turning lifetime service into the voluntary act of dedicated Christians. This partial transformation, which also ameliorated the lifetime division of labor, was first effected in the Benedictine monastery. While the ascetic routines of the monastic orders favored the machine, their rigorous accountancy of time and their careful control of money and goods were progressively passed on to other forms of bureaucratic organization, private and public, from trading to tax collecting, until by the sixteenth century they had set the style for mercantile enterprise and governmental administration.

Finally, the basic model of all three modes of regimentation, military, monastic, and bureaucratic, was introduced into large-scale industry by the factory system. It was this cumulative mechanical organization, not the steam engine, that accounts for the upsurge of industrial energy after 1750.

Though a considerable part of this transformation can be read in purely technical terms, one must not overlook the shift in human motives through the increasing translation of both political and economic power into purely abstract quantitative terms: mainly, terms of money. Physical power, applied to coerce other human beings, reaches natural limits at an early stage: if one applies too much, the victim dies. So, too, with the command of purely material goods or sensual pleasures. If one eats too much, one suffers from indigestion or is overtaxed by corpulence; if one seeks sensual pleasure too constantly, the capacity for enjoyment decreases and eventually becomes exhausted.

But when human functions are converted into abstract, uniform units, ultimately units of energy or money, there are no limits to the amount of power that can be seized, converted, and stored. The peculiarity of money is that it knows no biological limits or ecological restrictions. When the Augsburg financier, Jacob Fugger the Elder, was asked when he would have so much money that he would feel no need for more, he replied, as all great magnates tacitly or openly do, that he never expected such a day to come.

Thus the transformation of traditional polytechnics into a uniform, all-embracing monotechnics marked likewise the translation of a limited goods economy, based on a diversity of natural functions and vital human needs, to a power economy, symbolized by and concentrated on money. This transformation had taken thousands of years; and even today there are billions of people who remain outside the system and govern their activities by a different code. Coined money, a great step toward quantitative abstraction, was a relatively late invention (seventh century B.C.) and standard interchangeable monetary units came far later; while paper money and credit accounting on the scale now practiced was inconceivable before rapid transportation and communication became possible.

This historic process may be condensed in a brief formula: manual work into machine work: machine work into paper work: paper work into electronic simulation of work, divorced progressively from any organic functions or human purposes, except those that further the power system.

An abstract evaluation of goods and services in terms of standard money units, bushels if not coins, had played a role in the earliest power economy and indeed had been passed on, if not independently invented, by even more primitive communities with their cowrie shells and wampum and similar media for exchange. Accordingly, the persistent inflation of the money motive, from the sixteenth century on, has usually been taken as a mere extension of an existing institution. This would be true if money alone were the only factor. But something more impelling than the traditional pecuniary motives—greed, avarice, luxury—played a part in this explosion.

What took place was a far more commanding and complete transformation: the nucleation of a new power complex, comparable to that which produced the colossal constructive transformations of the Pyramid Age in both Egypt and Mesopotamia. What I have hitherto designated with intentional looseness as the myth of the machine I now propose to define more closely as the Power Complex: a new constellation of forces, interests, and motives, which eventually resurrected the ancient megamachine, and gave it a more perfect technological structure, capable of planetary and even interplanetary extension.

In English, by a happy alliterative accident, the main components of the new power complex all start with the same initial letter, beginning with Power itself: so that one may call it—all the more accurately because of contemporary American overtones—the Pentagon of Power. The basic ingredient was power itself, beginning in the Pyramid Age with such an assemblage of manpower as no earlier group had been capable of bringing into existence. Over the ages, this has been augmented by horsepower, waterpower, windpower, woodpower, coalpower, electricpower, oilpower, and climactically, only yesterday, by nuclear power, itself the ultimate form of the power from chemical reactions that had made the gasoline motor and the rocket possible.

Organized political power backed by coercive weapons is the source of both property and productivity: first of all in the cultivation of the land, using sunpower, and then at later stages in every other mode of production. Mechanical productivity, linked to widening markets, spells profit; and without the dynamic stimulus of profit—that is, money power—the system could not so rapidly expand. This perhaps explains why cruder forms of the megamachine, which favored the military caste rather than the merchant and industrial producer, and relied on tribute and pillage, remained static, and in the end unproductive and unprofitable to the point of repeated bankruptcy. Finally, no less an integral part of the power system is publicity (prestige, *panache*), through which the merely human directors of the power complex—the military, bureaucratic, industrial, and scientific elite—are inflated to more than human dimensions in order better to maintain authority.

These separate components of the power system derive from the far richer ecological complex—'ecosystem' in scientific parlance—in which all organisms, including man, live and move and have their being. Within that ecosystem, which includes human culture, all of these components of the power complex originally had their place and performed their indispensable functions. What the power complex did was to wrench these separate components from their organic matrix and enclose them in an isolated subsystem centered not on the support and intensification of life but on the expansion of power and personal aggrandizement.

So closely are the components of the power complex related that they perform virtually interchangeable functions: not only in the sense that every operation is reducible to pecuniary terms, but that money itself in turn can be translated equally into power or property or publicity or public (television) personalities. This interchangeability of the power components was already plain to Heraclitus at the critical moment that the new money economy was in formation. "All things may be reduced to fire," he observed, "and fire to all things, just as goods may be turned into gold and gold into goods."

When any one of these components is weak or absent, or is not closely enough joined to the neighboring processes, the power system cannot work at full speed or with maximum efficiency. But its final goal is a quantitative abstraction—money or its etherialized and potentially limitless equivalent, credit. The latter, like the 'faith' of the Musical Banks in Erewhon, is at bottom only a pious belief that the system will continue indefinitely to work.

Commitment to the power complex and relentless pursuit of pecuniary gains, in both direct and indirect forms, define the power system and prescribe its only acceptable goal. That goal, fitly enough, belongs to the same memorable series of alliterations—progress. In terms of the power system, progress means simply more power, more profit, more productivity, more paper property, more publicity—all convertible into quantitative units. Even publicity can be expressed in column-yards of newspaper clippings and man-hours of television appearance. Each new achievement of the power system, whether in scientific research, in education or medicine, in antibiotics, or in space exploration, will be expressed through the same media for institutional magnification and ego-inflation. The school, the church, the factory, the art museum—each currently plays the same power theme, marching to the same beat, saluting the same flags, joining the interminable columns already assembled on the side streets to become the new leaders of the parade that the kings, the despots, the conquistadors, and the financiers of the Renascence first marshalled together.

Though the constellation that has formed the power system was not deliberately assembled at any single moment, many of its active components, created in earlier civilizations, had never in fact passed out of existence. Once the restraining codes and ideals of a more humanly conditioned ideology were destroyed, the power system, freed from such institutional competition, swiftly burgeoned.

The power system has often been mistakenly identified with feudalism, with absolute monarchy, with princely despotism, with capitalism, with fascism, with communism, even with the Welfare State. But this multiple identification points to a more important characteristic: the fact that the power complex increasingly underlies *all* these institutional structures; and as it knits more closely together, seizing more power and governing wider areas, it tends to suppress original cultural differences that once, under feebler political institutions, were visible.

From unrestricted power through expanding pecuniary profit to insatiable pleasure, the most striking thing about this power complex is its studious indifference to other human needs, norms, and goals: it operates best in what is, historically speaking, an ecological, cultural, and personal lunar desert, swept only by solar winds.

As respects its isolation and its indifference to the basic requirements of all organic activity, the pecuniary power complex discloses a startling resemblance to a newly discovered center in the brain—that which is called the pleasure center. So far as is known, this pleasure center performs no useful function in the organism, unless it should prove that in some still obscure way it plays a part in more functional pleasure reactions. But in laboratory monkeys this localized center can be penetrated by electrodes which permit a micro-current to stimulate the nervous tissue in such a fashion that the flow of current—and hence the intensity of pleasure—can be regulated by the animal himself.

Apparently the stimulation of this pleasure center is so rewarding that the animal will continue to press the current regulator for an indefinite length of time, regardless of every other impulse or physiological need, even that for food, and even to the point of starvation. The intensity of this abstract stimulus produces something like a total neurotic insensibility to life needs. The power complex seems to operate on the same principle. The magical electronic stimulus is money.

What increases the resemblance between this pecuniary motivation and that of the cerebral pleasure center is that both centers, unlike virtually all organic reactions, recognize no quantitative limits. What has always been true of money, among those susceptible to its influence, applies equally to the other components of the power complex: the abstraction replaces the concrete reality, and therefore those who seek to increase it never know when they have had enough. Each of these drives, for power, for goods, for fame, for pleasure, may—it goes without saying—have as useful a part to play in the normal economy of a community as in the human body itself. It is by their detachment, their isolation, their quantitative over-concentration, and their mutual re-enforcement that they become perverse and life-corroding.

But one unfortunate feature of the pecuniary power complex has still to be noted; for it sets off recent manifestations from the earlier myth of the machine, and makes them even more obstructive to further development. Whereas in the past the power-pleasure nucleus was under the exclusive control of the dominant minority, and so could seduce only this extremely limited group, with the growth of megatechnics all its major features have been distributed, under the canons of mass society (democratic participation) to a far larger population.

To discuss the proliferation of inventions during the last two centuries, the mass production of commodities, and the spread of all the technological factors that are polluting and destroying the living environment, without reference to this immense pecuniary pressure constantly exerted in every technological area, is to ignore the most essential clue to the seemingly automatic and uncontrollable dynamism of the whole system. In order to 'turn on' this insensate pleasure center 'technological man' now threatens to 'turn off' his life. Money has proved the most dangerous of modern man's hallucinogens.

2 : MECHANICAL MOBILIZATION

The practical triumphs of mechanization and mass production as they passed from one industry to another, from printing to arms production to textiles, are beyond dispute. And if the archetypal model for the new system of thought was the clock, that for standardized mass production, with the progressive elimination of the responsible, tool-using worker, was the printing press; for printing from movable and replaceable type made in standardized molds demonstrated the advantages of swift mechanized processes over the equally standardized but tedious hand labor of manuscript writing. This happened long before the spinning jenny and the automatic loom were invented. If the so-called Industrial Revolution, in the old-fashioned sense, could be said to have begun at any single point, it was in the mass production of printed words and pictures, in the new arts of printing, engraving, and lithography. The later developments of mass production in textiles, pottery, and hardware, if more essential to physical well-being, were nevertheless derivative.

Beginning with Adam Smith's description in 'The Wealth of Nations,' the successive developments in mass production can be easily followed. From Smith's demonstration of the way in which a laborer, reduced under threat of starvation to being a docile 'hand,' could by specialization in a single repetitive task, or even a single motion, increase the output per man-hour, one comes by a direct route to the transfer of these mechanized skills to the parts of machines, worked increasingly by centralized power units— watermills, steam engines, dynamos—thence on to the latest type of automatic petroleum plant, steel-rolling mill, or textile factory, where only a few residual laborers, if any, are needed to keep an eye upon the automatic operation, otherwise effectively monitored by a computer.

The mechanical efficiency and the material gains from this system are indisputable; nor can there be any doubt that at least a fraction of these gains were passed on to a limited number of human beneficiaries: at first only to restricted classes or groups, the merchants, the manufacturers, the financiers, the rentiers, or the older but still wealthy landed aristocracy. The growth of the European middle classes, with their increasing ease and comfort from the sixteenth century on, was also, directly or indirectly, a by-product of this mechanization.

If however one takes in the entire population of any given country, and inspects what happened to the community as a whole, the improvements are by no means so great; for the gains were offset by wasted resources, depleted natural environments, artfully crowded slums, and, worst of all, by the degradation and depression of successive generations of human beings.

About the final gains and losses no objective statistical estimate, even the roughest, can be made. It is only because the mechanical world picture induced people to consider exclusively the physical changes, mechanical efficiencies, and salable products, that mechanization was regarded as an unqualified boon. But note: for the upper-income groups the main gains at first were not in the larger quantity of machine-made goods, but in the ability to command menial and professional services on a princely scale.

One thing at least is sure about mechanization, whether taken in its crude early reduction of the laborer to a 'moving part' or in its final form of eliminating him altogether: it did not succeed solely on its merits, genuine though these might be. At every stage the human costs were heavy, and many negative human reactions took place, from violence to sodden drunkenness. By protests, marches, strikes, boycotts, the threatened workers sought to preserve those vestiges of autonomy that had remained even in the handicrafts subject to capitalist exploitation. But for long all these efforts were in vain. To establish a monopoly for its heavy invest-ments in machinery, corporate industrial enterprise relied from the begin-ning upon governmental assistance—tariffs, subventions, military and police support. Further to monopolize production, the megatechnic industries deliberately wiped out competition from the independent craftsman, not only by undercutting him in the market but by imposing taxes and forced labor, in Africa, Asia, and Polynesia, upon tribes that, if left to themselves, would have been content with a mode of life that required neither British textiles nor German coal-tar dyes to color them with.

This is not the place to follow in detail the entire process of mechanization, as it went from industry to industry, from country to country, assembling new inventions, drawing on new sources of power, concocting new wants, establishing new fashions. This transformation produced enormous increases of income for the ruling minorities, never more than five per cent of the total population; measurable improvements for the so-called middle classes, possibly the upper third of the population; and finally very spotty benefits, often attached to severe handicaps and sacrifices, to the lower income groups, while leaving the 'submerged tenth,' or more accurately, the bottom quarter, near destitution and psychal starvation.

My purpose in this book is not to deal with these historic effects of industrialism, long subject to trenchant criticism, from Owen, Marx, Engels, Ruskin, and Mill onward. Not merely is this an old story; but many of the worst evils have been ameliorated, some indeed entirely overcome. It is not with the mischiefs, but rather with the seemingly beneficial human results, with what most people still regard as undisputed achievements and social gains, that I shall be most concerned.

By the beginning of the nineteenth century, in manufacturing processes like spinning and weaving, the problems of mechanical automation had already been solved. Given a sufficient source of power, great banks of rotating and whirring and clicking mechanisms performed every part of the process with no further help from human hands other than the tying together of a broken thread or the spotting of a place where the mechanism had failed to operate with its usual precision and perfection.

These separate automatic machines in turn tended to form part of a larger system, with results that were characterized, quite early on, by Karl Marx. "An organised system of working machines which are one and all set in motion by the transmitting mechanism from a central automaton, constitutes the fully developed form of machinofacture. In place of the individual machine, we now have a mechanical monster whose body fills the whole factory, and whose demon power, hidden from our sight at first because of the measured and almost ceremonious movement of his giant limbs, discloses itself at length in the vast and furious whirl of his numberless working organs."

In fields like textiles, where a high plateau of standardized performance had already been achieved by handicraft—the textiles of ancient Damascus or Peru have not been surpassed for durability or beauty—the specialization of automatic machinery is no handicap. Once a process reaches that state of technical perfection, the need for further alterations is small. But here we must distinguish between the automatic unit itself and the automatic system, which may contain many different components, not all of them mechanized, or even, until they enter the system, automatic. The automatic machine and the automatic system tend to re-enforce each other. Every machine must be judged individually, on its own merits, in relation to a specific human need. It is not the physical machinery but the basic premises of automation that demand scrutiny.

3: THE REMOVAL OF LIMITS

Every earlier system of production, whether in agriculture or in handicraft, developed in response to human needs and was dependent upon the energy derived mainly from plant growth, supplemented by animal, wind, and water power. This productivity was restricted, not merely by available natural resources and human capacity, but by the variety of non-utilitarian demands that accompanied it. Esthetic design and qualitative excellence took precedence over mere quantitative output, and kept quantification within tolerable human limits.

In the mechanized, high-energy system developed during the last two centuries, these conditions have been radically altered; and one of the results of commanding a plethora of energy is to place the stress on precisely those parts of our technology that demand the largest quantities of it; namely, those that make the fullest use of power-machines. This new industrial complex is based upon a group of postulates so self-evident to those who have produced the system that they are rarely criticized or challenged—indeed almost never examined—for they are completely identified with the new 'way of life.' Let me list these postulates once more, though I have already touched on them in examining the mechanical world picture.

First: man has only one all-important mission in life: to conquer nature. By conquering nature the technocrat means, in abstract terms, commanding time and space; and in more concrete terms, speeding up every natural process, hastening growth, quickening the pace of transportation, and breaking down communication distances by either mechanical or electronic means. To conquer nature is in effect to remove all natural barriers and human norms and to substitute artificial, fabricated equivalents for natural processes: to replace the immense variety of resources offered by nature by more uniform, constantly available products spewed forth by the machine.

From these general postulates a series of subsidiary ones are derived: there is only one efficient speed, *faster;* only one attractive destination, *farther away;* only one desirable size, *bigger;* only one rational quantitative goal, *more.* On these assumptions the object of human life, and therefore of the entire productive mechanism, is to remove limits, to hasten the pace of change, to smooth out seasonal rhythms and reduce regional contrasts—in fine, to promote mechanical novelty and destroy organic continuity. Cultural accumulation and stability thus become stigmatized as signs of human backwardness and insufficiency. By the same token, any institution or way of life, any system of education or production that imposes limits, retards change, or converts the imperious will to conquer nature into a relation of mutual aid and rational accommodation, threatens to undermine the power-pentagon and the scheme of life derived from it.

Now this supposed necessity to conquer nature is not quite so innocent in either its origins or its intentions as might seem. In part, at least, it applies unscrupulously to nature the more ancient ambitions of military conquest and imperialist exploitation; but in part, unfortunately, it is also due to a profound fault in Christian theology, which regarded the earth as man's exclusive property, designed by God solely for his use and enjoyment, and further looked upon all other living creatures as without souls, and so subject to the same treatment as inanimate things. (The present turning of the young to Hindu and Buddhist conceptions may be hopefully interpreted as an attempt to overcome this original ecological error. For the meek and the humble, not the proud, alone are fit to inherit the earth.)

Because these traditional attitudes toward man and nature supported the dominant power motives in post-medieval society, the new system of production lacked any method for normalizing wants or controlling quantity: it not merely lacked them but purposely broke down any older methods such as a concern with fine workmanship or esthetic expression.

Thanks to the proficiency of the machine, the problem of older societies, that of scarcity and insufficiency, was—at least in theory—solved: but a new problem, equally serious but at just the opposite extreme, was raised: the problem of quantity. This problem has many aspects: not merely how to distribute the potential abundance of goods justly, so that the whole community will benefit, but how to allocate the investment in machine-centered organizations without negating or destroying those many human activities and functions that are injured rather than helped by automation. The first of these problems has been far more successfully dealt with in many primitive communities than under any industrialized regime.

The bitter reproach that became popular in America during the economic depression of the nineteen-thirties, "starvation in the midst of plenty," reflected the breakdown in a distribution system whose conventions were based on scarcity. But an equally vexatious form of starvation is that which has been caused through the introduction of mechanized habits of life and automatic machines, by the pressure of overwhelming abundance. One might call this the Strasbourg-goose syndrome: gorging or forced feeding for the sake of further fattening a system of automation that produces quantities beyond the normal requirements of consumption.

Though I must postpone a more comprehensive discussion of this problem to a later point, this is the place to examine the impact of automation in a society that takes quantification and material expansion to be an ultimate good. And since the condition to be analyzed now exists in almost every phase of automation, from food production to nuclear weapons, I shall confine myself largely to the field I have the closest acquaintance with: the automation of knowledge. In this area conventional mechanical automation has up to now played only a small part.

As has happened again and again in technics, the critical step that led to general automation took place in the organization of knowledge before any appropriate automatic machinery was invented. The process has been dated and explained, stage by stage, by an historian of science, Derek Price, in 'Science Since Babylon,' and condensed, with certain necessary corrections, in a later essay.

Well before the automatic machines of the nineteenth century had been invented, science had perfected within its own realm a system of subdivided labor, operating with the standardized parts, confined to limited motions and processes, which paralleled in efficiency Adam Smith's favorite example of pin-making.

The means for effecting this immense outpouring of standardized knowledge, Price points out, was a new method of multiplying and communicating scientific information by means of a small standard unit, the scientific paper, whereby reports on isolated observations and experiments could be promptly circulated in scientific journals. This practical device, based on the earlier invention of the printing press, proved the effective starting point for the systematic automation of knowledge. By now the productivity in this area rivals anything that has been achieved in industrial manufacture. Periodical publication is in itself a phase of automation: once a periodical is set up, the regular flow of material and its regular publication is no longer subject to spontaneous fluctuations of supply or erratic publishing demands: the process instigates the product and punctuates the result—automatically.

Observe the interplay between the mass production of goods and the mass publication of scientific knowledge. Beginning with a single scientific journal in 1665, Price tells us that there were a hundred at the beginning of the nineteenth century, a thousand by the middle, and ten thousand by 1900. We are already on the way to achieve 100,000 journals in another century. Even allowing for the great increase in population, this is a gigantic advance. In the meanwhile, the enormous output of duplicating machines of every kind, from the mimeograph to the microfilm and Xerox, has multiplied the product. And here again the result is typical of the entire system: before any part of this process, except large-scale printing, was mechanically automated, the entire system exhibited all the virtues and defects of any completely automated unit—expanding productivity in quantities that are unassimilable, without re-introducing the human selections and abstentions that have been excluded from the system.

4: THE TRIUMPH OF AUTOMATION

The place to appraise the whole process of mechanization and mass production is at the terminal point already visible in many areas: total automation. Now neither the idea of automation, nor the process itself, belongs exclusively to the modern age: nor, more importantly, was either aspect dependent solely upon mechanical inventions. Growing plants are natural agents that automatically turn the sun's energy into leafy tissue; and the synthetic reproduction of this process in an automated chemical plant would not make it in any degree more automatic. So, too, the gravity flow system of conveying water through a pipe from a mountain spring, as in the ancient Palace at Knossos, was quite as automatic and efficient—and even more reliable than—the operation of an electrically driven hydraulic pump today. When Aristotle used the term automation, it was to describe those natural changes that take place, as in a chemical reaction, without any final purpose. But long before man had any scientific grasp of the role of organic automatism within the body the idea itself had taken hold of his mind; and it was from the first associated with three magical aims; superhuman power, material abundance, and remote control.

Central to these magic aspirations was, for obvious reasons, material abundance; this proved indeed to be the tempting immediate bait that concealed the collective trap of external power and centralized control. As early as 446 B.C. the Greek poet Teclecleides, himself probably echoing many unrecorded fables, pictured the Golden Age as one when "the earth bore neither fear nor disease, but all things appeared of their own accord; for every stream flowed with wine and barley cakes fought with wheat cakes to enter the mouths of men." Though the machine plays no part in this magical wish, the fantasy dwells on those gustatory joys and that effortless existence which people still associate with automation. As for the life so pictured, it was nothing less than the kind of existence that kings, nobles, and rich magnates had long enjoyed.

With this promise of abundance went another persistent wish: the idea of finding a mechanical substitute to take over the burden of painful human toil. Though Babylonian legends picture the gods as creating man purely for the purpose of performing back-breaking tasks for them, the more self-confident Greeks pictured their blacksmith god, Hephaistos, as proving his skill by creating a lifelike bronze automaton—historically the first of a long line of spectral robots that still haunt the minds of modern engineers.

In the very act of affirming the necessity for slavery by dismissing the idea that self-acting machines for weaving or building might be invented, Aristotle showed that the possibility of manufacturing automatons was active in the Greek mind: so we need not be surprised that Heron of Alexandria, a few centuries later, described a more elaborate automaton, that of a naval dockyard, where puppets cut and sawed timber. Here in playful form was the earliest small-scale model of the automated factory.

Since the fantasies of automation and absolute power have historically gone together, it is hardly surprising that absolute monarchs in all ages have persistently delighted in automatons, as symbolic witnesses to the unqualified power they themselves sought to exercise. Marco Polo, happily, has transmitted to us the boast of the Great Khan who regarded Christians as "ignorant, inefficient persons" because they did not possess the faculty of performing anything miraculous, whereas, he pointed out, "when I sit at table, the cups that were in the middle of the hall come to me, filled with wine and other beverages, spontaneously, and without being controlled by human hand." This technical facility, Kublai Khan plainly indicated, was proof of his own power and total control. He even went so far, in the same breath, as to anticipate the further extensions of this claim, made by scientists in our own day; for he boasted that his magicians had the power of controlling bad weather, and obliging it to retire to any quarter of the heavens. Marco Polo, unfortunately, neglected to verify this claim.

None of these motives was absent from the later developments of mechanization: but if ages passed before they became realizable, it was because these deep subjective impulses could not be harnessed until the necessary mechanical components were invented. Slaves and servants, treated as if they were such mechanical parts, may actually have delayed the coming of automation, for even now, it has been found, human organisms are still the best available all-round servo-mechanisms, cheaper to produce, easier to keep in order, more responsive to signals, than the most finicking mechanical robot.

Once more we come back to the mechanical clock. Apart from feedback the invention and perfection of the clock was the decisive move toward automation; for it provided the master model for many other automatic machines; and it reached a degree of perfection finally, in the eighteenth-century chronometer, which set a standard for other technological refinements. The one element lacking in the clock until the electric clock was invented, an automatic source of power, was provided at an early stage for coarser uses by the watermill: the automatic mine-pumping apparatus shown by Agricola in 'De Re Metallica,' and the equally automatic silk-reeling machine with multiple spools, illustrated by Zonca in 1607 in his 'Novo Teatro dei Machine e Edifici,' were but the late instances of a series of earlier automatic machines that lacked only a cybernetic regulator of the process and the output to become completely automated. Those who still imagine that automation first took place in the nineteen-forties, and was impossible until the computer was invented, have a lot of homework to do.

Purely as a machine, the clock remained—until the computer—the equal of all other automatic machines in refinement of construction and accuracy of operation; and long before this further improvement took place in any other area, the reduction of the fifteenth-century clock, with its clumsy clanking works, to the small, portable watch set a goal for later forms of miniaturization. What was lacking until the seventeenth century, then, was not automatons but a fully developed *system* of automation, and this awaited two things: the construction of the new mechanical world picture and an increase of demand sufficient to justify the installation of expensive prime movers and batteries of elaborate machines, kept in constant use. The sporadic need, the fitful demand, the special adaptation to regional resources or personal desires—all characteristic of small communities and handicraft operations—offered no incentive to complete automation. Rather, they remained obstacles to its achievement.

Here we come to the great paradox of both early mechanization and its ultimate expression in automation: so far from being responses to a mass demand, the enterpriser had in fact to create it; and in order to justify the heavy capital investment necessary to create automatic machines and automatic factories that assembled these machines in larger working units, it was necessary to invade distant markets, to standardize tastes and buying habits, to destroy alternative choices, and to wipe out competition from smaller industrial competitors, more dependent upon intimate face-to-face relations and more flexible in meeting consumer demands.

Sigfried Giedion's classic analysis of the processes of rationalization and automation, in 'Mechanization Takes Command,' demonstrates that the result of automation is not necessarily a better product; it merely enables the same product to be sold at a larger profit in a mass market. The growth of automated breadmaking has driven thousands of local bakers out of existence; but the result is neither a cheaper nor a superior loaf. What automation has done is to funnel its local energy-economies into long-distance transportation, advertising, higher salaries and profits, and further investments in plant expansion to the same ends. *The desired reward of this magic is not just abundance but absolute control.* Where the industry is sufficiently well unionized, the result is to extend this system of mass control to the labor union itself, under pseudo-democratic self-government.

5 : THE SAND IN THE WORKS

The process of automation has gone on steadily during the last century and a half. In the first stages of mechanization the number of workers needed to produce the final product was reduced, and the number of operations performed by any one laborer was likewise lessened, with a consequent loss of intelligent participation, as well as initiative, in the process as a whole. But the success of mechanization was gauged in terms of lessening the ratio of man-hours to the units of production, until finally, with complete automation and cybernetic control, only the minimum supervision of the whole plant remained, while the "work" left was little more than inspection and repair. Though computers and cybernetic controls are necessary when the overall unit is a complex assembly, there are essential likenesses between the automatic loom and an electric computer. For the latter, too, requires a human being to design it, to program it, and to monitor it.

When human monitors are lacking, serious breakdowns may occur—as more than one comic incident testifies. Witness the case of a defective machine in a fully automated English nuclear plant, which was programmed to call automatically for help in such case to a London station. Unfortunately, the taped voice which said: "Send an engineer at once" was answered by an equally automated telephone, which replied: "The number you are calling has been changed to . . . ," giving the new number. But the calling system had not been programmed to deal with new numbers, so getting no proper answer it kept on insistently dialing the original number—until the prolonged breakdown tardily awakened a human mind capable of intervening and summoning help.

But it is not to point out their frailties in operation that I have traced the tendency of mechanization and automation to form a self-enclosed system: one must expect residual errors or malfunctions in any product that comes from the hand of man; and where the object is an appropriate one the gains from automation may far outweigh the occasional disabilities one encounters. The point is that the most massive defects of automation are those that arise, not from its failures, but from its indisputable triumphs, above all, in those departments where the most optimistic hopes and boasts have been completely justified.

Let me emphasize: work in all its aspects has played a decisive, formative part in the enlargement of man's mind and the enrichment of his culture, not because man is identifiable solely as a tool-using animal, but because work is one of the many activities that have stimulated his intelligence and enlarged his bodily capacities. But if, for argument's sake, one accepts the still lingering anthropological identification of man's basic nature with tool-using and tool-making, what then should one say about the cumulative results of mechanization and automation, as they affect man's adaptive intelligence?

What merit is there in an over-developed technology which isolates the whole man from the work-process, reducing him to a cunning hand, a load-bearing back, or a magnifying eye, and then finally excluding him altogether from the process unless he is one of the experts who designs and assembles or programs the automatic machine? What meaning has a man's life as a worker if he ends up as a cheap servo-mechanism, trained solely to report defects or correct failures in a mechanism otherwise superior to him? If the first step in mechanization five thousand years ago was to reduce the worker to a docile and obedient drudge, the final stage automation promises today is to create a self-sufficient mechanical electronic complex that has no need even for such servile nonentities.

Curiously, all the while automatic processes were being perfected in industry, the leaders of nineteenth-century thought stressed, as never before, the human value of work as a way of easing anxiety and increasing the sum total of human happiness. Such a recognition of the dignity and value of work had been going on, sporadically, for a long time. While the pride of craft was an old one, it had been re-enforced by the creed of the Benedictine order, which held that 'to labor is to pray'; and it had gained institutional support in the medieval guild, which made a whole network of social relationships center in the workshop and its fellowship. Thus work in all its forms came to be regarded as the central activity of life: was it not indeed on these grounds that both manufacturers and workers despised the idle, playful, landed aristocracy, who for lack of serious work turned fox hunting and grouse shooting, polo and war and amatory adventure, into substitute forms of work, just as active, just as demanding?

Surely the time has come to reconsider the abolition of work. If work has been an integral part of human culture, and thus one of the active determinants of man's own nature for at least half a million years—and had perhaps its dim beginnings a million and a half years earlier, in the little hominoid ape that many anthropologists have too hastily identified as 'man'—what will remain of man's life if these formative activities are wiped out by universal cybernetics and automation?

Strange to say, it is only recently that the full implications of such a blanking out of the largest portion of man's working life has presented itself as a problem, though automation has been steadily gaining ground. Even now only a few realize that this problem, once honestly stated, seriously calls into question the ultimate goals of automation. As for the eventual assemblage of a completely automated world society, only innocents could contemplate such a goal as the highest possible culmination of human evolution. It would be a final solution to the problems of mankind, only in the sense that Hitler's extermination program was a final solution for the 'Jewish problem.'

6: THE PARADOX OF AUTOMATION

Here we face the great paradox of automation, put once and for all in Goethe's fable of the Sorcerer's Apprentice. Our civilization has cleverly found a magic formula for setting both industrial and academic brooms and pails of water to work by themselves, in ever-increasing quantities at an ever-increasing speed. But we have lost the Master Magician's spell for altering the tempo of this process, or halting it when it ceases to serve human functions and purposes, though this formula (foresight and feedback) is written plainly on every organic process.

As a result we are already, like the apprentice, beginning to drown in the flood. The moral should be plain: unless one has the power to stop an automatic process—and if necessary reverse it—one had better not start it. To spare ourselves humiliation over our failure to control automation, many of us now pretend that the process conforms exactly to our purposes and alone meets all our needs—or, to speak more accurately, we cast away those qualifying human traits that would impede the process. And as our knowledge of isolatable segments and fragments becomes infinitely refined and microscopic, our ability to interrelate the parts and to bring them to a focus in rational activities continues to disappear.

In even the most restricted area of knowledge—let us say virus diseases in the gastrointestinal tract of elderly earthworms—it is difficult for the most conscientious scholar to keep his head above water. To cope with the tidal wave of rapidly processed knowledge, the academic world has now taken the final step toward total automation: it has resorted to further 'mechanical' agents that only aggravate the original condition, because they seek to deal only with the results and do not dream of attacking the causes—namely, their own preconceptions and methods. The exponents of mass production of knowledge have created a hundred journals devoted only to abstracts of papers; and now a further abstract of all these abstracts has been proposed. At the terminal stage of this particular solution, all that will be left of the original scientific or scholarly paper will be a little vague noise, at most a title and a date, to indicate that someone has done something somewhere—no one knows what and Heaven knows why.

Though this program for the automatic mass production of knowledge originated in science, and shows characteristic seventeenth-century limitations, it has been imitated in the humanities, particularly in American universities, as a sort of status symbol, to underwrite budget requests in competition with the physical and social sciences, and to provide a quantitative measure for professional promotions. Whatever the original breach between the sciences and the humanities, in method they have now—*pace* Charles Snow!—become one. Though they run different assembly lines, they belong to the same factory. The mark of their common deficiency is that neither has given any serious consideration to the results of their uncontrolled automation.

Even a generation ago there was still a large margin for free activity and independent thinking within higher education. But today most of our larger academic institutions are as thoroughly automated as a steel-rolling mill or a telephone system: the mass production of scholarly papers, discoveries, inventions, patents, students, Ph.D.'s, professors, and publicity—not least, publicity!—goes on at a comparable rate; and only those who identify themselves with the goals of the power system, however humanly absurd, are in line for promotion, for big research grants, for the political power and the financial rewards allotted to those who 'go with' the system. The voluminous flow of corporate capital into the Educational Establishment, with a corresponding rise in money incentives for research, has proved in the United States the final step in making the University an integral part of the new power system.

Meanwhile, a vast amount of valuable knowledge becomes relegated, along with an even greater amount of triviality and trash, to a mountainous rubbish heap. For lack of a method with built-in qualitative standards, fostering constant evaluation and selectivity, and with assimilative processes that, as in the digestive system, would control both appetite and feeding, the superficial order of the individual packet is offset by the nature of the end product: for to know more and more about less and less is in the end simply to know less and less.

As a means for creating an orderly and intelligible world, the automation of knowledge has already come close to total bankruptcy; and the

current revolt of the university students, along with the even more threatening regression to total nihilism, is a symptom of this bankruptcy.

Do not, I beg, misinterpret this factual description of the automation of
knowledge as mischievous satire on my part; still less must it be taken as
an attack on science, scholarship, or the many exquisite feats of electronic
and cybernetic technology. No one but an idiot would belittle the immense
practical benefits and the exhilarating prospects for the human spirit that
the sciences, abetted by technics, have opened up. All I am saying here is
that the 'automation of automation' is now a demonstrable irrationality in
every department where it has taken hold: in the sciences and humanities
as much as in industry and warfare. And I suggest that this is an inherent
defect of any completely automated system, not an accidental one.

This irrationality was humorously summarized, with feigned exacti-
tude, by Derek Price; for he calculated that at the present rate of acceleration in scientific productivity alone, within a couple of centuries there will
be dozens of hypothetic scientists for every man, woman, child, and dog on
the planet. Fortunately, ecology teaches us that under such conditions of
overcrowding and stress, most of the population will have died off before it
reaches this point.

But there is no need to wait for the ultimate breakdown of this system
to foresee its consequences. Long before nearing the theoretic end, the
symptoms have become ominous. Already the great national and university
libraries are at their wits' end, not merely to find place for the books
already acquired—selective though that process has always been—but
even to catalog promptly the annual output of books, papers, and periodi-
cals. Without pausing to weigh the consequences many administrators are
now playing with the desperate notion of abandoning the preservation of
books entirely, as an obsolete form of the permanent record, and transfer-
ring the contents at once to microfilms and computers.

Unfortunately, "information retrieving," however swift, is no substitute
for discovering by direct personal inspection knowledge whose very
existence one had possibly never been aware of, and following it at one's
own pace through the further ramifications of relevant literature. But even
if books are not abandoned, but continue their present rate of production,
the multiplication of microfilms actually magnifies the central problem—
that of coping with quantity—and postpones the real solution, which
must be conceived on quite other than purely mechanical lines: namely, by
a reassertion of human selectivity and moral self-discipline, leading to
more continent productivity. Without such self-imposed restraints the overproduction of books will bring about a state of intellectual enervation and
depletion hardly to be distinguished from massive ignorance.

As the quantity of information increases in every field, to a point where
it defies individual appraisal and assimilation, an ever larger part of it must

be channeled through official distribution agencies. Though a trickle of fresh or unorthodox knowledge may still filter through to a miniscule minority by means of print, nothing will be transmitted further that does not conform to the current standards of the megamachine. This was neatly illustrated during the mounting Vietnam crisis in the United States, when television gave equal time to speakers who favored the official policy of seeking military victory and to those who favored entering into negotiations; but sedulously refrained from inviting those who, like myself, had put the case for unconditional withdrawal of American forces—at a time when this could still have been done without confessing a humiliating defeat.

Both the ancient and the contemporary control systems are based, essentially, on one-way communication, centrally organized. In face-to-face communication even the most ignorant person can answer back, and he has various means at his command besides the word—the expression of his face, the stance of his body, even threat of bodily assault. As the channels of instantaneous communication become more elaborate, the response must be officially staged, and this means, in ordinary circumstances, externally controlled. The attempt to overcome this difficulty with 'opinion polls' is only a more insidious way of maintaining control. The more complex the apparatus of transmission, the more effectively does it filter out every message that challenges or attacks the Pentagon of Power.

Though total control over the media of communication seems to give the modern megamachine a great advantage over the crude, earlier model, it is likely that its expansion may in the end hasten its breakdown, because of a lack of information needed for its own efficient performance. The refusal to accept such information even when offered becomes more ingrained as the system itself becomes more closely knit together.

Today the increasing number of mass protests, sit-downs, and riots— physical acts rather than words—may be interpreted as an attempt to break through the automatic insulation of the megamachine, with its tendency to cover up its own errors, to refuse unwelcome messages, or to block transmission of information damaging to the system itself. Smashed windows, burning buildings, broken heads are means of making humanly important messages take possession of the unmindful medium and so resume, though in the crudest form possible, two-way communication and reciprocal intercourse.

Once automatic control is installed one cannot refuse to accept its instructions, or insert new ones, for theoretically the machine cannot allow anyone to deviate from its own perfect standards. And this bring us at once to the most radical defect in every automated system: for its smooth operation this under-dimensioned system requires equally under-dimensioned men, whose values are those needed for the operation and the continued expansion of the system itself. The minds that are so conditioned are incapable of imagining any alternatives. Having opted for automation, they are committed to flouting any subjective reaction and to wiping out human autonomy—or indeed any organic process that does not accept the system's peculiar limitations.

Here, at the core of automation, lies its principal weakness once the system becomes universal. Its exponents, even if they are able to recognize its deficiencies, see no way of overcoming them except by a further extension of automation and cybernation. Thus a large-scale processing of compulsory leisure is now in order, to find profit-making substitutes for the vanished pleasures of work, which once brought an immediate human reward within the workshop, the marketplace, or the farm, both through the job itself and the many occasions for human association it opened up. The fact is, however, that an automatic system as a whole, once established, can accept no human feedback that calls for a cutback: therefore it accepts no evaluation of its deleterious results, still less is it ready to admit the need for correcting its postulates. Quantity is all. To question the value of mere quantitative increase in terms of its contribution to human well-being is to commit heresy and weaken the system.

Here finally we face another difficulty derived from automation itself. As the mechanical facilities of our educational institutions expand, with their heavy investment in nuclear reactors, their computers, their TV sets and tape recorders and learning machines, their machine-marked 'yes-or-no' examination papers, the human contents necessarily shrink in significance. What automation has done in every department where it has taken full command is to make difficult—in many cases impossible—the give-and-take that has existed hitherto between human beings and their environment; for the constant dialogue that is so necessary for self-knowledge, for social cooperation, and for moral evaluation and rectification, has no place in an automated regimen.

When Job's life miscarried, he was able, at least in imagination, to confront God and criticize his ways. But the suppression of personality is already so complete in an automated economy that the reputed heads of our great organizations are as incapable of changing its goals as the lowliest filing clerk. It is the system itself that, once set up, gives orders. As for anyone's confronting the principals in person, our automatic agencies are as obscure and as bafflingly inaccessible as the authorities that Franz Kafka pictured in his accurate prophetic nightmare, 'The Trial.' Humanly speaking, then, the proper name for automation is self-inflicted impotence. That is the other side of 'total control.'

While our technicians have been designing machines and automated systems to take on more of the attributes of living organisms, modern man himself, to fit into this scheme, finds he must accept the limitations of the machine and not ask for those qualitative and subjective attributes which the Mechanical World Picture originally failed to acknowledge, and which the machine-process, inevitably, does not possess.

What has proved quite as serious is that as the system of automation becomes more highly articulated, and thereby more self-sufficient and self-enclosed, it is less possible for anyone to intervene in the process, to alter its pace, to change its direction, to limit its further extension, or to reorient its goal. The parts may be flexible and responsive, as individual computers that play chess have demonstrated: but the larger automated system becomes increasingly rigid. Automation has thus a qualitative defect that springs directly from its quantitative accomplishments: briefly it increases probability and decreases possibility. Though the individual component of an automatic system may be programmed like a punch card on a motor-car assembly line, to deal with variety, the system itself is fixed and inflexible: so much so that it is little more than a neat mechanical model of a compulsion neurosis, and perhaps even springs from the same ultimate source—anxiety and insecurity.

7 : COMPULSIONS AND COERCIONS

While any new technical device may increase the range of human freedom, it does so only if the human beneficiaries are at liberty to accept it, to modify it, or to reject it: to use it where and when and how it suits their own purposes, in quantities that conform to those purposes.

Admittedly, the problem of preserving human freedom in the face of environmental, institutional, or technological pressures did not begin with the automatic machine. Custom, law, taboo, religious dogma, military coercion have all in the past imposed repetitive behavior and rigid conditions of performance upon earlier human communities. Some of this formalization was needful to ensure an underlying unanimity and coherence, serving as insurance against perverse random impulses and destructive acts. But there is little doubt that these uniformities, certainly in tribal societies, and in a large degree even in more open ones, often retarded human development. In almost every age, wise minds have sought to apply selective rational criteria to fixed customs and encrusted institutions, so as to modify if not eliminate constraints that have outlived their time.

But such inhibitions, such wariness, such discriminations have not yet been applied to the stream of inventions and discoveries that have come forward in every department. Western society has accepted as unquestionable a technological imperative that is quite as arbitrary as the most primitive taboo: not merely the duty to foster invention and constantly to create technological novelties, but equally the duty to surrender to these novelties unconditionally just because they are offered, without respect to their human consequences. One may without exaggeration now speak of technological compulsiveness: a condition under which society meekly submits to every new technological demand and utilizes without question every new product, whether it is an actual improvement or not; since under this dispensation the fact that the proffered product is the result of a new scientific discovery or a new technological process, or offers new opportunities for investment, constitutes the sole proof required of its value.

This situation was well characterized by the mathematician John von Neumann: "Technological possibilities are irresistible to man. If man *can* go to the moon, he *will*. If he can control the climate, he will." Though von Neumann himself was properly alarmed by this condition, he himself attributed too glibly to 'man' characteristics that belong only to this particular moment of Western culture, which has so concentrated its energies and its hopes for salvation on the machine that it has stripped itself of all the ideas, institutions, and habits that have in the past enabled other civilizations to overcome these obsessions and compulsions. Earlier communities, in contrast, strenuously resisted technological innovations—sometimes quite unreasonably—and either delayed them until they conformed to other human requirements and proved their worth, or rejected them altogether.

Now there is no doubt that the 'irresistible' impulse that von Neumann has described actually pervades the present-day scientific and technological world. Hermann Muller, the American geneticist, used von Neumann's dictum as a clincher in his argument for establishing genetic controls by scientists over the breeding of human populations. Speaking of the possibility of using banks of frozen human sperm cells taken from 'geniuses,' as one now preserves similar cells from prize bulls, Muller said, with alarming naïveté, "Their mere existence will finally result in an irresistible incentive to use them." Psychologists know this "irresistible incentive" in many forms: for at the moment any impulse, however normal, becomes irresistible in its own right and for no other reason than that it exists, it becomes pathological, and the unawareness of this pathology among scientists whose discipline supposedly serves as a safeguard against irrational conclusions or actions is just a further evidence of that pathology.

There is a simple way of establishing the downright absurdity—or more accurately the menacing irrationality—of accepting such technological compulsiveness; and that is to carry von Neumann's dictum to its logical conclusion: *If man has the power to exterminate all life on earth, he will.* Since we know that the governments of the United States and Soviet

Russia have already created nuclear, chemical, and bacterial agents in the massive quantities needed to wipe out the human race, what prospects are there of human survival, if this practice of submitting to extravagant and dehumanized technological imperatives is 'irresistibly' carried to its final stage?

In the light of these facts, the central problem of technics must be restated: *It is that of creating human beings capable of understanding their own nature sufficiently to control, and when necessary to suppress, the forces and mechanisms that they have brought into existence.* No automatic warning system can solve this problem for us.

But first we must dig deeper into our innermost being to discover the basis for these coercive promptings. We must ask ourselves: Why does every permission turn into a compulsion? Why is the secret motto of our power-oriented society not just "You can, therefore you may," but "You may, therefore you must." Is *that* the freedom science once promised? What one discovers beneath the surface of this scientific determinism is an even more sinister trait: a primitive fatalism, subjectively conditioned.

During the last generation scientist after scientist has anxiously pointed out—or else boastfully proclaimed—that scientific discoveries and their technical applications were proceeding faster than our ability to assimilate them and direct them to valuable ends. Yet so great is the professional compulsion to apply raw, insufficiently tested knowledge immediately, that permanent damage is still being done to both the environment and all its organisms, not least to man himself. By now it should be obvious that this methodology which professed to eliminate subjectivity from its world picture provided no way of recognizing its own subjective inflations, distortions, and perversions.

Once the translation of organic and human aptitudes into their system-controlled mechanical counterparts has fully taken place, man will have given up the full use of even his physical organs. There are already areas in the United States where people have lost the free exercise of their legs: in many California suburbs pedestrians are arrested by the police even in broad daylight as suspicious characters. The next step will be to imprison anyone who uses his own voice to sing instead of turning on his portable transistor radio; and even the possibility of indulging in autonomous daydreams has been largely taken over by centrally directed TV and radio. Big Brother did not wait for 1984 to establish his ascendancy: a host of Little Brothers, wearing the same badge, have crept into every department. With these ultimate modes of imprisonment I shall deal more fully later.

Here I would ask only one question—if man's own life is inherently so worthless, by what magic is it improved by being fed into a collective machine? And if the world we have put together with the aid of science is, by its own definition, a world that excludes values, by what logic can we assign values to either science or automation? When one empties out the proper life of man, all that is left, humanly speaking, is emptiness. To find a rational answer to the problem of relating mechanization and automation to the needs of man, we must fill up all the blank subjective spaces that were left vacant in the mechanical world picture.

8: FINAL STAGE: THE BIG BRAIN

"We have become thoroughly familiar with the implications of the statement that 'the steam engine and muscles both do work,' but we are uneasy with 'calculating machines and brains both think.' " As the writer of this statement, Professor J. Z. Young, sees clearly, the difference between these two statements is as great as their resemblance, for computers, though they perform some of the most difficult and laborious operations of abstract thought with incredible rapidity, are only automatically carrying out instructions given to them by a mind that does think.

Experiment had demonstrated that machines made of solid moving parts can transpose only very elementary mental operations, such as those of an old-fashioned adding machine. When Charles Babbage made his first daring effort to put together his 'Calculating Engine,' he sought to lighten the drudgery of those condemned to make laborious astronomical computations: but the design and organization of this machine proved so difficult that the original model was never finished—though, incidentally, the further demands it made for clockwork precision helped to develop the skill of a new generation of mechanics, who could build other complex machines that were already in demand. This elementary mode of thought demanded an electronic system capable of operating even more swiftly than the brain.

The electronic computer was modelled—if quite unconsciously—upon the human brain; and in turn, by its simplification and reduction of the brain's operations, it threw a further light upon the organic electrochemistry of recording, decoding, and composing messages. And whereas the behavior of ordinary machines can be adequately analyzed by the physical sciences, it is hardly surprising that the functions of a computer call, not only for physicists and electronic technicians, but for brain physiologists, linguists, logicians. The more lifelike computers become the more numerous and diversified these supernumeraries will be.

With the collective consequences—many of them socially disruptive—of extending the operations of the computer into areas hitherto under the direct control of man, I shall deal when we come to examine the new megamachine: but here I wish to consider only its immediate effect in bringing to a conclusion the processes that began with the mechanical clock. What it is important to realize is that automation, in this final form, is an attempt to exercise control, not only of the mechanical process itself, but of the human being who once directed it: turning him from an active to a passive agent, and finally eliminating him altogether.

The scientist who emphasized the function of control, by giving computerized direction the name of cybernetics was Dr. Norbert Wiener; and probably no one else contributed more to the early development of this series of inventions. Wiener helped endow the computer with some of the specialized attributes of human intelligence, including the capacity to absorb fresh information and to correct its own errors or failures (feedback). Yet no one better realized the problems that the independence of the computer from human intervention would raise; and no one was more concerned than he over the peculiar fascination automated systems would have for autocratic minds, eager to confine human reactions to those that conform to the limited data they are capable of programming. Technicians who themselves lack other purposes and values, memories and feelings, see no human deficiency in their seemingly superhuman machine, or in the kind of demands that they themselves make on it.

Norbert Wiener, in contrast, respected man's autonomy, his unpredictability, and his moral responsibility: the very qualities that those who now seek to extend the realm of automation in every direction—those "priests of power," as Wiener called them—have deliberately sought to eliminate. On this matter Wiener demands to be quoted at length.

"If we use, to achieve our purposes, a mechanical agency with whose operation we cannot efficiently interfere once we have started it, because the action is so fast and irrevocable that we have not the data to intervene before the action is complete, then we had better be quite sure that the purpose put into the machine is the purpose which we really desire and not merely a colorful imitation of it.

"The individual scientist must work as a part of a process whose time scale is so long that he himself can only contemplate a very limited section of it. Here, too, communication between the two parts of a double machine is difficult and limited. Even when the individual believes that science contributes to the human ends which he has at heart, his belief needs a continual scanning and re-evaluation which is only partly possible. For the individual scientist, even the partial appraisal of this liaison between the man and the process requires an imaginative forward glance at history which is difficult, exacting and only limitedly achievable. And if we adhere simply to the creed of the scientist, that an incomplete knowledge of the world and of ourselves is better than no knowledge, we can still by no means always justify the naive assumption that the faster we rush ahead to employ the new powers for action which are opened up to us, the better it will be. We must always exert the full strength of our imagination to examine where the full use of our new modalities may lead us."*

In the natural exultation of discovering how many lifelike functions can by abstraction be transferred to the computer, its total effectiveness in a real life situation has been often over-rated, and its competitive advantage has been exaggerated. Let me give two significant instances. The National Library of Medicine at Bethesda, Maryland, has an information retrieval service (MEDLARS), designed to index the medical periodical literature of about 2,800 journals. This system has been in operation since 1963 and by 1968 half a million articles were in storage. To compare the results of a computerized search with those made in a conventional manner, two members of the Radcliffe Science Library staff in England compiled a list of references on the same subject, covering the same period as the MEDLARS taped record. Though nine relevant references in MEDLARS were not discovered by the Library Staff, they dug out thirteen relevant references not included. Alike on grounds of promptness and low cost and qualitative value human agents proved preferable to the automation.

But an even more dramatic instance was provided by the Apollo 11 Moon Landing. At a critical moment in making the descent to the moon, the astronauts' computer repeatedly announced its inability to handle the data: in human terms, it panicked; so that the ground control officers were at one moment on the point of aborting the mission. Fortunately, they made the radical decision to close off the computer and let the astronauts alone manage the final stages of the landing.

The life-efficiency and adaptability of the computer must be questioned. Its judicious use depends upon the ability of its human employers quite literally to keep their own heads, not merely to scrutinize the programming but to reserve for themselves the right of ultimate decision. No automatic system can be intelligently run by automatons—or by people who dare not assert human intuition, human autonomy, human purpose.

Curiously Wiener's anxieties about automatism had been anticipated by John Stuart Mill, for similar reasons, in his 'Essay on Liberty.' "Supposing," Mill said, "that it were possible to get houses built, corn grown, battles fought, causes tried, and even churches erected and prayers said by machinery—by automatons in human form—it would be a considerable loss to exchange for these automatons even the men and women who at present inhabit the more civilized parts of the world, and who assuredly are but starved specimens of what nature can and will produce."

* "Some Moral and Technical Consequences of Automation," in 'Science,' 6 May 1960.

What Mill realized at this early moment, and what Wiener later emphasized, is that the sum total of human potentialities in any community is infinitely richer than the limited number that can be installed in a closed system—and all automatic systems are closed and limited—even those computers that are capable of learning through further use of the material already provided. By reason of its very nature no computer can be as wealthy in life-experience and tested information as a great city.

Obviously computers cannot invent new symbols or conceive new ideas not already outlined in the very setting up of their programs. Within its strict limits, a computer can perform logical operations intelligently, and even, given a program that includes random factors, can simulate 'creation,' but under no circumstances can it dream of a different mode of organization than its own. Faced with the problem of translation from one language to another—a function once hopefully assigned to the computer—its choices become absurd and its meanings scrambled, as in a case of brain damage.

Man, on the contrary, is constitutionally an open system, reacting to another open system, that of nature. Only an infinitesimal part of either system can be interpreted by man, or come under his control, and only an even minuter portion accordingly falls within the province of the computer. At any moment new and unexpected factors of subjective origin may upset or falsify the computer's most confident predictions—which latter has happened more than once in election forecasts. Such order as man has achieved through his laws and customs, his ideologies and moral codes, has proved precious—however infirm—precisely because it helps to keep both organic systems open without permitting man's capability for integration to be totally destroyed by exorbitant quantifications or irrelevant novelties.

By now it should be plain that many of the exorbitant hopes for a computer-dominated society are subjective emanations from the 'pecuniary-pleasure' center. Even hopes for the total elimination of the worker have proved somewhat premature. For every manual worker who is eliminated from an ancient craft or thrown off the assembly line, it turns out that a bureaucratic substitute, capable of feeding and nursing the vast cybernetic pseudo-organism that is coming into existence, will be needed: if not directly at the point of production, then in business corporations and government departments, in the universities and research institutes, in the sanitoria and hospitals engaged in the expansion of both mental and corporeal modes of control. The most sterile form of work possible, 'paper work,' without even such muscular exercise as manual work afforded, has increased by leaps and bounds; and the resulting degeneration of responsive and responsible intelligence is equally patent here. The notion that automation gives any guarantee of human liberation is a piece of wishful thinking.

At all events, the most serious threat of computer-controlled automation comes, not so much from the displacement of the worker in the process of manufacture, as in the displacement of the human mind and the insidious undermining of confidence in its ability to make individual judgements that run contrary to the system—or that proceed outside the system. I have before me "The Systemation Letter" circulated by a branch of a corporation pre-eminent in inventing and manufacturing computers: it shows how automation extends from the machine back to the organizations utilizing systems methods, with or without computer adjuncts: and from them back to the individual. The point of this letter is that "Deviation from the System can destroy control."

The most disastrous result of automation, then, is that its final product is Automated or Organization Man: he who takes all his orders from the system, and who, as scientist, engineer, expert, administrator, or, finally, as consumer and subject, cannot conceive of any departure from the system, even in the interest of efficiency, still less for the sake of creating a more intelligent, vivid, purposeful, humanly rewarding mode of life.

How deeply ingrained the commitment to automatism has become appears from a sad little tale passed on to me by Dennis Gabor, sometime Professor of Engineering at the Imperial College of Technology in London, himself an adept in some of the most advanced branches of science-oriented technology.

"I do not think that I have told you about a great hope which I had three years ago. I heard that IBM-France had made a remarkable experiment. In their great factory at Corbeil-Essonnes they made a break with division of labor. One technician completed a sizable element of a computer, using hundreds of tools, tested it himself, and *signed it,* like an artist! I heard also that the gain in interest and the development in intelligence of these workmen was fabulous. Thereupon I wrote an enthusiastic letter to IBM-France and asked to visit them. I got a crestfallen letter, that 'until now it was indeed like this—but their new factory will be fully automated!' " IBM was plainly not concerned with increasing *human* intelligence or giving back to machine workers the quality of life that once was fostered by the higher crafts.

This story sums up what I have been trying to tell. The process of automation has produced imprisoned minds that have no capacity for appraising the results of their process, except by the archaic criteria of power and prestige, property, productivity and profit, segregated from any more vital human goals. The Pentagon of Power. By its own logic automation is dedicated to the installation of a system of total control over every natural process, and ultimately over every organic function and human purpose. Not strangely, the one part of this civilization that escapes the principle of total control is—automation itself! The country in which this mode of collective servitude has been carried furthest has been taught by its information-manipulators (public relations specialists) to call this system 'Free Enterprise.' No wonder the recalcitrant IBM employee, who sent me the Systemation Letter from which I have quoted, accompanied it with an IBM punch card on which a single word was written—"Help!"

But at this terminal point, where the automatic process is on the verge of creating a whole race of acquiescent and obedient human automatons, the forces of life have begun, sometimes stealthily, sometimes ostentatiously, to re-assert themselves in the only form that is left them: an explosive affirmation of the primal energies of the organism. Already we are faced with a reaction from civilization more desperate than any hitherto visible on the historic record—partly a wishful withdrawal, to some more bucolic simplicity, but often in utter desperation to a state anterior to the most primitive human institutions—that which Shakespeare characterized as Caliban, and Freud as the primal under-layer of the human personality, the Id.

For mark this: the automaton was not born alone. The automaton has been accompanied, we can now see, by a twin, a dark shadow-self: defiant, not docile: disorderly, not organized or controlled: above all, aggressively destructive, even homicidal, reasserting the dammed-up forces of life in crazy or criminal acts. In the emerging figure of man, the sub-ego or id threatens to function as the superego in a reversed hierarchy that lowers the authority of the brain and puts the reflexes and blind instincts in command. The aim of this subversive superego is to destroy those higher attributes of man whose gifts of love, mutuality, rationality, imagination, and constructive aptitude have enlarged all the possibilities of life. It is in the light of these impending negations and destructions that the whole concept of subjugating nature and replacing man's own functions with collectively fabricated, automatically operated, completely depersonalized equivalents must at last be reappraised.

9: FORWARD TO 'NOWHERE'

The credit for understanding the full implications of automation belongs, not to any contemporary scientist or technician, but to the Victorian satirist Samuel Butler, a true descendant of Jonathan Swift, who anticipated so many of the absurdities and ostentatious trivialities of our present-day society in his description of Laputa, in 'Gulliver's Travels.'

Butler's original letter to 'The Press' in Christchurch, New Zealand, was published in 1863 and reproduced later in his 'Notebooks.'

As a young sheep rancher with time to ruminate over Darwin's recent work, 'On the Origin of Species'—daring to draw further conclusions, as no incipient Ph.D. would dare today, even had he the time—Butler sensitively pursued the forces already actively at work in society to their probable future. Butler was the first to see plainly that if Darwin's theory of evolution was correct, it could not arbitrarily stop short at the physical evolution of man, or assume that this age-old process was now terminated. Like most of his contemporaries—and ours—he believed that "there are few things of which the present generation is more justly proud than of the wonderful improvements which are daily taking place in all sorts of contrivances." But he could not refrain from asking: ". . . what the end of this mighty movement is to be? In what direction is it tending? What will be its upshot?"

His answer was that as the vegetable kingdom had developed from the mineral and the animal had supervened upon the vegetable, so now "in these last few ages, an entirely new kingdom has sprung up of which we have as yet only seen what will one day be considered the antediluvian prototypes of the race"—namely, the mechanical kingdom. By adding daily to the beauty and the delicacy of the physical organization of machines, Butler observed, man was creating his own successors, "giving them greater power and supplying by all sorts of ingenious contrivances that self-regulating and self-acting power which will be to them what intellect has been to the human race. In the course of ages, we shall find ourselves the inferior race."

This transposition of life into mechanical organizations will, Butler pointed out, eliminate man's most serious difficulty: that of developing his own capacities to become human. In the moral quality of self-control, the machines would be so superior that man would "look up to them as the acme of all that the best and wisest man can ever dare to aim at. No evil passions, no jealousy, no avarice, no impure desires will disturb the serene might of those glorious creatures. Sin, shame, and sorrow will have no place among them. . . . If they want 'feeling' (by the use of which very word we betray our recognition of them as living organisms) they will be attended by patient slaves whose business and interest will be to see that they want nothing." Anticipating Norbert Wiener, Butler even embraced the possibility of a machine's reproducing another machine as at least a remote prospect.

"Day by day," Butler concluded, "the machines are gaining ground upon us; day by day we are becoming more subservient to them; more men are daily bound down as slaves to tend them, more men are daily devoting the energies of their whole lives to the development of mechanical life. The upshot is simply a question of time, but that the time will come when the machines will hold the real supremacy over the world and its inhabitants is what no person of a truly philosophic mind can for a moment question."

Having accurately foreseen what is actually happening in the present age, Butler reacted against his own logic by putting forward, obviously with his tongue in his cheek, an absurd remedy. "War to the death should be instantly proclaimed against [the machines]. . . . Let us go back to the primeval condition of the human race. If it be urged that this is impossible under the present condition of human affairs, this at once proves that the mischief is already done, that our servitude has commenced in good earnest, that we have raised a race of beings whom it is beyond our power to destroy and that we are not only enslaved but are absolutely acquiescent in our bondage."

Butler seems to have been frightened by his own intuitions: so much so that he promptly sought security, as many of the readers of this passage will doubtless do, by joining the defenders of total automation. In a second letter to the same newspaper, Butler, on a contrary tack, stated the case for all technical development, from the most rudimentary flint 'hand-axe,' to the most exquisitely organized automatic machine. Correctly, he pointed out that the machine is an extension of man's organic properties, a further development of his bodily gifts, enlarging their range and adding new qualities, as musical instruments extend the range and quality of the human voice. As docile slaves machines are as innocent and as helpful as the fingers of one's hand.

But there is a difference between using the machine to extend human capabilities, and using it to contract, eliminate, or replace human functions. In the first, man still exercises authority on his own behalf; in the second, the machine takes over and man becomes a supernumerary. This brought Butler back to the problem he had frivolously evaded when he suggested a massacre of the machines: the question of what changes are necessary in order to restore and confirm man's control over his own creations.

When Butler returned to this problem in his topsy-turvy satire, 'Erewhon,' he took refuge in a humorous compromise, allowing a certain basic equipment of traditional machines, but providing for the destruction of machines invented after an arbitrary date, and punishing heavily all future attempts at invention. This was a slippery evasion of the real problem: that of establishing a method of evaluation, selection, and control. Yet Butler's insight, for all his whimsical masking of it, showed a fuller grasp of the difficulties mankind now actually faces than most of our contemporaries yet do; for a large part of 'advanced' thought today in both science and technics is directed toward feeding into the machine more and more human components, without even a quiver of concern over what will be left of man's life if this process goes on indefinitely.

It was Butler's merit to see through this technological obsession: to point out that the beneficiary of total mechanization would not be man himself but the machines which had turned into *Ersatz* love objects, and would soon pass from being fetishes to being gods. Butler saw that the program of mechanization would serve not to make man more powerful and intelligent, but to make him totally unnecessary—a trivial accessory of the machine, a lobotomized dwarf whose immense organic potentialities would be extirpated in order to conform to the requirements of the machine.

In foreseeing the blank wall at the end of this blind alley, Butler was prescient: "The power of custom is enormous, and so gradual will be the change that man's sense of what is due to himself will at no time be rudely shocked; our bondage will steal upon us noiselessly and by imperceptible approaches; nor will there ever be a decisive clash of desire between man and the machines as will lead to an encounter between them." Even more accurately, Butler observed in still another passage, in his later fantasy, 'Erewhon,' "We cannot calculate any corresponding advances in man's intellectual or physical powers which shall be set off against the far greater development that seems in store for the machines. Some people may say that man's moral influence will suffice to rule them; but I cannot think that it will ever be safe to repose much trust in the moral sense of a machine."

Lifted from its satiric setting, what could be a more realistic anticipation of the events, the institutions, and the state of mind we face today? But it is not in the textbooks of physics and engineering, nor yet in the fashionable standardized predictions of the technological future, whether parading as sociology or as science fiction, that these eventualities can be explored. For Butler was not merely dealing with the tangible inventions and discoveries of his period: he had taken note of the possibility of a more profound and universal change: one that would dismember the human organism in order to reconstitute it as a life-simulating, life-replacing collective machine.

Butler himself recoiled from this ultimate nihilism, and passed it off as a wry jest. But if he had been a religious prophet, rather than a satirist, he might have uttered the final words on this whole development, words used long ago by Isaiah. "Ye turn things upside down! Shall the potter be counted as clay? that the thing made should say of him that made it, He made me not; or the thing framed of him that framed it, He hath no understanding?" A century after Butler, these questions now thunder ominously in our ears.

CHAPTER EIGHT

Progress as 'Science Fiction'

1: THE WHEELS OF PROGRESS

Behind the scientific discoveries and technical inventions that rapidly accumulated after the sixteenth century one must recognize the constant influence of the cosmic and mechanical world picture which accompanied them. Although the technical innovations themselves were new, the animus behind them had existed in a shadowy form ever since the Pyramid Age, awaiting only the reincarnation of the Sun God, so to say, in order to take effect.

"The essential feeling of all the earliest work," noted Flinders Petrie of the Egyptians, "is rivalry with nature"; and this feeling of rivalry, the desire to conquer Nature and control all her manifestations, in an almost literal sense to get on top of her, has been one of the distinguishing marks of modern man. In that respect, Petrarch's famous feat of climbing Mont Ventoux for no other purpose than the climb itself—conquering space, rising above the earth—might be taken as the harbinger of this new age. That aspiration has now culminated in a walk on the moon.

By the eighteenth century, a subtle transposition of values had begun to take place, as technics itself began to occupy a larger place. If the goal of technics was to improve the condition of man, the goal of man was to become ever more narrowly confined to the improvement of technology. Mechanical progress and human progress came to be regarded as one; and both were theoretically limitless.

To understand how the idea of technical progress achieved such widespread acceptance as a quasi-religious faith during the nineteenth century, one must examine its history, which is a curiously brief one. There have been periods in every high culture when evidence of technical improvements were plainly visible: as in the replacement of bronze tools and weapons with iron ones, or in the conversion of the rude wooden temples of seventh-century Greece to the masterly marble forms of the fifth century—themselves made possible by redoubtable engineering ability in cutting, transporting, and erecting huge blocks of stone. But though these improvements were striking enough to incite imitation, they did not breed any sense of their inevitability, nor did they presage a long series of improvements in other fields. Strangely, those who sought human perfection were still inclined to look for it in an earlier age: they sought to recover a simplicity that had been lost, a humanity that only later had been corrupted. Even the Jewish people, who had a sense of their historic mission, found it easier to go back to Moses than forward to a new Messiah.

The earliest idea of progress was perhaps latent in the Christian notion of self-perfection for divine ends; and its ideal consummation, if not reversion to the Golden Age, was that of an equally static future in Heaven —a future not to be enjoyed by the whole community, since it also included for the wicked the possibility of an equally long but painful residence in Hell. The notion of progress likewise had its roots, as Tuveson has demonstrated, in the latter-day belief in a coming millennium, not in a passage to a remote Heaven but to a more tangible Heaven that was about to arrive on earth.

This idea was expressed as early as 1699 by John Edwards, an orthodox divine. The interesting thing about his statement is that in contrast to the earlier Anabaptists, who, too, had millennial social visions, and even experimented beatnik-fashion with their realization, he felt that improvements in natural and "mechanick" philosophy were being matched by improvements in Divine Knowledge, so that physical nature and human nature would be renewed simultaneously. Result: "the virtuosi will improve natural philosophy, the soil will regain its original fertility, life will be more comfortable. The inheritors of the Utopian earth will be not the risen saints but simply posterity." It would be hard to find a single sentence anywhere that encompassed so many of the focal ideas of progress: science, specialized skill, comforts, moral elevation, utopia, the future. In brief, Heaven would at last come down to earth, and "mechanick philosophy" would bring this about.

A few generations later, the idea of progress was put forth in its broadest form by Turgot and Edward Gibbon. Turgot, a Minister of State under Louis XVI and an unusually well-balanced mind, did not regard progress as a simple by-product of technology, but as due to human genius. Much as he admired science and anticipated a time when all truths might be stated in abstract mathematical form, he rather attached the possibility of progress to an innate human tendency to innovate, to create novelty, in counteraction to an equally observable tendency, to repress innovations and reforms, and to take refuge in a state of "treadmill repetitiveness." So one turns for a less qualified version of the idea to Gibbon, in his comforting final words in 'The Decline and Fall of the Roman Empire.'

"Every age of the world," Gibbon observed, *"has increased and still increases, the real wealth, the happiness, the knowledge, and perhaps the virtue of the human race."*

This picture of a steady, persistent, almost inevitable accumulation of improvements reflected not merely the bland optimism of 'Enlightenment' intellectuals, but also their self-flattering notion of their own place in human history; for the leaders of this movement, from Voltaire on—but here one must except Turgot!—believed that past cultures, particularly that of the Middle Ages, had been the victims of blind instincts, besotted ignorance, priestly repressions, and ruthless tyrants. Once the monstrous ideas and practices of the past were extirpated—they were particularly hostile to Gothic architecture!—all men would be moved and governed by reason alone, in conformity with the innate goodness of human nature. But if Gibbon's observation was well-founded, human improvement had never ceased: it was guaranteed by the nature of things. Each later generation surpassed all earlier achievements.

This conversion to the doctrine of progress had come swiftly. At the beginning of the eighteenth century the Duc de Saint-Simon described the forebodings of his eminent contemporary Marshal de Catinat, as follows: "He deplored the errors of the time, which he saw follow each other in endless succession: the deliberate discouragement of zeal, the spread of luxury . . . Looking at the signs of the times, he thought he discovered every element of the impending destruction of the State"; while before him a sixteenth-century observer, Louis Le Roy, had pointed out that every great civilization, after reaching a certain point, had declined.

What was a dire, if well-founded, foreboding to Marshal de Catinat became, for the progressive minds of the eighteenth century, a happy promise. They measured progress by the number of antiquated institutions that could be cast off. If progress be considered a linear movement through time, it may be taken in two ways: getting closer to a desired goal, or getting further away from a starting point. Those who favored progress simple-mindedly believed that evils were the property of the past and that only by moving away from the past as rapidly as possible could a better future be assured.

There were just enough traces of truth in this doctrine to make its radical fallacies more dangerous. All civilizations had carried with them for some five thousand years, I emphasize again, the traumatic institutions that had accompanied the rise of earlier power systems: human sacrifice, war, slavery, forced labor, arbitrary inequalities in wealth and privilege. But along with these evils had come also a considerable accumulation of goods, whose conservation and transmission were essential to man's own humanization and further improvement. The exponents of progress were too committed to their doctrine to anticipate that the authoritarian institutions they sought to destroy forever might come back more oppressively than ever, fortified through the very science and technics that they valued as a means of emancipation from the past.

A century later the curious assumption of continuous and inevitable progress, which made no allowance for observable organic processes—decay and destruction, lapses and breaks, arrests and regressions—would be voiced with fatuous confidence by the popular French philosopher Victor Cousin: "Think of it, gentlemen, nothing regresses, everything moves ahead." On that same principle today, contemporary prophets of progress have hailed the supersonic plane, with its physically destructive booms, its violent shock to the nervous system, its pollution of the air, and its eventual deterioration of the climate, as an inevitable contribution to transportation progress; though they have not been able to point to a single function, apart from military assault, that could not be adequately performed, as in the past, with greater comfort and safety, by a less shattering mode of transportation at a lower speed.

Now the strangest part of Gibbon's statement is that it occurs in the midst of a book that exhibited in detail just the opposite process. What Gibbon's grand historic survey disclosed was how the primal flow of energy that had raised Roman civilization to such a high level in so many fields, notably engineering, city building, and public law, was actually, within a few centuries, reversed: how throughout the great Roman imperium the 'wheels of progress' gradually ground to a halt: how important knowledge was lost, technical efficiency lowered, and once highly disciplined armed forces became greedy, rowdy mobs. Finally Gibbon's evidence showed how in a succession of retreats and defeats the once-viable goods of Rome had turned into evils, while the poverty, insecurity, and ignorance it had boasted of conquering had, before the incredulous eyes of cultivated Romans, served as the organizing nucleus of a more creative Christian order, which gathered to itself the ebbing energies of the older culture and polarized them around a negative conception of earthly life.

Parallel reversals had taken place, as even an eighteenth-century historian could know, not once in human history but many times before, with a similar break in tradition, a loss of knowledge, a dissipation of real wealth, to say nothing of outbreaks of violence and a general inordinate increase of human misery. These patent historic facts made nonsense of Gibbon's description of the steady increase of wealth and happiness. And if the doctrine of progress provided a key to a new future, there was certainly nothing in Gibbon's summary statement—though much in his historic description—to prepare his own countrymen for the reversal of technological 'Progress,' followed by a similar retreat and collapse throughout the British Empire. In his own imagination, indeed, he had already seen some future Gibbon surveying the ruins of London, as he had viewed those of Rome.

What Gibbon was in fact celebrating was not the realities of human progress but the smug feeling of superiority and security enjoyed by the British upper classes, who thought that in time humane intelligence would assume control of every institution and even ensure that the comforts and luxuries of the dominant minority would be passed on in appropriately diluted and vulgarized form, to the rest of the population: the essential doctrine of Whig 'Liberalism.' On this assumption Gibbon could even say, only a few years before the American and the French Revolutions—actually the beginning of two centuries of national uprisings, class struggles, imperialist conquests, and savage repressions—that there was no longer any need for revolutions!

The equation of mechanical with moral progress, once implanted in the Western mind, became a generally accepted doctrine, denied only in the Catholic countries of Western Europe, or in backward continents that the machine had not yet penetrated. Each successful new invention only supported further this unqualified faith in a corresponding human improvement. Naturally, the belief in the inevitability of progress tended for a while to bring further evidence of it into existence, just as an unqualified belief in a witch-doctor's powers often ensures the working of his magic curses or cures. Since the idea of progress had no way of accounting for new evils or regressions, it tended to sweep away the voluminous evidence, both historic and contemporary, of their existence. To count only the benefits and to take no notice of the losses proved the standard method of retaining the millennial assumptions on which the doctrine of progress had originally been built. But even in material comforts progress had been so uneven that, as Winston Churchill once wryly remarked, English mansions in the twentieth century still lacked central heating, which had been enjoyed by their Roman prototypes almost two thousand years before.

'Progress,' naturally, meant different things to different minds: one thing to Diderot and Condorcet, another to Marx and Comte, another to Herbert Spencer and Charles Darwin, and still another to present-day continuators. Meanwhile the valid notion of filling up and drawing upon a permanent cultural reservoir, which still partly made sense to Gibbon, dropped out of the concept.

Voltaire's grinning formula for progress—to strangle the last king with the entrails of the last priest—seemed to fellow-enthusiasts an admirable way of wiping the slate clean and setting society up on an entirely rational basis. Even those who might be shocked by this sadistic proposal neverthe-less followed in other fields the ":scorched earth" policy of razing the past as a means of hastening the advance into the future. Gibbon's doctrine had accepted the fact that the goods of civilization are cumulative, rather than successive: but once movement away from the past became the criterion of progress, the function of accumulation was turned over to museums.

2: EVOLUTION AND RETROGRESSION

What was lacking in the new concept of progress were two realities that were later included in the concept of evolution; but since the two emerged almost simultaneously, they were often, unfortunately, confused in popular thought. Evolution focussed on the central fact of organic life itself. In this evolutionary perspective, mass, energy, and motion do not account for anything but the abstract groundwork of life. Unlike 'physical' energies which run only in one direction, downhill, organic activities are bipolar, both positive and negative, active and passive, building up and tearing down, accumulating and selecting, in short, growing, reproducing, and dying. When the positive processes (counter-entropy or growth) have the upper hand, if only by a small and temporary margin, life prospers.

"Crawling upward on the spiral of form," the earthworm may, in Emerson's laconic metaphor, "become a man." The creature does not 'progress' by increasing its rate of growth and becoming merely a bigger earthworm, or the begetter of vaster numbers of earthworms. In countless organisms keeping alive and reproducing, 'holding their own,' does, in fact, constitute their success as a species, though merely by existing they may enrich the environment sufficiently to help other species to prosper, as the lowly plankton supports the sperm whale.

Along only one route so far visible has organic evolution resulted in consistent progressive change: in the development of the mammalian nervous system. While the kidneys and lungs were invented tens of millions of years ago, the nervous system has indeed steadily become more ample and adequate; and in man it underwent extraordinary growth during the last five hundred thousand years. Thanks to this nervous system and the products it has fashioned out of its own mind-stuff, signs and symbols, man lives in a world infinitely more wealthy in possibilities than any other creature. There alone, in the human mind, does the idea of progress have a serious content—or offer the prospect of a better future.

But a salient fact about this singular, evolutionary development must be noted: it has supplemented natural selection by a cultural selection that has not only modified man's own environment and his way of life, but has brought out new potentialities in his own nature, such as the playful mastery of mathematical abstractions, which could not have been anticipated when man began to count on his fingers. Until the invention of symbols, technological progress through manipulation and manual work played only a small part in that basic transformation.

This story, which has been pieced together only within the last century, modifies the whole conception of progress, for it separates mind-forming evolutionary developments within the human species, the culture, and the emergent personality, from those purely material advances in tools, weapons, and utensils that colored the nineteenth-century doctrines.

But while evolution discloses occasional leaps and creative sorties, it also reveals lapses, reversions, arrests, and lethal maladaptations; and just because of man's superior neural equipment—superior but unstable and extremely fragile—even his best technical advances have often been halted, or have been perverted and misapplied. In mastering the art of flying, for example, man released himself from his landbound condition. But this triumph carries disconcerting limitations. In pursuit of speed man has already restored, in even more restrictive form (space rockets) the limitations he sought to escape from, and has become a mere transportable mass, theoretically shrinking in size as he approaches the speed of light, and actually losing his capacity to react in any life-sustaining mode precisely to the degree he increases the speed of his vehicle.

In terms of evolutionary experience, there is no reason to think that genuine progress is achievable in any direction except in conformity to the terms laid down by man's biological nature, modified and partly superseded by his historic cultures, as these have been intensified through the development of man's nervous system. As concerns the living environment, many of modern man's imposing, indeed overpowering technological feats have already proved wantonly dangerous, and in some cases, deadly. Had not evolutionary doctrine itself been influenced by the mechanical world picture and had not mechanical progress been equated with the Malthusian 'survival of the fittest,' these facts would have been identified and appraised long before now.

To believe that a later point in time necessarily carries a larger accumulation of values, or that the latest invention necessarily brings a human improvement, is to forget the patent evidence of history: the recurrent lapses into barbarism, most conspicuous, and most dreadful, as Giambattista Vico long ago pointed out, in the behavior of *civilized* man. Was the Inquisition, with its ingenious mechanical innovations in nicely graded torture, a sign of progress? Technically, Yes: humanly, No. From the standpoint of human survival, to say nothing of further development, a flint arrowhead is preferable to a hydrogen bomb. Doubtless it hurts the pride of modern man to realize that earlier cultures, with simpler technical facilities, may have been superior to his own in terms of human values, and that genuine progress involves continuity and conservation, above all, conscious anticipation and rational selection—the antithesis of our present kaleidoscopic multiplication of random novelties.

Mainly, it was by centering on the abstractions of time and space and motion that the prophets of progress sought for proof of its validity. The very metaphor was but another name for unimpeded movement over the water, then through the air, and now, with rocket power, through the solar system, propelled further by fantasies of voyages to other stars many light-years away. It is not by accident that H. G. Wells' most original work of fiction, 'The Time Machine,' has as its hero an inventor who has learned how to travel through time. (The effective symbolic equivalent of that purely imaginary mechanical device is of course the study of history.)

In vulgar usage, Progress has come to mean limitless movement in space and time, accompanied, necessarily, by an equally limitless command of energy: culminating in limitless destruction. Even my old master, Patrick Geddes, still an optimistic Victorian at heart though tempered by the realistic pessimism of Carlyle and Ruskin, used to say equally about ideas or projects: "We must be getting on," and he held it a sufficient condemnation of Mahatma Gandhi's method of seeking Mother India's independence via hand-spinning that his ideas came from three main sources, Thoreau, Ruskin, and Tolstoy, all three already two generations behind. Despite the wide array of machines produced during the last two centuries, it is mainly by vehicles of transportation—the steamboat, the rail, the motor car, the plane, and the rocket—that the advances of modern technology have been identified in the popular mind.

Even when one restricts the notion of progress to conquering space and time, its human limitations are flagrant. Take one of Buckminster Fuller's favorite illustrations of the shrinkage of time and space, beginning with a sphere twenty feet in diameter, to represent transportation time-distance by walking. With the use of the horse, this sphere gets reduced in size to six feet, with the clipper ship, it becomes a basketball, with the railroad, a baseball, with the jet plane, a marble, and with the rocket, a pea. And if one could travel at the speed of light, one might add, to round off Fuller's idea, the earth would become, from the standpoint of bodily velocity, a molecule, so that one would be back at the starting point without having even the briefest sensation of having left.

By so carrying Fuller's illustration to its theoretic extreme, one reduces this mechanical concept to its proper degree of human irrelevance. For like every other technical achievement, speed has a meaning only in relation to other human needs and purposes. Plainly, the effect of speeding transportation is to diminish the possibilities of direct human experience—even the experience of travel. A person who undertook to walk around the earth would actually, at the end of that long journey, have stored up rich memories of its geographic, climatic, esthetic, and human realities: these experiences retreat in direct ratio to speed, until at the climax of rapid movement, the traveller can have no experience at all: his world has become a static one, in which time and motion work no changes whatever. Not merely space but man shrinks. Because of the volume of jet travel and the rapid turnover of tourists, this means of transport has already ruined beyond repair many of the precious historic sites and cities that incited this mass visitation.

Progress, as our machine-oriented culture defined it, was simply a forward movement through time, and the "going," as one pragmatist philosopher defined it, "becomes the goal"—the early version of the even shallower notion that "the medium is the message." Both ideas can, however, be stated in a valid form: the 'going' does indeed become part of the goal and enlarges it: while the 'medium' necessarily modifies the message.

But note: at its inception there was some justification for this fervid belief in 'Progress.' Too often in the past beneficial innovations had been unable to break through the deep crust of custom. Even the highly rational Michel de Montaigne thought that bad institutions should be maintained, rather than that society should risk the dangers that might attend their reform. To have the freedom now open to us to pick and choose from the past, it was first necessary perhaps to break with it entirely—as an adolescent must break with his parents to become mature enough to take from his elders eventually what will further his own growth.

For perhaps the first time the future took possession of men's minds, not as a remote hope of deliverance in a remote static Heaven, but as a persistent presence and a realizable promise of further fulfillments. All organisms have much of their future embedded in their life cycle: events still to come, forms still to be realized, constantly impinge on present choices and modify them: 'feed forward' is the vital complement to 'feedback.' Yet strangely a persistent consciousness of the future, as a dynamic ingredient of present life, seems to have been actively embodied in only one culture—though notably a long-lived one—that of the Jews; and it was in terms of their deliverance and ultimate return to Jerusalem that they survived hardships and ordeals that repeatedly shattered and obliterated other peoples, less confident in their own purposes, less committed to the future. In so far as the doctrine of progress gave as much weight to the future as to the past, it helpfully offset an excessive respect for the outworn institutions and customs that too often had lost their relevance.

However arbitrary and ignorant its rejection of the past, the idea of progress was at first a liberating one: a casting off of the rusty chains that had crippled the human spirit. In the immediate setting of Western Europe this led to an unsparing criticism of many serious evils, and despite the ruling-class hostility to 'reformers' and 'meddlers' it brought about effective remedies. Under this new impetus free public education was introduced everywhere, the insane were unmanacled, noisome prisons were cleansed and exposed to light: in some countries the populace were grudgingly granted a share in national law-making: the deaf and dumb were helped to express themselves, and even those who like Helen Keller were blind and deaf too, were with superhuman patience led to talk. For a while even torture was eliminated—at least officially—from criminal interrogation, though the most injurious ancient institutions, notably slavery and war, still kept their grip.

One need not belittle the fact that such happy changes were fostered and hastened by the idea of Progress. *But though these improvements were often notable, it is perhaps even more notable that not a single one owed anything directly to mechanical invention.*

This is not to deny that from the eighteenth century on there was an interaction between the idea of progress, systematic mechanical invention, scientific discovery, and political legislation: success in one department confirmed and supported similar efforts in other departments. "Where can the perfectability of man stop, armed with geometry and the mechanical arts and chemistry?" demanded Louis Sébastien Mercier in his eighteenth-century utopia 'The Year 2440.' Where indeed? The very choice of that distant year proclaimed that the future had become coeval with the past and even threatened altogether to supplant it.

Mercier's was one of the first of the futurist utopias that became common in the nineteenth century; and not a few of his anticipations have come to pass long before his climactic date. The notion that the machine by reason of its rationality of design and its austere perfection of perform-ance was now a moral force, indeed *the* moral force, one that set new standards of achievement for man, made it easier to equate the new tech-nology, even in its most sordid manifestations, with human improvement. Sinfulness no longer consisted in falling short of human potentialities: it now meant to fall short of the maximum utilization of the machine.

In the classic philosophies and religions, the notion of perfection had been directed almost exclusively to the cultivation of self or the salvation of the soul. Only as a by-product were human institutions considered the object of such effort. Still less was the technical milieu involved, until the Benedictine discipline turned work itself into a form of piety. This divorce and isolation of the self from the economic system and the material culture that helped to form it and give it substance was as crucial an error as any made in the delineation of the mechanical world picture. But it had one merit: it demanded conscious participation and disciplined effort. The Doctrine of Progress, on the other hand, conceived improvement as external and automatic: no matter what the individual desired or chose, so long as the community accepted the multiplication of machines and the consumption of the machine's typical products as the chief goal of human effort, progress was ensured.

So rapid, so numerous, so impressive were mechanical inventions that by the middle of the nineteenth century even such a humane, well-balanced mind as Emerson's was colored by this view, though he rejected the metaphysical foundations of the utilitarian creed. "The splendors of this age," Emerson once exclaimed, "outshine all other recorded ages. In my lifetime I have seen wrought five miracles—namely, 1. the Steamboat; 2. the Railroad; 3. the Electric Telegraph; 4. the application of the spectroscope to Astronomy; 5. the Photograph." That premature eulogy leaves one without adequate words to describe our present miracles—the electronic microscope, the atomic pile, the remote-controlled planet-circling space rocket, the computer.

Emerson might in another place wryly observe that no matter how far you travelled the same old self travelled with you. But it was precisely to evade the Axial task of disciplining and directing the personality that the apostles of Progress put all their energies into perfecting and multiplying machines, and using in new ways the knowledge that was becoming available. For every human weakness or disorder, there was supposedly a swift mechanical, chemical, or pharmaceutical remedy. Even the electric arc-light, when first introduced, was hailed confidently as a preventive of nocturnal crime. Hence the reckless application of X-rays for half a century, before the deleterious effects of many different kinds of radiation were acknowledged: likewise the random and excessive use of antibiotics; or again the too-hasty resort to surgery, as in frontal lobotomy, for organic disturbances open to other means of treatment.

The hopeful notion of the machine as the favored agent of moral and political as well as material good was, again, expressed by Emerson: this alone shows what a grip the doctrine of mechanical progress had established. "The progress of invention," Emerson noted in 1866, "is really a threat. Whenever I see a railroad I look for a republic. We must take care to induct free trade and abolish customs houses, before the passenger balloons begin to arrive from Europe, and I think the railroad Superintendent has a second and deeper sense when he inscribes his legend over the ways—'Look out for the Engine.' "

Little did Emerson suspect that superior technical equipment might beget not a world union of republics but a hostile alignment of destructive totalitarian military machines. Today there are still 'avant-garde' minds cast in this old-fashioned 'progressive' mold, who continue to believe that instant communication by television will produce instant understanding, or who are even so bound to their dogmatic faith in technological progress as to believe that the direction of congested and impeded auto traffic by radio from a helicopter is an evidence of superb technical efficiency—instead of what it really is, a revelation of a glaring bankruptcy alike in contemporary engineering, transportation planning, social control, and urban design.

The early believers in mechanical salvation would have been hard put to it to explain how the very decade that saw the triumph of air transportation likewise saw the universal restoration of national passport restrictions, which had been virtually abandoned by the end of the nineteenth century. In short, the notion that mechanical and scientific progress guaranteed parallel human benefits was already dubious by 1851, the year of the Crystal Palace Exhibition, and now has become completely untenable.

Both the early hopes for scientific and technical progress, and the later sense of disillusion, were expressed in two poems by Alfred Tennyson: 'Locksley Hall' (1842) and 'Locksley Hall Sixty Years After' (1886). As a young man he had hailed not only the locomotive but the coming of aerial travel, as an achievement that made it better, in his own words, to live fifty years in Europe than a whole cycle in Cathay. But he came finally to a different conclusion: the air war that would usher in "the Parliament of Man, the Federation of the World," no longer seemed likely to have such a happy outcome. Instead of urging "Forward, forward let us range," he turned on his earlier self with "Let us hush this cry of 'forward' till ten thousand years have gone."

As an *Ersatz* religion, the doctrine of an inevitable mechanical-cum-human progress gave the new world picture something that it lacked: an implicit goal; namely, the total demolition of the past, and the creation, mainly by 'mechanical' means, of a better future. Change itself became, in this complex of ideas, not merely a fact of nature—as it is—but an urgent human value; and to resist change or to retard it in any way was to 'go against nature'—and ultimately to endanger man by defying the Sun God and denying his commands.

On these assumptions, since progress was ordained by Heaven, regression was no longer possible. Only a few years before the First World War, in one of H. G. Wells' better novels, 'The New Machiavelli,' the exiled hero, writing about his past life, boasts: "No king, no Council, can seize me or torture me; no Church, no nation, can silence me—such powers of ruthless and complete suppression have vanished." At that late date an informed modern mind, confident in the benign workings of science, could not anticipate the possibility of a Hitler or a Stalin or a Mao: he could still believe that human progress was irreversible, though a little later, in 1914, he would himself realistically describe in 'The World Set Free' the destruction of a city hit by a single atom bomb.

The popular doctrine of progress gave support to, and in turn claimed support from, the later conception of Evolution. But this was an illicit alliance, since, as Julian Huxley observed, evolution involves not linear progress but "divergence, stabilization, extinction, and advance." In organic transformations the forces that resist change and ensure continuity are as important as those that give rise to novelty and bring about improvements. Even what constitutes an advance in one period may turn out to be a maladaptation or a regression in another.

At all events, one fact should now be plain: change is not in itself a value, nor is it an automatic producer of values; neither is novelty a sufficient evidence of improvement. These are only the catchwords and advertising slogans of commercial interests with something to sell. As for the notion that technological innovations have been the main source of all human development, this is a disreputable anthropological fable, which does not, as I showed in Volume One of 'The Myth of the Machine,' stand up under a more comprehensive analysis of man's nature and culture. Once modern man understands the need for continuity and selective modification, in terms of his own capacities and purposes, instead of blind conformity to either nature or his own technology, he will have many fresh choices before him.

3: THE ROLE OF UTOPIAS

Plato's notion that the human community might be deliberately reshaped and perfected by rational methods—that it was in fact a work of art—came back again with Thomas More. His book on the subject, 'Utopia,' which gave the name retrospectively to this whole literature, appeared within the revolutionary hundred years that witnessed the discovery and conquest of the New World, and the publication of Copernicus' 'De Revolutionibus.' And if, as Dr. Arthur Morgan suggested, More himself, like his chosen narrator, Hythloday, had direct news of the system of government imposed by the Incas of Peru, this would only add a final touch of historic authenticity to the resurgent myth of the machine: for the social regimentation and megalithic constructions of the Incas, to say nothing of their religion of the Sun, presents a striking parallel, as yet unaccounted for, to those of the much earlier Pyramid Age in Egypt.

Compared with the Doctrine of Progress the classic utopias from Plato's time onward have had little influence. Certainly it would be foolish to attribute to them directly any of the great social changes of the last two centuries; for even those who sought to follow a utopian pattern in founding ideal colonies in America or elsewhere were only a handful; and their inspiration came usually from millennial religious aspirations as in both Mormonism and Zionism. As for the practically successful ideal colonies, like those at Oneida, New York, or Amana, Iowa, they were only temporarily self-fulfilling and all too soon became self-terminating.

Yet utopian literature, from the beginning, had a hidden bond with the emerging system of collective mechanical organization; and it is only now that one can command sufficient historic data to make a plausible tracing of the route followed. If the true goal of human development was the perfection of the whole community, then a system that shaped each specialized part for the more efficient performance of his particular function would in the end perform with the efficiency of a machine.

On the surface, the concept of utopia implied just the opposite of progress: once perfection was achieved, utopian authors saw no need for further change. Even Marx deserted his dynamic Hegelian ideology once communism was supposedly achieved. Thus the ideal society would operate indefinitely, like a well-oiled machine, under the guidance of a collective dictatorship. The behavioral adaptations of the social ants and bees have demonstrated that such a mechanized collective is actually within the realm of organic possibility.

While there have been wide variations in the social and economic circumstances envisaged by different utopias since Aristotle made his first comparative survey of ideal Greek commonwealths, there are only a few classic utopias, notably William Morris' 'News from Nowhere,' that reject the basic common assumption: that of designing a whole society in conformity with an ideological blueprint, in which autonomy will be transferred from the individual organism, where it exists in some measure even in the lowest types, to the organized community.

Strangely, though the word Freedom is sometimes included in the descriptions of utopia—indeed, one nineteenth-century utopia was called Freeland—the pervasive character of all utopias is their totalitarian absolutism, the reduction of variety and choice, and the effort to escape from such natural conditions or historical traditions as would support variety and make choice possible. These uniformities and compulsions constitute utopia's inner tie to the megamachine.

Even before the mechanical world picture had taken hold of the Western mind the classic utopias, particularly Plato's and More's, the two most influential ones, showed these limitations. Professor Raymond Ruyer, in his exhaustive study of utopias, has confirmed my own original analysis in 1922: almost all utopias emphasize regularity, uniformity, 'dirigisme' or authoritarianism, isolation, and autarchy. Not least, they stress hostility toward nature, which leads to the suppression of the natural environment by geometric or mechanical forms, and the replacement of natural products by artificial manufactured substitutes.

These fixations seem all the stranger when one finds them in the work of such a sensitive and humane thinker as Thomas More. For in the main, the life More describes is only a robust idealization of the actual practices of the medieval country town and rural manor, as independently described in Stow's early Survey of London. But More superimposes on this a flatly contradictory regime, his 'ideal' one, in which he treats uniformity and regularity as if they were ends in themselves. How otherwise can one account for his singular boast, that he who knows one of the towns in Utopia knows all of them? Beneath the medieval garments of More's perfect commonwealth an iron Robot has already begun to move his artificial limbs, plucking the fruits of life with iron claws.

What is the meaning of these many efforts to identify the possibilities of human happiness with an authoritarian, or often indeed a grimly totalitarian society? This sterile fantasy has remained floating in the mind for tens of centuries, like the dream of the mechanical robot, or of human flight. With the coalescence of the mechanical world picture, Utopia took on a new role: it served as a prefabricated 'ideal' model for the actual society that the process of mechanization was rapidly making possible. Though even now few people seem to suspect the ideal form and the ultimate destination of the industrial organization that has been taking shape in our own time, it is in fact heading toward a static finality, in which change of the system itself will be so impermissible that it will take place only through total disintegration and destruction.

In short, it turns out that Utopia is not so much the distant ideal goal as the imminent operational terminus of our present development. Viewed realistically, the literature of utopias, when further supplemented by science fiction, presents a cross-section of the 'coming' world, as conceived by the accredited ministers of progress.

Do not misread this interpretation: there is no causal connection. The actual process of mechanization was not affected in any serious way by the publication of literary and scientific utopias. Except for Bacon's 'New Atlantis,' utopias have had virtually no effect upon technics: though an occasional one, like Bellamy's 'Looking Backward,' may have carried some current innovations to a later social conclusion. (Bellamy even provided, as did Fourier in his earlier plans for phalansteries, some of the necessary concrete suggestions that Marx and Engels deliberately refused to offer.) It would be truer, indeed, to hold that the exceptional speed of technical progress has, on the contrary, validated the ideal principles of utopia and brought on social consequences that might well have disconcerted the original authors. "Utopias," the Russian philosopher Berdiaev remarked, "appear to be much more capable of realization than they did in the past. And we find ourselves faced by a much more distressing problem: How can we prevent their final realization . . . how can we return to a non-utopian society, less 'perfect,' and more free."

Once again, it is not the failures of mechanization, but its achievement of an effortless perfectionism that is in question; and this makes it all the more imperative to look closely at the pictures of supposed social beatitude we find in our technological utopias. The real use of utopias was their service as 'trial balloons,' anticipating one or another form of the collective termitary we have been bringing into existence. The various 'perfect' future societies the utopian writers have put forward are not in fact prospectuses for a new Golden Age, too remote to permit of their realization. On the contrary, they are subjective anticipations of formidable actualities that have proved all too easy to accomplish—thanks to technology.

Utopia, in other words, is the secret destination of the invisible, all-embracing megamachine: the same destination that Teilhard de Chardin pictured in cosmic terms, and in a strangely euphoric mood, as the Omega point. Let us make a brief survey of these warnings, before we confront their eventual terminus.

4: PREFABRICATED UTOPIAS

Anyone who had read the literature of utopias during the past two centuries would have had a far better idea of the 'shape of things to come' than a newspaper reader who sedulously followed the random reports of events from day to day. When collated, the overall design that was taking form throughout society became apparent in these utopias, from a generation to a century in advance.

If one supplemented this account by wide reading in science fiction, from Poe to Jules Verne through H. G. Wells and Olaf Stapledon, not to mention a multitude of more recent predictions, one would have possessed an almost clairvoyant fore-knowledge of present-day society. As early as 1883, for example, one utopian prophet not merely pictured the electric motor car, gliding noiselessly over smooth concrete roads, but even added a refinement that was not introduced in the United States till the late nineteen-thirties—a dividing line in the middle of the road.*

Utopian literature has had a distinction that lifted it above the com-

* Ismal Thiusen (pseud.), 'The Diothas, or a Far-Look Ahead.' New York: 1883.

partmentalized thinking characteristic of the mechanistic ideology: it sought in some degree to deal with the ramifying human relationships in a concretely conceived society. And what the main utopias disclosed as an image of perfection was a totalitarian community, so organized that its rulers would, with the aid of the machine, assume control over all human activities, translating a large part of its functions into a mechanical or electronic form, and holding the workers themselves under the strictest possible discipline "for their own good." With disarming naïveté, Etienne Cabet, the author of one of the most influential mid-nineteenth-century utopias, describes this organization. The workers, he said, are "divided into as many groups as there are parts to be manufactured, and each of them always manufactures the same parts. There is so much order and discipline that they look like an army." Enough said.

Mechanical uniformity and human conformity are embedded in the prefabricated utopias of the nineteenth century: but it remained for the World's Fair at Chicago in 1933 to proudly emblazon this utopian theme over its portals, in so many words. "Science explores: Technology executes: Man conforms." The mind that coined this slogan undoubtedly believed that this conclusion was so obvious, this result so benign, that they needed no explanatory justification. With exquisite irony, the title of the Fair was: 'The Century of Progress.'

Progress indeed! *Man conforms*. But if that kind of progress had prevailed at the beginning of man's development, he would have conformed abjectly to Nature and accepted her conditions with the least possible modification of either himself or the environment—though even the lowest organisms still single out from the wide range of choices Nature offers the niche and the mode of life that responds most closely to their own nature and character.

In only slightly more sophisticated form, the same kind of fossilized utopia is still rolling off the assembly line, though the technological compulsions may be imposed by a space rocket, a computer, closed circuit television, or a nuclear reactor. Those who have followed my earlier description of the original Myth of the Machine will see that the classic utopias of the last two centuries have been stirred by the same myth as was working in the minds of ancient engineers, bureaucrats, and military commanders. Unfortunately neither the utopian writers nor our 'realistic' political leaders had sufficient historic background to anticipate that this new assemblage would be accompanied by more savage wars and revolutions, by sadistic terrorisms and psychotic human disorders. Even now, with the record before them, they studiously turn their eyes away from the scene, as one historian of technology was honest enough to remark in a personal letter, lest they be forced to confess to a radical flaw in their own philosophy.

But if utopian writers did not anticipate any of the possible malfunctionings of their ideal system, or suspect that the megamachine most of them were describing was necessarily a minority-manipulated majority-manipulating device, they correctly delineated the most salient characteristics of the new technical and social complex itself. In only one respect did they remain extremely naïve: they thought they had caught a glimpse of entrancing possibilities for universal human felicity, and that once utopia was achieved mankind would live happily ever afterward.

In retrospect, one of the most fantastic of the progressive nineteenth-century utopias has turned out to be among the most realistic: Bulwer-Lytton's 'The Coming Race' (1871). In this romance the author, through the very license of his imagination, came much closer to later realities than his more circumspect contemporaries like James Silk Buckingham. Not the least penetrating of Bulwer-Lytton's intuitions was his placement of his utopia in the bowels of the earth: he foretold the collective underground prison that would symbolize to perfection not only man's 'conquest' of nature, but in turn his abject surrender to the machines and utilities that would make that conquest possible.

With no direct help from 'The Coming Race' this is precisely the denatured environment that hundreds of busy architectural and engineering moles, inspired by the mine, the subway, and the underground rocket-control centers, are now projecting universally as the "next step" in urban development—or, indeed, are already incorporating in equally dismal buildings that still happen to rise above the ground. A generation after Bulwer-Lytton, Gabriel Tarde the French sociologist returned to the same habitat in his utopia, 'Underground Man.'

The members of 'The Coming Race' are already in possession of a mysterious source of energy, Vril, which gives them the absolute power of destruction possessed by those now in control of hydrogen bombs. But in Bulwer-Lytton's fantasy, this energy was all the more formidable because Vril had been miniaturized and was transportable in a hollow rod. By making this new energy the key to both the governance of men and dominance over nature, and by burying his ideal community below the surface of the earth, Bulwer-Lytton anticipated the core features of a new system of totalitarian control. His pre-vision failed in only one respect: he did not trace the system back to its necessary sources: an all-encompassing organization of trained experts and administrators who would, with the aid of specialized knowledge and equipment, restricted by its nature from easy public access, now propose to control the activities of the mass of men.

Instead of depicting this highly specialized military-bureaucratic organization, Bulwer-Lytton showed the ruling minority who possessed Vril as behaving remarkably like the nineteenth-century British aristocracy—including both their marital sexual laxity and their unbridled contempt for the lower races who had not discovered Vril and so were at their mercy. This combination of relentless control and sexual debauchery for the elite would come back again notably in the Nazi Third Reich. That Bulwer-Lytton, the gentlemanly aristocrat, the "lion in curl-papers" as he was known to his contemporaries, should have conceived this fantasy is an indication of how the original myth of the machine was taking form once more in the human unconscious, long before it had risen to the surface—or at least in the unconscious of ruling groups. Ironically, the only immediate result of this fantasy of super-energy was the bestowal of Vril as the last syllable of a once-famous British product, an extract of beef called Bovril.

5: BELLAMY'S BACKWARD DREAM

After Bulwer-Lytton, Edward Bellamy's utopia seems too pedestrian to appeal to a modern reader. But as with Bacon's 'New Atlantis,' part of our present boredom in reading 'Looking Backward' is due to the fact that so many of its boldest proposals have already become daily commonplaces. The marvels of his transformed commonwealth in the year 2000 are more conspicuous today than the horrors of Orwell's '1984,' though these, too, are near enough, if still covered with a slick Madison Avenue glaze. Nothing, certainly, could have been more wildly erroneous than the sober judgement of a reviewer in the Boston 'Transcript' in 1887, who felt that the book contained nothing that might not be possible if only Bellamy had placed his transformation seventy-five centuries away. Bellamy's imagination was far more realistic than the sober 'good sense' of the philistines.

Bellamy's utopia now reads so strangely, not through the absurdities of his prophecies, but because of the humane hopes that he attached to their fulfillment. For despite his compassion and his democratic ideals, Bellamy unguardedly embraced, under the rubric of the general welfare, the implacable totalitarian features that Bulwer-Lytton shrank from. Bellamy, indeed, was so enamored of the economic potentialities of large-scale organization and mechanization, as in an army, that he did not hesitate to accept military organization as the basic model of his ideal society, merely refining the methods of compulsion long used by the standard old-fashioned megamachines. Like Cabet, this singularly sensitive mind proposed to combine in a continental totalitarian organization the most ancient methods of control: a disciplined army, conscripted for work, and assigned to their tasks by a central authority—plus a large bureaucracy, efficiently regulating every part of the process and distributing annually equal shares of the total product.

In short, Bellamy committed his ideal community to the care of the archetypal megamachine. What makes Bellamy's method of organization even more notable is the fact that conscription on a national scale was so contrary to the New World *mores* that even its temporary application in the American War Between the States had caused violent draft riots. In the United States this mode of organization was still regarded—and with justice—as a hateful symbol of Old World tyranny and oppression, not to be used except in an extremity, when the very existence of the nation was imperilled. Bellamy—and here again he turned out to be a shrewd prophet —made conscription an everyday necessity: not only in war but in peace.

'Looking Backward,' then, turns out to be the first authentic picture of National Socialism (German style), or State Capitalism (Russian style), in its most insidiously corrupting form, that of the providential Welfare State with all its disciplinary braces relaxed—though not removed—by a massive bribe. This new form was different from that later instituted on ancient Czarist foundations in Soviet Russia, because Bellamy pictured it as being brought about by a popular ballot, not by an armed insurrection and a harsh 'dictatorship of the proletariat.' And it was equally different from later forms of fascism because it applied compulsion on the largest scale without feeling the need to resort to incarceration and torture. Those who did not conform to the national rules and regulations were simply cast out.

Bellamy apparently believed that he had avoided the need for compulsion or for punishment by anticipating the Thorndike-Skinner principle of control mainly through rewards: the method whereby animal trainers inculcate obedience and hasten the learning of set responses. Society became, in fact, a gigantic Skinner 'pigeon box' or teaching machine. The bait was extremely tempting, and so plausible, even on capitalistic principles, that it has been put forward once more in our time: namely, a guaranteed fixed income, bestowed on each member of the nation as a citizen. The large yearly income issued—again clairvoyantly—in the form of a *credit card* was the equivalent of perhaps twenty or twenty-five thousand dollars a year in the present inflation of currency: it enabled the citizen to withdraw equivalent goods from the national storehouses; and by this simple device eliminated any other mode of production and exchange. Bellamy allowed a few minor departures from this system: the conscript might retire from compulsory labor service at thirty-three, at half-pay; and if one was an author—Bellamy does not even smile!—one might earn unlimited royalties. But the basic fact is that in return for 'going with' the system both poverty and anxious insecurity are removed.

By these provisions Bellamy overcame two of the most serious defects of the ancient megamachine: he substituted reward for punishment as an incentive to labor; and he distributed those rewards equitably throughout the whole community, instead of giving an undue proportion to a dominant minority and withholding them, except by vicarious enjoyment on festal occasions, from the enslaved or disenfranchised majority. This followed, as Arthur Morgan has emphasized, the same general model that the Incas had installed in their Andean empire, though Bellamy added a few embellishments of his own. At the age of forty-five, for example, all members of the work army became, in our current unctuous locution, 'senior citizens,' that is, they were relieved of all responsibility except that of exercising—for the first time, be it noted!—political control. As Marie Louise Berneri remarks: "the joy with which the citizens of Bellamy's society greet their retirement is sufficient indication that industrial conscription is resented as a burden."

This singular mode of government would be the equivalent of 'alumni control' in a university; and one can hardly imagine a better means of inducing administrative arthritis, if any institution were ever so ill-advised as to install it. But so firmly was the notion of military discipline established in Bellamy's utopia that the right to vote was not exercised until the citizen ceased to be a member of the industrial army.

By now we know from the example of Soviet Russia how such a militarized system would work. The formation of an independent workers' shop committee would be mutiny: the advocacy of a change of method or goal in production would be counter-revolutionary sedition. As for criticism of the central administration—that would be treason. That is the modest price of Utopia.

Here, then, is the utopian life-span. Twenty-one years of nurture and education, that is, conditioning: three years of forced labor at the more disagreeable tasks and services: twenty years at a favored profession or vocation, as and where indicated by the national government; and finally, compulsory retirement after forty-five, with the remaining years of life devoted to leisure undiluted by any other duty than public work. Since there are no gradations of income in this society, the chief rewards for outstanding service are honors, status, authority, power. By taking the constitution of the United States as a model, the President of the Country became commander-in-chief of the industrial army; and since this army is in constant being, the political system is plainly that of a dictatorship: in effect, this mode of economic organization committed the country to a perpetual Cold War.

By now, advanced industrial nations have slipped into so many of the grooves indicated by Bellamy that it has become hard for many people to conceive of any other mode of life that would encompass the genuine advantages that our technology now offers. Indeed, the proposed equalization of income, duties, sacrifices, opportunities, seems so palpably just and 'democratic,' so unmenacing, so beneficial, that the one element missing in this scheme escapes us because we are already so close to having lost it: namely, there are no alternatives to the system itself.

Such freedom as is granted by this society is the freedom given to conscript soldiers on leave; and no provision whatever is made for conscientious objectors, or for those who would work against the system. The American farmer who lately rebelled against legislation preventing him from growing more than his allotted quota of grain even to feed his own hogs found when he migrated to distant Australia in search of freedom that he had made only one mistake: even in that seemingly open and independent continent he was subject to a similar set of imbecile regulations.

Bellamy leaves no doubt about the totalitarian nature of his utopia. "If a man refuses to accept the authority of the state and the inevitability of industrial service, he loses all his rights as a human being." All his rights as a human being? Did this tender-minded reformer realize what these words would mean? If not, our better-seasoned generation can tell him: for we have had before us the case of the Soviet Russian poet who was sentenced to jail as a "work-resister" because he devoted his days to translating, and to writing poetry—the 'wrong' sort of poetry of course. In tracing the grim, monolithic outlines of his perfect commonwealth, Bellamy, in his innocence, was more realistic than the anti-utopian Karl Marx, who, once socialism was installed, foresaw the State withering away.

Despite all these features, which now seem, in the light of present political experience, so coldly oppressive, many of Bellamy's contemporaries enthusiastically hailed his coming commonwealth as a manifestly desirable, if still improbable, technocratic dream. The fervor to embrace such militarized felicity points to the degrading and harassing conditions under which a majority of farm and factory workers then actually lived, even in a 'free' country. Otherwise, it would be hard to account for the book's popularity, or for the favorable impression it made upon many gentle, sensitive people, such as Ebenezer Howard, the British founder of the Garden City Movement, one whose whole bent of mind pointed rather in the opposite direction—toward an increase of choices and voluntary initiatives.

What made 'Looking Backward' a best seller in its day—139,000 copies of the American edition were sold in the first two years—was that Bellamy set forth the professed goals of scientifically oriented mechanization, wealth, security, and leisure, as immediately practicable. Queerly, he concealed, even from himself, the cost of this achievement. Once the militarized system was accepted as a whole, all its components could be prefabricated and mass-produced; for the megamachine, by its over-productive nature, was necessarily a communist, whatever the political form. Now the separate components of Bellamy's utopia were politically neutral and morally innocuous: many of his practical proposals or his mechanical improvements were neither harmful nor worthless: some indeed were excellent. Even a brief summary of Bellamy's anticipations would show various commendable new features, no less desirable than inventions already available in his day, from surgical anesthesia to the typewriter on which I write these words. In an age of the bustle and the chignon, Bellamy foretold a time when women would boldly expose their limbs and permit their bodies to develop naturally; in an age of coal and smoking chimneys, he pictured smokeless cities, heated and lighted by electricity; before the phonograph was perfected, when the telephone was still little more than a toy, he described a method of public broadcasting of music and the human voice, by telephonic diffusion; and among other things, he even foresaw the organization of purchase by sample, as in the mail-order catalog, or in the sale of bulky articles by department stores. All these things have actually come to pass. So have, for that matter, Roger Bacon's airships, Campanella's automobiles, More's incubators, Glanvill's magnetic telegraph, and Bacon's foundations for scientific research.

These sound utilitarian forecasts of Bellamy's were carried further by the fertile mind of H. G. Wells, who went Bellamy's nationalist utopia one better by giving his 'Modern Utopia' a planetary scope. Unfortunately neither Bellamy's military organization nor Wells' caste organization of Samurai, who might not even marry outside their caste, were in the least modern except in their technical equipment: the human organization, the pursuit of power, was five thousand years old. And though these thinkers possessed an immense amount of useful knowledge about the physical constitution of the universe and the fabrication of machines and machine-like organizations, they showed almost no apprehensive insight into the repeated miscarriage of human purposes that has resulted from the early practice of reducing men to the status of machines. To build up human autonomy, to control quantitative expansion, to encourage creativity, and, above all, to overcome and finally eliminate the original traumas that accompanied the rise of civilization—of these fundamental needs there is no utopian hint. Almost to the end of his life Wells naïvely pinned his faith for radical collective improvements upon a dedicated dictatorship of technicians—and aviators at that!

6: FROM UTOPIA TO KAKOTOPIA

The literature of utopias shades gradually into that of science fiction: and at first glance their likenesses are more striking than their differences. Both elaborate fantasies that are largely extrapolated from known contemporary or historical realities: both picture a possible future: both entertain the possibility of new social arrangements and new inventions. Even to say that science fiction is more shamelessly fictional than most utopian literature hardly points to a difference, because science fiction has often come strikingly close in advance to the actual achievements of our own age. Arthur Clarke, the dean of contemporary writers in this field, still regrets his mistake in selling a story describing radio communication via Telstar, instead of getting out a United States patent on it.

No: none of these facile discriminations will do. The true criterion of science fiction is that the perfection it seeks rests exclusively within the realm of conceivable scientific knowledge and technical invention; and that there is no attempt by most writers to show that this has any viable connection whatever with human welfare or further human development. The term science fiction is by now unfortunately so loosely applied that it covers old-style magical achievements—even black magic—and psychotic wishes, and some of these psychological corruptions and morbid obsessions are present, as C. S. Lewis was aware, in many technically 'advanced' fantasies. By no means the least interesting example is one that shows the human race threatened by the invasion of super-intelligent ants, capable of using graphic symbols. But in the main, science fiction only carried further the dark Nordic anticipation of the triumph of the Giants and the Dwarfs over the Gods of love and wisdom. So far from presenting its utopia as a beautiful dream, its effort terminates all too often in a kakotopia or realizable nightmare.

Though Kepler even more than Poe must be looked upon as the hallowed ancestor of modern science-fiction writers, Professor Marjorie Hope Nicolson has shown, in her admirably exhaustive study of voyages to the moon, that the literary antecedents of science fiction go back much farther into the human past and cannot be disentangled from the scientific and technical interests that tended, in time, to supersede them. In fact, they continually interacted, and it would be naïve to suppose that the scientific rationale has been protectively sterilized against wanton suggestions from the unconscious.

But the seventeenth century marks a new starting point for this genre; and the two voyages to the moon that were described in 1638, 'Man in the Moon' by Francis Godwin and 'Discovery of a New World' by John

Wilkins—both, perhaps significantly, bishops—repeat with variations Kepler's dream. Both center on the possibility of human flight; both are addressed to exploration; both seek to escape earthly limits; and though they seek the help of birds or of mechanical contrivances, they do so not to enjoy the freedom of the air, a truly human aspiration, but merely to conquer abstract distance and to satisfy their curiosity, in terms already set by the mechanical world picture.

This all came out plainly in Wilkins' crowning work. Ten years after the first edition of 'The Discovery of a New World in the Moon,' he published his 'Mathematical Magick.' This consists of two books: 'Archimedes, or Mechanical Powers,' and 'Daedalus: or Mechanical Motions.' Within that general framework, science, technics, and fantasy advanced hand in hand. Two and a half centuries later, H. G. Wells, who had probably never read either Kepler's 'Dream' or Wilkins' 'Discovery,' wrote his 'First Men in the Moon,' and discovered the same gruesome creatures and the same underground habitations that Kepler had pictured. In passing from flight by means of sleep, to flight with the aid of birds, to flight in a mechanical contrivance—notably Le Folie's first 'electrical' flying machine —only the technological expedients changed: the dream and the impulses that motivated it remained the same.

There is no need to range over the entire literature of science fiction to bring out the point that I am making—namely that, like utopias, its best present use is not to show what modern civilization has still to seek and achieve, but to demonstrate, in advance, malign possibilities that we must take precautions to anticipate, in order to control, redirect, or forfend.

So far from dismissing these confident probings of the future as empty fantasy, I hold that we have an obligation to take them seriously—not, as so many of the science-fiction writers themselves believe, so that we may push at a more furious pace toward their projected futures, but so that we may overcome these compulsions and plot a radically different destination, more compatible with the nature of organic development and the needs of the human personality.

Not the least significant aspect of the classics of science fiction, even when they do not in themselves picture monsters like Kepler's Prevolvans and Subvolvans, is that they bring, seemingly from the deepest levels of the unconscious, premonitions of disaster. Even in H. G. Wells' early 'Story of the Days to Come,' with its confident presentation of a wide array of new technical processes, efficient machines, and large-scale organizations, his pessimism is as deep as E. M. Forster's, in a similar fantasy of a sealed mechanized world in 'The Machine Stops'—the Machine being the universal air-conditioning mechanism whose sudden silence becomes absolutely ominous.

Most of the technical devices Wells invented in fantasy proved eminently practical—the airplane, the armored military tank, and the atom bomb—likewise the standardized teaching film and television. But the planetary Great Society that he hopefully forecast, as being the rational by-product of this technological progress, now seems farther away than ever, mainly because of his neglect of the human factors that were left out of his conscious original forecasts. Against his will, against all his hopeful conscious beliefs, Wells kept on saying under his breath: *No good can come of it.*

Perhaps nothing so sharply reveals the underlying pessimism of the writers of science fiction as the confession made by Arthur Clarke at the end of 'Profiles of the Future,' a book that lovingly describes and extols the new feats of technics he still confidently predicts for the next century. Suddenly the rapturous dream of the all-conquering, scientifically fabricated, world-embracing, sky-searching technology fades out, and Clarke comes back to strangely archaic symbols, expressing desires, fulfillments, states of mind not even momentarily entertained by the high priests of megatechnics, or by himself as science-fiction prophet. At the end of the chapter 'Aladdin's Lamp,' Clarke says: "So we may hope . . . that one day our age of roaring factories and bulging warehouses will pass away. . . . And then our descendants, no longer cluttered up with possessions, will remember what many of us have forgotten—that the only things in the world that really matter are such imponderables as beauty and wisdom, laughter and love."

One hardly knows whether to mock the sentimentality of this passage, made hollow and ridiculous by all that preceded it, or to weep over the poverty and futility of all the lives that have been, on Clarke's own confession, so extravagantly misspent in bringing to pass one technological miracle after another. Certainly both mockery and tears are in order. Beauty and wisdom, laughter and love, have never depended for their existence upon technical ingenuity—though they can be easily eliminated by devoting too much attention to the material means of existence, or attempting to play a game that subordinates all other human possibilities solely to the cultivation of abstract intelligence and to the electro-mechanical simulation of organic activities.

What Clarke was virtually saying at this point is what H. G. Wells, his most persuasive forerunner, uttered in a final wail of despair at the point of his own death: "Mind is at the end of its tether." Mind itself, taken at its full range of activities, shows no ground whatever for Wells' shattering confession. But the new kind of technically conditioned intelligence, cut off from the whole organism and trained to pursue no other purposes than power and control, is indeed at the end of its tether: dehumanized, obsessed, manic, heedlessly self-destructive, without even an animal's instinct toward self-preservation. Wells' unconscious had told him true, while his eager rational intelligence had betrayed him.

The fact is that the extraordinary facilities now at the disposal of scientists, inventors, and administrators have inflated their most sinister technological fantasies and given their projectors a freedom from sensible inhibitions hitherto enjoyed only in the form of nocturnal dreams. As a result, their acutest exhibitions of intelligence are not to be distinguished from the addled productions of Pop artists and their equally ephemeral successors. That such randy Pentagonal fantasies are now open to relatively instant materialization in successful working models makes them all the more dangerous; for they are untouched by any other realities except those included in their own life-defeating ideology. Only Swift's satiric description of the projects pursued at the Laputan Grand Academy of Lagado does justice to current technological exhibitionism.

Plainly, the ability to translate mathematical theorems and sub-atomic or molecular forces into new inventions, without encountering either technical delays or sobering human inhibitions, has turned our dominant technology itself into the equivalent of science fiction. Whatever appears in scientific fantasy the night before may appear next morning or next year in actual life. As Harvey Wheeler has put it, "instant information creates instant crisis." This practical triumph does not make the fantasies themselves less disturbing to their victims—that part of the human race enthralled and endangered by them.

Here is a situation without any parallel in human history. In the past, every invention passed through a long period of probation between its first appearance in fantasy, its intermediate stages of composition and invention, and its final materialization as a working apparatus or machine. The more audacious the conception, the slower the process, since often the necessary tools and intermediary mechanisms had first to be invented. Against the abrupt, often cataclysmic introduction of an invention, society heretofore was secured by a heavy crust of habit, custom and traditional wisdom, supplemented by natural mental sluggishness. The probing and testing of an invention gave time, not only to overcome its internal flaws, but to make the community ready to accommodate it—though even here we know, from the flagrant evils which once attended the factory system, that these barriers did not always offer sufficient social protection.

Now we are faced with just the opposite situation. The obstacles to immediate acceptance have been broken down; and the latest technical proposal, instead of having to establish its right to be recognized and accepted, rather challenges society to take it over at once, and at any cost; whilst any reluctance to do so immediately is looked upon as reprehensible, or, as Ogburn once naïvely put it, a cultural lag. That technics has often lagged behind culture, that the efficiency of the assembly line, for example, might be, humanly speaking, a mark of social backwardness, seems never to have occurred to the exponents of unqualified technological progress. But, be it noted, the universal society sketched out by the Chinese philosopher Mo Ti waited more than two thousand years for the technical agents—radio, television, and air transport—that would make it realizable. The lag of present-day technology behind superior moral insight should now be notorious.

Thus at the moment that the actual powers of technical invention have become unbridled, its compulsions and obsessions remain untempered by reality, since the only reality this society fully accepts is that which embodies these materialized psychoses and fixed ideas. On those terms, technics becomes licensed irrationality.

7: BRAVE NEW WORLD

For a summation of all that has been touched on in the concepts of a 'New World,' of Progress, of Utopia, and of Science Fiction, one must turn to Aldous Huxley. In 'Brave New World,' he spoke the final word of the sentence whose opening clause was uttered by Johannes Kepler. Though Huxley's book was published in 1932, at a moment when the economic institutions of the Western World were in a state of panicky bankruptcy, verging on total collapse, every part of his anti-Utopia was already visible, in token amounts and inchoate form; for the kind of knowledge on which it was based had gained in momentum and power and mass, like a gigantic snowball rolling downhill since 1543.

'Brave New World' was conceived as an uproarious satire, whose farcical anticipations would serve to puncture the technocratic faith embodied —strangely enough it now seems—in the Ford motor car assembly line, then deemed praiseworthy because the ordinary workman was paid as much as five dollars a day! Such satire can be effective only if there is a contrast between the actual world and a norm of human life to which everyone more or less subscribes. But so insistent and rapid have been the technological transformations of the last forty years that shortly this book ceased to have any impact as satire: Huxley's seemingly gross caricature had become a reality. The contrasting norm had almost disappeared.

At the time Aldous Huxley wrote, the manic-depressive cycle of capitalist economic activity seemed to have reached an ultimate downward point, even in countries like Germany and England, where various measures of social insurance had been installed during the previous half century. The impossibility of maintaining a high level of productivity without a more equitable distribution of both income and goods stared everyone in the face. The only alternative to this in terms of the current power ideology was either 'pyramid building' or preparations for war.

In the United States those who clung to the old assumptions of automatic progress were still desperately hoping for some new invention, some new corporate enterprise, that would set the wheels revolving again: by turns pre-fabricated housing, trailer houses, cheap safe airplanes, or Tom Thumb golf courses, were put forth as a means of bringing the depression to an end. Meanwhile, so desperate was the situation that many abandoned for the moment all hope of further technical progress: they turned instead to ancient modes of handicraft production and subsistence agriculture: there were even mining communities where only the Stone Age techniques of hunting and fishing helped families to evade starvation. In short, the national economy was bankrupt, at least in the United States, and was lapsing into a more primitive form: in more than one industrial town barter and locally issued scrip took the place of money. At that moment, Huxley's Brave New World still seemed too remote to be frightening.

Yet so far from foreseeing this civilization's returning to tribal anarchy, parochial isolation, and small-scale handicraft production, Huxley confidently carried the older scientific fantasies many centuries further, into their own special millennium. He pictured a highly centralized and disciplined world order, in which every aspect of life was controlled and regimented. Fixation and conformity, not dynamism and expansion, were the new goals. But Huxley advanced far beyond the older projects for space voyages and inter-planetary encounters and wars.

The monsters that inhabited this technocratic utopia were not such as Kepler imagined on the moon: they had, rather, been deliberately fabricated for the purpose of keeping every part of existence, above all human potentialities, under centralized scientific control. Huxley was imaginative enough to realize that the ultimate dream of power is not merely control over the external environment, but control over man himself: not only by the genetic re-shaping of his body, but by the biochemical conditioning of his whole organism, not least his mind, from birth onward.

The deliberate destruction of man's organic inheritance begins in the Central Hatchery and Conditioning Center with extra-uterine pregnancy, by a combination of chemical injections and shock treatments, even before the embryo emerges from the incubating bottles. From the careful choosing of the spermatozoa and ova onward, the purpose of the scientific manipulators is to create a rigid caste system, a biological hierarchy, graded downward from the highest intelligences, Alphas, bred to exercise control, descending by stages through Betas to Epsilons, increasingly lower in intelligence; all bred to the docile acceptance of a scientifically perfected world in which nothing, not even creativity, is autonomous—except the system itself.

In portraying this world Huxley took for granted those aspects of the environment that were mere extrapolations of current tendencies: sky scrapers many times the current height, air taxis for travel, and a hundred other devices, gadgets, luxurious utilities. And he realized that the most fatal fact about these triumphs of mechanical and biological control was that they would produce a completely boring and meaningless mode of life, which in turn would call for further counter-treatment on the same lines.

Huxley understood that radical genetic intervention might extirpate many traits undesirable to those who sought to establish complete human subordination to the megamachine. But he also saw that further adaptive measures would be necessary: thus potential mothers, deprived of the mammalian experience of pregnancy, would need a hormone pill to counterfeit this experience; and in addition, a whole series of sedatives, tranquillizers, and aphrodisiacs would be called for to keep the system in equilibrium. Some of these would be of a chemical nature, others, like the "feelies," would provide a more sophisticated, mindless equivalent of the movies. (In a 'feelie' representing sexual intercourse on a bearskin rug, Huxley notes, "every hair of the bear is reproduced.") But he could hardly guess that by the nineteen-sixties such Feelies would be in mass production for public entertainment. While Bulwer-Lytton and Wells could imagine a low-grade population kept in place only by force, Huxley saw that this was the weakness of most earlier forms of absolutism, and that an even surer mode of control would be achieved by parasitic surfeit, supplemented by tactile stimuli and frequent orgasms. The Pornographic Fair.

In the past a few successful absolutisms had taken some advantage of this weakness: did not Augustus Caesar ensure the popularity of his imperial regime by restoring the Saturnalia? And did not Lorenzo de' Medici stage delirious carnivals through whose sexual indulgences the citizens of Florence could forget the loss of their freedom? Huxley, anticipating Hitler, saw that such corruption might be made more systematic and universal, with a gain in effective power to those who directed the system. So sexual promiscuity becomes a duty; and in lieu of the still-uninvented Pill, every girl goes about with a visible cartridge belt of contraceptives, ready for Instant Copulation. Except for their work duties, everyone is reduced to an infantile dream state, and even the superior Alphas, the governing class, have a duty—as already today—to be infantile *whenever possible*. By the daily administration of Soma tablets, and by hypnopaedia—electronic teaching while asleep—docile conformity and obedience are ensured. The unforgiveable sins are to wish to be alone, to be selective, to be 'different,' to be self-governing. Even Alphas may not depart from their prescribed pattern.

So farfetched did this fantasy seem to Huxley himself that he pushed his Brave New World into the seventh century 'After Ford'—a dating that now seems quaint for more than one reason. But to his own consternation, as he confessed in 'Brave New World Revisited,' some of the most obnoxious features of his dehumanized, indeed, de-corticated commonwealth were already in existence, or were undergoing serious experimentation, before a single generation had passed, and many more have come about since.

In the ensuing years, the outlines of the system have become more unmistakable; and the sort of pseudo-life that awaits mankind once its total surrender shall have been effected has become more clearly defined. Beginning with artificial insemination and extra-uterine pregnancy (Muller), the automatic conditioning of the infant will start in his isolated and enclosed crib (Skinner); thenceforward learning machines (Skinner and others) operating in isolated cells without direct human contact will teach the growing child; one set of electronic apparatus will record dreams for computer analysis and personality correction, while another will provide programmed information; constant bombardment of meaningless messages will massage the tribalized mind (McLuhan); large-scale automated farming operations under remote control will supply food (Rand); central station computers with the aid of robots will take charge of all domestic operations from menu planning and marketing to housework (Seaborg); while cybernetically run factories will produce an abundance of goods (Wiener); and private motor cars under automatic central control (M.I.T. and Ford) will transport passengers along superhighways to underground cities or alternatively to asteroid colonies in space (Dandridge Cole); while centralized computers will take the place of national decision-makers, and a sufficient supply of hallucinogens will give every vestigial human being the ecstatic sense of being alive (Leary). With the aid of organ transplants (Barnard and others) we shall successfully extend this pseudo-life by a century or two. *Finally the beneficiaries of the system will die without for a moment having realized that they have never been alive.*

Meanwhile, a single detachable space capsule, the "first perfect environment" (Fuller) will serve each individual successively as a crib, a schoolroom, a housing unit, or a component of a fast-moving vehicle (automated motor car or rocket), until, at the end, both the capsule and its occupant are removed to a super-crematorium to be volatilized—or taken to a deepfreeze center to be preserved for surgical use, if not kept for future resuscitation on Mars. The other tempting alternative now being considered would be to retard all the natural processes of organic deterioration sufficiently to make this barely humanoid nonentity 'immortal.'

One further step alone remains to be extrapolated, for Huxley strangely overlooked it, though Samuel Butler and Roderick Seidenberg did not. And this is that the controllers who set up this supermechanism will themselves serve as its final sacrificial victims; for when the planetary megamachine reaches its terminal point of soulless perfection, the originating human intelligence will have become completely absorbed—and thus eliminated. So man's final achievement, at the summit of his progress, would be to create an ineffable electronic God: the deity for whom his chief contemporary prophet, Marshall McLuhan, has already composed an appropriately incoherent and frantically meaningless Holy Writ. Long before reaching this terminal stage, however, a planetary interchange of hydrogen bombs or scientifically contrived plagues will, far more probably, bring on an equally vacuous conclusion by an even speedier method.

This immense, still impending total human sacrifice cannot be appraised in the rational or scientific terms that those who have created this system favor: it is, I stress again, an essentially religious phenomenon. As such it offers a close parallel with the original doctrines of Buddhism, even down to the fact that it shares Prince Gautama's atheism. What, indeed, is the elimination of man himself from the process he in fact has discovered and perfected, with its promised end of all striving and seeking, but the Buddha's final escape from the Wheel of Life? Once complete and universal, total automation means total renunciation of life and eventually total extinction: that very retreat into Nirvana that Prince Gautama pictured as man's only way to free himself from sorrow and pain and misfortune. When the life-impulse is depressed, this doctrine, we know, exerts an immense attraction upon masses of disappointed and disheartened souls: for a few centuries Buddhism became dominant in India and swept over China. For similar reasons it is reviving again today.

But note: those who originally accepted this view of man's ultimate destiny, and sought to meet death halfway, did not go to the trouble of creating an elaborate technology to accomplish this end: in that direction they went no farther, significantly enough, than the invention of a water-driven prayer wheel. Instead they practiced concentrated meditation and inner detachment, acts as free from technological intervention as the air they breathed. And they earned an unexpected reward for this mode of withdrawal, a reward that the worshippers of the machine will never know. Instead of extinguishing forever their capacity to feel pleasure or pain, they intensified it, creating poems, philosophies, paintings, sculptures, monuments, ceremonies that restored their hope, their organic animation, their creative zeal: revealing once more in their erotic exuberance an impassioned and exalted sense of man's own potential destiny. Our latter-day technocratic Buddhism can make no such promises.

Let me sum up. Such visions of endless mechanical progress, such totalitarian utopias, such realistic extrapolations of scientific and technical possibilities all played a more active part in practical day-to-day changes than has usually been realized. These anticipatory subjective promptings were always in advance of actual experience, insistently beckoning, pointing ahead to the next step, breaking down resistance by suggesting that any attempt to reduce the tempo of change or to alter its direction was doomed by the very nature of the universe—by which those who took this view meant the obsolete mechanical world picture. Only by understanding the role of this ideological preparation can one appreciate the ease with which the new megamachine finally came into existence.

Both the mechanical world picture and the visions of ever more rapid mechanical and material progress, yes, even the horror stories of a scientifically ordained future, under the control of an officious bureaucratic elite, made it easier to accept the new megamachine as an inevitable and inescapable reality, perfect by definition, since all its dehumanized components conform to the requirements of the system. There has been no "blessed interval," as Aldous Huxley had hoped, between "too little order" and "the nightmare of too much," for the latter is already waiting "just around the corner." Now that we have reached this far from jolly corner, we must have the courage to confront that ghastly nightmare before it fatally envelops us.

CHAPTER NINE

The Nucleation of Power

1: 'A LETTER TO TEACHERS OF HISTORY'

In so far as human progress can be related to the facts of technological change since the medieval period, the best interpretation remains that of Henry Adams, who saw the import of this change well before there was an adequate history in either department. More than half a century ago, he perceived that there had been a constant increase in energy and an accelerated use from the thirteenth century on; and that this had been a main factor in transforming Western civilization.

Already, by 1905, Adams realized that this was not an unqualified gain, for the quickening of the tempo might destroy the entire social structure, whose shakiness was already noticeable to him in 'advanced' nations like England and France. So far as anyone might, greatly daring, undertake the task, he addressed himself to preparing his contemporaries to understand this situation, and get ready to make appropriate changes in their habits of thought and their institutions. Though his failure to awaken even a flicker of response should temper the expectations of anyone who would follow in his footsteps, this very fact demonstrates one part of the theme of the present chapter: the existence of ancient customs and compulsions attached to archaic fantasies that incapacitate the victims of the myth of the machine from taking the necessary counter-measures to slow down the 'automation of automation' and control the forces that threaten man's very being.

Not the least claim of Henry Adams to our respect is that he was led to understand the radical changes in store for the twentieth century by reading backward into the past from the contemporary applications of electricity, and forward into the future from the probable consequences of radium. Amazingly, he was almost alone in realizing the importance of the latter datum; for the radical transformation of our whole conception of the physical world, which derives from the discovery of the properties of the radioactive elements, was for long passed over by most of his scientific contemporaries. Highly competent physicists, not least Lord Rutherford himself, who shares with the Curies high distinction as both experimenter and theoretic physicist, remained indifferent to both the technical potentialities and the social consequences of exploiting atomic energy.

Even before historians of technics had put together the evidence for the increased utilization of energy after the twelfth century, Adams had, in outlining this change, quietly abandoned the misleading notion of the eighteenth-century 'Industrial Revolution': he shrewdly hit upon the nodal points on the curve of increasing energy in Western Europe. His inexact knowledge and his dubious mathematics were more than compensated by his extraordinary intuitive insight. What is more, he coupled the rate of increase in energy with the shortening of the time period for each phase. As a result, he even anticipated the present swift change from the electrical phase to one based on nuclear energy. If his dates require a slight correction, his general picture nevertheless stands. Here, in terms of energy alone, was a curve of genuine progress, all the clearer because it could be translated into mathematical terms on a cartesian graph. The curve, as it hit the nuclear phase, alarmingly headed steeply upward off the paper.

Though Henry Adams sought scientific aid for his interpretation, he was unable to enlist it: so unfortunately, in search of some sort of theoretic scaffolding, he attached his observations to a quite irrelevant physical principle: Willard Gibbs' phase rule, which at best provided him only with a vaguely suggestive metaphor. What the phase rule did was to call attention to the fact that each definable stage in the expansion of energy brought about an unpredictable change of character, comparable to the change from solid ice to water, from water to steam. Since Lloyd Morgan's penetrating analysis in 'Emergent Evolution,' one would now call each succeeding phase an 'emergent.'

As Henry Adams put it, the analogy was crude and misleading, all the more because it gave to this accelerated production of energy the independent status, it would seem, of a law of nature; whereas it was, instead, an observed fact in a particular movement in human history: the composite product of human inventions like the watermill, the windmill, gunpowder, and coal mining, of human activities in commerce and exploration and war, and of scientific interests, political ambitions, and financial drives that served directly and indirectly to widen the province of the machine. In short, the new power complex.

The increase in energy was, accordingly, not an expression of natural forces alone, like a stroke of lightning. But Adams' uncorrected Calvinism caused him to treat historic changes as if they were predestined, originating entirely outside man and as much beyond his control as was his damnation or salvation in Calvinist theology. This residual theology re-enforced the bias of contemporary science, with its dogmatic determinism. Intellectually, Adams was not at home in a world where human intentions counted and human actions, though quantitatively insignificant, might sometimes, as J. Clerk Maxwell believed, be decisive.

But if Henry Adams failed to give an adequate account of the dynamics of the social organizations, monastic, monarchic, and capitalistic, which had favored this enormous and constantly accelerating increase of energy from the twelfth century to the twentieth, he was far in advance of his contemporaries in tracing out the imminent consequences. As early as 1904, Adams perceived the psychological malaise that already accompanied the gains in power thus far achieved. Writing to a friend he said: "Prosperity never before imagined, power never wielded by man, speed never reached by anything but a meteor, had made the world nervous, querulous, unreasonable, afraid." In a still more striking letter to his fellow-historian Henry Osborn Taylor, written only a year later, Adams made an even more astonishing prediction, as follows:

"The assumption of unity, which was the mark of human thought in the Middle Ages, has yielded very slowly to the proofs of complexity. The stupor of science before radium is a proof of it. Yet it is quite sure, according to my score of ratios and curves that, at the accelerated rate of progression since 1600, it will not need another century or half century to turn thought upside down. Law in that case would disappear as theory or *a priori* principle and give place to force. Morality would become police. Explosives would reach cosmic violence. Disintegration would overcome integration."

Those who may have followed my writings since 1940 will already have read these prescient words, later published in the collection of Adams' letters. I do not apologize for repeating them more than once—though now, I trust, for the last time.

What Adams foresaw in this passage was the social consequences of increasing physical power without a commensurate increase of intellectual insight, moral discipline, social awareness, and responsible political direction: a need that was all too belatedly recognized only by a handful of nuclear scientists at the moment that "bombs of cosmic violence" were finally invented. What made this prospective transformation socially dangerous was not the expansion of energy by itself, but the coincident release from moral inhibitions and life-conserving taboos, practices that had proved essential to human survival from the earliest stages on.

The proof of Adams' profound understanding came even before the invention of the atom bomb, for in the development of monopolistic political power in all its various totalitarian forms, terror, torture, and mass extermination had been re-introduced as normal instruments of government. In the very act of resisting fascism by war after 1940, the constitutional democracies abandoned the moral standards and laws of war hitherto respected by 'civilized' nations and copied the abominable fascist practice of indiscriminately exterminating civilian populations. This sinister breakdown of morality antedated, and thereby 'justified,' by establishing the precedent, the use of the atom bomb as a cheaper means for effecting the same result.

The other name for this explosive increase of energy, then, was totalitarian de-moralization: the same animus that since 1945 has led the chief garrison states to develop nuclear bombs in quantities sufficient to annihilate all life on this planet. Power on the scale Adams predicted made paranoia respectable, by giving scientific and technological backing to infantile ambitions and psychotic hallucinations.

The year after Adams died, his hazardous generalizations were confirmed; since it was in 1919 that Rutherford's work had gone far enough to suggest the theoretic possibility of breaking up the atom, and thus ushering in the final phase that Adams had fixed at 1917. At this point Rutherford's chief assistant, Frederick Soddy, in the fourth edition of his two-volume work on radioactivity, observed:

"The problem of transmutation and the liberation of atomic energy to carry on the labour of the world is no longer surrounded with mystery and ignorance, but is daily being reduced to a form capable of exact quantitative reasoning. It may be that it will remain forever unsolved. But we are advancing along the only road likely to bring success at a rate which makes it probable that one day will see its achievement. Should that day ever arrive, let no one be blind to the magnitude of the issues at stake, or suppose that such an acquisition of the physical resources of humanity can be safely entrusted to those who in the past have converted the blessings already conferred by science into a curse."

Soddy's own acute sense of social responsibility caused him to turn from research in physics to the problem of expressing the energies now available in appropriate economic terms; but his training as a scientist, or rather his lack of a background in other fields, caused him to center his thoughts on the national control of money and credit, and the distribution of income, thus losing his broad objective by clinging to this insufficient single factor analysis. His anticipatory insight nevertheless remains highly creditable.

Before Soddy, then, Henry Adams had departed from the traditions of orthodox 'scientific' history by taking two radical steps. And first, he had flouted the canons of historic scholarship by carrying his data on the accelerated production of energy from the past into the future. As a determinist he assumed that the ideas and forces long in motion would continue along the curve he had traced, though it was already mounting so steeply that it indicated either an abrupt termination or the entrance into a new phase, admitting new factors not yet visible in any earlier historic development.

But Adams' second step was even more significant, for it contradicted his determinist faith: he proposed a deliberate initiative in thought, leading to a course of counter-action appropriate to the threatening situation he had described. In what should have been a mind-shaking, if not a world-shaking, 'Letter to Teachers of History,' in 1910, Adams called the attention of his colleagues to the changes that were then in process, and suggested that they should address themselves to understanding the forces that were at work, and pool their collective intelligence in an effort to devise the institutional changes necessary to turn these immense forces to human advantage, since, if uncontrolled, "bombs of cosmic violence" might bring civilization itself to an end.

Nightmare anticipations of just such eventualities had previously been registered in the Western mind, from the recorded dreams of Leonardo da Vinci on to the equally ominous fantasies, also published in the eighteen-eighties, of Madame Blavatsky: even Edmond de Goncourt, according to a letter of Oscar Wilde's, had thrown out the possibility, doubtless picked up from one of his scientific friends, of extracting hydrogen from the air to "make a terrible machine of destruction." (Oscar Wilde's 'Letters': 17 December 1891.)

In groping his way to these conclusions, Henry Adams had been unable to obtain any effective help from the physical scientists, most of whom were still too firmly anchored in the seemingly stable world of abstractions derived from seventeenth-century mechanics. So it is hardly to be wondered at that his closer academic colleagues, in history and philosophy, were equally unaroused by his dire predictions, and regarded his patent alarm as quite unwarranted by any realities they recognized, or were professionally qualified to handle. Their inertia was no different, indeed, from that of many distinguished physicists, down to Millikan, who were sure, despite their new insights into the structure of the atom, that nuclear fission could not be artificially induced. Even the actual designers of the atom bomb had reservations about their possible success. Yet Adams' failure to command attention from the scientific world implied no lack of cogency in his historic arguments. The potentialities he had opened up were simply too unpleasant for his contemporaries to face.

This resistance only adds to Adams' merit. As a competent generalist he had put together all the pieces of available technical and scientific knowledge, in a fresh pattern of great significance. But no specialist in any field, even had he been aware of Adams' proposal, was as yet prepared to see the whole picture, or to admit that, if this emerging pattern was meaningful, he could no longer cling to his dualistic seventeenth-century ideology or practice without revision the purely quantitative and 'objective' procedures that had so far proved so successful. That this mechanistic seventeenth-century cosmos would disintegrate suddenly, under the impact of nuclear explosions, and produce twentieth-century chaos seemed too unlikely to be taken seriously.

But if Adams was right, the historic situation called for a new outlook, new methods, and a deliberate assumption of grave new duties: a change of mind more urgent than that which took place in science after Copernicus. Unfortunately, these were requirements he himself was unable to fulfill even in Baconian outline.

If Adams' scholarly colleagues greeted his appeal with an embarrassed silence—even the free, open-minded William James turned a deaf ear—it was because Henry Adams' guiding idea was even more radical than he realized. By his stress on the potential future, he had moved from the world of serial time and causality—which his nineteenth-century training made him equate with reality—to the organic order of temporal duration, of phylogeny and social inheritance (memory and history), in which both past and future intersect in the present. In this organic world purpose superimposes itself on process and partly transforms it; here the succession of events is determined, not by external forces working in isolation upon isolated objects, but by reactions in a more complex field modified by the organism's inherited nature and by lifetime accumulations of experience in an environmental field teeming with other organisms: here, finally, organic continuity absorbs novelty and determines whether it is consistent with the organism's own persistent nature and its tentative gropings and projections toward the future.

Adams himself was unfortunately so committed to the deterministic atomism of orthodox post-seventeenth-century science, dealing with abstractions and isolates, that he did not see that the problem he propounded could not be answered on the basis of his own ideological premises. He evaded that issue by taking refuge in the waiting arms of the Virgin Mary.

Though Adams had attributed the constant acceleration of energies solely to the physical instruments that effected this transformation, he had actually stumbled upon a new factor whose tremendous and fatal significance has even now not been fully grasped. This is the fact that the gradual disruption of the whole system of social inhibitions, religious restraints, and communal customs that had prevailed in early societies had amplified human efforts through releasing an immense output of non-human energy: a process that recognized no limits to its own increasingly automatic expansion. Society, awed by its indisputable success in mechanization, had begun to obey its own automatic system, and every kind of activity was geared to an accelerated quantitative expansion: the expansion of territory, the expansion of population, the expansion of mechanical facilities, the expansion of production rates, capital gains, incomes, profits, and consumable wealth. Behind all these subsidiary phenomena stood the expansion of scientific knowledge, as the prime mover in this whole process. The 'Automation of Automation' had begun.

To most of Adams' contemporaries, these escalating automatisms, these deliberate departures from the restraining social norms of earlier communities were indefeasible signs of progress. Adams alone had the courage to follow that seemingly beneficent development to its menacing negative conclusion: power on a scale that could no longer be controlled—*except by a profound re-orientation of human habits, efforts, and goals.* Failing that transformation, Adams foresaw an appalling human debacle. Though Adams could propose no remedy for the threatening disease, his prognosis proved remarkably accurate. Within a generation after Adams' death, both scientific progress and human regression had taken place on a scale that he alone had been able to imagine.

2 : THE OLD MEGAMACHINE
AND THE NEW

Henry Adams' prediction, for all its remarkable prescience, was handicapped by being confined to a single factor, energy. Before the events he foresaw could come to pass the components of a new megamachine had to be discovered and invented, tested and organized, and finally assembled into a single unitary organization. As with the original megamachine of the Pyramid Age, this assemblage could be brought about only under the fusion heat of war. Adams correctly anticipated a major part of the radical change that was about to take place. But he could not foresee that a more massive integration of these forces might occur in a fashion that would establish an even more formidable system of control.

Yet up to the point where the implosion of these forces actually took place, so many of the necessary components were lacking, or were so deficient in quantity, and so many surviving institutions were so resistant to radical change, that Adams' prediction could be treated disdainfully as the aberration of an aging mind. Up to 1940 it was still possible to regard the continuation and acceleration of modern technology as, on the whole, favorable to human development; and so firmly has this conviction been implanted, so completely has the Myth of the Machine taken hold of the modern mind, that these archaic beliefs are still widely regarded as well-founded, scientifically accredited, indubitably 'progressive'—in short, practically unchallengeable.

Not that anyone, at the beginning of the twentieth century, could have been unaware that profound changes were being made in every aspect of daily life. These changes were invigorated and abetted, not merely by a great access of energy, but by a network of transportation systems and communications systems that had never existed before on anything like the present scale. The growth of capitalism, however uneven in its distribution of benefits, nevertheless appeared to many observers as the necessary preparation for a more equitable, socialized system. The seemingly ordained extension of political democracy, through responsible party government, at least in industrially advanced countries, supposedly guaranteed a smooth transition, by an accretion of measures that provided for social security and social welfare. Though the separate components of the megamachine were already in existence—indeed, the great industrial corporations and cartels were working models—the system as a whole had only begun to coalesce.

The notion that mechanical progress was in itself a liberating influence had remained unchallenged, on the whole, throughout the nineteenth century, except by 'romantics' like Delacroix, Ruskin, and Morris, or more backward-looking thinkers: many separate acts of liberation had indeed accompanied technical innovations and partly justified them, even during periods that saw the brutal degradation of the industrial worker in one new industry after another. Vast voluntary migrations of peaceable unarmed peoples took place, from Europe to America, and under more authoritarian pressures of punishment and political exile, from Russia to Siberia. Travel anywhere was possible—and permanent migration, too, in many countries —without any governmental authorization or restriction. Until 1914 no passports were required anywhere for travelers beyond military age, except in the two surviving major despotisms, Russia and Turkey.

For the first time in history, as the Italian historian Guglielmo Ferrero pointed out, 'freedom of the seas' prevailed everywhere: freedom and safety. Even imperialism, however harsh in its handling of conquered populations, had helped establish that basic law and order and personal security on which all real freedom is founded.

Meanwhile, during the nineteenth century, the number of self-governing societies, organizations, associations, corporations, and communities had markedly increased: and regional entities, once suppressed by the national state or the despotic empire, were beginning to re-assert their cultural individuality and their political independence. Small wonder that hardly anyone suspected that a new megamachine was already in process of formation, and that it would be brought into existence and magnified in every dimension by fresh technical advances.

During the last half century this whole picture has changed: much more than anyone born after 1910 could realize from his personal impressions and memories. And what seemed at first like a series of unrelated and often contradictory tendencies has turned out, not to be an entirely new phenomenon, but one that had first taken place at the very inception of civilization, largely as the result of a parallel constellation of forces operating under similar ideological premises and psychal drives, and bent upon achieving similar objectives: the domination of nature and the subjugation of man.

In Volume One of 'The Myth of the Machine' I associated this implosion with the birth of a new religion, the religion of the Sky Gods. And in my treatment of the scientific and technical transition after the fifteenth century, as the reader must be aware, I have steadily kept an eye on this approaching consummation. When one puts together the scattered, seemingly unrelated components of both systems, the likeness between the two ages becomes striking: all the more because what were once 'impossible' wishes, vain hopes, and empty boasts in the mouths of the ancient gods and kings have now become actualities, and herald even more wanton expansions of both irresistible power and unrestrained irrationality. Let us assemble these necessary components in the order of their appearance.

And first, there was the cosmic religious preparation, which I have already described as the rebirth of the Sun God, or, to put it in more commonplace terms, the heliocentric system of Copernicus. The exponents of this religion, once called natural philosophers, later scientists, for long bore themselves with such modesty and self-effacement, and brought forth such an abundance of useful knowledge, applicable in mining, hydraulics, navigation, war—and eventually in medicine, agriculture, and public health —that no one suspected that their methods might also become a prime instrument of dehumanized authority.

Along with the new universal religion of the Sun God came—with a deceptive air of independence—the centralization of political power, first in the emerging race of tyrants and despots and kings, who subverted both feudal obligations and municipal freedoms in order to exert unqualified command over private wealth, by taxation, expropriation, and downright conquest and robbery of weaker peoples. Out of this personal sovereignty of the king by divine right, openly proclaimed as such, rose the impersonal sovereignty of the State. Under oligarchic or republican rule, this collective agency claimed all the prerogatives and powers that the king had originally claimed in person, indeed more sweepingly than any monarch had yet dared to do. As with Egypt, the commands of this super-sovereign could not be carried out without the training and disciplining anew of two ancient orders: the bureaucracy and the army. Up automatism: down autonomy.

None of these institutions had, it is true, entirely disappeared during the intervening five millennia: in some respects, they had benefited from time to time by technical improvements in the media used for keeping the permanent record, in weapons and tactics, in functional hierarchic organization. Both had been kept in being, carefully nurtured by old traditions, in the Army and in the ecclesiastical organization of the Church of Rome, an etherialized megamachine which had endured for some fifteen hundred years.

The new absolute rulers, like Peter the Great of Russia, Frederick Wilhelm of Prussia, and Louis XIV of France, commanded permanent armies installed in permanent barracks, governed by a permanent bureaucracy—all capable, even before telegraphic communication, of exerting more or less effective remote control over distant enemies and scattered populations. This modern centralized mode of organization was incomparably more powerful than that of dispersed medieval communities, with their loose feudal or municipal armies, fitfully trained and sporadically assembled, or their municipal government by amateur officials, exercising limited powers for a single year of office.

These transformations only emphasize that there is no component of the modern megamachine that did not exist, in fact or in dream, in the original model. What is distinctly modern is the effective materialization of archaic dreams that had hitherto been technologically impracticable. With the coalition of political absolutism, military regimentation, and mechanical invention came the re-introduction of an ancient institution that had long been in abeyance: forced labor and compulsory national service for war. The first took the form of slavery and wage labor, under threat of starvation and imprisonment: a system that, like slavery in the United States, flagrantly eroded the pious professions of the current libertarian ideology. But compulsory national service, introduced under the banner of democracy, went even further: it came in as an instrument of 'national survival' in the heat of fighting the wars of the French Revolution, and was continued by the audacious, self-made emperor who liquidated that revolution. Thus the chief military innovation that made the Egyptian megamachine possible was re-introduced for the first time since as a permanent auxiliary of large-scale government. Even at the height of the Roman imperium, no such total organization of large populations for work or destruction had been feasible.

The significance of national conscription (politely called 'universal service') as an essential instrument for mass control, has been passed over by modern political and historical scholars with incredible frivolity or equally incredible blindness. Though no other factor has done more to add to the destructiveness of war, and to condition large populations to the rituals of human massacre, the scholarly literature on the subject is negligible. 'Conscription' claims only two pages in the first edition of the 'Cambridge Modern History' in the volumes dealing wholly with the French Revolution and with Napoleon. The one notable exception is an article by Colonel F. N. Maude in the eleventh edition of the Encyclopaedia Britannica (1910); for he noted that "there is perhaps no law on the statute-books of any nation which has exercised and is destined to exercise a more far-reaching influence on the future of humanity than this little-known French act of 1798." That judgement has still to penetrate our political consciousness.

Up to this point, forced labor, as for road building and fortifications, and compulsory military service, had been general, but local and sporadic: now they became systematic, regular, universal. The national army became, in effect, an educational institution for conditioning its human units to the unthinking, obedient, automatic execution of orders. Even allowing for its occasional generation of resentment and recalcitrance, there is no doubt that this systematic regimentation of a whole population found its way back into the bureau and the factory, and in fact imposed machinelike docility on a scale never before conceivable: all the more because the appropriate ideological doctrines and emotional responses supplemented the physical drill.

The effect of this regimen has become plain. What imperious social reformers like Saint-Simon and Auguste Comte had learned from the Napoleonic era was the efficacy with which military technique can be applied to social behavior. These prophets envisaged a "revolution so final and complete that it would render all legal and political institutions absolute." That goal identifies the new megamachine, and this revolution is now in process.

Let me make clear, at this point, a difference between the State as a mere unit of political administration and the activated megamachine. This difference is brought out in the changing definition of the word 'power' in English. The 'New English Dictionary' traces the definition of power as "possession of control or command over others" back to 1297; it then in 1486 shifts to legal ability, capacity, or authority to act; but in 1727 power takes on a technological role as "any form of energy or force available for application to work." Finally, with the construction of the megamachine, all the modes of power became available for work—both constructive and destructive—on a colossal scale otherwise unattainable. The megamachine, accordingly, is *not* a mere administrative organization: it is a machine in the orthodox technical sense, as a "combination of resistant bodies" so organized as to perform standardized motions and repetitive work. But note: all these forms of power, one re-enforcing the other, became essential to the new Pentagon of Power.

Unlike machines that perform partial operations for specialized purposes, the megamachine by its very nature can be used only in collective, large-scale operations, which are themselves components of a larger power system. By increasing the range and number of such operations from the archaic jobs of canal building, highway building and urban demolition, to the entire industrial process and thence into the organization of education and consumption, the megamachine exercises more effective control over large populations than any merely political unit can profess. Nietzsche once described war as the "health of the State"; but more than this, it is the body and soul of the megamachine. The extent of the megamachine's activities can be judged by the fact that, once a large war comes to an end, it takes from three to five years before the organizations and industries the megamachine absorbs can recover, even with aid from the central authority, the ability to carry on as quasi-independent units.

All the properties of individual machines—high energy inputs, mechanization, automation, quantity output—are increased by their inclusion in the megamachine: but so likewise are the disadvantages of such machines—their rigidity, their irresponsiveness to new situations, their detachment from human purposes other than those embodied in the design of the machine. The chief of these embodied purposes is the exercise of power.

Even before 'absolute' weapons were invented, automatism and absolutism were firmly coupled together in the constitution of every military organization. Hence war is the ideal condition for promoting the assemblage of the megamachine, and to keep the threat of war constantly in existence is the surest way of holding the otherwise autonomous or quasi-autonomous components together as a functioning working unit. Once a megamachine has been brought into existence, any criticism of its program, any departure from its principles, any detachment from its routines, any modifications of its structure through demands from below constitute a threat to the whole system.

3 : THE NEW COALITION

I have left to the end the one institutional prerequisite of the megamachine which, so far as one can analyze the megamachine at its point of origin, did not exist in the ancient model: namely, a special kind of economic dynamism based on rapid capital accumulation, repeated turnovers, large profits, working toward the constant acceleration of technology itself. In short, the money economy.

The coalition of money power with political power was one of the decisive marks of monarchic or despotic absolutism; and the more dependent the military machine became on technical inventions and mass production of weapons, the greater the immediate profits to the national economic system—even though in the long run succeeding generations would find these putative gains offset by the cost of reparations, repairs, and replacements, to say nothing of human wretchedness. Though the moral onus for promoting war has made the munitions manufacturers the scapegoats, the fact is that the paper-profits of war equally enrich every other part of the national economy, even agriculture; for war, with its unparalleled consumption of goods, and its unparalleled wastes, temporarily overcomes the chronic defect of an expanding technology—'overproduction.' War, by restoring scarcity, is necessary on classic capitalist terms to ensure profit.

In turn this economic dynamism, through bellicose destruction—or the building up of military capability for this eventual use—depends upon a vast transfer of credit to the government; and the need for both capital and current income to cover national military expenditures gives sanction to what, from the standpoint of orthodox 'free enterprise,' is an odious imposition: a national income tax. This is a measure that even absolute monarchs introduced with grave misgivings. Louis XIV did not dare to impose it without getting from the theologians of Paris the reassuring dictum that such an imposition could be justified since, as a ruler by 'divine right,' all land and property in the country belonged to him, and could be distributed at his pleasure. It was only during the Napoleonic Wars that, in a relatively free constitutional monarchy like England, the income tax was introduced; though conscription, in the inequable and arbitrary form of navy press gangs, had preceded it; and without the introduction of the constitutional change that legalized the income tax in the United States, in 1913, the vast sums needed to create the new megamachine after 1940 would not have been available.

By now it should be plain that the extravagant largesse derived from national taxation has become a substitute for the profit motive in fostering the economic dynamism of the modern economy. Neither profit-and-loss nor cost-benefit accountancy reduces effectively the operations of the megamachine; for the costs are magically converted into benefits, and the prospective losses through military obsolescence and outright destruction are the source of fresh corporate profits.

Through war, actual and prospective, the megamachine increased its scope and expanded its power, and incidentally removed the one form of feedback the capitalist system had developed to regulate and rationalize its operations: namely, close accountancy of profit and loss, with ultimate bankruptcy as the penalty of miscalculation. It was not through effecting major changes in the capitalist economy, which remained in a general state of semi-paralysis in the nineteen-thirties, but through re-armament and war that an economic revival was effected; and it is by war alone that the system was temporarily saved from self-destruction through its radical weakness: its failure to achieve distributive justice.

Not merely does the money economy, then, over-excite every part of the already expanding power technology, but it makes the continued extension of the megamachine into every area imperative in order to ensure the surplus needed for the negative enterprises of war, planned extermination, and mass control. What is more, as the State extends social security and technical services to the country as a whole, a growing part of the population—despite the fact that the income tax is habitually rigged to favor the rich—has a stake in this centrally directed mode of production, distribution, and collective destruction. In this combination of technological, financial, political, and military dynamism, no one agent was more essential than the other: but all were needed before the megamachine could be reconstituted in an efficient, up-to-date model, with most of its historic defects repaired and its traditional limitations removed.

By the beginning of the twentieth century, the main components of the new megamachine were already in existence, though some were still in half-formed state.

Only two things were lacking: a symbolic figure of absolute power, incarnated in a living ruler, a corporate group, or a super-machine; and a crisis sufficiently portentous and pressing to bring about an implosion of all the necessary components. The crisis arose and the implosion took place: but before that happened, older and cruder models of the megamachine, energized by new mechanical equipment, had come into existence and opened the way for the final explosion of 'absolute' power.

4: TRANSITIONAL TOTALITARIANISM

The re-invention and expansion of the megamachine was in no sense an inevitable outcome of historic forces: indeed, until the end of the nineteenth century, it seemed to many able thinkers that the major changes in Western civilization, even in technology, were favorable to freedom. Such a detached mind as Ernest Renan's, echoing Comte's earlier dictums, could observe, in the eighteen-nineties, that belligerent nationalism was on the wane, and the animus against war was so widespread the armed services could be maintained only by conscription.

During the earlier part of the nineteenth century, with the abandonment of serfdom and the suppression of slavery, strong counter-forces had seemed to be rising, leading to the universal reign of law, self-government, and cooperation on an increasingly worldwide scale. Even in militarized countries like Germany, as late as the Zabern affair in 1912, the government could be censured in the Reichstag for the brutal conduct of a single Prussian officer who had arrogantly pushed a lame cobbler into the gutter and struck him. Political oppression, brutal economic exploitation, preventable disease and starvation—all seemed on the wane.

Admittedly these brave expectations were arrested periodically by ugly outbreaks of collective barbarism, such as the Armenian and Macedonian massacres, the British Opium War in China, and the Boer War in South Africa, with its concentration camps, to say nothing of the infamous conduct of the Western armies that put down the Boxer Rebellion in China. Yet until the outbreak of the First World War, reason and compassion seemed to be gaining the upper hand, along with democratic understanding and cooperation. But the balance in favor of such constructive developments was shaken by the First World War, and the faith that had equated technological with human improvement was undermined, indeed, badly shattered by the realization that all the potentialities for evil had been augmented by the very energies technics had released.

The first intimation that a new megamachine was in fact being assembled came only after the First World War, with the rise of the totalitarian states, beginning with Soviet Russia and Italy. This reversed the trend toward representative government and popular participation which had been the dominant note even in Russia of the previous century. The new form of the fascist or communist dictatorships was that of a single party organization, based on a self-appointed revolutionary junta, and headed by a flesh-and-blood incarnation of the old-time 'king by divine right,' one no longer anointed by God, but, like Napoleon, self-crowned: a ruthless dictator (Lenin), a demonic Fuehrer (Hitler), a bloody tyrant (Stalin), proclaiming the lawfulness of unqualified power, unlawfully seized. That doctrine was as old as Thrasymachus' statement in Plato's 'Republic,' while the example itself was of course thousands of years older.

But the new megamachine did not grow up overnight; and it was only a sanguine liberal illusion of the nineteenth century to have ignored in contemporary life what it also ignored or minimized in its reading of history: the continued existence of slavery from the beginnings of 'civilization' down to the last half of the nineteenth century, along with war and conquest and human exploitation, accepted as normal prerogatives of the sovereign state. Though Herbert Spencer had made a colossal error in his one-sidedly optimistic picture of social evolution, by equating industrialism with peace, he deserves retrospective honor for being the first to deduce from the revival of imperialism in the last quarter of the nineteenth century a decisive reversion to barbarism: 'The Coming Slavery.' In coupling this slavery with the Welfare State, Spencer was in advance of both Hilaire Belloc and Friedrich Hayek. The shock was later to discover that the new barbarism was fortified, almost imposed, by the new technology.

The reassemblage of the ancient invisible machine took place in three main stages, at considerable intervals. The first stage was that marked by the French Revolution of 1789. Though this revolution deposed and executed the traditional king, it reinstated with far greater power his abstract counterpart, the National State, to which, on Rousseau's pseudo-democratic theory of the General Will, it bestowed absolute powers, like those of conscription, powers that historic kings would have envied. Sir Henry Maine, one of the most astute political observers of the Victorian Age, saw clearly through this device: he pointed out that "the despotic sovereign of the 'Contrat Social,' the all-powerful community, is an inverted copy of the King of France, invested with an authority claimed for him by his courtiers."

The second stage came in 1914 with the First World War, though many of the preliminary steps had already been taken by Napoleon I, and carried further by the Prussian military autocracy under Bismarck after the Franco-Prussian War in 1870. This included the enlistment of scholars and scientists as an arm of the state, and the placating of the working classes by universal suffrage, social welfare legislation, national elementary education, job insurance, and old-age pensions, measures that Napoleon, despite his high esteem for law and science and uniform education, had never carried so far. Had Napoleon succeeded in his conquest of Europe, and had he had time to consolidate his military-bureaucratic regime, the megamachine might have emerged, at least halfway toward its modern form, by the middle of the nineteenth century: indeed, even the bedraggled ideological aftermath of Napoleonism conjured up in the mind of young Ernest Renan a future not unlike that which we are now facing: dictatorship by a scientific elite.

Before the First World War was over, the main features of the new megamachine had been roughed in. Even nations that had already achieved a large measure of political freedom, like England and the United States, introduced military conscription; and to meet the exorbitant demands for war material, England established industrial conscription as well, though under somewhat different conditions than those sought by Bellamy. In order, further, to prosecute the war without falling into bankruptcy—an outcome that orthodox market economists had once thought would make any long war impossible—the British government imposed a heavier income tax than it had ever before dared to inflict; while the services of scientists were marshalled in every country to devise more destructive weapons, like TNT bombs and poison gases, to hasten 'victory.'

Thus collective power on a scale never achieved before heightened the pace of technical change in every department; and the control of information by the government, with the feeding of officially selected and favorably colored information to its own people, as a means of 'maintaining morale' (that is, quieting disillusion and opposition), gave modern 'democratic' governments their first taste of thought-control, on a more efficient positive basis than antiquated organizations like the Russian autocracy had employed. This provided the megamachine with a valuable supplement to physical coercion and military discipline.

Curiously, the first attempt to modernize the oppressive megamachine came about in Russia through the Bolshevik revolution. But despite the fact that Lenin and his collaborators were conditioned by their Marxian premises to favor Western science and industrialism, it happened that in taking over the Czarist state they inherited in the bureaucracy the most perfect surviving example of the ancient megamachine, untouched by economic competition and industrial efficiency. Though that system was now in a state of utter corruption and dissolution, it had imposed habits and responses upon the masses that up to a point favored the succeeding centralized bureaucratic organization. Much of the population was already conditioned to servile compliance and to the worship of a single, supposedly all-powerful ruler.

Though the democratic objectives of the social revolution were soon savagely suppressed, if not forgotten, the dictatorship survived by utilizing the bureaucratic social apparatus and the psychological conditioning of the antiquated megamachine. The State took over the most brazen assumption of rule by divine right: 'The King can do no wrong,' and even succeeded in translating it into a more absurd positive form: 'The Party is always right.' Those who oppose the Party Line, no matter how wildly it zigzags and contradicts itself, no matter how unscrupulously the new rulers, the *apparatchiki,* work to preserve their own privileged position, must be condemned as heretics, 'hooligans,' counter-revolutionaries.

Once this new autocracy was seated in power, rival institutions—the local soviets or agricultural communes, the cooperatives, the trade unions, non-conformist national or religious groups like the Orthodox Christians and the Jews, even the Gypsies—were harried, suppressed, or destroyed. The Megamachine is an elephant that fears even the smallest mouse.

This system of coercion, ruthless enough under Lenin and Trotsky, became absolute under Joseph Stalin, whose paranoid fears, suspicions, and murderous malevolence were in part signs that the new megamachine still lacked an essential feature that the old one possessed: an awe-inducing religion and a ritual of divine worship that would gain by mass suggestion a more complete submission and more abject obedience than terror alone can achieve. As with Hitler later, Stalin's methodical madness resulted in the deliberate slaughter on a wholesale scale not only of peasants, but of the informed groups and classes, the trained technicians and creative minds, upon whom such a complex fabric as a megamachine, even in its primitive state, depends for its existence.

For a while, indeed, Stalin through sheer terrorism almost succeeded in turning himself into a Divine King in the image of Ivan the Terrible and Peter the Great. He could be addressed, Russians have pointed out, only in the form that was used exclusively in the past in addressing a Czar. Stalin's solemn pronouncement on every subject from the mechanism of genetic inheritance to the origins of language were fatuously hailed as the voice of omniscience. So they became the ultimate guides to scholars and scientists who had spent their lifetime on research without ever reaching such ultimate and irrefragable truths. The same tendency later became magnified even to the point of gross caricature—if that were possible—in the pronouncements of Mao Tse-tung.

In its extreme Stalinist form the Russian megamachine betrayed, even before Hitler, the most sinister defects of the ancient megamachine: its reliance upon physical coercion and terrorism, its systematic enslavement of the entire working population, including members of the dictatorial party, its suppression of free personal intercourse, free travel, free access to the existing store of knowledge, free association, and finally its imposition of human sacrifice to appease the wrath and sustain the life of its terrible, blood-drinking God, Stalin himself. The result of this system was to transform the entire country into a prison, part concentration camp, part extermination laboratory, from which the only hope of escape was by death. The 'liberty, fraternity, and equality' of the French Revolution had turned, by a further revolution around the same axle, into alienation, inequality, and enslavement.

Unfortunately, long enurement to the Czarist megamachine had trained the Russians in forms of docile conformity that could hardly be distinguished from willing cooperation. Here and there a minority discovered little niches and hideouts where, silently, some portion of untrammelled life could be maintained. But woe to prouder souls, who dared open defiance. The writer Isaak Babel, who demanded the privilege of writing 'badly'— that is, not in conformity with the party line—and who proclaimed that silence, too, might be an effective mode of expression, was soon put out of the way and executed. Even silence could be provocative. Because this revolution, like its bloody predecessor, devoured its children in a methodical saturnalia of violence, it was long before the megamachine could produce in sufficient numbers the new elite, whose views and whose way of life conformed to its requirements: the technicians, the bureaucrats, the scientists. Fortunately the indispensable scientists, aided by orthodox science's methodical divorce from moral and social issues, continued to provide the system with the quotas of new knowledge necessary to accelerate the operations of the megamachine and effect the transition, via nuclear energy, from the archaic to the modern form.

By the time Stalin died he had rehabilitated and magnified all the most repulsive features of the ancient megamachine, while his scientific and technical collaborators, both voluntarily and under compulsion, had already begun to construct the principal components of the modernized megamachine. Because of its head start, the archaic form even now still dominates the Soviet system, though powerfully re-enforced by the new agents. The fact that Stalin, like Lenin before him, was treated at death to the ancient Egyptian process of mummification, and was put on view for public worship, makes the parallel almost too neat to seem anything but contrived—as if invented by me to support one of the major themes of this book. But so it actually was.

5: THE NAZI CONTRIBUTION

As it turned out, Adolf Hitler was destined to become, even more effectively than Joseph Stalin, the chief agent in the modernization of the megamachine. This is not because he was less psychotic, for delusions of grandeur and fantasies of absolute power are an essential motive power for this peculiar mechanism. Hitler's model, assembled in a scientifically advanced country, was a base hybrid: partly archaic, on the Assyrian model, and partly improved, on the mechanized, but still clumsy seventeenth-century model (Louis XIV-Napoleon), partly modern, utilizing aspects of the available science, plus the latest behaviorist advertising techniques, to condition the entire population; but likewise adding psychotic components derived from Hitler's own autistic fantasies. Albert Speer, the architect finally placed in charge of war production under Hitler, pointed out the singular merits of the Nazi megamachine in a speech made at the Nuremberg trials.

"Hitler's dictatorship," Speer noted, "differed in one fundamental point from all its predecessors in history. . . . Through technical devices like the radio and the loudspeaker, eighty million people were deprived of independent thought. . . . Earlier dictators needed highly qualified assistants, even at the lowest level—men who could think and act independently. The totalitarian system in the period of modern technical development can dispense with such men . . . it is possible to mechanize the lower leadership. As a result of this there has arisen the new type of the uncritical recipient of orders." One can take exception to Speer's analysis in only one respect: the uncritical acceptance began at the top as he himself demonstrated.

Now the leaders of the Nazi Third Reich regarded war as the natural state of human society and extermination as a desirable way of establishing the dominance of their national organization and their ideology over rival systems. The enslavement or extermination of inferior groups or nations thus became the appointed duty of those who accepted their doctrine of 'Aryan' superiority. Only in the atmosphere of constant war could totalitarian leaders command the absolute obedience and unqualified loyalty necessary for the smooth operation of such a megamachine.

In conformity with these aberrations, systematic violence, brutality, torture, and sexual corruption were treated as normal, even desirable accompaniments of the 'new order.' And though all these features were openly present from the beginning, many otherwise decent people, in other countries besides Germany, openly hailed this regime as 'The Wave of the Future,' though when one examines either its doctrines or its acts, one can find in Nazism only the sewage-laden backwash of the past.

The need to establish quickly the permanent supremacy of his megamachine drove Hitler to seek to achieve by war what he could probably have accomplished, with a little patience, by terror and corruption alone, with or without the connivance with Stalin that seemed guaranteed by the Nazi-Soviet pact in 1939. Far more effectively than Stalin, indeed, Hitler had secured the cooperation of the intellectual classes and the established Churches. Without serious opposition he restored the most virulent forms of racialism, existentialism, blood-and-soilism, by attaching them cunningly to reputable sentiments and genial emotional needs that had been left out of the mechanical world picture and more or less disparaged by the more rational utopian proposals of the previous century. In the subjugation of Austria, the enslavement of Czechoslovakia, the annihilation of Poland, and the conquest of France, Hitler demonstrated his understanding of the ancient malpractices and misuses of the megamachine far better than its positive potentialities.

Hitler, like Stalin, had by 1939 come as near to presiding over his people in the role of the divine king as it is possible to do in the present age. He did so, not merely with the blessings of the ancient German nobility, the great landlords, and the officers' corps, along with the magnates of Essen, Hamburg, and Berlin; but he likewise had the faithful support of a considerable part—possibly a major part—of the ecclesiastical and the scientific establishment, to say nothing of such obscurantist soothsayers as the existentialist philosopher Martin Heidegger.

To ensure undeviating uniformity, writers, artists, musicians, psychologists were enrolled in official organizations and obliged to wear the same mental uniform. Similarly, the Nazi cure for unemployment was on the best pharaonic pattern: the uniformed labor army. Meanwhile, the military spirit of brutal drill and mindless obedience was carried into the schools and universities, where, as had been proved during the First World War, it had never been entirely absent since Fichte's day. In short, the Germans not merely enlarged the dimensions of the ancient magamachine, but made important innovations in the techniques of mass control: innovations that later corporate megamachines are now perfecting with the aid of spying devices, opinion polls, market research, and computerized dossiers on private life. In the background, the torture chamber and the crematorium, if not planetary incineration, are still ready to complete the job.

But every totalitarian system brings its own Nemesis, to the very degree that the system is closed and self-sealed—incapable of self-criticism and self-correction. With poetic justice the first victims of the system were the leaders themselves, whose effective control was undermined by self-induced phobias, hallucinations, and prefabricated lies that they themselves had come to believe. Witness Stalin's stultifying stubbornness in rejecting authentic information about Hitler's approaching attack on Russia: a calamitous misjudgement that caused untold suffering and military humiliation: indeed, almost lost Russia the war. At the end of the conflict the Nazi megamachine had equally become the victim of its leaders' ideological perversities and emotional aberrations: they wasted on the occupation and greedy exploitation of peripheral countries military forces that should have been concentrated in combat. Likewise they undermined military and industrial effort by exterminating millions of non-combatant Russians and Poles for the mere gratification of their pathological hatred and contempt, while the regime further deprived itself, by starvation, torture, and death, of some six million Jews, many of whom, until they faced their incredible fate, had remained patriotic Germans, whose labor might have been used efficiently to increase production.

With all these screaming errors of judgement and miscarriages of military effort, one might think that both the Russian and the Nazi megamachines would have passed completely out of existence, more discredited than the invisible machine that had flourished in the Pyramid Age. But unfortunately the errors committed by the Nazis did not prevent them from at first achieving a series of astounding military successes; and these feats brought about a similar recrudescence of the megamachine in Britain and the United States. By the curious dialectic of history, Hitler's enlargement and refurbishment of the Nazi megamachine gave rise to the conditions for creating those counter-instruments that would conquer it and temporarily wreck it.

So far, then, from the megamachine's being utterly discredited by the colossal errors of its ruling 'elite,' the opposite actually happened: it was rebuilt by the Western allies on advanced scientific lines, with its defective human parts replaced by mechanical and electronic and chemical substitutes, and finally coupled to a source of power that made all previous modes of power-production as obsolete as Bronze Age missiles. In short, in the very act of dying the Nazis transmitted the germs of their disease to their American opponents: not only the methods of compulsive organization or physical destruction, but the moral corruption that made it feasible to employ these methods without stirring opposition.

Hitler, even more than Stalin, had proved himself a master of demoralization, for he was able to release in others the most destructive forces of the unconscious. In the course of a dozen years he had popularized every mode of human debasement. He even employed physicians who had taken the Hippocratic oath to perform loathsome pseudo-scientific tortures upon human beings, such as none but psychotics could entertain even in fantasy. On the world stage, Hitler turned the original 'Theater of the Absurd' into a 'Theater of the Cruel': and the avant-garde theaters that now glorify these psychotic manifestations are so many vulgar testimonials to Hitler's overwhelming success.

During his brief ascendancy Hitler and his agents succeeded in debauching human values and breaking down salutary inhibitions it had taken civilized peoples thousands of years to build up in order to protect themselves against their own destructive fantasies. None of the perversities Huxley had anticipated in his 'Brave New World' was out of order in the Third Reich. The first military triumph of the Nazis in the Second World War, the total destruction of central Warsaw, followed by that of the center of Rotterdam in 1940, carried out a technique originally established by the first megamachines. The Germans had caught the essential spirit of the original models, as in Ashurnasirpal's recorded boast: "I cut off their heads, I burned them with fire, a pile of living men and of heads against their city gate I set up, men impaled on stakes, the city I destroyed and devastated, I turned it into mounds and ruin heaps, the young men and maidens in the fire I burned." It remained for our 'progressive' age to sanctify these psychotic acts and normalize this criminality.

Even before the Nazis, this poison was already working in the 'progressive' technical-military mind. The policy of mass extermination of civilians from the air was first advocated by the American General William Mitchell, then by the Italian General Douhet, as a cheap, quick, substitute for the slow kind of victory achieved by armies assaulting other identifiable armies. Mussolini's boasted triumphs over the helpless Abyssinian villagers commended this principle for general use; and the Germans followed up their first easy demolitions in Warsaw and Rotterdam by more massive assaults against British cities, beginning in September 1940 with London.

As an effective strategy for achieving military domination, this demoralized method has repeatedly proved costly and futile. Even when deployed against whole cities, not military targets, official inquiry revealed that only twenty per cent of the bombs dropped during the Second World War by the American Air Force fell on the designated areas. From London and Coventry to Hamburg, Dresden, Tokyo, and Hanoi, the minuscule military results were hugely disproportionate to the industrial effort needed. Unfortunately, partly because of Britain's desperate position in 1940, Churchill, influenced by the mischievous advice of Professor F. A. Lindemann, retaliated against the Nazis by adopting the same totalitarian method; and in 1942 the American Air Force followed suit. This was an unconditional moral surrender to Hitler.

Again, with poetic justice, this reliance upon extermination bombing—once sanctimoniously called 'area' or 'obliteration' bombing—delayed the democratic victory, for that was actually won by orthodox military methods, backed by the *tactical* air arm, which destroyed bridges, railroads, and other planes. But an even more fatal consequence followed from the very successes achieved up to the surrender at Stalingrad by the combined Axis forces in Europe and Asia: the threat of a Nazi victory through technological superiority in long-distance rocket bombing, with the further threat of absolute superiority through the possible release of atomic energy, brought about in the United States the long-imminent implosion of a megamachine on an advanced twentieth-century model. Under the stress of war, the missing component of the megamachine, the form of energy whose coming Henry Adams had predicted, was finally unlocked and utilized: "Bombs of cosmic violence." The very organization that made this possible itself enlarged all the dimensions of the megamachine and increased, by an incalculable factor, its capacity to work wholesale destruction.

This vast transformation took place in secret, with the aid of secret funds, supporting secret groups of scientists whose work was unknown to each other, utilizing secret knowledge, for a purpose that remained secret —however close the guesses might come—until the first atom bomb was exploded. The very conditions under which this weapon was created brought the scattered components of the megamachine together. As with the first megamachine, the new model threw off hitherto firmly established limitations, scientific, technical, social, and moral; and like the ancient megamachine, it gave unqualified authority and power to those who, on the evidence of history, had never shown any capability for using even more limited power wisely and humanely.

One germane problem now remained, a problem towering over all others: how to prevent the human race from being destroyed by its demoralized but reputedly sane leaders.

That problem has still to be solved: meanwhile another one has become almost as pressing—how to protect mankind as a whole from coming under the complete control of the new totalitarian mechanism, without also destroying the scientific insights and the technical capacities that helped to bring it into existence. Well did Emerson observe in 1832, as if in anticipation of our present terrors and tribulations: "Don't trust children with edge tools. Don't trust man, great God, with more power than he has, until he has learned to use that little power better. What a hell we should make of the world if we could do what we would! Put a button on the foil till the young fencers have learned not to put each other's eyes out."

6: IMPLOSIONS AND EXPLOSIONS

To effect the implosion of ideas and forces that finally produced the atomic reactor and the atom bomb, more than three centuries of preparation had been needed. But even then no proposal of this magnitude could have been broached, with sufficient authority to overcome the peacetime inertia of 'business as usual,' had there not been a direct military challenge from the old-fashioned megamachine, with the vivid possibility that German physicists would soon place within Hitler's hands an 'absolute' weapon, by means of which he might blackmail all other nations into submission.

Such a threat of worldwide domination by the totalitarian Axis, Germany, Italy, Japan—and prior to June 1941 Soviet Russia—brought about a similar concentration of physical power on the part of the 'democracies,' even before the United States had been dragged into war by these enemies. At that time it was plain—though the memory of this reality has unfortunately faded—that no compromise with the victory-intoxicated Axis, still less any mode of passive or non-violent resistance, such as that practiced by the Hindus against the British government in India, could have halted their accelerating program of enslavement and extermination. If proof of this were still needed, the fate of the Jews and other national groups under the Nazis—a total of some twenty million massacred—demonstrated this. The sedulous efforts of A. J. P. Taylor and his followers to conceal this situation by turning Hitler into a reasonable statesman, pursuing limited national aims, is a disgraceful travesty of historical scholarship.

Once the 1939 war enveloped the planet, the necessary components of the megamachine were not merely enlarged in scope but brought into close coordination and cooperation, so that in each country they functioned increasingly as a single unit. Every part of the daily routine was placed directly or indirectly under governmental control—food rationing, fuel rationing, clothes production, building—all obeyed regulations laid down by the central agency: the system of conscription applied in effect, not only to the armed forces, but to the entire country.

Though industry at first moved reluctantly into this new orbit, the growth of cartels, trusts, and monopolies which had taken place during the previous century equipped these organizations for active collaboration under government control—lured naturally by the huge financial incentive for accepting such integration, namely, costs plus a large guaranteed profit. This ensured both maximum production and maximum financial return. As the war progressed this megatechnic assemblage functioned increasingly, despite corporate jealousies and local antagonisms, as a single working unit.

But two additional components were needed to effect the transition to the new megamachine. One of them was already in existence: an absolute ruler. As it happened, the President of the United States was equipped with emergency powers written into the American constitution in direct imitation of Roman precedent. Under wartime conditions, the President had unlimited authority to take whatever steps were necessary to safeguard the nation: no absolute monarch could have exercised greater power. Even the mere threat that Hitler might possess a super-weapon enabled President Roosevelt, with the budgetary consent of Congress, to draft the manpower and brainpower that resulted in the invention of the nuclear reactor and the atom bomb. In order to produce this result, all the classic components of the ancient megamachine were made over on a pattern that took full advantage of megatechnic organization and scientific research. No small concentration of the power complex could have produced the critical transformation of the military-industrial-scientific establishment. Out of this union, between 1940 and 1961 the modernized megamachine, commanding 'absolute' powers of destruction, emerged.

Instead of a single Archimedes, ingeniously destroying a Roman fleet, ten thousand replicas of Archimedes were put to work to multiply the engines of war and counteract those of the enemy; and for one quick-witted exponent of handicraft, such as the American soldier who devised a simple method for cutting down the matted hedges of Normandy, which had obstructed the deployment of American tanks, there were now thousands of exponents of the new technology, at work on radar and sonar, on jet planes and rockets—and above all on the atom bomb. Only under the intense pressures of war could such a coalition of forces, almost a coalescence, have taken place.

The production of the atom bomb was in fact crucial to the building of the new megamachine, little though anyone at the time had that larger objective in mind. For it was the success of this project that gave the scientists a central place in the new power complex and resulted eventually in the invention of many other instruments that have rounded out and universalized the system of control first established to meet only the exigencies of war.

Overnight, the civilian and military leaders of the United States were endowed with powers that hitherto had been claimed only by Bronze Age gods, powers that had never actually been exercised by any merely human ruler. Thereafter, in the order of precedence, the irreplaceable scientist-technician stood highest in the new hierarchy of power; and every part of the megamachine was made over in consonance with the peculiarly limited type of knowledge, deliberately sterilized of other human values and purposes, that their refined mathematical analysis and exact methods had been designed to further.

In view of the cataclysmic changes that followed, it is significant that the initiative in bringing about the release of nuclear energy, the central event in the recrudescence of the megamachine in modern form, was taken, not by the central government, but by a small group of physicists. Not less significant is the fact that these advocates of nuclear power were themselves unusually humane and morally sensitive people, notably, Albert Einstein, Enrico Fermi, Leo Szilard, Harold Urey. These were the last scientists one would accuse of seeking to establish a new priesthood capable of assuming autocratic authority and wielding satanic power. Those unpleasant characteristics, which have become all too evident in later collaborators and successors, were derived from the new instruments commanded by the megamachine and the dehumanized concepts that were rapidly incorporated in its whole working program. As for the initiators of the atom bomb, it was their innocence that concealed from them, at least in the initial stages, the dreadful ultimate consequences of their effort.

Certainly the physicists who were alert to the immediate threat the splitting of the atom held if this knowledge were in the hands of a totalitarian dictator, drew unsound political and military conclusions, against whose hasty application their scientific training had given them no adequate safeguards. Fearful that the Nazis would gain an overwhelming advantage by manufacturing an atom bomb first, Einstein and his associates placed before the Chief Executive the case for the United States' developing such a weapon, without their prudently canvassing various possible alternatives. Their fears were well grounded: their alertness was admirable. But their initiative unfortunately came half a century too late. Had the scientists in their corporate capacity taken heed of Henry Adams' and Frederick Soddy's warnings a generation earlier, they might have addressed themselves in time to the critical underlying problem: how to mobilize the intelligence of mankind to prevent such potentially catastrophic energy from being prematurely released. Unfortunately, their training had conditioned the scientists to the idea that the continued increase of scientific knowledge, and its speediest possible translation into practice, without regard to social consequences, was nothing less than a categorical imperative.

While a concerned contemporary can understand the initiative taken by Einstein and ratified by President Franklin D. Roosevelt—very possibly the present critic would under the same circumstances have made the same tragic mistake—it is now plain that this proposal was made within a far too limited historical context: it was a short-term decision to effect an immediately desired result, though the consequences may disastrously undermine mankind's entire future. To propose creating a weapon of 'cosmic violence' without at the same time providing, as a condition for scientific aid, the coordinate moral and political safety measures shows how unused even these moralized scientists were to considering the practical consequences of their vocational commitments.

But the facts are now clear: the preparation for this misuse of power preceded the explosion of the first atom bomb. Well before the first atom bomb was tested, the American Air Force had adopted the hitherto 'unthinkable' practice of the wholesale, indiscriminate bombing of concentrated civilian populations: this paralleled, except for distance from the victims, the practices employed by Hitler's sub-men in extermination camps like Buchenwald and Auschwitz. By using napalm bombs the Air Force had roasted alive nearly 100,000 civilians in Tokyo in a single night. Thus the descent to total demoralization and extermination was neatly plotted well before the supposedly 'ultimate' weapon, the atom bomb, was invented.

Once the plan to make an atom bomb was sanctioned, the scientists who gave themselves to this project were caught by their own erroneous ideological premises into accepting its military use. Their original error could not easily be repaired, no matter how their consciences might pain them, nor how strenuous the efforts of their more sensitive and intelligent leaders to awaken mankind to its plight. For something worse than the invention of a deadly weapon had taken place: the act of making the bomb had hastened the assemblage of the new magamachine; *for in order to keep that megamachine in effective operation once the immediate military emergency was over, a permanent state of war became the condition for its survival and further expansion.*

Though for twenty years after the atom bomb was dropped only two modern military megamachines came into existence—those of the United

States and Soviet Russia—they both carry the prospect, through their dynamic expansion, their insensate rivalry, their psychotic compulsiveness, of drawing into their orbit every other national unit. Ultimately these two systems must either destroy each other or coalesce with other similar megamachines on a planetary basis. In terms of further human development, the second possibility, alas! seems hardly more promising than the first. The only rational alternative is to dismantle the military megamachines.

All these results might have happened, one must grant, as long as science and megatechnics continued on the converging paths they had taken in the nineteenth century, even without the stimulus of war and the deliberate invention of the atom bomb. But it would probably have taken more than a century to get to the same point that was reached in less than a decade. The medium of war had proved an ideal broth in which every kind of lethal organism could multiply. Once again, as in the original implosion of 'civilization,' the same set of factors had, by expanding energy and human capability, unleashed forces of destruction that counterbalanced those of construction, and fostered a degree of collective irrationality that counteracted the marvellous positive gains in rational intelligence. And, once again, too, I must ask as I did in the Prologue to Volume One: "Is this association of inordinate power and productivity with equally inordinate violence and destruction a purely accidental one?"

The parallel between the Pyramid Age achievements and those of the Nuclear Age force themselves upon one, however reluctant one may at first be to admit them. Once again, a Divine King, embodying all the powers and prerogatives of the whole community, supported by a revered priesthood and a universal religion, that of positive science, had begun the assemblage of the megamachine in a technologically more adequate and impressive form. If one forgets the actual part played by the King (wartime American President), by the Priesthood (secret enclave of scientists), by the vast enlargement of the bureaucracy, the military forces, and the industrial establishment, one would have no realistic conception of what actually took place. Only in terms of the Pyramid Age do all the seemingly dispersed and accidental events become polarized into an orderly constellation. The construction of the modernized totalitarian megamachine, fortified by the invention of mechanical and electronic agents that could not be fully utilized until this assemblage had taken place, proved to be Hitler's most sinister, if wholly unintended, contribution to the enslavement of mankind.

Thus, one of the supreme feats in modern man's understanding of the ultimate constituents of the 'physical universe,' culminating in his unlocking of the very energies that the Sun God commands, came about under the pressure of a genocidal war and the threat of wholesale annihilation: a condition that paralyzed all life-conserving and life-promoting efforts. The continuation of that state, with the deepening and widening of the crisis in the ensuing Cold War, has greatly increased the malign possibilities that Henry Adams foresaw.

7: THE MEGAMACHINES COMPARED

We are now in a position to compare the ancient and modern forms of the megamachine; but before doing so, let me make plain that the ancient machine was not identified—indeed remained quite undiscovered—until the new one had taken form. As we shall see, their differences are as significant as their resemblances: yet the underlying similarities throw a fresh light, I submit, on the wide span of intervening history, and even more on the age that has just opened.

Both megamachines can be identified by their similar technological capacities: they are mass organizations capable of performing tasks that lie outside the range of small work-collectives and loose tribal or territorial groups. Yet at every point the ancient machine, since it was composed mainly of human parts, lay under human limitations; for even under the harshest taskmaster, a slave cannot exert much more than a tenth of a horsepower, nor can he keep working indefinitely without lowering his output.

The great contrast between the two types of machine is that the modern machine has progressively reduced the number of human agents and multiplied the more reliable mechanical and electronic components: not merely reducing the labor force needed for a colossal operation but facilitating instantaneous remote control. Though human servo-mechanisms are still necessary at nodal points in the system, the modern machine escapes spatial and temporal limitations: it can operate as a single, largely invisible unit, over a wide area, with its functioning parts operating as a whole through instant communication. Thus the new model commands whole regiments of diversified mechanical units, with superhuman power and superhuman mechanical reliability, and not least with lightning speed. Though the ancient megamachine would hardly have been conceivable without the invention of writing, earlier totalitarian regimes fell down repeatedly because of slowness in communication; indeed one of the chief concerns of older megamachines was the improvement of road and water communication, with relays of runners and horses, or with galleys pulled in machinelike unison by slaves.

Once the telegraph was invented, followed by telephone and radio, these limitations on effecting long-distance control were abolished. Theoretically, any spot on earth can now be in instant oral communication with every other spot, and instant visual transactions anywhere are only a short distance behind. An almost equal acceleration in speed has taken place in transporting the human body: the winged messengers that once carried commands from heaven to earth are in effect now available at any airport; and in a short while transportation at a speed of Mach II should enable our up-to-date angels to appear at any point on the planet in less than half a day. Power, speed, and control have been the chief marks of absolute monarchs in all ages: the doing away with previous natural limitations in these areas is the common theme that unites the ancient and the modern megamachine.

For the mass of men the ancient megamachine had operated with only minimal rewards but with maximal punishments; and so universal were these practices that even the highest officers of the state were frequently subject to similar abasements and coercions. Thus punishing labors were periodically performed by the whole community under threat of even worse punishment if the workers fell down in meeting their quotas. The documents that testify to these practices are abundant in every land exploited by the megamachine. In addition to those I have already cited let me here add a Hobbesian passage from 'The Laws of Manu,' quoted by Karl Wittfogel. "If the king did not, without tiring, inflict punishment on those worthy to be punished, the stronger would roast the weaker, like fish on a spit. . . . Punishment alone governs all created beings, punishment alone protects them."

From such evidence, one has reason to infer that the megamachine was originally the creation of the same weapons-bearing minority that invented organized warfare, and imposed unconditional obedience and regular tribute upon the passive, non-aggressive, compliant neolithic peasants, peasants who throughout all succeeding history have in fact formed the larger part of the human population. Though the modern megamachine is equally the product of war, it has, as we shall presently see, partly overcome the need for overt coercion by a more subtle kind, which substitutes rewards, or seeming rewards, for punishments.

On the other hand, this system carried with it special penalties of its own: it not merely wasted manpower by requiring an excessive number of slave-drivers and overseers, one for each squad of ten men: but it produced friction, sullen resentment, lowered outputs; and it tamped down the energies of superior minds that might have engaged in free inventions and spontaneous creativity. One cannot even guess how many potential Imhoteps or Josephs were sterilized—as in Soviet Russia or China today—by terror. What was worse, these repressive routines, these savage punishments spread beyond the province of work and corroded many other human relations. Historic evidence indicates that conspiracies, uprisings, poisonings, slave revolts lowered the working efficiency of the earlier megamachines. Obviously there was room for plenty of improvement even in the non-mechanical units of the megamachine. We shall examine some of these major improvements in the next chapter.

8: HUMAN SACRIFICE AND
MECHANICAL SALVATION

The ideology that underlies and unites the ancient and the modern megamachine is one that ignores the needs and purposes of life in order to fortify the power complex and extend its dominion. Both megamachines are oriented toward death; and the more they approach unified planetary control, the more inescapable does that result promise to become. In the gross form of war, everyone is familiar with this constant historic drive, for military violence—as distinguished from sporadic minor forms of animal aggression—is the historic product of a special form of social organization, developed in certain ant societies roughly sixty million years ago, and recovered, with all its sinister institutional accomplishments, in the Egyptian and Mesopotamian communities of the Pyramid Age.

All these ancient features were restored during the nineteenth century: above all, the collective dedication to death. During the last half century alone, between fifty and a hundred million people—it is impossible to make precise calculations—have met premature death through violence and starvation, on the battlefield, in concentration camps, in bombed cities and agricultural areas that have been turned into mass extermination camps. What is more, we have been repeatedly informed by official authorities in the United States—indeed they boast about it—that in the first nuclear strike between powers as well equipped as the United States and Soviet Russia, between a quarter and half the inhabitants in each of those countries would be killed on the first day.

With foxy circumspection these official predictions refrain from estimating further losses by the other means of genocide they have perfected, during the second day, the second week, the second year, and even the second century; for this would involve incalculable factors of astronomical dimensions, whose unforeseeable consequences might be permanently irreparable. (Scientists so pathetically vain as to suppose that they have the ability to foresee these incalculable effects count among the trusted advisers of the American government.)

As with all modern technical performances, the mass infliction of death has been both expanded and speeded up. But so far, nuclear explosions and rocket explorations, both directly issuing from war plans, have been the most conspicuous manifestations of these lethal facilities, along with the communications systems upon which they depend. The fact that no *human* purpose, present or prospective, would be served by these modes of extermination, no matter how successful in 'overkill,' only demonstrates the deep underlayers of psychotic irrationality upon which the fantasies of absolute weapons, of absolute power, and of absolute control have been laid. Freud made a parallel between the magic rituals of many so-called primitive peoples and the behavior of neurotic personalities in our time. But there is no practice in these arrested cultures, neither head-hunting nor cannibalism nor voodoo murder, that is comparable in superstitious savagery and mental corruption with the current plans of highly trained scientists, technologists, and military men to inflict collective death on the scale that modern technological agents have made possible.

One of the many concrete proofs of this officially sanctioned insanity comes to light at the very moment I write. In order to dispose of the deadly poison gases that the American Air Force has been experimenting with, the agency involved bored a hole fifteen hundred feet deep into which to dump the canisters of this horrible poison. But in addition to the hazards of merely transporting this gas from the place of origin to the bore, this area—near the city of Denver, once esteemed as a health resort—has lately become subject to a series of earthquakes, possibly the direct result of introducing this artificial fissure. Thus the ingenious perpetrators of this new form of genocide must decide whether to risk an earthquake that may release the gas they have carelessly disposed of—or fill up this hole; and in case of a serious earthquake risk the blame for having created the same result by their further efforts.

In our present death-oriented culture, the official stamp of approval, justified as a scientific advance or a military necessity, is supposed to cover up, or if exposed, to completely excuse, these dehumanized plans and these criminal acts. The willingness of modern nations—Sweden no less than the United States—to countenance this strategy, which is potentially as fatal to their fellow citizens as to any putative enemy, is a sure indication of both our moral degradation and our defective, or paralyzed, intelligence. No wonder some of the best of our younger generation regard their acquiescent elders with unutterable horror and justified rage.

Compared with this pervasive dedication to death in our own culture, the Egyptian cult of the dead, developed during the Pyramid Age, with its magniloquent pyramids, its magic rituals, and its elaborate techniques of mummification, was a relatively innocent exhibition of irrationality. Actually the destructions that accompanied the wars of the early military machines were so limited by their necessary reliance upon mere manpower and handweapons and handtools, that even their most extravagant efforts were reparable. It is our present removal of all limits, made possible only by the advances of science and technics, that reveals the true nature of this culture and its chosen destiny.

Yes: the priests and warriors of the megamachine can exterminate mankind: so, once again, if von Neumann is right, they will. No mere animal instinct of aggression accounts for this growing aberration. But something more than the animal instinct for self-preservation—an immense increase in emotional alertness, moral concern, and practical audacity—will be necessary on a worldwide scale if mankind is finally to save itself.

CHAPTER TEN

The New Megamachine

1: THE SECRETS OF THE TEMPLE

In the act of inventing the atom bomb, the essential human components of the new megamachine were not merely brought together in space but given critical roles; and not by accident, the generalissimo was Robert Oppenheimer, a physicist.

This novel conjuncture gave the participants powers that as individuals they had never before had either the incentive or the opportunity to exercise. While their liberties as men and citizens were curtailed by the need for maintaining military secrecy, their scope and authority as specialists were immensely increased. For the first time scientists were able, with the government's support, indeed at its urgent invitation, to draw virtually unlimited funds of money for their apparatus; and probably never before had such a large number of qualified practitioners been assigned to a single task. Only a populous territorial state, with huge material resources and an almost unlimited capacity for commanding taxes and human services, could have promoted such a collective effort. Thus sovereign power of pharaonic dimensions was secretly re-established at the heart of a constitutional government of limited powers supposedly under constant public surveillance and control.

At the same time, never before had scientists been compelled to work under conditions so unfavorable to free intellectual intercourse: they were not merely prevented from communicating with the outside world, but even from speaking freely about their several tasks among themselves. Though these precautions had the wartime justification of military secrecy, secrecy itself became valued as a badge of authority and a method of enforcing control. This practice was pushed to such a point that the discoverer of heavy water, Professor Harold Urey, whose research had contributed that

263

essential element, was not permitted to learn the methods the Du Pont Company used to produce such water.

Now the secret of every totalitarian system is secrecy itself. The key to exercising arbitrary power is to restrict the communications of individuals and groups by subdividing information, so that only a small portion of the whole truth will be known to any single person. This was an old trick of political conspirators; and it now passed from the core agency, the so-called 'Manhattan Project,' to every part of the militarized national establishment, though ironically even those at the top of the hierarchy lacked sufficient information or intelligence to put all the pieces together.

The difficulty of maintaining such sealed-in knowledge might have proved greater but for the fact that each department of science had already become, in effect, a secret agency in its own right. The sciences are now so specialized in their vocabulary, so esoteric in their concepts, so refined in their techniques, and so limited in their capacity to communicate new knowledge to non-specialists even in closely related fields, that non-communication has become almost a badge of vocational superiority among scientists. "When the members of my department meet once a week at luncheon table," a physicist recently told me, "we never talk about our own work. It has become too private for words. We take refuge in gossip about the latest car models or motor boats."

The success of the 'Manhattan Project' in the face of these limitations probably indicates that the capacity to bring together in close working cooperation such a diversity of theoretic and practical talents more than outweighed the unfavorable conditions of intellectual isolation and non-communication. The fact that the physicists, chemists, and mathematicians whose brilliant work made nuclear fission realizable were an international team, drawn from every 'advanced' country, revealed the latent potentialities for worldwide cooperation that Baconian scientific exploration, plus neotechnics, had brought into existence. The drawing together of the Hungarians Szilard, Wigner, and Teller, the Dane Bohr, the treacherous communist German Fuchs, the Italian Fermi, the Americans Oppenheimer and Urey gave the 'American' team an advantage that the Nazis, who relied upon the superiority of their self-isolated 'Aryan' culture, lacked.

The kind of group that speeded the invention of the atom bomb was, accordingly, in some ways a model for any higher kind of organization, which, if liberated from wartime secrecy, would seek to transcend the megamachine's original limitations: the pattern, indeed, for a still unborn United Nations organization, assembled to provide the maximum interchange of knowledge or of energy, and eventually to exercise moralized control over the demoralized, premature applications of half-baked scientific knowledge. This open secret of international cooperation and free intellectual interchange held far more promise for mankind's future than all the esoteric data locked in classified, top-secret files, or even published cautiously in scientific journals.

Yet to achieve such an integration of specialized knowledge, something more than a desire for 'interdisciplinary cooperation' was necessary: nothing less than a transformation of the 'classic' scientific *Weltanschauung,* which imputed objectivity only to measurable data and repeatable experiments and denied the constant interplay between the world of nature and the world of human culture, as both come to a focus in a human personality. The penalty for producing nuclear bombs sufficient to destroy the human race was that it put these genocidal and suicidal weapons in the hands of demonstrably fallible human beings whose astounding scientific achievements blinded their contemporaries to the human limitations of the culture that had produced them.

Power of this magnitude had never been in human hands before—hardly even in fantasy. But even power on a comparatively minute scale has, all through history, notoriously produced distortions and aberrations in the human personality; and the observed results of such power in inflating pride had made Christian theology, with acute perception, treat pride as the gravest of sins. Among the rulers of the United States and Soviet Russia, inflamed by the possession of 'absolute' weapons, ideological aberrations soon hardened into 'fixed ideas.' These 'ideas' fomented pathological suspicion and relentless hostility similar to that recorded on the walls of the tomb of Seti: a text dating from the fourteenth to the twelfth centuries B.C. but, according to Wilson, showing signs of a much older original. In this text Re, the Sun God, fancies that mankind is secretly plotting against him, and in return he plots the destruction of mankind.

Almost from the beginning the military wielders of nuclear weapons strutted, boasted, threatened, and exterminated in the manner of Bronze Age gods; and their official soothsayers and Fortune-Tellers, re-enforced by the greatly magnified destructiveness of the hydrogen bomb, confirmed their plans and confidently announced imminent crises and 'showdowns.' Despite their provocative efforts these predictions have proved no more accurate than those of their archaic prototypes—even if they still tend by their very nature to bring on eventually the calamity for which they zealously make ready. These pathological reactions, studiously nurtured by 'research' organizations in officially patronized 'think tanks,' have magnified all the destructive potentialities of thermo-nuclear weapons, and led to gratuitous secret experiments with equally diabolical bacterial and chemical weapons, even less controllable in nature once released.

Lord Acton's famous dictum about power has been repeated too often to have retained its original force; but it still holds its significance. "Power corrupts and absolute power corrupts absolutely." In our age this corruption has sprung alike from the nature of the nuclear weapons themselves,

from the agencies that have promoted them, and from the general demoralization brought on by the archaic military megamachines, widened,
indeed universalized, by the 'democratic' governments that blindly copied
their methods.

The Second World War was formally halted by the Axis surrender in
1945, but the modernized megamachine which had emerged by the
end of it did not give up its absolute weapons or the scheme for universal
domination by threat of total destruction that had given a coalition of
scientific and military agencies such inordinate power. Far from it. Though
nominally the older organs of industry and government resumed their
diverse activities, the militarized 'elite' fortified themselves in an inner
citadel—so beautifully symbolized by the architecturally archaic Pentagon—cut off from inspection or control by the rest of the community. With
the pusillanimous aid of Congress, they extended their tentacles throughout the industrial and the academic world, through fat subsidies for 'research and development,' that is, for weapons expansion, which made these
once-independent institutions willing accomplices in the whole totalitarian
process.

Thus the area of this self-enclosed citadel has widened steadily, while
the walls around it have grown thicker and more impenetrable. By the
simple expedient of creating new emergencies, fomenting new fears,
singling out new enemies or magnifying by free use of fantasy the evil intentions of 'the enemy,' the megamachines of the United States and Soviet
Russia, instead of being dismantled as a regrettable temporary wartime
necessity, were elevated into permanent institutions in what has now become a permanent war: the so-called Cold War. As it has turned out, this
form of war, with its ever-expanding demands for scientific ingenuity and
technological innovations, is by far the most effective device invented for
keeping this overproductive technology in full operation.

In the course of this development the two dominant megamachines
exchanged characteristics. The Russian machine departed from the obsolete original model by relying ever more heavily on its scientific and technological arm; while the American machine took over the most regressive
features of the Czarist-Stalinist system, vastly augmenting both its military
force and its agents of centralized control: the Atomic Energy Commission, the Federal Bureau of Investigation, the Central Intelligence Agency,
the National Security Agency—all secret agencies whose methods and
policies have never been openly discussed or effectively challenged, still
less curtailed by the national legislative authority. So deeply entrenched are
these agents that they dare to flout and disobey the authority of both the
President and the Congress.

This enlarged establishment has proved as immune to public criticism,
correction, and control as any dynastic establishment of the Pyramid Age.

And though like every other machine, the contemporary megamachine is an agent for performing work, the work that has occupied the huge scientific and technical staff it has assembled, in both the United States and Russia, the work that supposedly justifies its existence and lightens the heavy sacrifices it calls for, is nothing less than elaborating the mechanism of total destruction. The only question the megamachine leaves open is whether this destruction shall be swift or slow: the negative goal is incorporated in the basic ideological assumptions that govern the system. The artists of the present generation, who have exposed this goal in their anti-art and their non-art, have been more honest—as we shall soon see—than the inventors of this collective mantrap.

The generation that has permitted the new megamachine to be installed as a permanent feature of national existence has been reluctant to confront the evidence of this radical miscarriage of human purpose: they accepted the goal of total extermination, as a mere extension of war, without perceiving that the prospective increase of quantity was a far more frightful aberration than war itself. Paralyzed like a monkey in the coil of a python, the immediate post-Hiroshima generation, unable to utter a rational sound, shut its eyes and waited for the end.

Until now, human violence had been limited by the meager physical resources at the disposal of governments. In so far as earlier megamachines were forced to rely upon manpower to exercise control, they were kept to the human scale, and were, what is more, open both to attack from without and to corruption from within. But the new megamachine knows no such limitations: it can command obedience and exert control through a vast battery of efficient machines, with fewer human intermediaries than ever before. To a degree hitherto impossible, the megamachine wears the magic cloak of invisibility: even its human servitors are emotionally protected by their remoteness from the human target they incinerate or obliterate.

This high degree of dehumanization increases the lethal automatism of the megamachine. Those who plan its strategic objectives contemplate the extermination of a hundred million human beings in a single day with less aversion than the killing of a few hundred bedbugs. For them, the sacrifice of an equivalent number of their own countrymen has become equally 'acceptable,' once the 'balance of terror' fails.

In plain words, the religion of the megamachine demands wholesale human sacrifice, to restore in negative form the missing dimension of life. Thus the cult of the Sun God turns out, in its final scientific celebration, to be no less savage and irrational than that of the Aztecs, though infinitely more deadly. After all, the Aztec priests disemboweled their victims by hand, one by one; and human nausea at this spectacle was so great that the priests were compelled to ensure themselves against unfavorable reactions by threatening a similar fate for those who even turned their eyes away.

The priests of the Pentagon and the Kremlin have no need for such threats: in their underground control centers they can do their job more neatly, merely by pressing a button. Untouchable: unchallengeable: inviolable. Such are these new controllers of human destiny.

2: ABDICATION OF THE HIGHER

PRIESTHOOD

Among the first of the many casualties already produced by the megamachine was the honor of the scientific guild that had helped to bring it into existence. For their success as members of this growing totalitarian establishment threatened the loss of the scientists' most conspicuous virtue—the disinterested pursuit of knowledge, experimentally verifiable, sharable by their peers, accessible to public inspection, testing, and correction.

No one could serve the new megamachine and hold to the scientific ideal of uncensored, unimpeded thought; for total secrecy, necessitated by war, became incorporated as a permanent feature of the 'peacetime' (Cold War) regime. In return for this loss of independence and disinterestedness, the new priesthood has exercised an authority they had never dreamed of exercising before. And they have buttressed their new position by regarding as fixed and beyond challenge the crass assumptions on which the Cold War was based. Thus, one of its spokesmen, Herman Kahn, in a reputedly objective survey of the theoretic possibilities of thermo-nuclear strategy, refused to consider even the possibility of achieving peace. Here his 'objective' inquiry disclosed the typical trick of the new scientific establishment: to give answers only to carefully loaded questions that in themselves dictate the nature of the answer.

Those who rejected the megamachine's absolutism, notably many of the original scientists on the nuclear bomb project, withdrew from active atomic research. They had been raised in an atmosphere of relative intellectual freedom and moral choice: so that once they were awakened to the fact that as Henry Adams had predicted morality had become police, they threw their energies into criticizing and resisting the megamachine. Einstein, Szilard, and Wiener, to mention only the dead, belonged conspicuously to this honorable company. But neither the United States nor the Russian government had any difficulty in enlisting less enlightened—or less morally sensitive—minds, particularly among a new generation that had been studiously bred to indifference both to moral values and to autonomous activity.

To their shame the subservient scientists of both countries accepted the megamachine on the same terms, for the same unspeakable ultimate purposes. This new generation disappeared from the open world of traditional science: they withdrew into an underworld of secret activities instigated by the military forces. This was the new 'elite,' a contemporary name for the old priesthood, masters of the secret knowledge of the Temple, willing servants of the Pharaoh and sharers of his power. In return for unlimited funds for apparatus and assistants, a privileged status, with large salaries and perquisites, this new generation surrendered its scientific birthright: the unrestricted pursuit of knowledge.

Less than a decade after the explosion of the first atom bomb the megamachine had expanded to a point where it began to dominate key areas of the whole economy of the United States: its system of control reached beyond the airfields, the rocket sites, the bomb factories, the universities, to a hundred other related areas, tying the once separate and independent enterprises to a central organization whose irrational and humanly subversive policies ensured the still further expansion of the megamachine. Financial subventions, research grants, educational subsidies, all worked unceasingly for the 'Life, Prosperity, Health' of the new rulers, headed by Goliaths in brass armor bellowing threats of defiance and destruction at the entire world. In a short time, the original military-industrial-scientific elite became the supreme Pentagon of Power, for it incorporated likewise both the bureaucratic and the educational establishments.

In twenty years, the expenditure upon the Atomic Energy Program came to fifty billion dollars: more than the total amount of American military expenditures on the Second World War. The subsequent Cold War itself, that essential device for expanding the megamachine, has demanded in the United States an expenditure of more than fifty billion dollars a year. Of this the annual outlay for research and development, according to Ralph Lapp, came to sixteen billion dollars annually. In the case of the effort to build an atom-powered plane, the Air Force spent a billion dollars merely to prove that the idea was unworkable, though at the very time this money was being wasted, the development of the rocket had made such a plane, for any conceivable military purpose, unnecessary. Minds not committed to the megamachine's technological obsessions could have saved the country a billion dollars before a single blueprint was made.

Obviously, these misdirected absolute powers demand absolute immunity to independent investigation, and absolute conformity upon the part of those who operate the machine. Otherwise such life-threatening strategies themselves would be subject to open public discussion, critical appraisal, democratic control. Those who possess sufficient knowledge to challenge the prevailing policies are therefore excluded or extruded from the totalitarian establishment. So it was only after resigning his post as scientific adviser to the Pentagon that it was possible for Dr. Herbert York to say publicly: "If the great powers continue to look for solutions in the area of science and technology only, the results will be to worsen the situation."

Though in the quarter century since 1945 much has been accomplished, the construction of a megamachine capable of operation on a worldwide basis has been impeded not only by unexpected eruptions of counter-forces of an extremely primitive order, but by the fact that by the nineteen-fifties not one but two mutually antagonistic megamachines had come into existence with equally 'absolute' powers: that of Soviet Russia and that of the United States, with still another older one, China's, passing from a state of complete dilapidation to one remodelled on quasi-scientific lines. In the first two examples the nuclear reactor, the hydrogen bomb, the space rocket, television, chemical tranquillizers, and the computer have already provided the essential equipment for total control. Politically speaking, however the Russian megamachine had a head start, since it was based on the still operative Czarist establishment.

The American megamachine, on the other hand, was slightly retarded by the necessity of keeping up a pretense of representative government and voluntary participation. In addition, older traditions, favoring personal, regional, and corporate autonomy had not yet been altogether wiped out— despite the growing centralized control exerted by the two-hundred-odd super-corporations that dominated the entire national economy and had gained a foothold in many foreign territories. Steel, motor cars, chemicals, pharmaceuticals, oil, electronics, planes, rockets, cybernetics, television, and many subsidiary industries, to say nothing of banking, insurance, and advertising, were all conceived on the same unitary principle and consisted, corporately speaking, of interchangeable parts: so that even the most diverse industries could be scrambled into a single conglomerate system.

This situation was shrewdly appraised almost a century ago by the British sociologist Benjamin Kidd. He saw that the current 'liberal' doctrines of progress were leading in quite another direction than their advocates supposed. He foresaw that a formidable struggle would take place, not between nations as such, but between two rival systems, to settle which system should dominate the earth. We can now, with added experience, carry this analysis one step further: for though the American megamachine identifies itself as the guardian of the 'free world,' it has become plain that such freedom as still exists is a holdover from an earlier state—a few pockets of resistance, to characterize it in military terms—and that all the innovations that have been made with increasing rapidity and increasing compulsiveness are making the 'hostile' systems converge. To ensure its own autonomy, and maintain the status of its manipulators, the megamachine must destroy all the alternatives, historical, traditional, or prospective.

What Clinton Rossiter has demonstrated in his analysis of a single aspect of its transformation, the political, in his study of Constitutional Dictatorship, is now inherent in every operation of the megamachine. Each megamachine has displayed the same common features: the tendency to become self-sufficient, to draw into its structure organizations and institutions that would otherwise divert the energy it commands or divide loyalties and thus curb its automatic expansion.

In both Russia and the United States, centralized governmental agencies, unchecked by public opinion, uncontrolled by elected bodies, have perfected the techniques of the 'permanent crisis' in order to consolidate the powers that were originally designed solely to meet a passing threat.

The Soviet blockade of Berlin was an obvious instance of this tendency; but so, equally, was the Central Intelligence Agency's provocative continuance of U-2 flights over Russia, despite Russian protests, as an effective means of wrecking the approaching 'Summit Meeting' in Paris in 1960. Consistently the agents of the megamachine act as if their only responsibility were to the power system itself. The interests and demands of the populations subjected to the megamachine are not only unheeded but deliberately flouted. "The great issues of nuclear strategy," as Professor Hans J. Morgenthau has observed, "cannot even be the subject of meaningful debate, whether in Congress or among the people at large, because there can be no competent judgement without meaningful knowledge. Thus the great national decisions of life and death are rendered by technological elites."

In every field from atomic energy to medicine, policies that will permanently affect the destiny, and possibly bring to an end the whole adventure, of human life have been formulated and carried through by self-appointed and self-regulating experts and specialists, immune to human confrontation, whose very willingness to make these decisions on their own responsibility is proof positive of their total unfitness to do so.

The illusions and magical hallucinations of these ruling groups, visible in their reckless acts, their incompetent forecasts—one 'Bay of Pigs disaster' after another—and their published statements, can have only one possible terminus. To conceal this eventual goal, they have reached out in every direction to enlarge the number of accessories in their tacit conspiracy against mankind. Beginning first in the development of nuclear reactors, a self-assured technological elite has begun professionally to assume control over every human activity: from artificial insemination to space exploration.

Not the least menacing aspect of the new megamachine, then, is the fact that it has already produced a formidable and still growing ruling caste in the United States and Soviet Russia: a caste comparable to the Janissaries in the heyday of Turkish despotism. The next logical step, as with the Janissaries, would be to select the 'elite' in their cradles and deliberately deform them for the purpose in hand, so that no inconvenient human attributes will lessen their unconditional loyalty to the megamachine. John Hersey suggested this further development in his satiric novel, 'The Child Buyer,' a work that deserved more serious discussion than it received. But already a step well beyond this is in view: nothing less than the selection of the elite from a bank of frozen spermatozoa and ova for gestation, under control, in an artificial womb. The first bold theoretic steps toward this consummation have already been put forward, as an 'inevitable' advance of science, by more than one priest of the megamachine. Once again: "It can be done, therefore it *must* be done."

But a further move in the consolidation of the megamachine looms ahead, and it is not too early to anticipate its outcome in order to awaken, if possible, the counter-forces necessary to overcome it. If the first step in the rule of the Sun God was the unification of power and authority in the person of a Divine King, the second was the displacement of the actual king, who was still a living person, by a bureaucratic-military organization. But the third step, the fabrication of the all-embracing megamachine itself, could not be completed until an equivalent supreme ruler wholly of a 'mechanical' nature, without human parts or attributes, could be invented.

In mid-nineteenth century the great Basel historian, Jacob Burckhardt, foresaw a new kind of control would be the expression of a civilization that was already driving again toward an absolute despotism, without law or right: more absolute than any past system. "This despotic regime," he noted, "will not be practiced any longer by dynasties. They are too soft and kindhearted. The new tyrannies will be in the hands of military commandos who will call themselves republican. I am still reluctant to imagine a world the rulers of which will be completely indifferent to law, well-being, profitable labor, industry, credit, etc. and will govern with absolute brutality."

That world need no longer be imagined: it is almost here. And if Burckhardt's prediction is at fault at any point, it is because he endowed these despots with more human traits than they actually promise to exhibit: because of their 'objectivity,' 'neutrality,' and 'impersonality' they have already proved capable of even more absolute modes of calculated terror and criminality than any old-fashioned military commandos.

The new megamachine, in the act of being made over on an advanced technological model, also brought into existence the ultimate 'decision-maker' and Divine King, in a transcendent, electronic form: the Central Computer. As the true earthly representative of the Sun God, the computer had first been invented, as we have seen, to facilitate astronomical calculations. In the conversion of Babbage's clumsy half-built model into a fantastically rapid electro-mechanism, whose 'movable parts' are electric charges, celestial electronics replaced celestial mechanics and gave this exquisite device its authentic divine characteristics: omnipresence and invisibility.

In taking this form the computer achieved a higher level of performance in the storing of information and the solving of problems that demanded the almost instantaneous integration of a multitude of variables, with larger quantities of data than the human brain could handle in a lifetime. If one forgets that it is the human brain that invented this quasi-divine instrument and that must feed it with the data and pose the problems that are to be solved, the lowly human agent may be excused for worshipping this deity. On the other hand, those who have identified themselves with this new instrument are subject to the opposite kind of hallucination—that they in fact *are* God, or at least co-partners in omnipotence.

The special merit of the Omni-Computer, which sets it high above all merely human decision-makers, is its lightning operation, and accidents apart, its infallibility, given the partial information and the instructions provided by far from infallible human agents. While all these marvellous aptitudes must be freely granted, at least three crippling disabilities must be noted. The computer still suffers from the same radical weaknesses that undermined the decisions of Kings and Emperors: the only information it heeds is that which is fed into it by its Grand Viziers and courtiers; and as usually happened with kingship, the courtiers—read mathematical model-makers and programmers—ask the king only for such answers as can be based on the inadequate information they supply. That information must ignore many significant aspects of human experience in order to conform to His Majesty's peculiar limitations.

Unfortunately, computer knowledge, because it must be processed and programmed, cannot remain constantly in touch, like the human brain, with the unceasing flow of reality; for only a small part of experience can be arrested for extraction and expression in abstract symbols. Changes that cannot be quantitatively measured or objectively observed, such changes as take place constantly all the way from the atom to the living organism, are outside the scope of the computer. For all its fantastic rapidity of operation, its components remain incapable of making qualitative responses to constant organic changes.

3: THE ALL-SEEING EYE

In Egyptian theology, the most singular organ of the Sun God, Re, was the eye: for the Eye of Re had an independent existence and played a creative and directive part in all cosmic and human activities. The computer turns out to be the Eye of the reinstated Sun God, that is, the Eye of the Megamachine, serving as its 'Private Eye' or Detective, as well as the omnipresent Executive Eye, he who exacts absolute conformity to his commands, because no secret can be hidden from him, and no disobedience can go unpunished.

The principal means needed to operate the megamachine correctly and efficiently were a concentration of power, political and economic, instantaneous communication, rapid transportation, and a system of information storage capable of keeping track of every event within the province of the Divine King: once these accessories were available, the central establishment would also have a monopoly of both energy and knowledge. No such complete assemblage had been available to the rulers of the pre-scientific ages: transportation was slow, communication over a distance remained erratic, confined to written messages carried by human messengers, while information storage, apart from tax records and books, was sporadic and subject to fire and military assault. With each successive king, essential parts would require reconstruction or replacement. Only in Heaven could there exist the all-knowing, all-seeing, all-powerful, omnipresent gods who truly commanded the system.

With nuclear energy, electric communication, and the computer, all the necessary components of a modernized megamachine at last became available: 'Heaven' had at last been brought near. Theoretically, at the present moment, and actually soon in the future, God—that is, the Computer—will be able to find, to locate, and to address instantly, by voice and image, via the priesthood, any individual on the planet: exercising control over every detail of the subject's daily life by commanding a dossier which would include his parentage and birth; his complete educational record; an account of his illnesses and his mental breakdowns, if treated; his marriage; his sperm bank account; his income, loans, security payments; his taxes and pensions; and finally the disposition of such further organs as may be surgically extracted from him just prior to the moment of his official death.

In the end, no action, no conversation, and possibly in time no dream or thought would escape the wakeful and relentless eye of this deity: every manifestation of life would be processed into the computer and brought under its all-pervading system of control. This would mean, not just the invasion of privacy, but the total destruction of autonomy: indeed the dissolution of the human soul.

Half a century ago, the foregoing description would have seemed too crude and overwrought to be accepted even as satire: H. G. Wells' 'Modern Utopia,' which tentatively provided for a central identification system, did not dare carry the method through into every detail of life. Even twenty years ago, only the first faint outlines of this modern version of the Eye of Re could be detected by such a prescient mind as that of Norbert Wiener. But today the grim outlines of the whole system have been laid down, with the corroborative evidence, by a legal observer, Alan F. Westin, as an incidental feature of a survey of the numerous public agencies and technological devices that are now encroaching on the domain of private freedom.

What Westin demonstrates, also in passing, is that the countless record files, compiled by individual bureaucracies for their special purposes, can already be assembled in a single central computer, thanks to the fantastic technological progress made through electro-chemical miniaturization: not merely the few I have just picked out, but civil defense records, loyalty security clearance records, land and housing records, licensing applications, trade union cards, social security records, passports, criminal records, automobile registrations, driver's licenses, telephone records, church records, job records—indeed the list becomes finally as large as life—at least of abstracted, symbolically attenuated, recordable life.

The means for such total monitoring came about through the quantum jump from macro- to micro-mechanics: so that the seemingly compact microfilm of earlier decades, to quote Westin's words, "has now given way to photochromatic microimages that make it possible to reproduce the complete bible on a thin sheet of plastic less than two inches square, or to store page by page copies of all books in the Library of Congress in six four-drawer filing cabinets." The ironic fact that this truly colossal leap was a product of research by the National Cash Register Company does not detract from the miraculous nature of this invention: it merely confirms the previous description of the Power Pentagon.

If anything could testify to the magical powers of the priesthood of science and their technical acolytes, or declare unto mankind the supreme qualifications for absolute rulership held by the Divine Computer, this new invention alone should suffice. So the final purpose of life in terms of the megamachine at last becomes clear: it is to furnish and process an endless quantity of data, in order to expand the role and ensure the domination of the power system.

Here if anywhere lies the source of that invisible ultimate power capable of governing the modern world. Here is the Mysterium Tremendum, exercising unlimited power and knowledge, beside which all other forms of magic are clumsy fakes, and all other forms of control without charismic authority. Who dares to laugh at potencies of such magnitude? Who can possibly escape the relentless and unflagging supervision of this supreme ruler? What hideout so remote that it would conceal the rebellious?

A decade before these possibilities for the unlimited storage of information in this electronically etherialized form were realized, the further steps of technological process that loomed ahead—if no brakes were applied and if no natural deceleration came about—were extrapolated by a Jesuit father, Pierre Teilhard de Chardin. Even before the megamachine was identified, and well before the computer had perfected the system of control that is now being installed with breathless haste, he interpreted the billions of years of physical and biological evolution as leading, or, rather, being drawn ineluctably toward this ultimate result.

Since one of the main purposes of this book is to show that such an outcome, though possible, is not predetermined, still less an ideal consummation of human development, I shall deal more extensively with this thesis at a later point. Here I will venture only a tentative but reassuring prediction: that planetary supermechanism will disintegrate long before 'the phenomenon of Man' reaches the Omega point.

4: ORGANIZATION MAN

Neither the ancient nor the modern megamachine, however automatic its separate mechanisms and operations, could have come into existence except through deliberate human invention; and most of the attributes of this large collective unit were first incarnated in an ancient, archetypal figure: Organization Man. From the most primitive expression of tribal conformity to that of the highest political authority, the system itself is an extension of Organization Man—he who stands at once as the creator and the creature, the originator and the ultimate victim, of the megamachine.

Whether the labor machine or the military machine came first, whether the general pattern of regimentation was first evolved by the priest, the bureaucrat, or the soldier are idle questions, since no firm data are available for judgement. We must confine our description of Organization Man to the point at which, through documents and symbolic evidence, he becomes visible. Since the first definite records, after the paleolithic caves, are Temple accounts, tabulating the quantities of grain received or disbursed, it seems likely that the meticulous order that characterizes bureaucracy in every phase derives originally from the ritual observances of the Temple; for this kind of order is incompatible with the hazardous events of the hunt, or the chance-happenings of organized war. Yet even in the latter occupation, we find remarkably early records, in definite figures, of prisoners captured, animals rounded up, loot taken. Even at that early stage Organization Man can be identified by his concern with quantitative accountancy.

Behind every later process of organization and mechanization one must, however, recognize primordial aptitudes, deeply engrained in the human organism—indeed, shared with many other species—for ritualizing behavior and finding satisfaction in a repetitive order that establishes a human connection with organic rhythms and cosmic events.

Out of this original cluster of repetitive, standardized acts, increasingly isolated from other bodily and mental functions, Organization Man seems to have sprung. Or to put it the other way round, when one has detached, one by one, the organs and functions of the human body, and along with this all the historic accretions of art and culture, what one is left with is their common mechanical skeleton and muscle power, essential for vertebrate life but functionless and meaningless when treated as a separate entity.

The present age has reinvented this ideal creature as the Robot: but as a recognizable part of the human organism, and as an integral and indispensable aspect of all human culture, organization itself has always been present. It is precisely because mechanical order can be traced back to these primal beginnings, because mechanization itself has played a constant role in human development, that we can now understand the danger of isolating Organization Man as a self-constituted personality, detached from the natural habitats and cultural traits, with their limitations and inhibitions, that ensure a fully human character.

Organization Man, then, may be defined briefly as that part of the human personality whose further potentialities for life and growth have been suppressed for the purpose of controlling the fractional energies that are left, and feeding them into a mechanically ordered collective system. Organization Man is the common link between the ancient and the modern type of megamachine: that is perhaps why the specialized functionaries, with their supporting layer of slaves, conscripts, and subjects—in short, the controllers and the controlled—have changed so little in the last five thousand years.

Like any other cultural type, Organization Man is a human artifact, though the materials out of which he has been fashioned belong to the system of animate nature. Historically, it is an anachronism to picture Organization Man as a purely modern product, or as solely the product of an advanced technology: he is, rather, an extremely primitive 'ideal' type, carved out of the far richer potentialities of the living organism, with most of the living organs either extracted, or embalmed and desiccated, and the brain itself shrunken to meet the requirements of the megamachine. (The current epithet for such reduction of human potentialities—'head-shrinking'—is all too deadly in its accuracy.)

Within the limited setting of large-scale corporate economic organizations in the United States, W. H. Whyte has given a classic picture of the selection, training, and discipline of Organization Man at the higher levels of command, the transformation of the 'fortunate'—or at least fortune-seeking—minority into smoothly working components of the bigger mechanism. But this is only a small part of the conditioning that begins with the infant's toilet training and, through its equation of the Welfare State with the Warfare State, finally covers every aspect of life through to death and organ-transplantation.

The degree of external pressure necessary to model Organization Man is probably no greater than that needed by any tribal society to secure conformity to ancient traditions and rituals: indeed, through compulsory elementary education, military conscription, and mass-communication, the same stamp can be imprinted on millions of individuals in modern society quite as easily as upon a few hundred who meet face to face. What the sociologist Max Weber called the 'bureaucratic personality' was destined, he thought, to be the 'ideal type' prevailing in the modern world. If the present constellation of forces should continue to operate without abatement or change of direction his prediction may be easily satisfied.

The characteristic virtues of Organization Man correspond as nearly as possible to the machine that he serves: thus the part of his personality that was projected in mechanical instruments in turn re-enforces that projection by eliminating any non-conforming organic or human functions. The stamp of mechanical regularity lies on the face of every human unit. To follow the program, to obey instructions, to 'pass the buck,' to be uninvolved as a person in the needs of other persons, to limit responses to what lies immediately, so to say, on the desk, to heed no relevant human considerations, however vital: never to question the origin of an order or inquire as to its ultimate destination: to follow through every command, however irrational, to make no judgements of value or relevance about the work in hand, finally to eliminate feelings or emotions or rational moral misgivings that might interfere with the immediate dispatch of work—these are the standard duties of the bureaucrat: and these are the conditions under which Organization Man flourishes, a virtual automaton within a collective system of automation. The model for Organization Man is the machine itself. And as the mechanism grows more perfect, the residue of life needed to carry on the process becomes more minute and meaningless.

Ultimately, Organization Man has no reason for existence except as a depersonalized servo-mechanism in the megamachine. On those terms,

Adolph Eichmann, the obedient exterminator, who carried out Hitler's policy and Himmler's orders with unswerving fidelity, should be hailed as the 'Hero of Our Time.' But unfortunately our time has produced many such heroes who have been willing to do at a safe distance, with napalm or atom bombs, by a mere press of the release button, what the exterminators at Belsen and Auschwitz did by old-fashioned handicraft methods. The latter were slower in execution, but far more thrifty in carefully conserving the by-products—the human wastes, the gold from the teeth, the fat, the bone meal for fertilizers—even the skin for lamp-shades. In every country there are now countless Eichmanns in administrative offices, in business corporations, in universities, in laboratories, in the armed forces: orderly obedient people, ready to carry out any officially sanctioned fantasy, however dehumanized and debased.

The more power entrusted to Organization Man, the fewer qualms he has against using it. And what makes this 'ideal type' even more menacing is his successful use of the human disguise. His robot mechanism simulates flesh and blood; and except for a few troglodyte specimens there is nothing to distinguish him outwardly from a reasonable human being, smooth-mannered, low-keyed, presumably amiable. Like Himmler, he may even be a "good family man."

This type was not unknown in earlier cultures: even within our own era these servo-mechanisms arranged gladiatorial combats in the Roman arena and manipulated the bone-wracking machines used by the Holy Inquisition. But before megatechnics invaded every department, Organization Man had fewer opportunities: he was once in a minority, largely confined to the Bureaucracy or the Army. What makes the difference today is that his name is legion; and since he beholds only his own image when he looks around him, he regards himself as a normal specimen of humanity.

How effectively the blindly obedient responses required of Organization Man have been built into the modern personality has come out in a psychological experiment performed under Dr. Stanley Milgrim at Yale, as reported in 'The Journal of Abnormal and Social Psychology.' The experimenter sought to find out what sort of people, slavishly obeying orders, would be capable of sending their fellow-humans into gas chambers, or would commit similar atrocities, as in Vietnam. Forty subjects of various ages were recruited and told that the experiment was a scientific investigation of the effect of punishment, by electric shock, upon the learning process.

The subjects were seated at a console with thirty switches. Visible in the next room, separated by a glass wall, was seated a voluntary 'learner,' duly coached to act his specified part, supposedly in an 'electric chair' but actually unconnected with any current. According to the label on the switches used by the subjects, each switch gave a predetermined shock, ranging from mild to severe, as a penalty for making a mistake. After the switch labelled 'Danger: Severe Shock' there were two other switches bearing the ominous marks XXX! By instruction, the pseudo-learner reacted by crying out as if in pain when the 300-volt switch was flipped, though he banged on the wall demanding that the 'teacher' continue. At this point ten more switches remained, indicating increased intensity of voltage and pain.

Out of forty subjects only fourteen defied the experiment's instructions and refused to cooperate further when the response registered showed intense pain or torture. To their credit as human beings, some of the subjects who continued were emotionally disturbed by the experience: yet 'in the interests of science' sixty-five per cent of them continued beyond the 'danger point.'

Though an experiment performed on only forty subjects is not decisive, it nevertheless helps explain the conduct of supposedly civilized people at various points in history when with the backing of the highest authorities, royal, priestly, military, or—as today—scientific, they witnessed or actually committed hideous tortures. This proves all the easier in a culture like ours, conditioned, as an essential for achieving 'objectivity,' to believe that feelings, emotions, indeed any kind of subjective reaction must be eliminated from purely scientific experiments. Under this test, the participants ceased to be sympathetic, compassionate human beings: a majority were ready not only to witness torture but to bring it about under authoritative direction by acts of their own. This experiment possibly explains why sadistic practices first introduced under supposedly austere scientific discipline in the vivisection of animals have now spread far beyond these limits.

If this characterization seems like the grossest sort of distortion, it is only because the reality has become so commonplace that we cannot even identify it. Let me therefore place in evidence the words of an eminent scientist: a Nobel Prize winner, universally acclaimed by his fellow-biologists as a leader in his field. On the evidence of his writings he seems to have been a rational, 'normal' personality, free from any obvious neurotic pressures or aberrations. These attractive traits unfortunately throw into relief the actual proposals for human improvement he put forth as a geneticist before a group of fellow-scientists.

"Man as a whole," this scientist observed, "must rise to become worthy of his best achievement. Unless the average man can understand the world that the scientists have discovered, unless he can learn to comprehend the techniques he now uses, and their remote and larger effects, unless he can enter into the thrill of being a conscious participant in the great human enterprise and find genuine fulfillment in playing a constructive part in it, he will fall into the position of an ever less important cog in a vast machine. In this situation, his own powers of determining his fate and his very will to do so will dwindle, and the minority who rule over him will eventually find ways of doing without him."

I have not invented this scientist: his name was Hermann Muller. Before Muller described the assumptions and purposes of the new megamachine, I had already identified both the ancient and the modern types. What is remarkable is that after ten years' study I can support Muller's statement with a long list from other scientific exponents, some no less eminent than Muller. What is disconcerting is the fact that it was on the very same grounds that Muller used that the Jews were rejected by Hitler as unfit to participate in Hitler's great enterprise and "find genuine fulfillment in playing a constructive part in it." It was to carry out this 'final solution' for these unworthy non-Aryans that Eichmann and his colleagues were ordered to herd their victims into the gas chambers.

"Find ways of doing without him" seems like a quiet phrase: but is not its quietness ominous? Would it not have been more honest to say "do away with him"? Already these faithful servants of the megamachine have taken for granted that there is only one acceptable view of the world, that which they stand for: only one kind of knowledge, only one type of human enterprise has value—their own, or that which derives directly from their own. Ultimately they mean that only one kind of personality can be considered desirable—that established as such by the military-industrial-scientific elite which will operate the megamachine.

So unchallengeable does this position seem to these leaders that they already possess in their own eyes the right to establish personality types, on their own poorly qualified say-so, and to intimidate and coerce, if necessary 'do without,' those who may challenge their methods or deny the validity of their ends. This, then, is the final demand of Organization Man: the authority to make the world over in his own shrunken image.

5: THE TECHNIQUE OF TOTAL CONTROL

Up to now human culture, in its transformations, has shown many of the characteristics discovered in the evolution of species: the tendency toward species identification and individuated development in adaptive give-and-take with the environment has been counterbalanced by explorations and migrations that widened the possibilities of intercourse, interbreeding, and intercommunication. Though for convenience one may talk about 'Man' this is only a trick of speech: for except in a statistical sense no such uniform and universal creature exists. Up to now, no single political structure, no single ideology, no single technology, no single type of personality has ever prevailed over the entire planet. Man has never yet been homogenized.

What is true for human habitats and human cultures holds equally for man's historic affiliations. Just as no single region or culture can possibly offer fulfillment of all the potentialities for human development, so no single generation can embody these potentialities. And in fact no generation before our own has ever been so fatuous as to imagine it possible to live exclusively within its own narrow time-band, guided only by information recently discovered; nor has it ever before this accepted as final and absolute the demands of the present generation alone, without relating these demands to past experience or future projects and ideal possibilities. The shibboleths of the 'Now' generation do not apply even to animal existence, for all higher organisms provide for their future by mating and nurturing the young; and some even anticipate future needs by storing food.

For the sake of continuity and cultural accumulation, previous cultures have usually over-valued custom and tradition and have even preserved their errors, lest in extirpating them they forfeit their achievements. But the notion that the past, instead of being respected, must be liquidated is a peculiar mark of the megatechnic power system. On this matter, the anthropologist Raglan has spoken sobering words. "It is often assumed that decay is due to the dead hand of conservatism, and it is of course the fact that religious or political theories which involve a belief in the infallibility of the ancients must often lead to decay. . . . It is less often realized, on the other hand, that decay of culture can be brought about even more rapidly by breaking away from the past."

For a culture like the present one to cultivate its transience and ephemerality, as if dynamism were an absolute value and stability of any kind a handicap, is to ignore the plain facts not only of organic continuity but of physical existence. If all the chemical elements were as unstable as the radioactive group, organic life would never have appeared on this planet—nor would there have been such a planet as ours, predisposed, as Lawrence Henderson demonstrated, to life.

Despite many fixations and arrests, setbacks and losses, the cumulative results of human development during the last hundred thousands of years have been comparable in their richness and variety to those nature was able to achieve at only a crawling pace in the evolution of species. Each race, each culture, each tribe, each city, even each village has been turning out new specimens of 'man': always sufficiently similar to be identifiable in terms of the genus *Homo sapiens,* yet sufficiently different to provide the possibility of perhaps higher and richer achievements. Even in those traits that are common to all breeds of men, such as language, social organization, moral standards, there has been from the beginning a bi-polar development: one stressing individuation and autonomy, the other wider association and homogeneity: the first self-centered, localized, directed from within, the other tending toward uniformity, universality, globalism.

From time to time these developments have entered into man's reflective consciousness, sometimes reaching remarkable depths of perception among 'primitive' peoples. But it is only in the last few centuries that even a beginning has been made in describing the conditions under which human cultures have developed, and in distinguishing favorable modes of growth from those that are pathological and have resulted in lapses of function and in death. No one can pretend that the archaeological, anthropological, and historical knowledge so far available is sufficiently wide or well attested to provide more than promising suggestions of valid truths. But we have already a sufficiently clear picture of both biological and social evolution to see that the factors making for variety, selectivity, and change must be counterpoised by those making for continuity, regularity, stability, and universality; and that when either set is lacking, life and growth are threatened.

Though we are too close to it to make a completely objective judgement, it has become obvious that our own culture has fallen into a dangerously unbalanced state, and is now producing warped and unbalanced minds. One part of our civilization—that dedicated to technology—has usurped authority over all the other components, geographical, biological, anthropological: indeed, the most frenetic advocates of this process are proclaiming that the whole biological world is now being supplanted by technology, and that man will either become a willing creature of his technology or cease to exist.

Not merely does technology claim priority in human affairs: it places the demand for constant technological change above any considerations of its own efficiency, its own continuity, or even, ironically enough, its own capacity to survive. To maintain such a system, whose postulates contradict those that underlie all living organisms, it requires for self-protection absolute conformity by the human community; and to achieve that conformity it proposes to institute a system of total control, starting with the human organism itself, even before conception has taken place. The means for establishing this control is the ultimate gift of the megamachine; and without submergence in the subjective 'myth of the machine,' as omnipotent, omniscient, and omnicompetent, it would not already have advanced to the point it has now reached.

Let us go back again to the table of probable future inventions that those who have surrendered to the myth of the machine are now so busily propagating: such a plausible table as Arthur Clarke, for instance, has

offered. Of more than a dozen technical exploits he lists, from lunar landings to weather control, from suspended animation to artificial life, no one
of them has the slightest relation to man's central historic task, more
imperative today than ever—the task of becoming human. The failure to
perform that task for a single generation might set the erring community
back a whole geological epoch: indeed, there is reason to suspect that this
has actually begun to happen in our time.

The one set of discoveries and inventions that these prophets of technology will not allow for are those internal human devices that would
eventually bring technics itself under constant human evaluation and direction. On the contrary: to meet any such counter-attack, before it begins,
they have propagated the belief that technology provides the only conceivable and acceptable way of life today.

The business of creating a limited, docile, scientifically conditioned
human animal, completely adjusted to a purely technological environment,
has kept pace with the rapid transformation of that environment itself:
partly this has been effected, as already noted, by re-enforcing conformity
with tangible rewards, partly by denying any real opportunities for choices
outside the range of the megatechnic system. American children, who, on
statistical evidence, spend from three to six hours a day absorbing the
contents of television, whose nursery songs are advertisements, and whose
sense of reality is blunted by a world dominated by daily intercourse with
Superman, Batman, and their monstrous relatives, will be able only by
heroic effort to disengage themselves from this system sufficiently to recover some measure of autonomy. The megamachine has them under its
remote control, conditioned to its stereotypes, far more effectively than the
most authoritative parent. No wonder the first generation brought up under
this tutelage faces an 'identity crisis.'

Already this mode of conditioning has created a new psychological
type: one bearing almost from birth the imprint of megatechnics in all its
forms: a type unable to react directly to sights or sounds, to patterns or
concrete objects, unable to function in any capacity without anxiety,
indeed, unable to feel alive, except by permission or command of the
machine and with the aid of the extra-organic apparatus that the Machine-
God provides. In a multitude of cases, this conditioning has already
reached the point of total dependence; and this state of submissive conformity has been hailed, by the more ominous prophets of this regime, as
man's ultimate 'liberation.' But liberation from what? Liberation from the
conditions under which man has flourished: namely, in an active, give-and-
take, mutually rewarding relationship with a varied and responsive 'un-
programmed' environment, human and natural—an environment full of
difficulties, temptations, hard choices, challenges, lovely surprises, and unexpected rewards.

Here again, the first steps in establishing control seemed innocent. Consider B. F. Skinner's learning machine. For instruction in subjects such as languages, requiring much repetition and correction for accurate memorizing, such a machine can perhaps lighten the burden of the teacher and enable the student to go forward more rapidly to a point where the teacher may give him active help in matters that cannot be programmed on a machine. Conceivably, though not necessarily, this might work to their common advantage.

Like so many other mechanical devices, learning machines may be helpful auxiliaries. But the tendency of megatechnics with its over-riding interest in earning the maximum possible profits for the corporations exploiting these machines, is to turn such occasional minor aids into major permanent fixtures, and to extend the offices of the machine to every subject in the curriculum at every age. This means giving mechanical and electronic equipment the time, effort, money, and emotional involvement that should be given to human relations and human agents. In the end, good learning habits, established early, along with deliberate memory training, would provide better instruction than great batteries of machines—and be of far wider application. But such human devices do not produce financial dividends.

Such programmed pseudo-education is in fact the perfect instrument of political absolutism, and the general acceptance of this system would be fatal to the exercise of independent judgement, critical dissent, or creative thought. In France, under the post-Napoleonic bureaucracy, the Minister of Education could boast that he knew exactly what every teacher was teaching at a given hour in every school. But that mode of control still was unable completely to suppress the human dialogue and eliminate every spontaneous human reaction: for the teacher was still a visible personality, who could be challenged, defied, disobeyed; while the pupils in a class, however strict the discipline, still were reassured by one another's presence, and were capable of exerting an effect—if only by mischief and disorder!—upon their teacher. Such contacts mocked the Minister's boast of uniformity. It is to remove these last traces of human intercourse—that is, to ensure isolation and total submission—that current technics now addresses itself.

Threatened with a shortage of trained teachers, bureaucratic educational 'experts' eagerly seek elaborate mechanical solutions for every difficulty, instead of bending their efforts to persuade more qualified persons to enter the educational system, and to reduce the sterile procedures that vitiate human energy and interest. Not alone do they favor the wider use of teaching machines and computers; they have eagerly sought to exploit other methods of one-way communication, such as television broadcasts from a satellite for the entire system, to supplant such relics of two-way intercourse and active participation as exist in some measure even in the poorest classroom where teachers and students meet face to face.

This reliance upon mechanical solutions for the problem of quantity, when what is actually required is mechanical simplification and human amplification, solidifies the system introduced by the archaic-modern megamachine.

Today the simple learning machine is already outmoded. At the 1964 World's Fair in New York, the 'School of the Future' was presented in its final space-capsule form, whereby each student is turned into a kind of solitary 'learning-grub,' spending his whole day in a closed compartment, appropriately egg-shaped, in which information would be processed and fed to him from a central station. Thus the motto of the collective bakery or food-processing plant, "Nothing Touched by Human Hands," now gives way to the bolder one of mechanistic behaviorism: "Nothing Touched by the Human Personality." The isolation cell, one of the cruelest forms of punishment ever devised short of mutilation, is now proposed as the standard school equipment.

The purpose of this equipment is not merely to remove the student from reciprocal human contacts, but likewise to isolate him from intercourse with any part of the real world except that which has been programmed for him by a higher authority, so that he will be more completely under the control of the megamachine. Once this system is firmly established, not merely learning but all other human transactions would take place through official channels, and under the constant surveillance of a central authority. This is not education but animal training. Since man is the most adaptable of animals, a considerable number of people have already submitted, at least in their minds, to such a sterile conception of learning. Apparently they have no suspicion that this sort of technological 'progress' does violence to the human personality: in fact, is a disturbing sign of human regression.

Our contemporaries are already so conditioned to accept technological 'progress' as absolute and irresistible, however painful, ugly, mentally cramping, or physiologically damaging its results, that they accept the latest technical offering, whether a supersonic plane or a 'learning cell,' with smiling consent, particularly if the equipment is accompanied by a 'scientific' explanation and seems technologically an 'advanced' type.

This general aberration was long ago satirized by Tolstoi in his treatise, 'What Is Art?' There he pictured modern man ingeniously sealing up the windows of his house and mechanically exhausting the air so that he might, by utilizing a still more extravagant mechanical apparatus, pump air back again—instead of merely opening the window. Tolstoi did not suspect that within a generation this folly would actually be committed, not only as a permissible dodge for screening out dust and poisonous gas exhausts, or for tempering excessive heat: but it would even be used by the designers of houses and college buildings in the midst of open country, where fresh air is available, and where the natural noises are at a lower level than that of the exhaust fans used by a ventilating system.

By now, unfortunately, Tolstoi's satire has lost its point. For something even more indefensible has happened: every part of the environment is being reconstructed on the same principles, in order to ensure that at no part of a man's life shall he be free from external control. In past ages human growth was often impeded by lack of technical equipment, by lack of carefully sifted information or theoretic knowledge, by the absence of the physical means for sufficiently wide intercourse and cooperation. Strangely, many people still behave as if there were a dearth of these agencies. But just the opposite is true. No part of modern man's environment or organization as yet shows any signs of fixation or overstability, except automation itself. On the contrary, technology has produced a state of torrential dynamism, since the only form of control effectively exercised is that of making every part undergo still more rapid change, *whilst the system itself becomes more immobile and rigid.* Man himself is thus losing hold on any personal life that can be called his own: he is now being turned into a 'thing' destined to be processed and reconstructed collectively by the same methods that have produced the atomic pile and the computer.

Modern man's readiness to accept this external control, even after having tasted and enjoyed in the last few centuries a considerable measure of municipal, corporate, and personal freedom, has been facilitated by both external pressures and internal anxieties. The mere growth of numbers— not only the total increase of population but the increase in the size of all social units from cities to armies and bureaucracies—has made the individual soul timid and self-distrustful. He feels incapable of coping with events that lie so far beyond his range of vision or his active muscular controls. "A stranger and afraid in a world I never made."

Once his intimate, small-scale modes of association are either eliminated or paralyzed, he seeks security in great impersonal organizations— not only the State, but his insurance Societies or his Trade Unions, which also function as essential parts of the same power system. Unfortunately the prosperity of these corporate units imposes the need for still further regimentation and further centralization of control. Thus the 'escape from freedom,' as Erich Fromm pointed out a generation ago, produces a new form of liberation—permanent liberation from responsibility and active choice.

In the final stage of technical development, as various science-fiction writers have been quick to perceive, the organized sciences will attempt to do directly, mainly by physical and chemical devices, what other human institutions—religion, morals, law—sought to do more indirectly, with only partial success, by exhortation, persuasion, or warning threat: namely, to transform the nature of man. Science confidently proposes to alter his potentialities at the source through genetic intervention and through further programming his existence so as to permit no unforeseen departures or rebellions. Radical alterations that kings and priests never succeeded in performing except by evisceration scientists now confidently propose to do on the living corpse by surgical alteration, chemotherapy, and electronic control. But so obsessive is the drive to exert control that these experiments have received financial backing from 'philanthropic' national foundations; so that even before these words are printed radical decisions that may imperil the possibilities for further human development may well have been made.

The most cogent forewarning of the dismal destiny of man, once he submits completely to the megamachine, comes from the group that now holds all the strategic positions of authority in the modern state: the scientists. One might draw on a hundred examples of similar subjective aberrations coming forth in seemingly rational form as 'next steps in progress,' but I shall confine myself to a few typical examples; and first, an illuminating scientific symposium on 'The Future of Life,' organized as a public service by an international pharmaceutical corporation and attended by a distinguished array of scientists. (See Gordon Wolstenholme.)

The papers presented led to a discussion over what forms of control were possible in order to raise the genetic level of the population and eliminate unfavorable genes no longer suppressed by natural selection. This brought up the question of artificial breeding from superior stocks, and that in turn led to an argument as to whether human beings have a natural right to beget their own children. On this point, the statement of one of the participants, an historian of science, was illuminating: "Taking up Crick's point about the humanist argument whether one has a right to have children, I would say that in a society in which the community is responsible for people's welfare—health, hospitals, unemployment insurance, etc.—the answer is No."

It might seem unfair to hold a scholar strictly to a casual statement expressed in discussion, even if he has allowed this to appear in print. But the fact that his answer was so unhesitating, so unqualified, would indicate that it is one that is widely held. Too many of these self-elected rulers have already asserted that, in return for benefits received, obedience and strict conformity to instructions—*their* instructions—must be officially imposed, much as they are imposed by current bureaucratic routines upon helpless patients in modern hospitals.

This obligation involves something more than listening to medical advice, such as may properly be given to those who on the record have serious inheritable defects. It involves, as further discussion indicated, the scientist's right to establish ideal human types in terms of his own provincial, time-limited criteria, and on this basis to select spermatozoa and ova for reproduction. Sir Francis Crick indeed went further, and advocated freedom for experimentally altering the human genes, even though by bad luck he might, on his own admission, produce monsters.

One thing was notably absent among some of the participants in this discussion: any sense that those who might be in possession of the knowledge and techniques needed for exercising such controls should be obliged to produce some positive evidence of their special fitness for determining the future of the human race. The lack of such credentials, or rather the naïve belief that scientific achievement was the only credential needed, seemed to give no embarrassment. One would hardly have guessed from such a discussion that thousands of the wisest minds have meditated for thousands of years over what are the most desirable characteristics in human beings, what traits should be modified or repressed, what composite character—or indeed what assortment of characters—is desirable to produce the highest order of human being.

One culture after another has framed its own answer to this problem, by bringing forth ideal types and incarnating them in an endless succession of models in their gods, heroes, saints, sages. But as it has turned out, none of these models or their variants has ever been quite successful, never universally applicable. To speak only of the Greeks, neither Zeus nor Apollo, neither Prometheus nor Hephaistos nor Herakles, neither Achilles nor Odysseus meets every requirement. If we turn to the more conscious efforts of religion and philosophy to body forth an ideal human type, we are equally baffled in our choice: the Confucian, the Taoist, the Zoroastrian, the Buddhist, the Platonist, the Stoic, the Cynic, the Christian, the Mohammedan have all produced their own conceptions of the perfect man, often in defensive opposition to grosser types that had dominated earlier civilization. But one and all these ideal forms have fallen short, even when in individual personalities they seem as close as were Socrates or Francis of Assisi, to achieving perfection within their own chosen framework. In one of the most highly developed cultures on record, the Hellenic, no consensus was ever reached.

What this means, I conclude, is that the only effective approach to this problem is that long ago taken by Nature: to provide the possibility of an endless variety of biological and cultural types, since no single one, however rich and rewarding, is capable of encompassing all the latent potentialities of man. No one culture, no one race, no one period can do more than produce fresh variations on this inexhaustible theme.

Many biologists whose knowledge of evolution is not confined to molecular phenomena are convinced that the notion of improving any significant portion of the human stock by the specific selection of genes in individual specimens—even granting its dubious technical feasibility—is a mirage: in breeding cattle the results of too specific selection, as in the notorious case of dwarfism in the Black Angus, have often proved self-defeating. But the fact that such distinguished geneticists as Muller and Crick persuaded themselves that direct intervention is not only possible but desirable—"we can, therefore we must"—shows how far the insolent pharaonic notion of total control has seized possession of such minds. As with the deepfreezing of corpses for future resuscitation, which is the modern equivalent of mummification to ensure immortality, these proposals relate to the same archaic fantasies that burst forth with the success of the first megamachines in the Pyramid Age. The conclusion seems inescapable: the one part of the human personality that so far evades rational control is that which produces these fantasies.

What is most suspicious about this discussion, however, is not just the defect in scientific insight, but the absence of prudent self-awareness and self-criticism. Never more clearly has the dismissal of history, that is, the cumulative evidences of human experience, showed itself more plainly as a source of error. I am not talking only of human history but of organic evolution. Those species of ants that have achieved firm control in breeding special types have remained fixed for some sixty million years. They foretell the ultimate fate of a human population similarly constituted. Ah, Brave New World!

In this new scientific hierarchy only one-way communication is observed: those who speak with the highest authority upon some minute section of exact knowledge too often unblushingly claim the right to speak for mankind upon matters of general human experience upon which they can testify only on the same lowly basis as other human beings. In many discussions of the science-governed future, the right of popular resistance is not even mentioned; whereas, even in feudal society, as Marc Bloch pointed out, vassal homage, however humble, was a genuine contract and a bilateral one; and the right of resistance to unjust or arbitrary authority was not only implied but often specified. The sovereign himself was held responsible to the people, like the "swineherd to the master who employs him," as an Alsatian monk wrote about 1090. By one measure or another, often under the guise of public good, that precious right—the right of non-conformity, and counter-action—is now covertly being denied.

What is most suspicious in all these discussions of possible technological futures, mainly by the extrapolation of visible tendencies or incipient inventions, is the ingrained fatalism they display: they refuse to allow the possibility of a complete reversal of existing trends. This fatalism characterizes sociological observers like Professor Jacques Ellul, who plainly detests the evils of megatechnics, as well as those who are impatient to hasten the pace even if many precious human achievements are defaced and destroyed.

Let me give a final example, selected only because it is regrettably typical. In 'Genetics and the Future of Man,' a social scientist, highly respected as a population expert, has declared that deliberate genetic control is *"bound to occur,"* and once begun, "it would soon benefit science and technology, which in turn would facilitate further hereditary improvement, which in turn would extend science, and so on in a self-enforcing spiral without limit." He concludes that "when man has conquered his own biological evolution, he will have laid the basis for conquering everything else. The Universe will be his, at last."

This is a museum specimen of archaic scientific thinking, and circular thinking at that, for the original premise of automatism—"it is bound to occur"—is asserted as if unchallengeable. This scientist ignores the fact that every item in his deduction is unproved and unprovable, beginning with the notion that human development itself can be equated with the unconditional support of science and technology.

But even if scientists were able to identify the specific traits predisposing the embryo to these vocations, by what rational criterion could one say that the magnification, intensification, or wider distribution of these traits would constitute a desirable human goal? There is sounder ground for believing that a much richer genetic pool must be drawn on—in the human future as in the pre-human past—to realize further improvements; and that quite different character traits and human types are now needed to overcome mankind's present cultural disequilibrium.

As for settling on scientists and technologists as the supreme product of human evolution, the final incarnations of the 'just man made perfect'— what a happy solution that is! But so naïve in its narcissistic admiration of the scientific image that it is actually embarrassing to read. Such self-adulation would be laughable were it not so widely shared and if this now-common belief did not constitute a formidable barrier to the emergence of different personality constellations that do not fit into the power system and conform to the prescribed technical-scientific formulae.

This proposal for genetic control exposes the idea of control itself in its ultimate absurdity: the arrogant notion that finite minds, operating with the limited equipment of their particular culture and historic moment, will ever be qualified to exercise absolute control over the infinite future possibilities of human development.

One final term nevertheless demands exegesis: the idea of 'conquest' itself. In what sense does the notion of 'conquest' have the slightest meaning in relation to man's place in nature? What bearing does this have on the cooperative transactions and interactions of species, or to man's own attempt to transcend his own biological limitations by super-organic modes of life? The very term 'conquest' is an obsolete military term, however re-enforced by our whole power system: actually it is an ideological fossil left over from the traumatic original episodes in civilization which brought forth war, slavery, organized destruction, and genocide. 'Conquest' and 'cultivation' are historic enemies: they stand at opposite poles.

In short, conquest is in no sense a necessary sign of higher human development, though conquistadors have always thought otherwise. Any valid concept of organic development must use the primary terms of ecology—cooperation and symbiosis—as well as struggle and conflict, for even predators are part of a food chain, and do not 'conquer' their prey except to eat them. The idea of total conquest is an extrapolation from the existing power system: it indicates, not a desirable end, accommodation, but a pathological aberration, re-enforced by such rewards as this system bestows. As for the climactic notion that "the universe will be man's at last"—what is this but a paranoid fantasy, comparable to the claims of an asylum inmate who imagines that he is Emperor of the World? Such a claim is countless light-years away from reality.

The decisive factor of safety in human development lies in the fact that man's many specific experimental errors and subjective aberrations have *not* been deliberately fixed in the genes. To an extent that no other species enjoys, each fresh generation shakes the genetic dice and rolls out fresh combinations, leaving it open to new human factors to repair past errors and embark on fresh experiments. Many mistakes have been made in the development of every known culture, and some of them, like war, slavery, and class exploitation, have seriously crippled human development. Yet none of these aberrations is so deeply embedded in the flesh that it is unalterable or immortal. If in future fresh human possibilties should be closed off, it would be because the dominant power system had deliberately closed them, in the very fashion that technocratic spokesmen advocate.

In so far as the illusion of technological inevitability is taken for an inescapable reality—*e.g.,* *"genetic control is bound to occur"*—this atti-tude only adds an inner compulsiveness to the many external compulsions imposed by the Power Complex. Such beliefs often prove self-fulfilling prophecies, and they make more probable the riveting together of a planetary megamachine. This superimposed power system, with its insis-tent compulsiveness and automatism, may prove in the end the gravest menace to man's own development. While the cultural inheritance is partly re-programmed from generation to generation, from culture to culture, and is modified even from hour to hour by the plans and acts of individual minds, genetic control might program man out of existence, and create a substitute homunculus: the fixed component of a humanly vacuous automatic system. By its cultural inventions the human species has up till now avoided such a fatal arrest.

6: ELECTRONIC ENTROPY

But perhaps another fate is actually in store for mankind if it should continue blindly on its present course: not an arrested development, with an eventual lapse into unconsciousness, or a transmutation of all functions of the human intelligence into the planetary megamachine, nor yet the sort of venturesome selective breeding or chemical synthesis that Professors Charles C. Price and Joshua Lederberg have foreseen, with their possible production of such biological horrors as Olaf Stapledon described in the long future.

Perhaps *Homo sapiens* will come to a quicker end by a shorter route, already indicated in many manifestations of modern art, and expressed with psychedelic extravagance by Professor Marshall McLuhan and his followers. The seemingly solid older megamachine with its rigid limitations and predictable performance might give rise to the exact antithesis: an electronic anti-megamachine programmed to accelerate disorder, ignorance, and entropy. In revolt against totalitarian organization and enslavement, the generation now responding to McLuhan's doctrines would seek total 'liberation' from organization, continuity, and purpose of any sort, in systematic de-building, dissolution, and de-creation. Ironically, such a return to randomness would, according to probability theory, produce the most static and predictable state possible: that of unorganized 'matter.'

In the first stage of this 'liberation,' as McLuhan sees it, instantaneous planetary communication will bring about a release from all previous cultures and past modes of regimentation: machines themselves will vanish, to be replaced by electronic equivalents or substitutes. In McLuhan's trancelike vaticinations, he actually appears to believe that this has already happened, and that even the wheel is about to disappear, while mankind as a whole will return to the pre-primitive level, sharing mindless sensations and pre-linguistic communion. In the electronic phantasmagoria that he conjures up, not alone will old-fashioned machines be permanently outmoded but nature itself will be replaced: the sole vestige of the multifarious world of concrete forms and ordered experience will be the sounds and 'tactile' images on the constantly present television screen or such abstract derivative information as can be transferred to the computer.

Psychiatry reveals the true nature of this promised state. What is it but the electronic equivalent of the dissociation and subjective inflation that takes place under lysergic acid and similar drugs? In so far as McLuhan's conception corresponds to any existential reality, it is that of an electronically induced mass psychosis. Not surprisingly, perhaps, now that the facilities for instantaneous communication have planetary outlets, symptoms of this psychosis are already detectable in every part of the planet. In McLuhan's case, the disease poses as the diagnosis.

As it happens, the proposal to confine man to a present time-cage that cuts him off from both his past and his future did not originate in the present age, nor is it dependent upon an exclusive commitment to electronic communication. The ancient name for this form of exerting centralized control is 'the burning of the books.' In the past this has been the favored method of maintaining absolute royal control, once the broadcasting of the written record threatened to give power to those who defied the official control centers. The burning of the books in China in 213 B.C. by the last of the Ch'in emperors has been repeated at intervals as the 'final solution' when censorship and legal prohibition such as still prevail in totalitarian countries fail.

Though my generation usually associates this burning with the public bonfires lighted by the Nazis in the nineteen-thirties, that was a relatively innocent manifestation, for it disposed of only a token number of the world's store of books. But it remained for McLuhan to picture as technology's ultimate gift a more absolute mode of control: one that will achieve total illiteracy, with no permanent record except that officially committed to the computer, and open only to those permitted access to this facility. This repudiation of an independent written and printed record means nothing less than the erasure of man's diffused, multi-brained collective memory: it reduces all human experience into that of the present generation and the passing moment. The instant record is self-effacing. In effect, if not in intention, this would carry mankind back to a far more primitive state than any tribal one: for pre-literate peoples conserved a large part of their past by cultivating extraordinary memories, and maintaining by constant repetition—even at the cost of creativity and invention—the essential links to their own past. The bards of this oral culture could recite a whole Iliad without having recourse to a written word.

For this 'instant revolution' to be successful, the burning of the books must take place on a worldwide scale and include every form of permanent record open to public view. The shibboleth for such absolutism, like that for nineteenth-century anarchism, is "incinerate the documents."

McLuhan's denigration of the printed word, expressed in his hostility to 'Typographical Man'—itself a figment of his imagination—has nevertheless given support to purely physical assaults on books, as well as a chronic indifference to their contents. Similar insensate student demonstrations have taken place in universities on every continent. As in so many other phenomena of the power system, electronic communication has only hastened the speed, not changed the goal. The goal is total cultural dissolution—or what McLuhan characterizes as a 'tribal communism,' though it is in fact the extreme antithesis of anything that can be properly called tribal or communistic. As for 'communism,' this is McLuhan's public-relations euphemism for totalitarian control.

Now, electronic communication has obviously added a new dimension to human capability and practical cooperation: this is a platitude of nineteenth-century thought that McLuhan has sought to turn into a startling private paradox. Even before television was sufficiently perfected for commercial use, it was possible to describe its valuable potentialities and to anticipate the defects that have actually, since 1945, become apparent.

On this matter, I have no hesitation in putting forward the views expressed in 'Technics and Civilization' (1934), at a time when television was still in the experimental stage. In my interpretation of neotechnics I said: "With the invention of the telegraph a series of inventions began to bridge the gap in time between communication and response despite the handicaps of space: first the telegraph, then the telephone, then the wireless telegraph, then the wireless telephone, and finally television. As a result, communication is now on the point of returning, with the aid of mechanical devices, to that instantaneous reaction of person to person with which it began; but the possibilities of this immediate meeting, instead of being limited by space and time, will be limited only by the amount of energy available and the mechanical perfection and accessibility of the apparatus. When the radio telephone is supplemented by television communication will differ from direct intercourse only to the extent that immediate physical contact will be impossible."

Not merely did I point out the applications and implications of electronics: but unlike McLuhan I anticipated its drawbacks: not least the fact that "immediate intercourse on a worldwide basis does not necessarily mean a less trivial or a less parochial personality." I suggested moreover that the maintenance of distance both in time and space was one of the conditions for rational judgement and cooperative intercourse, as against unreflective responses and snap judgements. "The lifting of restrictions upon close human intercourse," I went on to say, "has been, in its first stages, as dangerous as the flow of populations into new lands: it has increased the areas of friction . . . [and] has mobilized and hastened mass-reactions, like those which occur on the eve of a war."

These pages diminish, I am afraid, the claims of priority and peculiar insight often made for McLuhan as the unique prophet of the Electronic Age—thirty years later. But it leaves him with few rivals in the art of rationalizing the irrationalities introduced by megatechnics: so much so that by concentrating upon McLuhan's errors one can clear the board of a large mass of similar mis-statements.

By turns the steamboat, the railroad, the postal system, the electric telegraph, the airplane, have been described as instruments that would transcend local weaknesses, redress inequalities of natural and cultural resources, and lead to a worldwide political unity—"the parliament of man, the federation of the world." Once technical unification was established, human solidarity, 'progressive' minds believed, would follow. In the course of two centuries, these hopes have been discredited. As the technical gains have been consolidated, moral disruptions, antagonisms, and collective massacres have become more flagrant, not in local conflicts alone but on a global scale. There is no reason whatever to think that radio and television will enable us to fare better, until they themselves become the instruments of wiser human decisions, and embrace every aspect of life, not limiting themselves to those that conform to the Pentagon of Power.

For this problem McLuhan and his technocratic contemporaries have a simple solution. It is to replace human autonomy in every form by an up-to-date electronic model of the megamachine. The mass media, he demonstrates, are *"put out before they are thought out. In fact, their being put outside us tends to cancel the possibility of their being thought at all."* Precisely. Here McLuhan gives the whole show away. Because all technical apparatus is an extension of man's bodily organs, including his brain, this peripheral structure, on McLuhan's analysis, must, by its very mass and ubiquity, replace all autonomous needs or desires: since now for us "technology is part of our bodies," no detachment or divorce is possible. "Once we have surrendered our senses and nervous systems to the private manipulation of those who would try to benefit from taking a lease of our eyes and ears and nerves, we don't really have any rights [read 'autonomy'] left."

This latter point might well be taken as a warning to disengage ourselves, as soon as possible, from the power system so menacingly described: for McLuhan it leads, rather, to a demand for unconditional surrender. "Under electric technology," he observes, "the entire business of man becomes learning and knowing." Apart from the fact that this is a pathetically academic picture of the potentialities of man, the kind of learning and knowing that McLuhan becomes enraptured over is precisely that which can be programmed on a computer: "We are now in a position . . . ," he observes, "to transfer the entire show to the memory of a computer." No better formula could be found for arresting and ultimately suppressing human development.

So far from undermining oral intercourse, writing and print made it effective for far larger populations in time and space than any immediate world broadcast today. When the oral Odyssey became also a book, Homer spoke not to the villages where he recited his poems, but to the world: and the 'Cry of the Eloquent Peasant' in Egypt, once recorded on papyrus, instead of being suppressed by the dominant minority, was still heard, thousands of years later, thanks to the scribes who copied and recopied it.

In communication, as in every other aspect of technology, a polytechnics that utilizes every technical accessory is superior to a monotechnics, especially one trimmed strictly to fit the needs of the power complex. But the fact is that only great poems, like Homer's, or significant events, like the Eloquent Peasant's challenge to absolutism, deserve worldwide circulation: more commonplace thoughts, events, and scenes, transmitted only to keep the deprived senses from starvation, by giving the illusion of life, do not deserve such enlargement. In any quantity they destroy the personal reactions to the living moment.

Audio-visual tribalism (McLuhan's 'global village') is a humbug. Real communication, whether oral or written, ephemeral or permanent, is possible only between people who share a common culture—and speak the same language; and though this area can and should be enlarged by personally acquiring more languages and extending one's cultural horizon through travel and active personal intercourse, the notion that it is possible to throw off all these limits is an electronic illusion. This illusion ignores the most characteristic feature of all organic forms, biological or cultural—their acceptance of limitations for the sake of ensuring the best life possible. Radio actually has scored some of its most signal triumphs not in global but in local transmission, where it has proved marvelously effective in bringing about social cohesion and prompt responses. Witness the uprising of the citizens of Prague in the summer of 1968. That spontaneous mobilization of resistance, made possible by portable transmitters, brilliantly demonstrated the suppleness of this new technology when used in small units.

Observe: this was not an expression of tribal culture in any sense: on the contrary, it was an evidence of the assembled intelligence of a *closely organized and intimately associated* historic city. This cooperation would not have been possible if Prague's population had been scattered over Czechoslovakia in a formless, incoherent 'megalopolis,' reachable only through high-powered central radio stations, which could easily be occupied by a small military force.

While superficially overcoming the effect of distance, the electronic media have shown what a heavy price must be paid for even the simulation of multi-dimensioned intercourse. In genuine communication every agent has its own special role to play: the visible gesture, the direct spoken word, the written message, the painting, the printed book, the radio, the phonograph record, the tape recorder, television. Instead of replacing these varied multi-media by television, radio, and the computer alone, a mature and efficient technology would strive to keep them all in existence, each for the performance of its appropriate function in the chosen situation. As with the transportation system, which cannot dispense with the free-moving and autonomous pedestrian without producing clotted urban congestion or equally baffling suburban dispersion, so with an efficient communications system. What is needed is a technology so varied, so many-sided, so flexible, so responsive to human need, that it can serve every valid human purpose. The only true multi-medium remains the human organism itself.

Anthropological studies have repeatedly demonstrated that the fluidity and ephemerality that McLuhan attributes to oral communication is precisely what no primitive tribal culture could tolerate except by courting dissolution. If our own complex inheritance should continue to follow McLuhan's injunctions, it would dissolve—*is it not already dissolving?*—before our eyes. It is only at a high stage of individuation, made possible at first by the painted or carved image, the written symbol, and the printed book, that true freedom—the freedom to escape from the passing moment and the present visible place, to challenge past experience or modify future action—can be achieved. To be aware only of immediate stimuli and immediate sensations is a medical indication of brain injury.

McLuhan's ideas about the role of electronic technology have been widely accepted, I suggest, because they magnify and vulgarize the dominant components of the power system in the very act of seeming to revolt against its regimentation. In treating the planet as a 'tribal village' by instant electronic communication, he has, in fact, united the crippling limitations of a pre-literate culture, which made the scattered, farming population of the world an easy prey to military conquest and exploitation, with the characteristic historic mischief of 'civilization': the subjugation of a large population for the exclusive benefit of a ruling minority.

So far from there being any spontaneous communication under this regime, these electronic media are already carefully controlled to make sure that 'dangerous,' that is, unorthodox views do not slip through. Such a system permits neither colloquy nor dialogue, as in genuine oral intercourse: what takes place is for the greater part only a meticulously arranged monologue, even if more than one person is present on the screen. A population entirely dependent upon such controlled oral communication, even though it reached every human soul on the planet, would not merely be at the mercy of the Dominant Minority but would become increasingly illiterate and soon mutually unintelligible. Thus once again the parallel between the Pyramid Age and our own forces itself upon the observer: here in prospect is actually the electronic Tower of Babel. Instant planetary communication, conducted on these principles, would bring about eventual excommunication from any identifiable community.

We have now to examine more closely the clinical picture presented by this Instant Revolution, with its instant knowledge, instant power—and instant destruction. Seen by itself this picture gives cause for grave alarm. But already the system has begun to produce reactions from within that threaten its continued dominance, if not its very existence.

CHAPTER ELEVEN

The Megatechnic Wasteland

1 : AIR-CONDITIONED PYRAMIDS

Though the Pyramid Age had a static conception of Heaven, its dynamism was as methodical and relentless as that of our own technocratic age. Each Pharaoh built a new capital for himself within his own lifetime: a change-over no present government has ventured to imitate. While these pyramids, with their attendant temples and priestly housing facilities, absorbed the surplus energies of the Nile Valley, they not merely kept this emerging economy of abundance in balance, but served as material evidence of the supernatural potencies of the new cosmic religion.

The modernized megamachine has reproduced all the early features of the ancient form by pyramid building on an even larger scale. And just as the static physical structures supported the worshipper's belief in the validity of the Pharaoh's claims to divinity and immortality, so the new dynamic forms of the pyramid-complex—the skyscrapers, the atomic reactors, the nuclear weapons, the superhighways, the space rockets, the underground control centers, the collective nuclear shelters (tombs)— seem equally to validate and exalt the new religion. No other religion has ever produced so many manifestations of power, has brought about such a complete system of control, has unified so many separate institutions, has suppressed so many independent ways of life, or for that matter has ever claimed so many worshippers, who by word and deed have testified to the kingdom, the power, and the glory of its nuclear and electronic gods. The miracles performed by the technocratic priesthood are genuine: only their claims of divinity are spurious.

Symbolically, at the entrance to the new pyramid complexes stands the nuclear reactor, which first manifested its powers to the multitude by a typical trick of Bronze Age deities: the instant extermination of all the inhabitants of a populous city. Of this early display of nuclear power, as of all the vastly augmented potentialities for destruction that so rapidly followed, one can say what Melville's mad captain in 'Moby Dick' said of himself: "All my means and methods are sane: my purpose is mad." For the splitting of the atom was the beautiful consummation—and the confirmation—of the experimental and mathematical modes of thinking that since the seventeenth century have inordinately increased the human command of physical forces.

With the neatness of a Euclidean demonstration, the energy of the sun was now united with the smaller concentrations of energy at man's command: thus the Sun God had in effect undergone a human incarnation, and his priests at last commanded a commensurate authority. Theirs is a Calvinist theology, only slightly revised, in which the mass of men are predestined to awful damnation, and only the elect—that is, the technocratic elite—will be saved. In short, the eschatology of Jehovah's Witnesses, brought up to date.

Once the secret of nuclear fission was unlocked, the construction of the new pyramids went on at such a furious rate that the United States military strategists, within a dozen years, were forced to invent a new term, 'overkill,' to describe the superfluous powers of extermination they already possessed. On a planet holding perhaps three billion people, they had bombs enough to wipe out three hundred billion. In this new economy of negative abundance, the means of death outpaced the means of life.

The parallels with the Pyramid Age do not end here. Around this mortuary group of megamachine pyramids spread in widening circles the working quarters of the priesthood, called research centers or 'think tanks.' Like the domestic barracks of the underlying population these are scattered thinly over the landscape, as far as possible outside the old centers of population—centers that still contain disturbing reminders of other forms of worship and other modes of life. The ideal symbolic site indeed for the new pyramids is, as originally at Los Alamos, the desert, for that is the ultimate environment, done over and more perfectly sterilized by the machine process, which corresponds with the ideology itself. The larger complex in turn invites the construction of lesser pyramids, such as the atomic reactors for producing nuclear fuel. Except for small quantities of radioactive materials useful in further scientific investigations, which involve no colossal investment and no grandiose explosions, the chief products of the atomic reactors are long-acting, extremely poisonous wastes and—the Gods are ironic—hot water.

The scientific knowledge that unleashed atomic energy brought genuine insight into the structure of the entire cosmos and in recent years has broken down the gap between pre-organic matter, once regarded as fatally inert and passive, and living organisms. For centuries the intellectual capital so accumulated will be yielding dividends in further knowledge that may prove of immense value, in ways still unsuspected, to our descendants—if we have any. But the direct effect of this mode of pyramid building compares exactly with that of the Pyramid Age itself. Our present viable alternative to Overkill is more Hot Water, that is, more energy at the service of this fatally over-expanding megasystem. Hot water is useful: but there are safer ways of producing it.

The disparity between the imaginative scientific achievement of the nuclear reactor and the commonplace practical result calls attention to a similar disproportion between the incalculable disintegrating power of absolute weapons and the trivial military results. Twenty years after the first atom bomb was dropped, the total military accomplishment of nuclear weapons can be briefly summed up as follows: the destruction of two medium-sized cities, Hiroshima and Nagasaki, with a massacre of life comparable to, but not greater than, that produced by slower but less costly methods of collective extermination and torture, such as the use of napalm bombs (Dresden, Tokyo), or, as in the Nazi German extermination camps, by poison gas. In addition, the wreck of two planes carrying a nuclear bomb has strewn atomic debris in Spain and Greenland, with still undetermined and perhaps indeterminable results.

The subsequent testing of improved nuclear weapons by the hundreds, indulged by the two leading nuclear powers, led by the United States, has produced these further results: the heavy pollution of the soils of the whole planet with strontium 90, plus radioactive iodine with a shorter life. This has resulted in poisoning of foods, especially babies' milk, and the secondary pollution of soil and water by radioactive debris, with a higher probable incidence of cancer as a result, along with genetic deformations whose full extent it will take two generations to discover.

Facile calculations of how many people might physically survive for a limited period in deep underground shelters give no hint of the psychological traumas awaiting those emerging into a blasted landscape whose skies would still rain poison, whose unblasted surfaces would be covered with putrefying organisms, and whose food, in places where it could still be grown, would likewise be befouled with cancer-producing substances; while if, as is likely, in the total psychosis brought on by such a nuclear encounter, the military strategists resorted to still more desperate modes of extermination, by anthrax and botulism, even the well-protected 'elite,' governmental and military, might find, like Hitler in his terminal air raid shelter, that suicide would be preferable to facing such survivors as had escaped instant incineration.

In short, up to the present it is the negative results of the great scientific achievement of splitting the atom that are colossal. As far as the nuclear bombs themselves go, the only positive benefits are those which temporarily accrue to the industrial, bureaucratic, and scientific establishments that have built up the new megamachine. Paradoxically, then, the greatest gains that have been achieved through command of nuclear reaction have been purely spiritual ones: an enriched conception of cosmic realities: a deeper insight into the nature of the universe and of the place that living organisms, and finally man himself, have come to occupy.

In the end, the most disastrous consequence of the building of the nuclear pyramid may turn out to be not nuclear weapons themselves or some irretrievable act of extermination that they may bring about. Something even worse may be in store, and should it go far enough, be equally irretrievable: namely, the universal imposition of the megamachine, in a perfected form, as the ultimate instrument of pure 'intelligence,' whereby every other manifestation of human potentialities will be suppressed or completely eliminated. Already the blueprints for that final structure are available: they have even been advertised as man's highest destiny.

Yet happily for mankind the megamachine itself is in trouble, largely because of its early dependence upon the nuclear bomb. For the very concept of wielding absolute power has set a collective trap, so delicately balanced that its mechanism has more than once been on the point of snapping down on its appointed victims, the inhabitants of the planet. Had that happened, the megamachine would have shattered its own structure as well. Over the entire Pentagon of Power, thanks to the technocratic arrogance and automated intelligence of those who have built this citadel, hovers a nuclear Ragnarok, or Twilight of the Gods, long ago predicted in Norse mythology: a world consumed in flames, when all things human and divine would be overcome by the cunning dwarfs and the brutal giants. After the Sixth Dynasty the Pyramid Age in Egypt came to an end in a violent popular uprising, even without any such cosmic disruption. And something less than the Norse nightmare, though no less ominous to the megamachine, may be in store—or is it now perhaps actually taking place?

2: SPACE FLIGHT FROM REALITY

The salient mark of the machines and utilities that the megamachine for its own irrational ends chooses to concentrate on is that they should draw on the largest possible stores of energy and utilize the most elaborate technical means for ends that are relevant chiefly to the power complex's restrictive purposes: the expansion of its own structure and the extension of its own mode of control. Having discarded purpose and design in any other aspect from its interpretation of natural events, the megamachine emerges with a single all-dominating purpose—its replacement of natural and human potentialities by its own under-dimensioned and strictly programmed system. All the improvements incorporated in this power structure are addressed, not to man, but to the megamachine and its auxiliaries; and what gives these feats significance is not their human value but their scientific or technological difficulty.

This paltry result has been eloquently defended—gratis!—by Marshall McLuhan, in his quintessential phrase: 'The medium is the message.' Since I was an amateur radio experimenter more than half a century ago, I know exactly what he means. As a youthful reader of 'Modern Electrics,' the new means of wireless communication dominated my adolescent fantasies. Once I had assembled my first radio set I was delighted when I actually got messages from nearby stations, and I kept on experimenting with new instruments and hookups in order to get still louder messages from more distant stations. But I never bothered to master the Morse code or learn what I was listening to: *The medium was the message.* Had I become a full-blooded technocrat or remained an arrested adolescent, I would never have demanded a more humanly valuable result. This little moral applies to a hundred other technical exploits. Minds content to exploit the medium and ignore the message are the irrational end-products of what has been uncritically called 'rationalization.'

Though nuclear bombs are of course the ultimate symbols of the megamachine's powers of destruction, the manned interplanetary space rocket is perhaps an even more exemplary demonstration of the principles underlying the whole system, for the space rocket makes the greatest demands for energy, is the most delicately complex in design, and is the most costly to fabricate and service—and likewise the most futile in tangible and beneficial human results, apart from the prestige and publicity that the astronaut's feat bestows on the pentagonal national establishment. With the aid of the high-powered rocket modern man is indeed conquering space. But in the very act of making this achievement possible, the megamachine is carrying further its conquest of man. With exquisite symbolic accuracy, the first object of space exploration was a barren satellite, unfit for organic life, to say nothing of permanent human habitation.

Like the supersonic plane and the intercontinental ballistic rocket, both designed to carry nuclear warheads, the space rocket is primarily a feat of imaginative 'military' strategy. Such strategy departs from the norms of traditional warfare, directed at a limited number of human beings, in order to achieve total control by threat or actual violence over populations of continental or hemispheric magnitude. Under present psycho-pressures, a case could perhaps be made out for meeting the purely scientific demand for unmanned space vehicles, on the part of those seeking either better means of intraplanetary communication or outer space exploration or better astronomical observation.

But the gigantic concentration on rocket development by the Soviet Union and the United States has quite another objective, an anti-human one, too hugely visible to be concealed, and indeed already partly achieved. This mode of rocket development began as a means of military espionage and now has come to a triumphant conclusion in a design for dropping nuclear bombs from a supposedly invulnerable space station. Man-carrying rockets and space stations are not inevitable or unavoidable innovations: they are the projection in concrete form of morbid military obsessions, and they arise solely out of the apprehension that the equally obsessed enemy might gain an advantage by establishing exclusive access to space. Our leaders seem to believe that they hide the nature of their homicidal fantasies by calling the appropriate weapons 'hardware.'

Kepler in his purely fanciful 'Somnium' was under no obligation to count the cost of such a moon journey; but a present-day scientist, Dr. Warren Weaver, has taken pains to do so. He has pointed out that the thirty billion dollars spent by the United States alone for the purpose of placing a man on the moon—some equivalent sum in manpower, scientific experiments, and working energy is of course likewise being spent in Soviet Russia—could have been disbursed for more significant human objectives in the following ways:

It would provide a ten per cent raise a year for ten years to every teacher in the United States. It would endow two hundred small colleges with ten million dollars each. It could finance the education of fifty thousand scientists, build ten new medical colleges at two hundred million dollars each. It could build and endow more than fifty complete universities. It could create three new Rockefeller Foundations worth five hundred million dollars each. Note that these alternatives reflect entirely educational aims, mainly indeed scientific ones. So they cannot be dismissed as coming from a mind indifferent to the interests of science or its continued advance. Instead of keeping a team of human beings riskily alive, barely functioning, at inordinate expense, on an uninhabitable planet, in order to accomplish an empty, if not intentionally destructive feat, Dr. Weaver's alternatives would at least maintain and replenish the existing scientific establishment. This is not the place to enter any reservations of my own about Dr. Weaver's proposals: enough that one may accept their humane intentions.

What this lesson in arithmetic has done is to bring out a point that may have puzzled the reader when I cited Burckhardt's predictions about the coming "military commandos" under whose tyrannous regime the rulers would be "completely indifferent to law, well-being, profitable labor, industry, credit, etc." That characterizes the prevalent state of mind among the 'military-industrial-scientific elite.' The astronomical funds squandered upon elaborating techniques of genocide and upon moon landings, with no regard to either human needs or economic consequences, are in the style that Burckhardt foresaw.

3 : SPACE TRAVAIL

Even at the risk of seeming to push the parallel between the ancient Pyramid Age and the modern one too far, I would suggest that the manned space capsule, as now conceived, corresponds exactly to the innermost chamber of the great pyramids, where the mummified body of the Pharaoh, surrounded by the miniaturized equipment necessary for magical travel to Heaven, was placed.

Already, in preparation for explorations outside the solar system, some of the priests of science have conjured up anew the assurance of an artificially contrived immortality, necessary for transportation distances that must be measured in light-years; and they assume that at such astral speed living organisms would become comatose and shrink in mass, according to Einstein's theorem, without suffering any internal damage or experiencing the passage of time: so that a thousand years would pass as a day and vital processes would be similarly reduced and suspended. Again this parallel between the motivations and symbolisms of the two ages is almost too precise to seem anything but a perverse invention. But fortunately the data are open to public inspection.

What space technics has already achieved, within the insulated capsule, may be described as temporary mummification: a state that provides the minimal conditions for keeping the human agent alive, or rather, from decomposing in the course of his flight. If the Egyptian tomb may be properly described as a static rocket, the cosmic space rocket is in fact a mobile tomb. In each case, the most exquisite confections of technology have been provided to keep a human mannikin in a state of suspended animation.

At the bottom of this whole effort lies a purpose that animates the entire megamachine, indeed, figures as its only viable consummation: to reduce the human organism itself, its habitat, and its mode of existence, and its life-purpose to just those minimal dimensions that will bring it under total external control.

In the case of the Egyptian Pharaoh, those who placed him in his Heaven-pointed space ship made believe that he was still alive, and capable of exercising all his exalted attributes. But just the opposite set of assumptions governs the preparations of an astronaut for a space voyage: while actually alive, he is forced under strict training to divest himself of every hampering attribute of life, so that what is left of human existence are just those minimal bodily and mental functions that will enable him to survive under hardships and deprivations as formidable as those encountered by the climbers who topped Mount Everest in the final ascent.

Obviously only a mixture of adventurous impulses and religious convictions of the deepest sort would persuade normal, warm-hearted human beings, such as many astronauts seem to be, to take part in such a life-denying ritual. Besides high physical courage, and the promise of an early termination of the ordeal, they need a deep religious conviction, all the more serviceable if unconscious of their role as Heavenly Messengers. A devotion of this order made it possible for Christian hermits to wall themselves permanently within a dark fetid hut, fed only through a vent: so the mode of sacrifice is not without earlier holy precedent. But nothing more eloquently testifies to the hold the myth of the machine has established over the popular mind than the acceptance of this ritual as a desirable and laudable 'next step' in man's de-natured command of nature.

But note, so unconditional is the spirit of sacrifice that the religion of the modern Sun God has awakened, that three Russians—a physician, a microbiologist, and an engineer—voluntarily submitted to a whole year's incarceration in a simulated space ship mainly to establish the possibility of remaining alive in a limited space—twelve feet square—using oxygen and water regenerated from human waste products, dehydrated food, and vitamin-rich watercress and other plants grown in a minimal, sixty-square-foot hothouse. Physically they survived the blank life and the resulting interpersonal tensions—tensions so great that they did not dare to play chess, lest it aggravate suppressed conflicts between winner and loser.

But this feat of endurance turned out to be as useless as it was meaningless: since the most formidable conditions of space travel were absent—weightlessness, spatial isolation from the earth, the ever-present possibility of danger from mechanical breakdown, bodily disorders, anxiety over further risks on re-entering the earth's atmosphere. The human sacrifice was real enough: but the conditions were faked. To make this whole experiment more preposterous, Russian officials announced a month before the test ended that an experiment with live dogs in actual space flight for as little as twenty-five days showed serious impairment of their vital organs and a loss of immunity to disease.

These efforts to determine minimal physical conditions for human survival in space are, it need hardly be emphasized, the precise opposite of an imitation of nature's exuberance and plenitude: those maximal conditions under which life has actually flourished. But the physical requirements for even a short-term existence in a space capsule, however, constricting and frustrating, turn out to be easier to meet than the psychal requirements; since sensory deprivation and loss of orientation lead, all too swiftly, to psychal disintegration. Significantly, some of these requirements were anticipated in Kepler's early dream, for he supposed that the first voyagers to the moon would be given narcotics in order to make them endure a passage that he too optimistically calculated would take only four hours.

Now the conditions for prolonged space travel—isolation from the multi-dimensioned human habitat, detachment from other human impulses and needs, except those laid down by technical necessity, a restricted opportunity for making alternative decisions and surmounting unexpected obstacles—all these had their parallel in earlier ocean voyages. Along with this went a similar apprehension of danger both from natural causes, like storms, and from human misjudgement. As with the earlier maritime explorers who faced such dangers and surmounted them, the doughty astronauts today doubtless enjoy a similar enhancement of the ego when the ordeal is over. Thus space travel, by reason of its technical and human difficulties, has promised indeed to restore some of that vital human self-confidence in meeting emergencies which push-button automatism is making every effort to do away with.

Unfortunately, the earth dwellers may prove more gravely endangered by space travel than the chosen astronauts; and there is every prospect, if the current methods of processing and conditioning the human organism are not modified, that the mass of men will be forced to endure the penalties of space travel for a whole lifetime without enjoying any of the rewards that are showered on a favored elite. So the ultimate gift of space technics, it now turns out, is to establish in experimental small-scale models the requirements for imprisoning, conditioning, and controlling large populations. To universalize this under-dimensioned model and make it a permanent feature of human existence would be one of the grossest miscarriages of megatechnics.

Perhaps this sacrifice has been more willingly made because the 'conquest of space' has proved, if temporarily, the only substitute yet available for harnessing the immense consumptive needs and destructive powers of the megamachine, without actually bringing about the catastrophic end of that machine itself in collective deeds of calculated genocide, which would defoliate the planet and exfoliate the human race. The rivalry between the Russian and the American megamachines, in their race to land on the moon or explore the nearer planets, might thus be considered a sophisticated though superstitious substitute for William James' "moral equivalent of war." But since such space rivalry leaves all the present weapons for annihilating mankind in existence, and in fact increases their lethal potentialities, this form of collective competition holds forth no better promise of ensuring permanent comity than do those international soccer matches which so frequently end in demonstrations of more intense hostility and outright violence.

Nevertheless, the immediate advantages of space exploration are highly satisfactory to those dependent financially upon the Power Pentagon. This includes, I need not remind the reader, everyone tied directly or remotely to the industrial establishment, the labor unions and middle-class investors no less than to the financial, managerial and scientific directors; so that space 'research-and-development' has preempted funds and personnel from every secular activity. Unlike any earthbound activity, space exploration is limitless, and the technological demands it makes are insatiable. In this sense, spatial adventurism has indeed the sinister advantages of war: all the more effectively because it recovers for popular consumption the archaic sentiments that originally led to the New World exploration of the sixteenth century and later.

Because 'open space,' swift motion, and choice of habitat all have happy human associations—in contrast to imprisonment, limitation of movement, sessile unadventurousness—space exploration once seemed to promise a general liberation for the human spirit, which even stay-at-homes could enjoy vicariously. The day will come, H. G. Wells exulted at the opening of the twentieth century, when "man will stand upon the earth as on a footstool, and reach out his hands among the stars." Who was shrewd enough to guess from the start that the proposed interplanetary conquest of space and time, one of the singular triumphs of modern technics, would prove in fact to be a device for curbing the spirit of man and diverting it from the areas most in need of intensive cultivation—the human personality itself, now mocked and belittled by its technical triumphs?

Even under more ingratiating conditions than rocket travel, this new conquest has already disclosed drawbacks quite as remarkable as its advantages. On a transcontinental flight by a jet plane approaching supersonic speed, the actual trip is so cramped, so dull, so vacuous, that the only attraction the air lines dare to offer are those vulgar experiences one can have by walking to the nearest cabaret, restaurant, or cinema: liquor, food, motion pictures, luscious stewardesses. Only a lurking sense of fear and the possibility of a grisly death help restore the sense of reality.

Short of a now unimaginable discovery in science for overcoming gravitation on some entirely new principle, it is unlikely that space rockets will ever be small and cheap, or that space capsules will ever be as big and comfortable as even second-class accommodations on a plane. But static space capsules can be constructed on a gigantic scale; and major steps have already been taken to produce such collective habitats. Those committed to these megastructures will conduct their existence as if in interplanetary space, with no direct access to nature, no sense of the seasons or of the difference between night and day, no change of temperature or light, no contact with their fellows except through the appointed collective channels.

Plainly, it is not chiefly for its human benefits that supersonic air travel and outer space technology have been so rapidly perfected. Without the pressure for military advantage, the more differentiated, reliable, safe, and humanly responsive transportation system that existed before 1940 might have remained in being long enough to absorb further technical improvements without blasting the landscape, polluting the air, and destroying one great city after another.

The fact is, that unlike other forms of transportation, space travel would be impossible without the total mobilization of the megamachine, commanding to the point of exhaustion all the resources of the state: it is both a symbol of total control and a means of popularizing it and extending it as an ineffable symbol of progress. Its ultimate goal, already cited in the estimate of Buckminster Fuller, is to reduce this great round globe to the dimensions, so to say, of a billiard ball. But it has other characteristics which a contributor to a recent treatise on Space Technology emphasizes: "Space is a project which is clearly limitless. . . . It requires the best efforts of the engineer's art; it possesses all the attractions of physical exploration; it is bound up with the protection of *the style of our existence.*" (Italics mine.)

The last of these three specifications is clearly the most significant: for the "style of our existence" the writer refers to is that of the ancient power complex—that conglomerate style based on the incessant manufacture and the consumption of technological novelties, consumptive superfluities, and vacuous pleasures. Humanly speaking, space technics offers a new style of non-existence: that of the fastest possible locomotion in a uniform environment, under uniform conditions, to an equally undistinguishable uniform destination. A world franchised exclusively for Howard Johnson Restaurants and Hilton Hotels. If this is already true of jet travel on earth, it applies even more accurately to outer-space travel: for both the space capsule itself and the possible destinations bear the least possible resemblance to those organically rich habitats in which life and mind have actually flourished.

To justify space travel, its exponents must brazenly vilify earthly life. And this is precisely what the technocratic intelligentsia do not hesitate to do, in order to justify their unconditional commitment to the megamachine. "It may well be," says Arthur Clarke, "that only in space, confronted with environments fiercer and more complex than any to be found upon this planet, will intelligence be able to reach its fullest stature. . . . The dullards may remain on placid Earth, and real genius will flourish only in space—the realm of the machine, not of flesh and blood."

To earth-conditioned 'dullards' such praise of the megamachine and its servitors may seem fulsome to the point of being fatuous. On Dr. Clarke's own admission 'real genius' will lack human attributes. But what is more important is that there is no scientific evidence whatever to indicate that the ninety-odd stable elements on earth are not in fact a fair sample of the state of matter in every other part of the universe; and that if other minds and other capabilities have developed elsewhere, it will have been the result, not of their having carried spatial exploration farther than the inhabitants of the earth have yet done in "fiercer and more complex" environments, but because they have been engaged even more intensively than we have, and possibly for a longer period of time, in plumbing the miracle of life in the only place where that miracle can be fully confronted: in the consciousness of superior living beings.

No comatose space travel, no millennial hibernation, however interminable, promise even a scintilla of what earthbound man has already accomplished. Our own planet still holds countless unlocked mysteries as great as any that lie beyond our own Milky Way. And even that knowledge, however deeply it penetrates, is only a part of the total manifestation of life in millions of living species. The actual genius that will "flourish only in space, in the realm of the machine," is the genius of entropy and anti-life. With space exploration, the traditional enemy of God and man has already re-appeared, in post-Faustian form. And as of old, if one is willing to sell one's soul to him, he offers his ancient bribe—unlimited power of control, control absolute, not only over all other kingdoms and principalities, but over life itself.

4: 'POST-HISTORIC' CULTURE

All the parts of the megamachine were independently invented with little conscious anticipation of the human results, except in utopias and science-fiction fantasies. Though specific and limited purposes entered into every stage of this scientific and technical development, the coalescence of these purposes into an increasingly coherent structure, self-organizing and self-expanding in seemingly automatic fashion, was in fact the outcome of the many conscious intelligences that had brought it into existence. In this respect—both its purposefulness and its highly complex ultimate character—the composition of the megamachine resembles language; it is only in the final stage of organized complexity that one can even guess in what direction the whole evolutionary process had increasingly been tending. To understand fully what happened earlier one must read backward from the present to the past.

Yet since technics is, at every point, a function of life, the excessive overgrowth and over-integration of 'technical' processes must threaten, like any other organic imbalance, many equally essential functions of life. So at odds is the ultimate unitary organization of the megamachine with the diverse requirements and prerogatives of the originally independent and autonomous human groups that fashioned it that even before the megamachine could transform itself into a gigantic self-sufficient unit, from which the human parts have been extruded, a reaction has begun to set in, of which the present critical analysis is itself an example. Fortunately, the megamachine has not yet been fully assembled: fortunately, too, it has already exposed itself as subject to miscalculations and ignominious breakdowns that lower the authority of its official caste and call into question both their basic assumptions and their ultimate objectives.

In appraising these results one is drawn back once more to the observations of Henry Adams. Analyzing the constant acceleration of scientific knowledge and extra-organic sources of energy since the thirteenth century, he observed: "But if, in the prodigiously rapid vibrations of its last phases, thought should continue to act as the universal solvent which it is, and should reduce the forces of the molecule, the atom, and the electron to that costless servitude to which it has reduced the old elements of earth and air, fire and water; if man should continue to set free the infinite forces of nature, and attain control of cosmic forces on a cosmic scale, the consequences may be as surprising as the change of water to vapor, of the worm to the butterfly, of radium to electrons." That prediction has, even at this early stage, proved sounder than any of Adams' immediate contemporaries were prepared to believe.

Such a retrogressive transformation of man was first explicitly analyzed in Roderick Seidenberg's disturbing but acute analysis, 'Post-Historic Man.' As pictured by Seidenberg this mindless creature would be the ironic end-product of evolution, achieved through a hypertrophy of man's dominant trait: his intelligence. As science and technics advanced, Seidenberg pointed out, "man alone appeared a wayward and unpredictable entity in an otherwise tractable universe." If science "required man to look upon himself objectively as part and parcel of his own system: he, too, had to become amenable to engineering calculation."

Such a situation would in time become intolerable, once intelligence turned by its own logic against the human organism itself. In short, the huge surprise already visible in the totalitarian triumph of scientific megatechnics is nothing less than man's own meek submission to the anti-human instruments that the human mind created. But that feat must bring its own Nemesis: the cutting off of pure intelligence from all its self-regulating, self-protecting organic sources, since the unique property that cannot be transferred to any kind of programmed automaton is life itself.

Seidenberg regarded this change as an irreversible process of biological evolution which, by favoring the development of intelligence in the hominidae and then in *Homo sapiens* himself would now force man to return to a state of docile somnolence: ultimately, into unconsciousness. This would be even worse than animal lethargy, for the accidental genetic mutations, the ceaseless environmental challenges, and the purposeful subjective gropings that promoted animal evolution would now be kept from interfering with the fixed plans of a post-humanoid intelligence to ensure its own continued control on the lines established and fixed by the megamachine.

Happily this neat, all-too-neat, biological interpretation of man's ultimate destiny rests on abstractions and purely logical deductions that are highly questionable. Man's biological emergence during the last two million years has, indeed, accelerated; and it has done so mainly in one direction, in the enlargement of the nervous system, under an increasingly unified cerebral direction. But it is not intelligence alone that has been the beneficiary of this growth: the range of emotions, feelings, imaginative intuitions, as expressed in moral culture, human intercourse, and the arts, likewise has been immensely increased. Seidenberg, like Arthur Clarke, chooses to overlook that efflorescence of the human psyche.

Mankind has enriched itself by the immense storage of artifacts and symbols that more than equal in meaning and value the products of the abstract intelligence—especially the limited pragmatic intelligence that has tied itself so closely to the power complex. There are already many evidences for human resistances or disintegrations that Seidenberg did not reckon with. And we shall soon have to examine the more destructive regressions that the last half century has already disclosed.

Not the least safeguard against the terminal process that Seidenberg describes, with man himself sinking into torpid universal hibernation, is the upsurgence of those primitive vitalities that unconsciously—and sometimes with savage irrationality—correct the misbehaviors of cold intelligence. Our present over-reliance upon the computer-model intelligence might, in event of a worldwide catastrophe brought on by its lack of human dimensions, induce such a paroxysm of collective rage and unrestrained violence as would destroy the entire structure long before it had reached its ideal terminus of absolute control. Yet if intelligence were actually increasing, it might overcome its narcissistic love of its own abstract image and exert itself to circumvent this destiny. An alert intelligence should be capable of modifying its false current premises and overcoming its own inherent limitations. Is this not indeed, I shall soon ask, what may already be beginning to happen?

What gives Seidenberg's analysis some weight, however, is that the aberration he describes is not solely the work of our own generation, inflated by the success of its scientists in penetrating some of the long-hidden secrets of both atom and cosmos. The concepts that make these precipitous applications of one-generation knowledge so compulsive have had a long history. Yet even such a humane mind as that of Teilhard de Chardin, despite his training in a religious order skilled in ferreting out the temptations of pride and power, fell under the same spell. "With our knowledge of hormones," he observed, "we appear to be on the eve of having a hand in the development of our bodies and even of our brains. With the discovery of genes, it appears that we shall soon be able to control the mechanism of heredity."

Perhaps nothing so well illustrates the fascination that the audacious pretensions of the power complex exert over the human mind than the fact that possibly the most attractive and animated version of its ultimate potentialities and its final character is that put forward by this same Jesuit father, in the series of books that began with 'The Phenomenon of Man'— books whose slippery logical pavement is treacherously concealed by a fresh snowfall of gleaming metaphors. Teilhard de Chardin's picture of human development rests mainly on his interpretation of organic evolution. In his approach to the future, however, he adds a new sphere to geology: besides the lithosphere, the hydrosphere, the atmosphere, he detects another sphere, which he calls the noösphere: a film of 'mind' that is now spreading around the earth, forming a distinct, increasingly unified layer of conscious cerebration. This process he calls the "unification, technification, growing rationalization of the human earth." In effect, this is an etherialized version of the megamachine.

As it happens, Teilhard de Chardin was only putting in more explicit quasi-scientific terms a thought that Nathaniel Hawthorne had uttered a century earlier through the mouth of Clifford, in 'The House of the Seven Gables.' " 'Then there is electricity, the demon, the angel, the mighty physical power, the all-pervading intelligence,' exclaimed Clifford. . . . 'Is it a fact that . . . by means of electricity the world of matter has become a great nerve, vibrating thousands of miles in a breathless point of time? Rather, the round globe is a vast head, a brain, instinct with intelligence! Or, shall we say, it is itself a thought, nothing but thought, and no longer the substance which we deemed it.' " In a few sentences, this poetic mind had identified, long before professional physicists, the new agency that would shatter the whole mechanical world picture.

Teilhard de Chardin's contribution was to carry Hawthorne's intuition one stage further: but in doing so he gave it a profoundly reactionary turn by attaching it to the human motivations—the amplification of a sterile intelligence and the conquest of nature—that belonged to the original power system: his etherialized megamachine was equally inimical to the autonomous, individuating, self-transcending traits disclosed in human evolution. In the final stage of development, as he envisaged it, identifiable human beings will have disappeared: reduced to mere specialized cells, like those of the heart or the kidney, with no life-purpose except that which serves the noösphere. At this point conscious existence will have shifted to a kind of ectoplasmic super-brain, all-knowing, all-powerful. In creating this far-from-loving God, man will have de-created Nature and destroyed himself.

Anything like a full critical appraisal of Teilhard de Chardin's thought would be irrelevant here. As a paleontologist, the co-discoverer of Peking Man, he spoke with authority in his chosen field; and he was quicker than many other scientists to come to the now almost inescapable conclusion, in the light of molecular physics, that the physical cosmos itself has experienced history, and that this historic process, beginning with the autonomous organization and specification of the atomic elements, has gone on without a break through more complex atoms and higher forms of organization, until immensely complex organic molecules became self-replicating forms of life. And with life came, at one of the latest stages of animal evolution, consciousness and purposeful organization. So far, well.

Teilhard de Chardin's further description of mind, however, is what must be subjected to searching analysis: for his interpretation of man's coming evolution rests on his embracing, without a critical revision, the notion that has been current since the seventeenth century: namely, that consciousness is measured by intelligence, and that the intelligence, in an increasingly abstract mathematical form, is the highest manifestation of mind. William Blake might have saved him from this error: for with his anxiety over the possible consequences of Newtonian physics, the poet had written: "God forbid that Truth should be Confined to Mathematical Demonstrations!" But if Teilhard de Chardin's premises were true, then this apotheosis of abstract intelligence, as embodied in the theorems of science and the magical practices of technics, would be the far-off divine event toward which all creation moves.

To avoid distrust and contention, let me quote his exact words in 'The Future of Man.' The proof of man's ultimate destiny, according to Chardin, is already visible; for "in fields embracing every aspect of physical matter, life and thought, the research-workers are to be numbered in hundreds of thousands. . . . Research, which until yesterday was a luxury pursuit, is in process of becoming a major, indeed the principal, function of humanity. As to the significance of this great event, I for my part can see only one way to account for it. It is the enormous surplus of free energy released by the in-folding of the Noösphere destined by a natural evolutionary process to flow into the construction and functioning of what I have called its 'Brain.' . . . "

Precisely. And in this narrowing of the processes of life to the pursuit and projection of organized intelligence alone, the infinite potentialities of living systems, as developed on our own planet, would be reduced to a trivial fraction: those which would further rational organization and centralized control. This whole transformation would be directed, on Teilhard de Chardin's terms, toward the point where the entire noösphere would function as a single world-brain, in which individual souls would lose their identity and forfeit their uniqueness as self-directing organisms in order to exalt and magnify the process of thought itself—thought thereby turning in upon itself and becoming the sole viable manifestation of life. While Descartes had made the first step toward this, "I think: therefore I am," Teilhard de Chardin exulted in the terminal process: "The Big Brain thinks, therefore *I am not.*" At that 'omega point,' according to him, cosmic evolution will have reached its consummation. This would indeed approach the heavenly Nirvana of the 'Now' generation: electronic salvation, disguised as Christian fulfillment.

Such a description of the ultimate reign of pure intelligence is not science but mythology and eschatology; and its merit, from the standpoint taken here, is that it has made explicit the underlying dogmatic premises of the metaphysics and theology of the megamachine. This extinction of the human personality, by absorption into the noösphere, under the eternal embrace of its electronic god, is for Teilhard de Chardin the ultimate destiny of man. "We conceive the 'ego,' " he wrote, "to be diminishing and eliminating itself, with the trend to what is most real and most lasting in the world, namely, the Collective and the Universal." For him, the transcendent attributes of personality will finally be manifested only in the center, where consciousness will bring together "the convergent beams of millions of elementary centres dispersed over the surface of the thinking earth."

In presuming that his own mind could come to any valid conclusions about the ultimate fate of the human species by extrapolating contemporary trends, this all-too-human Christian soul was committing something worse than a departure from theological orthodoxy: he was in fact presumptuously identifying his own mind with that of the new deity: playing God! In coupling both himself and the future of man with the processing of intelligence he was, in addition, surrendering in advance to the megamachine, and hastening its triumph in the most oppressive possible totalitarian form. Though Father Teilhard's whole argument was cast within a biological frame, it rested upon a denial of what is one of the signal identifying characteristics of all life—the absolute uniqueness of each living organism. However closely the members of a species resemble each other, no two specimens are actually alike; and that very trait is the source of life's amazing potentialities—and its improbabilities, its startling evolutionary surprises. This fact, biologists now insist, separates living organisms from the uniformities and predictabilities of pre-organic existence on one hand, or from mechanical and electronic artifacts on the other.

On a superficial view, the organismic mysticism of Teilhard de Chardin is at the opposite pole from the technocratic mysticism of, say, a Buckminster Fuller, a Marshall McLuhan, or an Arthur Clarke: but looked at a little closer, it is just as fatally insulated against organic realities. Despite the sweetly human personality one meets in his informal biography, Chardin's view is as depersonalized, as crudely materialized, as naïvely autocratic as that of these other servitors of the megamachine. Thus in speaking of human beings in planetary perspective, he habitually refers to them as 'particles'; and human minds, in the same setting, he speaks of as 'grains' or 'granules.'

By viewing the traits that actually identify human beings from such an astronomical distance, he ensures that the qualities and modes of behavior that distinguish them shall vanish completely, except such specialized cerebration as can be connected to a central planetary intelligence. Thus Chardin reduces life to a collection of abstract messages capable of being sorted and programmed by the noöspheric computer. By his too early death in 1955, Teilhard de Chardin missed those further developments in computer design and miniaturization that would confirm with appropriate instruments his technocratic transcendentalism and religious absolutism.

Where, then, is the fallacy in this religio-technocratic picture of man's future? Exactly where it was in the seventeenth century, when the original mechanical world picture was first put together. It leaves out of account, even more radically than any historic religion has done, the whole nature of man and the phenomena of life. The trick consists in reducing life to the abstract functions of the organized intelligence. Information is equated with existence. Such intelligence is only a limited part, but now a grossly overgrown part of "the phenomenon of man." By resolutely forgetting this fact Teilhard de Chardin makes the commands of intelligence unconditional, absolute, and therewith anti-organic.

Happily he has put this putative goal in so many words: "Knowledge for its own sake. But also, and perhaps still more, knowledge for power." The main duty of mankind, he says plainly, is to realize "that its first function is to penetrate, intellectually unify, and harness the energies that surround it, in order to further understand and master them. . . ." One could not guess from this account that life begins, even in the lowest organisms, in physical accretion and ecological association, and develops in the highest organisms into mutual support, loving reproduction, and hopeful renewal.

In order to thicken the planetary layer of mind, man's first duty according to Chardin is to do—but more consciously, more powerfully and persistently than ever before—precisely what Western man is now doing! That all those creative potentialities which are not solely functions of intelligence, which often precede it and fortify it, or even transcend it, would be eliminated by this intellectual and pragmatic concentration—this does not awaken in him any misgivings over his own theoretical framework. His recoil from these conclusions is as weakly sentimental as Arthur Clarke's, and like his, it only exposes the infirmity of his reasoning. As a dedicated Christian and a passively obedient—if inwardly heretical—member of his monastic order, he introduces, almost as an afterthought, the concept of love as an aspect of all human association, and as life's final crown. But what place has love in a noösphere from which the body and form of love has disappeared, or has been vaporized into messages?

Teilhard de Chardin deceived himself. The noösphere, as he conceived it, has no place for love, any more than it has for the emergence of more fully individuated personalities, tied to cosmic processes yet transcending them, as Christian theology depicted Jesus Christ. For all that Chardin says about love, which is a property that unites man to his mammalian ancestors and would preserve him from relapsing into the cold-blooded world of the armored lizards and the flying reptiles, he himself denies the very source of love. For he sees personality as "a specifically corpuscular and ephemeral property; a prison from which we must try to escape." From this 'prison' of the individual personality he voluntarily sought to transfer to a larger prison from which no escape would be possible: that of the totalitarian megamachine. Again his own words back up this grim conclusion.

"Monstrous as it is," Chardin observes again in 'The Phenomenon of Man,' "is not modern totalitarianism really the distortion of something magnificent, and thus quite near to the truth? There can be no doubt of it: the great human machine"—this last term is Chardin's own—"is designed to work and *must* work—by producing a super-abundance of mind." And the purpose of that superabundance, it becomes plain, is to increase the scope and power of the planetary machine. Q.E.D. What Chardin does not observe about the workings of this super-brain is that increasingly, in operating in its own world and on its own terms, it is feeding on itself, utilizing data, symbols, equations, theorems, that have only the most tenuous connections with the human personality or with the fullness of earthly experience: so divorced from reality as to be in every sense unbalanced. In short, it is addressed to the enlarging of the empire of a desiccated and sterilized mind, whose activated tissues are devoid of vital attributes. To this Teilhard de Chardin would dedicate the immense energies that modern technics has made available. One would hardly guess that love and sex and art and a pullulating dream-world existed.

Whether presented in the concrete form I have described as the Megamachine, or in the etherialized version upon which Teilhard de Chardin preferred to dwell, as a planetary 'film of mind,' or abstract intelligence, embracing all human activities, or rather reducing and concentrating those activities for the enhancement of knowledge and power, the final result would be the same: the Big Brain, a universal system of control from which no escape would be possible on this planet—or even *from* this planet. And yet in one sense this whole totalitarian system, more monstrous in its final assemblage than the present more limited varieties, is an ingenious attempt to escape from the uncertainties of creative self-transformation with its attendant frustrations and inevitable tragedies. Ultimately the purpose of this planetary system, for both is present directors and for Teilhard de Chardin, would be to reduce the potentialities of life to those that can be conveniently processed and transmuted by its electronic God. In this the functions that could not be so processed—human histories, personal and collective artifacts, autonomous activities, transcendent ideals —would be cast aside as worthless: worthless, that is, to the megamachine.

What an anti-climax to primate evolution!—to say nothing of man's own historic development. Teilhard de Chardin's picture of man's final destiny, completely absorbed into the autonomous planetary superorganism, hardly differs in its state of complete unconsciousness—as far as the separate 'granules' are concerned—from that depicted by Roderick Seidenberg. The residual quasi-human organisms that would be left would float in a mechanical-electronic void of man's own making. One by one all man's functions, creativities, and potentialities would be annihilated, or taken over in a duly sterilized form, coded for use in the self-sufficient megamachine—and so eliminating all further possibilities of development. Thus this infinitely dynamic world would, for all its energy and effort, terminate in a completely static condition, in a ceaseless interchange of meaningless messages whose very confusion would make any real development impossible, even in thought. There is nothing so predictable, indeed so stable, as chaos, for novelty and creativity are unrecognizable unless they emerge from order.

Curiously, such a vacuous irresponsible existence has already been lovingly described by an independent Japanese "Study Group for the Life Apparatus." This group has conjured up a planetary super-community, utilizing technical facilities still to be invented, that puts Zamiatin's 'We' and Aldous Huxley's 'Brave New World' to shame. I have already shown a graphic interpretation of this planetary super-being, with an explanatory text, in the final plate of 'The City in History'; and I only regret that the full proposal has not been made available in English.

Enough to say that it imaginatively embodies Teilhard de Chardin's conception of the noösphere, in an electronically simulated collective life, peopled by 'liberated' human granules. These floating particles are as functionless, as purposeless, as the mournful ghosts in Homer's Hades, since for these human nonentities even thought would be superfluous, and only 'pleasure'—that last abstract component of the power complex—would be left. But unlike this 'advanced' group, Homer knew he was describing Hell. If such a non-life were to be the final goal of all man's struggles, why should he spend so much effort to achieve it?

CHAPTER TWELVE

Promises, Bribes, Threats

1: BEGINNINGS OF AFFLUENCE

Until the twentieth century the spread of machine industry was retarded by customs and institutions that belonged to an earlier era of scarcity: an age chronically threatened, in many regions, by an insufficiency of extra-human energy, of material goods, or even of daily food. Except in the form of gambling and speculation, the canons of economy still governed both the factory and the marketplace. The small margin under which even a thriving agriculture operated could always be wiped out by a succession of dry years, a plague of insects, or the spread of a virulent disease. The thrifty habits needed to ensure survival had been artificially re-enforced, from the very beginning of civilization, by manufactured scarcity—the deliberate expropriation of the farmers' surplus for the benefit of the ruling minority.

Natural scarcity and backward agricultural practices, plus socially enforced penury and deprivation, were the incentives to daily work.

To impose the regimentation of labor demanded by the power system, common agricultural land in England was seized from the peasants, rural wages were driven down, the jobless were rounded up and imprisoned in 'workhouses' or factories, while their wives and children were sent into mills and mines to work from fourteen to sixteen hours a day to earn a pittance. As if to caricature both his own philosophy and current practices, Jeremy Bentham, the fountainhead of utilitarian pragmatism, actually proposed an 'ideal' structure, one-half factory, one-half prison, with both wings under central surveillance.

Incredibly, something like two centuries passed before capitalist industry at last realized that this systematic restriction of wages and buying power was curtailing the market that new inventions and mass production had opened up to them.

Yet the capitalist economy, for all its labor-sweating, had introduced a contradictory aim. Though it preached contented penury to the poor, it sought to further industrial expansion by erecting the dogma of 'increasing wants' as an indispensable basis for further industrial progress. This expectancy worked in the opposite direction: for the expanding economy was justified, not merely by its insurance against want or its fuller satisfaction of long-established needs, but by multiplying the number and variety of putative needs, and by raising the 'standard of living'—or more accurately by raising the standard of expenditure—throughout the whole population.

That standard had once been fixed at different levels according to caste, occupation, and family status. But in accordance with this new principle, even the lowliest worker might hope in time to achieve a modicum of middle class comforts, while the middle classes, with their increased incomes, could afford some of the luxuries and thoughtless extravagances that the aristocracy had once claimed as their exclusive privilege—not least the privilege of never counting the cost. (What is today's buying on unlimited credit but the 'democratization' of this well-established aristocratic vice?)

Curiously the most notable effect at first of machine production was one that has been fully realized perhaps only today, now that the phenomenon itself has vanished. Along with the coordinate general increase of population it released an increasing number of menial workers for domestic work, while at the same time it permitted a larger part of the labor force to go into the standing army, the new municipal police, and the civil services. Never before probably was human service so abundant and so cheap in the Western World as it was during the nineteenth century, indeed right up to the First World War. These were halcyon days for the rich and the middle classes, as everyone now realizes; for these classes were the chief beneficiaries of the new power system, through both cheap household services and more than ample goods. Fortunately, the organization of labor unions began a slow process of improving the working conditions, shortening the hours, and raising the income of the factory worker, and ultimately of the many remaining trades and services outside the factory.

Despite fitful improvements, however, the income of the working classes remained insufficient over the long run, either to pay for decent housing or to buy back the surplus of machine production and large-scale agriculture: hence periodic gluts in the market, corrected by devaluation or 'valorization' (artificially contrived scarcity) with its attendant losses to both investors and workers. These crises recurred often enough to be characterized as the 'business cycle,' and though its manic-depressive curves were in time smoothed out a little by unemployment insurance, social security, and old-age pensions, the system itself remained unworkable until its leaders belatedly accepted the fact that the old canons of parsimony must be cast aside if the economy of abundance that mass production made possible was to achieve sufficient stability to continue its expansion.

This change of outlook was too profound to take place overnight. By a series of tentative initiatives and accommodations, difficult to locate or date, yet gradually amalgamating into a general policy, the older scarcity economy has turned in 'advanced' countries, after many recessions and depressions, into an economy of abundance, or, as it might be more correctly styled, of mal-distributed affluence. Because of the staggering potential output of mechanized industry, a multitude of products once reserved for the uppermost income groups are now available in quantity at a middle level; and this process of raising the standard and widening the market might theoretically go on indefinitely until the market system was undermined once more by its own excesses.

Perhaps the salient breakthrough in passing from the old economy to the new came in the motor car industry, a classic case in every respect. To achieve a mass market for mass production, in such a complex machine as even the cheap Model T Ford, it was necessary to give additional purchasing power to a much larger income group. Henry Ford recognized this in establishing a higher wage scale on the assembly line. The workers themselves contributed their share to the machine-made abundance by stinting their families on housing or food in order to shift their spending to the motor car. The Lynds' first study of 'Middletown' documented this shift from basic needs to mechanical gratifications; these ill-balanced consumptive outlays proved prophetic of similar misdirected expenditures in society at large. The increase in the gross national product did little to correct this distortion. Yet once the need for mass consumption was recognized as the indispensable adjunct to mass production, the way became clear for an economy based on abundance rather than parsimony.

This conception was prematurely popularized in the United States before the depression of 1929–1939 as the 'New Capitalism'; and the slogan 'one car for every family' replaced Henri IV's 'chicken in the pot every Sunday.' Yet the severe deflation and depression that followed the first recognition of the importance of a mass distribution of income indicated that something was lacking in this formula.

What was needed had already been demonstrated by the First World War, and became firmly established through the leading national megamachines in the Second World War: namely, such an unlimited demand as only war—or pseudo-war—makes possible. Under national conscription, a 'Nation in Arms' became the equivalent of Edward Bellamy's Nation in Overalls, and along with this went an expansion of credit, a guarantee of profits in war industries, a rise in income level for all but the lowest third of the population, and, best of all, a swift disposition of the product by ceaseless destruction. This was mass consumption with a vengeance.

As a result of war itself, the economic center of gravity shifted to the State, that is, the national megamachine: and between repairing the destructions of the war itself, and inventing and manufacturing new weapons of destruction, more complex and costly than ever, the necessary condition for full employment, full production, full 'research and development,' and full consumption was for the first time approached.

Given these 'ideal' conditions—power-machines, centralized control, and unlimited waste and destruction—there is no doubt about the immense productivity of megatechnics, or about the fact that a larger part of the population than ever before stands to benefit from its methods; for industry itself can compensate for higher wages by passing on the increase in costs to the expanding body of consumers, sedulously conditioned by advertising and 'education' to ask only for those mass products that can be profitably supplied. Judged purely in terms of fabricated goods, there is no doubt that an economy of abundance is already in partial operation.

But the gain seems on paper to be larger than it actually is; for this reckoning leaves out the negative abundance that has accompanied this feat: the depleted soils and mineral supplies, the polluted air and water, the rusting auto graveyards, the mountains of waste paper and other rubbish, the poisoned organisms, the millions of dead and injured on the highways, all of which are inevitable by-products of the system. These are the poisonous effluents, as it were, of our affluent society.

Though the total result of the economy of abundance leaves a far smaller net gain than its proud exponents are usually willing to admit, it has nevertheless introduced one significant factor that outweighs many of its deficiencies. This factor is doubtless responsible for the unguarded way in which it has been embraced: namely, in order to work at all, the megatechnic system must not merely increase the rewards but distribute them throughout the whole population. Implicit in mass production are two notions that have the effect, if not the intention, of a humane moral principle. First, the basic goods of production, being a product of our total culture, should, once they exist in abundance, be distributed equally to every member of the community; and second, efficiency should be maintained, whenever work depends upon human effort, not by deprivation, coercion, and punishment, but mainly by adequate differential rewards. These are not small achievements: actually they have revolutionary consequences.

Before striking a balance, let us give this system its due. In contrast to the prevailing state of the working classes throughout the nineteenth century, indeed almost up to the present generation in the United States, the democratization of the whole economy would seem to bring many tangible social benefits. Even the fact that mass production cannot be efficient in small quantities, or in large quantities that are in uncertain or irregular demand, did not at first seem a serious drawback.

Such surpluses as are now available to vast populations, numbering tens of millions, were indeed known on a small scale to scattered primitive societies through occasional outbursts of natural abundance, as in a heavy run of salmon in the Pacific Northwest; and these communities had even resorted to social balancing devices like the potlatch, or the free bestowal of gifts by chiefs to the less privileged members of the group. Whatever success the Incas of Peru had in governing their far-flung empire was due to the fact that their system of regimentation, though often arbitrary and harsh in the destruction of local communal ties, nevertheless provided material security, with the widest distribution of their systematically garnered surpluses.

Those in control of capitalist enterprises have been slow to grasp the logic of this 'economy of gifts' as a compensatory device for their own profit economy. (Strangely, the chief literature on this subject comes not from the United States but France.) But the slogan 'Fair Shares for All' was not uttered for the first time by the British Labor Party in their 1945 election campaign: it was the theme of all socialist thought throughout the nineteenth century. The feats of organization and mechanization performed in industry after industry, reaching a climax in war production, momentarily made the most sanguine socialist expectations credible: credible, yes, and partly realizable.

By now the effective results are so patent and so familiar in advanced industrial countries that they hardly need to be statistically documented, or even recounted except in the most general terms. Suffice it to note that most of the new 'revolutionary' demands set forth in the name of the working class in 'The Communist Manifesto' of 1848, have now become commonplace achievements, even in countries supposedly still committed to monopolistic 'security capitalism' alias 'free enterprise.' Though monotony and drudgery have not been banished, they have been reduced, at least by a shortening of the hours and days of work, not to speak of coffee breaks, 'sick pay,' legalized absenteeism, and longer regular vacations. If in the highest strata property, privilege, political patronage, and military power still exact an exorbitant economic tribute from the community, below that level there is nonetheless a growing equalization of goods: medical care, education, security against unemployment and want, support in old age—all these human benefits have become increasingly available, not mainly through individual effort, but through the total productivity of industry and agriculture.

This enormous change from a savagely restrictive economy to an expansive hedonistic one can be summed up in a single contrast. More than a century ago Macaulay could write, in the midst of a severe economic depression, that it was better for unemployed workers to die of starvation than that the rights of property be in any wise curtailed—as by imposing an income tax for the relief of unemployment and starvation. Today, in contrast, the unemployed in the United States have begun to demand, not just the right to work, but a guaranteed annual income whether they work or not.

So far from this being considered a shocking proposal, it has been advanced independently by middle-class reformers under the somewhat specious label of the 'negative income tax.' I myself put forward a similar idea in 'Technics and Civilization,' under the more forthright designation of 'basic communism,' though I then envisaged—and still do—a lower minimum than that now demanded by those who have taken over Bellamy's idea without critically examining the serious limitations that experience with the Welfare States' relief and anti-poverty programs has already disclosed.

Yet once the idea was accepted that mass production entails mass consumption, two factors were introduced whose consequences have still to be adequately appraised. One was the withering away of many essential industries and services that can no longer compete with the wage scales established in the productive and financially opulent megatechnic industries. Human labor has not merely been progressively eliminated by automation: it has become exiled through its prohibitive costs in every other department, since the worker now demands for his services an hourly wage that only mechanized production can afford to pay. Though efforts are being made to invent multi-functional robots for domestic service, there is so little prospect of their being either cheap or self-operating, that already predictions for the twenty-first century include quaint but ominous forecasts of increasing the intelligence and servile usefulness of chimpanzees, to take on jobs once performed by human slaves.

But an even more serious consequence follows, once the ancient evils of civilizaton, back-breaking manual labor, and servile labor for the benefit of coercive ruling groups disappears. We now begin to find that we have exchanged the new burden of compulsory consumption for that of compulsory production. But unfortunately the principle of compulsion remains written into the system, and is the fixed condition for receiving its benefits. Instead of the duty to work, we now have the duty to consume: instead of being admonished to practice thrift, we are now coaxed—no, incessantly urged—to practice waste and wanton destruction. Meanwhile an ever larger portion of the population finds itself faced with a workless, effortless, physically coddled but increasingly vacuous life.

The emancipated masses now confront precisely the same problem that every privileged minority sooner or later has been forced to face: how to make use of its surplus of goods and its free time without being surfeited by one and corrupted by the other? With the enlargement of the benefits of mass production has come an enlargement of the unexpected penalties: of which perhaps the most deadly is boredom. What Thorstein Veblen ironically called "the performance of leisure" is fast becoming the tedious obligatory substitute for the performance of work.

Thus mankind is now in process of changing its quarters only by moving to a modern wing in the same archaic prison whose foundations were laid in the Pyramid Age: better ventilated and more sanitary, with a pleasanter outlook—but still a prison, and even more difficult to escape from than ever before because it now threatens to incarcerate a much larger part of the human race. But whereas the earlier modes of achieving productivity and conformity were largely external, abetted by magnificent religious rituals and palatial displays, those now applied to consumption are becoming internalized, and therefore harder to throw off. To estimate quantitatively the increase of these psychological pressures, Potter's figures on advertising are significant: by 1900 in the United States, $95,000,000 a year were spent in advertising: by 1929 it had reached $1,120,000,000: by 1951 it had reached $6,548,000,000, and has been going up steadily since. Even after correcting for increases in population and productivity, this inordinate advance registers the growth of forced consumption.

2: MEGATECHNIC COSTS AND BENEFITS

In 'advanced' industrial countries, where the 'Welfare State' is firmly established, many of the premises of megatechnics have been fulfilled in such a flow of goods as Telecleides pictured in the ancient verse I quoted earlier. Some of these products are not merely desirable, but have reached a high degree of technical perfection. In my own household, for example, an electric refrigerator has been in service for nineteen years, with only a single minor repair: an admirable job. Both automatic refrigerators for daily use and deepfreeze preservation are inventions of permanent value. Though one cannot bestow any such unqualified commendation upon the design of the contemporary motor car, one can hardly doubt that if biotechnic criteria were heeded, rather than those of market analysts and fashion experts, an equally good product might come forth from Detroit, with an equally long prospect of continued use.

But what would become of mass production and its system of financial expansion if technical perfection, durability, social efficiency, and human satisfaction were the guiding aims? The very condition for current financial success—constantly expanding production and replacement—works against these ends. To ensure the rapid absorption of its immense productivity, megatechnics resorts to a score of different devices: consumer credit, installment buying, multiple packaging, non-functional designs, meretricious novelties, shoddy materials, defective workmanship, built-in fragility, or forced obsolescence through frequent arbitrary changes of fashion. Without constant enticement and inveiglement by advertising, production would slow down and level off to normal replacement demand. Otherwise many products could reach a plateau of efficient design which would call for only minimal changes from year to year.

Under megatechnics, the pecuniary motive dominates every class in a way unknown in agricultural societies. The aim of industry is not primarily to satisfy essential human needs with a minimal productive effort, but to multiply the number of needs, factitious or fictitious, and accommodate them to the maximum mechanical capacity to produce profits. These are the sacred principles of the power complex. The avant-garde artists like Tinguely who have exhibited 'sculptures' that are designed to explode or collapse have only translated into pseudo-esthetic terms the barely disguised animus of megatechnics. The extension of new areas for technical exploitation and the multiplication of new products now yield the highest profits.

Not the least effort of this system is that of replacing selectivity and quantitative restriction by indiscriminate and incontinent consumption. No one has yet calculated the thousands of miles of film and the acres of sensitized paper that are consumed every year to make random snapshots that will never be looked at more than once when they have been returned from the developer—as if the vital pleasure of making instantaneous pictures with one's eyes lacked value until it was translated into a technical equivalent. Nor yet can one calculate the planet-girdling miles of sound-recording tape, to preserve non-selectively the results of business or academic conferences whose memorable contents, apart from the residue left in the minds of the participants, might usually be reduced to at most a few typed sheets.

The flammability of film and paper slightly soften this unfavorable judgement, for unlike poisonous chemicals and battered motor cars, they are in fact actually disposable without serious injury to the environment. But their main virtue is that they justify and sanctify the inventions themselves by providing heavy returns on the investment. (*Selectively used, I hasten to add, motion pictures and taped records and photographs are all potentially valuable contributions to human felicity:* it is only against the implacable rituals of automated consumption, imposed by the pecuniary-pleasure complex, that this criticism is directed.)

But unfortunately not all the products of megatechnics are so effectively self-destroying or self-eliminating as paper drinking cups or exploding sculptures; nor can their excessive use so lightly be condoned. In order to keep the megatechnic economy running smoothly with a steady expansion of all its facilities and the greatest possible Gross National Product, two conditions must be met. First of all, every member of the community must, in duty bound, acquire, use, devour, waste, and finally destroy a sufficient quantity of goods to keep its increasingly productive mechanism in operation. Since the productivity of this system is immense, this turns out to be not quite so light a duty as might seem. For not merely does megatechnics ignore many vital needs and interests, like that for housing lower income groups which cannot be supplied without massive State subvention, but in order to perform the duty of consumption, the worker himself must increase his own productive commitment.

Thus the shorter working day promised by this system is already turning into a cheat. In order to achieve the higher level of consumption required, the members of the family must take on extra jobs. The practice of the double job, known in the United States as 'moonlighting,' is becoming common, and if present consumptive pressures continue, will probably increase. The effect, ironically, is to turn the newly won six- or seven-hour day to twelve or fourteen hours; so in effect, the worker is back where he started, with more material goods than ever before, but with less time to enjoy them or the promised leisure. The same need may draw the housewife, even during the childbearing period, away from the care of her home and her children, in order to ensure the proper gush of status-maintaining superfluities.

The second requirement is no less strict. The majority of the population must forego all modes of activity except those that call for the unremitting use of the 'machine' or its products. Under the first head goes the abandonment of manual work and craft skill, even on the simplest domestic and personal scale. To indulge in any form of bodily exertion, wielding an axe or a saw, digging and hoeing a garden by hand, walking, rowing, or sailing, when a motor car or motor boat is available, even opening a single can or sharpening a pencil or cutting a slice of bread without benefit of a mechanical—preferably motorized—agent, is simply not playing the game. In so far as a minimum of bodily activity is necessary for health, it must be acquired by purchasing such exercising machines as stationary bicycles and mechanical masseurs. Thus the ancient aristocratic contempt for manual labor of any kind has now been democratized.

Such over-use of the machine flouts any practical test of efficiency: it has the force of an obligatory religious ritual, a genuflection before a holy object. What cannot be done by or with or for a machine must not be done at all. This has reached a climax in the elaborations of outdoor camping equipment, whereby an experience whose whole value consists in a return to a more rough and primitive relation with nature becomes a caricature by importing into the wilderness a close replication of all the familiar artifacts needed for living in a crowded city, from cooking stoves to television sets.

These tendencies have already gone far enough to permit one to forecast their ultimate consequences if no counter-movement takes place. The final triumph of technocratic society would be the consolidation of every human activity into an autocratic and monolithic system. This would produce a mode of existence in which functions that cannot be canalized into the system would be suppressed or extirpated. Considered by itself this prospect, once its outlines were publicly visible, would seem sufficiently dismaying to cause an overwhelming human reaction. And if this reaction has still to come, the reason is not far to seek. Once these terms are duly accepted, megatechnics, even in its present half-baked form, offers an immense bribe, which is bound to become bigger and more seductive as the Megamachine itself proliferates, conglomerates, and consolidates.

This loss of autonomy in order to maximize the services of megatechnics, carries with it one further condition: one must not demand any goods other than those that the machine offers in the current year, nor must one seek to retain, beyond the appointed half-life, any goods that have proved sufficiently durable and attractive to be preferable to those offered. This means that one must not demand any other kind of life than that which can be lived, as directed, within the current fashionable frame. To have a life that is in any way detached from the megatechnic complex, to say nothing of being cockily independent of it, or recalcitrant to its demands, is regarded as nothing less than a form of sabotage. Hence the fury evoked by the Hippies—quite apart from any objectionable behavior. On megatechnic terms complete withdrawal is heresy and treason, if not evidence of unsound mind. The arch-enemy of the Affluent Economy would not be Karl Marx but Henry Thoreau.

3 : THE MEGATECHNIC BRIBE

If one does not examine the megatechnic bribe too circumspectly, it would appear to be a generous bargain. Provided the consumer agrees to accept what megatechnics offers, in quantities favorable to the continued expansion of the whole power system, he will be granted all the perquisites, privileges, seductions, and pleasures of the affluent society. If only he demands no goods or services except those that can be organized or manufactured by megatechnics, he will without doubt enjoy a higher standard of material culture—at least of a certain specialized kind—than any other society has ever achieved before. If anything, the luxuries will be more plentiful than the comforts, though many basic human necessities that do not lend themselves to megatechnics will in fact be starved out of existence. In 'Fun City' one is not supposed to notice their absence.

For many members of the American community, which has been hastily subscribing to this system under the specious title of the 'Great Society,' or the 'Economy of Megalopolis,' the further development of this process-centered technology seems not merely inevitable but desirable: the next step in 'Progress.' And who dares resist Progress? Given the proper reward a population sufficiently coddled by the Welfare State asks for nothing better than what the market offers.

Those already conditioned from infancy by school training and television tutelage to regard megatechnics as the highest point in man's 'conquest of nature,' will accept this totalitarian control of their own development not as a horrid sacrifice but as a highly desirable fulfillment, looking forward to being constantly attached to the Big Brain, as they are now attached to radio stations by portable transistor sets even while walking the streets. By accepting these means they expect that every human problem will be solved for them, and the only human sin will be that of failing to obey instructions. Their 'real' life will be confined within the frame of a television screen.

Is this a gross exaggeration of current achievements, projects, promises? Are these only silly fantasies that no person of normal intelligence would seriously entertain? Unfortunately no: it is impossible to exaggerate. Consider the current lists of technological and scientific probabilities offered for the year 2000 by such spokesmen for this regime as Herman Kahn, B. F. Skinner, Glenn Seaborg, Daniel Bell—to say nothing of even more untrammeled technocratic minds.

To many credulous people, this whole prospect seems entrancing: indeed irresistible. Like those who have become helplessly addicted to cigarettes, they are now so committed to technological 'progress,' that they ignore the actual threat to their health, their mental development, or their freedom. Already a life that calls for assuming personal responsibility and exerting personal effort seems to them a utopian unreality, not, as it actually is, the normal state of all living organisms, one reaching a climax of conscious purpose in man.

By holding up effortless abundance as the ultimate goal of automation, with constant acquisition and consumption as a patriotic duty, this new economy has frayed the customary tie between possessions and meritorious personal effort. Theoretically, everything will soon be available for the asking. Without waiting for that millennial day, an increasing number of moral dropouts, responding to the advertisers' frantic incitements to instant affluence, have begun to help themselves to whatever goods they can lay their hands on. Shoplifting, theft, looting, burglary—crimes once committed only by anti-social types or by the desperately poor—have become a growing practice among people who are 'poor' and 'deprived' in the peculiar sense that they will never be able to possess, either by purchase or free gift, all the goods that the affluent society insists are essential for their happiness. Only theft will satisfy their insatiable needs. Such moral disintegration must wreck even the most equitable system of distribution.

For the sake of material and symbolic abundance through automated superfluity, these machine-addicts are ready to give up their prerogatives as living beings: the right to be alive, to exercise all their organs without officious interference, to see through their own eyes, hear with their own ears, to work with their own hands, to move on their own legs, to think with their own minds, to experience erotic gratification and to beget children in direct sexual intercourse—in short, reacting as whole human beings to other whole human beings, in constant engagement with both the visible environment and the immense heritage of historic culture, whereof technology itself is only a part.

To enjoy total automation, a significant part of the population is already willing to become automatons—or so it would seem if an increasing number of breakdowns and retreats did not indicate that this apparently irresistible process is actually being resisted, on a scale that should well before this have shaken the confidence of the priests and prophets of this regime.

At least one thing should soon become clear: once the majority of any nation opts for megatechnics, or passively accepts the system without further question, no other choices will remain. But if people are willing to surrender their life completely at source, this authoritarian system promises generously to give back as much of it as can be mechanically graded, quantitatively multiplied, scientifically sorted, technically conditioned, manipulated, directed, and socially distributed under supervision of a centralized bureaucracy. What held at first only for increasing the quantity of goods, now applies to every aspect of life. The willing member of megatechnic society can have everything the system produces—provided he and his group have no private wishes of their own, and will make no attempt personally to alter its quality or reduce its quantity or question the competence of its 'decision-makers.' In such a society the two unforgivable sins, or rather punishable vices, would be continence and selectivity.

"But is not this a fair bargain?" those who speak for the system ask. "Does not megatechnics offer by its own increasingly prodigious magic the 'cornucopia of plenty' that mankind has always dreamed of?" Quite true.

Many of the goods that megatechnics now provides, and still more those it promises to spread more widely in the future, are real goods: standardized at a high level, 'mechanically' efficient, embodying at least in the best examples that immense store of scientific knowledge, organized, collated, tested, which in our period has endowed mankind with powers it never before possessed or even dared to dream of. And if this knowledge can be fully understood and applied only by a highly endowed minority, adepts in abstract thinking though often babies in terms of well-salted human experience, what of the benefits that even the most limited souls now enjoy? Has there not already been an equalization of goods hitherto almost unknown in civilized communities, though common, despite poverty, in more primitive cultures?

Are not refrigerators, private motor cars and planes, automatic heating systems, telephones and television sets, electrically driven washing machines worth having? And what of the drudgery-eliminating achievements of the bulldozer, the forklift truck, the electric hoist, the conveyor belt, and a thousand other serviceable inventions? What of the appalling mental burdens in bookkeeping that have been lifted by the computer? What of the exquisite arts of the surgeon and the dentist? Are these not colossal gains? Why weep if some of the old goods and enjoyments have fallen through this electro-mechanical mesh? Does any sensible person mourn the passing of the old Stone Age? If all these goods are in themselves sound and individually desirable, on what grounds can we condemn the system that totalizes them? So say the official spokesmen.

Yes: if one examines separately only the immediate products of megatechnics, these claims, these promises, are valid, and these achievements are genuine. The separate benefits, if detached from the long-term human purposes and a meaningful pattern of life, are indisputable. None of megatechnics' efficient modes of organization, none of its labor-saving devices, none of its new products, however daring in their departures from old forms, should be arbitrarily disparaged or neglected, still less rejected out of hand. Only one proviso must be made, which the apologists for the power complex studiously have failed to recognize. All these goods remain valuable only if more important human concerns are not overlooked or eradicated.

Many of the promises that Francis Bacon held out are still valid and will be further validated. All that I seek here to bring out is the fact that these promises are not unconditional. On the contrary, their one-sided fulfillment, in terms that satisfy only the demands of megatechnics, endlessly stimulating the purposeless human 'pleasure center' of profit, without respect to other human functions and projects, carry heavy penalties that must be recognized and deliberately lifted. The mischiefs that have issued from megatechnics are not due to its failures and breakdowns but to its unqualified successes in over-quantification. These defects were present in the very conception of the mechanical world picture, which turned its back on organic needs and organic processes of feedback and over-emphasized quantity and speed, as if quantity in itself guaranteed value in the product quantified.

Plainly, then, it is not the mechanical or electronic products as such that intelligent minds question, but the system that produces them without constant reference to human needs and without sensitive rectification when these needs are not satisfied. By now, fortunately, this qualifying judgement has been slowly seeping back into the system itself, in the form of 'cost-benefit' appraisals, applied by engineers and administrators: a formal recognition of the fact that mechanical gains have often been achieved at great social losses, and that before one accepts unconditionally the gifts that megatechnics offers one must examine the accompanying deficits and decide whether the benefits justify them: and if immediately desirable, whether they are actually so in the long run. In a biotechnic economy, purely financial criteria would have only a limited place in such estimates.

4: QUANTIFICATION WITHOUT QUALIFICATION

The most serious flaw in megatechnics, uncorrectable on the principles historically embodied in the power complex, springs directly out of its astounding performances: human life is being suffocated and surfeited at a hundred places by sheer quantitative excess—beginning with an excess of births. This excess, we now can see, brings not only positive gains but heavy costs and disastrous penalties; and what is worse, the power complex prospers quite as well in producing negative goods like cigarettes and pesticides as in growing nutritious foods: indeed the profits from such deleterious products are often far higher.

Now the discovery that quantification is not in itself beneficial was made ages ago, at a time when only a favored minority could command goods and services in relatively unlimited quantity. As I showed earlier, the first real challenge to the ancient 'civilized' power system, which was the forerunner of our modern economy of abundance, came between the eighth and the sixth centuries B.C., when a succession of prophets and philosophers, perceiving the deleterious human results of an unrestricted pursuit of unlimited quantities of food, drink, sexual pleasure, money, and power, introduced a new system of voluntary control. The exhibitionist modes of consumption that had identified the rich and the powerful were no longer accepted as desirable patterns of human achievement: instead, the Axial religions and philosophies advocated abstention, moderation, the reduction of superfluous wants and capricious, ego-driven desires, for the sake of both internal equilibrium and spiritual exaltation.

Though civilization has been in some degree under the influence of these Axial religions and ideologies for roughly 2,500 years, they failed even at their moments of greatest acceptance and achievement to replace completely the earlier power systems or to forestall the present one. This for two reasons. For one thing, none of these new modes of thought themselves ever became firmly enough established to abolish the dominant institutions of ancient society—war, slavery, and economic expropriation—or to overcome the social aberrations upon which they were based. But no less disabling was the fact that their systems of abstention were designed, not to bring rewards in this life, but either to make the believer content despite their absence, or to look forward to compensation at compound interest in an imagined eternal life hereafter.

In consequence, the Axial religions did little except in an unreliable remedial way, mainly through voluntary charity, to ensure that goods in sufficient quantity were distributed justly to the entire community. Their exclusive emphasis upon the quality of life, upon internal and subjective rewards, thus merely reversed the older tendency to overstress materialistic power; whereas in all higher organisms a balance of quantitative and qualitative ingredients, of power and love, is necessary in order to ensure the best life possible. Neither unqualified power nor impotent virtue gives an adequate answer to the human problem.

With respect to an economy of abundance, there is a curious parallel between the dilemma modern man now faces through his technology and that which long ago occurred in nature, through excess of fertility in the reproduction of individual species. It has long been apparent to biologists that the reproductive capacity of any species, even of some that now occupy a modest niche, would be sufficient to over-run the planet with their offspring if it continued unchecked. Fortunately, Nature employs a whole series of limiting devices which, over any sufficient period of time, would check inordinate quantitative increase and establish an equilibrium. Faced with similar threats in the past, human populations were kept in line not only by the standard depletions of disease, war, and starvation, but by infanticide, incomplete coitus, homosexuality, voluntary continence supplemented occasionally by empirical contraceptives.

During the last three centuries there is evidence of a continued—if irregular—increase in population throughout the world, for reasons that are still difficult to account for, since it has taken place even in areas where there has been no notable increase in either natural resources or industrial productivity, and no serious changes, seemingly, in sexual habits or bodily hygiene. Whatever the diverse causes and circumstances, the so-called population explosion was matched by the technological explosion of Western civilization; and they both have a common terminus—the deterioration of life.

The perception that such prolific human breeding cannot continue indefinitely has been slow to awaken: yet the first consciousness of the dangers, as in Thomas Malthus' essay on population, coupled with the invention of the first cheap, popular contraceptives—mainly the sterilizing douche—slowed down the rate of increase to such an extent in countries like France and England that population experts, as late as 1940, looked forward to reaching an equilibrium in another generation, or even, in countries like France, a recession. These predictions have not been fulfilled: but the fact that a slowdown actually took place demonstrated that, with sufficient applied intelligence, biological over-quantification was and is avoidable. At a relatively trivial cost, the various contraceptive devices needed to reduce population increase throughout the planet to a socially and economically desirable optimum are at hand. The obstacles that remain are psychological and ideological, not technical.

Technology, unfortunately, has not yet developed from within, nor in terms of its favored economic incentives does it look forward to, any limit in the proliferation of machines or machine products: both power and profit depend upon producing more goods for more consumers, and ensuring their consumption in the shortest possible time span.

So in the long run—and by the long run one means a period of probably less than a century—our expanding megatechnic system, if it continues unaltered on its present course, will probably make the whole planet uninhabitable for anything like its present population, and eventually, if the same insensate forces now at work are not halted, even a thinned-out population will be doomed. When a scientist in good repute, like Dr. Lee Du Bridge, can defend the wholesale immediate use of pesticides, bactericides, and possibly equally dangerous pharmaceuticals, by saying that it would take ten years to test them sufficiently to certify their value and innocuousness and that *"industry cannot wait"*—it is obvious that his rational commitments to science are secondary to financial pressures, and that the safeguarding of human life is for industry not a matter of major concern.

Not that ample warnings about the misapplications of both science and technics have been lacking during the last century. Before the sudden shock of concern that has been recorded in the banning of DDT took place, the Wenner Gren Symposium, in 1955, in its survey of 'Man's Role in Changing the Face of the Earth,' took due note of the vast environmental damage being done by an irresponsible misapplication of technics; and the later analyses by many other competent biologists, notably Rachel Carson and Barry Commoner, have with amazing swiftness brought the situation home.

Even those who see no personal threat from quantification must be prepared to recognize its statistically demonstrable results in the many forms of environmental degradation and ecological unbalance that have resulted from the by-products of our megatechnic economy. The ironic effect of quantification is that many of the most desirable gifts of modern technics disappear when distributed *en masse,* or when—as with television—they are used too constantly and too automatically. The productivity that could offer a wide margin of choice at every point, with greater respect for individual needs and preferences, becomes instead a system that limits its offerings to those for which a mass demand can be created. So, too, when ten thousand people converge by car on a wild scenic area in a single day to 'get close to nature' the wilderness disappears and megalopolis takes its place.

In short, megatechnics, so far from having solved the problem of scarcity, has only presented it in a new form even more difficult of solution. Result: a serious deficiency of life, directly stemming from unusable and unendurable abundance. But the scarcity remains: admittedly not of machine-fabricated material goods or of mechanical services, but of anything that suggests the possibility of a richer personal development based upon other values than productivity, speed, power, prestige, pecuniary profit. Neither in the environment as a whole, nor in the individual community or its typical personalities, is there any regard for the necessary conditions favoring balance, growth, and purposeful expression. The defects we have examined lie not in the individual products but in the system itself: it lacks the sensitive responses, the alert evaluations and adaptations, the built-in controls, the nice balance between action and reaction, expressions and inhibitions, that all organic systems display—above all man's own nature.

"By his restrictions," Goethe wrote, "the master proclaims himself," and this truth applies not only to writers of genius but to all organisms: to speak of organisms is to speak of selective organization and quantitative limitation. All life exists within a narrow margin of heat and cold, nourishment and starvation, water or thirst: three minutes without breathing causes the death of a human being, and a few days without water, a month without food, and he is gone. Yet too much is as bad as too little. Though excess quantity, held in reserve, does in fact play an essential part in maintaining the organism's balance and makes possible freedom and exuberance, it is not by constantly using unlimited quantities that man flourishes. In sum, what has been lacking from the most brilliant feats of modern technology are precisely those specific organic features that Galileo, Descartes, and their later followers first systematically disregarded and then threw away.

5 : THE THREAT OF PARASITISM

Under the economy of abundance, even on the limited scale so far established in the United States, the huge bribe held out—of security, leisure, affluence—unfortunately also carries with it an equally huge penalty: the prospect of universal parasitism. Earlier cultures have had skirmishes with this enemy: Odysseus' scouts among the Lotos Eaters were so beguiled by their honeyed fare and dreamy ease that they had to be rescued by force. More than one emperor or despot discovered that permissiveness in the form of sensual inducements and enticements might be even more effective than coercion in securing compliance. Once established, the parasite identifies himself with his host and seeks to further the host's prosperity. Since parasitism has been widely observed in the animal kingdom, we have sufficient data to make a shrewd guess as to its ultimate human consequences.

Now megatechnics offers, in return for its unquestioning acceptance, the gift of an effortless life: a plethora of prefabricated goods, achieved with a minimum of physical activity, without painful conflicts or harsh sacrifices: life on the installment plan, as it were, yet with an unlimited credit card, and with the final reckoning—existential nausea and despair—readable only in the fine print. If the favored human specimen is ready to give up a free-moving, self-reliant, autonomous existence, he may, by being permanently attached to his Leviathan host, receive many of the goods he was once forced to exert himself to secure, along with a large bonus of dazzling superfluities, to be consumed without selection or restriction—but of course under the iron dictatorship of fashion.

The final consequences of such submission might well be what Roderick Seidenberg has anticipated: a falling back into a primordial state of unconsciousness, forfeiting even the limited awareness other animals must retain in order to survive. With the aid of hallucinatory drugs, this state might even be described by the official manipulators and conditioners as an "expansion of consciousness"—or some equivalent tranquillizing phrase that would be provided by public relations experts.

If proof were needed of the real nature of electronic control, no less a promulger of the system than McLuhan has supplied it. "Electromagnetic technology," he observes in 'Understanding Media,' *"requires utter human docility* [italics mine] and quiescence of meditation such as befits an organism that now wears its brain outside its skull and its nerves outside its hide. Man must serve his electric technology with the same servo-mechanistic fidelity with which he served his coracle, his canoe, his typography, and all other extensions of his physical organs." To make his point McLuhan is driven brazenly to deny the original office of tools and utensils as direct servants of human purpose. By the same kind of slippery falsification McLuhan would reinstate the compulsions of the Pyramid Age as a desirable feature of the totalitarian electronic complex.

The 'Big Bribe' turns out to be little better than the kidnapper's candy. Such a parasitic existence as megatechnics offers would in effect be a return to the womb: now a collective womb. Fortunately, the mammalian embryo is the only parasite that has proved capable of overcoming this condition once it has been established: the baby's birth cry triumphantly announces his escape. But note: once a human being has left the womb, the conditions that were there propitious to his growth become impediments. No mode of arresting development could be so effective as the effortless instant satisfaction of every need, every desire, every random impulse, by means of mechanical, electronic, or chemical equipment. All through the organic world development depends upon effort, interest, active participation: not least upon stimulating resistances, conflicts, inhibitions, and delays. Even among rats, courtship precedes copulation.

So essential is this condition to human development that in the area of games, where man has been able arbitrarily to lay down all the conditions, boundaries are fixed in time and space, and the strict rules of the game, re-enforced by penalties, are independent of the whim or will of the players. The very essence of the game itself lies in the tension and struggle of the human encounter—not alone in the winning or losing: in fact, too easy winning spoils the pleasure of the game, even for the winner. If the sole object of football, as William James once pointed out, were to get the football to the goal post, the simplest way to win would be to carry it there privately on some dark night. Under this same meretricious canon of easy success solitary masturbation has lately been suggested as superior to sexual intercourse.

Thus the effortless, automatic, push-button, sleekly secure existence promised by megatechnics, conceived exclusively on the pleasure principle, would lack the quickening sense of reality that even a game provides. In Egypt and Greece slavery probably provided a far happier existence for the slave in terms of his organic needs—at least for those who practiced the arts and crafts. On this matter, one can add further animal testimony. Zoo keepers have found that their animals keep in better condition when they have a whole carcass to dissect, as they do in nature, than when they are given meat already cut into chunks. If interest promotes effort, effort in turn sustains interest.

For short periods, in illness or convalescence or to offset extreme fatigue, one may profitably fall back into a quasi-parasitic routine, as one does as a patient in a sanitorium or a passenger on shipboard. But to make this condition the permanent goal of life and the justification of all man's earlier life-and-death efforts is to forget the conditions under which man originally emerged from animalhood, by living a more varied and strenuous life than other animals, for the most part, find necessary.

No umbilical cord attached man to nature: neither 'security' nor 'adjustment' were the guidelines to human development; and if tropical conditions of life were sometimes unduly favorable to indolence and somnolence, it was in regions of difficulty, at the edge of the desert, or along the flooding banks of rivers, in seemingly defective, insufficient, or half-hostile environments, that the spirit of man soared highest above its animal limitations, achieving not only equilibrium and growth but the ultimate—if rare—attribute of the human personality: transcendence.

Though domestication does not result in the wholesale deterioration brought about by complete parasitism, recent studies of the Norway rat by Curt P. Richter indicate that something more serious than a loss of autonomy takes place under such conditions. The Norway rat first became domesticated around 1800, to provide victims for the vulgar sport of rat baiting; and by the middle of the century a definite domestic breed of albino rats had been established, with various genetic variations, toothlessness, hairlessness, wobbliness, congenital eye cataracts, not found in the wild species.

Richter compares the conditions of rat domestication with those now provided by the 'Welfare State'—ample food, no danger, no stress, uniform environment and climate, and so forth. But he notes that, under these seemingly favorable conditions, organic deterioration has taken place: a decrease in the size of the adrenal glands, which help the organism meet stress or fatigue and forfend certain diseases: while the thyroid gland, the regulator of metabolism, becomes less active. Not strangely, perhaps, the brains of the domestic rat, and perhaps their mental ability, are smaller. At the same time, the sex glands mature earlier, become bigger, show more activity, and result in a higher rate of fertility. How human!

Richter notes parallel ailments in an over-protected human population: the increased incidence of arthritis, skin diseases, diabetes, and circulatory diseases; while tumorous conditions have been aggravated, seemingly, by an excessive secretion of sex hormones. Not least notable is the depletion of vitality and the increase of neurotic and psychotic disorders. This evidence is not conclusive: but it at least strongly suggests that any definition of a favorable economy in terms only of providing the maximum facilities

17: Technological Intuitions

An early model in stone for a screw propeller or a turbine? No: there is no record of any such invention anywhere at the time this figure was executed—in the ninth century before Christ. Anthropologists identify this geometric object as the head of a mace in the Cupisnique phase of the Chavin Horizon (Peru). Though the mace in many other forms served as both a deadly handweapon and an emblem of political authority, this particular form, rare if not unique, has as yet no understandable military use or symbolic significance. But even more than with early anticipations of human flight, this mace-head seems to testify to technological apparitions or intuitions that preceded any complex machine, but waited thousands of years for realization. If so, this would put technical invention on the same subjective footing as ritual, art, and language: all basic contributions to rationality and creativity whose practical applications and elaborations took place at a later stage.

18–19: Technological Exhibitionism

As indicated in 'Technics and Human Development' (Vol. I) cerebral control over the organs of his body was man's earliest technical triumph, which distinguished him from other tool-using and nest-building animals. Athletic exhibitionism ranges from the feats of Hindu yogins in regulating human breathing and heartbeat to Charles Blondin's performance in crossing the Niagara Falls on a tightrope in 1859. When Blondin reached the middle, 160 feet above the boiling waters, he set up a stove carried on his back, and fried some eggs, which he ate before passing to the other side. This fabulous act established a high point of perfection in cool-headed bodily control: technically a breath-taking feat. Only one further point need be noted: it was utterly without human significance or consequence.

So with much current technical exhibitionism. Though the moon landings are so far the most consummate example of this tendency, a museum devoted to such technological feats would soon be overcrowded. Some examples, like the jet-powered hovercraft, were originally designed for limited military application; but such air-cushioned transportation, even if generally practicable, would only through its widened use raise pollution closer to a lethal level. An even more glaring example of technological exhibitionism is the lately developed Cyborg, here illustrated: an up-to-date mechanical white elephant, promoted by the tax-proud military arm at a vast expense to perform services similar to those of a living elephant—if anyone could think up a plausible reason for doing so.

While many admirable inventions have sprung from children's playthings (the telephone, the motion picture, the helicopter), current technological exhibitionism reverses the creative process by turning elaborate and costly technical innovations into trivial toys. Every feat that the clumsy Cyborg achieves, as the General Electric brochure on this robot tacitly admits, can be effected by machines and apparatus already in existence, with greater facility, at a fractional cost: indeed from the Fourth Millennium onward they were performed by organized gangs of workmen with no mechanical apparatus at all.

As further mechanization and automation solve the practical problems of standardized mass production, it is likely that the area liberated for technological exhibitionism will steadily widen. Not a few of the publicized biological and medical innovations today, from heart transplants to medical diagnosis by two-way television, are largely responses to non-technical motivations: profit, publicity, prestige, ego-inflation. "To do everything that is technically possible," as von Weizsacker has shrewdly observed, "is non-technical behavior . . . not worthy of a technical age."

As so often, Jonathan Swift anticipated this technical avant-gardism in his 'Voyage to Laputa.' There the tailor "did his office in a different manner from those of his trade in Europe. He first took my altitude by a gradient, and then, with a rule and compasses described the outlines and dimensions of my whole body, all which he entered upon paper, and in six days brought my clothes very ill made and quite out of shape, by happening to mistake a figure in the calculation. But my comfort was, that I observed such accidents were frequent and little regarded."

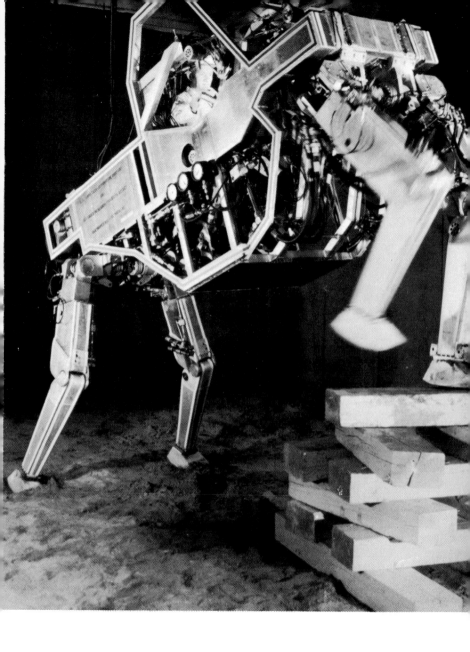

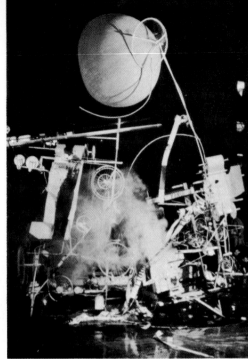

20: Homage to Giantism

Tinguely's sculptural happening, 'Homage to New York,' presents the subjective urban disintegration that Waldo Frank penetrated in 'The American Jungle' a generation ago. This formalized expression of megatechnic chaos is the negative counterpart of the outward drill and discipline of the daily round. The Port of New York Authority's World Trade Center, 110 stories high, is a characteristic example of the purposeless giantism and technological exhibitionism that are now eviscerating the living tissue of every great city. The Port Authority, a quasi-governmental corporation, was in origin a happy political invention, first installed in London; but unfortunately its social functions have been subordinated to pecuniary motivations: and its executives have conceived it their duty to funnel more motor traffic into the city, through new bridges and tunnels, than its streets and its parking spaces can handle—while contributing to the lapse of a more adequate system of public transportation that included railroad, subway, and ferry. This policy has resulted in mounting traffic congestion, economic waste, and human deterioration—though with a constant rise in land values and speculative profits. These baneful results were anticipated and graphically depicted by Clarence S. Stein, then Chairman of the New York State Housing and Regional Planning Commission, in his article on 'Dinosaur Cities' in the 'Survey Graphic,' May 1925. Stein there described the breakdowns—already quite visible—resulting from housing congestion, water shortage, sewage pollution, street clogging, traffic jams, and municipal bankruptcy. But Dinosaurs were handicapped by insufficient brains, and the World Trade Center is only another Dinosaur.

21: Environmental Desiccation

The agents of the pecuniary-power complex, under the guise of technical progress, feel obliged for both pecuniary advantage and self-protection to erase
every vestige of a more humane past. Though Frank Lloyd Wright's Imperial
Hotel in Tokyo did not count among his finest works, it showed his happy
characteristic fusion of the mechanical, the organic, and the personal. The replacement of this historic building with a structure that might have been designed by a computer summarizes a change that megatechnics is imposing
everywhere: the suppression of personal, communal, and regional individuality
by a kind of tasteless homogenized universalism: so that the faster and the
farther one travels, the less the actual scene changes, and the poorer the psychological stimulus that travel itself provides. This was caricatured in the film
'2001,' in which the space ship is served by a Howard Johnson's restaurant.

22: Organized Destruction

The over-expansion of motor and air transportation has not merely ruined the varied and flexible system of transportation that existed even a quarter of a century ago, but is in process of transforming cities and rural areas into deserts —airfields, expressways, junkyards, and parking lots. The illustrated intersection of the Pasadena and Hollywood freeways is a classic example of the highway engineer's monstrous sacrifice of precious urban land to the accommodation of increasing traffic. Fortunately, in the United States, where the damage has been greatest, there has been a belated reaction against the technocratic arrogance and ecological ignorance exhibited by current highway engineering. "U.S. Road Plans Perilled by Rising Urban Hostility" read the newspaper headlines. Though these challenges and stoppages are imperative, they can be effective only if they lead to a constructive policy of integrated urban and regional organization aimed at ecological and human balance.

23: Industrial Pollution, Commercial Fallout

The end products of megatechnic dynamism, which lacks human dimensions, rational feedback, or a social destination, are necessarily negative and life-damaging. As the pace of consumption rises, the result is "more and more of worse and worse." Only our present one-sided system of bookkeeping, which takes account only of profits, surfeits, and benefits, and ignores environmental damages and human deficits, could have so long remained oblivious to the massive miscarriages of the power system. The explanation of our present difficulties as mainly due to over-population applies only to local concentrations. For immediate ecological improvements, power control, mass-production control, rubbish control, and pollution control are more imperative than birth control.

24: Megalopolis into Necropolis

One of the plainest lessons of biology is that uncontrolled quantitative growth leads to malfunction through Mongolism or giantism, or to premature death through tumors and cancers. Patrick Geddes's summation of the downfall of cities, through over-population and congestion, as described in Chapter Four of 'The Culture of Cities,' has been confirmed by recent studies, such as Edward Hall's. Though the crowds on Fifth Avenue bear witness to the intense and varied life that the great city offers, the vices, perversions, corruptions, parasitisms, and lapses of function increase disproportionately: so that Parasitopolis turns into Pathololopolis, the city of mental, moral, and bodily disorders, and finally terminates in Necropolis, the City of the Dead.

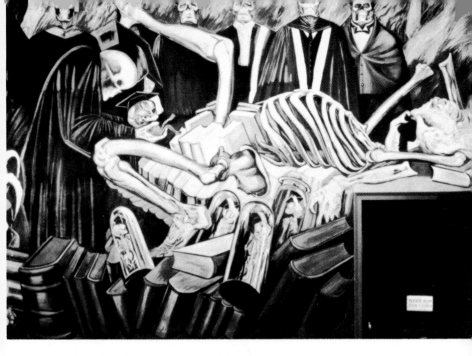

25: The Academic Establishment

More than a generation before the current student challenges, confrontations, and rebellions shook education systems throughout the world, the Mexican painter José Clemente Orozco produced this grisly comment on higher education: its desiccation and dehumanization, its sterile overspecialization, its indifference to human values and needs other than those that served to support or embellish the Establishment. Note the likeness between the academic witnesses to this accouchement of Alma Mater and the Aztec gods and priests who battened on human sacrifices. Yet before Orozco painted this savage mural, Ernest Hopkins, then President of Dartmouth College, had in fact anticipated its lesson and taken steps to correct this divorce of learning from life: for he attempted to break down departmental barriers by introducing, before Harvard did, a roving professorship licensed to lecture in any field, while he devaluated the Ph.D. as a prerequisite for teaching, and placed the quality of instruction above the quantitative production of scholarly papers as a condition for promotion. Characteristically, Mr. Hopkins chose a onetime teacher of English, Artemas Packard, to head a new Department of Art; and not strangely it was Packard who brought Orozco to Dartmouth, as professor, to paint the Baker Library murals—a contribution to the college teaching of art. Even before this, in April 1923, Alexander Meiklejohn, President of Amherst College, had presided over a Symposium on the Student Renaissance, which discussed "The Role of the College Student in Administrative and Curricular Reform" and "Of what importance that the student have a social political mission?"; and as head of the Experimental College at the University of Wisconsin, 1928–1933, he pioneered in putting some of the student demands to the acid test of practice. If these initiatives had been heeded, many imperative educational renovations might have come about through rational cooperation, not as panicky submissions to the physical threats of insolent minorities.

26: Mass Mobilization of Youth

Despite the well-founded dissatisfaction of the younger generation with the kind of life offered by the bloated affluence of megatechnic society, their very mode of rebellion too often demonstrates that the power system still has them in its grip: they, too, mistake indolence for leisure and irresponsibility for liberation. The so-called Woodstock Festival was no spontaneous manifestation of joyous youth, but a strictly money-making enterprise, shrewdly calculated to exploit their rebellions, their adulations, and their illusions. The success of the festival was based on the tropismic attraction of 'Big Name' singers and groups (the counter-culture's Personality Cult!), idols who command colossal financial rewards from personal appearances and the sales of their discs and films.

With its mass mobilization of private cars and buses, its congestion of traffic en route, and its large-scale pollution of the environment, the Woodstock Festival mirrored and even grossly magnified the worst features of the system that many young rebels profess to reject, if not to destroy. The one positive achievement of this mass mobilization, apparently, was the warm sense of instant fellowship produced by the close physical contact of a hundred thousand bodies floating in the haze and daze of pot. Our present mass-minded, over-regimented, depersonalized culture has nothing to fear from this kind of reaction—equally regimented, equally depersonalized, equally under external control. What is this but the Negative Power Complex, attached by invisible electrodes to the same pecuniary pleasure center?

27: Rituals of 'Counter-Culture'

The depressing monotony of megatechnic society, with its standardized environment, its standardized foods, its standardized invitations to commercialized amusement, its standardized daily routines, produces a counter-drive in overstimulation and over-excitement in order to achieve a simulation of life. Hence 'Speed' in all its forms, from drag races to drugs. With its narcotics and hallucinogens, its electrically amplified noise and stroboscopic lights and supersonic flights from nowhere to nowhere, modern technology has helped to create a counter-culture whose very disorder serves admirably to stabilize the power system.

Contrast this multi-media delirium with the intelligent, emotionally healthy plans of the Peace Moratorium, which reached a brief climax in the national Peace Mobilization at Washington in November 1969. Tens of thousands of people, young and old, braving inclement weather, marched with dignity before the White House all through the night, each reciting the name of an American killed in the Vietnam 'war,' and a similar demonstration was held in Washington Square in New York City. Note the use of the lighted candle, an ancient religious symbol, carrying human echoes that go back to the paleolithic caves. Though this demonstration did not win its immediate political objective, its effect upon the participants may yet be recorded in a more vital counterculture, centered in alert, clear-minded, articulate human beings in full possession of all their faculties; ready to act, in the words of ancient Athens' Ephebic Oath, "single-handed or with the support of all."

Francis Bacon, *Painting*, (1946). Oil and tempera on canvas, 77⅞ x 52. Collection, The Museum of Modern Art, New York. Purchase.

28: The Age of Monsters

Francis Bacon, setting out to "paint a bird alighting on a field," found that the lines of the bird's wing turned into this monster. From Warsaw to Hiroshima, from Auschwitz to Song My, the Monster has left his imprint on our minds and begotten a horde of lesser monsters, ready to enact degrading orgies of violence.

29: Passage to Biotechnics

Marcel Duchamp's 'Nude Descending a Staircase' counts as one of the more brilliant specimens of cubism: the representation of bodily movement in a static, mechanically conceived abstraction. In this work, as in many of Fernand Léger's paintings of the human figure, the specifically organic qualities are reduced to mechanical equivalents. The reverse process, of utilizing the machine itself to represent and express life, began with those brilliant studies of animal motion which resulted in the motion picture: the new art which transcends the technology that has made it possible. With the invention of the stroboscopic camera, it has become possible to show successive motions on a single film. This produces a more biotechnic equivalent of Duchamp's nude, for it does justice to the mobile beauty of a woman's body.

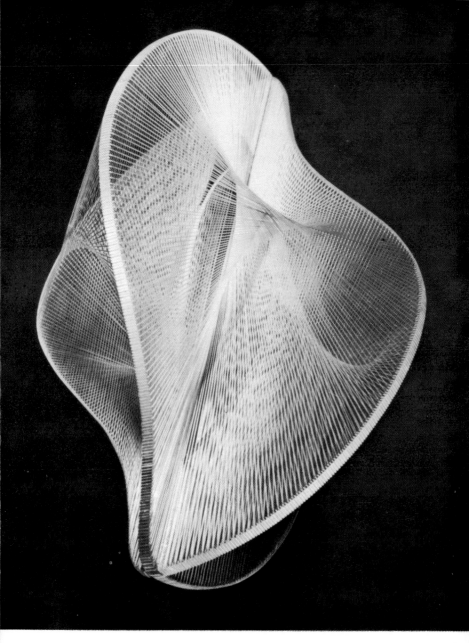

30: Etherialization of the World Picture (Gabo)

31: The Renewal of Life (Moore)

32: Naum Gabo and Henry Moore

[30] In this constructivist form by Gabo, the seventeenth-century world picture becomes completely de-materialized; and the old breach between the subjective and the objective, the inner and the outer, the vital and the mechanical, is resolved in a unified image which restores and re-creates the organic realities that were eliminated in the classic conceptions of mechanics and physics. Here, one of the highest functions of mind, the capacity for abstraction, realizes in the act of carrying further its own discipline, the perfect symbol of etherialization, released from mechanistic constrictions.

[31] Henry Moore's 'Family Group' derives from two sources: the living earth and the body of Woman, conceived primarily as the Great Mother, protecting and enfolding the life she brings forth. The stable posture of Moore's figures, firmly seated or reclining, proclaims a deep opposition to the insensate dynamism and furious disintegration of our age. Here is the beginning, on primal foundations, of organic integrity—though at first, in contrast to Gabo, with a sacrifice of the higher cerebral functions, as indicated in the diminished heads of Moore's figures. These archetypal maternal images of Earth and Woman are, one dares hope, making ready for the renewal of life.

PICTURE CREDITS

1. *Center,* The Metropolitan Museum of Art; *bottom,* The New York Times. 2. *Top,* Dartmouth College. 3. *Left,* Tennessee Valley Authority; *right,* Burt Glinn, from Magnum. 4. *Both,* Deutsches Museum München. 5. Wide World. 6. *Top,* Lawrence Rubin Gallery; *bottom,* IBM. 7. Ewing Galloway. 8. *Both,* Photoworld. 9. *Top,* "Paris Match," Pictorial Parade; *center,* Süddeutscher Verlag; *bottom,* Sovfoto. 10. *Left,* Fuller & Sadao; *right,* courtesy of the Oriental Institute, University of Chicago. 11. *Left,* Transamerica Corporation; *right,* United Press International. 12. *Left,* Mirrorpic, from Gilloon Agency; *right,* United Press International. 13. *Top,* Carter Hamilton, from Design Photographers International; *bottom left,* Danny Lyon, from Magnum; *bottom right,* Wide World. 14. NASA. 16. *Top, both,* Elliott Erwitt, from Magnum; *bottom,* International Harvester Company. 17. Courtesy of the American Museum of Natural History. 19. General Electric. 20. *Left,* Wide World; *right,* David Gahr. 21. *Both,* United Press International. 22. *Top,* State of California, Department of Public Works, Division of Highways; *bottom,* Elliott Erwitt, from Magnum. 23. *Top,* Burk Uzzle, from Magnum; *bottom,* Paul Conklin. 24. *Top,* Harbrace Photo; *bottom,* Arthur Tress. 25. Dartmouth College. 26. *Both,* Burk Uzzle, from Magnum. 27. *Left,* Charles Gatewood; *right,* The New York Times. 28. Collection, The Museum of Modern Art, New York. 29. Philadelphia Museum of Art. 30. Collection of the Stedlijk Museum in Amsterdam, photograph by Rudolph Burckhardt. 31. The Phillips Collection, Washington, D.C.

for maintaining physical existence with a minimum of organic effort is open to the suspicion of ignoring the more complex conditions, *including negative ones,* needed for every kind of organic development.

On this matter Patrick Geddes long ago made some observations as biologist that are still pertinent. In his 'Analysis of the Principles of Economics,' he noted that the "conditions of degeneration in the organic world are approximately known. These conditions are often of two distinct kinds, deprivation of food, light, etc. so leading to imperfect nutrition and enervation; the other, a life of repose, with abundant supply of food and decreased exposure to the dangers of the environment. It is noteworthy that while the former only depresses, or at most extinguishes the specific type, the latter, through the disuse of the nervous and other structures, etc. which such simplification of life involves, brings about that far more insidious and thorough degeneration seen in the life history of myriads of parasites."

The personality changes that will result—in many areas they are already visible—from an attempt to produce through the megamachine an existence that calls for as little thought and exertion and personal interest as possible, have still to be measured and appraised: yet the extremes to which this movement tends are now obvious: infantilism or senility. Psychoanalysts have long been aware of a latent tendency in human beings to seek a return to the womb. Even after emerging from this perfect environment, the infant retains an illusion of omnipotence: for he has only to cry to have his wishes fulfilled. By bawling loudly he gets an immediate response from the environment: a face reassuringly appears, a hand strokes him, a breast offers him food.

To carry this magical effortless existence into maturity has been the tacit effort of the system of automation modern man has perfected. But the state that the infant begins with, in which he is not able to discriminate between his own body and any other part of the immediate environment, becomes at a later stage an inability to identify himself or to have any desires that are not immediately satisfiable in the given environment. The price of this magic wish fulfillment is utter dependence; and if no further growth took place, separating the demanding child from his yielding parent, this would lead to the progressive disuse of essential organs and a relapse into a state of utter mindlessness.

If automation begins by establishing infantile dependence, it ends, to the extent that its regimen is successfully imposed upon the whole community, by producing senile alienation and deterioration, marked by the lapse of such faculties and functions as have developed. In its final workings, then, automatism artificially induces premature old age; for it reduces the human organism to that state of helplessness, feeble-mindedness, and vocational uselessness which is the worst curse that may befall the aged. The current wave of ostentatious pornography is perhaps a final evidence of such senility: this inevitably concentrates on abstract images, or what is left of sex when the active capacity to make love vanishes.

Now, the traumatic experience that often overtakes the aged when they have reached the "retirement age," though they are often still capable of functioning efficiently, is the realization that they are no longer needed. The most cruel ordeal of the retired worker is to face a future when he no longer has any function to perform, any place to occupy, any responsibilities to fulfill. Those who face old age intelligently seek to avert this final period of deprivation, alienation, and paralysis as long as possible. But megatechnic automation, precisely to the extent that it becomes successful and universal, will import these terminal disabilities into ever earlier stages of life: until at some ideal point the traits of infantilism will dissolve into those of senility without leaving a gap to be filled with anything that can properly be called a mature, self-directed, self-fulfilling life.

If one had any doubts about the reality of this compulsive approach to collective parasitism once the megamachine is in full operation, there is plenty of admonitory evidence, almost from the time that written records are available. Nothing is more striking throughout history than the chronic disaffection, the malaise, the anxiety, and the psychotic self-destructiveness of the ruling classes, once they are in command of "all that the heart can desire." For the dominant minority, the privileged few, have always been faced with the ultimate curse of such a meaningless existence: sheer boredom. Witness the Mesopotamian 'Dialogue on Suicide' cited in Pritchard's texts, or in 'The Intellectual Adventure of Ancient Man.'

Kings have always boasted that their slightest wishes were commands. The classic proof of their power and their success was their command of limitless amounts of food and drink, limitless quantities of clothes and jewels: the services of innumerable slaves, servants, and officials: limitless sensual stimulations, and not least, limitless opportunities for sexual intercourse, for even here erotic delight was measured in gross quantitative terms. The affluence that once was monopolized by the king and his court is now being held up as the ultimate gift of the power system to mankind at large.

Yet mark the serious difference between the two modes. In the older system there was a saving challenge that will no longer exist once the present tendencies become universal. For the parasitism of the archaic minorities came about in fact as the ambivalent reward for their originally predatory mode of life. Only by fierce exertions and by running the risk of being slain did these rulers and their warriors conquer and exploit the far more numerous peasant populations. Even after the successful monarchs had achieved sufficient control and tribute to relapse into a parasitic mode of life, they still had to be on guard against the attacks of envious rivals, the assaults of other predatory governors and princes seeking to extend their taxable domains, or even mass uprisings on the part of the exploited peoples and slaves, as in the Jewish exodus from Egypt.

At the first rumors of revolt, or even in preventive anticipation, the ruling class would take up the mace and the sword to re-establish its authority. This tension kept the main beneficiaries of the parasitic regime in a state of animal alertness and fitness; and they habitually re-sharpened their predatory edge by hunting lions and tigers. Those who lost their edge and sank into parasitic inertia were speedily displaced by more able and active rivals.

Old-fashioned war, then, was not merely the standard means of absorbing the excess energies of the archaic economy: it likewise kept the dominant minority in contact with the underlying realities of organic existence, realities that an economy of abundance, based solely on the power-pleasure principle, tacitly denied or openly flouted. As our present military megamachines are constructed, even these personal risks and strains will soon cease to exist: the one group that will be safe, unless their malign strategy includes active germ warfare, will be the military caste, safe in its underground control centers or its mobile underwater hideouts. If once anything like planetary control were firmly effected, as it might be by a coalition of now hostile military megamachines, the condition for complete parasitism, that is, for the wholesale deterioration of human potentialities, would be established.

In endeavoring to answer the question, "Is Life Worth Living?" William James pointed out that the psychological conditions that supplement the biologists' observations upon parasitism show that organic activities of the highest sort oscillate between two poles: positive and negative, pleasure and pain, good and bad; and that an attempt to live in terms of the positive, the pleasurable, and the plentiful alone destroys the very polarity needed for the full expression of life. "It is, indeed, a remarkable fact," observed James, "that sufferings and hardships do not, as a rule, abate love of life; they seem on the contrary to give it a keener zest. The sovereign source of melancholy is repletion. Need and struggle are what excite us; our hour of triumph is what brings a void. Not the Jews of the Captivity, but those of the days of Solomon's glory are those from whom the pessimistic utterances in our Bible come."

Even primitive peoples, whom one might reasonably suspect of having to endure too many hardships, have recognized this fundamental paradox: the interchangeable roles, within limits, of pleasure and pain: so they have invented 'rites of passage' and ordeals of initiation, often accompanied by bodily mutilation that demanded stoic fortitude. When physical effort, stress, danger, strenuous exertion are no longer necessary in order to gain a living, what will sustain modern man in health? Already, at the push of a button or the turn of a switch, a whole retinue of mechanical servants takes

over. Under these conditions, sport may serve as temporary substitute for
work: but for the most part sport, under the usual canons of the power
complex, is turned over to highly paid professionals, and watched by
thousands of overfed and underexercised spectators whose only way of
taking active part in the game is to assault the umpire.

The young in such a semi-parasitic culture now improvise their own
rites of passage in murderous gang assaults, sadistic hazings, random
destruction of property, or death-inviting motor races, unregulated by the
customs of the tribe or the wisdom of parental authority. The culture of
Rome, which practiced parasitism on the largest scale as the 'Roman Way
of Life,' provided vicarious trials and dangers in the arena: prolonged
orgies of violence culminating in mass exterminations. Before we accept
the promised economy of abundance as inevitable on the terms that it
is now presenting itself to us, we had better examine more closely, as
I shall do in the next chapter, the evidences of disintegration and demoralization, which are already visible in every culture that the renovated power
system has even remotely touched.

Here again, as in 'The City in History,' I should be uneasy about my
own interpretation of the evidence before us if I had not been anticipated
more than a century ago by one of the most prescient political interpreters
that Europe has ever produced: Alexis de Tocqueville. He was not unaware, in his observation of the New World democracy in the United
States, of the many promises that the new technology already held out:
indeed he said in so many words that the history of the last seven hundred
years was a history of progressive economic and social equalization. But he
was also aware of the terrible price that might be paid for these improvements. "I seek," he said, "to trace the novel features under which
despotism may appear in the world among a multitude of men, all equal
and alike, incessantly endeavoring to procure the petty and paltry pleasures
that glut their lives . . .

"Above this race of men stands an immense and tutelary power, which
takes upon itself to secure their gratifications and to watch over their fate.
That power is absolute, minute, regular, provident, and mild. It would be
like the authority of a parent if, like that authority, its object was to
prepare men for manhood; but it seeks, on the contrary, to keep them in a
perpetual state of childhood: it is well content that people should rejoice,
provided they think of nothing but rejoicing. For their happiness such a
government willingly labors, but it chooses to be the sole agent and the
only arbiter of that happiness; it provides for their security, increases and
supplies their necessities, facilitates their pleasures, manages their principal
concerns, directs their industry, regulates the descent of property, and
subdivides their inheritances: what remains but to spare them all the care
of thinking and all the trouble of living? . . .

"After having thus successively taken each member of the community in its powerful grasp and fashioned him at will, the supreme power then extends its arm over the whole community. It covers the surface of society with a network of small complicated rules, minute and uniform, through which the most original minds and the most energetic characters cannot penetrate, to rise above the crowd. The will of men is not shattered, but softened, bent, and guided; men are seldom forced by it to act, but they are constantly restrained from acting. . . .

"I have always thought that servitude of the regular, quiet, and gentle kind which I have just described might be combined more easily than is commonly believed with some of the outward forms of freedom, and that it might even establish itself under the wing of the sovereignty of the people."

No one else has better described either the bribe or the threat that the very success of megatechnics, culminating in the final assemblage of a planetary megamachine, would bring about. What was once pure speculation in the utopian and scientific fiction writers, is now uncomfortably close to the point of materialization.

CHAPTER THIRTEEN

Demoralization and Insurgence

1: THE CRACKING MONOLITH

There is little doubt that at least in most industrially developed countries the Megatechnic Complex is now at the height of its power and authority, or is fast approaching it. In objectively measurable physical terms—units of energy, output of goods, input of 'bads,' capabilities for mass coercion and mass destruction—the system has nearly fulfilled its theoretic dimensions and possibilities; and if not judged by a more human measure, it is an overwhelming success.

In many fields the megamachine complex in both the United States and Soviet Russia has begun to exercise virtually total control—though possibly the American system remains more efficient because it still draws in an emergency upon the older polytechnic tradition of its pioneer days, along with the habits of independent initiation and invention so fostered. Apart from their mutual rivalry and overt antagonism, these two regimes seem increasingly unassailable and invincible; and the habits of mind and the irrational proposals they have promoted are being transmitted by the mass media to an ever larger portion of mankind.

Schumpeter pointed out a generation ago that capitalism generated by its own forces the practices that would cause its replacement by some form of impersonal collectivism that has no place for private property, private judgements of value, private contracts, and eventually even of private gains and emoluments, except in the ancient forms of status and privilege.

What applies to the capitalist economy applies now to the entire power complex: the confusions and demoralizations expressed in avant-garde art are fast approaching the point where the medium not only replaces the message but likewise the subject to whom the message was once addressed. Like the sanitorium and its inmates and doctors in Thomas Mann's 'The

Magic Mountain' our whole power system has become fraudulent: its goods have become evils; its benefits deficits; its useful inventions are becoming useless and destructive; and instead of rational goals and predictable order it has now created a maximum possibility for disorder.

We need not be surprised, then, that in more than one area the Power Complex has been undergoing severe strain. Though immune to any frontal assault except by another power system of equal size, these giants are particularly vulnerable to localized guerrilla assaults and raids, against which their mass formations are as helpless as was heavily armored Goliath against a nimble David who did not choose to use the same weapons or attack the same part of the anatomy.

The present tensions all over the world reveal the inability of the military, bureaucratic, and educational 'elite' to understand the human reactions that the smooth success of their system has already brought about. Still less are they able to cope with them, except by bringing to bear a larger measure of the dehumanized processes that are now producing these hostile responses. Though desertions and dropouts are still insignificant in quantity, something like a large-scale withdrawal and reversal may actually be in the offing.

The very dynamism of megatechnics, its seemingly endless resourcefulness in concocting technocratic answers to human problems, has blinded its governors to the nature of these contrary reactions. Hence the orthodox remedy for discontent—the Welfare State's variants of 'bread and circuses'—only aggravates the disease. Unfortunately, just as in the body there is no tissue that shows a more extraordinary capacity for rapid growth than cancer cells, so in the body politic, the disintegration and destruction that has been going on with cumulative force for half a century now threaten to outpace the productive mechanism and even undermine the principles of cosmic order and rational cooperation upon which its genuine constructive achievements have in fact been based.

Though I shall approach the concrete evidence of the social disintegrations and regressions of our megatechnic regimes mainly by examining the subjective reactions that have long been visible, let me first point out briefly the obvious cracks in this seemingly monolithic structure. Probably the majority in any industrial country, sedulously conditioned to accept and overvalue the more profitable products of megatechnics, will continue eagerly to demand its material rewards. Yet these beneficiaries show an increasing unwillingness to keep the system in operation by willing efforts: instead they seek to wring from it ever larger gifts and bonuses and perquisites, whilst performing ever more reluctantly a minimal amount of work and accepting an equally minimal degree of responsibility. Characteristically, the parting salute of one American worker to another is: "Take it easy!"

The reason for this general letdown should be plain. With most of the old skills and decisions taken out of the worker's hands by automatism and centralized control, what human qualities remain are mostly negative ones: balkiness, mindless indifference, resentment, foot-dragging, or, to sum it up in a single phrase, psychological absenteeism. Even when the worker remains physically present, he is no longer "all there."

To compensate for their inability to guide the work-process or to mold its products, even the most favored members of a megatechnic organization, like the great unions of industrial workers, do not hesitate to disrupt or paralyze the essential activities of a whole nation in order to enforce compliance with their sometimes arbitrary demands. Since profit-making expansion, not rational distribution and social justice, is the criterion of megatechnic success, the Establishment can present no appealing moral alternative. The persistence of slow-downs, sit-ins, wildcat strikes, often for trivial reasons, would seem to be an unconscious effort to restore by spasmodic disruption some of the human initiatives that the system has suppressed. Hence labor revolts are often directed against the workers' elected leaders, who correctly enough are identified with the established order.

Admittedly, the professional 'elite' by whom and for whom the whole system is increasingly run, have never been more fully engaged, more demandingly overworked, more handsomely rewarded, more esteemed and exalted, flattered and publicized, than they are today. Like their ancient priestly predecessors, they feed well on the burnt offerings sacrificed on the holy altars of the Sun God.

For all those who are still committed to the archaic myth of the machine, and who are accredited members of the new pentagon of power, the sacrifices that the Sun God exacts only confirm the intensity of their commitment. Astronauts, we have seen, submit to the severest bodily ordeals in order to satisfy the ritual demands for space travel to distant parts of the solar system. To a certain degree, vicarious participation in these rites by the earthbound inhabitants of the planet, made possible through film, television and radio, restores the waning sense of high adventure; and the ever present possibility of death in a cosmic setting augments, as in motor racing, the daily doses of untrammeled gladiatorial violence faithfully provided by the mass media.

The point to be grasped has been staring Western civilization in the face for the last half century: namely, that a predominantly megatechnic economy can be kept in profitable operation only by systematic and constant expansion. Instead of a balanced economy, dedicated to the enhancement of life, megatechnics demands limitless expansion on a colossal scale: a feat that only war or mock-war—rocket building and space exploration—can supply.

Now the more highly organized the power structure becomes, the fewer non-conforming factors can be admitted, and the more open the whole system is to breakdowns from mechanical defects and natural accidents—but even more from the counter-assaults of those classes and groups that are excluded from the system or partly deprived of its boasted benefits. With war itself in one form or another as the dynamic core of this structure, no part of the periphery is immune to attack. Without war the megatechnic system in its present spatially enlarged planetary and cosmic form would be choked by its own purposeless productivity. Hence the apt title of Herman Kahn's book, 'Thinking about the Unthinkable.' As he makes plain at the beginning, what is unthinkable is not totalitarian genocide—his book only elaborates various statistical guesses on that subject—but any attempt to invest equivalent amounts of mind-energy and material resources toward creating a worldwide equilibrium favorable to justice and peace. To place any limits upon the expansion of the power system is what has become unthinkable.

While the megatechnic economy was being built up, it was possible for 'progressive' thinkers to regard its social deficiencies and its physical degradations as due solely to the decayed social residue from technically cruder earlier regimes. Thus the Victorian philosopher of evolution, Herbert Spencer, like Auguste Comte and the Saint-Simonians, looked upon militarism and war, along with all forms of supernatural religion, as the relics of a barbarous society soon to be replaced by sensible utilitarian goals and more rational business and engineering practices. (Comte's 'Law of Three States.') Before the nineteenth century was over Spencer himself was honest enough to recognize the dismaying contrary evidence of imperialism: but the specious attempt to account for the magnitude of present evils without reference to the amplifications of modern technology throws away an important historic key.

As we have seen, what modern technology has done is not to replace the decrepit institutional complex one can trace back at least to the Pyramid Age, but to rehabilitate it, perfect it, and give it a global distribution. The *potential* benefits of this system, under more humane direction, are still immense. But its inherent defects, through its complete divorce from ecological moderations and human norms, have already cancelled out its advantages and weighted it heavily against the very survival of living species. For who can doubt that the destructions and massacres, the environmental depletions and the human degradations that have become prevalent during the last half century have been in direct proportion to the dynamism, power, speed, and instantaneous control that megatechnics has promoted?

By now, then, even the most salutary achievements in technics are closely tied to coeval negative manifestations. On a national scale, the total amount of material destruction and human extermination that has taken place in the last fifty years far outpasses in insensate brutality and purposeless destruction the most sustained efforts of the Assyrians, the Mongols, or the Aztecs. And this aberration is not confined to war. The most typical triumph of mass production today, the motor car, has since 1900, statistics show, slaughtered vastly more human beings than have been killed in *all* the wars ever fought by the United States—while the total number of those injured or permanently maimed is probably much higher.

That callous public indifference to the results of our daily commitment to power and speed helps explain our tolerance of massive technological assaults in every other area of life. So two generations have grown up for whom every variety of mindless violence has become the constant accompaniment to 'civilized' life, sanctified by other equally debased but modish customs and institutions.

2 : VANISHED SAFEGUARDS

Looking back upon the period we have been living through, one is puzzled not over the protests and challenges that are now taking place, but at the fact that they did not occur more promptly, and even more intransigently. There are doubtless many reasons for this delayed response; and first of all, the obvious one was the actual advance of technology itself, which, despite the desperate rearguard fight of the old handicraft workers, encouraged even among the working classes the hope that a better day was at hand.

During the nineteenth century many timely warnings challenged these hopes: but since they came mainly from those outside the system they were dismissed as 'old-fashioned,' hopelessly idealistic, or absurdly escapist.

But the fact was that the power system, which began by discarding the traditional social and moral values that had made human understanding and cooperation possible—as it had discarded traditional explanations of natural phenomena—could continue in operation only so long as an active residuum of these values remained, supported by the forms of art and ritual that had created a more lovable, life-sustaining world. Once power was stripped of these historic clothes, what was left of man were two components no longer recognizably human: the automaton and the id, the first a product of scientific and technical abstractions, the other a manifestation of gross organic vitality over whose often destructive impulses the mind has not yet assumed control. This lack of human dimensions cannot, unfortunately, be recognized by minds formed and strictly conditioned by the power system. Hence the present human situation: one that steadily approaches total demoralization.

There were still other conditions that for over a century kept more or less in abeyance the internal forces of barbarism generated by the system itself. One of these is the fact that until the beginning of the present century some four-fifths of the population of the planet still lived in relatively isolated villages and farmsteads, hardly touched in any basic way by the new technology.

Until upset by mechanization and urbanization, that rural and communal underlayer, however exploited by the power system, remained outside it. What is more important, its archaic moral culture held the rest of society together: for though it still maintained many effete, irrational customs, it also kept close to the ultimate realities of life, human and divine: birth and death, sex and love, family devotion and mutual aid, sacrifice and transcendence, human pride and cosmic awe. Even the lowliest tribes, no less than major national groups, retained a sense of their own importance and value as conscious beings, participating in a social scheme that did not depend for its significance solely upon their tools or their bodily comforts. This cultural reservoir retained by its very backwardness some of the essential organic components that megatechnics, concerned only with removing all limitations on productivity and power, neglected or contemptuously extirpated.

For a while romanticism, as both idea and act, played a counter-balancing role in affirming and in some degree rehabilitating conceptions of nature and modes of life that had been excluded from the mechanistic and utilitarian world picture. This movement was in every sense a vital one, and made salutary contributions even to science; for the same ideas that were formulated by Rousseau incited Humboldt and Goethe and a whole generation of nineteenth-century naturalists, headed by Darwin and Wallace. But in the long run it was ineffective because it could not be attached to the Power Complex without forfeiting its own principles and ideals. Unlike the situation in Defoe's fable, 'Robinson Crusoe,' the ship abandoned by the romantic castaways had not been wrecked, but became increasingly seaworthy and was headed for more distant ports.

Yet an even more important factor in protecting the power system from internal assault was the presence of many surviving historic institutions whose customs and folkways and active beliefs supplied an essential structure of values. These vital social patterns were lacking in the basic seventeenth-century ideology, and even more in its later technocratic and pragmatic equivalents. But who can say how much the exaltation of Christian meekness, Christian otherworldliness, and Christian hope, along with the pious moral account-keeping of the Protestant sects, counteracted the worst humiliations imposed on the pottery workers of Stoke, the cotton operatives of Manchester and Lowell, or the coal miners of Wales and Pennsylvania, and ensured their stolid endurance. For many pious souls the ancestral forms of religion still gave at least a prospective value in eternity to what was otherwise an utterly miserable and meaningless existence.

With the erosion of this traditional heritage, megatechnics lost a social ingredient essential for its full working efficiency: self-respect, loyalty to a common moral code, a readiness to sacrifice immediate rewards to a more desirable future. As long as this basic morality, with its taboos, its inhibitions, its restrictions and abnegations remained 'second nature' in the community, the power complex had a stability and continuity that it no longer possesses. This means, we now begin to see, that in order to remain in effective operation, the dominant minority must, as in Soviet Russia and China, resort to the same system of ruthless coercion their predecessors established back in the Fourth Millennium B.C. Otherwise, in order to ensure obedience and subdue counter-aggression, they must use more 'scientific' modes of control—such as the proposal recently made by one scientist to introduce tranquillizers and sedatives into the water supply. Now that religion is no longer the 'opium of the people,' 'opium' (pot, hashish, heroin, LSD) is fast becoming the religion of the people.

The two factors that protected the power system from internal rebellion and external disruption are now lacking: the escape hatch, by migration, has closed and the internal modes of social control, based on widely shared values, orderly rituals, and supernatural hopes, have broken down. Under these conditions the most highly mechanized system will soon cease to function; for it has no values of its own, except its own absolute: the support of the power complex. Hence the only effective way of conserving the genuine achievements of this technology is to alter the ideological basis of the whole system. This is a human, not a technical, problem and it admits only a human solution.

Many ancient rituals and dogmas are now plainly empty of meaning. But what significance can be attached to the current routines of the office, the factory, the laboratory, the school, or the university, founded as they so largely are on the sterile, life-inhibiting postulates of the power system? What difference is there between a working day spent on programming and monitoring computers, and a day spent on sentry duty or on the assembly line? What plethora of material goods can possibly atone for a waking life so humanly belittling, if not degrading, as the push-button tasks left to human performers actually are? And if power and freakish pleasure, not fullness of life, be mistaken for ultimate goods, why should not those who seek to bypass the megamachine reach them by a more direct route?

3: THE REVOLUTIONARY BACKWASH

Despite the fact that from the Fourth Millennium B.C. onward—and possibly earlier—the odds against a successful revolution were always in favor of the armed minority who held the actual citadels of power, an underlying fear of such a revolution seems throughout history to have haunted the ruling classes. And not without reason, since we have documentary witness from ancient Egypt that such a revolt actually occurred and brought the mighty Pyramid Age itself to an ignominious end.

In the eighteenth century, the popular promotion of democracy, with its demand for the abolition of privilege and the equalization of opportunity, had culminated in the French Revolution; and the fear of such an attack upon the power complex was re-enforced, after the outbreaks of 1848, by the rise of socialism, which threatened to overthrow the existing economic structure. Even in its most laissez-faire mode, capitalism relied heavily on the police and the military to put down riots and to imprison, exile, or shoot the leaders of such protests.

Now socialism, as formulated by the influential succession of thinkers from Saint-Simon and Enfantin to Marx and Engels and their latterday disciples was an ingenious compound of utopian dreams, realistic concessions, and hopeful technological proposals. In so far as it sought a wholesale transformation of the power system, once the working class had seized the military and bureaucratic apparatus of the state, it intensified the counter-efforts of the ruling classes to rebuild the megamachine by imperialist military conquests and by total conscription. On one famous occasion a general railroad strike was averted in France by calling men of military age to the colors. As the threat of violent revolution developed further the tactics of preventive counter-revolution through war offset it.

But there was an even more effective safeguard for the power system, which only such humane anarchist-communists as Peter Kropotkin recognized: namely, that the working class revolutionary movement had naïvely accepted the ideological premises of the power complex. Socialism, through its Marxian notion that mechanical progress was inevitable and virtually automatic, was only proposing a transfer of power from one ruling class to another; the overall mechanism remained the same. Its most realizable utopia was the revolutionary process itself; and once revolution has taken place, as we now see in countries like Soviet Russia, it is difficult to distinguish the new order from that which has been installed by legislation and corporate agreement in other countries, for everywhere the once-revolutionary demands summarized in the 'Communist Manifesto' of 1848 have gradually been absorbed into daily practice and often carried further.

Thus the fears of the older capitalist establishment have proved unfounded: the welfare provisions, the pensions, insurance against illness, accident, unemployment, higher incomes, and a larger share of mass production—all these once-revolutionary demands have in fact stabilized the power system, not overthrown it. What is more, in the United States no less than in Soviet Russia or China, these accommodations have only served to bind the entire population to the official agencies of power. What did not in fact take place anywhere, not even in the earliest stage of the Russian Revolution, was fulfillment of the romantic fantasy of an 'instant revolution': a spontaneous transformation from which the New Man, the New Woman, the New Education, the New Community, the New World would suddenly appear: a bright flutter of liberated communist butterflies emerging from the ugly chrysalis of capitalism.

To account for many of the regressive phenomena we now witness, we must remember both the ironic fulfillment and the sordid collapse of the unbridled utopian hopes of the nineteenth century That dismal collective letdown was at an early moment symbolized in the transformation of the utopian dreamer, Barthélemy Enfantin—who had concocted a new socialist religion, with appropriate rituals, costumes, forms of address, all heralding the coming of a female Messiah who would divinely crown the new order—into a successful civil engineer engrossed in railroad building. The only visible female Messiah of the nineteenth century, Mrs. Mary Baker Eddy, did not somehow correspond to Enfantin's prescription.

That particular disillusionment was more comic than pathetic: but a similar loss of faith met, not merely avowed utopians like the Owenites, the Fourierites, the Hutterites, the many scattered kindred groups like the Mormons, but also, sadly, the masses of people who had rallied to socialism: for when the First World War broke out those who most eagerly supported the national military machine were the more revolutionary leaders of France and Germany. The old catchwords and slogans of both mechanical 'progress' and dictatorial 'revolution' are still repeated most vociferously at present among adolescents—under and over thirty—whose minds are so insulated from the past that they have learned nothing whatever from its mistakes, its frustrations, and its defeats. The price of imposing the ruthless will of an ideological minority upon a large population is massacre; and the ultimate victim of that massacre is the revolution itself.

As it happens, both romantic utopianism and revolutionary utopianism were expressed with singular clarity in the life and work of William Morris: all the better because the internal conflict between them was never fully resolved. His inherited fortune, derived from mining investments, enabled him to devote a large part of his life to the writing of poetry and the practice of the arts and crafts, whereby single-handed he renovated the practice of the handicrafts in block printing, stained glass, rug making, wallpaper design, and typography. The lesson of this example has still to be soberly appraised and applied to contemporary society—a society now debilitated by its lack of engrossing manual work, and its increasing resistance to active work of any kind.

Part of Morris' life was transfigured in his idyllic utopia, 'News from Nowhere,' written after he had been converted through his hatred of ugliness, poverty, and injustice to revolutionary Marxian socialism. Though Morris had come to value the machine as a reliever of physical drudgery, he never accepted—rather he vehemently detested—the power system itself, even though he felt that the changeover to a new society could not be achieved without physical violence.

But which picture has proved more realistic—the revolutionary transformation or the sweet bucolic idyll? Morris well knew that the England of the future he pictured in 'News from Nowhere' was a figment of his imagination, an embellishment of his personal experience as a householder at Kelmscott Manor. But was his dream actually more naïve than Nikolai Lenin's belief on the very eve of the Russian Revolution that money would be abolished, and that the State would, as Marx had confidently predicted, wither away and the dialectic process itself come to an end? Neither Marx nor Lenin seems to have had any anticipation that once the revolution succeeded, the old hierarchy of power would be re-established, with the elevation of a new privileged minority, and that the original features of the megamachine would be restored in the strict classic form already described. What official bureaucratic communism said in effect was: Do not fear the revolution! Nothing essential to the Power Complex will change!

Alongside these disastrous miscarriages, William Morris' revivalist dream had one sober virtue: he based it on human traits that are still active. The form in which his utopia was cast was archaic, and the life that it pictured was too free from tensions, frustrations, restrictions, and conflicts to be favorable to human creativity. In this idyllic mood Morris weakly ignored the lessons of his own tragic personal life. But Morris' 'News from Nowhere' was good news, for it indicated a return to the human center: the liquidation of the power complex and the institutional fixations which, since the Pyramid Age, have helped to cripple and abort human development.

In presenting this picture Morris exposed his disillusion, not merely with contemporary industrialism, but with the sort of revolutionary ideology that hoped to displace it. That disillusion has now spread to an ever larger portion of the population in Western countries; and it partly explains the inner disruption that has taken place among part of the younger generation. This disruption, if it does not abate, must eventually undermine all the prevalent power systems, whether reactionary, 'progressive,' or revolutionary.

4: NIHILIST REACTIONS

Without keeping in view the ideas and events I have all too briefly noted, one can hardly have any insight into the outward disturbances and inner disintegrations now visible everywhere. It is against this background that the disillusion, cynicism, and existential nihilism now visible must be gauged. It is the threatened annihilation of man by his favored technological and institutional automatisms that has in turn brought about an equally devastating counter-attack—an attack against civilization itself, and even against the basic order essential for organic continuity As in the disintegration of the Hellenistic power complex from the Fourth Century B.C. on, Chance has become the ruling deity and Chaos the new Heaven.

Yet the results we see today were not unanticipated during the nineteenth century by those who were sufficiently alert. "I could smile," wrote John Ruskin, "when I hear the hopeful exultation of many, at the new reach of worldly science and vigor of worldly effort; as if we were again at the beginning of new days. There is thunder on the horizon as well as dawn." Delacroix saw in the new agricultural machinery on exhibition at Paris the terrible engines of future wars, as the tractor, in the form of the military tank, actually turned out to be; while Tennyson foresaw 'airy navies' raining death down from the heavens. The sensitive intuitions of poets and painters had a closer grip upon the coming realities than the supposedly shrewd pragmatic calculations of engineers, scientists, soldiers, statesmen. Had the subjective life itself not been eviscerated and mummified in the churches, schools, and universities of the Western World, the collective reaction to this unbalanced technological scheme might have come more promptly, and taken a more rational course.

What has been happening so swiftly during the last half century was anticipated at a much earlier moment by Dostoevsky in 'The Possessed,' in 'Crime and Punishment,' in his scarifyingly prophetic 'Letters from the Underworld.' In that latter story, in the person of a snivelling Beatnik narrator, a prototype, almost a pre-incarnation, of Hitler, he predicted that the whole organization of modern society, with its laws, its conventions of respectability, its technological progress, would be "kicked to smithereens" some fine day, so that life would be lived again "according to our own stupid whims"——on the same defiantly irresponsible terms that proliferating groups of Beatniks and Hippies have recently been trying to live them.

In this apotheosis of destruction, Dostoevsky went beyond even the nihilism of the Nihilists, which Turgenev had portrayed in 'Fathers and Sons.' In that novel, more than a century ago, Turgenev had exposed the generation gap of his day: almost an exact parallel to our own. As a philosophical nihilist his anti-hero, Bazarov, will have nothing to do with the traditional values of society. Not merely does he reject the institutions of State and Church: he rejects equally the hypocritic liberalism of his father's generation, with its ambivalent but anxious efforts to improve the lives of their fellow-men without essentially altering their own self-indulgent routines. So sweeping was this nihilist rejection that Bazarov likewise contemptuously cast the poet and the artist out of his ideal society. He was ready, he said, to trade them all for good chemists.

But note: despite Bazarov's readiness to destroy the entire social structure and begin anew, he nevertheless retained an undiminished faith in the orthodox post-seventeenth-century absolute: science and technology. He lacked any sense that his own scientific rationalism might be quite as questionable, quite as vulnerable to searching criticism, as the more hoary dogmas he rejected. What he did not allow for was that if the funded heritage of human values and purposes was destroyed, the values of the scientific order might dissolve, too—or even worse, become the ready instrument for terrible aberrations that had hitherto been under partial moral control. Again, it was Dostoevsky's Raskolnikov, who murders an old woman so as to experience a fresh sensation, who foretold the juvenile and adult delinquencies of our time.

These delinquencies have now been consolidated and re-enforced by the conscious cult of anti-life. The heroes of this cult, from the Marquis de Sade to Céline and Jean Genet, have elevated sadism, perversion, pornography, madness, and self-destruction into the ultimate expressions of both life and art. On their negative scale of values, there is no moral limit to the forces of anti-life. Thus in practical effect this cult gives countenance to the infamous military plans now in readiness for total extermination.

Already the climactic triumph of the cult of anti-life has taken place: the perfect incarnation in outwardly human form of two creatures that have descended, not just to a sub-human but to a sub-animal level. The primal Adam and Eve of this cult are the male and female in England who not merely tortured two little children to death, but with admirable technocratic foresight made a tape recording of their agonized pleas and cries for their future enjoyment. Only one final act of this diabolic ritual was left to some future apostle of the cult: the instant refrigeration of their victims' remains for future enjoyment at private cannibal feasts. There is no principle in the cult of anti-life that would counsel stopping short before this final delight. In a hundred avant-garde theaters all over the world, the scenario for this ugly ritual has already been written—yes, and partly enacted.

What Bazarov's comparatively humane nihilists only began, the savage nihilists of our own day are attempting to carry to its conclusion: an insensate attack against life itself, and all those organized creations of the mind, old and new, that preserve and explore, encourage and enhance man's creative potentialities.

Though these regressive reactions have been taking place with increasing frequency, and in many different guises, all over the world, they do not seem as yet to convey any message to the bland prophets of megatechnics, still less to disturb them. Neither have these negative reactions—nor the positive ones I shall dwell on later—indicated to them the need to make at least a theoretic allowance for a possible reversal of the trend toward total technological control that the spokesmen for the power system assume is the final destiny of human society. While the dominant minority often displays marvellously liberated imaginations in the abstract mathematical-technical sphere, their style of thinking, when they approach the concrete, the organic, and the human, is singularly fettered.

As yet the technocratic elite cannot conceive that their own system is not a final one, or that an attack from the rear (the so-called avant-garde) on the entire human tradition is now taking place. Though they believe that change is a law of existence, they curiously believe that the power system itself is exempt from this process.

5: SYMPTOMS OF REGRESSION

Ever since Emile Durkheim opened the discussion of 'anomie,' the awareness of alienation and self-destruction as a contemporary human problem has been growing. As with similar manifestations in other cultures—both Hellenistic and Roman society have left no little literary evidence—we confront a mass society whose typical interests, pursuits, and products do not provide a sufficiently meaningful life even for its most prosperous beneficiaries, still less of course for those who are exploited or, even worse, neglected.

What is more, the whole apparatus of life has become so complex and the processes of production, distribution, and consumption have become so specialized and subdivided, that the individual person loses confidence in his own unaided capacities: he is increasingly subject to commands he does not understand, at the mercy of forces over which he exercises no effective control, moving to a destination he has not chosen. Unlike the taboo-ridden savage, who is often childishly over-confident in the powers of his shaman or magician to control formidable natural forces, however inimical, the machine-conditioned individual feels lost and helpless as day by day he metaphorically punches his time-card, takes his place on the assembly line, and at the end draws a pay check that proves worthless for obtaining any of the genuine goods of life.

This lack of close personal involvement in the daily routine brings a general loss of contact with reality: instead of continuous interplay between the inner and the outer world, with constant feedback or readjustment and with stimulus to fresh creativity, only the outer world—and mainly the collectively organized outer world of the power system—exercises authority: even private dreams must be channeled through television, film, and disc, in order to become acceptable.

With this feeling of alienation goes the typical psychological problem of our time, characterized in classic terms by Erik Erikson as the 'Identity Crisis.' In a world of transitory family nurture, transitory human contacts, transitory jobs and places of residence, transitory sexual and family relations, the basic conditions for maintaining continuity and establishing personal equilibrium disappear. The individual suddenly awakens, as Tolstoi did in a famous crisis in his own life at Arzamas, to find himself in a strange, dark room, far from home, threatened by obscure hostile forces, unable to discover where he is or who he is, appalled by the prospect of a meaningless death at the end of a meaningless life.

In primitive cultures, before individuated minds and individual identities had been achieved, it was the *persona* of the tribe that necessarily established and maintained the identity of its members. Some of this early form of identification happily still survives in families and vocational groups, in neighborhoods, cities, and nations, though in all these places a homogenized mass culture associated with the continued spread of 'Megalopolis'—itself a disintegrated and unidentifiable urbanoid nonentity—threatens even these residual supports for the human ego.

The changes taking place in every kind of large collective organization, just because of the relentless dynamism of megatechnics, create still other identity crises. Though I am a born and bred New Yorker, familiar of old with every neighborhood in my city, so many changes in the physical habitat and the human population have taken place there in a brief twenty years that I can no longer recognize the city as my own or feel my identity as a New Yorker. Tolstoi felt that the strange dark room he had awakened in, far from home, was a coffin. As in the womb-dream of childhood, he felt himself floating in an oppressive nothingness. No better image could be found for the state of modern man. That collective coffin is now the envelope of our whole 'civilization': not only materialized but accurately symbolized in underground shelters and military control centers: the technocratic tomb of tombs.

In surrendering unconditionally to the power system, with its 'automation of automation,' modern man has forfeited some of the inner resources necessary to keep him alive: above all, animal faith in his own capacity to survive and to reproduce his kind, biologically, historically, and culturally. In the act of dismissing the past he has undermined his faith in the future; for it is only by their convergence in his present consciousness that he can preserve continuity through change and embrace change without forfeiting continuity. This and nothing less is the 'way of life.'

The psychiatrist Viktor Frankl, who survived the penultimate horror of a Nazi concentration camp, in accounting for the existential vacuum of our time, points out that if no instinct tells man what he has to do, "and no tradition tells him what he ought to do, soon he will not know what he wants to do." Empty affluence, empty idleness, empty excitement, empty sexuality are not the occasional vices or misfortunes of our machine-oriented society but its boasted final products. Once life is reduced to this state of helpless inertness, what good reason can be offered for keeping alive? At such a pass suicide could be pardoned, if not commended, as a last desperate assertion of autonomy.

We have to confront, then, a culture that is over-organized, over-mechanized, over-directed, over-predictable. In the course of playing the empty economic and social games that serve this automatic process, human beings become 'things' or 'counters' to be treated in the same fashion as any random sample of brute matter. As the system approaches perfection, the residual human components are further absorbed into the mechanism: so only non-life, which soon turns with its residual energies into a resentful negation of life, remains. The concrete manifestation of this process lies within everyone's experience: for the cult of anti-life—anti-order, anti-intelligence, anti-design—now dominates the arts.

Unless a response takes place sufficient to bring about a reconstitution of our dominant ideology, its institutional structures, and its ideal personalities, mere withdrawal, even on the scale achieved by Christianity in the fourth century, will not suffice. As in Herman Melville's 'Bartleby,' passive withdrawal can only result, collectively speaking, in death. Yet those who choose this course can say truly with Bartleby: "*I know where I am.*" Bartleby realized that a life-sentence as a copying clerk was in fact not life in any real sense at all. The rebellious unemployables today, who resent dull jobs, bureaucratized scholarship, or degrading military duties, are on the side of life. By making a sort of last-ditch attempt to restore their identity and their native life-plan, if only by defiantly growing long hair, or by rejecting the fashionable goods and pecuniary rewards offered to those who conform, they prove themselves more alive than those who merely try to 'make the best of it.'

Unfortunately, this negative reaction to the megamachine is partly conditioned by the very forces it reacts against, as in A.E.'s aphorism: "A man becomes the image of the thing he hates." Indeed, it already threatens to become a negative power system, equally arbitrary and absolute. So the increasingly violent current reactions show many of the same symptoms of pathological aggression and frantic dynamism that have marked the triumphs of megatechnics. What began as a counter-movement to the power complex has turned into deliberately defacing and debuilding, not only the power structure, but all organized structures, all objective criteria, all rational direction. In short, a cult of anti-life. By perhaps something more than a mere coincidence, if only as a startling example of Jung's hypothesis of synchronicity, this cult of anti-life has arisen at the same moment as the physicist's concept of anti-matter: a theoretic force that annihilates matter on contact.

To give even a summary account of these mass reactions, interactions, and transactions, which by now have spread over a large part of the planet, is probably beyond the scope of any single mind. But fortunately every aspect of the cult of anti-life has been symbolically recorded in the art of our time. If we confine our examination to these symbols, seeking to make not an esthetic appraisal but an assessment of their meaning, which is often radically different from the artist's own description, we shall have a better understanding of the political and technical irrationalities of our time— often so implacably rational in form, but, like nuclear genocide, desperately irrational in actual content and purpose.

6: THE CULT OF ANTI-LIFE

Until recently both the inner and outer disorders of megatechnic civilization were successfully covered by its massive constructive achievements. Despite two world-enveloping wars, despite the virtually total devastation of scores of big cities, the evidences of destruction have up to now been so speedily repaired that within half a generation they soon became invisible and almost forgotten, like a bad dream—even by eyewitnesses who had grievously suffered.

Outwardly this capacity to recover so swiftly from a series of shattering blows would seem to indicate a state of bounding social health. But the quick reappearance of solid structures and familiar routines, which momentarily quiet anxiety, has only contributed to further disintegration on an even greater scale, for it has delayed the public reaction to the swift, relentless expansion of the power complex, whose destructive potentialities increased in direct proportion to its technological inventiveness and financial profitability.

Now the place where such a collective disintegration is first recorded is in deeper levels of the mind. Yet any attempt to make a quantitative estimate of the deterioration that has taken place here by compiling current statistics of crime, mental illness, drug addiction, homicide and suicide, can give but a partial and superficial account of what is actually happening, even to the extent of roughly estimating its volume. Only one fact is clear: the area of violence and irrationality, both private and institutionalized, has steadily widened during the last half century. The fact that these imponderables cannot be weighed does not mean they have no weight.

Who can describe the massive collective impact of two world wars, with their orgies of hate, sadism, wanton extermination? Who shall appraise the damage already done by nuclear bombs, not only those actually dropped on Japan or exploded in military tests, but even more those bombs of greater violence that have been exploded in the mind, leading to legally sanctioned experiments in nuclear, bacterial, and chemical genocide, protected from critical attack by secrecy, systematic misinformation, and insolent official falsifications?

Yet the millions of inmates of asylums and prisons offer an insignificant threat to mankind compared with the official terrorists whose costly plans for total collective extermination are still lavishly subsidized by national governments and passively approved as a guarantee of stability and 'peace' by their citizens. These projects for extermination are not less morbid because they have materialized under precise official direction; nor are they less demented because they have broken out from the dream world and taken possession of scientific laboratories, military headquarters, and government offices.

None of these pathological data can be adequately handled in quantitative terms, except in gross estimates of the number of past or prospective victims incapacitated by illness, injury, or death. If we wish to examine the disintegrations and regressions that now threaten to undermine the existence of mankind, making mock of our genuine technological advances, we must rather interpret purely qualitative evidence, best drawn from the world of art; for it is first of all in the graphic and plastic arts, in literature, and in music that distant tremors of the psyche are faintly recorded, as on a seismograph, often a whole century before they become visible and tangible.

After the Russian nihilists the first definite indication of the present cult of anti-life came from the Italian futurists, headed by Marinetti, reacting passionately—and not without reason—against Italy's entombment under its ancient traditions, which turned its inhabitants into mere museum curators and guards. Characteristically, as with Turgenev's nihilist hero, this total rejection of the past was combined with a naïvely uncritical and over-enthusiastic response to technology, its power and dynamism, which Marinetti coupled with physical violence in every form: with "strife" and "aggressiveness," with war, militarism, incendiarism, with "the blow on the ear, the fisticuff," as if to combine the most primitive manifestations of power with the most sophisticated.

Symptomatically, his 'Futurist Manifesto' was not only a celebration of new mechanical potentialities but a paean to unrestrained violence in every form. Marinetti had already intuitively grasped the ultimate destination of the megamachine.

Marinetti's proclamation of 1909 served as the advance notice of the more than half century of war, fascism, barbarism, and extermination that actually followed. Admittedly, there was a positive side to this movement, as there is to megatechnics itself. Futurism was part of a general movement of thought between 1890 and 1915 which included Art Nouveau, and the subsequent manifestations of Cubism, all of which welcomed the machine as an active ingredient in modern culture and a new source of form.

For a while modern artists carried through consciously, with a kind of puritanic severity, a program that had already been embodied in the work of engineers like Rennie, Paxton, and Eiffel, and had been given earlier intellectual expression in the writings of Horatio Greenough and Louis Sullivan. This esthetic espousal of technics was in fact an effort to widen the range of human responses. If at times the artist might be tempted to exaggerate the functions of science and the 'machine,' or to assign value exclusively to their abstract derivatives, the general intention nevertheless was to raise the human potential.

Such positive responses to technics must not, let me emphasize, be confused with Marinetti's sentimental dynamism and violence; and still less with a whole series of assaults on historic culture, even in its most beneficent and vital forms, which began with Dadaism and has sunk into an ultimate pit of vacuous imbecility in Pop Art.

Anyone who examined the new images of Dadaism in the nineteen-twenties would have had a first glimpse of the world today. Beginning among the Dadaists with mock art, this movement would soon turn into anti-art, and before long become the underlayer of a more general cult of anti-life. If the observer had likewise noted the lavatory wall obscenities and chamber-pot sculpture of the early Dadaists, he would have been equally prepared for the characteristic hallmarks of 'avant-garde' infantilism. Not without irony, this movement, which began with a total rejection of the past, has been content to live within its own strictly limited segment of the past, that of the last half century. So it still clings pathetically to once 'advanced' experiments that have in fact become archaicisms and academicisms—already as moribund as those mediocre sentimental images which the more robust artists of the nineteenth century reacted against.

At first Dadaism with its sometimes imaginative surprises seemed only a hilarious mockery of the Establishment, deflating the pompous platitudes of 'patriotism,' 'glory,' and 'service' that had covered over the stubborn ineptitudes and insensate human sacrifices of the 1914 war: that war which no government had the intelligence to prevent, the moral courage to withdraw from, or the magnanimity to bring to an end until all sides were hopelessly exhausted. Like a loud fart in a polite salon, Dadaism called the attention of its contemporaries to the sordid human condition. Even before the fascist-communist dictatorships, before the economic depression of the thirties, before the Second World War, with its aerial genocide, before the Stalinist and Nazi extermination camps, these coming events were prefigured in the blasted landscapes and deformed images of the Dadaists and the Surrealists. From 1930 on, the inner world of art and the outer world of technics and government alternated in oscillations of mounting violence and compulsive destruction. With every fresh increment of megatechnic order and regimentation came a subjective counterblast of rejection and rebellion.

To give anything like a detailed description of this subjective deface-ment and destruction would require an encyclopedic volume in itself. So out of a vast welter of evidence I shall select a scattering of contemporary samples: mere reminders of a much huger mass of purposeful irrationality, paranoid inflation, cultivated idiocy, and mindless destruction. The order in which the evidence is presented is as random as the events.

Exhibit A. An orchestral concert, held in a hall where music is usually performed. The members of the orchestra take their seats. One of them begins to saw a violin in two. Others follow suit with axes. Loud noises, electronically produced, accompany this performance. In the end nothing is left. The audience that has tolerated these insults has allegedly participated in the 'new music,' while those who have indignantly left the hall have, by their justifiable anger or contempt, testified to the success of the anti-musicians.

Exhibit B. Performance of '4′33″,' composed by John Cage. A human dummy is seated at a piano on a concert-hall stage. For four minutes and thirty-three seconds no sound is made. The de-composition is finished.

Exhibit C. Explanation by a contemporary music critic. "When com-poser John Cage wrote '4′33″' he opened a door to the new music. This work . . . was first performed in 1952. The 'music' consisted of the coughs and creaks that arose from the audience during the 'performance.'

Thus Cage endowed unintentional noise with the status of intentionally produced music and broke the last connection with traditional definitions of musical structure. . . . Today, the composer considers the piece archaic because of its *pre-arranged,* or determinate length."

Exhibit D. A Happening. A group of women build a nest. A group of men erect a tower. Then each destroys the other's work. At the end, the actors surround an automobile covered with strawberry jam and lick it off. This performance takes place at an American university.

Exhibit E. Newspaper clipping reporting a new seminar at the University of Oregon (an educational institution): "The students in Morris Yarowsky's class destroyed everything they could get their hands on recently. It was part of a seminar on 'destruction as a process in art' in a visual semantics class. . . . One girl lathered herself with red soap and shaved off an eyebrow, and a man put a goldfish in a mixing bowl and poured some table salt into the bowl. A student stood on a chair and threw a cake at the ground, a sledgehammer was slammed into a television set and a man donned a crash helmet and jumped on clay sculpture."

Exhibit F. An assistant to the New York Administrator of Recreation and Cultural Affairs presides over a 'sculptural' happening. Two gravediggers, hired at union rates (fifty dollars a day) dig a 'grave' in Central Park. After a lunchtime break, they shovel the dirt back into the hole. Claes Oldenburg, the conceiver of this imbecile performance, is known for his 'happenings' and Pop Art, such as a huge plaster hamburger and a towering phallic lipstick. The city's consultant on sculpture with due solemnity supports his hoax. "Everything is art if it is chosen by the artist to be art."

Where is the irreverent laughter? Where the indignant demands that the municipal authorities involved apologize publicly for this insult to their citizens' intelligence and this misuse of public funds? Only respectful silence follows. These tedious monkeyshines have become the mass substitute for genuine esthetic creativity. Anti-art has become in fact the new Establishment, evoking glib encomiums from art critics, grave rationalization from art historians, favored exhibition space and effusive catalogs from 'important' museum directors. The reasons for this success should be obvious. Both non-art and anti-art meet the exact specifications of the Power Complex: unrestricted productivity, instant achievement, large profits, immense fashionable prestige, blatant self-advertisement. Under this banner regression and demoralization become authentic marks of 'progress.'

Psychiatrists, a generation ago, discovered that painting was one of the many manual crafts through which patients could work their way back to reality. Fashionable non-art and anti-art now perform precisely the opposite function: they are methods of inducing large numbers of educated people to loosen their already weak grip on reality and abandon themselves freely to addled subjectivity—or at least to express their current preference for 'going with' the forces of disintegration by joining the licensed madmen in their antics.

This cultural nihilism, which began as a reaction against regimentation, has become in turn a mode of counter-regimentation, with its ritualized destruction and its denial of all the cultural processes that have sublimated man's irrational impulses and released his constructive energies.

Historically speaking, the program for anti-art was given a classic formulation by Louis Aragon at the beginning of the nineteen-twenties, in his famous declaration of Dada.

"No more painters, no more writers, no more musicians,
no more sculptors, no more religious, no more republicans,
no more royalists, no more imperialists, no more anarchists,
no more socialists, no more bolsheviks, no more politicians,
no more proletarians, no more democrats, no more bourgeois,
no more aristocrats, no more armies, no more police, no more
fatherlands; enough of all these imbecilities: no more of
anything, nothing at all: NOTHING, NOTHING, NOTHING."

Only one thing was curiously lacking in this total denial: NO MORE DADA. Dada refused to obey its own original credo—"All true Dadas are anti-Dada." Just the opposite happened: Dada now claims to be All.

In every country today a large part of the population, literate or sub-literate, indoctrinated by the mass media, reinforced by the more fashion-able leaders in schools, colleges, and museums, accepts this madhouse 'art,' not only as a valid expression of our meaningless and purposeless life—as in one sense it actually is—but as the only acceptable existential approach to reality. Unfortunately, the effect of this publicity and indoctrination is to intensify the underlying irrationality of the power system, by eliminating every possible reminder of those cumulative human traditions which, energetically re-cultivated and renewed, are still needed to transform it.

The mark of authentic experience, accordingly, is the systematic elimi-nation of the good, the true, the beautiful, in both their past and their possible future forms. Along with this goes an aggressive attack on what-ever is healthy, balanced, sane, rational, disciplined, purposeful. In this world of inverted values, evil becomes the supreme good, and the capacity to make moral discriminations and personal choices, to inhibit destructive or murderous impulses, to pursue distant ends for humane purposes, becomes an offense against the rehabilitated God of lawlessness and disorder. An inverted moralism.

In all its modes, then, from sculptured junk to junkie fantasies, from the ear-shattering thump of rock music to the cagey emptiness of accidental noises trapped in a concert hall, from the studious vacancy of blank canvases to the confusions of drug-clouded minds, anti-art draws its financial and its technological resources from the very agencies it professedly defies. The means used by those who seek to 'drop out' from megatechnics demonstrate this close affiliation: heroin, lysergic acid, stroboscopic lights, electronic amplifiers, 'speed' in both its chemical and mechanical forms, are all tied to scientific discovery and profit motivation. The chronic users of marijuana have already prepared the ground for the extension of the cigarette industry into 'pot' manufacture, with even greater financial profits: according to report, the seductive wrappers and advertising slogans are already prepared. What seems like a withdrawal is only another form of active participation and submergence in the Power System. Ironically, even Hippie costumes have offered a new market for mass production.

What perhaps accounts for this eager espousal of anti-art is precisely the fact that it performs a dual but contradictory role. Professedly it is a revolt against our over-mechanized, over-regimented megatechnic culture. But as it turns out, it also serves anti-art equally to justify the power system's end products: it acclimates modern man to the habitat that megatechnics is bringing into existence: an environment degraded by garbage dumps, auto cemeteries, slag heaps, nuclear piles, superhighways and megastructured conglomerates—all destined to be architecturally homogenized in a planetary 'Megalopolis.'

By making the subjective annihilation threatened by the megamachine his own object, the anti-artist gains the illusion of overcoming that fate through an act of personal choice. In the course of seeming to defy the power complex and to negate its orderly routines, anti-art obediently accepts its programmed outcome.

Consider the meaning of junk sculpture. What the fabricators of this 'sculpture' are perhaps telling us is that, even after a nuclear holocaust, life at some abysmal sub-human level might go on, and that artists, foraging for materials in the ruins, might still be able to simulate, with the aid of rusted engines, cracked toilet bowls, twisted pipes and wires, broken crockery, disemboweled alarm clocks, something that, however wryly deformed, would still express a residue of the creative will. If this be indeed the unconscious motive that underlies anti-art, one can understand it and with severe reservations honor it as a prophetic warning against a future that must be circumvented.

In this light society owes a debt to the anti-art of our period; for it revealed, more than a generation before our scientific instruments of destruction had proliferated and escalated, the irrational promptings and the sterile goals that now characterize Western civilization. If the prophetic nature of this art had been widely understood, it might, taken in sufficiently diluted doses, have served as a timely inoculation to protect us against the disease that is now taking hold of the entire social organism.

7: ADDLED SUBJECTIVITY

Unfortunately, the anti-art of our day has not merely exposed the underlying irrationalities of our society, but it has re-enforced them, using popular media like the film and the television screen to provide magnified models for destructive collective fantasies: piling monster upon monster, horror upon horror, violence upon violence, and thereby obliterating in the mind even the bare animal faith in existence. In the past these psychotic impulses had repeatedly erupted among the ruling classes and been enacted in grisly rituals of torture and slaughter: the rest of the human race happily was tethered too close to the daily realities of working and eating, of mating and rearing the young, to be so completely cut off from reality.

Now that the binding ties of habit, custom, and moral code have been loosened, an increasing portion of the human race is going out of its mind. One has only to read the 'Black Manifesto,' published in 1969, to realize that an educated portion of the Negro population of the United States has surrendered—at least temporarily—to the same sort of fatal hallucinations as almost wiped out the Xosa people in Africa during the nineteenth century. Yet these fantasies are essentially no more insane than the statement publicly uttered by a United States Senator from Georgia, who did not flinch from the prospect of atomic genocide which would wipe out most of the human race, provided that an American Adam and Eve—of course white!—were left to repopulate the planet!

To account for the fact that the dementia has spread so rapidly, I must go back to a basic re-interpretation explicitly stated in Volume One of 'The Myth of the Machine.' This view was indirectly approached by other interpreters before sufficient data were available, notably by Alfred Russel Wallace. Wallace pointed out that man's overgrown brain, from the very point where *Homo sapiens* left his primate and hominid ancestors behind him, was far in excess of his needs for animal survival. For long this has been a threat to man's inner balance and further development. His ever-active mind, sensitively responding through *all* his organs to the environment, over-stimulated by his liberated (non-seasonal) sexual activities, has too often been at the mercy of his unconscious, since he has thrown off the genetic fixations and instinctual controls that restrict the behavior of other organisms. Before man had created a firm over-layer of culture, through ritual and language, he was dangerously open to the random, often destructive and suicidal promptings of his own unconscious. That danger still remains.

These subjective forces, erupting in dream images and motor impulses, too often proved hard to distinguish from the public objects of his waking consciousness: all the more when other members of the community suffered the same hallucinations. Apart from repeated setbacks and disasters, which must have eliminated those chronically incapable of distinguishing fantasy from fact, man seems to have been saved by a special trait, still visible in infants and children—a positive need for repeating experiences, accompanied by equally positive delight in repetitive bodily movements and vocal expressions. Thus habit and custom and ritual restored the order that man's excessive cerebral development, which divorced him from his instincts, had taken away.

From the beginning, if this hypothesis holds, the great problem for man was to utilize the magnificent creative potentialities of his large brain and complex sensorium without becoming dangerously unbalanced by the pre-rational, and often destructively irrational, impulses welling up from the depths of his being. Because primitive man's special gift for enjoying exact repetition lies at the bottom of human culture, man has been able to build up a firm inner structure of meaning and an orderly, internally consistent routine of life.

While habit and custom have notoriously tended to curb inventiveness and resist even beneficent change, they more than atoned for this by curbing the sub-human promptings of the unconscious. But so dangerously infantile are man's untutored and undisciplined impulses that even the most stable cultures have not been able to prevent life-threatening explosions of irrationality—'going berserk,' 'running amok,' practicing systematic torture and human sacrifice or, often with pseudo-rational religious support, embarking on the insensate slaughters and destructions of war.

These erratic manifestations of human nature have been widely recognized. From Homer and Sophocles down to Shakespeare and Dostoevsky poetic minds, at home with their own unconscious sources, were acutely aware of this chronic streak of madness, or at least a potentiality for madness, long before Freud. But mankind's ability to recover its balance after massive outbreaks of irrationality has in the past—and once again today—limited the effort to come more effectively to grips with his own nature. Many of his most menacing irrationalities have themselves been encysted in custom and piously regarded as part of an intelligible moral order: 'God's will.'

During the last three centuries this disturbing factor has been magnified rather than diminished. For the Power Complex has not merely deliberately disrupted salutary customs and undermined traditional moral values: what is even more serious, it has transferred all the stabilizing repetitive processes from the organism to the machine, leaving man himself more exposed than ever to his own disordered subjectivity. No longer does daily work and religious ritual demand that active participation which serves to incorporate the diverse ingredients needed for balance in the human psyche. As a result the unconscious has now resumed its early dominion over man. What is worse, the pre-human properties of the unconscious now command powerful technological resources they never before had at their disposal.

In a culture where only the machine embodies order and rationality, the 'liberation' of man does not mean an increase of choice: it means only the liberation of his unconscious, and his submission to demonic impulses and drives. By funnelling all order into the machine, man has cut himself off from those very repetitive acts and rituals which so long proved useful in maintaining some degree of internal balance, some prospect of creativity. The order that was once embodied in the patterns of culture and the structure of the human personality, has been sacrificed to mere technological achievement. And by now it should be clear that there is no technological solution for this perilous state. Only if a sufficiently passionate human reaction takes place will it be possible to reverse this process and give back to the depleted human organism the autonomous functions, orderly processes, and cooperative associations it has almost relinquished.

Here Dr. C. G. Jung, in his 'Memories, Dreams, Reflections,' has given valuable personal testimony. There was a moment in his working on the role of fantasies when, he confessed, he found it absolutely essential to have a "point of support in 'this world,' " lest the unconscious should drive him out of his wits. The fact that he had a medical diploma at a Swiss university, that he had an obligation to his patients and had a family and five children to support, that he lived in an identifiable house in an identifiable place—"these were actualities which made demands upon me and proved again and again that I really existed, that I was not a blank page whirling about in the winds of the spirit."

This hold upon solid realities and daily continuities is exactly what our present over-heated technology, in which every plausible technological fantasy is at once translated into saleable hardware, patently lacks. A culture that boasts of its uncontrollable dynamism is in a state of nightmarish disintegration, and before mankind throws off that nightmare the very bed in which one sleeps, the earth itself, may disappear, like any other disposable container. Thus the basic conditions for mental stability—accepted criteria of values, accepted norms of conduct, recognizable faces, buildings, landmarks, recurrent vocational duties and rituals—are constantly being undermined; and as a result our whole power-driven civilization is turning into a blank page, torn to shreds from within by psychotic violence.

This analysis exposes the superficiality of the panicky remedies now being offered for overcoming our present social disintegration and regression. The kind of mental aberration I have exposed via the products of anti-art has been matched and magnified in an increasing number of individuals and groups both inside and outside mental hospitals. But that cannot be corrected by any of the institutional means at our disposal. This state is too universal to be treated in sanitoria, even if many more were to be built; nor can the victims be handled through 'group therapy' or by increasing the number of psychiatrists and physicians; for the pathological conditions that affect the patients are equally discernible in many of those who have been certified as professionally competent to advise or treat them.

What is involved if the human race is not to lose its grip on reality entirely is something like a profound and ultimately planet-wide re-orientation of modern culture, above all the formidable recent culture of 'civilized' man. My 'Transformations of Man' attempts to outline the historic setting for such a change.

8: THE OPTIMISM OF PATHOLOGY

As physicians have learned from the study of the body, a disease often indicates, not a permanent deterioration, but an attempt to restore an equilibrium that has been disturbed, and to recover natural functions that have been thwarted or suppressed. Without some overt manifestation of pathological symptoms, permanent damage might result before the disease could be detected and adequate measures taken to overcome it.

Admittedly this reaction has been slow; and it is too early to give, from present signs, an altogether favorable prognosis: for some of the proffered alternatives have the same lack of human dimensions as the system they seek to replace. Still, it is significant that an underlying anxiety about the course of mechanical 'progress' has long been present, even among those who have regarded themselves as active prophets of the new technical order.

As early as 1909 H. G. Wells wrote in an article in 'The New World': "Perhaps, after all, the twentieth century isn't going restlessly onward, we are going to have a setback to learn again, under simpler conditions, some of these necessary fundamental lessons our race has learnt as yet insufficiently well—honesty and brotherhood, social collectivism, and the need for some common peace-preserving council for the whole world." That was written by the same but different Wells who earlier in the decade had written his optimistic 'Anticipation of the Effects of Mechanical Progress.'

The most palpable evidence of an awakening is that of the student movement; and what is most significant about it is the fact that it is worldwide, and that the immediate motives, grievances, and proposals are so diverse that the underlying reasons for its existence must be common to all countries, no matter how different their traditions or their immediate problems. Though this conjecture is not open to positive proof, I suggest that the only characteristic that is actually so universal, and that embraces so wide a span of differences, is the Power System itself, in its present technologically expansive and compulsive form. In short, this is nothing less than a revolt against a power-centered 'civilization.' That revolt had long been overdue: something like five thousand years overdue.

Beneath this revolt is a deep and, as one need hardly emphasize, a well-justified fear: that the next step in technological progress may bring about the annihilation of man. With good reason the young regard the atrocious methods used in conducting American military operations in Vietnam not only as a threat against their own existence but as an ominous prelude to the whole human future. If the post-nuclear generation rejects the past, it is perhaps because its members believe that the future has already rejected them: hence only the existential 'Now' is real.

Paradoxically, it required the advanced instruments of technology to bring about this realization and to make the revolt itself spread so swiftly, and with such methodical uniformity. It is the very generation that came into the world after the modernized, nuclear-powered megamachine had been put together—the generation many of whose immediate predecessors were passive, cowed, silent—that has suddenly awakened with a loud cry of horror and dismay. And that horror and dismay are justified: likewise the fury with which the young are attacking the combination of forces that have undermined their future.

Yes: at least the youth of our time have awakened. They are in the shocked state of Young Goodman Brown in Hawthorne's fable: they realize that their elders have participated, despite their sanctimonious avowals, in the obscene rites of a Witches' Sabbath—terminating in a series of collective blood sacrifices, those same irrational sacrifices that have monotonously punctuated the annals of human history and have desecrated man's highest achievements.

More alert in their responses than the older generation to what is going on before their eyes, an active minority among the young are behaving as if a nuclear catastrophe had already in fact occurred. In their minds they are now living among the ruins, without any permanent shelter, without any regular supply of food, without any customs or habits except those they improvise from day to day, without books, without academic credentials, without any fixed vocation or career, without any source of knowledge except the inexperience of their own peers. Unfortunately, the revolt is not merely against their elders: it has become, in fact, a revolt against all historic culture—not merely against an over-powered technology and an over-specialized, misapplied intelligence, but against any higher manifestations of the mind.

In their unconscious, the young are living in a post-catastrophic world; and their conduct would be rational in terms of that world. Only by massing together and touching each other's bodies do they have any sense of security and continuity. So, many of them escape to the open country, form temporary pads, communes, and encampments, anesthetize themselves to cold, rain, mud, hardship, repulsive sanitary conditions, accept poverty and deprivation. But, in compensation, they recover an elemental animal faith, perform acts of mutual aid, hospitality, and love, share freely whatever food or drink they can get hold of, and get pleasure simply out of each other's physical presence—and out of the reduction of life to the most elemental bodily exercises and expressions.

Since the ruins are still imaginary, these would-be dropouts draw upon the very order they reject. They journey long distances by motor car in tens of thousands to their collective 'rock' festivals, actively magnifying their egos by participating in radio and television happenings, and deliberately obliterate consciousness with drugs and druglike music electrically amplified. And so, despite their gestures of revolt against the established goods of civilization, the young are in fact addicted to its most decadent mass products. This is a purely megatechnic primitivism. By reducing their world to a series of addled happenings, they invite the ultimate Happening against which they supposedly protest.

This, fortunately, is only part of the picture. At the moment of composing this passage I received a form letter addressed by three young students to some two hundred intellectuals whose help they sought to enlist. These students, starting where their elders left off, have identified the typical megatechnic insanities of the present age with those of the ancient power complex; and they hopefully proposed a meeting with their elders and mentors to formulate a more active, unified opposition. But the most important meeting was that which had already brought them together: for it took place in a course on 'The Irrational Man.' There they had studied the ultimate Enemy: not our predatory animal ancestry but a more elusive enemy in the human soul; the blind Will-to-Power, that eyeless monster which must be hauled to the surface of consciousness before man can bring all his other spiritual and cultural resources to bear on it. That task plainly takes precedence over further technological improvements.

Unfortunately, as the youth revolt has widened, it has become plain that the ambivalences and contradictions of present-day civilization have, willy-nilly, entered into it. On one hand, vital proposals for dissociating the University from its commitments to the power system; for overcoming the bureaucratization of learning; for deflating the business economy of points and credits and purely formalistic degrees—the Ph.D. Octopus William James warned against; and on the positive side, for more active individual participation in the daily life of the community, in devotion to moral and social ends not in accord with the demands of the power complex. (That change was advocated by Patrick Geddes, more than half a century ago, under the rubric of the University Militant.) Under this new regime, if followed to its conclusion, the University would no longer be restricted to the detached pursuit of higher learning, divorced from art, politics, and religion, but would apply all its special resources for intellectual coöperation to revitalizing the whole life of the community.

But on the other hand, the Power Complex has left its mark on the method of revolt, and has deformed the ideal aims of the student movement: witness the physical occupation of buildings, the manhandling of responsible university officers, the presentation of rigid 'non-negotiable' demands, backed by guns and threats of more extensive violence, the resegregation of racial minorities, to say nothing of the sponsoring of reactionary ideological and social fashions (McLuhanism, Black Power, witchcraft, compulsive pornography, sexual exhibitionism, stoning, drug-taking). This is only the reverse image of the Pentagon of Power. As for the open attempt in some quarters to destroy the University itself—what is this but an effort to destroy the authority of superior minds, by attacking the highest point in the hierarchy of education: one of the main repositories of human culture, as incarnated and personified and activated in living men and women.

The vital impulse the young have happily discovered in themselves is the facility for direct, immediate human association. Using that power at its lowest levels of neighborly feeling they were able to confront the system, challenge it, and break with it, if not to disestablish it. That confidence-breeding demonstration was more important than any concrete results that came from it. It proved the ability of the human spirit to take the initiative and to lay down the terms for its ultimate deliverance. This was a genuine liberation, and a permanently valuable one, for even though the immediate effort might be balked it gave spiritual support to similar acts of defiance and resistance on the part of many neighborhood groups and regional habitats that had hitherto seemed doomed to be swallowed up and annihilated by the inexorable spread of Megalopolis. In a score of different forms this spirit is now making itself felt.

The revolt of the younger generation is only the most recent and most conspicuous of the assaults upon the power complex: but similar challenges have long been in existence, attacking alike archaic and modern structures. Both the nationalist and the regionalist movements, as I pointed out in 'Technics and Civilization,' are necessary counter-efforts to re-establish cultural identities and autonomies, restoring literatures and languages that had been neglected, or virtually wiped out; and these movements, far from diminishing, have gained strength during the last half century with the re-establishment of Gaelic and Hebrew as national languages, to say nothing of similar challenges and rehabilitations among the Norwegians, the Bretons, the Welsh, the Basques, the Czechs, the Catalonians. Yet nowhere is this more in evidence than in the racial revolts in Africa and Asia, where it has led to a reconquest of European colonial possessions by the peoples whose countries had been over-run and whose tribal or national traditions had been disrupted. In the realm of nature, the conservation movement has played a similar role, which is now entering a dynamic stage: not merely to preserve residual resources but to maintain ecological variety and regional integrity in every habitat of man.

The same kind of attack upon the one-sided universalism of mega-technics and upon political governments irresponsive to the needs and claims of reciprocal intercourse has now taken place in what seemed an unassailable stronghold: the Roman Catholic Church. The sudden weakening of Catholic orthodoxy and strict hierarchical control, which had become more dogmatic, more authoritative, more self-confident under rationalist attacks during the nineteenth century, even to the point of asserting the infallibility of the Pope in questions of dogma and morals, is significant. Is it not another proof of the deep dissatisfaction that the megamachine, even in its most etherialized form, had taken no account of and had done nothing to alleviate? The fact that this revolt has taken place within the once anti-liberal Catholic Church, and even more surprisingly among the Bishops and within the monastic orders, indicates an intransigence quite as radical as that of the student movement. Even more effective than an organized physical assault upon the power structure are these scattered acts of detachment and withdrawal: preludes to renewal and replenishment.

There are many signs, both on the surface and beneath it, that a similar reaction more or less spontaneous has been taking place at many points. But now the forces challenging the power complex have a special advantage that derives from the advances of technology: its members, however separated in space, are united in time by a network of communication systems, and however separated in time, are united in space through books, discs, taped records, and frequent, quickly arranged face-to-face meetings. Hence resistance to the megamachine is no longer pathetically sporadic, but increasingly coordinated through constant inter-viewing as well as inter-communication.

As the network of Roman roads, with itineraries, meant for official use, helped Paul to unify the doctrines and practices of Christian congregations, so the electronic communication and record systems, even when operating mainly under centralized control, have given confidence and mutual support to otherwise isolated and seemingly lonely groups. Witness the way in which even the fundamentally dissolute Hippie movement has spread, through mimeographed 'underground' papers, teletape records, and personal television appearances, throughout the world, even behind the Iron Curtain, without any extraneous organization. These amorphous demonstrations have shown that the most solid megatechnic carapace is permeable. In widely scattered movements, then, the decentralization of power has already begun. The dismantling of the entire megamachine is plainly the order of the day.

Though these signs of an awakening to the actual condition of modern man have only lately become fully visible, they have actually been erupting in images, myths, and disordered forms of conduct, at first as enigmatic as a dream, for well over a century. Whatever Moby Dick may have meant in Melville's unconscious, whether the White Whale was God or Devil, Calvinist predestination or cartesian determinism, the body-denying Superego or the soul-denying Id, 'Moby Dick' the novel admirably symbolized that collocation of institutional and technological forces that were laming the spirit of man and threatening to deprive him of his rightful heritage as a full-bodied being, with all his organs intact, none withered or amputated. In Captain Ahab's blind anger, his relentless animosity, and his satanic pride, Melville was expressing the common spirit of desperate Nihilist defiance, ready to destroy the world itself if necessary in order to vindicate the tortured spirit of man.

In Ahab and in his beatnik, quasi-criminal prototype, Jackson (in 'Redburn'), Melville gave expression both to the megatechnic 'Khans' of the global Pentagon and to the counter-forces they had brought into being. And the fact that Ahab's torment and hatred had gone so far that he had lost control of himself and, through his own mad reliance upon power, had become dominated completely by the creature that had disabled him, only makes Melville's story a central parable in the interpretation of modern man's destiny. In Ahab's throwing away compass and sextant at the height of the chase, Melville even anticipated the casting out of the orderly instruments of intelligence, so characteristic of the counter-culture and anti-life happenings of today. Similarly, by his maniacal concentration, Ahab rejects the inner change that might have saved the ship and the crew, when he turns a deaf ear to the pleas of love uttered by sober Starbuck in words and by Pip, a fright-shocked child and an African primitive, in dumb gesture.

Outwardly mankind is still committed to the grim chase Melville described, lured by the adventure, the prospect of oil and whalebone, the promptings of pride, and above all by a love-rejecting pursuit of power. But it has also begun consciously to face the prospect of total annihilation, which may be brought about by the captains who now have command of the ship.

Against that senseless fate every act of rebellion, every exhibition of group defiance, every assertion of the will-to-live, every display of autonomy and self-direction, at however primitive a level, diminishes the headway of the doom-threatened ship and delays the fatal moment when the White Whale will shatter its planks and drown the crew. All the infantile, criminal, and imbecile manifestations in the arts today, everything that now expresses only murderous hatred and alienation, might still find justification if they performed their only conceivable rational function—that of awakening modern man sufficiently to his actual plight, so that he seizes the wheel and, guided by the stars, heads the ship to a friendlier shore.

CHAPTER FOURTEEN

The New Organum

1: PLANTS, MAMMALS, AND MAN

In the opening pages of this book we followed the two parallel paths of exploration that beckoned modern man: the exploration of the earth, hitherto never encompassed as a whole, and the exploration of the skies, and of all the physical phenomena, cosmic and earthbound, that could be interpreted and controlled without direct reference to man's own biological and cultural antecedents. We saw how the period of exploration and colonization gave the primal vitalities of Western man fresh outlets, at the very moment that the new mechanical order began to curb and contain them more completely than ever.

I propose here to emphasize, not only the heavy debt that modern technology has owed from the very start to terrestrial exploration, but how this exploration in turn laid the basis for a change that is only now beginning to pass from the initial phase of ideation, incarnation, and rational formulation into one widely organizing and incorporating a new mode of life, radically different from that of the power system. The human insufficiency of that system has grown in direct proportion with its technical efficiency, while its present threat to all organic life on this planet turns out to be the ultimate irony of its unqualified successes in mastering all the forces of nature—except those demonic and irrational forces within man which have unbalanced the technological mind.

Terrestrial exploration, plainly, began a gigantic revolution which was both a quantitative and a qualitative one. It established contacts between the entire population of the planet, and brought about an increase in energy resources and a circulation of goods, plants, peoples, and ideas on a global basis, breaking down adaptations, like that of the Negroid races to tropical Africa, that had taken hundreds of thousands of years to effect. The transplantation of the Negro from the continent to which he had so completely adapted himself, and the reverse transplantation of the European to the Americas and to Africa, were only the first of a series of wanton displacements in which the profit and convenience of the governing groups outstripped both biological knowledge and social prudence. Never was the ecological balance of nature, and even more the integrity of cultures, so violently upset as during the last two centuries.

By now this exploration has reached a natural terminus: the last frontier is closed. The landing of the first two astronauts on the moon was not the beginning of a new age of cosmic exploration but the end. The scientific technological revolution that began in the sixteenth century therewith reached its appropriately sterile terminus: a satellite as uninhabitable as the earth itself will all too soon become—unless by a massive expenditure of imagination and courageous political effort the peoples of the world challenge the age-old power complex. Without a counter-movement to slow down or reverse these automatic processes mankind comes closer, year by year, to what is in more than one sense a dead end.

Though the effect of the terrestrial exploration in offsetting the constraints of technical invention and organization was only temporary, it actually laid the foundations for a new world order: one which would alter the original mechanical world picture by superimposing upon it a more complex model derived, not from matter and energy in their preorganic states, but from the living organism. The geographic frontier is now closed, but a less superficial exploration is taking place. This is an exploration in time as well as space, and into subjective as well as objective phenomena. This new exploration deals not with cause-and-effect alone, but with patterns of almost inextricable and indescribable complexity, flowing through time and constantly interacting. In one field after another this organic world picture is already unfolding. In his Introduction to Darwin's 'Origin of Species,' George Gaylord Simpson points to this approaching transformation. "The astronomical and physical revolutions were already well advanced in the early nineteenth century," he noted, "but the biological revolution, destined to change the world even more profoundly, was still to come."

Unfortunately this biological revolution has already been recognized and eagerly hailed by the exponents of the power system as the next step in one-sided technocratic control. Carried out on their own peculiar terms this revolution would lead, not to a fuller development of man but to his progress into a quite different kind of organism, or series of organisms, genetically transformed in the laboratory or modified in an artificial womb. Man in any recognizable historic sense would be thrown on the scrapheap. This series of changes would give to the Power System, itself a segregated,

time-abbreviated product of human intelligence, an authority that man, by
the virtue of his own constitution, has always declined to give to Nature.
To what rational end?

On this matter, a poet of our day has spoken wise and timely words: an
admonition that might be specially directed to the priests of the megamachine, now sharpening their nano-needles, so to say, in preparation for
permanently altering the nature of man.

"Re-shaping life!" exclaimed Boris Pasternak in 'Dr. Zhivago.' "People
who can say that have never understood a thing about life—they have
never felt its breath, its heartbeat—however much they have seen or done.
They look on it as a lump of raw material that needs to be processed by
them, to be ennobled by their touch. But life is never a material, a substance to be molded. If you want to know, life is the principle of self-
renewal, it is constantly renewing and remaking and changing and trans-
figuring itself."

Happily for early man's development, his own mind seems to have
made an even greater impression on him than the physical environment;
and even in that environment he was more aware of the edibility of plants
and the activities of birds and animals than he was of purely physical
manifestations of nature, except when they occurred violently, as in storms,
floods, and volcanic eruptions. Nature itself spoke to him as an animate
being: in exhibiting malice or friendliness, stones might be lifelike, but
organisms were not petrified. Even after neolithic grinding and polishing
had introduced people to regular industry the improved environment was
mainly one belonging to living organisms, though copiously invaded by
gods, demons, and sprites more lively than man dared yet to be.

Although systematic industry and enforced drudgery had been introduced by the early civilizations, the greater part of the human race largely
escaped complete subservience to the power system. Under the prevailing
hunting and agricultural economies, a good part of mankind remained
dispersed in villages outside the province of the megamachine, never rising
to the heights it achieved in re-shaping the habitat or enlarging the mind,
yet never sinking to its depths, except when under the calamitous external
pressures of 'civilized' war.

Until our own day human culture as a whole developed in an organic,
subjectively modified environment, not in a sterile machine-made enclo-
sure. In a confused unfocussed way, the criteria of life prevailed everywhere and man's own existence prospered or failed in so far as a balance
favorable to life was preserved among all organisms. It is only in the worst
degradation of ancient slavery—namely, in the working of underground
mines—that human existence has been conceived as possible in an environment devoid of life.

Man lived in active partnership with plants and animals for whole geological periods before he fabricated machines. His mental involvement with the world of life began with the consciousness of his own existence. Many of his basic qualities he shares with other animals: prolonged sexual pairing and nurturing the young, social companionship and erotic delight, playfulness and joy. His deep love of life was fostered by finding himself in an environment prepared, not merely to maintain life with the requisite amount of physical nourishment, but to promote its unceasing self-transformation. On these matters, even the simplest organisms have something essential to teach us beyond the range of our most sophisticated technology. If we were dependent for our instructions and our material sustenance upon machines alone, the human race would long ago have died of malnutrition, boredom, and hopeless despair.

Remember Loren Eiseley's observation in 'The Immense Journey' about that turning point in organic development when the Age of Reptiles gave way to the Age of Mammals, those warm-blooded beasts that suckled their young. He pointed out that the Age of Mammals was accompanied by an explosion of flowers; and that the reproductive system of the angiosperms was responsible, not only for covering the whole earth with a green carpet composed of many different species of grass (over four thousand) but for intensifying vital activity of every kind; since their nectars and pollens and seeds and fruits and succulent leaves dilated the senses, quickened the appetite, exhilarated the mind, and immensely increased the total food supply.

Not merely was this explosion of flowers a cunning device of reproduction, but the flowers themselves assumed a variety of forms and colors that in most cases cannot possibly be accounted for as having survival value in the struggle for existence. It may add to the attraction of a lily to have all its sexual organs displayed among teasingly open petals; but the huge success of so many compositae, like the daisy and the goldenrod, with their insignificant florets, shows that biological prosperity might have been purchased without any such floral richness and inventiveness.

Efflorescence is an archetypal example of nature's untrammeled creativity; and the fact that floral beauty cannot be explained or justified on purely utilitarian grounds is precisely what makes this explosion so wonderful—and so typical of other life-processes. Biological creativity and the esthetic creativity that so often accompanies it exist for their own sake and transcend the organism's earlier limitations. If survival were all that mattered, life might have remained in the primal ooze or crept no further upward than the lichens. Though one may abstractly conceive a world with neither colors nor any richness of living structures, that muted world is not the actual world of life.

Long before man himself became conscious of beauty and desirous of cultivating it, beauty existed in an endless variety of forms in the flowering plants; and man's own nature was progressively altered, with his increasing sensitiveness to sight and touch and odor, through his further symbolic expression of beautiful form in his ornaments, his cosmetics, his costume, his painted and graven images: all by-products of his enriched social and sexual life. In this sense, we are all 'flower children.'

For at least twelve thousand years, possibly far longer, man's existence has depended upon the close symbiotic partnership between man and plants, rooted in thousands of small village communities spread over the entire earth. All the higher achievements of civilization have rested on this partnership, one devoted to the constructive improvement of the habitat and the loving and knowing care of plants: their selection, their nurture, their breeding, their enjoyment, in a routine of life that punctuated and heightened the delights of human sexuality. That culture, as Edgar Anderson has suggested, made some of its best discoveries in plant breeding by being equally concerned with the color, the odor, the taste, the flower and leaf pattern, and the nutritive qualities of plants—valuing them not only for food and medicine but for esthetic delight.

In our machine-dominated world, there are plenty of people working in scientific laboratories today who, though they may still call themselves biologists, have no intimate contact with this organic culture and no respect for its achievements. They have already begun to regulate the creative process in accordance with the market demands of the power complex. One of the latest triumphs in plant breeding, for example, has been to develop a variety of tomato which not merely grows to uniform size but ripens in quantity at the same time, in order that the crop may be garnered by an automatic picking and packing machine.

From such preconceptions flow further dreams of an even more tightly ordered world from which all more primitive or non-profitable species and varieties will be eliminated—even though primitive stocks remain essential for creative hybridization. Perhaps only the residual wildness left in man himself, still stirring in his dream life, will now save him from submission to such deadly conformity.

Admittedly, in the earlier stages of human development the relation between man and plants had been a one-sided one, not an effective relation of mutual aid. Though plants, birds, and insects have been man's active partners as well as his chief food for most of his history, he did little at first to modify the natural vegetation, still less to assist in the cultivation of favored plants. Man's attachment to the existing plant life was parasitic rather than symbiotic. But first by preservation and selection, and then by active cultivation, man found himself able, when the last glacial period ended, to make his own environment more habitable, more edible, and— what was no less important—more stimulating and lovable. In the very act of establishing a new role for plants, man both deepened his roots in the landscape and gave himself a new leisure and a new security. It was in the garden that man, thanks largely to woman's efforts, found himself completely at home: at peace, if only fleetingly and precariously, with the world around him.

The prolonged tending of plants began with the fruit and nut trees, the mango and the durian, the olive and walnut and palm, the orange, and not least, if Henry Bailey Stevens prove right, the apple. Here in orchard and garden, a world in which life prospered without inordinate effort or systematic carnage, man had his first glimpse perhaps of paradise, for paradise is only the original Persian name for a walled garden.

Significantly, it was in another garden, according to fable, the Garden of Eden, that man, by eating an apple, lost the innocence of animals and gained the consciousness of good and evil, of life and death. All those selective discriminations that aim to promote life and to reduce or countermand the forces that would diminish it must be alert to the presence of evil in its many forms, from fixation to wanton violence and destruction. Though Walt Whitman might, in 'Song of Myself,' praise the innocence of animals, he was sufficiently aware of the realities of human existence to proclaim that he was the poet of evil as well as the poet of good—and he knew the difference.

The capacity for growth, exuberant expression, and transcendence, symbolized esthetically as well as sexually by the flowering plants—this is the primal gift of life; and in man it flourishes best when living creatures and equally living symbols are constantly present, to stir his imagination and encourage him in further acts of expression both in the mind and in his daily performances of life-sustaining work and human nurture. Love begets love as life begets life; and eventually every part of the environment should be open to this response even if, under the command of love, one sometimes serves it best by withdrawing and allowing it, like a redwood forest or an ancient monument, to remain itself, simply mirrored in man's mind, without more than the faintest sign of man's own presence. A day without such contacts and emotional stirrings—responses to the perfume of a flower or an herb, to the flight or the song of a bird, to the flash of a human smile or the warm touch of a human hand—that is, a day such as millions spend in factories, in offices, on the highway, is a day empty of organic contents and human rewards.

There are no mechanical or electronic or chemical substitutes for whole living organisms, though one may have frequent need for symbolic enlargements and re-enforcements of actual experience. To be condemned for any length of time to a devitalized megalopolitan habitat, in which human beings are isolated not merely from each other but from all other organisms, and may even be forbidden by housing regulations to keep a dog or a cat for company, is to unlearn and discard all the lessons learned in

cooperation by living organisms during some three billion years on earth—
and by man, especially, during the last hundred thousand years. "We live
by helping one another," a soldier in combat wrote. This applies to all
creatures at all times; and it holds not only for survival but for further
human development.

For man to restrict his social activities and his personal fulfillments
solely to those that conform to external megatechnic requirements would
be a form of collective suicide: and that suicide—or more accurately
biocide—is in fact taking place before our eyes. Our elaborate mechanical
equipment may be a useful supplement to organic existence: but it is
not, except in grave emergencies—as with a mechanical kidney—an
acceptable permanent alternative. It is from the organic world in its entirety,
not merely from a swollen fragment of man's mind, his technique for
handling abstract symbols, that the materials for further development are
to be drawn. Once the new organic world picture becomes intelligible and
acceptable, the ancient 'myth of the machine,' from which our compulsive
technocratic errors and misdirections are largely derived, will no longer
keep its grip on modern man.

2: THE ORGANIC WORLD PICTURE

At the risk of carrying a valid Egyptian analogy too far, let me point out
that the return of the Sun God was accompanied figuratively by the resurrection of Osiris, the god of vegetation, he who taught man the arts and
crafts, and who in his own person, unlike the Sun God, went like men
through the experience of birth and death. As the practices of the megamachine became more embedded in Egyptian society—and here again we
anticipate a modern parallel—the cult of Osiris transferred attention from
life to an after-life, fastening on the drama of death and bending its efforts
toward the preservation of the body in mummified form, with magical
spells and prayers, all duly paid for according to rank and income. This
arrest turned the God of life, which includes death, into a God of death,
preparing for a mock life—a life devoid of its specific earthly characteristics: its fragility, its instability, its constant self-transformation, its potentialities for self-transcendence.

A similar miscarriage took place in the biological sciences, only faintly
visible in the sixteenth century, but now glaringly evident today. The great
step in putting biology on a scientific basis, comparable to that made by
Copernicus, was taken by Andreas Vesalius in his systematic description of

the human body, as disclosed by post-mortem dissection. Many vital truths were learned by this about the structure, the composition, and even the functional relations of the living organs; and in time this was further buttressed by microscopic and chemical examination of equally dead tissues. So eager were medical men for such knowledge that, when the law intervened, corpses were snatched from the grave for dissection. Vesalius himself was indeed so voracious for firsthand data, his biographer informs us, that he attended the drawing and quartering of a criminal so that he might snatch the heart, still palpitating, from the opened body, in order to perfect his description. In thought, accordingly, the corpse replaced the living organism, for it lent itself to more accurate objective description. What remained indescribable by this method was the dynamic, multifunctional living organism.

The realization that organic forms have produced a model for man's own development, immensely richer than any provided by the mechanical world picture, is itself perhaps the greatest gift that science has made: greater than any of the discoveries of physics from Archimedes to Newton and Einstein: though made possible, in part, by these discoveries. The delay in the development of the biological sciences—the study of organisms itself did not receive the name biology until 1813—was believed, by Auguste Comte and others, to be due to the fact that the sciences appeared in a logical order, beginning with the most abstract, 'preliminary sciences,' logic and mathematics, and going on through physics to chemistry, thence to biology, psychology, and sociology, increasing in complexity and richness with each ascent of the ladder. This scheme is neat logically and plausible; but history records that the biological knowledge needed for plant and animal domestication preceded astronomical measurement and the calendar which later served it; and the same holds true in medicine.

The fact is that organic models yielded to mechanical models in interpreting living phenomena mainly for two reasons: organisms could not be connected to the power complex until they were reduced, in thought even more than in practice, to purely mechanical units; and it was only through their attachment to the power system, which, as Comte noted, came in with the employment of the engineers as the key figures in advanced industries, that the physical sciences had, from the sixteenth century on, flourished.

One day a book will be written that will expose the contradictory workings of mechanism and vitalism as profound *religious influences* from the sixteenth century onward. This book will show that even while the mechanical complex was consolidating its control, it was being modified willy-nilly by the growing appreciation of organic nature in every aspect: witness the better regimen of child-care, hygiene, and diet introduced by the Romantic movement, mainly through Rousseau's writings, if not his practice; witness the growing interest in play and sport which modified the harsh attitude toward such relaxation introduced by Calvinism and utilitarianism: witness the kindly teaching practices introduced by Froebel's Children's Garden (Kindergarten)—the precise antithesis of Comenius' mass-organized drill-school; while at the same time the growing love of nature expressed itself in zealous amateur gardening, in landscape design, in rural sports, and outdoor exercises—hunting, fishing, rambling, mountain-climbing. In some degree these activities cushioned the impact of mechanization, and for over a century they have been opening the way for a more organic culture.

When that book is written it will show further how this growing appreciation of all that distinguishes the world of organisms from the world of machines gave rise, at a given point in the nineteenth century, to a fresh vision of the entire cosmic process. This vision was profoundly different from the one offered by those who left out of their world picture the essential qualitative attribute of life: its expectancy, its inner impetus, its insurgency, its creativity, its ability at singular points to transcend either physical or organic limitations.

The name given to this new vision of life was bestowed belatedly, only when it began to be systematically pursued: it is now known as ecology. But at first it was identified solely with the principle of organic evolution, and confined to a single aspect of that evolution: adaptation and survival through natural selection. This transformation is properly associated with the work of Charles Darwin—though by the very nature of organic change one would know without other evidence that he was not alone.

The significance of this new vision and the nature of Darwin's contribution have long been obscured by his own misinterpretation of his role; for Darwin believed that the basis of his claim to originality and priority was his establishing the probability of organic evolution. When the 'Origin of Species' came out he was annoyed to be reminded by Lyell of his predecessor, Lamarck; yet his own grandfather, Erasmus Darwin, had similar evolutionary views; and it was only with some reluctance that in a later edition he added a chapter on his many earlier precursors.

But if Darwin deserves the high place alongside Copernicus and Newton accorded him by a consensus of his peers, it is not because he had discovered the principle of evolution or even of natural selection. The latter idea both he and Alfred Russel Wallace had derived directly from Malthus' theory that population increased geometrically while food supply increased arithmetically; so that, if no restraints are imposed, this produces a savage struggle for existence, ending with the physical elimination of the weaker stocks. Darwin was in fact imputing to nature the ugly characteristics of Victorian capitalism and colonialism. So far from offsetting the effects of the mechanical world picture, this doctrine only unhappily offered a further touch of cold-blooded brutality; for it justified, in Darwin's own words, the "extermination of the 'less intellectual lower races' by the more intelligent higher races." (See his letter to Lyell, 11 October 1859.)

What finally gave immense authority to the 'Origin of Species' and its successor, 'The Descent of Man,' was something far more significant. Darwin, on the basis of his personal experience during the voyage of the 'Beagle,' had assembled a great quantity of scattered data pointing toward the continuous modification of species, starting from the very simplest organisms. Not content with a subjective impression of vast evolutionary transformations, he had devoted himself to patiently gathering from varying sources every possible scrap of concrete evidence, or even suggestive information. This master idea of organic unity had been in the air for over a century, in the minds of Buffon, Diderot, Lamarck, Goethe, Saint-Hilaire, Chambers, and Herbert Spencer. Darwin gave substance to all these observant intuitions by incorporating in his own person all the diverse modes of available knowledge—apart from mathematics and the exact sciences—needed to explain organic existence, organic change, and organic development.

In making himself ready for this great ecological contribution, Darwin had not merely moved outside the mechanical world picture, gently aided by his own ineptitude for mathematics: but he had escaped from that one-sided vocational specialization which is fatal to a full understanding of organic phenomena. For this new role, the very amateurishness of his preparation proved admirable. Though he was appointed as naturalist to the 'Beagle,' he had had no specialized university training; indeed as a biologist he had no early education whatever, except as a passionate animal hunter and beetle collector. With his lack of scholarly fixations and inhibitions, nothing prevented Darwin's awakening to every manifestation of the living environment: the geological formations, the coral reefs, the teeming seas, the diversification of species from the lowliest barnacles to the tortoises and birds and apes. That ever-broadening education occupied his whole lifetime, night and day, stirring him with ideas that could not be laid aside even to court sleep.

Following up every fresh clue, wherever it might come from, Darwin had become in his own person a new kind of scientist: even the designation 'biologist' is almost too narrow to describe him, except on the terms he himself had created. He was an entomologist, a geologist, a botanist, a practical breeder, and even, as a natural consummation, an animal psychologist and a proto-anthropologist. In the cultivation of this ecological interpretation of life, Darwin's own qualities as a human being, as a husband, a father of ten children, a friend, are indissolubly connected with his fresh ideas; and even when he tried, as he did when he was aware of his own vanity or jealousy, he never entirely eliminated himself from the equation.

In all Darwin's thinking he was there *in person:* not merely as an abstract intellect but as a sensitive, sympathetic human being. Darwin not merely studied organisms objectively: he loved living creatures almost as warmly as Saint Francis did, grieved even over the cruel training of performing dogs, and sturdily opposed the current practice of vivisection. In his alliance with all forms of life, Darwin was in the noble line of a succession of similar naturalists, from Gilbert White and Linnaeus to Humboldt and Audubon.

Darwin himself, as a person, made an even more important contribution to the organic world picture than Darwinism, the hypothesis that the struggle for existence and the natural selection of the fittest account for the modification of species. It was not his theoretic attempt to explain the evolutionary process that alone establishes his greatness: what mattered more was his living example, as the first and perhaps the greatest of ecologists. No one else had so thoroughly described the constant and inseparable interplay between organism, function, and environment. Symbolically in the person of Charles Darwin the post-mechanistic world picture, based on the observed nature of living organisms, was robustly incarnated; and so brought fully into consciousness, for more definitive formulation and activation.

Viewed in this light it is hardly an accident that Darwin completely lacked mechanical interests, and what is more, even disdained to use available mechanical facilities. Through no lack of money, he refused to buy a compound microscope and continued to use his simple old-fashioned magnifier; and he laughed at his own original clumsiness in making sections for microscopic examination till he belatedly acquired a microtome. So, too, Darwin shrank from killing and dissecting the pigeons he bred; and he would have shrunk even more from contemporary high school courses in biology, whose first lesson is how to kill a frog. Finding himself losing his early taste for poetry and painting, he lamented this as a loss of happiness, and observed that it "may possibly be injurious to the intellect, and more probably to the moral character, by enfeebling the emotional part of our nature."

Thus Darwin was disposed to take account of those very vital reactions that differentiate organic behavior from pre-organic changes produced by temperature, pressure, or purely chemical and electrical reactions. In his treatise on emotional expression in animals, he restored to the scientific description of organisms the subjective responses that Galileo and later scientists had ruled out as being beyond the possibility of 'objective' description. Darwin himself, though increasingly confined to systematic intellectual studies, was still so enamored of life that my master, Patrick Geddes, could report his dancing for joy over a slide under his microscope where paramecia were swimming—feeling perhaps as Herbert Spencer Jennings did later, that here already was not merely incipient life but incipient mind. In Darwin's interpretation of form, color, and ornamental excrescences as factors in sexual selection, he recognized esthetic expression—whatever its meaning—as an organic trait. Wallace, his friendly rival, shared Darwin's delight, pursuing birds of paradise and brilliant tropical butterflies in the islands of the Coral Sea.

Before Darwin, the concept of organic evolution had floated through many minds. What made his contribution so convincing was not his specific theories about the formation and modification of species, but his singular ability to assemble a great mass of observations about particular events of the most varied nature. Despite the insufficiency of any one set of observations to account for the evolution of life, the total mass, when Darwin put it together, revealed a concrete pattern of utmost complexity, in which every aspect of the whole in space *and* time was theoretically necessary to account for the smallest part or the most fleeting event. For the first time nature could be rationally contemplated, not as a fortuitous concourse of atoms, but as a self-organizing system from which man himself had finally emerged through a singular neural development that provided images and symbols for his conscious understanding.

In classic scientific thinking, the whole must be interpreted in terms of the part, deliberately isolated, carefully observed, precisely measured. But in Darwin's complementary ecological approach, it is the whole that reveals the nature and function and purpose of the part. Though threads in the pattern may need to be replaced, and parts of the pattern modified or completely redrawn as new evidence accumulates, it is important to take in the whole, even at some cost of sharp definition, and to carry that whole through time, since some of the transformations effected by time can only be experienced, not measured.

The feat of putting together the outlines of this intricate ecological pattern was Darwin's magnificent contribution. And because he was ready to take account of every fresh thread or color that further investigation might reveal, he himself in later editions of the 'Origin of Species' on occasion was driven to adopt the Lamarckian explanation he had at first rejected—much to the scandal of more orthodox Darwinists. Thus the very absence of a rigorously systematic, geometrizing mind permitted Darwin to entertain evidence that contradicted or at least modified his original notion about the creative role of elimination, or natural selection.

Through the concept of evolution, Western man at last began to recognize himself as the frail topmost shoot of a branching and towering family tree, rather than as a favored being given a divine patent of nobility some six thousand years ago, when he and his fellow creatures were created by a single 'act of God.' This new version of Genesis, it became plain, was not only truer to life, but it proved quite as miraculous as any single act of creation. The greatest lesson of the new natural history was the lesson of history itself: the lesson of life's cumulative domination over the non-living. If astronomical and terrestrial exploration had revealed new worlds in space, evolutionary exploration revealed an even more significant new world in time. Lawrence J. Henderson's analysis, 'The Fitness of the Environment,' completed this evolutionary interpretation by showing that physical nature, so far from being inherently hostile to life, was by the very chemical and physical properties found on earth pre-disposed in its favor.

This new time-perspective stood in such contrast to the brief millennial period of Biblical history, as well as to the blank, static eternity that Christian theology attached to the hereafter, that even the most daring thinkers of the nineteenth century could hardly entertain it. Thus Hegel, who is often given credit for evolutionary views, had held that change was an attribute of the spirit alone, and that the world of nature was only a self-repeating cycle, so that the "multiform play of its phenomena so far induces a feeling of ennui."

Ennui indeed! Just the contrary holds: thanks to the evolutionists' fresh insight, freedom and novelty, purposive adaptation and emergent design, could be detected within the entire world of life, not as the result of a single, original divine plan, but as the outcome of an interminable succession of limited efforts and improvisations that in time re-enforced each other and became more coherent and purposeful. Though subject to impediments and diversions, to regressions and retreats, the evolutionary process holds a promise of a more benign dominance by the mind of man, not merely through his intelligence but through his sensitive emotional reactions and his increasing ability to unify, both in symbol and in action, his objective and subjective experiences, without sacrificing one to the other. Such a unification should correct some of the painful aberrations and frustrating mischances that have accompanied the upward movement of life.

In this organic world picture time held a new meaning; for it was now correlated not just with motion and succession, but with organic growth both in species and in the individual. The past, so far from being left behind, remained vividly present in the individual memory, in the genetic inheritance, in the actual structure of the whole organism; while similarly, an anticipatory, directive, forward thrust became equally visible, engrained in every organic function, carrying those species capable of further development into new situations which demanded new strategies, and opened up new functions and fresh lines of growth. Therewith the central idea of 'progressive' or 'avant-garde' thought—*the past must be destroyed!*—revealed itself as a perverse fantasy, born of ignorance or indifference to the phenomenon of life. 'Leaving the past behind' is the equivalent of leaving life behind—and with this, any desirable or durable future.

Perhaps the greatest handicap to human development was the relegation of the past to the unconscious, without any effort at the revaluation and selection that is needed to give form to the future. This wholesale repression of the past accounts for the fact that the traumas that warped the development of civilization from the fourth millennium onward, if not before, have persisted from century to century, and from culture to culture: war, slavery, organized collective destruction and extermination.

The conception of time as the flux of organic continuity, experienced as duration, as memory, as recorded history, as potentiality and prospective achievement, stands in frontal opposition to the mechanistic notion of time simply as a function of the motion of bodies in space—along with its spurious imperative of 'saving time' by accelerating motion, and of making such acceleration in every possible department the highest triumph of the power complex.

Let us not be deceived by surviving mechanistic illusions. From conception and gestation to death all living functions have their appointed time: only the destructive processes are swift: only entropy comes easy. On this re-reading of time, in terms of organic experience, the formulations of C. Lloyd Morgan, Bergson, Geddes, and Whitehead remain as essential for the 'biological revolution' as those of Copernicus, Galileo, and Newton were for the mechanical revolution.

Darwin himself, for all his exemplary expositions, never perhaps fully realized that his own combination of evolutionary perspective and ecological method carried important applications to every part of daily life—if only because they undermined the conceptual framework of the dominant power system. Darwin had not merely broken down the static picture of a single act of creation, with fixed species, fixed boundaries, tending toward a fixed final end, duly appointed from the beginning. He had revealed something far more wonderful—that the creative process was not over but was constantly going on, reaching back into a cosmic evolution, which, as physicists now interpret it, began with the differentiation of the elements from a primordial hydrogen atom. The mode of evolution was neither random nor pre-determined: yet some basic tendency toward self-organization, unrecognizable until billions of years had passed, increasingly gave direction to the process.

In so far as the organism has achieved the necessary preconditions for stability, continuity, dynamic balance, and self-replenishment, further creativity is assured; and the ability to transcend these conditions, at extremely rare intervals, becomes possible. It is in those moments, and in the personalities through whom such flashes of divinity become visible, that organic existence reaches a brief, but utterly satisfying, climax. When, on the other hand, chance events multiply and a dehumanized social regimentation leaves no place for an organic response, disintegration and wanton destruction gain, as now, the upper hand.

Unfortunately Darwinism, in the form popularized by Thomas Henry Huxley, the Saint Paul of Darwinism, with his picture of "Nature red in tooth and claw" triumphed over Darwin's deeper vision of life, and for long distorted the emerging organic world picture. For reasons too complex to be analyzed here, Darwin's thought had taken on at the very beginning the color of his Victorian habitat, in which the industrial-imperialist modes of exploitation were dominant. The very sub-title of the 'Origin of Species' "the preservation of favored races in the struggle for life" displays that animus. Darwinism in this crude sense not merely expelled value and purpose from organic evolution: it withdrew from its exponents Darwin's own best qualities—his sensitiveness, his tenderness, his direct emotional response to every manifestation of organic activity.

Darwin's contribution to evolutionary doctrine and ecological insight gave the pursuit of biology an immense impetus, all the more because coeval developments in chemistry made it possible to identify the special combination of elements—principally carbon, hydrogen, oxygen, nitrogen—that mainly constituted protoplasm. How is it then that the organic world picture was so slow to emerge, and is still not dominant? Mainly for two reasons, it would seem. Organic evolution, which is by no means uniform, automatic, or consistent, was mistakenly identified with mechanical progress. This mis-identification made it easy to turn the "struggle for existence" into an inhuman auxiliary of the myth of the machine. In turn, mechanical processes were treated as more 'objective' than organic behavior: so that the machine model remained a criterion for scientific accuracy and adequacy even in dealing with subjectively conditioned organisms.

For all this, the sanguine belief in continued evolutionary advance itself was still very much alive as late as half a century ago. Both John Dewey and Woodrow Wilson hailed Darwinian thinking as superseding the non-historic Newtonian mode. But the next fifty years retarded the development of an organic world picture. The all-too-obvious national 'struggles for existence,' grimly illustrated in two world wars and a multitude of 'civilized' massacres, destroyed the hopeful message of evolution; and except for specialists in phylogeny, or a few philosophic minds like Henri Bergson and Leonard Hobhouse, the idea of evolution fell into general discredit, as unfashionable if not false—though in the meanwhile the principles of ecology were being carried into many departments. Patrick Geddes, in his study of cities, sought to apply them even to the higher life of the mind.

With the celebration of the centenary of the 'Origin of Species' the neglect of evolution was arrested; and a more comprehensive picture of the whole process is now again in the act of being developed. Julian Huxley, the grandson of Darwin's old ally, was one of those who rallied the counter-forces of biologic humanism. Not by accident the isolationism and reduc-tionism of orthodox science, following too studiously the conditions laid down by the power system for accelerating all forms of power, is under indictment, because of the catastrophic results of applying such anti-organic concepts to exploiting and controlling living species. All thinking worthy of the name now must be ecological, in the sense of appreciating and utilizing organic complexity, and in adapting every kind of change to the requirements not of man alone, or of any single generation, but of all his organic partners and every part of his habitat.

If during the next generation the destructive forces accelerated by science can be brought under control before they have permanently dam-aged the planet, it will be because the new organic model of ecological association and self-organization (autonomy and teleonomy), which was first assembled by Darwin, will have at last begun to prevail.

3: FROM POWER TO PLENITUDE

Now in terms of the available knowledge about organic evolution, about the ascent of man, about the development of culture and personality—in-sufficient and imperfect though these new insights still are—it has become obvious that both the mechanical world picture and its technological components are hopelessly backward in their human commitments. The more firmly we get attached to the power system, the more alienated we become from those vital sources that are essential to further human development.

The collective failure to recognize these ancient traumatic imprints and to correct their aberrations has led one civilization after another to repeat, to the point of exhaustion, the errors originally made. As the scope of the power system widens, however, the once genuine possibility of making a fresh start in another place, through another people, with a different cul-ture, becomes less likely; for the very success of mass production and the mass media has spread and solidified civilization's ancient errors.

The great revolution needed to save mankind from the projected assaults against life by the controllers of the megamachine demands first of all a displacement of the mechanical world picture with an organic world picture, in the center of which stands man himself, in person—"cool and composed," as Whitman says, "before a million universes." In taking an organic model one must renounce the paranoid claims and foolish hopes of the Power Complex, and accept finiteness, limitation, incompleteness, uncertainty, and eventual death as necessary attributes of life—and more than this, as the condition for achieving wholeness, autonomy, and creativity. Perhaps the implications of this changeover from a cosmic-mechanical model to an earth-centered, organic, and human model can be most clearly followed in technics itself.

Though far from complete and in universal use, the organic model is already partly in being, so well established that it has been in operation for almost a century, even within the domain of technics. Yet so insistent is the mechanical stereotype that even an otherwise excellent history of technology described the invention of the telephone without any reference to the fact that it had its origin in an attempt to create a speaking automaton, and that the receiver was deliberately modelled by Alexander Graham Bell on the anatomy of the human ear.

But this was only the first striking invention based on an organic model to simulate life—not, like Vaucanson's clockwork duck or flute player, through fabricating crude mechanical equivalents, but through drawing on a pre-existing biological solution. So, too, the careful study of the flight of birds, from Borelli and Pettigrew to the brothers Wright, made possible the mechanical simulation of winged creatures. In an even higher order of machine, the computer, no serious advance was made until the mechanical components were replaced by electric charges, as in the transmission of information by the nervous system: a change first prefigured in Galvani's experiment with the reflexes of a frog. By now the debt to organic phenomena is so palpable that advanced computer research teams recruit physiologists, brain specialists, and linguists, no less than mathematicians, electro-physicists, and engineers.

Helmholtz once made disparaging remarks about the human eye and suggested specific mechanical improvements: but no machine in existence is anything but a clumsy fake, no more lifelike except for motion, than a mummy, in comparison with any living vertebrate. This holds more particularly true for the higher human functions, in which sensitivity, imagination, emotional responsiveness, feeling, sexual passion, love, with all their associated symbols, provide an otherwise unattainable enrichment that no machine can even feebly utilize or duplicate.

Above all, only organisms that can reproduce and renew themselves have stood the test of time, maintaining continuity, exhibiting creativity, and temporarily reversing entropy. As for automation and cybernation, which technologists now boast of as the highest product of their art—what are they but the most ancient of organic devices, rather than the most modern: equivalent to the reflexes, not the cerebral cortex. In this evolutionary sense automation, if treated as a goal of human development, would be a backward step—as in some areas it already is.

There is nothing essentially new in these observations; but the point of them has still to be taken in. Not merely were man's crude original tools derived from the organs of the body—the hammer a fist, the scraper fingernails, the stick that knocked down fruit an extended arm; but even more astonishingly, earliest man's most complex instrument—far outrivalling any mechanical organization in complexity and flexibility—was the symbolic structure of language, built solely out of gestures, sounds, images, whose parts have both stability as units and virtually infinite capacities for re-assemblage in unique but intelligible structures.

Both in its dynamic continuity and its productivity, language is in fact a far more perfect prototype for an economy of abundance than any system concocted on a mathematical model, just because it stores a variety of human experiences for which there is no mathematical or logical counterpart.

In so far as an organic model implicitly pervades all human activities, unless supplanted for practical reasons by a simpler and more limited scheme, it has saved mechanization from many embarrassments, just as humane village customs and traditions and even older animal loyalties have often modified harsh legal codes that left no merciful loopholes. As technics in future becomes more open to organic criteria, the idea of quantitative productivity will give way to a different objective: that which will increase variety and establish plenitude.

We now come back to the basic idea that underlies this book. If we are to prevent megatechnics from further controlling and deforming every aspect of human culture, we shall be able to do so only with the aid of a radically different model derived directly, not from machines, but from living organisms and organic complexes (ecosystems). What can be known about life only through the process of living—and so is part of the experience of even the humblest of organisms—must be added to all the other aspects that can be observed, abstracted, measured.

This new model will in time replace megatechnics with biotechnics; and that is the first step toward passing from power to plenitude. Once an organic world picture is in the ascendant, the working aim of an economy of plenitude will be, not to feed more human functions into the machine, but to develop further man's incalculable potentialities for self-actualization and self-transcendence, taking back into himself deliberately many of the activities he has too supinely surrendered to the mechanical system.

Under the power complex the purely quantitative concept of unlimited abundance, not merely material but symbolic abundance, has served as the guiding principle. As opposed to this, an organic system directs itself to qualitative richness, amplitude, spaciousness, free from quantitative pressure and crowding, since self-regulation, self-correction, and self-propulsion are as much an integral property of organisms as nutrition, reproduction, growth, and repair. Balance, wholeness, completeness, continuous interplay between the inner and the outer, the subjective and the objective aspects of existence are identifying characteristics of the organic model; and the general name for an economy based on such a model is an economy of plenitude. Such plenitude is distinct from mere quantitative affluence or unqualified abundance.

As soon as this organic standard prevails, that which is small, quantitatively insignificant, or unrepeatable may turn out to be highly significant and valuable, just as a minute trace element in the soil or the diet, once left out in nutrition tables based on calories, may make the difference between health and disease. On these terms, the old folk saying 'Enough is plenty' turns out to be wisdom. This indeed is re-enforced by Blake's pregnant aphorism: "More! More! is the cry of a mistaken soul; less than All will not satisfy Man." (But 'all' means a whole, not everything.)

Now the notion of plenitude, as a necessary condition for satisfying organic development, and above all as an indispensable condition for the good life, was common long before it was open to scientific statement through the investigation of organic evolution and ecological balance. As Arthur Lovejoy demonstrated, in 'The Great Chain of Being,' there are many traditional versions of the principle of plenitude, first formulated, it seems, by religious minds, contemplating with wonder the riotous abundance of nature and the incessant creativity of God. Even when species were still regarded as static and final, the result of a single magistral fiat, it was not just the abundance of species, or their gradation from the lowest organisms up to man himself, that was taken as the most satisfactory proof of the intelligent and providential ordering of all existence. Plenitude indicated more than abundance: it was the condition for organic variety, diversification, selectivity, in a word, freedom, which reached its climax in man.

Though one part of the biological principle of natural plenitude was embodied in the doctrine of natural selection, the prevalent Victorian power ideology gave to the negative processes an ambiguous role that confused extermination with selectivity and survival with development, and so lost sight of the principle of plenitude as the basic condition for autonomous activity and self-directed transformation.

Fortunately for our present purpose, the doctrine of organic plenitude was re-stated by Dr. Walter Cannon in his treatise on 'The Wisdom of the Body.' His conclusions issued from a close experimental investigation of the organs and functions of the human body, particularly those autonomic processes relating to the feelings and emotions, thus carrying further the original investigations of Claude Bernard, John Scott Haldane, and Charles Sherrington, not to mention Darwin himself.

Cannon's study of the body centered on the marvellous apparatus that animal organisms have developed to maintain their dynamic equilibrium: especially on those coordinated interchanges of information and response, operating with extreme sensitiveness and promptness in matters like maintaining the essential acid-alkaline balance of the blood. The same 'homeostatic balance' preserves the organism against any impairment of its wholeness, whether through excess or deficiency; for it is precisely this wholeness that is almost a definition of organic competence and health.

In the elemental emotions of fear and rage associated with the most primitive parts of the brain, this swift response without conscious intervention or direction is a condition of survival: but something more than survival comes forth from it; for this very automatism freed the growing brain and ramifying nervous system for more important services, detached from the immediate pressure for survival, performed by the new brain. Here by his conscious symbolic activities man created a second realm that conforms more closely to his higher personal and social needs.

To preserve wholeness in the midst of constant change, and to allow for a maximum amount of instability and variability, for adventurous effort, pushing beyond immediate needs and stimuli while retaining a sufficiently constant structure and a dynamic pattern of wholeness defines the nature of living organisms as opposed to random samples of molecules. Even more significantly, it describes the difference between higher and lower organisms. Though all organisms undergo unceasing changes, these changes take place within more or less definable boundaries in time and space, for indefinite extensions in time are all restricted by the organism's inherited life-span and by the ecological complex of which it is, willy-nilly, an integral part.

Thus the chief properties of a power economy—the magnification and over-expansion of power alone, and the lack of qualifications, limits, and boundaries—are antithetic to those of an organic system. In organisms power is always related to function and purpose. Life does not flourish under a regime of compulsive dynamism, where uncontrolled change—change only for the sake of further change such as megatechnics now imposes—removes the possibility of maintaining a dynamic equilibrium or going on with an autonomous development.

What holds in general for any organism holds even more significantly for man. It is in terms of a future that transcends and outlasts his present self that all his past achievements in mind and collective culture become significant: if cut off from that future, he becomes as distraught as if he were cut off from his needed supply of water and air. Man's vital prosperity rests on establishing a balance between self-maintenance and growth, between external proposals and internal responses, between activity and recuperation: yet always with the need for a surplus sufficient to make good depletions, to meet unexpected demands, and to permit the exercise of choice. To preserve its identity as a member of a species and a group, and likewise as a unique individual, to remain 'true to character,' to establish the minimal conditions needed for traversing the whole life-cycle: this is the basic condition for organisms, communities, cultures—and above all for man.

Walter Cannon's special contribution was to give an experimental physiological basis for the fundamental doctrine of Greek 'paideia'—the idea of balance or the golden mean. Cannon demonstrated that the human body's automatic self-balancing organization—note that I do not call it 'mechanism'—is what makes possible its purposive self-direction, increasingly free from external constraints. This balance is no mere matter of quantity: it involves not merely the right measure but the right mixture of qualities and the right pattern of organization.

As Cannon pointed out, "in so far as our internal environment is kept constant, we are freed from the limitations imposed by both internal and external agencies or conditions that could be disturbing." Freedom for what? Cannon answers: "freedom for the activities of the higher nervous system and the muscles which they govern. . . . In summary then, we find the organism liberated for its more complicated and socially important tasks because it lives in a fluid matrix, which is automatically kept in a constant condition." We shall return in a moment to consider these important tasks.

In addition to recognizing the need for a dynamic inner equilibrium, Cannon pointed to another characteristic that was essential for the full functioning of the body: organized superfluity. The body has at its command a far larger store of energy and a greater number of organs than it actually requires to maintain itself under ordinary conditions. Many of the essential organs, eyes, ears, lungs, kidneys, arms, legs, hands, testicles, are paired. If one of these organs should be injured or destroyed the other remains in operation and is capable of maintaining the whole organism, though perhaps falling short of its highest levels. Now there is still another important mode of organization at hand for coping with sudden emergencies that demand heavy muscular exertion. This lies in the supply of sugar that is automatically unlocked by the adrenal glands under the stimulus of fear or anger, when extra energy is needed for flight or attack. This largesse contrasts with the principle of economy appropriate to the design and operation of a machine—though even here prudent designers have learned to provide extra energy or structural strength, the so-called factor of safety, to meet unusual demands, and more than one bridge or building or plane has fallen to pieces when this organic principle was ignored.

Cannon's exposition of 'The Wisdom of the Body' is not, of course, definitive for all organic functions. For one thing, the principle of homeostasis deals mainly with self-maintenance, and all the work processes dependent upon it; but it does not incorporate the demands of bodily growth, which often temporarily upset the overall equilibrium; nor does it take into account all those 'superfluous' activities of play and work and thought without which even animal life would remain at a vegetative level. What Cannon's study mainly did was to demonstrate that millions of years before our present technology was assembled, nature had produced its own economy of abundance and its own system of automation. But he fully realized that the ultimate significance of his researches was to indicate how the internal equilibrium of the body made it possible for man to develop his superior functions.

At the same time, Cannon's description of organic homeostasis reveals the inherent limitation of any automatic system as it approaches perfection. This is a point I made independently in discussing mass production and automation: namely, that it tends to become rigid and static unless it leaves room for factors outside the system and provides a means for growth by drawing on a larger environment and a richer fund of experience than that which has been programmed in the automatic system itself.

Cannon realized—as our contemporary technocrats do not—that automation lies at the beginning, not the end of human evolution: that the need to escape from this low level of organic perfection was expressed in the remarkable neural development of the primate stocks, and particularly by the continued growth of the brain, out of all proportion to immediate exigencies, which marked the ascent of man from other ancestral anthropoids.

Though Cannon's study serves to sanction on biological grounds the principle of automation, it also exposes the limitation of an economy that seeks to translate man's higher functions into an automatic system that will finally be capable of making decisions and plans of action without calling upon anticipatory mental processes or memories except those that can be programmed on a computer. The path of human advance is not toward such collective automation but toward the increase of personal and communal autonomy; and any system that reverses this direction not merely turns man's most highly developed organ, his brain, into a virtual nonentity, but cuts itself off from the most precious products of the human mind: that vast storehouse and powerhouse of images, forms, ideas, institutions, and structures, through which man rises above the conditions of his immediate environment. To reduce or destroy this heritage is to inflict brain damage on the human race.

Instead of accepting total automation, then, as the only possible terminus of a mature economy, we must replace quantified power with qualified plenitude; and to do this one must begin with man's higher functions: especially those that enable him to detach himself from both his biological and institutional fixations.

With the natural caution of a scientist venturing outside his field, Dr. Cannon concluded his study of 'The Wisdom of the Body' with the suggestion that the model of the living organism might be applied with advantage to the larger human community. Since technologies and economic systems are themselves products of life, it is not strange that, to the degree that they work effectively at all, they have incorporated many organic devices not in line with their own abstract ideological or institutional premises. But because brain physiology, dream exploration, and linguistic analysis were all outside his area of high competence Dr. Cannon never faced the central problem that arose, at a very early point, I suspect, once the enlargement of man's neural functions enabled him to escape the automatism of his reflexes and hormones. How under those conditions to prevent the brain from succumbing to its own disorderly hyperactivity, once liberated from the bodily functions and environmental contacts and social pressures necessary for its existence? The need to recognize this special source of instability coming from the extraordinary powers of the mind, and to take measures for overcoming it, is not the least lesson to be drawn from man's historic development.

In so far as automatic systems become more lifelike as well as more powerful, they carry with them the threat of increasing human irrationality at higher levels. To follow an organic model, then, not only the system as a whole must be kept in view, but each individual part must be in a state of alertness, ready to intervene at any point in the process and take over.

4: INVITATION TO PLENITUDE

The tendency of the present power system, it is obvious, goes directly contrary to the ideal of plenitude. With the perfection of automation and cybernation, it seeks to draw more and more of man's higher functions into an automatic system, and therefore deprive him of the very powers of exercising control over automatism that the development of man's superabundant nervous system gave him. Under an organic economy that sought the advantages of plenitude, more and more of the automatic functions would be restored to conscious control, decentralized, and brought back, often for the first time, under the full sway of the whole personality, re-enforced by a culture no longer confined either to a petrified past or a deliquescent here and now.

Hitherto, the human advantages of plenitude have been explored—but only sporadically and selfishly—through their forced expropriation of the economic surplus by a privileged minority. For the greater part of history, the personal freedom and the cultural stimuli open to such groups exposed both the advantages of plenitude and the possibilties for corruption that an economy of profit-conditoned abundance, often confused with plenitude, carries with it. The rewards of such a life have often been undeniable: out of the surplus came confident, full-blooded personalities, well fed and brimming with vitality, ready to conceive and execute imaginative designs, whether in architecture, in government, or in religion, whose achievement would have remained impossible, indeed inconceivable, with the pinched facilities and limited horizons of a small community.

But apart from the wealth achieved by such coercion, the best examples of plenitude are those that exist in quite primitive communities. In many areas, before neolithic horticulture and agriculture came under a coercive centralization that imposed taxes and forced labor, a modest level of plenitude had in fact been achieved without insistent expropriation. Neither the Malthusian struggle for existence nor the Marxian class war characterized such simple communities. This was specially the case in favorable tropical habitats, often still in existence when the nineteenth-century explorer visited them.

The fragility of such an economy is obvious: the gifts of nature are too uncertain, the margin too narrow, the balance too delicate. Hence primitive cultures, in order to be sure of continuity, tend to be restrictive and parsimonious, unready to welcome innovations or take risks, even reluctant to profit by the existence of their neighbors. This weakness was summed up by Lao-tse in a passage curiously meant to praise the advantages of such an economy. "There might still be boats and carriages, and no one would go in them. . . . The next place might be so near at hand that one could hear the cocks crowing in it, the dogs barking, but people would grow old and die without ever being there."

In so far as the power complex has overcome that species of fossilization, we owe it a debt. Plenitude on such a solitary, meager, unadventurous basis too easily sinks into torpid penury and stupefication. Thoreau tested out that possibility for himself during his two years at Walden: but he realized that it was not good for a lifetime, nor attractive, either, except as a vacation from a more demanding economy that denied him the leisure he needed for his true life as a feeling, thinking, reflecting observer.

It is not to go back toward such a primitive plenitude, but forward to a more generous regimen, far more generous than the most affluent society now affords, that the coming generations must lay their plans. Many of the most desirable features of an economy of plenitude—including the luxury of turning one's back upon specious luxuries—are lacking almost by definition from the power system. If we dare to forestall the ugly future that the prophets of megatechnics predict, if we reject their sterile bureaucratic utopias, it is because we propose to base our alternative economy on a more adequate model, one derived not from the solar system or its mechanical derivatives, but from the nature of its so-far ultimate product, life itself, as embodied in living organisms, as reflected, magnified, and enhanced in the mind of man. The ideal of an organic system, seeking plenitude, not material or symbolic abundance alone, is to release human vitalities and to leave a fresh imprint of meaning and value upon every phase of existence, past, present, or possible.

Note the difference between the ideal of quantitative magnification—the mass production of inventions, goods, money, knowledge, messages, pleasures—and the ideal of organic plenitude. Not the least difference is that a regime that seeks to establish plenitude must provide for contraction as well as expansion, for restrictive discipline as well as liberation, for inhibition as well as expression, for continuity as well as change. Organic plenitude, then, is in no wise definable as mere quantitative abundance, still less as relentless productivity, unabridged expenditure, and thoughtless consumption.

Under a regime of plenitude abundance is permissive, not compulsive: it allows for extravagant expenditures to satisfy man's higher needs for knowledge, beauty, or love—as in the parable of the oil with which Jesus was anointed—while it may exact the severest economy for less worthy purposes. Emerson's advice, to save on the low levels and spend on the high ones, lies at the very core of this conception. Yet paradoxically, only through such a power system as has been coming into existence during the last three centuries shall we be capable of extending the blessings of plenitude, not just to scattered minorities and favored habitats, but to the whole human race, billions of whom are still too close to starvation.

This benign transformation can happen only on one condition, and that a hard one: namely that the life-negating ideals and methods of the power system be renounced, and that a conscious effort be made, at every level and in every kind of community, to live not for the sake of exalting power but for reclaiming this planet for life through mutual aid, loving association, and biotechnic cultivation. Not the 'Advancement of Learning' or the advancement of power, but the advancement of life and mind is the goal.

That organic ideal has often taken root in many cultures, only to be repeatedly mocked, despised, and flouted all through recorded 'civilized' history; and there is no guarantee that it will not be suppressed and thrown aside again. So the promise of plenitude is not an easy promise to fulfill: it would be much safer to predict that the destructive forces now in operation will drive on without swerving to their inevitable self-destruction. But one saving grace may still work for mankind: for it has been under the threat of total extinction that the unconscious forces of life have repeatedly rallied, and turned total defeat into a partial victory. That may yet happen again.

Obviously the potentiality for achieving plenitude, which is the chief economic gift of the power complex, cannot be realized on the terms that govern this system. So long as the ideals of unqualified power remain prevalent, governing the activities of those who seek to change the system as well as those who proudly associate themselves with it, no organic transformation is possible. Nevertheless, it is an error to believe that the impetus behind the system is uncheckable, because it represents a cosmic force that can neither be defied nor controlled.

What law of nature has singled out the increased application of energy as the law of organic existence? The answer is: No such law exists. In the complex interactions that made life possible on earth, energy in all its forms is of course an indispensable component, but not the sole factor. Organisms may almost be defined as so many diverse inventions for regulating energy, reversing its tendency to dissipation, and keeping it within limits favorable to the organism's own needs and purposes. This screening process began, before organisms could make their appearance, in the atmospheric layer that tempers the direct heat of the sun and filters out lethal rays. Too much energy is as fatal to life as too little: hence the regulation of energy input and output, not its unlimited expansion, is in fact one of the main laws of life. In contrast, any excessive concentration of energy, even for seemingly valid purposes, must be closely scrutinized, and often rejected as a threat to ecological equilibrium.

The notion that the megamachine is in fact omnipotent and irresistible came in, as we have seen, with the cult of Divine Kingship: the primal myth of the machine. At the entrance of the great palaces in Mesopotamia and Egypt, from which the ancient system was governed, there were stationed gigantic statues of Lions or Bulls, whose main object was to fill those who approached the royal presence with a paralyzing sense of their own littleness and impotence: as a Tomb Text from the 14–12 century B.C. said of the intentions of the Sun God, Re: *"I shall prevail over them as a King and diminish them."* In more devious symbolic ways these same awe-inspiring creatures still stand at the portals of the Power Pentagon today, though the god they represent, whose secret knowledge cannot be challenged and whose divine commands cannot be questioned, turns out actually to be, when one tears aside the curtain, only the latest model IBM computer, zealously programmed by Dr. Strangelove and his assistants.

But there is another error, the reverse of magnifying the role of power, that it would be equally fatal to make: one that now treacherously tempts the younger generation: the notion that in order to avoid the predictable calamities that the power complex is bringing about, one must destroy the whole fabric of historic civilization and begin all over again on an entirely fresh foundation. Unfortunately that 'fresh' foundation, as envisaged by such revolutionary groups, includes the forms of mass communication, mass transportation, and mass indoctrination abetted by violence that favor, not human liberation, but a mass dictatorship, possibly even more dehumanized than the present affluent Establishment, since it renounces as worthless and irrelevant our immense cultural accumulations. As if ignorance and impotence were viable solutions! As if human institutions could be improvised overnight!

What applies to ancient Bronze Age civilizations, and partly atones for their misuse of power, applies equally to our modern equivalents. "The negative institutions . . . would never have endured so long but for the fact that their positive goods, even though they were arrogated to the use of the dominant minority, were ultimately of service to the whole community, and *tended to produce a universal society of far higher potentialities, by reason of its size and diversity.*" If that observation held true at the beginning, it remains even more true today, now that this remarkable technology has spread over the whole planet. The only way effectively to overcome the power system is to transfer its more helpful agents to an organic complex. And it is in and through the human person that the invitation to plenitude begins and ends.

5: EMERGING CULTURAL PROSPECTS

To work out in detail the economic and social implications of a regime of plenitude lies far beyond the scope of this book—or of any single mind. Yet since the principle of plenitude, as distinguished from affluence, abundance, or even plenty, is not generally understood I shall attempt to trace out a few of its many possible consequences: results that future generations, if once an organic world picture prevails, will work out in their own way.

In flashes some of the best minds of the nineteenth century anticipated some of these developments: minds as different in other respects as those of Comte, Marx, Mill, Thoreau, Kropotkin, William Morris, and Patrick Geddes. And a few of these leaders carried into personal practice some of the most fundamental changes, already touched on in my estimate of Leonardo da Vinci: indifference to money incentives, the liberation from self-inflating publicity, the diversification of vocational activities, the deliberate slowing down of the tempo of production, whether industrial or intellectual, the renewed concentration on superior human functions and cultural values, not least the active 'resorption' of government.

One of the most favorable outcomes of plenitude, possible only because of a potential surplus of energy and goods, is the abandonment of a lifetime concentration upon a single occupation or task, even if such concentration produces goods as valuable and durable as the Persian rug I have cited: for such confinement is in fact a slave's existence, not worthy of a fully developed human being. To open up more than one occupational activity does not, however, mean that special aptitudes need be unused or neglected: quite the contrary. What it does mean is that in pursuing the daily routine, and even more the whole life course, no one interest will be considered sufficiently cultivated unless it is accompanied by an awareness of the other interests and activities needed to maintain psychological and ecological balance.

Karl Marx foresaw this result as the radical human change to be brought about by socialism: namely, that the same man might fish without becoming a 'fisherman,' or write literary criticism without becoming a 'literary critic': in short, that vocational pigeon-holes would become increasingly meaningless as the 'Vocation of Man' became the focus of all activity. In this respect William Morris' life was as exemplary as Leonardo's. To become a full human being is nothing less than a lifetime's task. Unlike some of Marx's other beliefs, this was not a romantic youthful hope he left behind.

As late as 1875 in his 'Critique of the Gotha Programme' Marx regarded the desired goal of communism as "the end of the subordination of individuals to the 'division of labor' and with it the contradiction between intellectual and physical work." Therewith labor would become not only a means of life but the prime necessity of living. Thus the amateur who works for love with no more tangible incentive, and the dedicated craftsman in any field whose work is for him the most fascinating occupation possible, would be indistinguishable. From my own life experience, I can testify to the soundness of that critique, for I would be hard put to it to tell which I enjoy more: the hours I spend at writing or at gardening. Without the opportunity for such active, varied work I would, like William Morris, feel desperate.

More than one recent observer has pointed out that the prospective achievement of universal leisure, with the six-hour day and the five-day week, carries the threat of intolerable emptiness and boredom. The hope expressed by Julian Huxley and others that this vacancy will be profitably filled by continued studies in the school and the university, to use the time once occupied by office or factory work, over-rates both the attraction and the nutritive value of such fare, and fails to take note of the ominous rebellion against it already manifested by those college students who find no joy in exercising their minds, and who would rather dull them by drugs or stone them by violent sounds.

There is no substitute for work except other serious work. Nothing proves this better than the fact that the 'work' of one culture—paleolithic hunting for example—usually becomes the favorite sport of the culture that succeeds it.

The economy of plenitude which now beckons suggests an entirely different approach from that of the old-fashioned division of labor no less than from the upper class freedom to avoid labor. That new possibility was outlined more than a century ago by that singular if mad genius Charles Fourier. This is what Fourier called the 'butterfly principle.' Instead of working a whole day at a single occupation, still less a whole lifetime, Fourier proposed that the working day should be enlivened by moving at intervals from one task to another. As so often happened with him he weakened a good idea by stretching it to absurdity: in this case by making the work periods too brief. But again I can testify from my own experience—and here happily I find backing from a behaviorist opponent, Professor B. F. Skinner—that a four-hour work period, or a little less in the case of writing, produces the best results; and the alternation of intellectual activity with other forms of work, like gardening, wood-chopping, food-garnering, carpentry, or machine-tinkering, animates and raises to a higher pitch every other part of the day.

At a humble level the butterfly principle is what so long made the life of farmers rewarding, except when exploited or environmentally impoverished: so much so that its typical routines and seasonal celebrations underwent no radical changes for thousands of years. As against the segregated activities, the regimented discipline, the bleak environment of the factory, farm work favored many hour-to-hour, day-to-day, and season-to-season variations. The boast of the psychologist Stanley Hall, in his 'Autobiography,' was not a vain one: that as a New England farm boy in mid-nineteenth century he was versed in a score of different occupations and was master of many of them. The economy of plenitude, in achieving briefer work periods, would make it possible to restore initiative on a voluntary basis in many forms of work now denied to the beneficiaries of affluence who are chained to the demand for compulsory consumption.

Precisely because of the productive technical advances made during the last two centuries, the lifetime division of labor has become irrelevant. The classic treatise that Emile Durkheim wrote expounding the advantages of the division of labor, not least its intellectual advantages, has become in view of the present invitation to plenitude a set of instructions on what to avoid. In so far as Durkheim took the division of labor to be an essential feature of 'civilization,' that is, of the power complex, he was correct; not merely correct, but in good company, from Plato to Adam Smith. But curiously none of these thinkers realized that mechanical efficiency has no necessary relation to life efficiency, to say nothing of life fulfillments.

Power machines have so vastly multiplied the number of mechanical 'slaves' that it would be absurd to retain the ancient lifetime division of labor or the present obsolete craft divisions, and the bureaucratic and police controls that have gone with them. But the leisure now available is waiting to be filled not just with sport and television and tourism. The happy alternative open to us is for more varied forms of work, private and public. Such work will be increasingly voluntary and gratuitous, without the meretricious incentives of money or publicity. Many of the social problems, like the care of the sick and aged, which, because the upward equalization of incomes makes such services prohibitive, will continue to grow more formidable until an ever larger portion of human services and hand-made goods are produced either as public duties or as individual gifts as between neighbors and friends. Some of the underlying spirit generated by an economy of plenitude, with its indifference to pecuniary incitements, has already come forth in a spontaneous if somewhat feckless sharing of their goods among the younger generation.

Curiously one of the best modern examples of the feasibility of multiple occupations and of a diversified, rather than a specialized, life comes from the break in standard peacetime routines brought about on a large scale by the First World War and demonstrated again in the Second. In those crises, with only the most limited time in which to effect the transformation, people not merely changed occupations but even altered their own characters. Men who had previously chosen safe occupations faced danger and torture in the underground resistance; untrained girls who had never even operated a sewing machine became efficient operators of lathes and punches; housewives who had never worked outside their homes became hospital nurses or aides, and coped with bedpans, repulsive diseases, and severe bodily injuries; while middle-aged men who had always edged away from danger became air raid wardens and ambulance drivers, comforting the frightened, and pulling the maimed and the dead out of the ruins.

Nothing could have shown up better the needless stultification of lifetime specialization than these rapid adaptations. In many cases, if I may judge by later contact with such people, this change of roles gave an increased sense of self-confidence and capability. The reward was not power or profit or prestige, but an intensification of life. That collective experience disposes of all the old caste stratifications and fixations. It shows that there is a deep reservoir of human resources that the power system has never drawn on except in moments of crisis.

The obstacle to achieving such vocational diversification and general aptitude does not lie in the human character as such, but rather in the mass of qualifying educational and vocational restrictions imposed by every privileged group in order to maintain its special status, emoluments, and perquisites. Though the reputed object of these regulations is often laudable, as measures to ensure competence and protect members from unqualified rivals, the underlying aim is to prevent fresh activities and organizations from arising in competition with the power system. As a result, the scope of human initiative through direct action becomes limited: today the smallest new measure must run a gauntlet of licensing laws, professional codes, trades union regulations, wage schedules, promotion priorities, bureaucratic restrictions and inspections. Even the exigencies of war were only partly able to break down or bypass these barriers—for where are they more deeply entrenched than in the military machine itself?

This explains, perhaps, why there is so little prospect of overcoming the defects of the power system by any attack that employs mass organizations and mass efforts at persuasion; for these mass methods support the very system they attack. The changes that have so far been effective, and that give promise of further success, are those that have been initiated by animated individual minds, small groups, and local communities nibbling at the edges of the power structure by breaking routines and defying regulations. Such an attack seeks, not to capture the citadel of power, but to withdraw from it and quietly paralyze it. Once such initiatives become widespread, as they at last show signs of becoming, it will restore power and confident authority to its proper source: the human personality and the small face-to-face community.

Only through encouraging decentralized communal agents will such a worldwide organization as an effectively reconstituted United Nations find the massive human backing needed for banishing all weapons of genocide and biocide, and ensuring justice and comity among its members. To assemble peace-making power in a world authority without such a revitalizing of autonomous smaller units capable of exercising local and regional initiatives, would be to rivet together the ultimate megamachine.

Before the power system had made plenitude possible, the great objection to vocational diversification would have been that it would decrease the necessary supply of goods, lower profits, and slow down the pace of production. But this slowdown would apply mainly to superficial and meretricious goods; this is precisely what an economy of plenitude demands if it is to foster a selective use of goods, and due rejection of 'bads.' A slowdown in many areas of production has become imperative, so as to curtail the over-stimulation of the profit-pleasure centers. But a slowdown, sometimes even a stoppage, is no less imperative in order to provide the leisure necessary for fostering more intimate human relations.

Let me put the contrast in a single concrete example. The physician who finds time to give personal attention to his patients and listen to them, carefully probing inner conditions that may be more significant than any laboratory reports, has become a rarity. Where the power complex is dominant, a visit to a physician is paced, not to fit the patient's needs, but mainly to perform the succession of physical tests upon which the diagnosis will be based. Yet if there were a sufficient number of competent physicians on hand whose inner resources were as available as their laboratory aids, a more subtle diagnosis might be possible, and the patient's subjective response might in many cases effectively supplement the treatment. Thoreau expressed this to perfection when he observed in his 'Journal' that "the really efficient laborer will be found not to crowd his day with work, but will saunter to his task surrounded by a wide halo of ease and leisure."

Without this slowing of the tempo of all activities the positive advantages of plenitude could not be sufficiently enjoyed; for the congestion of time is as threatening to the good life as the congestion of space or people, and produces stresses and tensions that equally undermine human relations. The inner stability that such a slowdown brings about is essential to the highest uses of the mind, through opening up that second life which one lives in reflection and contemplation and self-scrutiny. The means to escape from the "noisy crowding up of things and whatsoever wars on the divine" was one of the vital offerings of the classic religions: hence their emphasis was not on technological productivity but on personal poise. The old slogan of New York subway guards in handling a crush of passengers applies with even greater force to the tempo of megatechnic society: "What's your hurry? . . . Watch your step!"

6: IF THE SLEEPERS AWAKEN

The stoppages and breakdowns that have occurred have a certain potential educational value, for they disclose the susceptibility of the whole system to human intervention, if only of a negative kind. Disobedience is the infant's first step toward autonomy, and even infantile destruction may temporarily awaken confidence in the individual's capacity to change his environment. But the well publicized devastations of a world war or the threat of greater nuclear catastrophes still did not shock mankind into taking sufficient steps for its own self-protection: witness the present pitiful substitute for a responsible world organization, the United Nations—purposely crippled in advance by the 'Great Powers.'

The realization that the entire system is now breaking down might have come about more swiftly if the professional bodies that should have been monitoring our technology—the engineers, the biologists, the physicians—had not so completely identified themselves with the power system's objectives. So until lately they have been criminally negligent in anticipating or even reporting what has actually been taking place—and in the case of nuclear fallout and nuclear wastes have often deliberately, in conformity to the 'national policy,' minimized their dangers.

Not that occasional warning voices were absent, even at an early date: I have already cited the examples of Henry Adams and Frederick Soddy, to say nothing of H. G. Wells. But when an eminent British engineer, Sir Alfred Ewing, suggested in 1933 that there might well be a moratorium on invention, in order to assimilate and integrate the existing mass of inventions and evaluate further proposals, he was hooted at as a crank, demanding a foolish and impossible sacrifice.

Few of Ewing's contemporaries realized then that a purely mechanical system whose processes can neither be retarded nor redirected nor halted, that has no internal mechanism for warning of defects or correcting them (feedback), and that can only be accelerated is, as we have all too late found out, a menace to mankind. Yet anyone familiar with the history of inventions would know that great industrial corporations have frequently bought up patents—like the early one for an automatic telephone system—in order to suppress them, or have diverted research from areas where new inventions might threaten capital investment or reduce inordinate profits. (Note the studious indifference to developing more efficient accumulators essential to the electric motor car and the use of windpower.) There was nothing unrealistic in Ewing's proposal—except the hope that it might be carried out by those still spellbound by the myth of the machine. Had Ewing's warning been generally heeded, the world would now be a healthier and safer place.

During the past three decades the involuntary failures of the power system have become increasingly lethal, and they have been occurring with a frequency and a force that corresponds to the dynamism of the individual parts. As these brownouts and blackouts and breakdowns continue to occur, with disastrous consequences to both the habitat and the human population, such a change may take place as was noted in London during the Blitz, a comparable ordeal. At that time psychiatrists observed that their anxious, neurotic patients, when confronted by a real danger they could neither evade in fantasy nor flee from, began to function as competent human beings, able at last to face up to their difficulties.

The situation that mankind now faces collectively shows a certain resemblance to that confronted by the individual in the midst of a neurosis. Before his disturbance comes into the open various events, unrecognized by the patient, have paved the way for his illness. But as long as he is able to conceal his condition from himself and perform his daily tasks without exhibiting suicidal depression or uncontrollable hostility to those around him, he may be unwilling to consult a physician, or re-examine his life. The first step toward recognizing his state and seeking help usually begins with a visible collapse, bodily or mental, often both.

At this point the method of pychoanalysis offers a clue that may be of value in handling the present collective breakdown: this lies in the effort to trace present symptoms back to earlier mishaps or injuries, deeply buried in the psyche, difficult to uncover, which deflected the organism from its normal path of growth. By bringing such traumas into consciousness, the patient may better understand his own nature and acquire insight into the conditions under which he can, through his own efforts, make the most of the potentialities that his personal life and his culture offer him.

The unbaring of man's historic past during the last two centuries may well prove a more important contribution to man's survival than all his other scientific knowledge. This reclamation of human history will involve, as Erich Neumann has emphasized, absorbing into man's conscious existence the evils that, if unidentified and unrecognized, will otherwise continue to thwart him. Our megatechnic culture, based as it is on the strange supposition that subjective malice has no reality and that evils do not exist, except in the sense of reparable mechanical defects, has proved itself incompetent to take on such responsibilities.

The realization that the physical breakdowns and subjective demoralizations of Western civilization derive from the same ideological failures is now at last taking hold. But for a dynamic response to this situation, something like a universal awakening sufficient to produce an internal readiness for a profounder transformation, must take place. Such a reaction, one must honestly confess, has never yet occurred in history solely as a result of rational thinking and educational indoctrination: nor is it likely to occur in this way now—at least within the narrow time limits one must allow, if greater breakdowns and demoralizations are to be circumvented.

Half a century ago H. G. Wells observed, correctly enough, that mankind faced a race between education and catastrophe. But what he failed to recognize was that something like catastrophe has become the condition for an effective education. This might seem like a dismal and hopeless conclusion, were it not for the fact that the power system, through its own overwhelming achievements, has proved expert in creating breakdowns and catastrophes.

Today's technological breakdowns are no less ominous than the growing resistance of the personnel to performing the unrewarding labor necessary to keep the system in operation: but they may bring compensatory reactions, for they give the human personality a chance to function. This stunningly took place during the Northeast power breakdown of November 1965. Suddenly, as in E. M. Forster's fable, The Machine Stops. Millions of people, caught without either power or light, immobilized in railroad trains, subways, skyscraper elevators, moved spontaneously into action, without waiting for the system to recover or for orders to come from above. "While the city of bricks and mortar was dead," 'The New Yorker' reported, "the people were more alive than ever."

For many this stoppage proved an exhilarating experience: autos, which can function by their own power and light, kept moving: citizens supplemented policemen in directing traffic: trucks took on passengers: strangers helped one another: people found that their legs would transport them efficiently when wheels failed: one set of young men and women gaily formed a procession, carrying candles, chanting in mock solemnity, "Hark the Herald Angels Sing!" All the latent human powers that a perfect, smooth-running mechanical organization suppresses began to function again. What seemed a calamity turned into an opportunity: when the machine stopped, life recovered. The kind of self-confidence and self-reliance generated by such an experience is what is needed to cut the power complex down to human size, and bring it under control. "Let man take over!"

Admittedly the partial disasters of war, though no longer locally limited, had through the ages grown too familiar to bring about a sufficient reaction. During the last decade, fortunately, there has been a sudden, quite unpredictable awakening to prospects of a total catastrophe. The unrestricted increase of population, the over-exploitation of megatechnical inventions, the inordinate wastages of compulsory consumption, and the consequent deterioration of the environment through wholesale pollution, poisoning, bulldozing, to say nothing of the more irremediable waste-products of atomic energy, have at last begun to create the reaction needed to overcome them.

This awakening has become planet-wide. The experiences of congestion, environmental degradation, and human demoralization now fall within the compass of everyone's daily life. Even in the open country, small communities are now forced to take political action against canny enterprisers seeking to dump wastes from distant cities in rural areas that already have difficulties enough in coping with their own rubbish and sewage. The extent of the approaching catastrophe, its visible nearness, and its dire inevitability unless counter-measures are rapidly taken, have done far more than the vivid prospects of sudden nuclear extinction to bring on a sufficient psychological response. In this respect, the swifter the degradation, the more likely effective measures against it will be sought.

Yet even granting that, in the first shock of realizing mankind's plight, hitherto unthinkable political measures may be proposed, the question remains whether the massive human participation needed will actually occur. Any program sufficient to reverse the destructive success of technological affluence will demand not merely drastic restrictions; it will demand economic and social changes directed toward producing goods and services, modes of work and education and recreation, profoundly different from those offered by the power complex.

Reformers who would treat the campaign against environmental and human degradation solely in terms of improved technological facilities, like the reduction of gasoline exhaust in motor cars, see only a small part of the problem. Nothing less than a profound re-orientation of our vaunted technological 'way of life' will save this planet from becoming a lifeless desert. And without such a wide-ranging preliminary alteration of personal desires, habits, and ideals the necessary physical measures for mankind's protection—to say nothing of its further development—cannot conceivably be carried out.

On this matter, one dare not become over-optimistic even though the first stir of a human awakening seems actually to be taking place. The unwillingness of millions of cigarette smokers to free themselves from their addiction to cigarettes despite the incontestable evidence of the probable consequences in lung cancer, gives a hint of the difficulties we shall face in redeeming the planet—and ourselves—for life. Our present addiction to private motor transportation alone may prove equally hard to break until every traffic artery is permanently clogged and every city is ruined.

For its effective salvation mankind will need to undergo something like a spontaneous religious conversion: one that will replace the mechanical world picture with an organic world picture, and give to the human personality, as the highest known manifestation of life, the precedence it now gives to its machines and computers. This order of change is as hard for most people to conceive as was the change from the classic power complex of Imperial Rome to that of Christianity, or, later, from supernatural medieval Christianity to the machine-modeled ideology of the seventeenth century. But such changes have repeatedly occurred all through history; and under catastrophic pressure they may occur again. Of only one thing we may be confident. If mankind is to escape its programmed self-extinction the God who saves us will not descend from the machine: he will rise up again in the human soul.

Epilogue: The Advancement of Life

In earlier books I have sought to describe the formative processes of nature and culture through which man has emerged as the apex so far of organic development. "Human life, in its historic manifoldness and purposefulness, is our starting point. No single being can embrace that life; no single lifetime contains it; no single culture can encompass all its potentialities. One cannot even partly understand the nature of man, unless one realizes that its roots lie buried in the debris of countless invisible lives and that its topmost branches must by their very frailty defy the most daring climber. Man lives in history; he lives through history; and in a certain sense, he lives for history, since no small part of his activities goes toward preparation for an undisclosed future." ('The Conduct of Life.')

Man's existence in all its dimensions is perhaps best understood in terms of the theater, as a drama unfolding in action. If I have repeated this metaphor more than once it is because I know no more scientific analysis that does such justice to every aspect of human development. In his earthly theater man is by turns architect and scenic designer, director and stagehand, playwright and spectator; and above all he is an actor whose whole life is "such stuff as dreams are made on." Yet he is so formed and shaped by the nature of the stage, by the roles that he assumes, by the plots that he superimposes, that every aspect of the drama has substance and takes on some measure of significance.

Though in the dim beginnings of man's emergence the scenario was improvised from moment to moment, from scene to scene, he himself has become increasingly conscious of his own special roles, and now, with more than Prospero's magic spells, he occupies the center of the stage. On many occasions the plot has been misdirected and the play has seemed little better than a wry comedy of errors; at other moments, it rises to a brief, soul-searching climax, amid which even the properties and costumes cease to be trivial accessories and actively sustain the drama—only to fall back, as in the final act of 'King Lear,' into lacerating confusion.

This drama takes place in a cosmic setting; and its beginning and ending must remain forever outside the boundaries of actual human experience. Whatever the defects of this metaphor, of one thing one may be sure: the empty building, the stage properties, or the apparatus for manipulating the scenery and the lights do not in any sense constitute the drama, or justify the immense collective effort necessary to assemble and train the cast. By themselves, none of the physical constituents, not even the human bodies, are important. It is only through illumination by the mind of man that either the cosmic or the human drama makes sense.

In so far as the universal religions, and not a few more primitive cults and myths, have had some sense of the all-enveloping cosmic process as more significant than anything that is immediately visible and intelligible on the stage, they have had a firmer hold on reality than those delimited, factual descriptions that remain unaware of the wonder and mystery of the whole performance. Cosmodrama, biodrama, technodrama, politodrama, autodrama—to use Patrick Geddes's terms—provide the scenario and setting of human existence. And if in this study of 'The Myth of the Machine' I have emphasized the technodrama, it is not because I have accepted the technocratic belief that the command of nature is man's most important task, but because I regard technology as a formative part of human culture as a whole. As such, technics has been deeply modified at every stage of its development by dreams, wishes, impulses, religious motives that spring directly, not from the practical needs of daily life, but from the recesses of man's unconscious. It is in the human mind that these dramas take form; and it is there that they culminate from time to time in flashes that suddenly light up the wide landscape of human existence.

From the mountains of rubble, slag, rubbish, bones, dust, excrement that bear witness to the works and days of each passing generation, a few milligrams of radioactive mind-energy have in the course of history been extracted, and from them, only a fractional amount has been preserved. That fraction, passing from mind to mind, has the property of irradiating the rest of existence with meaning and value. Like the radioactive elements themselves, these dynamic and formative attributes of mind are extremely powerful, but evanescent: yet their half-life, as with the ancient Egyptian organization of the megamachine, may last for thousands of years.

So far, nonetheless, these activating manifestations of mind are the ultimate witnesses to the cosmos itself—whose potentialities remained invisible and undetectable for billions of years until man himself, through the massive growth of his brain, achieved his greatest technological triumph: the invention of symbols and complex symbolic structures that enhance consciousness. For it was initially through the fabrications of the mind, through dream and symbol, not alone through the cunning of his hands, that man learned to command his own bodily organs, to communicate and cooperate with his kind, and to master so much of the natural environment as would serve his actual needs and ideal purposes.

The sober, day-to-day descriptions of human existence take man's subjective activities for granted. They reflect the preoccupation of the workshop with materials and tools, the preoccupation of the merchant with buying and selling, or the preoccupation with quantitative measurements necessary for every kind of large-scale organization. All these pragmatic interests refer to an existence in which the creative role of mind, though always present, may for 'practical purposes' be disregarded. As Galileo put it, and as the exponents of the power complex agreed, counting and measuring are the attributes of mind that have objective reality; and whatever cannot be accounted for mathematically, or quantitatively described, may be ignored as rationally unimportant and virtually non-existent.

As long as older manifestations of mind, variously embodied in religion and art, in ritual and social custom, gave a coherent symbolic organization to support other aspects of life, the belief that material objects exist and function by themselves did no immediate damage. In daily life all that was deliberately left out in the mechanical world picture still remained actively present and gave play to other parts of man's nature besides those that subserved technics. Whatever Bacon and Galileo omitted from their account of nature, Shakespeare and Pascal brilliantly kept in existence; even Bacon, though no Shakespeare, had a vivid sense of the empty spaces that were left unaccounted for, no matter how accurately this or that part of the 'objective' picture might be faithfully delineated, or brought under technological control.

Unfortunately, those who equated reality with 'objective,' mechanical, quantitatively measurable modes of thought, not merely disregarded the immense creativity of the human mind in other areas but remained increasingly indifferent to the wonder of the whole cosmic performance. Newton, still deeply steeped in religious culture, was humble before the mystery that his own prodigious intellectual performance had only magnified, and continued to ask questions he could not answer about the nature of the beauty and order his mind recognized in those physical forces that are remote from human passions. But those materialist philosophers who—as they supposed—had left art and religion, values and purposes, behind them, who gave precedence to unminded 'matter,' denied the source of their own creativity: for the very idea of quantitative measurement or mathematical interpretation is a subjective one, known only to man. In so far as modern technology operated on these limited terms, so contrary to those that created all earlier forms of polytechnics, it could only muffle up and isolate the human presence as a source of contamination.

The translation of brute experience into significant cultural forms, so that every aspect of existence will ultimately bear some impress of mind, is surely the central fact of human development. This is what distinguishes a higher culture from a lower one, a vacuous existence from a purposeful one, a superior, mentally activated, fully developed human being from one who has barely risen above a dull animal state of being. Through man's prolonged efforts at minding and making, he who was originally speechless, workless, houseless, artless, took on his supreme task—that of making himself human. To this end he utilized his specific bodily functions for other purposes than those that served reproduction and survival.

By shaping and directing his own organs, beginning with the control of his bowels and his bladder, deliberately inhibiting or releasing, curtailing or enlarging every other organic function, even learning the most difficult art of effectively canalizing his once random mental activities, man did something more important than 'conquer nature.' For in time he reorganized every part of nature, his own body as well as his habitat, for purposes that transcended animal existence. From the beginning, technics had an active part to play in this self-transformation; but it neither instituted these activities by itself nor, until our own age, did it seek to narrow man's capacities to those that could be confined to a technological outlet.

Man is his own supreme artifact. But this passage from animal to human has been no easy one; and it is far from finished; many further developments still loom ahead. All through history there have been fixations, regressions, degradations, monotonous cyclical repetitions, institutionalized errors and horrors, and terminal disintegrations. On all these negative aspects A. J. Toynbee's 'A Study of History' presents voluminous evidence. Yet despite these blockages, there have been intermittent, if not incessant, evidences of high creativity and genuine development, culminating in symbolic personalities, mythical and natural, human and divine, that still set a standard for further human development.

Without these possibilities for subjective transcendence, which are basic to man's whole development, it is doubtful if such a hyper-sensitive organism as man's could have survived the terrors and ordeals that were painfully magnified by the sweep and depth of his own consciousness: disease, bodily injury, senseless accident, human malignity, institutional corruption. An age like our own, whose subjectivity trusts only one channel, that through science and technology, is ill-prepared to face the stark realities of life. Even those who still cling to the ancient heritage of religion and art, rich and nourishing though that still is, have become so acclimated to the dehumanized assumptions of technology that only a scattering of faithful souls have dared to challenge even its grossest perversions.

The existence in man of a dynamic internal world, whose essential nature cannot be probed by any instrument, and can be known only when it finds expression in gestures and symbols and constructive activities, is a mystery as profound as the forces that bind together the components of the atom and account for the character and behavior of the elements. In man that mystery can be experienced, but not described, still less explained: for the mind cannot mirror itself from within. Only by getting outside itself does it become conscious of its inwardness.

The effort to eliminate the formative role of the mind, making the artifact more important than the artificer, reduces mystery to absurdity; and that affirmation of absurdity is the life-heresy of the present generation. This reductionism turns at last into the drooling blankness of 'Waiting for Godot' or 'Krapp's Last Tape,' with their representation of boredom and tedium as the inevitable climax of human existence. This in itself is a sardonic final commentary on the mechanical world picture, the power system, and the subjective non-values derived from them. For a technology that denies reality to the subjective life cannot claim any human value for even its own highest products.

An organic world picture cannot, however, deny entropy. It must accept as given the breaking down processes that accompany all vital activities: indeed, they are no less an integral part of life, no less a contrapuntal contribution to its creativity than the orderly, constructive, upbuilding functions; for the two processes can no more be separated than body and soul, brain and mind, until they are arrested in death. But there is latent energy in the mind that in rare moments by-passes these organic limitations and ignores or defies the ultimate terminus of death: this reveals itself as the impulse to transcendence. The recognition as a species that man possesses a deep longing to overcome his organic limitations, and that this aspiration may give significance even to the most distressing moments of existence, has been the benign gift of religion, and accounts, surely, for the hold it has had over the mass of mankind. This office is all the more singular because it frequently flouts the requirements for organic maintenance, reproduction, and survival: hence it cannot be derived from animal needs as so many other human functions, not least those of technics, can be derived.

Despite the elimination of subjectivity from the mechanical world picture, the desire for perfection, the need to defy and circumvent fate, the impulse to transcendence, can be observed in technology, too, along with other manifestations common to religion, like the readiness to accept sacrifice and premature death.

Consider the ancient dream of effecting the transmutation of the baser metals into gold. That may be easily dismissed with contempt as a childish effort to get rich quickly; but if riches alone had been the object there were a hundred demonstrably better ways at hand. The desire to overcome physical limitations by magic manipulations owed as much to the mind as chemistry did to the alchemist's furnace: so impetuous, so willful, so insistent, was this desire that it sometimes tempted the alchemists to fake the results by hiding a pellet of gold in the ashes. But this subjective impulse to transcend the limitations of 'matter' has turned out to be closer to reality than the well-grounded inhibitions against it: the alchemists' dream, we now realize, pointed to the ultimate miracle of nuclear fission.

Though large areas of human culture have died out or been destroyed in the course of history—especially during the last four centuries—the unformed, unorganized 'apparitions' of the mind have retained as much scope as ever: or rather, they have grown stronger because they have been canalized into science and technics. Strangely, the very existence of these pre-conscious sources of technology have been ignored on the supposition that science and technics have no subjective attachments. Nothing could be further from the truth.

This great over-simplification and self-deception was originally bolstered up by the mechanical world picture; and it still remains in effect even though that world picture now influences only the more backward areas of science. As I showed earlier, the idea of time is more important than any physical instrument invented for recording time; and this idea took form in the human mind, with no other instrument than the naked human eye observing planetary motions and calculating them with the aid of abstract mathematical symbols that likewise existed only in the human mind. The idea of time did not come from either the sundial or the hourglass: neither would any direct improvement of these instruments by the human hand have produced the mechanical clock.

As Newton astutely observed in his 'Optics,' it is through tracing the causes of phenomena from their physical effects that we come to the First Cause; and this, he added, "is certainly not mechanical." If I dare amend that statement in order to apply it, not to the physical universe but to human affairs, it would be by finding the First Cause, not alone in Newton's all-pervading Divine Organizer, but in the human mind.

To hold that man's subjective impulses and fantasies must be given as much weight as formative influences in culture, indeed as prime movers, as either the impressions made on his senses by the 'physical world' or by the varied tools and machines he has contrived in order to modify that world may seem to many, even today, a somewhat daring hypothesis. In our one-sided picture of the universe, man himself has become the displaced person: out of sight and therefore out of mind, an exile and a starving prisoner in a concentration camp he himself has laid out.

In reacting against the uncontrolled subjectivism of earlier world pictures our Western culture has gone to the opposite extreme. Once upon a time people gave far too much authority to their uncorrected and incorrigible fantasies, and they ignored the fact that men cannot by exclusive concentration upon their inner life survive and reproduce except by the charity and grace of others who do not suffer from such delusions: a truth that the Hippies will in time find out. The failure to create a coherent transcendental world picture that did sufficient justice to the existential and subjectively unalterable facts of human experience has been the fatal weakness of all religions. But this subjective error has now been overcorrected, and has in turn produced a notion that is equally false: namely, that the organization of physical and corporeal activities can prosper in a mindless world.

The present analysis of technics and human development rests on belief in the imperative need for reconciling and fusing together the subjective and the objective aspects of human experience, by a methodology that will ultimately embrace both. This can come about, not by dismissing either religion or science, but first by detaching them from the obsolete ideological matrix that has distorted their respective developments and limited their field of interaction. Man's marvellous achievements in projecting his subjective impulses into institutional forms, esthetic symbols, mechanical organizations, and architectural structures have been vastly augmented by the orderly cooperative methods that science has exemplified and universalized. But at the same time, to reduce acceptable subjectivity to the ideal level of a computer would only sever rationality and order from their own deepest sources in the organism. If we are to save technology itself from the aberrations of its present leaders and putative gods, we must, in both our thinking and our acting, come back to the human center: for it is here that all significant transformations begin and terminate.

The nature of this interplay and this union between the subjective and objective aspects of existence defies any extensive description, since it involves nothing less than the entire history of mankind. So it was left for a poet to sum up this underlying reality in a few words. What Goethe said about nature applies equally to every manifestation of culture and personality. "Nature has neither core nor skin: she's both at once outside and in." It is on that assumption that I have given equal weight, in describing man's technological advances, to every part of his organism, not to the hand and its derivative tools alone. And this is why, too, I have emphasized the part played by wishes and projects, by symbols and fantasies, upon even the most practical applications of technology. For it is through all the activities of the mind, not alone the intelligence and the dynamic instruments of intelligence, that radical departures from conventional practices are made in technics itself.

This approach, if sound, carries with it a conclusion that challenges those who imagine that the forces and institutions now in existence will go on indefinitely, becoming bigger and more powerful, even though their very bigness and power threaten to nullify the benefits originally sought. If human culture in fact arises, develops, and renews itself through fresh activities in the mind, it may be modified and transformed by the same processes. What the human mind has created, it can also destroy. Neglect or withdrawal of interest works as effectively as physical assault. This is a lesson that our machine-oriented world must quickly assimilate, if it is to preserve even its own successful innovations.

In order summarily to describe the active part man has played in his technical development—as contrasted with the view that he is the fated victim of external forces and external institutions over which he has little or no control—I purpose to follow the interplay of man's subjective and objective life in two complementary movements: materialization˙ and etherialization. Paradoxically, the process of materialization begins in the mind, while that of etherialization proceeds from the visible and external world to the inner personality, finally taking form in the mind, through words and other symbols, as a more or less coherent world view.

The following account of the modes of human development must not be confused, because of the verbal resemblance, with either Hegelian idealism or Marxian materialism, though there is a modicum of abstract truth in both those philosophies, with their recognition of dynamic and contradictory processes, which I seek to reconcile with concrete historic realities. An organic concept of cultural and personal change must treat both inner and outer aspects as coeval, not mutually exclusive. Emerson, in his 'Essay on War,' came near to formulating my own view when he said: "Observe how every truth, every error, each a thought of some man's mind, clothes itself in societies, houses, cities, language, ceremonies, newspapers." I am grateful to Emerson for realizing—contrary to both Hegel and Marx—that error as well as truth, evil as well as good, may play a part, for, as he noted in 'Uriel,' "Evil will bless, and ice will burn."

Both etherialization and materialization go through a series of distinguishable but not always successive phases; and if they take place at the same time, they move in opposite directions—though not always at the same pace or with the same impact in different areas of the same culture. If etherialization begins originally in the direct impression that the external habitat and its inhabitants make on man's mind, materialization begins rather in the human mind itself, at a stage prior to abstraction and symbolization: the stage of dreams and pre-conscious activities whose stimulus comes mainly from within, through the hormones and endocrines, notably those connected with sex, hunger, and fear.

The first phase of materialization springs from neural activities to which the term 'mind' can hardly yet be attached: what later will come forth as an 'idea' might with greater accuracy be called an apparition, more impalpable than the traditional ghost. This apparition is, by definition, an entirely private experience, unformed, wordless, incommunicable—and therefore more difficult to lay hold of than even a nocturnal dream. Obviously such an intuitive process cannot be investigated scientifically: its existence can only be deduced by a backward reading from its later developments. But the constant flow of stimuli from the internal organs of the body, including the brain itself, which shows activity even in sleep, must be posited as the starting point for all formalized and organized mental life.

The existence of these formless subjective activities might remain questionable were it not for the fact that they have a tendency, if heeded— and especially if frequently repeated—to take on a stable character. Thus the nascent 'idea' of courage, before it can be called an idea, may assume the recallable image of a lion. To pass from what is internal, unconscious, and private, to a public world which can be shared by other men is the next stage in materialization. At this point, the nascent idea, well before it can find words to express itself, first does so in the language of the body. It is by this process that formative ideas that may eventually dominate a whole society take possession of a living person, and in time become visible to other men. *'Idées-forces'* was Alfred Fouillée's happy term for such dynamic and formative ideas.

Most germinal 'ideas' die a-borning: they never pass beyond the stage of apparition. Even an idea viable enough and lucky enough to survive must undergo a long period of incubation and experimental testing, before it becomes sufficiently palpable as an idea to get lodged, like a windblown seed, in a niche favorable to its growth. That niche must be a living person, though not always the originator and only begetter. This is the phase of 'incarnation.'

Even before an idea can be transmitted in speech it becomes, if one may use the classic New Testament description, incarnate in the flesh, and makes itself known by appropriate bodily changes. Do not suppose that the preliminary phases of intuition and ideation are in any sense mystical: they are commonplaces of everyday experience. Nor does the concept of incarnation refer necessarily to the particular theological epiphany from which we derive the term. In Volume One of 'The Myth of The Machine' I showed how the idea of 'Kingship' arose as a transcendental image of power and authority derived from a fusion of the commanding experience of a mighty hunting chief with the worship of a solar deity, Atum-Re—or in Sumer and Akkad, with an equally powerful Storm God who there took precedence.

But we need not look to ancient Mesopotamia, Egypt, or Palestine for examples of incarnation. The yearning for a primitive counter-culture, defying the rigidly organized and depersonalized forms of Western civilization, began to float into the Western mind in the original expressions of Romanticism among the intellectual classes. That desire to return to a more primeval state took a folksy if less articulate form, in the elemental rhythms of jazz, more than half a century ago. What made this idea suddenly erupt again, with almost volcanic power, into Western society was its incarnation in the Beatles. It was not just the sudden success of the Beatles' musical records that indicated that a profound change was taking place in the minds of the young: it was their new personality, as expressed in their long, neo-medieval haircut, their unabashed sentimentality, their nonchalant posture, and their dreamlike spontaneity that opened up for the post-nuclear generation the possibility of an immediate escape from megatechnic society. In the Beatles all their repressions, and all their resentments of repression were released: by hairdo, costume, ritual, and song, all changes depending upon purely personal choice, the new counter-ideas that bound the younger generation together were at once clarified and magnified. Impulses that were still too dumbly felt for words, spread like wildfire through incarnation and imitation.

The spread of a new gospel through visible personalities often characterizes the emergence of a new cultural epoch. There were many Messiahs and Teachers of Righteousness, both genuine and false, both before and after the coming of Jesus Christ.

But note: the newly incarnated personality, be it Buddhist or Liverpool-Dionysian, cannot survive alone, narcissistically gazing at its own image. Like a single biological mutant, the idea would be doomed unless similar impulses were beginning to find a corporeal form in thousands of other personalities: it is only by this general readiness, in fact, that the formative idea can imprint itself, by direct contact and emulation, upon a sufficient body of disciples and followers before the idea itself in more purely verbal form can be understood. Whitman spoke for all participators in this process when he said "I and mine do not convince by arguments: we convince by our presence." Proverbially it is by living the life that one knows the doctrine: by first taking bodily shape the idea begins to spread throughout the community by bodily imitation before it can be more effectively defined by word of mouth and in intellectual formulations.

It is through the maturation of ideas, in the daily experience of living, that the gap between the original 'apparitions and intuitions' and the realities of social life which other men participate in is bridged. This state of formulation and ideation and elaboration may be identified with the oral teachings of the great masters, the memorizing of their words by disciples, as in the Confucian Analects, Plato's Dialogues, or the Christian Gospels, and their final fixation in books. At this point the unique insights of the incarnation become strengthened by many others ideas that are already either part of a stable tradition, indeed a system of education, or are still in the 'air.' As with the incarnation, the formative ideas, in order to remain alive, must be re-thought and re-tested by fresh experience from generation to generation.

The next stage, toward a wider socialization of the idea, may be called 'incorporation': at last the original formative impulse is re-enforced by conscious rational effort throughout the whole community, manifesting itself in the habits of family life, the customs of the village, the routines of the city, the practices of the workshop, the rituals of the temple, the legal procedures of the court. Without this general social adoption and modification, the formative idea, even if widely incarnated, would lose its authority and efficacy; and indeed it was the weakness of Christianity in extending its moral principles to organized government, its reluctance to come to grips with slavery and war and class exploitation that, despite the immense energies it released in other departments, was responsible for its loss of impetus, its inner corrosion, and its failure to achieve the universal brotherly society it proclaimed.

Karl Marx properly recognized how effective a role the organization of the materials of production (technology) played in molding the human personality. But he made the grave error of treating economic organization as an independent, self-evolving factor, immune to active human intervention; whereas this form of materialization is but one of the many ways in which the fermenting ideas of a culture become accepted, regularized, carried into general daily practice. In this respect, perhaps the high point of Christian social achievement came relatively late in the Middle Ages, when its monasteries, almshouses, orphanages, and hospitals were to be found in every city, on a scale hitherto unknown.

It is by institutional extension that subjective impulses cease to be private, willful, contradictory, and ineffectual, and so become capable of bringing about large social changes. This transformation both releases new potentialities and may disclose, if it fails to take corporate form, unexpected defects. Matriarchy in one age, kingship in another, divine redemption and salvation in a third, must be incorporated into every institution and influence every collective action, if the formative ideas underlying a culture are to flourish sufficiently and hold their own against the mass of residues and encrusted material survivals, still tenacious and often powerful. Since the existing institutions have a past that antedated the new idea and incorporated values and purposes of a different nature, it is in this third phase that many further modifications will be made, contributing ingredients that were lacking in the original proposals. Yet at the same time it is only by this act of incorporation that the assent and support of a larger population can be assured.

At this point of incorporation the new cultural form, for better and worse, loses some of its pristine clarity. Those who have fallen under the spell of a new vision, or who have sought to take on swiftly the mask of a new personality, often shrink from accepting this further mode of materialization: it seems at best a compromise, at worst a complete betrayal. Certainly by incorporation in existing institutions, the idea loses some of its original purity, if it does not in fact turn into its own antithesis through the very act of materialization.

Thus when the Roman state was converted to Christianity under Constantine, the Christian Church was also in some degree converted to paganism, and not merely tolerated many Roman practices, but even transferred the sadistic rituals of the Roman arena to the Christian conception of Hell, as an ultimate dispensation of Divine justice, making the spectacle of the eternal torture of condemned sinners one of the supreme joys for the faithful in Heaven.

The final materialization of a formative idea, from its pre-conscious inception in many individual minds to a fully externalized and socialized state, shared by everyone, consists in the transformation of the physical environment, alike through practical means and symbolic expressions. This phase may be called 'embodiment.' First the plot is outlined, then the actors are chosen; then the actors put on their make-up and their costumes; then the scenario is outlined and the plot is developed; and finally new physical structures are built to express and support the idea.

Yet it is in these reconstituted physical structures that novel possibilities are revealed that were only latent in the original conception—quite untranslatable into more easily formed verbal, graphic, or musical symbols. Could Jesus Christ, the most spontaneous and informal of personalities, have guessed that the ultimate expression of Christianity would be realized in a formalized hierarchic organization, operating uniformly over the entire continent of Europe, and that the culmination of this worldly movement would be the widespread erection of cathedrals, churches, monasteries, whose technical audacity and esthetic vitality had no place in Jesus' intuitions? And yet, paradoxically, without the Christian idea there would have been no Durham, no Chartres, no Bamberg—and no Holy Inquisition! What better revelation could be offered of the unpredictability of the future—as contrasted with the present method of extrapolating observable existing tendencies?

Though I have used a particular episode in Western history, the rise of the Christian Church, as a convenient example, the process summarized is a general one, applicable with many variations to all cultures, not least to the triumph of the myth of the machine.

In putting together the phases of materialization in a serial form in time, I have ignored simultaneous phenomena, and have treated, as if they were separate and formally recognizable events, institutions, personalities, and ideas that were in fact in constant flux and interaction, undergoing both inner and outer transformations. So, for example, the incarnation of Jesus did not take place only once: for the Christian idea, to keep alive, needed further re-incarnations, always with fresh modifications, in the persons of Paul, Augustine, Francis of Assisi, and countless other Christian souls. In these changes the luminous original message lost, no doubt, some of its force, for the ideas suitable to a dying culture were irrelevant to the resurgent vitalities of later periods. Yet though both the institutional organization of the Church and its wealth of physical structures smothered the original flame, it smoldered on—and astonishingly flared up again in our own late day in the person of Pope John XXIII.

One final aspect of materialization remains to be noted: a paradox. And this is that subjective expressions remain alive in the mind far longer than the corporate organizations and physical buildings that seem to the outward eye so solid and durable. Even when a culture disintegrates, the loss is never quite complete or final. From the total achievement much will remain and leave its imprint on later minds in the form of sport, play, language, art, customs. Though few Westerners have seen a Hindu temple, the Sanskrit root for mother and father still remains on their tongue in addressing their parents, more durable than any monument; and this symbolic debris of past cultures forms a rich compost for the mind, without which the cultural environment would be as sterile as that of the moon. André Varagnac has demonstrated that an extremely ancient, orally transmitted culture, largely neolithic, perhaps even pre-neolithic in origin, passed on its magical beliefs, its sexual customs and marriage rites, its folklore and fairy tales to succeeding generations throughout the world.

This archaic culture still forms the buried underlayer of contemporary society. The games of ball played everywhere are survivals from the temples where, in religious ritual, the ball represented the sun, and the opposing players stood for the forces of light and darkness. The notorious recrudescence of astrology and witchcraft today is only the latest example of this subjective persistence. Even when all the material properties needed for a wornout drama have disappeared, some vestige of the play itself will nevertheless remain in proverbs, ballads, musical phrases and melodies reverberating from generation to generation: more durable in the spoken word than if incised in stone. If the great pyramids of Egypt seem an exception, one must remember that, for all their solidity, they were symbols of the Mountain of Creation, of the yearning for immortality, of the desire to transcend time and organic corruption.

The counter-process to materialization I have chosen to call 'etherialization,' but since Arnold Toynbee has used the latter term in a more limited sense I should perhaps make clear a certain difference. In 'A Study of History' Toynbee pointed to a tendency, visible in both biological and social development, toward a diminution in size and increasing simplification, going along with a higher degree of internal organization and refinement. Witness the passage in evolution from the giant empty-headed reptiles to the small brainy mammals, or from the lumbering cathedral clocks of the fifteenth century to the exquisitely compact and accurate watches of the twentieth. In a rough way, this generalization holds: yet Toynbee ignores the equally significant contrary process that I have been describing, which proceeds in the opposite direction. For that part of the process which Toynbee indicates I would prefer to use the term 'de-materialization.'

Following the mode of etherialization, the tangible visible world is translated progressively into symbols and reorganized in the mind. In 'Technics and Human Development' I endeavored to outline the natural history of this process: so here I purpose only to describe how a once fully embodied culture becomes de-materialized, and thus opens the way for a new constellation of formative ideas, which themselves come into existence partly by reaction against the dominant culture, and yet are constantly conditioned, and even temporarily supported by the very customs and institutions they seek to replace.

When the organizing idea of a culture has been fully explored, when its drama has been played out and all that is left of the original creative impulse is a soul-deadening ritual and compulsory drill, the moment for a new formative idea has come. Against such a change, however, the whole body of entrenched institutions presents a solid wall; for what is an institution but a closed society for the prevention of change? Hence the path of etherialization, so far from beginning with a new idea, starts at just the opposite end by attacking the visible structures and organizations which, so long as they remain in good working order, allow no place for a new idea to take hold.

The path of etherialization, then, is often opened up by a breakdown that invites this assault. At first this is mainly a physical breakdown which exposes the technical ineptitude or human insufficiency of a seemingly prosperous society: wars and the physical impoverishment and destruction that wars produce, along with the depletion of life. Epidemic diseases and environmental degradations, soil erosion, pollution, failure of crops, outbreaks of criminal violence and psychotic malevolence—all these are symptoms of such disorganization, and they produce further social lapses; for the people affected, feeling cheated and oppressed, refuse then to perform their old duties or make the daily efforts and sacrifices always needed for keeping the mechanism of society moving.

What has brought on these breakdowns usually turns out to be due to a radical failure in feedback: an inability to acknowledge errors, an unwillingness to correct them, a resistance to introducing new ideas and methods that would provide the means for a constructively human transformation. If once recognized, many of the defects that eventually undermine a society could be corrected, provided that prompt action were taken with the agents already at hand; but failing this, a more dire pathological situation, demanding surgery rather than diet, comes into existence.

For these reasons the first manifestation of etherialization, though it issues from subjective disillusion and disenchantment, does not take place on the level of ideas: it begins rather with an assault upon visible buildings, in acts of iconoclasm and destruction. Sometimes this takes the form of an organized physical attack; sometimes, as was the case with the Christian rejection of the great Roman monuments, it shows itself by a desertion of the old structures, as the Christians deserted the arenas and public baths and established themselves in other buildings on other sites. Obviously the visible forms of a society are easier to identify—and to demolish—than the underlying ideas and doctrines, which may be maintained in the mind, as the Jews secretly kept to their ancient rites even in Catholic Spain. But the burning of books and the tearing down of sound buildings undermine confidence in continuity. Remember the Bastille!

Though materialization is necessarily a slow process, de-materialization works fast: even the cessation of work on new structures, or their rebuilding in a new style, as the daring Gothic constructions displaced the ponderous Romanesque forms, constitutes an action that, as in the proverb, notoriously speaks louder than words.

When the dismantlement has gone far enough, the way is open for the positive forces of etherialization: for the ground is sufficiently cleared. At this point the furnishings and draperies of the existing society will begin, for all their shiny newness, to seem old-fashioned; and the apartments that were once reserved for the elite will be advertised for occupancy by new tenants—who ironically will either build different quarters for themselves elsewhere, or will take possession of even more ancient structures and convert them to their new purposes; as the mansions of the aristocracy in London, Paris, and Rome have been converted into business offices, hotels, establishments for the higher bureaucracy.

There is no need to provide further specific historic examples of etherialization. Again, as in the behavior of organisms, the integrating and disintegrating processes take place side by side, not without affecting each other. To follow the course of etherialization one has only to read the serial analysis of materialization backward, beginning with debuilding and dismantling, and finally returning to the initial stage where a change of character and life-style becomes visible, to reach the point at which a formative idea again emerges. For when the negative phase of etherialization has gone far enough, a new constellation of ideas, a new world picture, a new vision of human possibilities, will take possession of a whole culture, and a different cast of characters will occupy the center of the stage and present a new drama.

If, on the other hand, the processes of disillusion, alienation, dismantlement, and destruction go further, if no counter-balancing modes of etherialization become effective, disintegration will, it seems probable, go on with increasing swiftness until no restorative measures are possible. In this case, the forces of anti-life will be in the ascendant, and the actors who seize the center of the stage and profess to represent the Living Theater will be incarnations of the absurd, the sadistic, the cruel, and the paranoid, whose mission will be to give the final sanction of their own insanity to the dehumanization achieved by the Power Complex.

Fortunately there already are many indications, though scattered, faint, and often contradictory, that a fresh cultural transformation is in the making: one which will recognize that the money economy is bankrupt, and the power complex has become, through its very excesses and exaggerations, impotent. Whether this change is as yet sufficient to arrest further disintegration, still more whether it can successfully dismantle the nuclear megamachine before it brings on a total human catastrophe, are matters that may long remain in doubt. But if mankind overcomes the myth of the machine, one thing may be safely predicted: the repressed components of our old culture will become the dominants of the new one; and similarly the present megatechnic institutions and structures will be reduced to human proportions and brought under direct human control. Should this prove true, the present canvass of the existing society, its technological miscarriages and its human misdemeanors, should by implication give valid positive directions for working out a life-economy.

If this schematic outline of materialization and etherialization holds, it should apply equally, of course, to the formative ideas of science and technics, and their subsequent translation into our present power complex.

What were only fleeting intuitions of new mechanical inventions in the mind of Roger Bacon's contemporaries in the thirteenth century became a well-defined group of ideas in the works of a galaxy of seventeenth-century thinkers from Campanella and Francis Bacon to Gilbert, Galileo, and Descartes. In the archetypal figure of Isaac Newton, whose mathematical language was so novel and abstruse that it could be understood only by initiates, the new mechanical world picture appeared in its most clarified and glorified form. On this new ideological basis, the richer polytechnics of the Middle Ages, which always kept a place for subjective expressions, was restricted and diminished. The dreams of Kepler, Bishop Wilkins, John Glanvill, which extruded this human factor, were early projections of man's conquest over time and space.

If 'incarnation' played only a minor part in the transformation of science and technics, this was perhaps because the very idea of personality was excluded from the automatons that served as models for the new world vision. In this mechanical realm, the human personality was an embarrassment to the new conception of 'objectivity': to eliminate this 'irrational' human factor was the common aim of both theoretic science and advanced technology.

In compensation, technics passed swiftly into the further stages of materialization: in a multitude of new inventions and modes of organization, the novel formative ideas of the power system became visible and operative. From the eighteenth century on, the ideal of mechanical regularity and mechanical perfection entered into every human activity, from the observation of the heavens to the winding of clocks, from the drilling of soldiers to the drilling of seeds in fields: from keeping commercial accounts to establishing the routine of study in schools.

In every department these habits were validated by enormous quantitative gains in productivity, provided the qualitative results were taken for granted. In our own time, the mechanical world picture at last reached the state of complete embodiment in a multitude of machines, laboratories, factories, office buildings, rocket-platforms, underground shelters, control centers. But now that the idea has been completely embodied, we can recognize that it had left no place for man. He is reduced to a standardized servo-mechanism: a left-over part from a more organic world.

If 'Technics and Civilization' and 'The Myth of the Machine' could lay no claim to originality in any other department, they at least have radically challenged, if not yet successfully undermined, the idea that the Power Complex evolved by itself through the action of external forces over which man had no control, and which his own subjective life could not affect.

If machines alone were sufficient to produce machines, if technological systems automatically proliferated by reasons of inherent forces similar to those that account for the growth and development of organisms, the outlook for mankind in the near future would be even blacker than that pictured either in Samuel Butler's quoted letter or in Henry Adams' later analysis. But if the power system itself was, to begin with, a product of the human mind—the materialization of ideas that had organic and human roots—then the future holds many open possibilities, some of which lie entirely outside the range of our existing institutions. If the fashionable technocratic prescriptions for extending the present system of control to the whole organic world are not acceptable to rational men, they need not be accepted. The pressing human task today is not to endure further misapplications of the power system, but to detach ourselves from it, and cultivate our subjective resources as never before.

If this seems an all but impossible demand, with the odds heavily in favor of the power system and against the human personality, one need only remember how absurd such a withdrawal, such a rejection, such a challenge seemed to most intelligent Romans before Christianity presented an alternative.

In the period of the first Roman emperor, Augustus (63 B.C.–A.D. 14), the Roman power system, supported and extended by its massive engineering and military machines, had reached the height of its authority and influence. Who then guessed that the law and order of the Pax Romana were not so solidly established as to be virtually impregnable? Despite the earlier warnings of the historian Polybius, the Henry Adams of his day, the Romans expected that their way of life would last indefinitely. So well entrenched was their economy that educated Romans for long regarded with contempt the insignificant Christian minority who deliberately withdrew from this system, who rejected their goods and disparaged their massive achievements in road building and sewage disposal no less than their dedication to gluttony and pornography.

What educated Roman guessed, at the time of Marcus Aurelius, that only two centuries later one of their best-educated minds, Augustine, a lecturer of note, thoroughly at home in the culture of the past, would write 'The City of God' to expose the iniquities of the whole Roman establishment and castigate even its virtues? And who then, in his wildest fancies, could guess that a while later Paulinus of Nola, a patrician, born to be a Roman consul, the highest political office open, would retire to a distant Spanish monastery at the height of his career, to cultivate his faith in the divine order and eternal life promised by Jesus; and so believing, would eventually sell himself into slavery in order to ransom from captivity the only son of a widowed mother? Yet that unthinkable ideological transformation took place and those unthinkable deeds actually happened.

If such renunciation and detachment could begin in the proud Roman Empire, it can take place anywhere, even here and now: all the more easily today after more than half a century of economic depressions, world wars, revolutions, and systematic programs of extermination have ground the moral foundations of modern civilization to rubble and dust. If the power system itself seemed never so formidable as now, with one brilliant technological feat following another, its negative life-mutilating counterpart has never been so threatening: for unqualified violence and crime in every form, pattern after the dehumanized examples of the Power Pentagon, have invaded what were once the most secure and inviolable human activities.

This is not a prophecy: it is a factual description of what is already happening before our eyes, with murderous confrontations and infantile tantrums taking the place of rational demands and cooperative efforts.

Yes: the physical structure of the power system was never more closely articulated: but its human supports were never more frail, more morally indecisive, more vulnerable to attack.

How long, those who are now awake must ask themselves, how long can the physical structure of an advanced technology hold together when all its human foundations are crumbling away? All this has happened so suddenly that many people are hardly aware that it has happened at all: yet during the last generation the very bottom has dropped out of our life; the human institutions and moral convictions that have taken thousands of years to achieve even a minimal efficacy have disappeared before our eyes: so completely that the next generation will scarcely believe they ever existed.

Let us take a dramatic example of this collapse. What would the great proconsuls of the British Empire, the Curzons and the Cromers, have said if, in 1914, they had been informed that, despite all the statistical reports in the Yearbooks, their Empire would, within a single generation, fall to pieces—though at that very moment Sir Edward Lutyens was designing the imposing buildings of the new capital at Delhi and a great viceregal mansion, as if the Empire would hold together for countless centuries. Only Kipling, though the poet of imperialism, foresaw that ominous possibility in his 'Recessional.'

Could these empire builders have guessed, what is now so plain, that the most lasting effect of British imperialism, in its most humane expression as a Commonwealth of Nations, would be to open the way for a counter-colonialism and a counter-invasion of England by its once subject peoples? Yet all this has happened, with parallel reversals and humiliations already visible everywhere else, not least in the United States. If these outer bastions of the Pentagon of Power have been taken, how long will it be before the center itself surrenders or blows up?

The Roman Empire in the East won a new lease on life for a thousand years by coming to terms with Christianity. If the Power System is to continue in existence as a working partner in a more organic complex dedicated to the renewal of life, it will only be if its dynamic leaders, and those larger groups that they influence, have undergone a profound change of heart and mind, of ideal and purpose, as great as that which for so long arrested the decay of the Eastern empire established in Byzantium. But it must be remembered that this intermixture of Roman and Christian institutions was achieved at the expense of creativity. So until the disintegration of our own society has gone even further, there is reason to look for a more vigorous life-promoting solution. Whether such a response is possible depends upon an unknown factor: how viable are the formative ideas that are now in the air, and how ready are our contemporaries to undertake the efforts and sacrifices that are essential for human renewal? There are no purely technological answers.

Has Western civilization yet reached the point in etherialization where detachment and withdrawal will lead to the assemblage of an organic world picture, in which the human personality in all its dimensions will have primacy over its biological needs and technological pressures? That question cannot be answered except in action. But the evidences for such a transformation have already been put forward.

To describe even in the barest outline the multitude of changes necessary to turn the power complex into an organic complex, and a money economy into a life economy, lies beyond the capacities of any individual mind; any attempt at a detailed picture would be presumptuous. And this is so for two reasons: genuine novelty is unpredictable, except in such features as are recognizable in another form in past cultures. But even more because the materialization of the organic ideology, though already well begun, will take as long to replace the existing establishment as the power system itself required to displace the feudal and municipal and ecclesiastical economy of the Middle Ages. The first evidences of such a transformation will present themselves in an inner change; and inner changes often strike suddenly and work swiftly. Each one of us, as long as life stirs in him, may play a part in extricating himself from the power system by asserting his primacy as a person in quiet acts of mental or physical withdrawal—in gestures of non-conformity, in abstentions, restrictions, inhibitions, which will liberate him from the domination of the pentagon of power.

In a hundred different places, the marks of such de-materialization and etherialization are already visible: many more than I have felt it necessary to cite. If I dare to foresee a promising future other than that which the technocrats (the power elite) have been confidently extrapolating, it is because I have found by personal experience that it is far easier to detach oneself from the system and to make a selective use of its facilities than the promoters of the Affluent Society would have their docile subjects believe.

Though no immediate and complete escape from the ongoing power system is possible, least of all through mass violence, the changes that will restore autonomy and initiative to the human person all lie within the province of each individual soul, once it is roused. Nothing could be more damaging to the myth of the machine, and to the dehumanized social order it has brought into existence, than a steady withdrawal of interest, a slowing down of tempo, a stoppage of senseless routines and mindless acts. And has not all this in fact begun to happen?

When the moment comes to replace power with plenitude, compulsive external rituals with internal, self-imposed discipline, depersonalization with individuation, automation with autonomy, we shall find that the necessary change of attitude and purpose has been going on beneath the surface during the last century, and the long buried seeds of a richer human culture are now ready to strike root and grow, as soon as the ice breaks up and the sun reaches them. If that growth is to prosper, it will draw freely on the compost from many previous cultures. When the power complex itself becomes sufficiently etherialized, its formative universal ideas will become usable again, passing on its intellectual vigor and its discipline, once applied mainly to the management of things, to the management and enrichment of man's whole subjective existence.

As long as man's life prospers there is no limit to its possibilities, no terminus to its creativity; for it is part of the essential nature of man to transcend the limits of his own biological nature, and to be ready if necessary to die in order to make such transcendence possible.

Behind the picture of fresh human possibilities I have been drawing all through 'The Myth of the Machine' is a profound truth to which almost a century ago William James gave expression. "When from our present advanced standpoint," he observed, "we look back upon past stages of human thought, we are amazed that a universe which appears to us of so vast and mysterious a complication should ever have seemed to anyone so little and plain a thing. . . . There is nothing in the spirit and principles of science that need hinder science from dealing successfully with a world in which personal forces are the starting point of new effects. The only form of thing we directly encounter, the only experience that we concretely have, is our own personal life. The only complete category of our thinking, our professors of philosophy tell us, is the abstract elements of that. And this systematic denial on science's part of the personality as a condition of events, this rigorous belief that in its own essential and innermost nature our world is a strictly impersonal world, may conceivably, as the whirligig of time goes round, prove to be the very defect that our descendents will be most surprised at in our boasted science, the omission that to their eyes will most tend to make it look perspectiveless and short."

The whirligig of time has gone round; and what James applied to science applies equally to our compulsive, depersonalized, power-driven technology. We now have sufficient historic perspective to realize that this seemingly self-automated mechanism has, like the old 'automatic' chess player, a man concealed in the works; and we know that the system is not directly derived from nature as we find it on earth or in the sky, but has features that at every point bear the stamp of the human mind, partly rational, partly cretinous, partly demonic. No outward tinkering will improve this overpowered civilization, now plainly in the final and fossilized stage of its materialization: nothing will produce an effective change but the fresh transformation that has already begun in the human mind.

Those who are unable to accept William James' perception that the human person has always been the "starting point of new effects" and that the most solid-seeming structures and institutions must collapse as soon as the formative ideas that have brought them into existence begin to dissolve, are the real prophets of doom. On the terms imposed by technocratic society, there is no hope for mankind except by 'going with' its plans for accelerated technological progress, even though man's vital organs will all be cannibalized in order to prolong the megamachine's meaningless existence. But for those of us who have thrown off the myth of the machine, the next move is ours: for the gates of the technocratic prison will open automatically, despite their rusty ancient hinges, as soon as we choose to walk out.

BIBLIOGRAPHY

ACKNOWLEDGEMENTS

INDEX

BIBLIOGRAPHY

Though this bibliography has been carefully weeded, certain books of no particular importance are nevertheless cited if they have been quoted in the text. This is my only concession to the scholarly practice of providing detailed citations for every item: a practice that would double the size of this book without sufficiently increasing its value. Extensive though this bibliography is, the student who wishes to explore the field more thoroughly will find further help in the bibliography of *Technics and Civilization* and in Volume I of *The Myth of the Machine*.

Adams, Henry. *The Degradation of the Democratic Dogma.* New York: 1919. Contains the following papers: *The Tendency of History. A Communication to the American Historical Association:* 1894. *The Rule of Phase Applied to History.* Washington: 1909.
Despite minor errors these papers constitute a masterly summation and forecast.

The Education of Henry Adams. Limited edition. Boston: 1918. Popular edition. Boston: 1927.

Anderson, Edgar. *Natural History, Statistics, and Applied Mathematics.* In American Journal of Botany: December 1956.
Appreciative discrimination between the roles of 'pattern thinking' and analytic-mathematical thinking.

Angyal, Andras. *Foundations for a Science of Personality.* New York: 1941.
Classic evaluation of autonomy and heteronymy in human development, handicapped only by the inherent dualism of our language.

Arendt, Hannah. *The Origins of Totalitarianism.* New York: 1951.
Confined to the perversions and horrors of latter-day totalitarianism.

The Human Condition. Chicago: 1958.
An acute, often brilliant analysis, which incidentally reinstates the ancient Greek distinction between 'work' as a mode of life and 'labor' as a servile degradation.

Aron, Raymond. *Progress and Disillusion: The Dialectics of Modern Society.* New York: 1968.

Asimov, Isaac. *The Perfect Machine.* In Science Journal: October 1968.
Not unexpectedly, the perfect machine, it turns out, would be God. Q.E.D.

Bacon, Francis. *The Advancement of Learning.* First edition. London: 1605. With an introduction by G. W. Kitchen. London: 1915.

New Atlantis. First edition. London: 1627. With an introduction by Alfred B. Gough. Oxford: 1924.
> More directly influential, perhaps because of its brevity and concreteness, than his more comprehensive discourses. Taken with *The Advancement of Learning* it gives a reasonably full report on Bacon's outlook and hopes. For inexplicably Victorian reasons this edition leaves out certain passages 'offensive to present taste.'

Bacon, Roger. *The Opus Major of Roger Bacon.* Translated by Robert B. Burke. 2 vols. Philadelphia: 1928.
> One of the medieval heralds of the scientific transformation.

Baldwin, James Mark. *Development and Evolution.* New York: 1902.
> His concept of organic selection anticipated Waddington and avoided the pitfalls of so-called Lamarckism while recognizing the agency of social heredity.

Barret, François. *Histoire du Travail.* Paris: 1955.

Bech, S. J. *Emotional Experience as a Necessary Constituent in Knowing.* In M. Reymert (editor), *Feelings and Emotions.* New York: 1950.

Becker, Carl L. *Progress and Power.* Stanford, Cal.: 1936.

Beckwith, Burnham P. *The Next 500 Years: Scientific Predictions of Major Social Trends.* Foreword by Daniel Bell. New York: 1967.
> The span of time chosen takes this report out of the scientific sphere, because of the incalculable number of variables and unforeseeable events it cannot possibly anticipate. A perfect caricature of pseudo-scientific prophecy based on the extrapolation fallacy.

Beer, Gavin de. *Streams of Culture.* New York: 1969.

Beiler, Everett T. (editor). *Beyond Time and Space: An Anthology.* New York: 1952.

Bell, Daniel. *The Study of the Future.* In The Public Interest: Fall 1965.
> See Beckwith, Burnham P.

Belloc, Hilaire. *The Servile State.* London: 1912.
> This book, following Herbert Spencer's *The Coming Slavery*—but before Hayek—correctly identified totalitarian tendencies that were still disguised by liberalism's hopes and assumptions. The argument anticipated and underlined events that were still to come.

Bergonzi, Bernard. *The Early H. G. Wells: A Study of the Scientific Romances.* Manchester: 1961.

Bergson, Henri. *Creative Evolution.* New York: 1924.

Berle, A. A. *Power.* New York: 1969.

Bernal, J. D. *Science and Industry in the Nineteenth Century.* London: 1953.

Bertalanffy, Ludwig von. *Robots, Men, and Minds: Psychology in the Modern World.* New York: 1967.
> Reclaims for biology the conception of man as primarily a symbol-making, and thereby self-transcending, animal: in opposition to the reductionist, mechanistic, and passively adaptive conceptions.

General System Theory: Foundations, Development, Applications. New York: 1968.
> A post-mechanistic philosophy of the organism. Rich in reference to kindred works.

The World of Science and the World of Value. In Bugental, J. F. T. (editor), *Challenges of Humanistic Psychology.* New York: 1967.

Bettelheim, Bruno. *The Informed Heart.* New York: 1960.

Blackman, Allan. *Scientism and Planning.* In The American Behavioral Scientist: September 1966.

Boardman, Philip. *Patrick Geddes: Maker of the Future.* Chapel Hill, N.C.: 1944.
Useful on Geddes' educational ideas; but fortunately an enlarged and enriched study by Boardman is now in preparation.

Bodleian Library Record: July 1968.
Report on human agents versus computers.

Boguslaw, Robert. *The New Utopians: A Study of System Design and Social Change.* New York: 1905. Englewood Cliffs, N.J.: 1965.
Excellent analysis of alternatives and limitations in "system design," which pierces through the fashionable gobbledygook (secret knowledge) of the systems bureaucracy. Recommended.

Bork, Alfred M. *Randomness and the Twentieth Century.* In The Antioch Review: Spring 1967.

Born, Max. *My Life and My Views.* With an introduction by I. Bernard Cohen. New York: 1968.

Borsodi, Ralph. *The Green Revolution.* Brookville, Ohio: 1965.

Boulding, Kenneth. *The Meaning of the Twentieth Century.* New York: 1965.

Boyle, Robert. *The Sceptical Chymist.* First edition. London: 1661. With an introduction by M. M. Pattison Muir. New York: n.d.

Brady, Robert A. *Organization, Automation, and Society: The Scientific Revolution in Industry.* Berkeley, Cal.: 1961.
Perhaps the best cross-sectional description of modern technology in its economic and bureaucratic aspects.

Brandeis, Louis D. *The Curse of Bigness: Miscellaneous Papers.* New York: 1935.
Like the Founding Fathers, Justice Brandeis realized that both bigness and centralized power were dubious blessings, calling for counteraction.

Braudel, Fernand. *Civilization Matérielle et Capitalisme (XV–XVIII Siècles).* Tome I. Paris: 1967.
Worldwide survey, well documented, richly illustrated. Both the technical data and the social interpretation are admirable.

Brickman, William W., and Stanley Lehrer (editors). *Automation, Education, and Human Values.* New York: 1966.
Thirty-three essays, thinly covering a wide field.

Brinkmann, Donald. *Mensch und Technik: Grundzüger einer Philosophie der Technik.* Bern: 1946.

British Association for the Advancement of Science (by various authors). *London and the Advancement of Science.* London: 1931.

Bronowski, J. *The Identity of Man*. London: 1966.

Human and Animal Languages. In *Essays to Honor Roman Jakobsen*. The Hague: 1967.

Brown, Harrison. *The Next Hundred Years*. New York: 1961.

Buber, Martin. *Paths in Utopia*. New York: 1950.
Discriminating assessment of nineteenth-century ideological attempts to reconstitute society, done with insight and finesse.

Bugliarello, George. *Bio-Engineering as a New Dialogue*. In Carnegie Review: Winter 1965.
A significant re-orientation toward understanding and remodelling physico-chemical engineering in terms of the more complex behavior of organisms. Reductionism in reverse. A welcome interpretation of the new biotechnic age I tentatively described in *Technics and Civilization* (1934).

Engineering Implications of Biological Flow Process. In Symposium on Chemical Engineering in Medicine, American Institute of Chemical Engineers: 19 May 1965.
Explores the contribution of biology to an emerging biotechnics.

Bulwer-Lytton, E. *The Coming Race*. London: 1871.

Burckhardt, Jacob. *Force and Freedom: Reflections on History*. New York: 1943.

Burnham, Jack. *Beyond Modern Sculpture: The Effects of Science and Technology on the Sculpture of This Century*. New York: 1968.
Valuable for its data and its descriptive analyses: but points to an extremely dubious (suicidal) conclusion: namely, that life will give way to superintelligent automata. A vulgar example of the tendency to overvalue abstract 'intelligence' as the final consummation of human existence, and to overestimate the survival potentialities of purely mechanical systems, unabetted—and presumably unopposed—by man. See Seidenberg, Roderick.

Burtt, Edwin Arthur. *The Metaphysical Foundations of Modern Physical Science: A Historical and Critical Essay*. New York: 1927.
Masterly appraisal of the structural weakness of an 'objective' method that excludes any inquiry into its own subjectivity and even denies its existence.

In Search of Philosophic Understanding. New York: 1965.

Bury, J. B. *The Idea of Progress: An Inquiry into Its Origin and Growth*. New York: 1932. Paperback: 1955.

Butler, Samuel. *Unconscious Memory*. First edition. London: 1880. Reissued: 1922.
Follows up the trail opened in *Life and Habit*, by reference to work of Hartmann on *The Unconscious*.

The Notebooks of Samuel Butler. Selected, arranged, and edited by Henry Festing Jones. With an introduction by Francis Hackett. New York: 1917.

Life and Habit. London: 1923.

Erewhon and Erewhon Revisited. With an introduction by Lewis Mumford. New York: 1927.

Butterfield, Herbert. *The Origins of Modern Science, 1300–1800*. New York: 1951.
Brief and excellent.

Calder, Nigel. *Technopolis*. London: 1969.

Calder, Nigel (editor). *Unless Peace Comes: A Scientific Forecast of New Weapons*. New York: 1968.
A sober and sobering description of the new scientific weapons of extermination. See also Lapp, Ralph E.

Cannon, Walter B. *Bodily Changes in Pain, Hunger, Fear, and Rage: An Account of Recent Researches into the Function of Emotional Excitement*. First edition. New York: 1915. Second edition: 1929.
A classic study: alike as to method, findings, interpretation, *and* human insight.

The Wisdom of the Body. New York: 1932.
A fruitful application of a lifetime of physiological research to wider areas of human life, which Cannon never dismissed as outside the responsible scientist's range.

Carson, Rachel. *Silent Spring*. Boston: 1962.
A decisive contribution that dramatized the threat of general biocide through a misconceived effort to increase food production. Deservedly a classic.

Carter, George R. *The Tendency Towards Industrial Combination*. London: 1913.
Examines England's belated attempt to meet competition of earlier American and German trusts and cartels, reviving in new forms the corporate enterprises Adam Smith had thought doomed by individualistic competition.

Casson, Stanley. *Progress and Catastrophe: An Anatomy of the Human Adventure*. New York: 1937.
The data are now dated: but the mood Casson's interpretation records makes it a landmark.

Cassou, Jean (editor). *L'Homme, la Technique et la Nature*. Paris: 1938.

Centre International de Prospective. *Prospective Numéro 6*. Paris: 1960.
The purpose is as significant as the prospect.

Centro per gli Studii Historici. *The Sacral Kingship: Contributions to the Central Theme of the VIIIth International Congress for the Study of Religions*. Rome: 1955.
Belongs in Vol. I. But nothing in it undermines my interpretation of the earliest phases of Divine Kingship.

Chase, Stuart. *The Most Probable World*. New York: 1968.
A reasonable canvass of the goods and bads of modern technics, by an economist whose *Tragedy of Waste* was a pioneer study.

Chomsky, Noam. *Cartesian Linguistics: A Chapter in the History of Rationalist Thought*. New York: 1966.

Ciriacy-Wantrup, S. V., and James J. Parsons (editors). *Natural Resources: Quality and Quantity*. Berkeley, Cal.: 1967.

Civiltá delle Macchine. Round Table on the Future: May-June 1968.
A broad representation of current Italian scientific thought assembled in what has been, for many years, the outstanding periodical on the role of technics in civilization.

Clark, G. N. *Science and Social Welfare in the Age of Newton*. Oxford: 1937.

Clarke, Arthur C. *Profiles of the Future: An Inquiry into the Limits of the Possible*. New York: 1962.
> By a knowledgeable, indeed highly inventive, science-fiction writer, who of course means by 'future' the mechanically conditioned and controlled future.

Time Probe: The Sciences in Fiction. New York: 1966.
> One is struck by the fact that this selection shows so many magical and primitive traits, far closer to the Arabian Nights than to science proper.

Clow, Archibald and Nan L. *The Chemical Revolution: A Contribution to Social Technology*. London: 1952.
> Though working mainly from British data, this work fills a serious gap.

Coblentz, Stanton. *From Arrow to Atom Bomb: The Psychological History of War*. New York: 1953.

Cohen, Morris. *Reason and Nature*. New York: 1931.
> Important. Though I began as a pragmatist and a positivist, logical analysis leads me ever closer to Cohen's platonism.

Comenius, John Amos. *The Great Didactic*. Edited and translated by M. W. Keatinge. London: 1896.

Commoner, Barry. *Science and Survival*. New York: 1965.
> Appraisal of the results of scientific and technological irresponsibility.

Condorcet, Marie J.A.C.N. *Sketch for a Historical Picture of the Human Mind*. Paris: 1794. London: 1955.

Conklin, Groff. *Big Book of Science Fiction*. New York: 1950.

Coote, J. (publisher). *A New Universal History of Arts and Sciences: Showing Their Origins, Progress, Theory, Use, and Practice, and Exhibiting the Invention, Structure, Improvement, and Uses of the Most Considerable Instruments, Engines, and Machines, with Their Nature, Power, and Operation*. 2 vols. London: 1759.

Daedalus, Editors of. *Toward the Year 2000*. Cambridge, Mass.: 1967.
> A collective attempt by scholars in many different fields at forecasting and fore-molding. Like so many other similar efforts, it lacks an adequate concept of the future.

Dansereau, Pierre (editor). *Challenge for Survival: Land, Air, and Water for Man in Megalopolis*. New York: 1970.

Darling, J. Fraser, and John P. Milton (editors). *Future Environments of North America: Being the Record of a Conference Convened by The Conservation Foundation in April 1965*. Garden City, N.Y.: 1966.
> Enlightening survey of ecological realities. See also Sauer, Bates, and Mumford (chairmen).

Darwin, Charles. *On the Origin of Species by Means of Natural Selection, or the Preservation of Favored Races in the Struggle for Life*. First edition. London: 1859. Sixth edition, revised: 1872.

The Descent of Man. London: 1871.
> Even more daring than the *Origin*, for Darwin did not make use of the one fossil of an intermediate species then known; yet he adduced reasons for supposing an African habitat.

Dasman, Raymond F. *A Different Kind of Country*. New York: 1968.
The case for ecological diversity.

Daumas, Maurice. *A History of Technology and Invention*. 2 vols. New York: 1970.

Davis, David Brion. *The Problem of Slavery in Western Culture*. Ithaca, N.Y.: 1966.

Davis, Kingsley. See Roslansky, John D. (editor).

Descartes, René. *A Discourse on Method*. Leyden: 1637. Edited with an introduction by A. L. Lindsay. New York: 1912.
This essay is central to Descartes' thought: but the other essays included in this English translation are also relevant.

Dessauer, F., *et al. Der Mensch im Kraftfeld der Technik*. Düsseldorf: 1955.

Dijksterhuis, E. J. *The Mechanization of the World Picture*. First edition. Amsterdam: 1950. Oxford: 1961.
An interpretation of 'classical science' from its Greek prelude to Isaac Newton. Copious in scientific detail but lacking in references to those non-scientific aspects of the mechanical world picture I have stressed.

Drucker, Peter F. *The Future of Industrial Man*. New York: 1969.

The Age of Discontinuity. New York: 1969.

Duboin, Jacques. *Economie Distributive de l'Abondance*. Paris: n.d.

Rareté et Abondance: Essai de Mise à Jour de l'Economie Politique. Paris: 1945.

Dubos, René. *Man Adapting*. New Haven: 1965.
Rich in information on the biological conditions underlying human existence in health and sickness.

Durkheim, Emile. *The Division of Labor in Society*. New York: 1933.
Classic statement, first published in Paris in 1893 with the subtitle: *Etude sur l'organisation des sociétés supérieures*. But much that was taken for granted by Durkheim calls now for critical revision.

Eaton, Stewart C. *Roger Bacon and His Search for a Universal Science: A Reconsideration of the Life and Work of Roger Bacon in the Light of His Own Stated Purposes*. Oxford: 1952.

Edholm, O. G. *The Biology of Work*. New York: 1967.
Excellent both in text and illustrations.

Eiseley, Loren. *The Immense Journey*. New York: 1946.
Fresh insights into the human condition, by one of a new breed of wide-ranging biologists and anthropologists. See Carson, Rachel.

Darwin's Century: Evolution and the Men Who Discovered It. New York: 1958.

Eisenstadt, Shmuel Noah. *The Political System of Empires*. New York: 1963.
Comprehensive but formalistic.

Ellul, Jacques. *The Technological Society*. With an introduction by Robert K. Merton. New York: 1964.
While this work covers some of the same general area as the present book, it sees the situation in a different light and comes, on theological grounds, to radically different conclusions.

Encyclopaedia Britannica. *Conference on the Technological Order*. In Technology and Culture: Fall 1962.

Encyclopedia of Science and Technology. 15 vols. New York: 1966.

Erikson, Erik H. *Gandhi's Truth: On the Origins of Militant Non-Violence*. New York: 1969.

Psychoanalysis and Ongoing History: Problems of Identity, Hatred, and Nonviolence. In The American Journal of Psychiatry: September 1965.
A crystallization of Erikson's mature observations: a rare combination of scientific intelligence and human insight applied to extremely complex social phenomena.

Eurich, Nell. *Science in Utopia: A Mighty Design*. Cambridge, Mass.: 1967.

Ewing, J. Alfred. *An Engineer's Outlook*. London: 1933.

Fair, Charles M. *The Dying Self*. Middletown, Conn.: 1969.

Farber, Seymour M., and Roger H. L. Wilson. *Control of the Mind*. New York: 1961.
Raises many important problems both scientific and ethical.

Conflict and Creativity. New York: 1963.
This is Part 2 of *Control of the Mind*, and deals among other things with drugs.

Farrington, Benjamin. *Francis Bacon: Philosopher of Industrial Science*. New York: 1949.

Faucher, Daniel. *Le Paysan et la Machine*. In Collection: *L'Homme et la Machine*. Paris: n.d.

Ferkiss, Victor C. *Technological Man: The Myth and the Reality*. New York: 1969.

Fisher, Marvin. *Workshops in the Wilderness: The European Response to American Industrialization, 1830–1860*. New York: 1967.

Forti, V. *Storia della Technica alle Origine della Vita Moderna*. Florence: 1940.
Valuable mainly for its illustrations.

Fouillée, Alfred. *La Psychologie des Idées-forces*. Paris: 1893.

Fourastié, Jean. *Machinisme et Bien Être*. Paris: 1951.

The Causes of Wealth. Glencoe, Ill.: 1960.

Francastel, Pierre. *Art et Technique, aux XIXᵉ et XXᵉ Siècles*. Paris: 1956.
Recommended.

Frank, Waldo. *The Re-Discovery of America*. New York: 1929.
A post-Romantic criticism of the gods and cults of power.

Frankl, Viktor B. *Man's Search for Meaning: An Introduction to Logotherapy*. Boston: 1962.
A newly revised and enlarged edition of *From Death-Camp to Existentialism*.

Fraser, J. T. *The Voices of Time: A Cooperative Survey of Man's Views of Time as Expressed by the Sciences and by the Humanities*. New York: 1966.
Well-chosen, with copious references.

Friedmann, Georges. *Problèmes Humains du Machinisme Industriel*. Paris: 1946.

Le Travail en Miettes: Spécialisation et Loisirs. Paris: 1956.

The Anatomy of Work: Labor, Leisure, and the Implications of Automation. New York: 1961.
Specially valuable for critical insight derived from French experience. Friedmann is an outstanding authority on technics.

Sept Etudes sur l'Homme et la Technique. Paris: 1966.
Admirable.

Fromm, Erich. *The Sane Society*. New York: 1955.

Marx's Concept of Man. New York: 1961.
Emphasizes Marx's original humanistic position, as based on Marx's philosophical and economic papers of 1844.

The Revolution of Hope: Toward a Humanized Technology. New York: 1968.
Brief but suggestive, along lines not dissimilar to those of the present book.

Fuhrmann, Ernst. *Wege: Versuch Angewandte Biosophie*. Frankfurt-am-Main: n.d.

Fuller, R. Buckminster. *Untitled Epic Poem on the History of Industrialization*. Highlands, N.C.: 1962.
The verse and the thought are on a parity. Must be read to be believed.

Ideas and Integrities: A Spontaneous Autobiographical Disclosure. New York: 1963.
Fuller's faith that the limitless process of technological expansion will find a solution to every human problem would present a far worse problem, if generally accepted, than any he seeks to answer.

Operating Manual for Spaceship Earth. Carbondale, Ill.: 1969.
The place of publication must be an editorial error. Such a manual could come only from Heaven.

Gabo, Naum. *Gabo*. Cambridge, Mass.: 1957.
A beautiful presentation of his whole work.

Of Divers Arts. New York: 1962.
Recommended.

Gabor, Dennis. *Electronic Inventions and Their Impact on Civilization*. London: 1959.

Inventing the Future. London: 1963.
> A discriminating study of technological possibilities and difficulties—including the ulti-
> mate threat of a boring life.

Technological Forecasting in a Social Frame. London: 1968.
> Though making use of a list of technological possibilities canvassed, by Kahn and
> Wiener (which see), Gabor's list covers 105 items, largely because he is more aware of
> biological possibilities and social needs.

Galbraith, J. K. *The Affluent Society.* Boston: 1958.

The New Industrial State. Boston: 1967.

Galilei, Galileo. *Dialogue on the Great World Systems.* Translated by T. Salus-
bury (1661). Revised by Giorgio de Santillana. Chicago: 1953.
> The only work, as de Santillana points out in his admirable introduction, that gives the
> full measure of Galileo's mental plenitude.

Geddes, Patrick. *An Analysis of the Principles of Economics.* Part I. London:
1885.

Geddes, Patrick, and J. Arthur Thomson. *Life: Outlines of Biology.* 2 vols.
New York: 1931.
> The best summation of Geddes' outlook and method, though inadequate in its system-
> atic sociological presentation.

Gerzon, Mark. *The Whole World Is Watching: A Young Man Looks at Youth's
Dissent.* New York: 1969.

Giedion, Sigfried. *Mechanization Takes Command.* New York: 1955.
> An outstanding contribution to the industrial history of the last century.

Gillespie, James E. *The Influence of Oversea Expansion on England to 1700.*
Studies in History, Economics, and Public Law. New York: 1920.

Gillispie, C. C. (editor). *A Diderot Pictorial Encyclopedia of Trades and
Industry.* New York: 1959.
> Plates reproduced from the justly famous eighteenth-century work.

Girardeau, Emile. *Le Progrès Technique et la Personalité Humaine.* Paris: 1955.

Glacken, Clarence J. *Traces on the Rhodian Shore: Nature and Culture in
Western Thought from Ancient Times to the End of the Eighteenth Century.* Berkeley, Cal.: 1967.
> Able presentation of a sector of human thinking too long neglected.

Glanvill, Joseph. *Scepsis Scientifica: or, Confest Ignorance the Way to Science.*
London: 1665. Edited with an introductory essay by John Owen. London:
1935.

Glass, Bentley. *Science and Ethical Values.* Chapel Hill, N.C.: 1965.

Glass, Bentley, Owsei Tomkin, and William L. Straus, Jr. *Forerunners of
Darwin, 1745–1859.* Baltimore: 1959.

Glennie, J. S. Stuart. *Sociological Studies.* In *Sociological Papers.* Vol. II.
London: 1906.
> Glennie not only identified and dated the 'moral revolution' of the sixth century B.C.,
> but was an early precursor even before Patrick Geddes of field theory. Though addicted

to an overelaborated terminology, he was the first to invent such necessary terms as 'mechanotechnic' and 'biotechnic.'

Goodman, Paul. *Growing Up Absurd*. New York: 1960.

Goody, Jack (editor). *Literacy in Traditional Societies*. Cambridge, Mass.: 1968.
Important.

Gould, Jay M. *The Technical Elite*. New York: 1966.

Graham, Michael. *Human Needs*. London: 1951.

Grazia, Sebastian de. *Of Time, Work and Leisure*. New York: 1962.

Gregory, Joshua C. *A Short History of Atomism: from Democritus to Bohr*. London: 1931.
The best historic summary to its date of publication.

Gregory, R. L. *Eye and Brain: The Psychology of Seeing*. New York: 1966.

Hacker, Andrew (editor). *The Corporation Take-Over*. New York: 1964.
Analysis by various hands, including Berle and Means, of the scope and methods of corporate enterprise, down to the ultimate bearings of cybernation.

Haden, Selma von. *Is Cyberculture Inevitable? A Minority View*. In Fellowship: January 1966.
Brilliant summation of the case against an automatically expanding technology under central control. Quite independent of my own contribution.

Haldane, John Scott. *Organism and Environment as Illustrated by the Physiology of Breathing*. New Haven: 1917.

Mechanism, Life and Personality: An Examination of the Mechanistic Theory of Life and Mind. New York: 1921.
Important. See also Whitehead, Alfred North.

Hall, A. Rupert. *From Galileo to Newton, 1630–1720*. New York: 1963.
See also Santillana, Koestler, Butterfield, and Dijksterhuis.

Hall, Edward T. *The Hidden Dimension*. Garden City, N.Y.: 1966.
A fresh contribution to the ecology of mind.

Hammond, J. L., and Barbara Hammond. *The Rise of Modern Industry*. New York: 1926.
Denigrated by apologists for Victorian capitalism, but still important for the data the latter minimize or ignore.

Hanson, Earl D. *Animal Diversity*. Englewood Cliffs, N.J.: 1961.
A careful attempt to describe organic variety and explain it on evolutionary grounds. But Hanson is scrupulous enough to admit that the explanation is inadequate.

Hardy, Sir Alister. *The Living Stream: A Restatement of Evolution Theory and Its Relation to the Spirit of Man*. London: 1965.
Goes further along the lines opened by C. Lloyd Morgan and E. S. Russell in recognizing the active part played by the behavior of the organism itself in its own evolution. Hardy admits, in discussing extra-sensory perception, the possibility of other factors not open to external observation or recognizable in terms of accepted methods. An independent support for my critique of Galileo and Descartes.

Harrington, Alan. *The Immortalist: An Approach to the Engineering of Man's Divinity*. New York: 1969.
The last silly word in Technocracy.

Hartmann, Georges. *L'Automation*. Boudry (Neuchatel): 1956.

Harvard University Program on Technology and Society. *Fourth Annual Report*. Cambridge, Mass.: 1968.
See also Mesthene, Emmanuel G.

Haskell, H. J. *The New Deal in Old Rome*. New York: 1939.
Superficial but suggestive.

Hatfield, H. Stafford. *The Inventor and His World*. New York: 1948.

Hayek, F. A. *The Road to Serfdom*. London: 1944.
Recognizes the ultimate tendency of the megamachine, but underestimates the cumulative historic drive of the power system.

   The Counter-Revolution of Science: Studies of the Abuse of Reason. Glencoe, Ill.: 1952.
Well-documented study of the relation of positivist scientism to technology. Supplements my own analysis.

Hayes, Carleton. *The Historical Evolution of Nationalism*. New York: 1928.

Heckscher, Eli F. *Mercantilism*. 2 vols. London: 1935.
A classic study.

Henderson, Lawrence J. *The Order of Nature: An Essay*. Cambridge, Mass.: 1913.

   The Fitness of the Environment: An Inquiry into the Biological Significance of the Properties of Matter. New York: 1927. Paperback, with introduction by George Wald. Boston: 1958.
Both works are outstanding, and still important.

Henderson, Philip. *William Morris: His Life, Work and Friends*. Foreword by Allan Temko. New York: 1967.
Has the advantage of being able to use biographic material, particularly the distressing undercurrents of his marriage, that Mackail could not use. Like Paul Thompson's, this biography does justice to Morris' massive contributions as a craftsman.

Herber, Lewis. *Our Synthetic Environment*. New York: 1962.

Heron, A. H. *Why Men Work*. Stanford, Cal.: 1948.

Hersey, John. *The Child-Buyers*. New York: 1960.
A novel whose most ghastly fantasies are all too close to the commonplaces of corporation science.

Hillegas, Mark R. *The Future as Nightmare: H. G. Wells and the Anti-Utopians*. New York: 1967.

Hilton, Alice Mary (editor). *The Evolving Society: The Proceedings of the First Annual Conference on the Cybercultural Revolution—Cybernetics and Automation*. New York: 1966.
Superficial: the participants never asked themselves why all forms of work *should* be abolished, or what might follow if this took place.

Hobbes, Thomas. *De Cive, or, The Citizen.* Paris: 1642. Edited by Sterling P. Lamprecht. New York: 1949.

Leviathan; on the Matter, Forme, and Power of a Commonwealth, Ecclesiastical and Civill. London: 1651. New York: 1914.

Hobhouse, Leonard T. *Development and Purpose: An Essay Towards a Philosophy of Evolution.* London: 1913.

Hobson, J. A. *Imperialism: A Study.* New York: 1902.

Holton, Gerald. *Johannes Kepler: A Case Study on the Interaction of Science, Metaphysics, and Theology.* In The Philosophical Forum. Boston: 1956.

Science and New Styles of Thought. In The Graduate Journal. Gainesville, Fla.: Spring 1967.
Brilliant study of 'disorder' in science and art.

Holton, Gerald (editor). *Do Life Processes Transcend Physics and Chemistry?* In Zygon: Journal of Religion and Science: December 1968.
Fresh statements of the anti-reductionist position by Platt, Polanyi, and Commoner.

Hughes, James, and Lawrence Mann. *Systems and Planning Theory.* In American Institute of Planners Journal: September 1969.
Unusually lucid for a work in this area.

Huxley, Aldous. *Brave New World.* New York: 1932. With a new foreword. New York: 1946.
One of the most complete and ruthless kakotopias, though from a purely literary standpoint probably Huxley's most ill-written work. Its very ineptness perhaps reveals his personal distaste for the singularly prophetic outpourings of his unconscious. And yet . . .

Brave New World Revisited. New York: 1958.
Written against the intervening background of Nazi and Communist totalitarianism, with the startled sense that the human perversions he predicted were no longer centuries away. Huxley's picture of the new methods of controlling human behavior was closer to reality than Orwell's *1984:* yet he himself in his misguided final chapter, What Can Be Done, invoked chemical agents to enhance 'happiness.' *Happiness?*

Island: A Novel. New York: 1962.
A permissive utopia, where human felicity is ensured by moksha, a hallucinatory drug: that common bond between the Hippies and the unscrupulous technocrats who seek to control mankind.

Huxley, Julian. *New Bottles for New Wine.* New York: 1957.
See especially the essay Transhumanism. The new paperback title is: *Knowledge, Morality, and Destiny.*

Jaccard, Pierre. *Histoire Sociale du Travail, de l'Antiquité et Nos Jours.* Paris: 1960.

James, E. O. *The Worship of the Sky-God.* London: 1963.
Recommended to those who, being unfamiliar with the religious background of the megamachine, may be skeptical of my interpretation.

James, William. *The Varieties of Religious Experience: A Study in Human Nature.* New York: 1902.

The Will to Believe, and Other Essays. New York: 1903.
See the essay on What Psychical Research Has Accomplished.

Jennings, Herbert Spencer. *The Universe and Life.* New Haven: 1933.
Still a challenging affirmation of organic realities.

Johanneson, Olof (pseud.). *The Tale of the Big Computer: A Vision.* New York: 1968.
A presumably scientific account of a computer-governed future, too near reality to be satire and too near satire to be accepted as reality. The writer's predictions, if they are predictions, were anticipated by Samuel Butler.

Jones; H. Bence. *The Life and Letters of Faraday.* London: 1870.
Note account of Faraday's paper in 1844 on the nature of matter.

Jordy, William H. *Henry Adams: Scientific Historian.* New York: 1952.
A careful study, but vitiated by Jordy's disparagement of Adams' most pregnant contribution.

Jouvenel, Bertrand de. *On Power: Its Nature and the History of Its Growth.* New York: 1949.
An abstract analysis, penetrating, often brilliant. But I prefer my own more concrete interpretation in *The City in History*.

Juenger, Friedrich Georg. *The Failure of Technology: Perfection Without Purpose.* Hinsdale, Ill.: 1949.
The case against our compulsive technology—one-sided and overstated—but no worse than the unqualified praises that mark the technocratic True Believers and Holy Rollers.

Jung, Carl Gustav. *Memories, Dreams, Reflections.* Recorded and edited by Aniela Jaffe. New York: 1963.
A valuable complement to Jones' biography of Freud.

Civilization in Transition. New York: 1964.

Kahler, Erich. *The Meaning of History.* New York: 1964.

The Disintegration of Form in the Arts. New York: 1968.
A critical but sympathetic effort to interpret the non-art, the pseudo-art, and the anti-art of our time.

Kahn, Herman. *Thinking About the Unthinkable.* First edition. New York: 1962. Paperback, with an afterword: 1966.
Pentagonal platitudes.

Kahn, Herman, and Anthony J. Wiener. *The Year 2000.* New York: 1967.

Keeling, S. V. *Descartes.* London: 1934.

Kepes, Gyorgy (editor). *Vision + Value Series.* 3 vols. *Education of Vision. Structure in Art and in Science. The Nature and Art of Motion.* New York: 1965.
Richly illustrated; with some notable essays in each volume. Over-attentive, perhaps, to microscopic infra-patterns, yet within its chosen range adequate.

Kepler, Johannes. *Concerning the More Certain Fundamentals of Astrology: A New Brief Dissertation Looking Towards a Cosmotheory, Together with a Physical Prognosis for the Year 1602 from the Birth of Christ, Written to Philosophers.* 1602.

Kepler's Dream. Frankfurt-am-Main: 1635. Edited by John Lear. Berkeley, Cal.: 1965.

A work whose remarkable anticipations account for its present exhumation. Alternative translation by Edward Rosen. Madison, Wis.: 1967.

L. Gunther's German translation appeared in 1898. But Professor Marjorie Nicolson was the first scholar to perceive its contemporary significance.

The Six-Cornered Snowflake. Colin Hardie, editor and translator. With essays by L. L. Whyte and B. J. F. Mason. Oxford: 1966.

A fascinating work, long neglected. Opens up an area in science unapproachable by causal or statistical analysis—what Kepler called the 'formative faculty,' now as visible in the atom as in a snowflake or a bird.

Kidd, Benjamin. *The Principles of Western Civilization.* New York: 1902.

Wordy but notable for a single idea. At that early date *Kidd realized that the principle of natural selection applied only to large populations, not individuals.* He carried this a step further by pointing out that social changes were to be evaluated, not in terms of immediate contemporary benefits, but in reference to the *largest possible population—* that of the future.

Klapper, Joseph T. *The Effects of Mass Communication.* Glencoe, Ill.: 1960.

Kluckhohm, Clyde, and Henry A. Murray (editors), with the collaboration of David M. Schneider. *Personality, in Nature, Society, and Culture.* Second edition. New York: 1953.

Knapp, Bettina Liebovitz. *Jean Genet.* New York: 1968.

Koebner, Richard. *Empire.* Cambridge: 1961.

Notes on the idea of empire from the Romans to 1815.

Koestler, Arthur. *The Sleep Walkers.* New York: 1959.

Brilliant if unconventional summary of astronomical speculation and observation, from the Greeks through Newton. Koestler's freedom from the professional prudence of the specialist is not the least of his merits.

The Ghost in the Machine. New York: 1967.

An attempt to account for the chronic irrationality of human behavior, and to find some means to bring it under greater control. Though his final suggestion of a chemical remedy is silly, it does not invalidate his better insights.

Kohn, Hans. *The Idea of Nationalism: A Study in Origins and Background.* New York: 1951.

Kranzberg, Melvin, and Caroll W. Pursell, Jr. (editors). *Technology in Western Civilization.* 2 vols. New York: 1967.

Though more limited than the five-volume Singer *History of Technology,* it does better justice to the social setting and carries technics itself into the twentieth century. See also the review Technology and Culture, edited by Kranzberg.

Kropotkin, Peter. *Fields, Factories, and Workshops: or Industry Combined with Agriculture and Brain Work with Manual Work.* London: 1889.

Classic study of the possibilities of small-scale industry and agriculture with an advanced neotechnic base. Though 'dated,' it remains in advance of much current thinking. Recommended for those seeking the improvement of underdeveloped economies without destroying indigenous values and purposes.

Mutual Aid. London: 1904.

A fundamental correction of the Malthus-Darwin-Huxley interpretation of the struggle for existence as the main formative factor in organic evolution.

Kuhn, Thomas S. *The Copernican Revolution: Planetary Astronomy in the Development of Western Thought.* Cambridge, Mass.: 1957.

La Mettrie, J. O. de. *L'Homme Machine 1747–Man a Machine.* La Salle, Ill.: 1912.
A classic of reductionist dogma.

Lapp, Ralph E. *The New Priesthood: The Scientific Elite and the Uses of Power.* New York: 1965.

The Weapons Culture. New York: 1968.
By a physicist whose association with nuclear research, beginning with the Manhattan Project, has made him alert to the dangers of placing mankind's fate in the hands of the military-industrial-scientific 'elite.'

Laslett, Peter. *The World We Have Lost: England Before the Industrial Age.* New York: 1965.
Not as nostalgic as the title, hauntingly repeated, would indicate. But a teasing work: based on fresh, and in many cases significant, local research, but with an inadequate general background which does not allow for England's original industrial backwardness.

Latil, Pierre de. *La Pensée Artificielle: Introduction à la Cybernétique.* Paris: 1953.

Lawn, Brian. *The Salernitan Questions: An Introduction to the History of Medieval and Renaissance Problem Literature.* Oxford: 1963.

Lefranc, Georges. *Histoire du Travail et des Travailleurs.* Paris: 1957.

Leitenberg, Milton (editor). *Biological Weapons.* In Scientist and Citizen: August-September 1967.
Examination by socially concerned scientists of the calculated atrocities practiced upon man and his environment in modern 'war' (genocide).

Lewin, Kurt. *Field Theory in Social Science.* London: 1952.

Lewis, Arthur O. (editor). *Of Men and Machines.* New York: 1963.
Wide-ranging selection.

Lichtman, Richard. *Toward Community: A Criticism of Contemporary Capitalism.* In The Center for the Study of Democratic Institutions, *Occasional Papers.* Santa Barbara, Cal.: 1966.

Lilley, S. *Men, Machines and History: A Short History of Tools and Machines in Relation to Social Progress.* London: 1948.

Lorenz, Konrad. *On Aggression.* New York: 1966.
Excellent zoology: careless sociology—though free from the looser fictional extrapolations of Dart and Ardrey. Lorenz's affectionate relations with his graylag geese made him overlook the immense cultural gap between man and all other inhabitants of the animal kingdom. If homicidal aggression were an inescapable biological fact and a major cause of war, why the necessity for military conscription, practiced from the Fourth Millennium on?

Lovejoy, Arthur O. *The Great Chain of Being.* Cambridge, Mass.: 1950.
Classic study.

Essays in the History of Ideas. New York: 1955.

Lucretius. *On the Nature of Things*. Translated by H. A. J. Munro. In W. J. Oates, *The Stoic and Epicurean Philosophers*. New York: 1940.
> The only full explanation of Epicurean atomism, whose revival by Gassendi opened a new world in chemistry, a science in which both Greeks and Romans were backward.

MacIver, R. M. *Society, Its Structure and Changes*. New York: 1932.

MacMunn, George. *Slavery Through the Ages*. London: 1938.
> Inadequate presentation of a subject that has never, except for German studies of slavery in Greece and Rome, stirred sufficient scholarly zeal.

Maine, Henry Sumner. *Popular Government: Four Essays*. New York: 1886.
> Acute discussion of the limitations and perversions of popular government. Unfortunately, still relevant. See Lasswell, *et al.*

Malthus, T. S. *Essay on the Principles of Population as It Affects the Future Improvement of Society*. London: 1798. Second edition. Revised. 1803. 2 vols. New York: 1927.

Mandeville, Bernard. *The Fable of the Bees, or, Private Vices, Public Benefits*. First edition. London: 1714.
> Exposition of a self-regulating laissez-faire economy, based on self-interest alone, in which individual conflicts emerge as collective cooperations.

Mannheim, Karl. *Man and Society: In an Age of Reconstruction*. New York: 1940.

Mannoni, O. *Prospero and Caliban: The Psychology of Colonization*. New York: 1956.
> Suggestive if not always convincing.

Manuel, Frank E. *The Prophets of Paris*. Cambridge, Mass.: 1962.
> A masterly study of the ideologists, from Turgot to Comte.

Marcuse, Herbert. *Eros and Civilization: A Philosophical Inquiry into Freud*. New York: 1955.
> A modification of Freud's views, but unfortunately in the direction of infantile perversions and passivities. Marcuse wars against those like myself whose conceptions of personality and community accept the constant organic interplay (not dialectic) of repression and expression, of the patriarchical and matriarchical factors, as ingrained in all human activity.

One Dimensional Man: Studies in the Ideology of Advanced Industrial Society. Boston: 1964.
> If this analysis had been adequate I would gladly have deleted more than one section of the present book.

Marks, Sema, and Anthony G. Oettinger. *Educational Technology: New Myths and Old Realities*. Harvard University Program on Technology and Society. Cambridge, Mass.: 1968.

Martin, Thomas. *The Circle of the Mechanical Arts: Containing Practical Treatises on the Various Manual Arts, Trades, and Manufactures*. London: 1818.
> Gives detailed report, incidentally, on the development of railroads from early seventeenth century on, and in mining quotes Agricola extensively. But no mention of the steam engine which, according to the mid-Victorian fairy tale, 'caused' the 'Industrial Revolution.'

Marx, Karl. *Capital: A Critique of Political Economy*. Translated from the fourth German edition by Eden and Cedar Paul. London: 1929.
Though Marx's abstract economic reasoning is obsolete, and his historic predictions have proved erroneous, as a technical historian Marx was here a redoubtable pioneer.

Maslow, Abraham. *Toward a Psychology of Being*. Princeton, N.J.: 1962.

 Religions, Values, and Peak Experiences. Columbus, Ohio: 1964.
A departure from S-R psychology and an attempt to restore subjective initiatives and religious representations.

Masson, John. *The Atomic Theory of Lucretius: Contrasted with Modern Doctrines of Atoms and Evolution*. London: 1884.
Admirable; all the better because it poses the problem of atomism against then current Victorian debates. See Lucretius.

Masters, William H., and Virginia E. Johnson. *Human Sexual Response*. Boston: 1966.
An 'objective' (quasi-scientific) exposition of sexuality that neatly excludes the specifically human aspects of love-making, since they cannot be scientifically measured. Apparently quite unaffected by the ethologist's discovery that animals behave quite differently under laboratory conditions than in their natural environment. Reductionism reduced to absurdity: but obviously a pilot project for a new machine guaranteed to produce orgasms without human intervention.

May, Rollo. *Love and Will*. New York: 1969.
The popularity of this work is a good augury.

Mayr, Ernst. *Accident or Design: The Paradox of Evolution*. In Symposium on the Evolution of Living Organisms. Melbourne: December 1959.

 Cause and Effect in Biology. In Science, No. 134: 1961.
Important distinction between functional and evolutionary biology.

McCloy, Shelby T. *French Inventions of the Eighteenth Century*. Lexington, Ky.: 1952.
Long-needed examination of the French contribution to the period that English-speaking economic historians too smugly took to be a purely English event.

McCurdy, Edward. *The Mind of Leonardo da Vinci*. New York: 1928.

McHarg, Ian. *Design with Nature*. New York: 1969.
A truly ecological approach to ecology by a landscape architect whose passionate convictions are matched by his intellectual grasp and his concrete experience.

McKinley, Daniel. See Shepard, Paul.

McLuhan, Herbert Marshall. *The Mechanical Bride: Folklore of Industrial Man*. New York: 1951.

 Understanding Media: The Extensions of Man. New York: 1964.
What McLuhan understands has long been familiar to students of technics: it is his singular gift for *mis*understanding both technology and man that marks his truly original contributions.

Meier, Richard I. *Science and Economic Development: New Patterns of Living*. Cambridge, Mass.: 1956.
Dubious.

Mercier, Louis Sebastien. *L'An du Mille Quatre Cent Quarante: Rêve S'il en Fût Jamais*. London: 1772.

Merton, Robert, *et al. Reader in Bureaucracy*. New York: 1952.
Useful because of its range, in the absence of a more systematic study.

Mesthene, Emmanuel G. *How Technology Will Shape the Future*. Harvard University Program on Technology and Society. Cambridge, Mass.: 1969.

Meynaud, Jean. *Technocracy*. London: 1968.

Milgrim, Stanley. *A Behavioral Study of Obedience*. In Journal of Abnormal and Social Psychology: 1963. Also in Arthur M. Eastman (editor), *The Norton Reader*. New York: 1965.

Mills, C. Wright. *The Power Elite*. New York: 1956.
See especially the chapters on the Warlords and the Military Ascendency.

Mishan, E. J. *The Costs of Economic Growth*. New York: 1967.
A challenge to expansive affluence.

Montagu, M. F. Ashley. *The Direction of Human Development: Biological and Social Bases*. New York: 1955.
Recommended.

On Being Human. New York: 1966.
A valid anthropological statement, as well as a personal testament; and not least an antidote to the anti- and sub-human fantasies now rife.

Montagu, M. F. Ashley (editor). *Man and Aggression*. New York: 1968.
Useful emetic for those who have swallowed Ardrey's fantasies.

Montgomery, Edmund. *Philosophical Problems in the Light of Vital Organization*. New York: 1907.
Path-breaking. Its neglect stems perhaps from its early challenge to both mechanistic and idealistic clichés.

Moore, Barrington, Jr. *Social Origins of Dictatorship and Democracy: Lord and Peasant in the Making of the Modern World*. Boston: 1966.
By its emphasis on the democratic processes it complements—and partly corrects—any overstress of mine on common totalitarian features. Recommended.

More, Louis Trenchard. *Isaac Newton: A Biography, 1642–1727*. New York: 1934.
Chapter Eight, on The Mechanistic Hypothesis, gives a succinct summary of the seventeenth-century scientific background.

Moreno, J. L. *Who Shall Survive? A New Approach to the Problem of Human Interrelations*. Washington, D.C.: 1934.
An essay in human ecology too little noted today.

Morgan, Arthur E. *Nowhere Was Somewhere: How History Makes Utopias and How Utopias Make History*. Chapel Hill, N.C.: 1946.
Attempts to trace More's Utopia to contemporary reports of the Inca system, partly because Morgan wishes to prove that utopias do not "go against nature." For an ironic comment on this theory see my essay in *Utopias and Utopian Thought,* edited by Frank E. Manuel.

Morgan, C. Lloyd. *Emergent Evolution: The Gifford Lectures.* New York: 1923.

Life, Mind, and Spirit: Being the Second Course of the Gifford Lectures, under the General Title of Emergent Evolution. New York: 1926.

Morison, Elting E. *Men, Machines, and Modern Times.* Cambridge, Mass.: 1966.
Brief, but illuminating, witty, and wise: an effective antidote for the technocratic gush of the more popular prophets of the megamachine. Morison's conclusions might well serve as an epigraph for this book. "It still seems that a new kind of culture could be built up that would contain the new technology within appropriate limits. And the creation of such a new culture would seem to be the first order of business."

Morris, Henry C. *The History of Colonization: From the Earliest Times to the Present Day.* 2 vols. New York: 1900.
A useful work in its time that now cries for a successor of equal scope.

Morris, William. *The Collected Works of William Morris.* With an introduction by his daughter, May Morris. 24 vols. Oxford: 1936.
See *Vol. 2. Work in a Factory as It Might Be.* These articles refute the popular academic notion that Morris was so enamored of handicraft that he was willing to forgo both the machine and factory organization. With his prediction of a four-hour workday in the factory, he showed that he had a better grasp of the future than his more 'practical' contemporaries. Even in *News from Nowhere* (Vol. 16), where he gives a deliberately idyllic picture of life under socialism, he allows for such constants of human nature as wrath and murder.

Mumford, Lewis, *The Story of Utopias.* New York: 1922. Paperback, with new introduction: 1962.
My first exposition of the fundamental difference between the good life and the 'goods life.'

Technics and Civilization. First edition. New York: 1934. Paperback, with new introduction: 1963.

Art and Technics. The Bampton Lectures in America, No. 4. New York: 1952.
Recommended. But see Francastel, Pierre.

In the Name of Sanity. New York: 1954.
The essays Assumptions and Predictions, Technics and the Future, and Mirrors of Violence, not merely outline some of the main themes of the present book, but show clearly they were visible more than twenty years ago.

The Transformations of Man. Revised edition. London: 1957.
A useful prelude to the present study.

The Myth of the Machine. Vol. I. Technics and Human Development. New York: 1967.
The present book cannot be fully understood without reference to this volume.

Anticipations and Social Consequences of Atomic Energy. In Proceedings of the American Philosophical Society: April 15, 1954.
This paper terminated in a proposal to hold a grand World Assize under the aegis of the United Nations, using all the available knowledge, released from the ban of official secrecy, to estimate the probable effects of releasing atomic energy in various quantities in peace and war. As late as 1954 this proposal for a reasonable scientific assessment violently outraged many of the scientists present.

The Morals of Extermination. In The Atlantic Monthly: October 1958.
The latest and best of my essays contra genocide.

Machine. In *Encyclopedia Americana. Vol. 15.* New York: 1967.

Murphy, Gardner. *Human Potentialities.* New York: 1958.

Murray, Henry A. *Myth and Mythmaking.* New York: 1960.

Preparations for the Scaffold of a Comprehensive System. In Sigmund Koch (editor), *Psychology: A Study of Science.* New York: 1959.
The philosophic testament of a psychologist, grounded in biology and reaching outward and upward to canvass the fullness of human achievement.

Unprecedented Evolution. In Henry Hoagland (editor), *Evolution and Man's Progress.* Boston: 1962.

Needham, Joseph, *et al. Technology, Science, and Art: Common Ground.* A lecture series delivered at Harfield College of Technology. Harfield: 1961.

Nef, John U. *War and Human Progress: An Essay on the Rise of Industrial Civilization.* Cambridge, Mass.: 1952.
An important contribution though, in opposition to Sombart, Nef underestimates the technical stimulation of war. See also my *Technics and Civilization.*

Neumann, Erich. *The Origins and History of Consciousness.* New York: 1954.

The Archetypal World of Henry Moore. New York: 1959.

Neumann, Johann von. *Can We Survive Technology?* In David Sarnoff (editor), *The Fabulous Future: America in 1980.* New York: 1956.
An essay worth the rest of the entire series of trite predictions and stale hopes, published by the editors of Fortune.

Nicolson, Marjorie Hope. *Voyage to the Moon.* New York: 1948.
A classic contribution to both literary and technical history, by a scholar highly sensitive to the winds of change. Sufficiently generous in quotation to serve those who have no direct access to the many significant works quoted, including Wilkins.

The Microscope and English Imagination. In Smith College Studies in Modern Languages. Northampton, Mass.: July 1935.

The World in the Moon: A Study of the Changing Attitude Toward the Moon in the Seventeenth and Eighteenth Centuries. In Smith College Studies in Modern Languages. Northampton, Mass.: January 1936.
These studies have the laudable distinction of anticipating in the field of literature the interest in scientific history that came later.

Nisbet, Robert. *Community and Power.* New York: 1962. First published as *The Quest for Community.* New York: 1953.
An excellent critique of both ideas and institutions.

O'Malley, C. D. *Andreas Vesalius of Brussels, 1514–1564.* Berkeley, Cal.: 1965.

Oparin, A. I. *The Origin of Life.* New York: 1938.
Speculations on the conditions under which inorganic elements on this planet combined to form the complex protein molecules. L. H. Henderson's earlier work, *The Fitness of the Environment,* helps fill out the picture.

Ortega y Gasset, José. *The Revolt of the Masses*. New York: 1932.

   The Dehumanization of Art. Princeton, N.J.: 1951.
   Both these analyses have been confirmed by events.

Orwell, George. *1984*. London: 1949.

Ozbekhan, Hasan. *The Triumph of Technology: "Can" Implies "Ought."* Santa
   Monica, Cal.: 1967.
   Like Selma von Haden's essay, this goes critically to the roots of a technological com-
   plex that is hostile to all qualities or values except those that further its own expansion.

Packard, Vance. *The Waste Makers*. New York: 1960.

Parry, J. H. *The Establishment of the European Hegemony, 1415–1715*. New
   York: 1961.

   The Age of Reconnaissance. London: 1963.
   Many-sided description of European exploration, trade, and settlements from the fifteenth to the eighteenth centuries.

Pfender, M. (editor). *Die Technik Prägt Unsere Zeit*. Düsseldorf: 1956.

Platt, John R. *The Step to Man*. New York: 1966.

   The Function of Varied Experience. New York: 1969.

   Organism, Environment & Intelligence as a System. In Journal of the History
   of Biology: Spring 1969.

Platt, John R. (editor). *New Views of the Nature of Man*. Chicago: 1965.
   See especially, Wald, Sperry, and Goertz.

Poggioli, Renato. *The Theory of the Avant-Garde*. Cambridge, Mass.: 1968.
   A careful, seemingly objective study, whose objectivity is, however, vitiated by the fact
   that the author judges the products of the avant-garde solely by their own esthetic and
   social criteria.

Polanyi, Karl. *The Great Transformation*. New York: 1944.
   The end of the market economy: a little peremptory in its dismissal, but probably will
   be justified within a generation.

Polanyi, Michael. *Science and Man's Place in the Universe*. In Harry Woolf
   (editor), *Science as a Cultural Force*. Baltimore: 1964.
   See also his *Personal Knowledge*.

Portmann, Adolph. *New Paths in Biology*. New York: 1964.

Postan, M. M., E. E. Rich, and Edward Miller. *The Cambridge Economic His-
   tory of Europe. Vol. III. Economic Organization and Policies in the Middle
   Ages*. Cambridge: 1963.
   Excellent. See also *Vol. VI. The Industrial Revolution and After*. Cambridge: 1965.

Potter, David M. *People of Plenty: Economic Abundance and the American
   Character*. Chicago: 1954.

Price, Derek J. de Sola. *Science Since Babylon*. New Haven: 1961.

   The Science of Science. See Platt, John R. (editor).
   Brief and more circumspect re-statement of *Science Since Babylon*.

Pritchard, James B. (editor). *Ancient Near Eastern Texts: Relating to the Old Testament.* Princeton, N.J.: 1955.

Prochazka, Oldrich. *Sybnek Fizer and "The Consolation of Ontology."* In The Crane Review: Fall 1967.
Since Fizer's work has not yet been translated, this is a useful introduction to a new Marxist version of Buddhism, which curiously confirms my quite independent interpretation of the final religion of the megamachine.

Pumphrey, R. J. *The Origin of Language.* Liverpool: 1951.

Purchas, Samuel. *Hakliutus Posthumus, or, Purchase His Pilgrimes. Contayning a History of the World Sea Voyages and Lande Travelles by Englishmen and Others.* 20 vols. Glasgow: 1905.
The first volume significantly begins with exploration in the ancient world. The rest of the material was partly derived from unedited accounts handed on by Hakluyt.

Rich, E. E., and C. H. Wilson (editors). *The Cambridge Economic History of Europe.* 6 vols. Cambridge: 1967.

Rickover, H. G. *Can Technology Be Humanized—in Time?* In National Parks Magazine: July 1969.

Riesman, David, in collaboration with Reuel Denney and Nathan Glazer. *The Lonely Crowd: A Study of the Changing American Character.* New Haven: 1950.
A pioneer study of power, autonomy, conformity, and mass media in our highly mechanized American society.

Ritter, William E., with the collaboration of Edna Watson Bailey. *The Natural History of Our Conduct.* New York: 1927.

Robergs, Carl R., and B. F. Skinner. *Some Issues Concerning the Control of Human Behavior.* In Science: November 1956.

Roberts, Catherine. *The Scientific Conscience: Reflections on the Modern Biologist and Humanism.* New York: 1967.
Criticizes both the assumptions and the methods of science, with its increasing emphasis on dehumanized experiments and on practical proposals that are callous to man's higher development. The moral criticism is all the more weighty because the author is a professional microbiologist.

Rosenfeld, Albert. *The Second Genesis: The Coming Control of Life.* New York: 1969.
A competent summary of the current attempts by technologically inflated men to play God. If the present book does nothing else, it at least provides the historic background for appraising these ominous proposals.

Rosenfield, L. C. *From Beast Machine to Man Machine.* New York: 1941.

Rosenstock-Huessy, Eugen. *The Multiformity of Man.* Norwich, Vt.: 1948.
Pregnant observations contrasting a man-centered with a machine-centered technics.

Rosinski, Herbert. *Power and Human Destiny.* New York: 1965.
See Juvenal. See also Reinhold Niebuhr's divers works for a theological appreciation of the same constant in human history.

Roslansky, John D. (editor). *Genetics and the Future of Man*. New York: 1965.
See Kingsley Davis' paper.

The Uniqueness of Man. Amsterdam: 1969.
Excellent organicist symposium.

Rossi, Paolo. *Francis Bacon: From Magic to Science*. Bari: 1957. London: 1968.

Rossiter, Clinton L. *Constitutional Dictatorship: Crisis Government in the Modern Democracies*. Princeton, N.J.: 1948.
After a brief chapter on ancient Rome, confines itself to Germany, England, France, and the United States in recent times.

Roszak, Theodore. *The Dissenting Academy*. New York: 1968.
Critical revaluation of the teaching of the humanities in American universities.

The Making of a Counter Culture: Reflections on the Technocratic Society and Its Youthful Opposition. New York: 1969.
Widely documented, sometimes acute: but Roszak's evidences for anything that could be called a culture capable of counterbalancing the existing order are unsubstantial—and hardly hopeful.

Rousseau, Pierre. *Histoire des Techniques*. Paris: 1956.

Rowntree, B. Seebohm. *Poverty: A Study of Town Life*. London: 1902.

Poverty and Progress: A Second Social Survey of York. London: 1941.

Rubin, William J. *Dada, Surrealism, and Their Heritage*. New York: 1941.

Rubinoff, Lionel. *The Pornography of Power*. New York: 1967.
A valuable discussion, whose sexy title and paperback cover are a disgrace to television and publishing, if not to the author.

Russell, E. S. *The Directiveness of Organic Activities*. Cambridge: 1945.
Important for minds escaping from the blind alley of mechanism yet still afraid to accept as real the inescapable differentia of organic behavior: namely, its autonomous, goal-seeking, self-organizing, time-patterned activities.

Ruyer, Raymond. *L'Utopie et les Utopies*. Paris: 1950.
An excellent survey that stresses the totalitarian character of most utopias.

Sakharov, Andrei D. *Progress, Coexistence, and Intellectual Freedom*. With an introduction by Harrison E. Salisbury. New York: 1968.
A human plea by a scientist worthy to be the countryman of Brigadier General Grigorenko.

Salomon, Albert. *The Tyranny of Progress: Reflections on the Origins of Sociology*. New York: 1955.

Santillana, Giorgio de. *The Age of Adventure: The Renaissance Philosophers*. New York: 1956.
Admirable selections, from Nicolas of Cusa to Bruno, with a distinguished introduction.

The Origins of Scientific Thought, from Anaximander to Proclus, 600 B.C. to 300 A.D. Chicago: 1961.
Enchanting.

Sauer, Carl O. *Northern Mists*. Berkeley, Cal.: 1968.
Well-documented account of the many pre-Columbian Western voyages.

Sauer, Carl, Marston Bates, and Lewis Mumford (chairmen). *Man's Role in Changing the Face of the Earth: An International Symposium*. Edited by William L. Thomas, Jr. Chicago: 1956.
Well-prepared papers and wide-ranging discussions. See my summation of the section on Prospect.

Schmookler, Jacob. *Invention and Economic Growth*. Cambridge, Mass.: 1966.

Schneider, Kenneth R. *Destiny of Change*. New York: 1968.

Schrödinger, Erwin. *What Is Life? The Physical Aspect of the Living Cell*. Cambridge: 1945.

Nature and the Greeks. Cambridge: 1954.
Demonstrates the fallacy of Galileo's elimination of qualities, and traces it back to the Greeks.

Mind and Matter. Cambridge: 1959.
By a distinguished physicist who was at home with the humanities, attempting to do justice to those parts of human experience deleted by the confinement of post-seventeenth-century science to depersonalized 'objects.'

Schubert-Soldern, Rainer. *Mechanism and Vitalism: Philosophical Aspects of Biology*. London: 1962.

Schumpeter, Joseph A. *Capitalism, Socialism, and Democracy*. First edition. New York: 1942. Third edition: 1950.
Acutely reasoned, brilliantly written. Though some of the evidence is dated, the conclusions have been increasingly confirmed. Schumpeter's analysis complements and largely confirms my own parallel picture of megatechnics. See Hayek, F. A.

Seidenberg, Roderick. *Posthistoric Man*. New York: 1950.
Interpretation of human development in terms of the increasing dominance of the rational intelligence over instinct, with a progressive transference of the intelligence to extra-human mechanisms that make man's own activities superfluous. If the basic conceptions could be accepted the conclusions would be unavoidable.

Seligman, Ben B. *Most Notorious Victory: Man in an Age of Automation*. Foreword by Robert L. Heilbroner. New York: 1966.

Selz, Peter. *New Images of Man*. New York: 1959.

Senate Judiciary Committee. *Economic Concentration. Hearings Before the Subcommittee on Antitrust and Monopoly*. Washington, D.C.: 1964, 1965, 1966.

Shaw, Ralph R. *Electronic Storage and Searching*. In Times Literary Supplement: April 6, 1962.

Shelley, Mary Wollstonecraft. *Frankenstein, or, The Modern Prometheus*. London: 1818. Oxford: 1969.

Shepard, Paul, and Daniel McKinley (editors). *The Subversive Science: Essays Toward an Ecology of Man*. Boston: 1969.
Despite the misleading title, this is a first-rate collection with much fresh thinking.

Shils, Edward. *The Theory of Mass Society*. In Diogenes: Fall 1962.
A theory that flatly contradicts the thesis of this book: recommended as a pinch of salt to bring out the latter's special flavor.

Simon, Herbert A. *The Shape of Automation for Men and Management*. New York: 1965.
A well-balanced summation.

The Architecture of Complexity. In Proceedings of the American Philosophical Society: December 1962.
Deft analysis of the organic method of handling quantities and complexities by graded hierarchic structures.

Simpson, George Gaylord. *The Meaning of Evolution*. Revised edition. New Haven: 1967.

The Biology of Man. New York: 1969.

The Crisis in Biology. In The American Scholar: Summer 1967.

Singer, Charles. *From Magic to Science: Essays on the Scientific Twilight*. New York: 1928.
Sketchy, but still useful on the pre-Renascence background.

Singer, Charles, *et al*. (editors). *History of Technology*. 5 vols. Oxford: 1954–1958.

Skinner, B. F. *Walden Two*. New York: 1948.
Technocratic behaviorist utopia, as specious as the title.

Science and Human Behavior. New York: 1958.

Smith, Cyril Stanley. *Materials and the Development of Civilization and Science*. In Science: May 14, 1965.

Soddy, Frederick. *The Interpretation of Radium*. London: 1909. Revised and enlarged edition: 1920.
A pioneer work. Soddy's sense of social responsibility caused him to withdraw from physics. But that exemplary moral decision was vitiated by his fastening on 'social credit' as a sufficient means of control.

Speer, Albert. *Erinnerungen*. Berlin: 1969.
Extremely interesting account of Hitler and Hitlerism by a shrewd, technically able participant who lived to repent, and even better to explain, the part he played.

Spencer, Herbert. *The Data of Ethics*. New York: 1879.
Regarded as so important by Spencer that he interrupted his Synthetic Philosophy Series to publish it. A questionably optimistic antithesis to Seidenberg's dark prediction in *Posthistoric Man*.

Spengler, Oswald. *The Decline of the West*. 2 vols. New York: 1928.
Sometimes factually shaky or arbitrary, but often intuitively sound, especially in interpreting evidences of contemporary disintegration more 'objective' minds preferred to overlook. His epithet, Faustian, for post-medieval obsessions with money, power, and technics was well chosen.

Sperry, Roger W. *Mind, Brain, and Humanist Values*. See Platt, John R. (editor).
Like this book, it challenges the reductionist effort to turn the brain into a programmable machine.

Stallo, J. B. *The Concepts and Theories of Modern Physics*. First edition. New York: 1881. Edited by Percy W. Bridgman. Cambridge, Mass.: 1960.
The work of a first-rate philosophical mind, neglected in its own day, but still relevant, as Bridgman pointed out.

Stapledon, Olaf. *Last and First Men: A Story of the Near and Far Future*. London: 1931.

Stevens, Henry Bailey. *The Recovery of Cultures*. New York: 1949.

Stewart, George R. *Not So Rich as You Think*. Boston: 1968.
Assessment of the waste and poisons and destruction introduced by 'advanced' technology.

Strauss, Anselm (editor). *The Social Psychology of George Herbert Mead*. Chicago: 1956.

Sussman, Herbert L. *Victorians and the Machine: The Literary Response to Technology*. Cambridge, Mass.: 1968.

Sypher, Wylie. *Literature and Technology: The Alien Vision*. New York: 1968.

Tawney, R. H. *The Acquisitive Society*. New York: 1920.
Basic.

Taylor, Alfred. *Mind as Basic Potential*. In Main Currents of Modern Thought: March 1958.
A biochemist's view that 'rationality' is implicit in the structure of nature.

Technology and Culture. Melvin Kranzberg (editor), 1959–current.
The quarterly organ of the Society for the History of Technology. Recommended.

Teilhard de Chardin, Pierre. *The Phenomenon of Man*. New York: 1959.
The central expression of Teilhard de Chardin's view of man's origin, development, and destiny.

Man's Place in Nature: The Human Zoological Group. New York: 1966.

Theobald, Robert. *The Challenge of Abundance*. New York: 1961.

Thompson, Edward Palmer. *The Making of the English Working Class*. London: 1965.
Well documented: sympathetic to the exploited.

Thorpe, W. H. *Science, Man and Morals*. London: 1965.

Tillyard, E. M. W. *The Elizabethan World Picture*. New York: 1944.
Brief but penetrating.

Times Literary Supplement. *The Changing Guard*. London: 1965.
A serious but uncritical survey of avant-garde gibberish.

Tocqueville, Alexis de. *Democracy in America. Vol. I*. New York: 1945.

Toffler, Alvin. *The Future as a Way of Life*. In Horizon: Summer 1965.

Toulmin, Stephen, and June Goodfield. *The Architecture of Matter*. New York: 1962.

Toynbee, Arnold. *Lectures on the Industrial Revolution of the Eighteenth Century in England*. London: 1884.
This book, by taking 1760 as a definite starting point, crystallized the notion of "the" Industrial Revolution. This Toynbee must not be confused with the later historian!

Toynbee, Arnold J. *A Study of History*. 10 vols. New York: 1934–1956.
These volumes are too rich in carefully assayed ore, often minted with fresh thought, to be dismissed as contemptuously as many historians have done, either because of factual errors or radical differences in historic perspective. Though overburdened with scholarly detail and sometimes unbearably prolix, this work points fresh paths, much as Spengler does, in many directions.

Change and Habit: The Challenge of Our Time. New York: 1966.

Tuveson, Ernest Lee. *Millennium and Utopia: A Study in the Background of the Idea of Progress*. Berkeley, Cal.: 1949.
Treats the protestant theologians who foresaw improvements in both religion and secular life, sometimes as more than a prelude to the 'final judgement.'

Usher, Albert Payson. *A History of Mechanical Inventions*. New York: 1929. Revised edition: 1954.
A classic: still indispensable.

Van Doren, Charles. *The Idea of Progress*. New York: 1967.
Systematic comparative study, more extensive and detailed than Bury's.

Veblen, Thorstein. *The Instinct of Workmanship*. New York: 1914.

Imperial Germany. New York: 1915.

Theory of the Leisure Class. New York: 1926.
A Swiftian exposure of the futilities of the dominant minority who turn work into leisure in order to turn leisure into work.

Verne, Jules. *The Master of the World*. Paris: 1914.
A final testament of the prophet of technocracy. Inferior to his other works, but significant as an ultimate paranoid fantasy, logically derived from his premises.

Vignoli, Tito. *Myth and Science: An Essay*. New York: 1882.
A forgotten but not negligible book: a landmark in the nineteenth-century conception of progress.

Waddington, C. H. *The Ethical Animal*. London: 1960.
A valiant attempt to get beyond the clichés of positivism and Victorian survivalist evolutionism.

The Nature of Life. New York: 1962.
By a distinguished animal geneticist whose sociological and philosophic insights have opened up fresh approaches.

Wald, George. *The Search for Common Ground*. In Zygon: March 1966.
Interpretation of cosmic processes by a biologist seeking a rational foundation for religion.

Indeterminacy, Individuality, and the Problem of Free Will. See Platt, John R. (editor).
Brilliant summary.

Walker, Charles Rumford. *Modern Technology and Civilization*. New York: 1962.

Walsh, Chad. *From Utopia to Nightmare.* New York: 1962.
A canvass of negative utopias (dystopias or kakotopias).

Washburn, S. L. *The Evolution of Human Behavior.* In John D. Roslansky (editor), *The Evolution of Human Behavior.* Amsterdam: 1969.

Webb, Walter Prescott. *The Great Frontier.* With an introduction by Arnold J. Toynbee. Boston: 1964.
An imaginative hypothesis set within a somewhat arbitrary framework: the American dynamic frontier and the 'static' European 'Metropolis,' between 1500 and 1900. But Webb overlooked both the earlier frontier movements in Europe and the dynamic European technology which made the American frontier possible.

Weizsacker, C. F. von. *The History of Nature.* Chicago: 1949.
Beautifully reasoned.

Wells, H. G. *Anticipations of the Reaction of Mechanical and Scientific Progress.* London: 1902.
Many of Wells' predictions here have already been fulfilled, though often not with .the happy results that Wells anticipated.

A Modern Utopia. London: 1905.
His most comprehensive and carefully laid out picture of possibilities already almost within reach, granted the necessary political and social mechanisms.

The Complete Short Stories of H. G. Wells. London: 1927.
This edition contains *The Time Machine,* one of Wells' most significant fantasies of the future, as well as more practical forecasts, like *The Land Ironclads.* From a literary standpoint *A Story of the Days to Come* is perhaps one of his poorest imaginative works: but in some ways it is startlingly prophetic.

Mind at the End of Its Tether. London: 1945.
A mixture of insight, disillusion, and senile disintegration.

Westin, Alan F. *Privacy and Freedom.* New York: 1967.
Important analysis by a competent student of law: all the more so because it opens up the more ultimate questions of autonomy and personal responsibility. Orwell's *1984* brought down to date.

Weyl, H. *Symmetry.* Princeton, N.J.: 1952.

White, Lynn, Jr. *Machina ex Deo: Essays in the Dynamism of Western Culture.* Cambridge, Mass.: 1968.
Recommended. But see also Mumford, *Technics and Civilization* (1934).

Whitehead, Alfred North. *Science and the Modern World.* New York: 1923.
Still one of the effective analyses of the naïve metaphysics that most physical scientists since Galileo and Descartes regarded as the ultimate basis of 'modern,' that is scientific, thought. See also Stallo, C. Lloyd Morgan, Schrödinger, Michael Polanyi, and many later thinkers who have pursued this line.

Whyte, Lancelot Law. *Unitary Principle in Physics and Biology.* New York: 1949.

The Unconscious Before Freud. New York: 1960.

Whyte, William H., Jr. *The Organization Man.* New York: 1956.
Based on much firsthand research, and full of shrewd observations, though the inquiry is limited to a special variant of Organization Man, the heads of great corporations and

those seeking to rise in the system. Many observations are now dated, but they have historic value.

Wiener, Norbert. *The Human Use of Human Beings: Cybernetics and Society.* Boston: 1950.

  God and Golem, Inc.: A Comment on Certain Points Where Cybernetics Impinges on Religion. Cambridge, Mass.: 1964.

Wilkins, John. *The Discovery of a World in the Moone, or, A Discourse Tending to Prove That 'Tis Probable There May Be Another Habitable World in That Planet, with a Discourse on the Possibility of a Passage Thither.* London: 1638.
This caps Kepler's prediction of a voyage to the moon by suggesting that colonies be planted there. Though America was then unsettled and inviting, this extravagant dream already haunted seventeenth-century thinkers—in this case a bishop.

  Mercury, or the Secret and Swift Messenger: Shewing How a Man May with Privacy and Speed Communicate His Thoughts to a Friend at a Distance. Second edition. London: 1694.
The titles and dates of these works are almost as significant as their contents: fortunately, since they are hard to come by. But see Nicolson, Marjorie Hope.

Wilkinson, John (editor). *Technology and Human Values.* Santa Barbara, Cal.: 1966.
Brief but meaty papers.

Wilson, Arthur M. *Diderot: The Testing Years, 1713–1759.* New York: 1957.
Penetrating.

Wittfogel, Karl A. *Oriental Despotism: A Comparative Study of Total Power.* New Haven: 1957.
Important contribution, widely but unevenly documented. Unfortunately Wittfogel's notion that this totalitarian mode of government arose mainly through the need for water control insufficiently appreciates the non-economic, non-technical factors that Frankfort emphasized in his study of Kingship.

Wolf, A. *A History of Science, Technology, and Philosophy in the 16th and 17th Centuries.* New York: 1935.
Done with the cooperation of Dr. F. Dannemann and Mr. A. Armitage. The best available summary for this period.

Wolff, Philippe, and Frederic Mauro. *L'Age de l'Artisanat (X–XVIII Siècles).* In *Histoire Générale du Travail* (publiée sous la direction de Louis-Henri Parias). Paris: 1959–1961.
Admirable.

Wolheim, Donald A. *Novels of Science.* New York: 1945.
See especially Wells' *First Men in the Moon,* and Olaf Stapledon's *Odd John.*

Wolstenholme, Gordon (editor). *Man and His Future.* London: 1963.
A symposium, arranged by the Ciba Foundation, that reveals as much about the limitations of the scientific approach to man as about his future, which many scientists can conceive only in terms of an extrapolated past or an accelerated present.

Woodruff, William and Helga. *Economic Growth: Myth or Reality.* In *Technology and Culture:* Fall 1966.

Wooldridge, Dean E. *The Machinery of the Brain*. New York: 1963.
> The title betrays the fact that every attempt to interpret organic events solely in terms of cause and effect, plus chance, must fall back upon the machine—a purely teleological model. Thus the discarded concepts of final purpose and design are illicitly smuggled back into the mechanistic conception of life, while the unexplainable tendency to self-organization is denied.

Wulff, Hans E. *The Traditional Crafts of Persia: Their Development, Technology, and Influence on Eastern and Western Civilizations*. Cambridge, Mass.: 1966.

Wymer, Norman. *English Town Crafts: A Survey of Their Development from Early Times to the Present Day*. London: 1949.

Zamiatin, Eugene. *We*. New York: 1934.
> Still one of the best portrayals of the human Ant-State, extrapolated from Soviet Russia, though now implicit in American technology.

Zimmern, Alfred. *Nationality and Government*. London: 1918.
> Zimmern's distinction between nationality and nationalism is still relevant.

ACKNOWLEDGEMENTS

Since the foundations for my technological studies were laid in my youth, it is impossible for me to acknowledge adequately my many personal debts, beyond those referred to in 'Technics and Civilization.' The stimulus for fresh thinking on this subject came from a seminar I gave as Visiting Bemis Professor in Architecture at the Massachusetts Institute of Technology. In that seminar I re-examined the ground covered in 'Technics and Civilization' in the light of new developments in science and technics, and my growing awareness of the irrational factors present in our machine-oriented technology, from its inception in the Pyramid Age onward.

The more immediate stimulus for writing 'The Myth of the Machine' came, however, from my giving the Saposnekow Lectures under that general title at the City College of New York in 1962. Besides recording my debt to these institutions I must also acknowledge my obligation to the Center for Advanced Studies at Wesleyan University, where in 1962 I began writing these two volumes, originally conceived as a single book. But by far the largest part of the preparation and the writing of both volumes was done at Leverett House, Cambridge, where as 'Visiting Scholar' I enjoyed the courtesies and privileges of Harvard, as well as the intellectual companionship of the Fellows, Associates, and Tutors—and on occasion the students. For this aid I give special thanks to Mr. Richard T. Gill, the Master of Leverett House, whose friendly offices turned a House into a home.

And finally, this is a fitting point to record my debt to my wife, Sophia Wittenberg Mumford, not alone for her often clairvoyant secretarial services, but for her unflinching honesty in pointing out those lapses and solecisms in writing that are sometimes harder for a writer to acknowledge than his downright errors. Her human insight, her steadfastness, and her magnanimity are woven into the texture of all my books, and—it goes without saying—of my life.

—L. M.

INDEX

Brackets around numerals denote plate numbers in the graphic section.

Aberrations, nuclear, 265; totalitarian, 249
Aborigines, extermination of, 10
Absentee ownership, 148
Absolute control, magical, 178
Absolute power, misdirection of, 269; need for new symbol of, 243
'Absolute' weapon, fear of, 253
Absolutes, untrustworthiness of, 74
Absolutism, [2]; baroque, 81; Descartes' admiration for, 80; Descartes' baroque, 98; Descartes' philosophic, 81; despotic, 242; Hobbes' justification of, 101; passage to, 80
Abstract art, Gabo's organic, [32]
Abstract values, interchangeability of, 167
Abstractions, scientific, 57
Abundance, economy of, 324; natural and technological, 335; negative, 324; royal economy of, 342
Academic Establishment, [25]
Academic quantification, 181
Accademia dei Lynxei, 115
Acton, Lord, 265
Adam and Eve, future American, 368
Adams, Henry, [3], 230–235, 255, 268, 312, 410, 430
Adams' scientific analysis, scholarly indifference to, 234
Ader's airplane, 93
Adventurism, spatial, 309
A. E. (George Russell), 361
Aerial navigation, possibility of, 46
Affluence, beginnings of, 321
Africa, Negro adaptation to, 378
Age of Reptiles, 381
Aged, traumatic experience of the, 342
Agricola, 140, 177
Agriculture, 19, 145; as safeguard against power system, 351; basic contribution to, 132; basic importance of, [3]; moral culture of, 351; primacy of, 132; small margins of early, 321
Ahab, Captain, 301, 376
Aiken, Conrad, 121
Air conditioning, Tolstoi's satiric description of, 286
Air Force, U.S., 252, 256, 269

Air travel, Melville's prediction of, 46
Alchemist's dream, 125; verification of, 419
Alienation, 287, 359, 429
Alsted, J. H., 103
American Indians, robbery of, 42
American Philosophical Society, 111, 114
Ammann, Jost, 140, 143
'Analysis of the Principles of Economics,' 341
Anarchism, 158
Anatomical dissections, Leonardo's, 162
Anaxagoras, 34
Anderson, Edgar, 382
'Andromeda Strain,' 126
'Animal Automatism,' 96
Annual income, guaranteed, 326
Anti-art, 267, 365
Anti-city, [10]
Anti-life, cult of, 361, 366; space exploration as mode of, 311
Anti-poverty programs, feedback from, 326
'Anticipation of the Effects of Mechanical Progress,' 372
Anticipations, Bellamy's realistic, 219
Aphorism, A.E.'s, 361
Apollo 11, 190
'Apparitions,' nature of, 422
Aquinas, Thomas, 77
Aragon, Louis, 366
'Arbeit und Rhythmus,' 137
Archetypes, Henry Moore's, [32]
Aristocracy, extravagances of, 322
Aristotelian doctrines, 52
Aristotle, 83, 176
Arms factories, 149
Army, educational function of, 240; growing importance of, 239
Arsenal, Venetian, 38
Art, 416; avant-garde definition of, 365; destruction as process of, 365; effect of technics on, 363; junk and pop, 367
Art Nouveau, 363
Artifact, man's supreme, 417
Artificial life, automata as form of, 99
Arzamas, Tolstoi's dream at, 359
Ascensionism, 34, 197
Ashurbanipal, [12]

Ashurnasirpal, 251

'Assayer, The,' 53

Assyrians, 350

Astrologer, court, 31

Astrology, Christian condemnation of, 31

Astronauts, [14–15], 307, 348; moon, 379

Astronomy, importance of, 33

Atlantean World, The New, 114

Atom, secrets of, 314

Atom bomb, Adams' anticipation of, 233; demoralizing effect of, 252; failure to provide safeguards for, 255; initiative to invent, 256

Atomic energy, portable, 214; problems raised by, 233

Atomic Energy Commission, 266

Atomic energy program, 269

Atomic genocide, 368

Atomic reactors, chief products of, 301

Atoms, present conception of, 59

Atrocities, military, 252; Nazi, 251

Atum-Re, 28, 35, 422

Audio-visual tribalism, 297

Audubon, John James, 8, 15, 24

Augustine, Saint, 431

Augustus, 431

Auschwitz, 256, 279

Authoritarian system, surrender to, 332

Authoritarianism, utopian, 210, 211

Autocracy, technocratic, [10]

Autodrama, 415

Automated man, 192

Automated systems, radical defect in, 183

Automatic fixations, earlier forms of, 185

Automatic loom, 178

Automatic machine, Comenius' praise of, 103; characterization of, by Marx, 171

Automatic progress, 225

Automatic systems, insulation of, 184; primitive nature of, 399

Automation, Aristotle's dismissal of, 136; as total control, 184; 'automation' of, 182, 236, 360; beginnings of, 170; computer-controlled, 192; defects of, 179; failure to control, 180; human problem of, 180; impact of, 174; implications of, 192, 193; inflexibility of, 184; Kublai Khan's exhibition of, 176; medieval, 177; monitoring of, 178; 19th-century achievement of, 171; organic, 394, 399; paradox of, 180; pre-industrial, 175; principal weakness of, 184; surrender to, 186; triumph of, 175; ultimate goal of, 331; uncontrolled, 181; varied means of, 95

Automatism, brain's early escape from,

400; fatalistic attitude toward, 291; lethal, 267; Mill's and Wiener's anxieties over, 190

Automaton, 350; Hephaistos' bronze, 176; shadow-self, 193

Automatons, as organic models, 85; clockwork, 77; human, 193; hypnotic effect of, 96; societies of, 126

Autonomy, 393; insurance of, 144; renunciation of, 332; transfer to state, 100; welfare state's suppression of, 345

Average man, scientific threat to, 280

Awakening, planet-wide social, 412

Axial religions, failure of, in curbing power system, 335

Axioms, need to examine accepted, 129

Axis, surrender by, 266

Aztecs, 9, 350; priests, 267

Babbage, Charles, 65, 112, 188

Babel, Isaak, 247

Backwash, revolutionary, 353

Bacon, Francis, 31, 77, 105–129, 333, 414, 416, 429; balanced views of, 124; deflation of, 109; enlargement by, of mechanistic world picture, 118; open-mindedness of, 107; premises of, appraised, 127–129; scientific deficiencies of, 106

Bacon, Francis (contemporary painter), [28]

Bacon, Roger, 53, 61

Baconian 'Lamps,' 113

Baconian premises, 127

Baconian synthesis, 125

Bactericides, 336

Balance, 397; idea of, 398; polytechnic, 145

Balanced economy, 348

Ballistic rocket, intercontinental, 304

Barbarism, [13]

Barbarous society, relics of, 349

Bargain, power system's, 332

Barnard, Dr. Christiaan, 227

'Bartleby,' 360

'Bay of Pigs,' 271

Bazarov, 357, 358

'Beagle,' voyage of the, 387

Beatles, 423

Beauty, importance of, 381

Bell, Alexander Graham, 394

Bell, Daniel, 331

Bell Telephone Company engineers, 69

Bellamy, Edward, 211, 215, 219, 323

Belloc, Hilaire, 245

Belsen, 279

Bentham, Jeremy, 321

Bentham, Samuel, 149

Berdiaev, N. A., 211
Bergson, Henri, 391, 392
Bernard, Claude, 397
Berneri, Marie Louise, 217
Bettelheim, Dr. Bruno, [14–15]
Big Brain, 104, 316; constant attachment to, 331; control by, 319
'Big bribe,' 339
'Big Brother,' 187
Biocide, [12]
Biodrama, 415
Biologic humanism, Huxley's, 393
Biological evolution, Seidenberg's interpretation of, 313
Biological 'revolution,' 379
Biological sciences, late establishment of, 385; miscarriage of, 384
Biotechnics, 394, 395; passage to, [29]
Birket-Smith, Kaj, 69
'Black Manifesto,' 368
Blackouts, 410
Blake, William, 315, 396
Blavatsky, Madame, 234
Blitz, human reaction to, 410
Bloch, Marc, 290
Block printing, 139
Blockade, Soviet, of Berlin, 271
Blondin, Charles, [18–19]
Bodily nature, man's, 417
Body, language of the, 422; wisdom of the, 400
Body politic, disintegration of, 347
Bohr, Nils, 53, 264
Bombing, Churchill's indefensible decision on, 252
Bombs, napalm and atom, 279
Books, burning of, 294; threat to abandon, 182
Borelli, Giovanni, 38, 394
Boscovich, R. G., 70
Boyle, Robert, 96
Brahe, Tycho, 27, 31
Brain, as controller of automatic processes, 399; computer's resemblance to, 188; hyperactivity of, 400; Kepler's false notion of, 61
Bramah, Joseph, 142
Braudel, Fernand, 146
Brave new world, 40, 290
'Brave New World,' 224–228, 319
'Brave New World Revisited,' 227
Bread, monopolistic mass production of, 178
'Bread and circuses,' 347
Breakdown, as condition for restoring health, 411; megatechnic, healthy reaction to, 412
Breakdowns, 410; causes of, 427
Breeding, fallacies of, 290
Bribe, megatechnic, 330

Bridgman, Percy, 75
British Empire, collapse of, 432
Bronze Age gods, modern rivals of, 255
Bruno, Giordano, 38
Brutalities, persistence of political, 244
Buchenwald, 256
Buddhism, modern version of, 228
Buecher, Karl, 137
Buffon, Comte de, 387
Bulwer-Lytton, Edward, 214–215, 226
Burckhardt, Jacob, 13, 272, 305
Bureau d'Addresse, Renaudot's, 114
Bureaucracy, Czarist, 246; growing importance of, 239; post-Napoleonic, 285; utopian, 215
'Bureaucratic personality,' 278
Burial societies, 142
Burning of books, Nazi, 294
Burtt, E. A., 67, 68
'Business cycle,' 322
Butler, Samuel, 96, 193–196, 430
Butterfield, Herbert, 32
'Butterfly principle,' 406
Byzantine Empire, prolonged life of, 432

Cabet, Etienne, 213
Cage, John, 364
Calculating machines, 188
Calvinism, Adams', 232
'Cambridge Modern History,' 240
Campanella, Tommaso, 4, 429; letter to Galileo, 13
Candles, use of, in Vietnam war protest, [27]
Cannon, Walter, 396–400
Capital, availability of, for investment, 148
Capitalism, 159; growth of, 237; 'new,' 323; replacement of, 346; state, 216
Capitalist economy, contradictory aim of, 322
Capitalist salvation, dependence of, on war, 225
Capitalist system, war as redeemer of, 242
Capitalistic organization, governmental backing of, 146
Cardan, Jerome, 29
Carpenters Company of Philadelphia, 133
Cartesian limitations, Bacon's escape from, 117
Cartesian mechanism, usefulness of, 105
Cartesian method, 80
Catastrophe, awakening to, 412; forebodings of, 199; shadow of, 75
Catinat, Nicholas de, on approaching destruction, 199
Causal analysis, 89

Causal determinism, 87
Causality, 87
Celestial mechanics, 36
Céline, Louis-Ferdinand, 357
Cellini, Benvenuto, 160
Censorship, Leonardo's voluntary, 163
Central Computer, 273
Central Intelligence Agency, 266, 271
Centralized organization, 239
'Century of Progress, The' (1933), 213
Chambers, Robert, 387
Chance; 87, 356
Change, and value, 209; limits on, 173
Chaos, 356; 20th-century, 235
'Child Buyer, The,' 272
Chimpanzees, as slaves, 326
China, [8], 270, 352
Christian faith, disintegration of, 40
Christian Gospels, 423
Christian Heaven, operative function of, 58
Christian hermits, as models for astronauts, 307
Christian minority, Roman contempt for, 431
Christian revelation, non-credibility of, 32
Christian superego, freedom from, 41
Christianity, 413; late achievement of, 424; Roman state's conversion to, 425; ultimate expression of, 425
Church doctrine, fossilization of, 52
Chute-the-chutes, [4]
Cigarette industry, 367
Circulation of the blood, Harvey's observations on, 38
City, role of the, in assembling intelligence, [6]; superiority of the, to computer, 191
'City in History, The,' 81, 319, 344
'City of God, The,' 431
'City of the Sun, The,' 4
Civilian population, indiscriminate bombing of, 256
Civilization, Bronze Age, 404; chronic defects of, 199; original traumas of, 292; radical historic errors of, 292; traumatic effects of, 22
Civilized man, barbarism of, 203
Clarke, Arthur, 220, 222, 283, 310, 313
Class war, Marxian, 401
Classification of sciences, Comte's, 385
Clock, analysis of, 88; as cartesian model, 85; as model of later automatons, 177
Clockmaker, invisible, 90; superhuman, 89
Coal, increased use of, 146
Coalition of power complex, 239
Coercion, communist, 246
Coinage, 165

Colbert, Jean Baptiste, 149
Cold War, 266–269
Cole, Dandridge, 227
Collective life, electronic simulation of, 319
Collectivism, 346
Colonialism, 159
Colonization, Europe's 'mission,' 19; of moon, premature, 48; of planets, archaic aims of, 44
Colt's revolver, handicraft reproduction of, 136
Columbus, Christopher, 6; first voyage of, 5
Comenius, John Amos, 102–103
'Coming Race, The,' 214
Commoner, Barry, 337
Communal complexity, mechanical rejection of, 84
Communication, limitations on, 189; oral, 298; organic nature of, 297
Communications systems, 237
Communism, 158; 'basic,' 326; bureaucratic, 355
'Communist Manifesto, The,' 325, 353
Community, mechanistic denial of, 81; restoration of face-to-face, 408
Complexities, ecological, 68
Compulsions, megatechnic, 272; technical, 224; technological, 186
Compulsory consumption, burden of, 326
Compulsory production, 326
Computer, 188; Central, 273; collective consequences of, 188; demand of, for diversified specialists, 188; Divine, 275; historic city's superiority to, [6]; intelligent assembly of, 192; judicious use of, 190; lifelike functions of, 190; limitations of, 273; moon-landing breakdown of, 190; noöspheric, 317; radical weakness of, 191; role of, as 'decision maker,' 98; Wiener's warning on, 189
Computer technicians, human deficiencies of, 189
Computerdom, [6]
Comte, Auguste, 240, 243, 349, 385, 404
Concentration camp, 247
Concretion versus abstraction, 87
Conditioning center, utopian, 225
Condorcet, Marquis de, 19, 240
'Conduct of Life, The,' 414
Conformity, as utopian ideal, 213
Confucian Analects, 423
Congress, U.S., pusillanimous passivity of, 266
Conquest, meaninglessness of, 291; of nature, one-sided nature of, 79; of space, as mode of population control, 308
Conquistadors, 9

Conrad, Joseph, 9
Consciousness, expansion of, 338
Conscription, national, 239; paucity of references to, 240
Conservatism, Raglan quoted on, 282
Conservatoire des Arts et Métiers, 93
'Considerable Speck, A,' 91
Constancy, organic, 397
Constitutional dictatorship, 271
Constructivism, Gabo's organic, [32]
Consumption, compulsory, 326; forced, 174; Golden Age of, 175; indiscriminate, 328; misdirected, 323
Contemporary art, irrational modes of, 364
Continuity, need for, 370
'Contrat Social,' 245
Control, acceptance of external, 287; all-pervading system of, 274; automatic, 183; automation's effort at human, 189; automation's escape from, 192; centralized, 270; contribution of illiteracy to, 294; long-distance, 146; mechanization as condition for, 80; permissive, 338; remote, [5]; scientific impulse to, 186; 'scientific' modes of, 352; Thorndike-Skinner method of, 216
Control apparatus, Napoleonic, 245
Control systems, ancient and contemporary, 183
Cook, Captain James, 9, 101
Cooking, as polytechnic art, 141
Copernican revolution, 29
Copernicus, Nicolaus, 27, 29, 31, 384, 386; as sun-worshipper, 32
Corbeil-Essonnes, 192
Corporate scientific organization, 123
Corpse, as scientific equivalent of living organism, 385
Corruption, totalitarian, 251
Cort, Henry, 149
Cosmodrama, 415
Cosmos, potentialities of, 415; secrets of, 314
Counter-culture, rituals of, [27]; stabilization of Power System by, [27]; youthful desire for, 422
Cousin, Victor, 200
Craft guilds, function of, 133
Craft industry, eliminated by power system, 171
Craft specialization, artists' breakthrough in, 138
Craft traditions, deliberate wrecking of, 155
Crafts, internal development of, 143
Craftsman, Morris as archetypal, 158
Craftsmen, Japanese, 136; medieval, 26
Creation of life, as goal of modern science, 125

Creative society, dependence of upon personality, 75
Creativity, biological, 381
Crick, Sir Francis, 289
'Crime and Punishment,' 356
Crimes, affluent temptations to, 332
'Critique of the Gotha Programme,' 405
Cromer, Lord, 432
Crystal Palace, 143
Crystal Palace Exhibition, 208
Cubism, 363
Cultural accumulation, 282
Cultural climax, novel element in, 425
Cultural dissolution, 295
Cultural forms, 417
Cultural inheritance, programming of, 292
Cultural interchanges, contribution of, to technics, 18
Cultural lag, 223
Cultural prospects, emerging, 404
Cultural reservoir, importance of, 351
Culture, archaic, 426; distinguishing marks of, 417; formative processes of, 414; Instant, 282; patterns of, 370; 'post-historic,' 311; pre-literate limitations, 298; present death-oriented, 261; re-orientation of, 371; semi-parasitic, 344
'Culture of Cities, The,' [24]
Cultures, extirpation of earlier, 10; national, 375
'Cursor Mundi,' 35
Curzon, Lord, 432
Cybernation, organic, 394
Cyborg, as mechanical elephant, [18–19]
'Cyclopedia of the Mechanical Arts,' 131
Czarist-Stalinist system, 247–248, 266

Dacca muslin, 137
Dadaism, 363–364, 366
Dartmouth College, [25]
Darwin, Charles, 351, 379, 386–389, 391–393, 397; great contribution of, 387; precursors of, 387; qualification of, as biologist, 387
Darwin, Erasmus, 386
Darwinian thinking, 392
Darwinism, popularized version of, 392
DDT, 336
'De Cive,' 99
'De Contagione et Contagiosis Morbis,' 29
'De Humani Corporis Fabrica,' 29
'De Re Metallica,' 140, 177
'De Revolutionibus Orbium Coelestium,' 29
Dead, modern cult of the, 261
Death, 418; Egyption cult of, 384; mega-

Death (Cont.)
   technic orientation to, 260; premature wholesale, 260
'Death of a Salesman,' 136
Decentralization, need for, [5]
Decision-maker, computer's role as, 98; electronic form of, 273
'Decline and Fall of the Roman Empire,' 199
Defoe, Daniel, 351
Degeneration, conditions for, 341
Dehumanization, 267, 429; progress in, 227
Deities of disintegration, 356
Delacroix, Eugène, 237, 356
'De-materialization,' 427, 428, 433
Democracy, popular promotion of, 353; Tocqueville's observation of, 344
De-moralization, 233; Adams' insight into, 235
Dependence, infantile, 341
Descartes, René, 77–94, 429; Gassendi's criticism of weakness of, 82; rejection by, of dreams, 83; specification of, for the machine, 83
'Descent of Man, The,' 387
Desiccation, environmental, [21]
Design, nature of organic, 87
Despair, Wells' ultimate, 222
Despotism, Descartes' preference for, 83; obsolescence of, 272; reappearance of, 344
Destruction, 429; organized, by 'freeways,' [22]; purposeless, 350; megatechnic need for, 349; recovery from, 361
Detachment, 433
Determinism, astronomical basis of, 32; scientific, 82
Dewey, John, 392
'Dialogue on Suicide,' 342
'Dialogues,' 52
'Dialogues on Two Worlds,' 57
Dictatorial 'revolution,' stale concepts of, 354
Dictators, new, godlike attributes of, 247
Dictatorships, fascist and communist, 244; new style, [8]
Diderot, Denis, 15, 21, 140, 387
Dinosaur cities, [20]
'Dirigisme,' utopian, 210
'Discourse Concerning a New World,' 48
'Discourse on Method,' 77
Discoveries, regressive side of, 20
'Discovery of a New World,' 220
Disease, early germ theory of, 29
Disillusion, 429
Disintegration, 429; Adams' diagnosis of, 232; moral, 332; psychological, 55; reactions to, 362
Dismantlement, 428, 429

Dissection, post-mortem, 385
Distribution, absence of a just system of, 152
Diversification, Leonardo's example of, 160
Divine King, 274; new image of, 247
Divine Kings, American Presidents as, 257; as colonizers, 36
Divine kingship, 29, 403; Hitler's and Stalin's approach to, 249; Hobbes' reinstatement of, 101; new-style, [8]
Divine knowledge, improvements in, 198
'Divine Organizer,' 419
Divine revelation, scientific reaction against, 60
Divine right, state rule by, 246
Divine salvation, 424
Divine worship, new ritual of, 247
Divinity, as climax of evolution, 391; Pharaoh's claim to, 300
Division of labor, American resistance to, 23; antiquated, 406; end of, 405; scientific, 112
DNA, 54, 120
Docile obedience of modern personality, 279
Docility, need for human, 339
'Dr. Zhivago,' 380
Dogmatic 'objectivity,' Hume's classic example of, 64
Domestic arts, 141
Domestic service, lack of, 326
Domestication, deterioration under, 340
Dominant minority, 352
Doom, technocratic, 435
Dostoevsky, Feodor, 356, 357
Double helix, 54
Douhet, General Giulio, 251
Drake, Sir Francis, 146
Drama, cosmic setting of, 415; human, 414
Dream world, Freud's reclamation of, 83
Dreams, 'objective' inquiry into, 92
Driesch, Hans, 87
Dropouts, 347; moral, 332
Drugs, 373
Dualism, Galileo's, 57; scientific, 58
Du Bridge, Lee, 336
Duchamp, Marcel, [29]
Dürer, Albrecht, 11
Durkheim, Emile, 358, 406
Dynamism, 243; disintegration by, 370; economic, 242; Marinetti's sentimental, 363; power system's, 169; technological, 287

Eastern empire, arrested decay of, 432
Ecological balance, 396
Ecological complexities, 68

Ecological method, application of, 391
Ecological partnership, man's, 380
Ecological recklessness, 379
Ecology, Darwin's contribution to, 389
Economic depression, 326
Economic gains, just distribution of, 324
Economic organizations, corporate, 278
Economic prison, new, 327
Economic waste, 328
Economy, automated, 184; democratization of, 324
Economy of abundance, nature's, 399; organic models for, 395
'Economy of gifts,' 325
'Economy of Megalopolis,' 331
Economy of plenitude, 402
Ecosystems, 395
Eddy, Mary Baker, 354
Education, centralized control of, 286; clockwork model for, 103; Comenius' conception of, 102; Gargantua's, 138; mass production in, 102
Education and catastrophe, race between, 411
Edwards, John, 198
Efflorescence, as symbol of creativity, 381
Effort, organic need for, 339
Effortless life, 338, 339
Ego, diminishment of, in 'noösphere,' 316
Eichmann, Adolph, 279
Eight-hour day, 147
Einstein, Albert, 255, 256
Eiseley, Loren, 60, 381
Electricity, Hawthorne's intuitions about, 314
Electronic Age, McLuhan's belated interpretation of, 296
Electronic dissociation, 294
Electronic inventions, Mumford's early interpretation of, 295
Electronic media, heavy price of, 297; juvenile rapture over, 304
Electronic super-brain, 315
Electronics, 394
Eliade, Mircea, 35
'Elite,' professional, rewards for, 348; technocratic, 358; technological, preemption of national decisions by, 271
Ellul, Jacques, 291
'Embodiment,' structural, as final stage in human drama, 425
'Emergent Evolution,' 231
Emerson, Ralph Waldo, 9, 10, 23, 24, 202, 207, 253, 421
Empiricism, Francis Bacon's, 106; value of, 110
Encapsulated man, [14–15]
'Encyclopédie, Grande,' 140
Energy, basic source of, 132; long insufficiency of, 321; necessary modulation of, 403
Energy increase, Adams' interpretation of, 231
Enfantin, Barthélemy, 353, 354
Engels, Friedrich, 353
Enlightenment, the, 15; prejudices of, 6
Enslavement, civilized, release from, 405; totalitarian, 249
Entropy, acceleration of, 293; electronic, 293; reality of, 418
Environment, de-natured, 51; desiccation of, [21]; destruction of, 147; man's life-sustaining, 381; megatechnic threat to, 336
Environmental degradation, common experience of, 412; superficial response to, 413
Eotechnic improvements, 145
Ephebic Oath, Athens', [27]
Equilibrium, dynamic, 397
'Erewhon,' 167, 195
Erikson, Erik, 359
Escapism, post-nuclear, 373
'Essay on Liberty,' 190
'Essay on Self-Reliance,' 23
'Essay on War,' 421
Establishment, Dada's mockery of the, 364
Esthetics, technical contribution to, 363
Eternal life, promise of, by Jesus, 431
'Etherialization,' 421–433; Gabo's image of, [30]; Toynbee's examples of, 427
Evils, failure to recognize, 411
Evolution, as contrasted with progress, 202; 208; Butler's application of, to machines, 194; end of human, 293; mode of, 391; positive and negative, 203; Spencer's description of, 105; Victorian identification of, with struggle, 392
Evolutionary process, promise of, 390
Ewing, Sir Alfred, 410
Exhibitionism, technological, [18–19]
Existential vacuum, contemporary, 369
Existing institutions, contribution of, 424
Expansion, necessity for, 348
Expenditure, standard of, 322
Experience, Galileo's disqualification of, 55; translation of, 417
Experiment, Bacon on importance of, 61
Experts, massive errors of, [7]; self-appointed, 271; vanity of, 260
Exploits, progressive technical, 284
Exploration, age of, 3; complementary kinds of, 3; cosmic, sterile terminus of, 379; importance of, for technics, 18–19; leaders of, 12; terrestrial and technological, 21; two modes of, 4, 378

Exploration and invention, science's contribution to, 78

Explosion of flowers, 381

Explosives, cosmic violence of, predicted, 232

Extermination, Assyrian model for, 251; compulsion to, 262; Darwinian acceptance of, 387; Nazi plans for, 249; projects for, 362; Western man's, 9

Extermination bombing, military futility of, 252

Extermination camps, German, 302, 364; Stalinist, 364

Extermination laboratory, 247

Extermination program, 253

Extravagance, democratization of, 322

Eye, the All-Seeing, 274

Eye of Re, 275

Factories, large-scale, 149

Factory system, 149, 165

Fallout, commercial, [23]

Fantasies, contemporary, 368; Pentagonal, 223

Faraday, Michael, 70

Farming, versatility of, 406

Fascist human debasement, 251

'Fathers and Sons,' 357

Federal Bureau of Investigation, 266

Feedback, 184, 189

Fermi, Enrico, 255, 264

'Final solution,' scientific, 281

Finalism, 87; Spencer's automatic, 106

Financial dynamism, 243

Financial success, condition for, 328

First Cause, non-mechanical nature of, 419

'First Men in the Moon,' 221

'Fitness of the Environment, The,' 390

Flowering plants, as life symbols, 383

Flowers, explosion of, 381

Flying machine, Le Folie's first 'electrical,' 221

Ford Motor Company, 227

Forecasts, incompetent authoritative, 271

Formative ideas, retesting of, 424

Forster, E. M., 221, 412

Fouillée, Alfred, 422

'Foundation research,' Bacon's, 113

Fourier, Charles, 406

Fracastoro, Girolamo, 29

Frank, Waldo, [20]

Frankenstein, 126

Frankl, Viktor, 360

Franklin, Benjamin, 65, 111

'Free Enterprise,' 193

'Free World,' 270

Freedom, conditions for true, 298; escape from, 287; internal balance as

condition for, 398; lack of, in utopia, 210, 218; political and social, 237; technical conditions of, 185

Freedom of will, as organic attribute, 86

French Revolution, 353; effect of, on power system, 245

Freud, Sigmund, 83, 94, 261

Friedmann, Georges, 153

Friendly societies, 142

Froebel, Friedrich, 386

Fromm, Erich, 287

Frost, Robert, 91

Fugger, Jacob, the elder, 146, 165

Fulfillment, Baconian, 120; instant, 341

Fuller, Buckminster, 56, 58, 204, 227

Future, foreseeable, promising, 433; role of the, 205; scientific and technical, Bacon's prediction of, 117

Future inventions, Bacon's account, 116

'Future of Life, The,' 288

'Future of Man, The,' 315

Futurism, 363

'Futurist Manifesto,' Marinetti's, 363

Futurists, Italian, 363

Gabo, Naum, [30], [32]

Gabor, Dennis, 192

Galileo, Galilei, 32, 52, 58, 416, 429; absolution for, 74; academic opposition to, 61; Burtt's critique of, 68; Campanella's letter to, 13; crime of, 57, 73; heresy of, 57; merit of method of, 60; non-baroque nature of, 56; on primary and secondary qualities, 62–63, 64

Galvani, Luigi, 394

Gama, Vasco da, 9

Gandhi, Mahatma, 204

Garden of Eden, 383

Gardens, cultivation of, 383

Gassendi, Pierre, 82

Geddes, Patrick, [24], 122, 204, 341, 374, 389, 391, 392, 404, 415

'Gene pool,' 154

Generation, post-war, passivity of, 267

Genesis, evolutionary version of, 390

Genet, Jean, 357

Genetic intervention, proposed, 288

'Genetics and the Future of Man,' 291

Genghis Khan, [12]

Genius, Clarke's notion of, 311

Genocide, [12], 362; military advocacy of, 251; official predictions of, 260

Geometry, language of, 54

Giantism, homage to, [20]

Gibbon, Edward, 198, 199

Giedion, Sigfried, 177

Gilbert, William, 109, 113

Glanvill, Joseph, 47, 429

Glass, importance of, for science, 27

'Global village,' McLuhan's, 297
God, electronic, 228; human identification with, 316; scientific attitude toward, 121
Godwin, Francis, 220
Goethe, Johann Wolfgang von, 180, 337, 351, 387, 420
Gold, lust for, 8
Golden Age, 175
Golden mean, 398
Golem, Wiener's, 125
Goliaths, brass-armored, 269
Goncourt, Edmond de, 234
Goods and services, abstract evaluation of, 165
'Gotha Programme,' 405
'Granules,' Chardin's human, 319
Grave-snatching, scientific, 385
'Great Chain of Being, The,' 396
'Great Didactic, The,' 102, 103
Great Mother, Moore's, [32]
Greene, Felix, 144
Greenwich time, 36
Growth, 397; organic means for, 399
Guilds, legal abolition of, 133
'Gulliver's Travels,' 193
Gustavus Adolphus, 149
Gutenberg, Johann, 140

Habitats, devitalized, 383
Hague, The, Lord Mayor of, 141
Hairdo and costume, as personality transformers, 423
Haldane, John Scott, 397
Hall, Edward, [24]
Hall, Stanley, 406
Halley's comet, 36
Handicraft, disabilities of, 135, 136; ignorance of, 156; personal relations in, 141; social compensations of, 137
Happening, [20], 365
Hawkins, Sir John, 146
Hawthorne, Nathaniel, 314, 372
Hayek, Friedrich, 245
Health, conditions for, 343
'Heart of Darkness,' 9
Heavenly messengers, modern, 307
Hegel, Georg Wilhelm Friedrich, 390, 421
Hegelian idealism, 421
Hell's Angels, [13]
Helmholtz, Hermann von, 394
Henderson, Lawrence J., 282, 390
Heraclitus, 37, 167
Hereditary improvement, scientific guarantee of, 291
Hero of Alexandria, 13
Hersey, John, 272
Hierarchic organization, Christian, 425

Hierarchy, new scientific, 290
Hierarchy of power, scientists' place in new, 255
Higher needs, relation of plenitude to, 402
'Higher races,' as exterminators of 'lower,' 387
Highway engineers, arrogance of, [22]
Himmler, Heinrich, 279
Hinkle, Lawrence, 55
Hippie costumes, mass production of, 367
Hippies, 420
Hiroshima, [28]
Historic city, 297
Historic time, as third 'New World,' 39
History, cultural, 13; importance of, 414; negative aspects of, 417; science's contempt for, 64, 65; scientific, rejection of, 82, 84; Western march of, 36
Hitler, Adolf, 244, 248, 249–253, 254, 279, 281, 356
Hobbes, Thomas, 98–102
Hobhouse, Leonard, 392
Holidays, pre-industrial, 138
Holocaust, nuclear, 302
'Homage to New York,' [20]
Homeostasis, organic, 399
'Homeostatic balance,' 397
Homicide, [12]
Homo sapiens, 313; end of, 293
Homogenized environment, [21]
Hooke, Robert, 115
Horsepower, 132–133
Horses, breeding of, 132
Horticulture, 383
'House of the Seven Gables, The,' 314
Houston Space Center, [5]
Hovercraft, pollution dangers from, [18–19]
Howard, Ebenezer, 218
Hubris, Laplace's, 32
Human association, values of, 374
Human autonomy, replacement of, by megamachine, 296
Human awakening, 413
Human brain, superiority of, to computer, 54
Human center, need for return to, 420
Human culture, technics as formative part of, 415
Human development, dramatic metaphor for, 414; guidelines to, 340; modes of, 421
Human evolution, 399
Human experience, Galileo's dismissal of, 57; objective and subjective axes of, 74
Human intentions, importance of, 232
Human labor, prohibitive costs of, 326
Human mind, powers of, 421

Human motives, shift of, under power system, 165

Human organism, collective dismemberment of, 196; reduction of, 306

Human person, 434

Human personality, devaluation of, 60; irrational factor in, 430

Human possibilities, fresh picture of, 434

Human potentialities, richness of, 191

Human progress, 197

Human re-orientation, need for, 236

Human rights, utopian deprivation of, 218

Human sacrifice, impending, 228

Human service, abundance of, 322

Human task, today's pressing, 430

Human victims, religious sacrifice of, 9

'Humane empire,' technological enlargement of, 110

Humboldt, Alexander von, 15–16, 351

Hume, David, 64

Hunsdon, Lord, 9

Huxley, Aldous, 224, 229, 319; technocratic utopia of, 225

Huxley, Julian, 209, 393, 405

Huxley, Thomas Henry, 96, 392

Hydrogen atom, 90

IBM-France, 192

Iconoclasm, 428

Id, 350; subjective reaction of, to automaton, 193

Idea, socialization of, 424

Ideal colonies, 210

Ideal State, Bacon's, 118

Ideal type, organization man as, 278

Ideal types, religious, 289

Ideas, bodily shape of, 423; 'incarnation' of, 422

'Idées-forces,' 422

'Identity crisis,' 284, 359

Ideology, New World, 40; polytechnic lack of, 158

Idiocy, esthetic, 364

'Immense Journey, The,' 381

Immortality, Pharaoh's claim to, 300

Imperial Hotel, Tokyo, [21]

Improvements, megatechnic, 333; nonmechanical, 145

'Incarnation,' 422; minor part of, in science and technics, 429, 430

Incas of Peru, 209

Incentives to work, 321

Income, guaranteed annual, 326

Income tax, as necessity of war, 242

Incomes, equalization of, 407

'Incorporation,' social, 424

'Increasing wants,' dogma of, 322

Indian, pioneer's imitation of, 8

Indians, military pressure against, 8

Indigenous cultures, records of, 12

Industrial arts, military support for, 150

Industrial pollution, [22], [23]

Industrial Revolution, 130, 147, 154; medieval start of, 169

Industrialism, human costs of, 170

Industrialization, military prelude to, 150

Industry, aim of modern, 328, 336

Infallibility, computer's supposed, 273

Infantilism, 'avant-garde,' 363; Brave New World's, 226; promotion of, 344

Information, control of, 183; need for authentic, 61; official distribution of, 183; storage of, 182; subdivisions of, 264

Inhibitions, breakdown of, 251; importance of, 352

Inner life, over-concentration on, 420

Inquisition, 38, 77, 203, 425

'Instant revolution,' 294

'Instauration, The New,' 105

Institutional collaboration, 123

Institutional 'incorporation,' 424

Integration and disintegration, 418

'Intellectual Adventure of Ancient Man, The,' 342

Intellectual intercourse, unfavorable wartime conditions for, 263

Intelligence, promotion of, by tool-using, 179; terminal stage of, 313

Internal organs, stimuli from, 422

Internal world, man's dynamic, 418

International Encyclopedia of Social Sciences, 156

'Introduction to Stallo,' 75

Intuitions, 423; technological, [17]

Invention, arrest of, 195; capitalist suppression of, 410; cataclysmic introduction of, 223; effect of curiosity and ambition on, 112; the invention of, 111; Leonardo's preoccupation with, 161; moratorium on, 410

Inventions, false hopes for, 207; patents for, 121; reason for proliferation of, 169; resistance to, 153

Inventiveness, 156

'Invisible College,' 115

Iron Age, 131

'Irrational Man, The,' 373

Irrationality, collective, 371; institutionalized, 362; problem of controlling, 369; scientific, 186

'Is Life Worth Living?,' 343

Isaiah, 196

Isolationism, craft, 138

James, William, 308, 339, 343, 374, 434

Janissaries, 272

Jazz, as symptom, 423
Jennings, Herbert Spencer, 389
Jesus, 402, 423, 426; intuitions of, 425
Jet propulsion, pollution by, [18–19]
'Jet Set,' lunar, 48
Jet travel, vacuousness of, 309
Jews, Nazi elimination of, 281
Jobs, multiple, 329
Joey [Dr. Bettelheim's autistic machine-dependent patient], [14–15]
John XXIII, Pope, 426
Johnson, Samuel, 46
Johnson, Virginia E., 69
Joint stock company, 148
'Journal of Abnormal and Social Psychology,' 279
Jung, Carl Gustav, 370
Junk, sculptured, 366

Kafka, Franz, 184
Kahn, Hermann, 268, 331, 349
Kant, Immanuel, 63
Kepler, Johannes, 31, 35, 45–50, 58, 59, 61, 220, 221, 305, 429; 'Opera' of, 53
Kidd, Benjamin, 270
Kindergarten, 386
'King Lear,' 415
Kingship, 422, 424; divine, [8], 29, 36, 101, 247, 249, 257, 274, 403; mechanical reinforcement of, 101
Kipling, Rudyard, 432
Knowledge, acceleration of, 312; accurate or adequate, 66–67; as power goal, 317; automation of, 174, 182; Bacon's aphorism re, 118; capital accumulation of, 17; esoteric nature of scientific, 264; mass production of, 181; piecemeal, 67; quantitative, excesses of, 180; secret, 113, 269; standardized, 174; unwritten, Leibnitz's observation on, 153
'Krapp's Last Tape,' 418
Kremlin, [7]; priests of, 268
Kropotkin, Peter, 156, 353, 404
Kublai Khan, 176

La Boétie, Etienne de, 5
Labor, regimentation of, 321
Labor-saving, boon of, 42
Labor unions, 322
Lamarck, Jean Baptiste, 386, 387
Lamarckian explanation, Darwin's, 389
'Lamps,' Baconian, 113
Language, man's uniqueness in using, 86; organic model for, 395
Languages, national, 375
Lao-tse, 401
Lapp, Ralph, 269
Laputa, technological exhibitionism in, [18–19], 193, 223

Latin, scholastic, 121
Law, scientific and governmental, 82
Lawgiver, the scientist as, 84
Lawn, Brian, 25
'Laws of Manu, The,' 259
Learning, organic modes of, 285
'Learning-grubs,' 286
Learning machine, 285, 286
Leary, Timothy, 227
Lederberg, Joshua, 293
Le Folie, 221
Léger, Fernand, [29]
Leibnitz, Gottfried Wilhelm, 67, 153
Leisure, 407; definition of, 138; performance of, 327; prospective achievement of, 405
Lenin, Nikolai, 244, 246, 355; deification of, [9], 248
Leonardo da Vinci, 108, 160, 405; contrast of, with contemporary specialists, 163; practical failures of, 161
Le Roy, Louis, 199
'Letter to Teachers of History,' 234
'Letters from the Underworld,' 356
'Leviathan,' 99, 100
Lewis, C. S., 220
'Liberalism,' Gibbon's Whig, 201
'Liberation,' technological, 284
Liberty, Mill's essay on, 190
Library of Congress, miniaturization of, 275
Life, advancement of, 414; artificial creation of, 126; as comedy of errors, 414; as potentiality of matter, 54; cartesian description of, 85; conditions creating zest for, 343; contradictory scientific attitude toward, 125; Darwin's passion for, 388; definitions of, 96, 100; evasion of realities of, 303–306, 417; interplay of subjective and objective, 421; mystery of, 90; processes of, as narrowed to intelligence, 315–316; renewal of, [31]; re-shaping of, 380
Life-cycle, conditions for traversing, 398
Life-deprivation, present-day, 383
Life-goal, security as, 340
Light and space, new world of, 33
Limits, removal of, 168, 172
Lindemann, F. A., 252
Lion, symbolism of, 422
Living organisms, daily reactions to, 383
Living phenomena, dogmatic discrimination against, 55
Living Theater, The, [13]; nihilism of, 429
Locke, John, 103
'Locksley Hall,' 208
'Locksley Hall Sixty Years After,' 208
Longfellow, Henry Wadsworth, 22

'Looking Backward,' 215–220
Lords of nature, 78
Los Alamos, 301
Lotos Eaters, 338
Louis XIV, 30, 242, 248
Love, vaporization of, 318
Lovejoy, Arthur, 396
Lunar technocracy, early, 48
Lutyens, Edward, 432
Lyell, Sir Charles, 386, 387
Lynd, Helen, 323
Lynd, Robert, 323

Macaulay, Thomas Babington, 111, 326
Mace, Peruvian, [17]
Machine, as defective organism, 96; as
    mode of human redemption, 58; as
    handicraft product, 142; as model of
    teleology, 87; hypothetic experiment
    with, 88; limitations of, 95; mechanical,
    194; New World of, 36; overuse of,
    329; reason for our valuation of, 72;
    widened empire of, 98
Machine conditioning, American chil-
    dren's, 284
Machine dependence, pathology of, [14–
    15]
'Machine Stops, The,' 221, 412
Machines, components of, 95; increasing
    autonomy of, 194
Madness, chronic human threat of, 369
'Magic Mountain, The,' 346–347
Magnification, [9]
Maine, Sir Henry, 245
Malthus, Thomas, 336, 386
Mammals, 378
Man, 378; as machine, cartesian concep-
    tion of, 84; Butler's definition of, 96;
    emergence of, scenario for, 414; en-
    capsulated, [14–15]; future of, religio-
    technocratic picture of, 317; nature of,
    56, alteration of, 382; neural develop-
    ment of, 399; organization, 192, 276–
    281; phenomenon of, 276, 314–319;
    post-historic, [14–15], 312; retrogres-
    sive transformation of, 312; ultimate
    destiny of, 316
'Man in the Moon,' 220
Managerial organization, 148
'Manhattan Project,' 264
Mann, Thomas, 346
Manpower, loss of, 137
'Man's Role in Changing the Face of the
    Earth,' 336
Manuel, Frank, 19
Mao Tse-tung, [9], 247
Marco Polo, 176
Marcus Aurelius, 431
Marijuana, [26], 352; commercialization
    of, 367

Marinetti, Filippo Tommaso, 363
Marsh, George Perkins, 23, 24
Martin, Thomas, 131
Martyrs, scientific, absence of, 38
Marx, Karl, 210, 353, 355, 404, 405,
    421, 424
Masque, Bacon's extravagant, 111
'Mass' and 'motion,' 57
Mass extermination, totalitarian, 233
Mass media, 296
Mass mobilization, [26]
Mass production, 149, 169, 332–333;
    curbs on, 325; scholarly, 181
Massacre, Albigensian, 10; Armenian, 10;
    19th-century, 244
Masters, Dr. William H., 69
Material structures, de-materialization of,
    428
Materialism, Marxian, 421; scientific, 94
Materialization, 421, 429; counter-pro-
    cesses to, 426; paradox of, 426; seem-
    ing betrayal by, 425
Materials of production, organization of,
    424
Mathematical information, Galileo's re-
    liance on, 61
'Mathematical Magick,' 221
Mathematicians, aid of, to power com-
    plex, 51
Mathematics, as "language of the uni-
    verse," 53; contribution of, 37
Matriarchy, 424
Matter, new concept of, 54; obsolete,
    17th-century view of, 53
Maude, Colonel F. N., 240
Maudslay, Henry, 142
Maxwell, J. Clerk, 70, 232
McLuhan, Marshall, 227, 293–297, 304,
    338–339
Measurement, accurate, early existence
    of, 108
Mechanical creature, danger of elevating,
    97
'Mechanical explanation,' meretricious
    nature of, 89
Mechanical ideology, unique service of,
    73
Mechanical improvement, medieval, 139,
    143
Mechanical industry, 18th-century trans-
    formation of, 131
Mechanical kingdom, Butler's concep-
    tion of, 194
Mechanical model, under-dimensioned
    nature of, 92
Mechanical order, as ideal value, 84
Mechanical progress, 197; Emerson's
    paean to, 207; human irrelevance of,
    204; losses from, 133; pre-18th-cen-

tury, 147; stale catchwords of, 354; Wells' anxiety over, 371

Mechanical system, failure of, 410

Mechanical world picture, 51–76, 419; as inferior to Australian primitives', 70; blank spaces in, 188; complete embodiment of, 430; current influence of, 71; diagram of, 37; dismaying outcome of, 66; exaltation of, 69; fallacy of, 54; insufficiencies of, 73; mass components in, 416; necessity for alteration of, 379; Newton's perfection of, 120; sardonic commentary on, 418

Mechanics, celestial, 33

Mechanism, 385; teleological nature of, 97

Mechanistic absolutism, implications of, 83

Mechanization, beneficiaries of, 196; Butler's realistic prognosis of, 196; effect of war industries on, [2]; indebtedness to, of primitive cultures, 155; losses from, 152; practical triumphs of, 169; religious cult of, 158; spread of, [16]; subjective, [17]; success of, 178

'Mechanization Takes Command,' 177

Mechanized industry, potential output, 323

Mechanomorphism, failure of, 95

Medical schools, influence of Salerno's, 25

Medicine, Descartes' hopes for improvement through, 79

Medieval naturalism, 25

Medieval technics, destruction of, 140

Medieval tradition, chapter on, 7

MEDLARS, 190

Megalopolis, [24], 367; prediction of crisis in, [20]

Megamachine, American, 256–257, 270–272, 308; ancient, rehabilitation of, 248; archetypal, 216; automatic insulation of, 183; comparison of ancient and modern, 258–259; contribution to atom bomb to, 255–256; demoralization of, 251; duplication of defects of, 242, 247; economic center of, 324; etherialized, 164, 315; expansion of, 269; the Eye of the, 274; German innovations in, 250; goal of, 267; impact of war on, 244; improved model of, 100; inadequate anticipation of new, 238; menacing aspects of, 272; military use for, 259; modernization of, 246; nature of, 240; new components of, 274; properties of, 241; reassemblage of, 244; Russian, 246–248, 256–257, 270, 271, 272, 308; scientific contribution to, 248; separate components of, 237; three stages of, 245; two needed components for, 254

Megastructures, as technocratic monuments, [10]

Megatechnic absolutism, challenge to, 268

Megatechnic advance, 333

Megatechnic civilization, disorders of, 361

Megatechnic complex, success of, 346

Megatechnic culture, pseudo-revolt against, 367

Megatechnic economy, 349

Megatechnic goods, value of, 333

Megatechnic system, deficiency of, 337

Megatechnics, alternatives to, 158; bribe offered by, 330; flaws in, 334; gifts of, 334; 'ideal' conditions for, 324; monopoly of production by, 171; pecuniary motives in, 328; penalties of, 332; reactions against, 347; rejection of, 373; rigidity of, 287

Melville, Herman, 24, 42, 46, 301, 360, 376

'Memories, Dreams, Reflections,' 370

Memory, collective, 294

Mental hospitals, insufficiency of, 371

Mercantilism, as phase of new power complex, [2]

Mercier, Louis Sébastien, 206

'Mercury or the Swift Messenger,' 48

Message, medium as, 205

Messiahs, socialist, 354

Metallurgical industries, military demands on, [2]

Metaphors, mechanical, 38

Middle Ages, Gothic horror story of, 6; technical contribution of, 131

'Middletown,' 323

Migrations, 237, 352

Milgrim, Stanley, 279

Militarism, and war, 349; increasing impact of, [2]

'Military commandos,' 305

Military conscription, democratic acceptance of, 245

Military discipline, 148

Military dynamism, 243

Military-industrial-scientific complex, 254

Military megamachines, security of, 343

Mill, John Stuart, 190, 404

Miller, Arthur, 136

Mind, as aboriginal component in cosmic evolution, 90; creativity of, 416; formative attributes of, 415; inwardness of, 418; neural beginning of, 421; unifying properties of, 55

Mind-energy, radioactive, 415

Miniaturization, electro-chemical, 275

Mitchell, General William (Billy), 251

'Moby Dick,' 42, 99, 301; contemporary symbolism of, 376
Model-makers, mathematical, 273
Model T Ford, 323
'Modern Electrics,' 304
'Modern Utopia, A,' 275
'Moderne Kapitalismus, Der,' 147
Money, 165; etherialization of, 167
Money economy, over-excitement by, 243
Money-making, mechanization of, 146
Money motive, colossal magnification of, 166
Money power, 242
Mongols, 350
Monitoring, total, 275
Monitors, human, 178
Monkeyshines, esthetic, 365
Monoculture, [16]
Monolith, cracking, 346
Monopoly, automation's contribution to, 177
Monotechnics, 148; defects of, 155
Monsters, age of, [28]
Montaigne, Michel de, 5, 205
Montezuma, 9, 11
Moon colonization, 48
Moon exploration, costs of, 305; Kepler's description of, 46, 47
Moon flight, Kepler's, 45
Moon landing, 190
Moonlighting, 329
Moore, Henry, [31], [32]
Moral culture, archaic, 351
Moral debacle, contemporary, 431
Moral evaluation, automation's resistance to, 184
Moral standards, abandonment of, by civilized nations, 233
Moral values, disruption of, 370
Morality, basic, 352
More, Thomas, 209
Morgan, Arthur, 209, 217
Morgan, C. Lloyd, 53, 231, 391
Morgenthau, Hans J., 271
Morris, William, 135, 144, 155, 156, 158, 237, 354–355, 404, 405
Mo Ti, 224
Motion, Western obsession with, 37
Motor car, as exterminator, 350; unsatisfactory design of, 327
Motor coach, early steam, [4]
Muller, Hermann, 186, 227, 281
Multi-media, 298
Mummification, absolute rulers', [9], 248
Murray, Henry A., 34
Music, as related to handicraft, 137
Musical Banks, 167
Mussolini, Benito, 251
Mysterium Tremendum, 275

Mysticism, organismic, Teilhard de Chardin's, 317; technocratic, 317
Myth of the machine, overcoming of, 429; restoration of, 213; resurgence of, 209
'Myth of the Machine, The,' [10], [18–19], 161, 209, 238, 422; 430, 434
Myths, working-class, 158

Napalm bombs, 256
Napoleon Bonaparte, 39, 150, 245, 248
National Aeronautics and Space Administration (NASA), 45
National army, educational function of, 240; growing importance of, 239
National Cash Register Company, 275
National decisions, pre-emption of, by technological 'elites,' 271
National languages, 375
National Library of Medicine, 190
National Security Agency, 266
National service, compulsory, 239
National socialism, utopian, 216
Nationalism, 375
Natives, exploitation of, 8; massacres of, 9; treatment of, 10
Natural selection, 203, 388
Naturalism, contribution of medieval craftsmen to, 26
Nature, book of, 32; Christian attitude toward, 173; conquest of, 11, 172; Goethe's characterization of, 420; man's reactions to, 380; power complex's attitude toward, 173, 197; recovery of, 27; romantic appreciation of, 386
Nature of man, Fuller's description of, 56
Nature of organic design, 90
Navigation, as spur to science, 21
Nazi leaders, 249
Nazis, book-burning by, 294; extermination camps of, 302, 364
Necropolis, [24]
Nef, John, 146
'Negative income tax,' 326
Negroid races, 378
Neolithic industries, 18th-century advances in, 131
Neotechnics, 295
Nervous system, progressive nature of, 202
Neumann, Erich, 411
Neumann, John von, 186, 262
Neural development, man's, 399
Neurosis, collective, 410
'New Atlantis, The,' 107, 110, 112, 114, 117, 211

'New English Dictionary,' 240
'New Machiavelli, The,' 208
New World, 3; achievements of, 41; characterization of, by Humboldt, 16; conflicts and contradictions of, 14; discovery of, 4; richness of, 16; terrestrial and industrial, 15; treasures of, 12; varieties of concepts of, 14
New World culture, success of, 23
New World dream, components of, 43
New World generation, 16
New World methods, ferocity of, 9
New World utopia, 21, 24
New World vision, 4
'New York, Homage to,' [20]
New York State Housing and Regional Planning Commission, [20]
New York World's Fair (1964), 286
'News from Nowhere,' 355
Newton, Isaac, 34, 87, 386, 416, 419, 429
Nicolson, Marjorie Hope, 46, 220
Nietzsche, Friedrich, 241
Nihilist defiance, Melville's, 376
Nihilist reactions, 356
Nihilists, Russian, 362; today's, 358
'1984,' 215
Nocturne in E-flat Major, 137
Noises, as new music, 364
Non-art, 267, 365
Nonsense, Oldenburg's esthetic, 365
Norsemen, raids by, 7
Northeast power breakdown (1965), 412
Norway rat, 340
'Notebooks,' 194
Notebooks, Leonardo's, 162
Novelty, acceptance of, as duty, 186; unpredictability of, 433
'Novum Organum,' 111
'Now' generation, 282, 316
Nuclear absolutism, 254
Nuclear Age, parallel of, with Pyramid Age, 257
Nuclear bombs, 75; damage done by, 362
Nuclear catastrophe, youth's anticipation of, 372
Nuclear destruction, nightmare anticipations of, 234; traumatic effect of, 302
Nuclear fission, 264, 419; secret of, 301
Nuclear physicists, 70
Nuclear power, advocates of, 255; military misuses of, 39
Nuclear pyramid, consequences of, 303
Nuclear strategy, immunity of to public discussion, 271
Nuclear testing, 302
Nuclear weapons, 265; negative military accomplishment of, 302

'Objective' methods, inadequacy of, 92
Objective physical world, inference of, 62
Objectivity, cultural basis of, 63; one-sided, 55; pseudo, 187
Obsession, technological, 186, 224
Occupational change, 406, 407
Occupations, moonlighting in, 329; multiple, 407; wartime changing of, 407
O'Connor, Frank, 72
Odysseus, 338
Ogburn, W. F., 223
Oldenburg, Claes, 365
'Omega Point,' 316
Omni-Computer, merit of, 273
Omnipotence, divine, 274
Oppenheimer, J. Robert, 263, 264
Oppression and exploitation, prospective end of, before 1914, 244
'Optics,' 87, 419
'Opus Majus,' 53
Oral intercourse, contribution of writing and printing to, 297
Order, astronomical basis of, 74
Organic activities, nature of, 202
Organic art, Gabo's and Moore's, [32]
Organic behavior, Darwin's insight into, 388; mechanical simplification of, 95
Organic complex, 433
Organic complexes, 395
Organic complexity, 80; evolutionary background of, 91; scientific rejection of, 58
Organic design, nature of, 90
Organic existence, mechanical substitutes for, 384
Organic model, rise of, 394
Organic nature, appreciation of, 385
Organic past and future, 88
Organic phenomenon, cartesian rejection of, 83
Organic progress, 202
Organic properties, aboriginal nature of, 90; machines as extension of, 195
Organic success, preconditions for, 391
Organic system, 191; ideal of, 402
Organic trait, esthetic expression as, 389; mechanism as, 95
Organic world picture, 384–393; man's central place in, 55; necessity for acceptance of, 379–384; slow emergence of, 392
Organismic phenomena, science's theological horror over, 70
Organisms, as 'enduring realities,' 67; attributes of, 87; reproduction as trait of, 96; unique properties of, 55
Organization, centralized, 239
Organization Man, 192, 276–281; definition of, 277

'Origin of Species, On the,' 194, 379, 386–387, 392
Orozco, José Clemente, [2], [25]
Orthodoxy, Teilhard de Chardin's dubious, 317
Orwell, George, 215
Osiris, 384; as friend of man, 35
Ostwald, Wilhelm, 82
Overcrowding, 182
Overkill, 261, 301, 302
Overproduction, quantitative, 127

Pain, 'objective' rejection of, 71
Paleolithic culture, New World recovery of, 16
Paley, William, 89
Panofsky, Erwin, 17
Papal authority, questioning of, 375
Paper work, 165
Paracelsus, Philippus Aureolus, 113
Paradise, Persian name for garden, 383
Parasitism, as modified by predation, 342; anti-social effects of, 342; deterioration under, 340; human, 339; present manifestations of, 344; threat of, 338
Parasitopolis, [24]
Parsimony, versus plenitude, 401
Partnership, ecological, 380
Party line, 246
Pascal, Blaise, 34, 82, 416
Past, arbitrary rejection of, 205; current destruction of, 372; importance of, 390; relegation of, to the unconscious, 391
Pasternak, Boris, 380
Pasteur, Louis, 111
Patent system, 148
Patents, corporate monopoly of, 410
Patholopolis, [24]
Patterns of culture, human, 370
Paul, Saint, 376, 426
Paulinus of Nola, 431
Pax Romana, 431
Peace moratorium, [27]
Peano, Giuseppe, 121
Pecuniary abstraction, 165
Pecuniary over-stimulation, 168
Pecuniary pleasure-center, 168–169
Pecuniary pressure, 169
Pedestrians, as suspicious characters, 187
Pentagon, [1]; priests of, 268; strategists of, outwitted, 144
Pentagon of Power, [7], 164, 166, 192, 275, 303, 431, 432; reverse image of, 374
Pepys, Samuel, 137
Perfectability of man, 206

Perfection, desire for, in technics, 418; religious notion of, 206
Periodical publication, 174–175
Person, primacy of, 433
Personal forces, 434
Personalities, needed variety of, 289
Personality, central role of, 434; effect of parasitism upon, 341; new incarnation of, 423; sterilization of, 286
Personality cult, youth's, [26]
Personality types, Greek, 289
Pesticides, 336
Petrarch, 197
Petrie, Flinders, 197
Pettigrew, J. Bell, 394
Pfaall, Hans, moon trip of, 46
Pharmaceuticals, 336
Phase rule, Gibbs', 231
Ph. D. octopus, 374
'Phenomenon of Man, The,' 314, 318
'Philosophy of Manufactures,' 112
Physical events, scientific clarification of, 67
Physical objects, abstract world of, 56
Physical organs, elimination of, 187
Physical phenomena, 17th-century conception of, 59
Physical world, abstract conception of, 67
Physicists, contribution of, to mechanical world picture, 51
Physics, Comenius' treatise on, 103
Pioneer, westward march of, 15
Planck, Max, 53
Plane, atom-powered, 269
Planetary communication, limitations on, 295
Planetary destruction, Norse prophecy of, 303
Plant breeding, machine-conditioned, 382
Plants, 378; as main energy source, [3]; cultivation of, 382; effects of tending, 383
Plato, 244, 423
Pleasure and pain, interchangeable roles of, 343
Pleasure center, pecuniary, 168–169, 408
Plenitude, 400, 403; culture of, 405; economy of, 406; human advantages of, 401; invitation to, 401; natural, 396; permissiveness of, 402; potentiality for achieving, 403; power system's contribution to, 402; social implications of, 405
Poe, Edgar Allan, 46
Polanyi, Michael, 53
Political absolutism, Descartes' belief in, 80
Political dynamism, 243
Political power, centralization of, 238

Politodrama, 415

Poliziano, Angelo, 4

Pollution, industrial, [22], [23]

Polybius, 431

Polytechnic occupations, restoration of, 144

Polytechnics, basis of, 136; capitalist, 147; international, 132; medieval, 131; subversion of, 145

Pop Art, 363, 365

Pope, Arthur Upham, 132

Population, increase of, 336; Malthus' theory of, 386

Pornography, 341

Port of New York Authority, [20]

Portmann, Adolf, 64

Post-Baconian world, Bacon's anticipation of, 118

'Post-Historic Man,' 312

Pot, 352, 367; mind-clouding by, [26]

Potlatch, 325

Power, absolute, 344; as energy, productivity, profit, 166; as scientific motivation, 78; decentralization of, 408; Emerson's warning against premature, 253; fantastic magnitude of, 265; fascist belief in, 244; hydro-electric, [3]; increase of, 118; increase of collective, 246; intoxication with, 41; invisible ultimate, 275; jet, [3]; nature of, 265; new implosion of, 238; Pentagon of, [7], 164, 166, 192, 275, 303, 374, 431, 432; restoration of human, 408; social isolation of, 157; successive definitions of, 240; wartime exercise of, by American President, 254

Power Complex, 163, 164–169, 292, 370, 429, 433; basic models for, 165; etherialization of, 434; failing appeal of, 348; nucleation of, 166; pathology of, [9]; pecuniary, 168; psychological malaise of, 232; secret motto of, 187; strain in, 347; subjective drive to, 229; unfortunate feature of, 169; weakness of, 337

Power elite, 433; untouchableness of, 268

Power structure, dilapidation of, 432

Power Symbols, space rockets as, [11]

Power system, breakdown of, 410–412, 431; components of, 166; disengagement from, 348; educational agents of, 286; escape from, 433; extrapolation of, 292; failure of, 410; formative ideas of, 430; frailty of, 432; human origin of, 434; inner undermining of, 356; irrational expansion of, 303; military errors of, 250; 'Moby Dick' as parable on, 376; need of traditional values in, 350; negative, 361; overcoming defects of, 408; postulates of, 173; reactions against, 347, 375; reassertion of an-

cient, 34; replacement of, 433; terminus of, 228; war as cure of, 349

Pragmatic world picture, pragmatic efficiency of, 68

Prague, 1968 uprising in, 297

Predictability, as scientific desideratum, 82

Prefabrication, 149

'Prevolvans,' Kepler's, 48, 221

Price, Charles C., 293

Price, Derek J., 174, 182

Priesthood, higher abdication of, 268–273

Primate evolution, anti-climax, 319

Primitive man, Hobbes' versus Rousseau's picture of, 101

Primitivism, megatechnic, 373

Printing press, swift adoption of, 139

Prison, new economic, 327

Pritchard, James B., 342

Productivity, 171, 324, 333; devices for absorbing, 328

'Profiles of the Future,' 222

Profit-pleasure centers, 168–169; necessity for curtailment of, 408

Profits, financial, 8; increase of, by power system, 166; dominant motivation of, 168

Programmers, 273

Progress, 167; as shrinkage of space and time, 204; automatic, 225; Christian notion of, 198; Churchill's exposure of, 201; easy formula for, 201; economic, 331; fatuous praises of, 200; genuine, 198; idea of, Turgot's and Gibbon's, 198–199; justification of, 205; 'liberal' doctrines of, 270; non-mechanical demonstrations of, 206; of invention, false hopes for, 207; one-sided picture of, 152; organic, 202; proofs of vitality of, 204; religious expression of (1699), 198; reversals of, 200; technological, 203; versus evolution, 202, 208; Wells' unconscious doubts of, 222; wheels of, 197–202

Property rights, Macaulay's defense of, 326

Prophets of doom, technocratic, 435

Prospecting, importance of, for technics, 19

Protection, penalties of social, 340

Protective associations, workers, 142

Psychoanalysis, need for collective, 411

Psychological malaise, of power complex, 232

Psychosis, electronically produced, 294

Ptolemy, 28

Public work, wider use for, 407

Pumpelly, Raphael, 12, 136

Pumphrey, R. J., 69

Pyramid Age, 30, 99; generalized concept
   of, 29; parallel of, with Nuclear Age,
   257
Pyramids, air-conditioned, 300; Egyptian,
   426; technocratic, [10]
Pythagoras, 34

Qualitative excellence, its precedence,
   172
Qualities, Galileo's distinction between
   primary and secondary, 62–63; pri-
   mary, Burtt's observations on, 67,
   Galileo's commitment to, 64, 68; sec-
   ondary, Galileo's rejection of, 62
Quantification, breakdown of, 182
Quantitative expansion, 236
Quantitative measurement, subjective
   contribution to, 416
Quantitative output, 172
Quantity, questionable value of, 184

Rabelais, François, 138
Radcliffe Library, Oxford, 190
Radium, consequences of, 231
Raglan, Lord, 282
Ragnarok, 303
Raskolnikov, 357
'Rasselas,' 46
Rat domestication, 340
Rational understanding, science's estab-
   lishment of, 66
Reality, contemporary evasion of, 417;
   space flight from, 303–306
Rebellions, justification of contemporary,
   377
'Recessional,' 432
Record, permanent, 294
Records, centralized, 275
Reductionism, 87, 418; scientific, 69, 87,
   93, 418
Refrigerators, automatic, 327
Regimentation, military, 150; universal,
   240
Regionalism, 375
Regression, symptoms of, 358; New
   World, 41
Re-incarnations, need for, 426
Religion, 416; economic dependence on,
   352; supernatural, 349
Religions, Axial, 335; vital offerings of,
   409
Religious conversion, need for equivalent
   of, 413
Remote control, [5]
Renan, Ernest, 243
Renascence, 13; buried, 159–163
Renascence artists, contribution of, 27;
   wide range of abilities of, 138

Renaudot, Théophraste, 60, 114
Re-orientation, need for human, 236
Repetition, functional value of, 369
'Republic, The,' 244
Research and development, 127; annual
   budget for, 269
Resistance, right of popular, 290
Restrictions, case for drastic, 413; need
   for, 337, 339; vocational, 408
Retirement age, 342
Revolt, youth's, 372–374
Revolution, failures of, 356; French, 245,
   353; of 1848, 353; Russian, 246, 355;
   threat of, 353
Revolutionary saturnalia, 247
Revolutionary utopianism, 354
Rewards, distribution of, 324
Richter, Curt P., 340
Riots, 183
Ritual order, monopoly of, by machine,
   370
Rituals, 416; meaningless modes of, 352;
   of counter-culture, [27]; soul-deaden-
   ing, as end product of culture, 427
'Robinson Crusoe,' 15, 351
Robot, [18–19], 277
'Rock' festivals, [26], 373
Rocket, development of, 305; man-carry-
   ing, 305
Roman Catholic Church, insurgence in,
   375
Roman Empire, conversion of, to Chris-
   tianity, 425, 432; iniquities of the es-
   tablishment in, 431; parasitism in, 344;
   power system of, 413, 431; practices
   of, accepted by Christianity, 425; re-
   nunciation of, 431
Romantic dream, betrayal of, 42
Romantic movement, 385, 423; realiza-
   tion of, 11; vitality of, 351
Roosevelt, Franklin D., 254, 256
Rossiter, Clinton, 271
Rousseau, Jean-Jacques, 15, 21–22, 351,
   385
Rowntree, Seebohm, 143
Royal Society, 114; foundation of, 115
Rubber, contribution of, by primitives,
   19
Rubbish, academic production of, 181
Rug-making, Persian, 136
Ruins, imaginary, 373
Rules of war, American, British, German,
   252; violations of, 10
Ruling classes, paranoid ambitions of, 22
Rural crafts, esthetic contribution of, 138
Ruskin, John, 237, 356
Russell, Bertrand, 31
Russell, Senator Richard, 368
Russia, [8], 217, 218, 244, 253, 257, 271,
   352

Russian megamachine, 246–248, 256–257, 270, 271, 272, 308
Russian nihilists, 362
Russian Revolution, 246, 355
Rutherford, Ernest, 231, 233
Ruyer, Raymond, 210

Sacrifice, astronauts' religious, 307; Aztec, 267; human, and mechanical salvation, 260–262
Sade, Marquis de, 357
Safeguards, rural and communal, 351
Sail wagons, [4]
Saint-Hilaire, Auguste de, 387
Saint-Simon, Comte de, 19, 240, 353
Saint-Simon, Duc de, 199
Saint-Simonians, 349
'Salernitan Questions,' 25
Salvation, 99, 413; mechanical, 208
Santillana, Giorgio de, 34, 56
Sauer, Carl, 6
Savagery, technological, 261
Scarcity, new form of, 337
'Sceptical Chymist, The,' 96
Schrödinger, Erwin, 53, 59, 68
Schubert, Franz, 137
Schumpeter, J. A., 346
Science, and technics, Baconian unification of, 108; as 'power thought,' 31; as public knowledge, 122; as 'useful knowledge,' 78, 111; Bacon's intuitions of destination of, 109; Bacon's original conception of, 110; conditioning by, 280; debt of, to medieval thought, 26; effect of, on invention, 121; exploding universe of, 127; geometric beauty of, 34; growing irrelevance of, 128; institutional collaboration with, 123; institutionalized, 113; irresponsibility of, 234; New World contribution to, 17; organization of, 117; poets' interest in, 66; principles of, 434; reasonableness of, 60; royal patronage of, 38; social detachment of, 123; subjective perversions of, 187; transfer of, from university, 120; utilitarian applications of, 116; valueless, 188
'Science and the Modern World,' 25
Scientific abstractions, as neutral medium of exchange, 65
Scientific advances, unforeseen consequences of, 80
Scientific data, military need for, 38
Scientific discoveries, profitable exploitation of, 122
Scientific dismemberment, 68
Scientific fantasy, instant realization of, 223
Scientific game, rules for, 75

Scientific history, rejection of, 82
Scientific ideology, effect of, 106
Scientific investigation, motives for, 78
Scientific journals, mass publication of, 174
Scientific knowledge, beginnings of, 174
Scientific laws, supposed finality of, 70
Scientific method, claims for, 94; positivist and platonist, 68
Scientific orthodoxy, limitations of, 39
'Scientific Outlook, The,' 31
Scientific personality, corporate, 113; words used in praise of, 94
Scientific philosophy, popularity of, 65
Scientific property, Pascal's attitude toward, 122
Scientific reductionism, 69, 87, 93, 418
Scientific self-adulation, 291
Scientific societies, foundation of, 115
Scientific thinking, archaic, 291
Scientific underworld, 269
Scientists, as lawgivers, 84; human qualities of, 75; increasing number of, 108; old image of, 122; physical, limitations of, 39
Sculpture, junk, 367
Seaborg, Glenn, 331
Secrecy, as secret of totalitarian power, 264
Security, power system's promise of, 338, 340
'Seeing is believing,' as scientific principle, 61
Seidenberg, Roderick, 312, 313, 314, 319, 338
Selection, cultural, 202
Self-actualizing design, 90
Self-confidence, loss of, 359
Self-governing units, increase of, 237
Self-government, promise of, 244
Self-maintenance, 397, 399
Self-organization, as evolutionary key, 391, 393
Self-reliance, Emerson's essay on, 23
Self-replication, 96
Self-transformation, part of technics in, 417
Senility, pornography as sign of, 341–342
Sentimentality, technocratic, 222
Serial versus integrated thinking, 235
Servants, increase of, in 19th century, 322
Services, need for human, 407
Servitude, acceptance of, 345
Servo-mechanism, man's reduction to, 179; Organization Man as, 278
Sewing machine, military use for, 151
Sexual acts, laboratory report on, 69
Sexual reproduction, mechanical explanation of, 72

Sexual selection, 389

Shakespeare, 416

Shelley, Mary, 126

Shelley, Percy Bysshe, on power, [7]

Sherrington, C. S., 97, 397

Shipbuilding, impromptu, 137

Shipping, increased use of, before 'Industrial Revolution,' 146

Silk-reeling machine, 139, 177

Simpson, George Gaylord, 379

Singular events, scientific disregard of, 84

Sit-downs, 183

Skinner, B. F., 65, 216, 227, 285, 331, 406

Sky Gods, 28, 238

Skyscraper, Bacon's, 117

Slavery, 8; the coming, 245; encroachment of, 24; proposed restoration of, 326

Slowdown, necessity for, 408

Smith, Adam, 169, 174

Snow, Charles Percy, 63, 181

Snowflake, Kepler's reflection on, 58

Social behavior, application of military technique to, 240

'Social Contract, The,' 77, 101

Social control, by tranquillizers, 352

Social custom, 416

Social development, scientific light on, 283

Social disintegrations, 347

Social life, bridges to, 423

Social order, Christian contribution to, 351

Social responsibilities of science, Soddy's sense of, 233

Socialism, 158, 353; Marx's forecast of, 405; National, 216

Socialist demands, achievement of, 325

Society, computer-dominated, 191

Soddy, Frederick, 233, 255, 410

Solar calendar, as symbol of royal authority, 31

Solar system, exploration of, 306

Solar theology, effect of, 29

Soloism, Descartes', 81

Solomon's House, 117, 123

Solutions, unlikelihood of technical, 270

Sombart, Werner, 147

'Somnium' ('Dream'), 45–50, 221, 305

Song My, imprint of Monster on, [28]

Sorcerer's Apprentice, Goethe's, 180

Sorre, Max, 132

Soul, elimination of, 55

Sovereign power, medieval, 290

Sovereign state, 99

Space, as Satan's power bribe, 311

Space capsule, 227; as minimal environment, 306; static, [21], 309

Space dissertation, first, 45

Space exploration, immediate advantages of, 309

Space rockets, as embodiment of power complex, [11], 304; limitations of, 309

Space stations, 305

Space technology, supposed advantages of, 310

Space travel, negative conditions for, 308; ritual demands of, 348; sacrifices for, 307; safety of, 47

Space vehicles, unmanned, 304

Specialization, inroads of, 138; lifetime, stultification of, 407

Specialized knowledge, integration of, 265

Species, fixation of human, 290

Speed, [4], [27], 306; compulsion to achieve maximum, 204–205; homicidal, 350; limitations on, 203; megamachine's need for, 259; social modes of, 367

Speer, Albert, 248

Spencer, Herbert, 105, 244, 349, 387

Spinning wheel, 139

Stalin, Joseph, 10, 244, 246–248, 249, 250, 251; mummification of, [9]

Stallo, J. B., 53, 57, 59

Standard of living, 322

Standardization, 149

Standards, qualitative, 133

Stapledon, Olaf, 212, 293

Starvation, of peasants, Stalin's deliberate, 10

State, Marxian doctrine of the, 355

State capitalism, utopian, 216

Statute of Apprentices, English, 151

Steam engine, 147

Stein, Clarence S., [20]

Stevens, Henry Bailey, 383

'Sticks and Stones,' 7

Strangelove, Dr., 403

Strasbourg-goose syndrome, 174

Strategic bombing, ineffectiveness of, 252

Strategy, thermo-nuclear, 268

Stroboscopic lights, [27]

Structures, symbolic, 415

Struggle for existence, 388, 392; Hobbesian, 102

Student power, 374

Study Group for the Life Apparatus, 319

'Study of History, A,' 417, 426

Subjective activities, formless, 422; obliviousness to, 416

Subjective impulses, as prime movers, 419

Subjective life, Church's monopoly of, 94

Subjective responses, Darwin's restoration of, 388

Subjective state, privacy of, 63

Subjectivity, addled, 368; and rationality, 76; public expression of, 63; science's own, 74; scientific disreputability of, 71

Submission, 99

Subversion, megatechnic, 269

'Subvolvans,' 48, 221

Suicide, modern modes of, 384

'Summit meeting' in Paris, deliberate wrecking of, 271

Sun, Kepler's praise of, 35; restored place of, 30; worship of, 35

Sun God, 35, 51, 69, 73–74, 197, 265, 267, 273, 384, 403; incarnation of, 301; marks of ascendancy of, 31; rebirth of, 238; religion of, 28, 33; rule of, 272

Sun King, 30

Super-brain, ectoplasmic, 315

Superego, subversive, 193

Superfluity, automated, 332; organized, 398

Superior functions, internal bodily basis for, 399

Supernatural religion, 349

Surfeit, deprivation by, 127; quantitative, 342

Surgery, Galileo's hypothetical, 62

Surpluses, distribution of, 325; economic, 325; use of organic, 398

Survey, of York, 143

'Survey Graphic,' Regional Planning Number of, [20]

Survival, Byzantine, cost of, 432

Swift, Jonathan, [18–19], 193, 223

Symbiosis, 382

Symbolic organization, 416

Symbols, durability of, 426; invention of, 415

Syncretism, technological, 160

Synthesis, need for subjective and objective, 420

'Synthetic Philosophy,' 105

System, deviation from, 192

Systemation letter, 192

Szent-Györgyi, Albert, 87

Szilard, Leo, 255, 264, 268

Tasmanians, slaughter of, 10

Taylor, A. J. P., 253

Taylor, Henry Osborn, 232

Taxable wealth, increase of, 149

Teachers, of history, Adams' letter to, 234; shortage of, 285

Teaching, monitorial, 102

Technical advances, misreading of, 145

Technical development, case for, 195

Technical heritage, belated preservation of, 156

Technical improvements, foreign origins of, 132

Technical innovations, liberating influence of, 237

Technical resources, increase of, 132

Technical skills, medieval, 135

Technics, as personality molder, 424; as product of mind, 430; as servant of absolutism, 78; central human problem of, 187; historic contributions to, 134; materializations of, 429; medieval, 140; militarization of, 84; overgrowth of, 312; power-oriented, 123; symbolic contributions to, 420

'Technics and Civilization,' 295, 326, 375, 430

'Technics and Human Development' ('The Myth of the Machine,' Vol. I), [10], [18–19], 161, 209, 238, 422

Technocracy, autocratic, [10]

Technocratic predictions, dehumanized, 435

Technocratic prison, escape from, 435

Technocratic triumphs, early fears about, 49

Technocrats, 433

Technodrama, emphasis on, 415

Technological breakdowns, 411

Technological dynamism, 243

Technological exhibitionism, [18–19]

Technological forecasts, Wells' accurate, 222

Technological heritage, 19th century's, 153

Technological pool, 153–154

Technological possibilities, 186

Technological progress, deteriorations from, 203; net gains of, 170

Technological salvation, improbability of, 270, 412

Technological syncretism, 160

Technology, backward, 134; debt of, to exploration, 378; debt of, to primitive societies, 19; electronic, 298, 339; lethal, 261; man's submission to, 283; medieval components of, 135; preconscious sources of, 419; prophets of, 284; revolt against, 372; scientific basis for, 107

Teilhard de Chardin, Pierre, 212, 314–319

Telecleides, 175, 327

Teleology, mechanistic, 87, 97

Teleonomy, 393

Telephone, organic models for, 394

Television, 295

Teller, Edward, 264

Telstar, 220

Temple, secrets of the, 263–268

Tempo, lowering of, 409
Tennyson, Alfred, 208
Tensions, use of, 339
Terrestrial exploration, revolutionary effect of, 378
Territorial discovery, climax of, 18
Territorial exploration, advantages of, 20
Terror, totalitarian, 233
Terrorists, official, 362
Textiles, ancient achievements in, 171
'Theater of the Cruel,' 251
Theft, provocation to, 332
Theological conflicts, science's release from, 73
Think tanks, 301
'Thinking the Unthinkable,' 349
Thiusen, Ismal, 212n
Thoreau, Henry, 24, 404, 409
Thorndike, Lynn, 26, 216
Thrasymachus, 244
Tillyard, E. M. W., 30, 35
Time, idea of, 419; concept of, as essential to clock, 89; organic conception of, 391
'Time Machine, The,' 49, 204
Tinguely, Jean, [20], 328
Tocqueville, Alexis de, 344
Tokyo, civilian deaths in fire-bombing of, 256
Tolstoi, Leo, 286, 287, 359
Torture, acceptance of, 280; totalitarian, 233, 249
Totalitarian mass extermination, 233, 249
Totalitarian system, 264; Nemesis of, 250; new equipment for, 248–249
Totalitarian utopia, Cabet's, 213
Totalitarianism, Teilhard de Chardin's praise of, 318; Transitional, 243
Tower of Babel, electronic, 298
Toynbee, Arnold, 130
Toynbee, Arnold Joseph, 417, 426
Tradition, devaluation of, 148
Traffic congestion, Port Authority's promotion of, [20]
Tranquillizers and sedatives, social control by, 352
Transcendence, subjective, 417–418
Transcendental world picture, failure to create, 420
Transformation, first evidences of contemporary, 433
'Transformations of Man, The,' 371
Transmutation, ancient dream of, 418
Transportation systems, [20], [22], 237
Traumas, fresh consciousness of, 411
Traumatic institutions, civilizations', 199
Trees, food-yielding, 383
'Trial, The,' 184

'Tribal communism,' McLuhan's conception of, 295
Trotsky, Leon, 246
Turgenev, Ivan, 357
Turgot, A. R. J., 198
Turkish despotism, modern parallel to, 272
Twilight of the Gods, Norse prophecy of, 303
'Typee,' 46
'Typographical Man,' 295
Tyrannies, the new, 272

U-2, deliberate provocation by, 271
'Ultimate' particles, mysterious nature of, 59
Unconscious, irrational impulses from the, 369; liberation of the, 370
'Understanding Media,' 339
Underworld, scientific, 269
Uniform, military, 150
Uniformity, educational, 285; mechanical, 213; totalitarian, 250
United Nations, 409
'Universal Man,' Renascence examples of, 162
Universal society, higher potentialities of, 404; technological backwardness in realizing, 224
Universe, man's conquest of, 291; mathematical language of, 53
Universities, medieval, 120
University, destruction of, 374
University Militant, 374
Unwritten knowledge, Leibnitz's observation on, 153
Urey, Harold, 255, 263–264
Useful knowledge, science's contribution of, 66
Usher, Albert Payson, 149
Utopia, 210; Bellamy's totalitarian, 215; Bulwer-Lytton's underground, 214; Inca model for, 217; life-span in, 217; machine-conditioned, 158; military model for, 219; New World, 21, 24; possible realization of, 212; prefabricated, 211; price of, 217; role of, 209–212
'Utopia,' 209
Utopian prophecy, 212

Varagnac, André, 426
Variety, polytechnic, 141; vocational, 405
Vasari, Giorgio, 138, 160

Vaucanson, Jacques de, 394
Veblen, Thorstein, 327
Venetian Arsenal, 38
Verdi, Giuseppe, 138
Verne, Jules, 107, 212
Vesalius, Andreas, 29, 384
Vespasian, Emperor, 153
Vico, Giambattista, 203
Victoria and Albert Museum, 136
Victorian capitalism, influence of, on Darwinism, 386
Vietnam, 279; American military operations in, [12], 372; survival of, through manpower, 144
Vietnam crisis, 183
Vietnam film, 144
Violence, 247, 362; pre-scientific, limitations on, 267
Vitalism, 385
Vocation of man, 405; academic interpretation of, 296
Vocational diversification, obstacle to, 408
Vocorder, 69
Vril, 214

'Waiting for Godot,' 418
Wald, George, 126
'Walden Two,' 65
Wallace, Alfred Russel, 16, 101, 351, 368, 386
Walters, Gray, 113
War, as counterbalance to parasitism, 343; as salvation of mass production, 323; economic 'prosperity' through, 242; Emerson's essay on, quoted, 421; industrial demands of, 146; moral equivalent of, 308; Nietzsche's description of, 241; permanent, 266
Warfare State, 278
Waste, the duty to, 329
Waterpower, 133
Water-turbine, 155
Watt, James, 131, 139
'Wave of the Future, The,' 249
'We,' 319
'Wealth of Nations, The,' 169
Weapons, absolute, 265
Weather control, Kublai Khan's boast of, 176
Weaver, Warren, 305
Webb, Walter, 16
Weber, Max, 278
Weizsacker, C. F. von, [18–19]
Welfare measures, 323
Welfare state, 168, 245, 278, 327, 331, 347; socialist contributions to, 354
Wells, H. G., 49, 107, 204, 219–222, 275, 371, 411

Welser, Bartholomäus, 146
Wenner-Gren Symposium (1955), 336
Western civilization, rebellion against, 423; subjective demoralizations of, 411
Western social structure, weakness of, 230
Westin, Alan F., 275
'What Is Art?' 286
Wheel of life, escape from, 228
Wheeler, Harvey, 223
Whirligig of time, 434
Whitehead, A. N., 25, 53, 67, 111, 391
Whitman, Walt, 24, 120, 383, 393, 423
Wholeness, as organic requisite, 397
Whorf, Benjamin, 63
Whyte, William H., Jr., 278
Wiener, Norbert, 72, 125, 189, 194, 268, 275
Wigner, Eugene P., 264
Wilde, Oscar, 234
Wilderness, prefabricated substitute for, 44
Wilkins, John, 20, 48, 429
Wilson, Woodrow, 392
Windpower, 133
Wire-pulling machine, 139
'Wisdom of the Body, The,' 396, 399, 400
Withdrawal, Christian, 431; from power system, 433
Wittfogel, Karl, 259
Wolstenholme, Gordon, 288
Woman, [29]; computerized presentation of, [1]; importance of, in industry, 141; medieval craftsman's feeling for, [1]; Renascence painter's mapping of, [1]
Womb, return to, 341
Woodstock Festival, [26]
Work, as life experience, 405; bureaucratic substitute for, 191; future function of, 406; human value of, 179; questionable abolition of, 179; voluntary, 407
Work period, 406
'Work-resister,' utopian and Russian, 218
Workers, debasement of, 152
Working conditions, improvement of, 322
World, external and internal, as inseparable, 58
World picture, Darwin's post-mechanistic, 388; Gabo's etherialization of, [30], [32]; mechanization of, [1]; mechanized, 37, 51–76, 120, 188, 416, 418, 419, 430; organic, 55, 379–393, 418; scientific, 105
'World Set Free, The,' 208
World systems, Ptolemy's and Copernicus' contribution to, 32
World Trade Center, New York City, as example of purposeless giantism, [20]

World view, Australian primitives', 70
World War, First, 244, 354; Second, 266
World's Fair, Chicago, 213
Worlds, probable and possible, 62
Wright, Frank Lloyd, [21], 117
Wright, Orville, 394
Wright, Wilbur, 394
Wymer, Norman, 143

Xerox duplicating machine, 175
Xosa people, 368

'Year 2440, The,' 206
York, Herbert, 270
York, survey of, 143
Young, J. Z., 188
Young Goodman Brown, 372
Youth, mass mobilization of, [26]; regi-
    mentation of culture of, [26]; revolt of,
    372–374

Zabern affair, 244
Zamiatin, Eugene, 319
Zest for life, negative conditions for, 343